Innovations in Database Design, Web Applications, and Information Systems Management

Keng Siau
University of Nebraska-Lincoln, USA

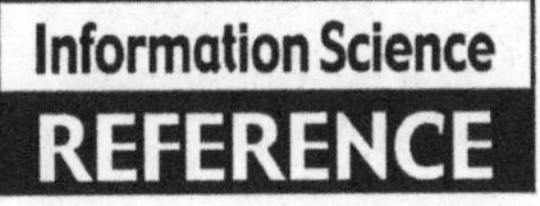

Managing Director: Lindsay Johnston
Editorial Director: Joel Gamon
Book Production Manager: Jennifer Yoder
Publishing Systems Analyst: Adrienne Freeland
Assistant Acquisitions Editor: Kayla Wolfe
Typesetter: Christy Fic
Cover Design: Jason Mull

Published in the United States of America by
Information Science Reference (an imprint of IGI Global)
701 E. Chocolate Avenue
Hershey PA 17033
Tel: 717-533-8845
Fax: 717-533-8661
E-mail: cust@igi-global.com
Web site: http://www.igi-global.com

Library of Congress Cataloging-in-Publication Data

Innovations in database design, web applications, and information systems management / Keng Siau, editor.
p. cm.
Includes bibliographical references and index.
Summary: "This book presents ideal research in the areas of database theory, systems design, ontologies and many more, including examples of the convergence of ideas from various disciplines aimed at improving and developing the theory of information technology and management of information resources"--Provided by publisher.
ISBN 978-1-4666-2044-5 (hardcover) -- ISBN 978-1-4666-2045-2 (ebook) -- ISBN 978-1-4666-2046-9 (print & perpetual access) 1. Database design. 2. Web site development. 3. Semantic Web. 4. Information resources management. I. Siau, Keng, 1964-
QA76.9.D26I564 2012
006.7--dc23

2012013141

British Cataloguing in Publication Data
A Cataloguing in Publication record for this book is available from the British Library.

The views expressed in this book are those of the authors, but not necessarily of the publisher.

Editorial Advisory Board

List of Reviewers

Table of Contents

Chapter 6
Multi-Level Modeling of Web Service Compositions with Transactional Properties 139
K. Vidyasankar, Memorial University, Canada
Gottfried Vossen, University of Muenster, Germany

Chapter 7
Service Composition and Interaction in a SOC Middleware Supporting Separation of Concerns with Flows and Views 171
Dickson K. W. Chiu, Dickson Computer Systems, Hong Kong
Qing Li, City University of Hong Kong, Hong Kong
Patrick C. K. Hung, University of Ontario, Canada
Zhe Shan, City University of Hong Kong, Hong Kong
S. C. Cheung, Hong Kong University of Science & Technology, Hong Kong
Yu Yang, City University of Hong Kong, Hong Kong
Matthias Farwick, University of Innsbruck, Austria

Chapter 8
Ensuring Customised Transactional Reliability of Composite Services 203
Sami Bhiri, National University of Ireland, Galway, Ireland
Walid Gaaloul, Telecom & Management SudParis, France
Claude Godart, LORIA-INRIA, France
Olivier Perrin, LORIA-INRIA, France
Maciej Zaremba, National University of Ireland, Galway, Ireland
Wassim Derguech, National University of Ireland, Galway, Ireland

Chapter 9
Leveraging Early Aspects in End-to-End Model Driven Development for Non-Functional Properties in Service Oriented Architecture 233
Hiroshi Wada, National ICT Australia, Australia
Junichi Suzuki, University of Massachusetts, Boston, USA
Katsuya Oba, OGIS International, Inc., USA

Chapter 10
Complementing Business Process Verification by Validity Analysis: A Theoretical and Empirical Evaluation 265
Pnina Soffer, University of Haifa, Israel
Maya Kaner, Ort Braude College, Israel

Chapter 11
Data Management and Data Administration: Assessing 25 Years of Practice 289
Peter Aiken, Virginia Commonwealth University, USA
Mark L. Gillenson, University of Memphis, USA
Xihui Zhang, University of North Alabama, USA
David Rafner, Richmond Group Fund Co., Ltd., USA

Detailed Table of Contents

Hyunjung Park, Seoul National University, Korea
Sangkyu Rho, Seoul National University, Korea
Jinsoo Park, Institute of Management Research, Seoul National University, Korea

The information space of the Semantic Web has different characteristics from that of the World Wide Web (WWW). One main difference is that in the Semantic Web, the direction of Resource Description Framework (RDF) links does not have the same meaning as the direction of hyperlinks in the WWW, because the link direction is determined not by a voting process but by a specific schema in the Semantic Web. Considering this fundamental difference, the authors propose a method for ranking Semantic Web resources independent of link directions and show the convergence of the algorithm and experimental results. This method focuses on the classes rather than the properties. The property weights are assigned depending on the relative significance of the property to the resource importance of each class. It solves some problems reported in prior studies, including the Tightly Knit Community (TKC) effect, as well as having higher accuracy and validity compared to existing methods.

Bo Xu, Fudan University, China
Zhangxi Lin, Texas Tech University, USA
Yan Xu, Del Mar College, USA

Open source software (OSS) has achieved great success and exerted significant impact on the software industry. OSS development takes online community as its organizational form, and developers voluntarily work for the project. In the project execution process, control aligns individual behaviors toward the organizational goals via the Internet and becomes critical to the success of OSS projects. This paper investigates the control modes in OSS project communities, and their effects on project performance. Based on a web survey and archival data from OSS projects, it is revealed that three types of control modes, that is, outcome, clanship, and self-control, are effective in an OSS project community. The study contributes to a better understanding of OSS project organizations and processes, and provides advice for OSS development.

To customize a data warehouse, many organizations develop concrete data marts focused on a particular department or business process. However, the integrated development of these data marts is an open problem for many organizations due to the technical and organizational challenges involved during the design of these repositories as a complete solution. In this article, the authors present a design approach that employs user requirements to build both corporate data warehouses and data marts in an integrated manner. The approach links information requirements to specific data marts elicited by using goal-oriented requirement engineering, which are automatically translated into the implementation of corresponding data repositories by means of model-driven engineering techniques. The authors provide two UML profiles that integrate the design of both data warehouses and data marts and a set of QVT transformations with which to automate this process. The advantage of this approach is that user requirements are captured from the early development stages of a data-warehousing project to automatically translate them into the entire data-warehousing platform, considering the different data marts. Finally, the authors provide screenshots of the CASE tools that support the approach, and a case study to show its benefits.

In this paper, the author investigates the effect on understanding of using business domain models that are constructed with Resource-Event-Agent (REA) modeling patterns. First, the author analyzes REA modeling structures to identify the enabling factors and the mechanisms by means of which users recognize these structures in a conceptual model and description of an information retrieval and interpretation task. Based on this understanding, the author hypothesizes positive effects on model understanding for situations where REA patterns can be recognized in both task and model. An experiment is then conducted to demonstrate a better understanding of models with REA patterns compared to information equivalent models without REA patterns. The results of this experiment indicate that REA patterns can be recognized with minimal prior patterns training and that the use of REA patterns leads to models that are easier to understand for novice model users.

Discovering services acquires importance as Service-Oriented Computing (SOC) becomes an adopted paradigm. SOC's most popular materializations, namely Web Services technologies, have different challenges related to service discovery and, in turn, many approaches have been proposed. As these approaches are different, one solution may be better than another according to certain requirements. In consequence, choosing a service discovery system is a hard task. To alleviate this task, this paper pro-

Web services are defined independently of any execution context. Due to their inherent autonomy and heterogeneity, it is difficult to examine the behaviour of composite services, especially in case of failures. This paper is interested in ensuring composite services reliability. Reliable composition is defined as a composition where all instance executions are correct from a transactional and business point of view. In this paper, the authors propose a transactional approach for ensuring reliable Web service compositions. The approach integrates the expressivity power of workflow models and the reliability of Advanced Transactional Models (ATM). This method offers flexibility for designers to specify their requirements in terms of control structure, using workflow patterns, and execution correctness. Contrary to ATM, the authors start from the designers' specifications to define the appropriate transactional mechanisms that ensure correct executions according to their requirements.

In Service Oriented Architecture (SOA), each application is designed with a set of reusable services and a business process. To retain the reusability of services, non-functional properties of applications must be separated from their functional properties. This paper investigates a model-driven development framework that separates non-functional properties from functional properties and manages them. This framework proposes two components: (1) a programming language, called BALLAD, for a new per-process strategy to specify non-functional properties for business processes, and (2) a graphical modeling method, called FM-SNFPs, to define a series of constraints among non-functional properties. BALLAD leverages aspects in aspect oriented programming/modeling. Each aspect is used to specify a set of non-functional properties that crosscut multiple services in a business process. FM-SNFPs leverage the notion of feature modeling to define constraints among non-functional properties like dependency and mutual exclusion constraints. BALLAD and FM-SNFPs free application developers from manually specifying, maintaining and validating non-functional properties and constraints for services one by one, reducing the burdens/costs in development and maintenance of service-oriented applications. This paper describes the design details of BALLAD and FM-SNFPs, and demonstrates how they are used in developing service-oriented applications. BALLAD significantly reduces the costs to implement and maintain non-functional properties in service-oriented applications.

This paper investigates the need for complementing automated verification of business process models with a validity analysis performed by human analysts. As business processes become increasingly automated through process aware information systems, the quality of process design becomes crucial. Although verification of process models has gained much attention, their validation, relating to the reachability of the process goal, has hardly been addressed. The paper investigates the need for model validation both theoretically and empirically. The authors present a theoretical analysis, showing that process model verification and validation are complementary in nature, and an empirical evaluation of the effectiveness of validity criteria in validating a process model. The theoretical analysis, which relates to different aspects of process model quality, shows that process model verification and validation are complementary in nature. The empirical findings corroborate the effectiveness of validity criteria and indicate that a systematic criteria-supported validity analysis improves the identification of validity problems in process models.

Data management (DM) has existed in conjunction with software development and the management of the full set of information technology (IT)-related components. However, it has been more than two decades since research into DM as it is practiced has been published. In this paper, the authors compare aspects of DM across a quarter-century timeline, obtaining data using comparable sets of subject matter experts. Using this information to observe the profession's evolution, the authors have updated the understanding of DM as it is practiced, giving additional insight into DM, including its current responsibilities, reporting structures, and perceptions of success, among other factors. The analysis indicates that successfully investing in DM presents current, real challenges to IT and organizations. Although DM is evolving away from purely operational responsibilities toward higher-level responsibilities, perceptions of success have fallen. This paper details the quarter-century comparison of DM practices, analyzes them, and draws conclusions.

The quality of conceptual models directly affects the quality of the understanding of the application domain and the quality of the final software products that are ultimately based on them. This paper describes a systematic literature review (SLR) of peer-reviewed conference and journal articles published

Chapter 15
A Meta-Analysis Comparing Relational and Semantic Models 394
Keng Siau, University of Nebraska – Lincoln, USA
Fiona Fui-Hoon Nah, University of Nebraska – Lincoln, USA
Qing Cao, Texas Tech University, USA

Data modeling is the sine quo non of systems development and one of the most widely researched topics in the database literature. In the past three decades, semantic data modeling has emerged as an alternative to traditional relational modeling. The majority of the research in data modeling suggests that the use of semantic data models leads to better performance; however, the findings are not conclusive and are sometimes inconsistent. The discrepancies that exist in the data modeling literature and the relatively low statistical power in the studies make meta-analysis a viable choice in analyzing and integrating the findings of these studies.

Chapter 16
Extending Agile Principles to Larger, Dynamic Software Projects: A Theoretical Assessment......... 410
Dinesh Batra, Florida International University, USA
Debra VanderMeer, Florida International University, USA
Kaushik Dutta, National University of Singapore, Singapore

The article evaluates the feasibility of extending agile principles to larger, dynamic, and possibly distributed software development projects by uncovering the theoretical basis for agile values and principles for achieving agility. The extant literature focuses mainly on one theory – complex adaptive systems – to support agile methods, although recent research indicates that the control theory and the adaptive structuration theory are also applicable. This article proposes that at least three other theories exist that are highly relevant: transaction cost economics, social exchange theory, and expectancy theory. By employing these theories, a rigorous analysis of the Agile Manifesto is conducted. Certain agile values and principles find theoretical support and can be applied to enhance agility dynamic projects regardless of size; some agile principles find no theoretical support while others find limited support. Based on the analysis and the ensuing discussion, the authors propose a framework with five dimensions of agility: process, design, people, outcomes, and adaptation.

Compilation of References 430

About the Contributors 468

Index.. 479

Preface

The book begins with "A Link-Based Ranking Algorithm for Semantic Web Resources: A Class-Oriented Approach Independent of Link Direction" by Hyunjung Park *et al.* The information space of the Semantic Web has different characteristics from that of the World Wide Web (WWW). One main difference is that in the Semantic Web, the direction of Resource Description Framework (RDF) links does not have the same meaning as the direction of hyperlinks in the WWW, because the link direction is determined not by a voting process but by a specific schema in the Semantic Web. Considering this fundamental difference, the authors propose a method for ranking Semantic Web resources independent of link directions and show the convergence of the algorithm and experimental results. This method focuses on the classes rather than the properties. The property weights are assigned depending on the relative significance of the property to the resource importance of each class. It solves some problems reported in prior studies, including the Tightly Knit Community (TKC) effect, as well as having higher accuracy and validity compared to existing methods.

Chapter 2, "A Study of Open Source Software Development from Control Perspective" by Bo Xu *et al.*, describes how open source software (OSS) has achieved great success and exerted significant impact on the software industry. OSS development takes online community as its organizational form, and developers voluntarily work for the project. In the project execution process, control aligns individual behaviors toward the organizational goals via the Internet and becomes critical to the success of OSS projects. This chapter investigates the control modes in OSS project communities, and their effects on project performance. Based on a web survey and archival data from OSS projects, it is revealed that three types of control modes, that is, outcome, clanship, and self-control, are effective in an OSS project community. The study contributes to a better understanding of OSS project organizations and processes, and provides advice for OSS development.

Next, Jesús Pardillo *et al.* investigate the customization of data warehouses. To customize a data warehouse, many organizations develop concrete data marts focused on a particular department or business process. However, the integrated development of these data marts is an open problem for many organizations due to the technical and organizational challenges involved during the design of these repositories as a complete solution. In this chapter, "An MDA Approach and QVT Transformations for the Integrated Development of Goal-Oriented Data Warehouses and Data Marts," the authors present a design approach that employs user requirements to build both corporate data warehouses and data marts in an integrated manner. The approach links information requirements to specific data marts elicited by using goal-oriented requirement engineering, which are automatically translated into the implementation of corresponding data repositories by means of model-driven engineering techniques. The authors provide two UML profiles that integrate the design of both data warehouses and data marts and a set of QVT transformations with which to automate this process. The advantage of this approach is that user requirements are captured from the early development stages of a data-warehousing project to automatically translate them into the entire data-warehousing platform, considering the different data marts. Finally, the authors provide screenshots of the CASE tools that support the approach, and a case study to show its benefits.

In the next chapter, "Understanding Business Domain Models: The Effect of Recognizing Resource-Event-Agent Conceptual Modeling Structures," Geert Poels investigates the effect on understanding of using business domain models that are constructed with Resource-Event-Agent (REA) modeling patterns. First, the author analyzes REA modeling structures to identify the enabling factors and the mechanisms by means of which users recognize these structures in a conceptual model and description of an information retrieval and interpretation task. Based on this understanding, the author hypothesizes positive effects on model understanding for situations where REA patterns can be recognized in both task and model. An experiment is then conducted to demonstrate a better understanding of models with REA patterns compared to information equivalent models without REA patterns. The results of this experiment indicate that REA patterns can be recognized with minimal prior patterns training and that the use of REA patterns leads to models that are easier to understand for novice model users.

In Chapter 5, Marco Crasso *et al.* conduct a review of research on "A Survey of Approaches to Web Service Discovery in Service-Oriented Architectures." Discovering services acquires importance as Service-Oriented Computing (SOC) becomes an adopted paradigm. SOC's most popular materializations, namely Web Services technologies, have different challenges related to service discovery and, in turn, many approaches have been proposed. As these approaches are different, one solution may be better than another according to certain requirements. In consequence, choosing a service discovery system is a hard task. To alleviate this task, this chapter proposes eight criteria, based on the requirements for discovering services within common service-oriented environments, allowing the characterization of discovery systems. These criteria cover functional and non-functional aspects of approaches to service discovery. The results of the characterization of 22 contemporary approaches and potential research directions for the area are also shown.

K. Vidyasankar and Gottfried Vossen describe "Multi-Level Modeling of Web Service Compositions with Transactional Properties." Web services have become popular as a vehicle for the design, integration, composition, reuse, and deployment of distributed and heterogeneous software. However, although industry standards for the description, composition, and orchestration of Web services have been under development, their conceptual underpinnings are not fully understood. Conceptual models for service specification are rare, as are investigations based on them. This chapter presents and studies a multi-level service composition model that perceives service specification as going through several levels of abstraction. It starts from transactional operations at the lowest level and abstracts into activities at higher levels that are close to the service provider or end user. The authors treat service composition from a specification and execution point of view, where the former is about composition logic and the latter about transactional guarantees. Consequently, the model allows for the specification of a number of transactional properties, such as atomicity and guaranteed termination, at all levels. Different ways of achieving the composition properties and implications of the model are presented. The authors also discuss how the model subsumes practical proposals like the OASIS Business Transaction Protocol, Sun's WS-TXM, and execution aspects of the BPEL4WS standard.

Next, "Service Composition and Interaction in a SOC Middleware Supporting Separation of Concerns with Flows and Views" by Dickson K. W. Chiu *et al.* explores Service-Oriented Computing (SOC), which has recently gained attention both within industry and academia; however, its characteristics cannot be easily solved using existing distributed computing technologies. Composition and interaction issues have been the central concerns, because SOC applications are composed of heterogeneous and distributed processes. To tackle the complexity of inter-organizational service integration, the authors propose a methodology to decompose complex process requirements into different types of flows, such as control, data, exception, and security. The subset of each type of flow necessary for the interactions with each partner can be determined in each service. These subsets collectively constitute a process view, based on which interactions can be systematically designed and managed for system integration through service composition. The authors illustrate how the proposed SOC middleware, named FlowEngine, implements and manages these flows with contemporary Web services technologies. An experimental case study in an e-governmental environment further demonstrates how the methodology can facilitate the design of complex inter-organizational processes.

Web services are defined independently of any execution context. Due to their inherent autonomy and heterogeneity, it is difficult to examine the behaviour of composite services, especially in case of failures. Chapter 8, "Ensuring Customised Transactional Reliability of Composite Services" by Sami Bhiri *et al.* is interested in ensuring composite services reliability. Reliable composition is defined as a composition where all instance executions are correct from a transactional and business point of view. In this chapter, the authors propose a transactional approach for ensuring reliable Web service compositions. The approach integrates the expressivity power of workflow models and the reliability of Advanced Transactional Models (ATM). This method offers flexibility for designers to specify their requirements in terms of control structure, using workflow patterns, and execution correctness. Contrary to ATM, the authors start from the designers' specifications to define the appropriate transactional mechanisms that ensure correct executions according to their requirements.

In the following chapter, Hiroshi Wada *et al.* write about "Leveraging Early Aspects in End-to-End Model Driven Development for Non- Functional Properties in Service Oriented Architecture." In Service Oriented Architecture (SOA), each application is designed with a set of reusable services and a business process. To retain the reusability of services, non-functional properties of applications must be separated from their functional properties. This chapter investigates a model-driven development framework that separates non-functional properties from functional properties and manages them. This framework proposes two components: (1) a programming language, called BALLAD, for a new per-process strategy to specify non-functional properties for business processes, and (2) a graphical modeling method, called FM-SNFPs, to define a series of constraints among non-functional properties. BALLAD leverages aspects in aspect oriented programming/modeling. Each aspect is used to specify a set of non-functional properties that crosscut multiple services in a business process. FM-SNFPs leverage the notion of feature modeling to define constraints among non-functional properties like dependency and mutual exclusion constraints. BALLAD and FM-SNFPs free application developers from manually specifying, maintaining and validating non-functional properties and constraints for services one by one, reducing the burdens/costs in development and maintenance of service-oriented applications. This chapter describes the design details of BALLAD and FM-SNFPs, and demonstrates how they are used in developing service-oriented applications. BALLAD significantly reduces the costs to implement and maintain non-functional properties in service-oriented applications.

Chapter 10, "Complementing Business Process Verification by Validity Analysis: A Theoretical and Empirical Evaluation" by Pnina Soffer and Maya Kaner, investigates the need for complementing automated verification of business process models with a validity analysis performed by human analysts.

As business processes become increasingly automated through process aware information systems, the quality of process design becomes crucial. Although verification of process models has gained much attention, their validation, relating to the reachability of the process goal, has hardly been addressed. The chapter investigates the need for model validation both theoretically and empirically. The authors present a theoretical analysis, showing that process model verification and validation are complementary in nature, and an empirical evaluation of the effectiveness of validity criteria in validating a process model. The theoretical analysis, which relates to different aspects of process model quality, shows that process model verification and validation are complementary in nature. The empirical findings corroborate the effectiveness of validity criteria and indicate that a systematic criteria-supported validity analysis improves the identification of validity problems in process models.

In "Data Management and Data Administration: Assessing 25 Years of Practice," Peter Aiken *et al.* take a retrospective view of Data Management (DM), which has existed in conjunction with software development and the management of the full set of information technology (IT)-related components. However, it has been more than two decades since research into DM as it is practiced has been published. In this chapter, the authors compare aspects of DM across a quarter-century timeline, obtaining data using comparable sets of subject matter experts. Using this information to observe the profession's evolution, the authors have updated the understanding of DM as it is practiced, giving additional insight into DM, including its current responsibilities, reporting structures, and perceptions of success, among other factors. The analysis indicates that successfully investing in DM presents current, real challenges to IT and organizations. Although DM is evolving away from purely operational responsibilities toward higher-level responsibilities, perceptions of success have fallen. This chapter details the quarter-century comparison of DM practices, analyzes them, and draws conclusions.

The quality of conceptual models directly affects the quality of the understanding of the application domain and the quality of the final software products that are ultimately based on them. "A Systematic Literature Review on the Quality of UML Models," by Marcela Genero *et al.*, describes a systematic literature review (SLR) of peer-reviewed conference and journal articles published from 1997 through 2009 on the quality of conceptual models written in UML, undertaken to understand the state-of-the-art, and then identify any gaps in current research. Six digital libraries were searched, and 266 papers dealing specifically with the quality of UML models were identified and classified into five dimensions: type of model quality, type of evidence, type of research result, type of diagram, and research goal. The results indicate that most research focuses on semantic quality, with relatively little on semantic completeness; as such, this chapter examines new modeling methods vs. quality frameworks and metrics, as well as quality assurance vs. understanding quality issues. The results also indicate that more empirical research is needed to develop a theoretical understanding of conceptual model quality. The classification scheme developed in this chapter can serve as a guide for both researchers and practitioners.

In "Semi-Automatic Composition of Situational Methods," Anat Aharoni and Iris Reinhartz-Berger define situational methods as approaches to the development of software systems that are designed and constructed to fit particular circumstances that often refer to project characteristics. One common way to create situational methods is to reuse method components, which are the building blocks of development methods. For this purpose, method components must be stored in a method base, and then retrieved and composed specifically for the situation in hand. Most approaches in the field of situational method engineering require the expertise of method engineers to support the retrieval and composition of method components. Furthermore, this is usually done in an ad-hoc manner and for pre-defined situations. In this chapter, the authors propose an approach, supported by a tool that creates situational methods semi-automatically. This approach refers to structural and behavioral considerations and a wide variety of characteristics when comparing method components and composing them into situational methods. The resultant situational methods are stored in the method base for future usage and composition. Based on an experimental study of the approach, the authors show that it provides correct and suitable draft situational methods, which human evaluators have assessed as relevant for the given situations.

The next chapter, "DocBase: Design, Implementation, and Evaluation of a Document Database for XML" by Arijit Sengupta and Ramesh Venkataraman introduces a complete storage and retrieval architecture for a database environment for XML documents. DocBase, a prototype system based on this architecture, uses a flexible storage and indexing technique to allow highly expressive queries without the necessity of mapping documents to other database formats. DocBase is an integration of several techniques that include: (i) a formal model called Heterogeneous Nested Relations (HNR), (ii) a conceptual model XER (Extensible Entity Relationship), (ii) formal query languages (Document Algebra and Calculus), (iii) a practical query language (Document SQL or DSQL), (iv) a visual query formulation method with QBT (Query By Templates), and (v) the DocBase query processing architecture. This chapter focuses on the overall architecture of DocBase including implementation details, describes the details of the query-processing framework, and presents results from various performance tests. The chapter summarizes experimental and usability analyses to demonstrate its feasibility as a general architecture for native as well as embedded document manipulation methods.

Keng Siau *et al.* develop "A Meta-Analysis Comparing Relational and Semantic Models" in the next chapter. Data modeling is the *sine quo non* of systems development and one of the most widely researched topics in the database literature. In the past three decades, semantic data modeling has emerged as an alternative to traditional relational modeling. The majority of the research in data modeling suggests that the use of semantic data models leads to better performance; however, the findings are not conclusive and are sometimes inconsistent. The discrepancies that exist in the data modeling literature and the relatively low statistical power in the studies make meta-analysis a viable choice in analyzing and integrating the findings of these studies.

The final chapter, "Extending Agile Principles to Larger, Dynamic Software Projects: A Theoretical Assessment" by Dinesh Batra *et al.* evaluates the feasibility of extending agile principles to larger, dynamic, and possibly distributed software development projects by uncovering the theoretical basis for agile values and principles for achieving agility. The extant literature focuses mainly on one theory—complex adaptive systems—to support agile methods, although recent research indicates that the control theory and the adaptive structuration theory are also applicable. This chapter proposes that at least three other theories exist that are highly relevant: transaction cost economics, social exchange theory, and expectancy theory. By employing these theories, a rigorous analysis of the Agile Manifesto is conducted. Certain agile values and principles find theoretical support and can be applied to enhance agility dynamic projects regardless of size; some agile principles find no theoretical support while others find limited support. Based on the analysis and the ensuing discussion, the authors propose a framework with five dimensions of agility: process, design, people, outcomes, and adaptation.

Keng Siau
University of Nebraska-Lincoln, USA

Chapter 1
A Link-Based Ranking Algorithm for Semantic Web Resources: A Class-Oriented Approach Independent of Link Direction

Hyunjung Park
Seoul National University, Korea

Sangkyu Rho
Seoul National University, Korea

Jinsoo Park
Institute of Management Research, Seoul National University, Korea

ABSTRACT

The information space of the Semantic Web has different characteristics from that of the World Wide Web (WWW). One main difference is that in the Semantic Web, the direction of Resource Description Framework (RDF) links does not have the same meaning as the direction of hyperlinks in the WWW, because the link direction is determined not by a voting process but by a specific schema in the Semantic Web. Considering this fundamental difference, the authors propose a method for ranking Semantic Web resources independent of link directions and show the convergence of the algorithm and experimental results. This method focuses on the classes rather than the properties. The property weights are assigned depending on the relative significance of the property to the resource importance of each class. It solves some problems reported in prior studies, including the Tightly Knit Community (TKC) effect, as well as having higher accuracy and validity compared to existing methods.

DOI: 10.4018/978-1-4666-2044-5.ch001

INTRODUCTION

The Semantic Web can be regarded as a smart web designed to understand the requests of people and machines to use Web contents (Berners-Lee, 2001), and one of the most common requests may be the ranking of Semantic Web resources. Therefore the Web had better have some understanding of the concept of ranking, and the ranking mechanism adequate for a specific domain could be defined in the domain ontology. However, there have not been many studies on ranking in the Semantic Web, while there have been extensive studies on the evaluation of the World Wide Web.

Traditionally, the importance of a particular Web page is estimated based on the number of keywords found on the page, which is subject to manipulation (Marchiori, 1997). In contrast, link analysis methods such as Google's PageRank (Brin et al., 1998; Haveliwala, 1999; Page et al., 1998) capitalize on the information that is inherent in the link structure of a Web graph. PageRank considers a page important if it is referred to by many other pages. The degree of importance also increases if the importance of the referring pages is high. Kleinberg's Hypertext-Induced Topic Selection (HITS) algorithm (Kleinberg, 1998) is another link-structure-based ranking algorithm for Web pages. The HITS algorithm differs from PageRank in that it utilizes two kinds of scores: an authority score and a hub score. If a page has a high authority score, it is an authority on a given topic and many pages refer to it. A page with a high hub score links to many authoritative pages. The link-structure-based ranking method has become an essential tool for using WWW, and its effectiveness and efficiency have been widely recognized.

On the other hand, information from the Semantic Web can be expressed using a Resource Description Framework (RDF) graph (Klyne et al., 2004; Manola et al., 2004). An RDF graph, in which a resource and a property are expressed as a node and a link, respectively, is similar to a WWW graph in which a Web page and a hyperlink are expressed as a node and a link, respectively. Consequently, research on methods for applying the link-structure-based ranking technique of WWW to an RDF graph of the Semantic Web has great significance. The WWW graph can be thought of as an enormous class of the Web pages with only one recursive property called a 'refer to' property, so to speak. An RDF schema, in contrast, can have various classes and properties, and each link corresponding to a property can have an opposite direction depending on whether it is an active or a passive voice. As a result, RDF schemas can have many different forms because the direction of each link is changeable, even if they describe the same thing, and the direction of an RDF link does not have the same meaning as that of a WWW hyperlink. In WWW, if a page is pointed to by a directing link, we can tell that the pointed page must have some useful information. PageRank and HITS are based on this basic assumption.

Although there were some attempts made to modify the HITS algorithm to rank query results retrieved from RDF knowledge bases (Bamba & Mukherjea, 2004; Mukherjea & Bamba, 2004; Mukherjea et al., 2005), this fundamental difference has been overlooked. These attempts used the objectivity and subjectivity scores of a resource, which correspond to the authority and hub scores of a page, respectively, from Kleinberg's algorithm. The objectivity score of a certain resource is calculated by summing up all the subjectivity scores of the resources linking to it after they are multiplied by appropriate property weights. The subjectivity score of a resource is calculated similarly. If the direction of a link in a triple is changed by a schema, the objectivity and the subjectivity of the triple are reversed, causing the objectivity scores and the subjectivity scores of the linked resources to be changed. Besides this unobserved problem, there is a reported limitation of the Tightly Knit Community (TKC) effect where resources that are less important but densely connected are given higher scores than those that are more important but sparsely connected in their approach.

In this paper, we examine the resource-ranking problem from a different perspective and propose a new algorithm. We argue for a class-oriented approach, which is independent of link direction. The property weights are assigned depending on the relative significance of the property to the resource importance of each class. The resulting algorithm alleviates problems resulting from the TKC effect and gives an explanation for other limitations described in previous studies. The experiment was designed to examine the validity of ranking results, and a mathematical analysis is given, which shows the convergence of our algorithm and allows the matrix calculation procedure to be simplified. The ranking algorithm proposed in this paper will be applicable to various domains, if they are thoroughly expressed with almost all the necessary classes and properties. Compared with the previous method, our approach relies on more structural federation and needs to be consolidated by domain experts. Our algorithm is appropriate for the domain where more objective ranking results are needed.

The paper is organized as follows. First, it briefly reviews essential literature pertaining to the previous research on ranking algorithms. It then explains the basic concepts of our proposed new algorithm. The proposed algorithm is tested against the previous algorithm and the results are discussed in light of future applications and possible improvements.

RELATED RESEARCH

Kleinberg's Authority Score and Hub Score

The PageRank and HITS algorithms, as mentioned above, can be regarded as representative ranking methods for assigning the degree of importance of each Web page by analyzing its link structure. The HITS algorithm uses two types of scores for ranking the Web pages: an authority score and a hub score (Kleinberg, 1998). An authority score describes the number and quality of other pages that link to the page being ranked; a hub score describes the number and quality of other pages linked to by the page being ranked. The authority score of a certain page is calculated by summing up all the hub scores of the pages referring to it. The hub score of a page is calculated by summing up all the authority scores of the pages it refers to. For example, the authority score of document a in Figure 1 is determined by adding up all the hub scores of pages ①, ②, and ③, and the hub score of a is determined by adding up all the authority scores of documents ④, ⑤, and ⑥.

Resource-Ranking Algorithm for the Semantic Web

The information space of the Semantic Web, having various objects that can be ranked, is much more complex than that of the WWW. Many researchers have investigated link structures with particular focus on the different types of ranked objects.

Maedche et al. (2001) and Maedche and Staab (2002) studied the ranking of query results retrieved from an F-Logic knowledge base depend-

Figure 1. Kleinberg's calculation of authority and hub scores

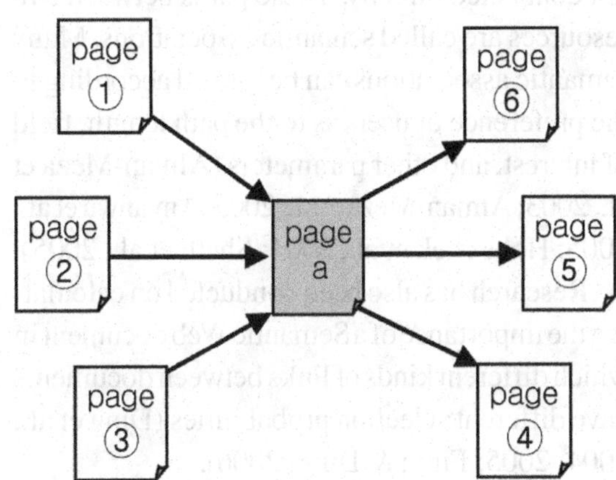

ing on the similarity of knowledge bases. Bamba and Mukherjea (2004), Mukherjea and Bamba (2004), and Mukherjea et al. (2005) studied the ranking of query results from an RDF knowledge base. Stimulated by the idea of Reverse PageRank, Wu and Li (2007) proposed a resource-ranking approach that applies an object-level link analysis ranking algorithm reversely to the direction of relations and consistently across the schema graph and data graph. Graves et al. (2008) proposed a graph-theoretic method to rank nodes in an RDF graph based on the notion of centrality. Hurtado et al. (2009) considered about querying semi-structured data such as RDF without knowing its structure and proposed an approximate matching framework to incorporate edit distance as well as certain RDFS inference rules, thereby capturing both syntactic and semantic approximations. Franz et al. (2009) modeled the Semantic Web by a 3-dimensional tensor that enables the seamless representation of arbitrary semantic links and presented TripleRank which captures the additional latent semantics of Semantic Web data by means of statistical methods for faceted authority ranking in an RDF knowledge base. Their measure could be used to sort the nodes returned by a SPARQL query or to find the important concepts in an RDF graph.

The ranking of semantic associations can be considered as a second group of objects. Two resources on an RDF graph can be connected through other resources and links lying on the path from one resource to the other, even if they are not connected directly. These paths between two resources are called semantic associations. Many semantic associations can be ranked according to the preference of users as to the path length, field of interest, and other parameters (Alman-Meza et al., 2003; Alman-Meza et al., 2005; Anyanwu et al., 2005; Halaschek et al., 2004; Sheth et al., 2005).

Research has also been conducted on calculating the importance of a Semantic Web document in which different kinds of links between documents have different selection probabilities (Ding et al., 2004, 2005; Finin & Ding, 2006).

All of these studies are related in that they are based on link structure. For example, if the degree of resource importance is determined, this information can be used as input for the ranking of semantic associations. This is based on the assumption that the more important the resources on a semantic association path are, the more important the path becomes.

RDF, RDF Schema, and RDF Query Language

The RDF is a data model used to describe a resource by expressing its properties, or the relationship between it and other resource with a Uniform Resource Identifier reference (URIref) (Klyne et al., 2004; Manola et al., 2004). The necessary vocabularies and basic assumptions for describing the composition of a domain and the interactions among classes can be defined using an RDF schema (Brickley et al., 2004).

The RDF resources can be searched using RDF query languages such as SPARQL (Prud'hommeaux & Seaborne, 2007). Although the W3C Candidate Recommendation for SPARQL has been published and SPARQL is contained in the Semantic Web layer cake published by Tim Berners-Lee (Berners-Lee, 2005), SPARQL does not have the capability to rank resultant dataset based on resource importance except for the text-oriented sorting function, like other RDF query languages.

Ranking Algorithm for Semantic Web Resources: Objectivity and Subjectivity Score

Bamba and Mukherjea (2004), Mukherjea and Bamba (2004), and Mukherjea et al. (2005) modified Kleinberg's algorithm and applied it to the ranking of query results from an RDF knowledge base by the degree of resource importance. As their studies are often referred to in this paper, we will refer to their studies as 'the prior research' or 'the prior algorithm', and their approach as 'the predicate-oriented approach' in this paper.

Mukherjea and Bamba (2004) introduced the weight concept when treating RDF graphs consisting of various properties to control the amount of increase in scores. They noticed that the weights for the objectivity and subjectivity scores may not be the same, but can vary depending on the 'predicate.' For the triple (INVENTOR, *invented*, PATENT) in Figure 2, the subjectivity and objectivity weights of *invented* are 1 and 0.4, respectively. The subjectivity score of the INVENTOR is the sum of the objectivity scores of the PATENT, while the objectivity score of the PATENT is obtained by multiplying the subjectivity score of the INVENTOR by the objectivity weight of 0.4. This is to restrain the objectivity score of a patent from getting higher in the same way as it did with the inventor, simply because there are many inventors included in the same patent. Figure 3 shows a portion of an RDF graph where the property weights have been set by this predicate-oriented approach.

If the objectivity and subjectivity weights are determined for each property based on the characteristic of the property, the weights of all the links on an RDF graph are set up accordingly. If the importance flows with the same proportion in both directions, the objectivity and subjectivity weights are all equal to 1. If the proportions are not the same in both directions, the stronger is set to 1 first, and the weaker is determined in comparison with the stronger, with the estimated relative ratio being varied depending on the user or context. As a result, the objectivity score of resource r is found by multiplying the subjectivity score of a resource by an objectivity weight and summing up weighted subjectivity scores for all the links connecting other resources to resource r. Similarly, the subjectivity score of resource r is found by multiplying the objectivity score of a resource by a subjectivity weight and summing up the weighted objectivity scores for all the links connecting resource r to other resources.

Figure 2. Weights of Invented

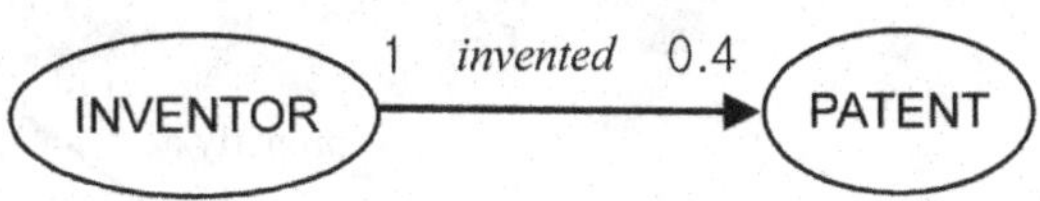

Mukherjea et al. (2005) reported the following limitations after applying their ranking algorithm to the Semantic Web systems such as Unified Medical Language System (UMLS), Biomedical Patent, and TAP. First, their algorithm is effective only when the Semantic Web system clearly states most of the information related to the domain. In other words, the ratio of links to nodes should be high, or resources should be described in detail for their algorithm to properly work. Second, in cases where there are many links connecting a group of nodes, the nodes in the group could receive a higher score than more important nodes that are more sparsely connected. This phenomenon is called the TKC effect and is one of the fundamental problems in designing a link analysis algorithm. Third, it is possible for a resource to receive a higher score, not because it is important, but simply because it is very common and, as a consequence, has many links pointing to it.

CLASS-ORIENTED WEIGHT ASSIGNMENT ALGORITHM

Basic Concepts

From the Predicate-Oriented to the Class-Oriented

To address the limitations of the predicate-oriented weight-setting method mentioned in the previous section, we propose a new resource-ranking algorithm using a class-oriented approach in which we shift focus from predicates-based to classes-based on the following ideas.

Figure 3. Weights from the predicate-oriented approach

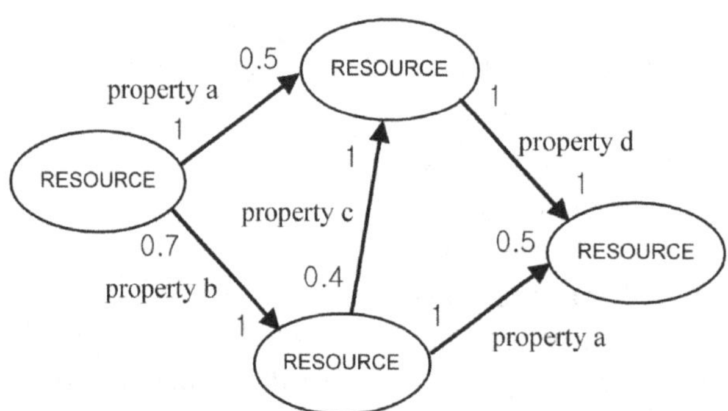

First, querying RDF knowledge bases will usually return numerous resources belonging to the same class, thus an evaluation standard for that class will be necessary. It seems valid to use one standard for the Web page ranking since the WWW can be regarded, so to speak, as one document class having a huge number of instances. In the Semantic Web, however, there are many heterogeneous classes, thus applying a different appraisal standard for each class is more reasonable.

Second, assigning weights with the class-oriented approach makes checking for missing information easier. A perfectly described class will have all the essential properties for determining the importance of a resource belonging to that class. Even if the prior algorithm only works well when the information is descriptive enough, it is difficult to decide whether the description is reasonable using the predicate-oriented approach. If many properties are connected to a resource, it may seem to be perfect, but many of them may be irrelevant to the importance of the resource.

Third, the predicate-oriented approach makes it difficult to express the difference between the case where two directly linked resources interact with the same high intensity, and the case where they interact with the same low intensity, since the weights are set to 1 in both cases. Additionally, there is a case where the weight of a property should be changed depending on the class the property is connected to. In Figure 4, the influencing power of the property '*graduated_from*' can vary depending on whether it relates to the class of PROFESSOR or the class of BUSINESSPERSON. It would be reasonable to assume that educational background is more important to a professor than to a businessperson.

Shifting the focus from predicate to class, we can set the weights of properties connected to a class, weighing their relative importance in determining the importance of the resources of that class. When doing this, we can assign a weight of 0 to a certain property if it has nothing to do with the resource importance for that class and does not cause the property to affect the overall importance of the corresponding resources. We expect this method could be a promising solution for the TKC effect.

Fourth, the class-oriented approach is similar to the evaluation method of humans where different items are assigned specific weights and then summed up to determine the weighted average. Most items, namely, properties, that have been used for various evaluations can be regarded as data-type properties that are unrelated to the link connection; however, there are some items for which a more objective and qualitative measure is needed rather than a simple quantitative one (Ren & Taylor, 2007). For example, when considering a paper for scholarly evaluation, analyzing the link structure in relation to other papers and

Figure 4. Property weights varying depending on the class

determining how much the paper is referenced by other papers would be more objective than assigning an importance score depending on the journal where it is printed. Therefore, in the Semantic Web where the link structure can be determined between resources, it is reasonable to keep the general evaluation method and consider a qualitative measure based on the link structure for each item. Examples for the class-oriented approach are shown in Figure 11 and Figure 19 in the Appendix.

Introduction of Interaction Concept for Overcoming Schema Diversity Constraints

Since an RDF graph can change depending on the directions of links in the RDF schema, Kleinberg's algorithm should be carefully applied to an RDF graph. If an RDF graph is changed, the objectivity and subjectivity score of each resource is also affected, even if the overall content of information remains the same. Figure 5 shows an example of such a situation. The property *'published'* is an active voice, while *'published_by'* is a passive voice. The directions of the links are opposite from each other, but each of the two triples has the same meaning. The RESEARCHER of the first triple plays the role of subjectivity, while it plays that of objectivity in the second triple. It is natural that the subjectivity score of the RESEARCHER is increased in the first triple, while the objectivity score of the RESEARCHER is increased in the second triple. If there is only one property, this will not matter – we can choose either of the two voices – and the comparison of objectivity or subjectivity score will be valid.

RDF schemas, however, include diverse properties and each property has its own direction, producing various link combinations. Therefore, we can get undesirable results if we separately compare the objectivity scores or subjectivity scores between resources, as Kleinberg did with the Web pages.

Even if the prior research tried to modify Kleinberg's to be better suited for RDF knowledge base, it does not seem to be a fundamental solution. Let us consider the schema in Figure 6. INVENTOR and PATENT are connected with the property *'invented'* in Figure 6. Suppose all the other links are outgoing from INVENTOR and PATENT. In this schema, the subjectivity score of INVENTOR will go up and the objectivity score of the PATENT will go down. Although they used a lower objectivity weight to reduce the influence power of the INVENTOR on the PATENT, the influence of the INVENTOR on the PATENT may be greater than that of PATENT on

Figure 5. Subjectivity and objectivity dependent on the statement voice of the property

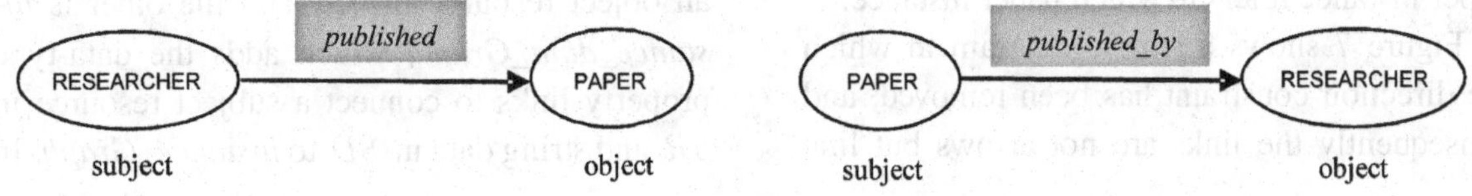

Figure 6. Varying influence depending on the schema rather than on the weight

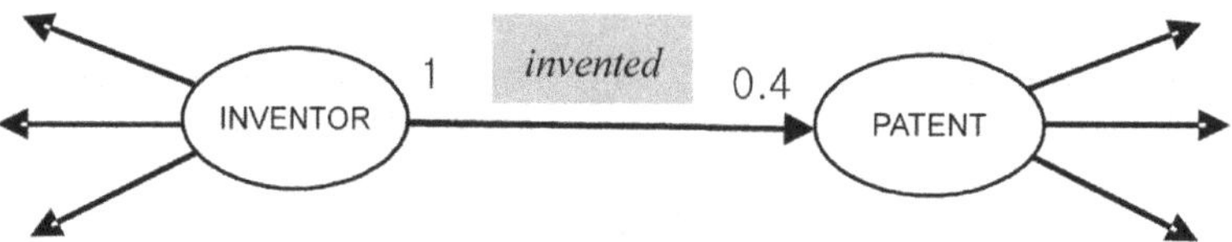

the INVENTOR because of the schema. Another significant problem is that when two resources in one triple give and receive the other's score, the score represents not the whole importance but the partial one; that is, the objectivity or subjectivity score, which varies with the schema.

The diversity of the RDF schema has been mentioned in the prior studies; however, in the end, they ranked resources comparing the objectivity or subjectivity score individually, or comparing the score gained by summing up the objectivity and subjectivity scores of a resource with an arbitrarily set ratio.

We introduce an entirely new concept. We compute only one overall importance score for a resource. When resources interact with one another, they use only one kind of score: the intensity of interaction being controlled by the property weights. The directions of links are of no concern in our method. In other words, whether a resource is objective or subjective is of little importance—it is just the linkage between a pair of resources that matters. But there is a case where the direction counts. If a property is recursive, namely, the domain and range of the property is the same class, it is necessary to clarify which instance is subjective or objective by the link direction. For example, for the *'refers_to'* property connecting two paper instances of the PAPER, if the link does not have an arrow, it would be difficult to distinguish between objectivity and subjectivity weights because there is no way to know which paper instance refers to which paper instance.

Figure 7 shows a simple diagram in which the direction constraint has been removed, and consequently the links are not arrows but line segments. In Figure 7, the importance score of a RESEARCHER is the sum of the importance score of the PAPER he/she published, the PATENT he/she invented, the BOOK he/she wrote, the UNIVERSITY he/she graduated from, multiplied by the surrounding weights 0.6, 0.2, 0.19, and 0.01, respectively, before being added together. But for ease of explanation, or for rapid readability, there will be cases when we use the phrase, objectivity weight or subjectivity weight, and arrows instead of line segments.

Resource-Ranking Algorithm and Matrix Operation

We have developed a resource-ranking algorithm based on our new concepts, as explained above. We calculate only one importance score for one resource instead of objectivity and subjectivity scores. The previous predicate-oriented weight-setting method will be referred to as 'Predicate-Two', and our class-oriented weight-setting method as 'Class-One' for the convenience of description.

Let (C, P, IR, SD) be the information space of the Semantic Web designated by an RDF schema, where C represents classes, P refers to properties, IR are instance resources of a class, and SD represents string data. We can extract two kinds of instance graphs from this space. One is *instance_Graph,* which includes only the object property links that connect a subject resource to an object resource in IR, and the other is *instance_data_Graph,* which adds the data-type property links to connect a subject resource in IR and string data in SD to *instance_Graph.* In

Figure 7. Weight-setting example of the properties of the RESEARCHER class

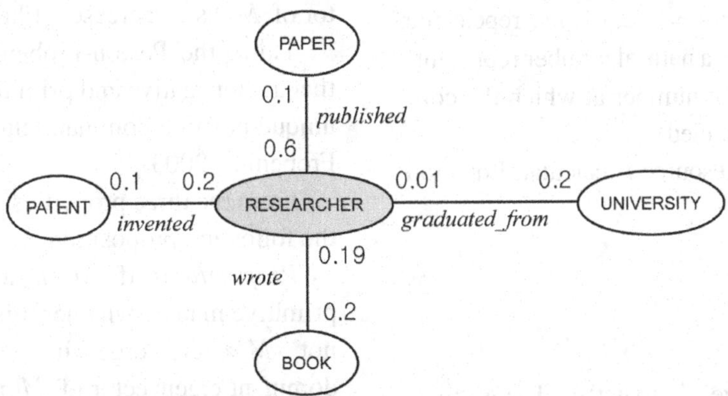

other words, in *instance_Graph*, resources in *IR* are expressed as nodes, and relationships formed among these resources as links. The *instance_data_Graph* is an expansion of *instance_Graph* for including significant data-type property links and the related data values as dummy nodes.

Calculation of Resource Importance

Weight Assignment of Properties

Equation 1 is an equation for *instance_Graph* in which property weights are assigned. On the RDF schema level, the objectivity and subjectivity weights are set according to the relative importance of the property to the class with which it is connected. Equation 1 is a condition for weight assignment of class C, $objWt_{(D,C)}$ being an objectivity weight of the property of which the domain is class D and range is class C, and $subjWt_{(C,D)}$ being a subjectivity weight of the property of which the domain is class C and range is class D. To distinguish from an instance, we use capital letters for class.

$$\sum_{D} objWt_{(D,C)} + \sum_{D} subWt_{(C,D)} = 1 \qquad (1)$$

Iterative Algorithm for Resource Importance Calculation

For *instance_Graph* $G = (V, E)$, let $V = \{1, 2, \cdots, N\}$ be a set of resources having N number of resources, and E be a set of directional links which links a resource r $(1 \le r \le N)$ in V to another resource k $(1 \le k \le N)$ in V. We can assign two kinds of property weights for each link in E in accordance with the property weights set on the schema earlier.

After setting the property weights, we assume the following calculation steps for our Class-One. At first, we can define the weight matrix M as follows:

$$M_{rk} = w_{rk},$$

where w_{rk} $(0 \le w_{rk} \le 1)$ is the weight to be multiplied with the importance score of resource k when calculating the importance score of resource r. The weight is set depending on the relative importance of the related property and can be an objectivity weight or a subjectivity weight for the link connecting resource r and k. In the following algorithm, g^r is the importance score of resource r $(1 \le r \le N)$, and g without the superscript is $(N \times 1)$ vector containing all the importance scores of N resources.

1. **Initialization:** $g_0^r = 1, (1 \le r \le N)$.
2. **Iteration:** For $i = 1, 2, \cdots, m$, repeat the following (m : a natural number representing the iteration number at which the convergence is attained).
   a. For each resource r, calculate Equation 2 below.

$$g_i^{\bullet r} = \sum_k g_{i-1}^k \times w_{rk} \qquad (2)$$

   b. Normalize $g_i^{\bullet}$, to get g_i. The normalization condition is the equation below:

$$\sum_r (g_i^r)^2 = 1.$$

3. Return g_m.

Convergence of the Iterative Resource Importance Algorithm

The iterative algorithm presented above is based on the property that the score vectors gained at each iteration step converge in a certain direction. If the direction of a vector converges, the ranking of the components of that vector will no longer change. In this way, the ultimate vector can be used for the ranking of resources. There are three proven properties related to the analysis of the convergence of our algorithm.

First, if M is a diagonalizable matrix with a unique dominant eigenvalue and z is not orthogonal to the dominant eigenvector of M, then $M^i z$ converges in the direction of the dominant eigenvector of M as i increases (Burden & Faires, 2001; Golub & Van Loan, 1989; Ehrlich, 1969).

Second, if M is a nondiagonalizable matrix with a unique dominant eigenvalue and z is not orthogonal to the subspace of eigenvectors and generalized eigenvectors of M associated with the dominant eigenvalue, then $M^i z$ also converges in the direction of the dominant eigenvector of M as i increases (Ehrlich, 1969).

Third, the Perron-Frobenius theorem states that a nonnegative and primitive matrix A has a unique positive dominant eigenvalue (Perron & Frobenius, 2003).

From the three properties above, we can infer the following proposition.

Proposition: If M is a nonnegative and primitive matrix, whether it is diagonalizable or not, $M^i z$ converges in the direction of the dominant eigenvector of M as i increases (M being diagonalizable, z should not be orthogonal to the dominant eigenvector of M, $_{\text{and}}$ M being nondiagonalizable, z should not be orthogonal to the subspace of eigenvectors and generalized eigenvectors of M associated with the dominant eigenvalue$_{)}$.

If we convert Equation 2 into a matrix form for N resources, it becomes $g_i^{\bullet} = Mg_{i-1}$. This becomes $g_1^{\bullet} = Mg_0$ when $i = 1$, resulting in $g_1 = n_1 Mg_0$ when n_1 is a constant multiplied during the normalization procedure. When $i = 2$ continuously, the matrix expression becomes $g_2^{\bullet} = Mg_1 = n_1 M^2 g_0$, resulting in $g_2 = n_1 n_2 M^2 g_0$ when n_2 is a normalization constant. If followed through to the ith iteration, as before, the importance score vector g_i becomes a unit vector to $M^i g_0$. M is a nonnegative weight matrix and can be considered to be primitive; according to the proposition, the ultimate importance score vector is found to be the unit dominant eigenvector of M, when g_0 is consistent with the respective conditions.

Example of a Class-Oriented Weight Matrix

Suppose a very simple domain containing only one instance per class, with classes constituted and property weight given as in Figure 8. The weight matrix M is constructed as shown in Figure 9 for the information given from Figure 8.

Figure 8. A class-oriented weight assignment

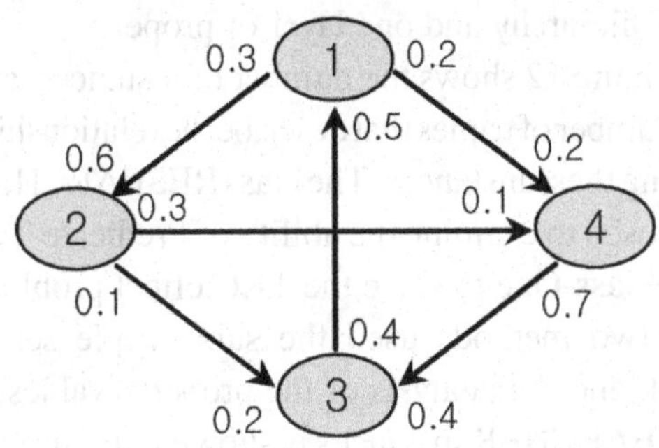

Implementation of the Class-Oriented Resource Importance Algorithm

Based on the results of mathematical analysis, we developed the following algorithm to determine the importance of a resource.

1. Assign the objectivity and subjectivity weights of properties for each class on the schema.
2. Create the weight matrix M for *instance_Graph.*
3. Calculate the resource importance score vector from the dominant eigenvector of the matrix M.

The first step above relies on Equation 1. The property weights can be varied depending on the context or user. If the case needs to be highly objective and the public criteria should be applied, careful consideration must be given to the selection of significant properties of each class and determination of weights for these properties. The regression coefficients can be used as the property weights (NRC, 2003) for cases in which independent variables are measurable items corresponding to property values extracted from factor analysis and the dependent variable is a qualitative evaluation score for a class instance rated by a domain expert. This kind of study, however, is beyond the scope of this paper, which aims to establish a robust framework that handles various set of weights, and probable weights are set by rule of thumb in the experiment.

Process Implementation

The process from the construction of the RDF knowledge base to the ranking of query results is shown in Figure 10. The RDF triples are assumed to have been extracted from *instance_Graph,* and triple data were composed using MS Excel. The weight matrices were created from this triple information using MS Visual Basic, and MatLab 7.0.4 was used to manipulate the weight matrices.

EXPERIMENT AND EVALUATION

This section will demonstrate the performance of our Class-One by applying it to practical domain. Class-One is compared with the previous method Predicate-Two.

Data Set

The subjectivity and objectivity weights of the predicates assigned are shown in Table 1 and Table 2. Two kinds of weight set A and B were used in Predicate-Two for a more complete and objective comparison. Arbitrary but probable values were assigned to the weights of weight set A and the weight set B has been derived from weight set A for the purpose of closing the performance gap

Figure 9. Matrix formation for the example

$$g_i^{\bullet} = Mg_{i-1}$$

$$\begin{bmatrix} g_i^{\bullet 1} \\ g_i^{\bullet 2} \\ g_i^{\bullet 3} \\ g_i^{\bullet 4} \end{bmatrix} = \begin{bmatrix} 0 & 0.3 & 0.5 & 0.2 \\ 0.6 & 0 & 0.1 & 0.3 \\ 0.4 & 0.2 & 0 & 0.4 \\ 0.2 & 0.1 & 0.7 & 0 \end{bmatrix} \begin{bmatrix} g_{i-1}^{1} \\ g_{i-1}^{2} \\ g_{i-1}^{3} \\ g_{i-1}^{4} \end{bmatrix}$$

between Class-One and Predicate-Two with weight set A. Some weights of weight set B corresponding to those equal to zero in Table 2 have been changed to 0.0001, a value close to zero (see the shaded cells in Table 1 and Table 2). The experiment with weight set B was conducted additionally but the results will be shown together with those of the original experiment. Class-One and Predicate-Two with weight set A were implemented in the original setting.

The experiment deals with a domain with a schema shown in Figure 11. The schema is simplified, and it is assumed that there is one layer of class hierarchy and one layer of property.

Figure 12 shows the number of instances, and the number of triples that describe the relationships among these instances. The class RESEARCHER is chosen to examine the ability of Predicate-Two and Class-One to solve the TKC effect problem. The two methods used the same triple set as input, and the analysis of the property values of RESEARCHER instances is shown in Figure 13. The fragment identifier form without URL and '#' were used as the name of instance and property for brevity when the triple information was composed.

Figure 10. Overall process

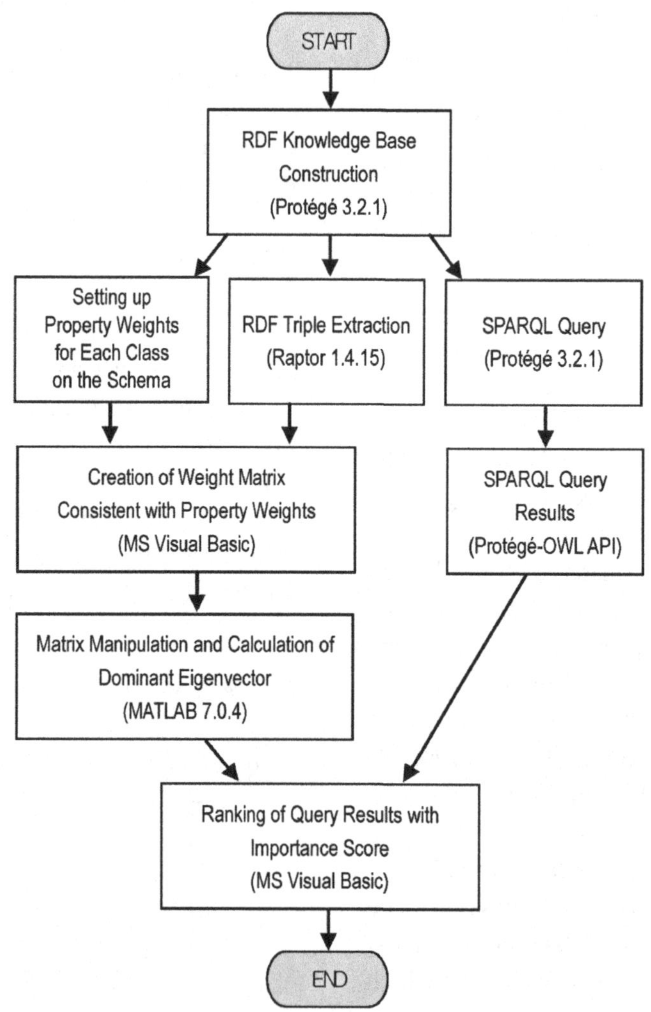

Figure 11. Class composition of experiment domain

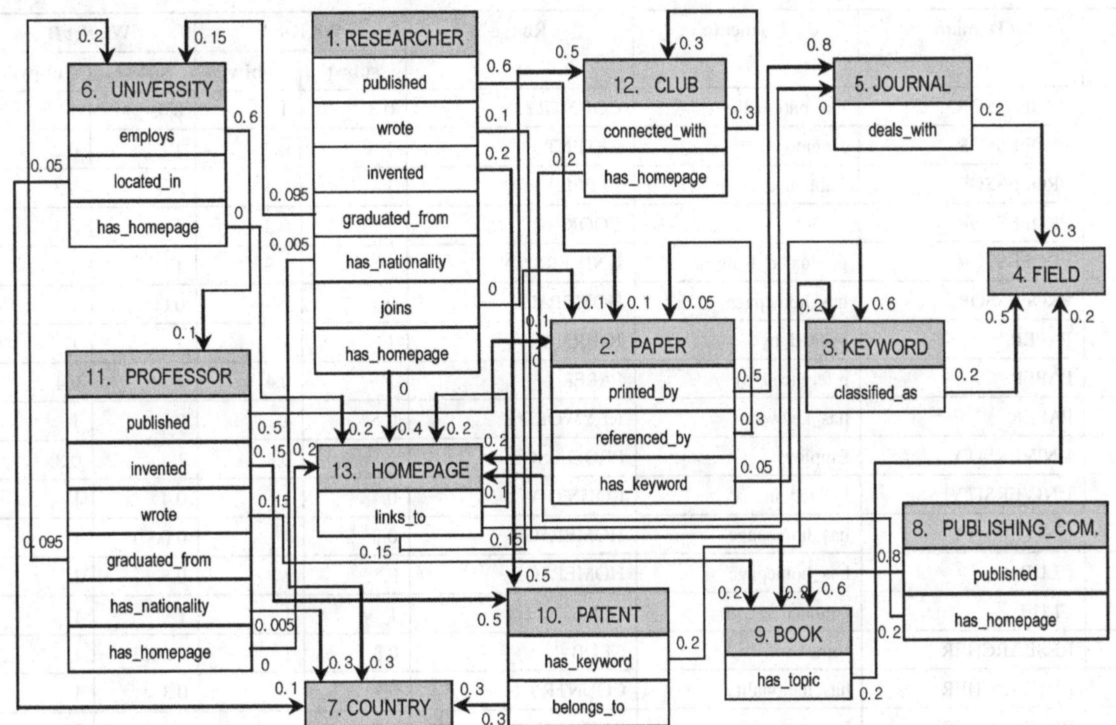

The form of the instance name is "(class name)(class number)-(instance number)." The dataset was designed for the smaller numbered instance to have the higher score according to Figure 19 in the Appendix, that is, the smaller numbered instance from a class has a significant relation with the smaller numbered instance from another class, and the number of significant relations between the smaller numbered instances is greater than that of relations between the larger numbered instances. As an example, Figure 13 shows data for a number of researchers: 'researcher 1-1' published ten papers, while 'researcher 1-25' did not publish any. The number of published papers decreases and the instance numbers of related papers increase, with the instance number of researchers increasing. To make a TKC, many links were created between 'researchers 1-21 to 1-25' and clubs according to the "RESEARCHER joins CLUB" relation; 'researchers 1-17 to 1-25' and homepages according to the "RESEARCHER has_homepage HOMEPAGE" relation; clubs and homepages according to the "CLUB has_homepage HOMEPAGE" relation; homepages and homepages according to the "HOMEPAGE links_to HOMEPAGE" relation, and so on. 'Researcher 1-25' joined five clubs, which should not affect the importance rating. On this dataset, the ranking results of the two algorithms will be compared.

We will also examine if the algorithm of the class-oriented approach makes the ranking results consistent with the designed triple information for each class, and check if the ranking score of the related resource goes upward or downward when the influential link is added or deleted.

Experiment Results

The ranking results of the RESEARCHER class by Predicate-Two and Class-One are shown in Figure 14. The ranking scores are calculated by summing up the objectivity and subjectivity

Table 1. Predicate-two: weights (predicate view)

	Domain	Predicate	Range	Wt. Set A		Wt. Set B	
				subwt	objwt	subwt	objwt
1	PROFESSOR	has_nationality	COUNTRY	0.3	1	0.3	1
2	PROFESSOR	Invented	PATENT	1	0.2	1	0.2
3	PROFESSOR	Published	PAPER	1	0.3	1	0.3
4	PROFESSOR	Wrote	BOOK	1	0.3	1	0.3
5	PROFESSOR	graduated_from	UNIVERSITY	1	0.8	1	0.8
6	PROFESSOR	has_homepage	HOMEPAGE	0.8	1	0.0001	1
7	PAPER	printed_by	JOURNAL	1	1	1	1
8	PAPER	referenced_by	PAPER	1	0.4	1	0.4
9	PAPER	has_keyword	KEYWORD	0.6	1	0.6	1
10	UNIVERSITY	Employs	PROFESSOR	1	0.8	1	0.8
11	UNIVERSITY	located_in	COUNTRY	0.4	1	0.4	1
12	UNIVERSITY	has_homepage	HOMEPAGE	0.8	1	0.0001	1
13	CLUB	has_homepage	HOMEPAGE	0.8	1	0.8	1
14	CLUB	connected_with	CLUB	1	1	1	1
15	RESEARCHER	Joins	CLUB	0.8	1	0.0001	1
16	RESEARCHER	has_nationality	COUNTRY	0.3	1	0.3	1
17	RESEARCHER	Invented	PATENT	1	0.2	1	0.2
18	RESEARCHER	Published	PAPER	1	0.3	1	0.3
19	RESEARCHER	Wrote	BOOK	1	0.3	1	0.3
20	RESEARCHER	graduated_from	UNIVERSITY	1	0.8	1	0.8
21	RESEARCHER	has_homepage	HOMEPAGE	0.8	1	0.0001	1
22	JOURNAL	deals_with	FIELD	0.4	1	0.4	1
23	BOOK	has_topic	FIELD	0.5	1	0.5	1
24	PUBLISHING_COM.	Printed	BOOK	1	0.7	1	0.7
25	PUBLISHING_COM.	has_homepage	HOMEPAGE	0.8	1	0.8	1
26	KEYWORD	classified_as	FIELD	0.4	1	0.4	1
27	PATENT	belongs_to	COUNTRY	0.2	1	0.2	1
28	PATENT	has_keyword	KEYWORD	0.6	1	0.6	1
29	HOMEPAGE	links_to	PAPER	1	0.8	1	0.0001
30	HOMEPAGE	links_to	JOURNAL	1	0.8	1	0.0001
31	HOMEPAGE	links_to	HOMEPAGE	1	0.8	1	0.8

scores for Predicate-Two. With the weight set A of Predicate-Two, 'researcher 1-25', who did not publish any paper was ranked higher than 'researcher 1-3' who published seven papers and wrote one book, or 'researcher 1-4' who published six papers, as shown in Figure 13. In addition, other researchers who were linked to clubs or homepages received high rankings. With the weight set B of Predicate-Two, the ranking of 'researcher 1-25' dropped a little and the ranking seems to be much better, but there remain some problems unsettled. For example, 'researcher 1-13' was

Table 2. Class-one: weights (predicate view)

	domain	predicate	Range	subwt	objwt
1	PROFESSOR	has_nationality	COUNTRY	0.005	0.3
2	PROFESSOR	invented	PATENT	0.15	0.5
3	PROFESSOR	published	PAPER	0.5	0.1
4	PROFESSOR	wrote	BOOK	0.15	0.2
5	PROFESSOR	graduated_from	UNIVERSITY	0.095	0.2
6	PROFESSOR	has_homepage	HOMEPAGE	0	0.2
7	PAPER	printed_by	JOURNAL	0.5	0.8
8	PAPER	referenced_by	PAPER	0.3	0.05
9	PAPER	has_keyword	KEYWORDS	0.05	0.6
10	UNIVERSITY	employs	PROFESSOR	0.6	0.1
11	UNIVERSITY	located_in	COUNTRY	0.05	0.1
12	UNIVERSITY	has_homepage	HOMEPAGE	0	0.2
13	CLUB	connected_with	CLUB	0.3	0.3
14	CLUB	has_homepage	HOMEPAGE	0.2	0.2
15	RESEARCHER	joins	CLUB	0	0.5
16	RESEARCHER	has_nationality	COUNTRY	0.005	0.3
17	RESEARCHER	invented	PATENT	0.2	0.5
18	RESEARCHER	published	PAPER	0.6	0.1
19	RESEARCHER	wrote	BOOK	0.1	0.2
20	RESEARCHER	graduated_from	UNIVERSITY	0.095	0.15
21	RESEARCHER	has_homepage	HOMEPAGE	0	0.2
22	JOURNAL	deals_with	FIELD	0.2	0.3
23	BOOK	has_topic	FIELD	0.2	0.2
24	PUBLISHING_COM.	printed	BOOK	0.8	0.6
25	PUBLISHING_COM.	has_homepage	HOMEPAGE	0.2	0.2
26	KEYWORDS	classified_as	FIELD	0.2	0.5
27	PATENT	belongs_to	COUNTRY	0.3	0.3
28	PATENT	has_keyword	KEYWORDS	0.2	0.2
29	HOMEPAGE	links_to	PAPER	0.15	0
30	HOMEPAGE	links_to	JOURNAL	0.15	0
31	HOMEPAGE	links_to	HOMEPAGE	0.1	0.4

ranked too low. On the other hand, we see that the serial number is in a close agreement with the rankings of Class-One and that 'researcher 1-25' is evaluated properly in Class-One. The ranking is not the same as the serial number, however, for instances after 'researcher 1-15'. This is because it is difficult to make the complex link connection required to create a TKC among researchers with instance numbers larger than 16.

In Figure 15, the first column (A) stands for the number order of instances, that is, the ranking results justified in terms of Table 2 or Figure 19 in the Appendix, while from the second to forth column represent the ranking order of Predicate-

Figure 12. Number of instances and triples

	Number of Instances
1. RESEARCHER	25
2. PAPER	100
3. KEYWORD	15
4. FIELD	5
5. JOURNAL	5
6. UNIVERSITY	3
7. COUNTRY	3
8. PUBLISHING_COM.	3
9. BOOK	15
10. PATENT	10
11. PROFESSOR	9
12. CLUB	5
13. HOMEPAGE	30
Total Number of Instances	228
Total Number of Triples	1160

Two and Class-One. The Spearman's rank correlation coefficients (Mendenhall et al., 1990) of weight set A and B of Predicate-Two were calculated as -0.328 and 0.608, respectively, and that of Class-One as 0.997. Since n equals 25, we can see that the weight set A of Predicate-Two represents the negative correlation at the significance level of 10%, and Class-One exhibits the strong positive correlation even when the significance level is 1% ($n=25$, $\rho=0.47$, p-value<0.01). This shows that the weight set A of Predicate-Two produces a result that is totally different from what a system user intends, especially when there is a TKC. By contrast, Class-One reflects the intention of users almost 100% even when there is a TKC.

When applying the weight set B to Predicate-Two, the Spearman's correlation coefficient was greatly improved from -0.328 to 0.608, though it is still much lower than the 0.997 of Class-One. As mentioned before, the weights of the properties known irrelevant to the resource importance through Class-One approach were set to 0.0001 in the weight set B to relieve the TKC effect. But if we see the resource ranking problem through the predicate oriented view, judging the irrelevancy or the relative significance of a property will be more difficult. As a result, even if more weights changed, there would be a limit, which cannot be overcome with the previous method. Moreover, even though some weight combinations to give a desirable ranking result may be found, should another new property be added, there will be too much uncertainty about the change of the ranking result.

The rank correlation coefficients of all the classes are shown in Figure 16. The ranking scores of Predicate-Two were calculated by adding up the objectivity and subjectivity scores for the purpose of comparison with Class-One. Because Predicate-Two was sensitive to the schema, FIELD class was not evaluated. In the case of class FIELD, two kinds of scores were calculated as 0. The reason for this is that the resource in the FIELD class can only be objectivity and, naturally, the subjectivity score is 0, as shown in Figure 11. The objectivity score is 0 because there is no outgoing link from the neighboring classes, JOURNAL, KEYWORD, and BOOK other than the link to FIELD and the subjectivity score of this link is 0. In this way, Predicate-Two has a weakness in that it fails to evaluate some classes in a particular schema. The last row shows the weighted averages of all the correlation coefficients except that of FIELD class by applying weight in proportion to the number of instances of each class. Class-One exhibits the best result of 0.952, and it also ranks the FIELD instances properly.

In Class-One, the importance scores increase or decrease as expected depending on whether a link connection is added or deleted. For example, if the link from 'researcher 1-1' to 'paper 2-1' is deleted, that is, if we suppose 'researcher 1-1' did not write 'paper 2-1', the importance score of 'researcher 1-1' goes down in Class-One. These results are not presented, however, because they are quite straightforward.

Figure 13. Brief analysis of property values of RESEARCHER instances

	# of papers (paper #)	# of books (book #)	# of patents (patent #)	graduation	nationality	# of clubs (club #)	homepage (homep. #)
researcher 1-1	10 (1~10)	4 (1~4)	3 (1~3)	university 6-1	country 7-1	0	no
researcher 1-2	8 (11~18)	3 (5~7)	2 (4~5)	university 6-1	country 7-1	0	no
researcher 1-3	7 (19~25)	1 (8)	0	university 6-1	country 7-1	0	no
researcher 1-4	6 (26~31)	0	0	university 6-1	country 7-1	0	no
researcher 1-5	5 (32~36)	0	0	university 6-1	country 7-1	0	no
researcher 1-6	5 (37~41)	0	0	university 6-1	country 7-1	0	no
researcher 1-7	5 (42~46)	0	0	university 6-1	country 7-1	0	no
researcher 1-8	5 (47~51)	0	0	university 6-1	country 7-1	0	no
researcher 1-9	5 (52~56)	0	0	university 6-1	country 7-1	0	no
researcher 1-10	4 (57~60)	0	0	university 6-1	country 7-2	0	no
researcher 1-11	4 (61~64)	0	0	university 6-2	country 7-2	0	no
researcher 1-12	4 (65~68)	0	0	university 6-2	country 7-2	0	no
researcher 1-13	4 (69~72)	0	0	university 6-2	country 7-2	0	no
researcher 1-14	4 (73~76)	0	0	university 6-2	country 7-2	0	no
researcher 1-15	4 (77~80)	0	0	university 6-2	country 7-2	0	no
researcher 1-16	3 (81~83)	0	0	university 6-2	country 7-2	0	no
researcher 1-17	3 (84~86)	0	0	university 6-2	country 7-2	0	yes(10)
researcher 1-18	3 (87~89)	0	0	university 6-2	country 7-3	0	yes(9)
researcher 1-19	2 (90~91)	0	0	university 6-3	country 7-3	0	yes(8)
researcher 1-20	2 (92~93)	0	0	university 6-3	country 7-3	0	yes(7)
researcher 1-21	2 (94~95)	0	0	university 6-3	country 7-3	3 (1~3)	yes(6)
researcher 1-22	2 (96~97)	0	0	university 6-3	country 7-3	3 (1~3)	yes(5)
researcher 1-23	1 (98)	0	0	university 6-3	country 7-3	3 (1~3)	yes(4)
researcher 1-24	1 (99)	0	0	university 6-3	country 7-3	4 (1~4)	yes(3)
researcher 1-25	0	0	0	university 6-3	country 7-3	5 (1~5)	yes(1,2)

We have observed that previous limitations such as the TKC effect, which are still problematic when using the Predicate-Two approach, are eliminated when property weights are determined using a Class-One approach. In the Class-One approach, the links that have no effect on resource importance can be treated as if they do not exist by assigning them weights of zero. We found that Class-One, using one kind of importance score instead of two, provides an attractive solution to problems caused by the diversity of RDF schemas and enhances the accuracy of evaluation by reflecting the whole resource importance. It is also expected to increase the efficiency of calculation by using one matrix instead of two for objectivity and subjectivity. In addition, this algorithm has been shown to produce proper ranking results for a given dataset and be insensitive to the schema depending on link directions.

An Application Using Class-One: Itgling.com

Itgling.com is a community service for sharing knowledge and opinions on current trends such as fashion, movies, social problems, and health

Figure 14. Ranking results of RESEARCHER class

Ranking	Predicate-Two		Class-One
	Wt. Set A	Wt. Set B	
1	researcher 1-1	researcher 1-1	researcher 1-1
2	researcher 1-2	researcher 1-2	researcher 1-2
3	researcher 1-25	researcher 1-3	researcher 1-3
4	researcher 1-18	researcher 1-4	researcher 1-4
5	researcher 1-17	researcher 1-5	researcher 1-5
6	researcher 1-20	researcher 1-6	researcher 1-6
7	researcher 1-19	researcher 1-7	researcher 1-7
8	researcher 1-24	researcher 1-9	researcher 1-8
9	researcher 1-21	researcher 1-8	researcher 1-9
10	researcher 1-22	researcher 1-25	researcher 1-10
11	researcher 1-23	researcher 1-17	researcher 1-11
12	researcher 1-15	researcher 1-18	researcher 1-12
13	researcher 1-16	researcher 1-10	researcher 1-13
14	researcher 1-14	researcher 1-20	researcher 1-14
15	researcher 1-3	researcher 1-19	researcher 1-15
16	researcher 1-4	researcher 1-24	researcher 1-18
17	researcher 1-5	researcher 1-22	researcher 1-16
18	researcher 1-6	researcher 1-21	researcher 1-17
19	researcher 1-7	researcher 1-23	researcher 1-19
20	researcher 1-8	researcher 1-15	researcher 1-20
21	researcher 1-9	researcher 1-16	researcher 1-22
22	researcher 1-10	researcher 1-14	researcher 1-21
23	researcher 1-11	researcher 1-11	researcher 1-23
24	researcher 1-12	researcher 1-12	researcher 1-24
25	researcher 1-13	researcher 1-13	researcher 1-25

information. Users write posts (similar to blog posts) on various topics and are encouraged to link their posts to other posts with related topics (similar to trackbacks). Each post is presented with linked posts. Each post has keywords assigned by its writer and post-notes, which other users may write after reading the post. Various relationships among users, posts, keywords, and post-notes are represented as triple forms. These triples are used to compute the rankings of users, posts, keywords, and post-notes with our algorithm. The weights of the properties are set in accordance with the ranking policies of the Itgling service. To mention one of the ranking policies, the importance score of a user mainly depends on the number and importance of the posts he/she wrote and the number and importance of other users who trust him/her. With a real data set, the weights were adjusted for the ranking results to be sufficiently reasonable by trial and error during the closed beta service. In addition, considering the users' tendency to give more attention to the lat-

Figure 15. Spearman's rank correlation coefficients of RESEARCHER class

A (Answer)	Predicate-Two		Class-One
	Wt. Set A	Wt. Set B	
1	1	1	1
2	2	2	2
3	15	3	3
4	16	4	4
5	17	5	5
6	18	6	6
7	19	7	7
8	20	9	8
9	21	8	9
10	22	25	10
11	23	17	11
12	24	18	12
13	25	10	13
14	14	20	14
15	12	19	15
16	13	24	17
17	5	22	18
18	4	21	16
19	7	23	19
20	6	15	20
21	9	16	22
22	10	14	21
23	11	11	23
24	8	12	24
25	3	13	25
Spearman's Coefficient	-0.328	0.608	0.997

est information, the weights are decremented by a predetermined function as time goes on. That is, the links representing the same property can have different weights depending on the time they were created.

The open beta of Itgling service is being provided to the public and it now has more than 2,000 users and has accumulated 8,000 posts, 12,000 keywords, 22,000 post-notes, and about one hundred thousand triples. It takes about 1 second for the present ranking system, consisting of two dual-core Intel Xeon CPUs with 16 GB memory and NVIDIA GPU with 1 GB graphic memory, to get the ranking vector from a square weight matrix of size 50,000 after about 500 iterations. Once the convergence is attained, the ranking order does not change even if more iterations are executed. The processing time needed for an experimental square matrix of size 10 million is less than 10 seconds. Even if the size of a weight matrix gets much larger, the processing time is not likely to matter, as we can see from PageRank ranking billions of pages

Figure 16. Spearman's rank correlation coefficients of all the classes

Class Number	Class (number of instances)	Predicate-Two		Class-One
		Wt. Set A	Wt. Set B	
1	RESEARCHER(25)	-0.328	0.608	0.997
2	PAPER(100)	0.512	0.479	0.946
3	KEYWORD(15)	0.989	0.989	0.925
4	FIELD(5)	not eval.	not eval.	1.000
5	JOURNAL(5)	1.000	1.000	0.900
6	UNIVERSITY(3)	-0.500	1.000	1.000
7	COUNTRY(3)	-0.500	1.000	1.000
8	PUBLISHING_COM.(3)	1.000	1.000	1.000
9	BOOK(15)	0.900	0.964	1.000
10	PATENT(10)	1.000	1.000	1.000
11	PROFESSOR(9)	0.927	1.000	0.988
12	CLUB(5)	0.600	-1.000	1.000
13	HOMEPAGE(30)	0.424	0.325	0.880
Weighted Average(FIELD excluded)		0.495	0.584	0.952

Figure 17. Main Page of Itgling.com

with similar matrix operations. Ranking data of users, posts, and keywords are used to determine the orders in which they are displayed in various parts of the service. For example, as shown in the main page of Itgling (see Figure 17), the top five posts of the day and the week are selected using the ranking data. With this system, blog posts of well-known blog sites can easily be linked as posts of Itgling service and other features can be added continuously. The overall structure of the ranking system is shown in Figure 18.

CONCLUSION AND FURTHER RESEARCH

The Semantic Web comprises many techniques that promise to dramatically improve the current WWW including ontology. There can be a great number of classes and properties in an ontology based on the RDF schema. The instances belonging to each class will be accumulated over time, and the ranking of instances will become increasingly necessary.

The class-oriented assignment of property weights, which reflects the relative importance of properties to the importance of a resource in a class, has much in common with the human cognitive process of evaluation. The users usually apply different ranking criteria to resources belonging to different classes, and the ranking result could be provided to the software agents for the Semantic Web whenever it is required. The class-oriented approach also provides an effective standard for deciding whether the information is descriptive enough or not, with which we can easily check if there is a significant property that is missing. Considering not only the number of neighboring nodes but also the actual importance of the node, it will be less susceptible to malicious manipulation, just as PageRank produces more objective importance scores than the traditional ranking technique with link structure.

Our algorithm, on the other hand, requires a considerably well-described schema and there

Figure 18. Handling process of the ITGLING ranking system

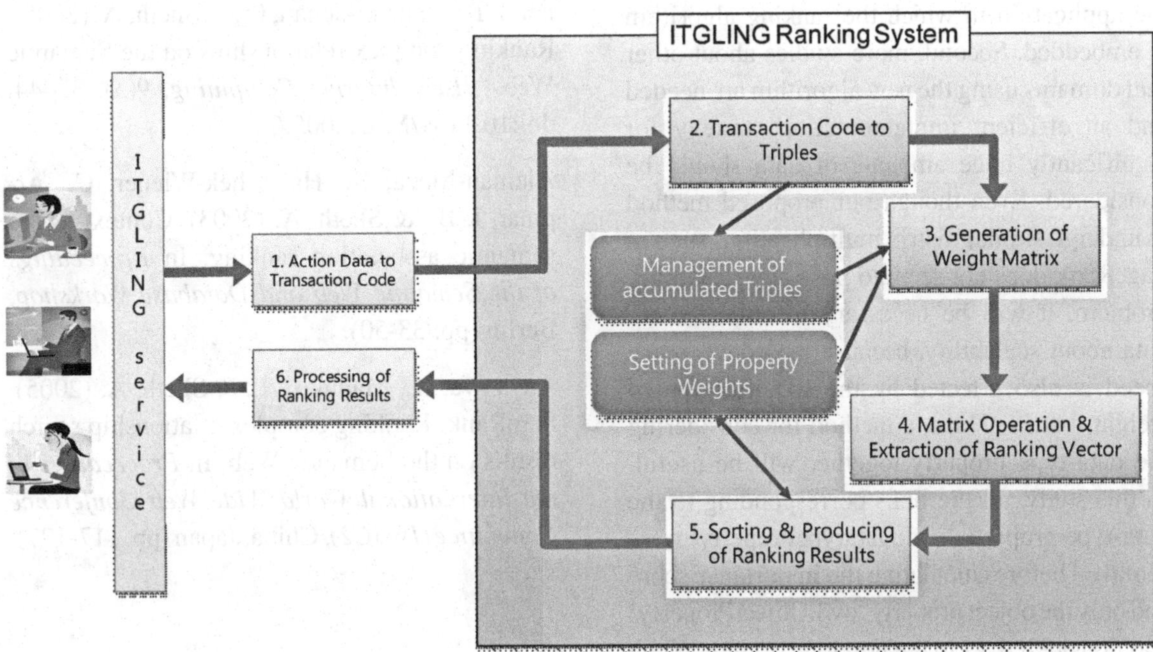

has to be some degree of interaction among the classes in the schema. Even if our approach is less sensitive to the structure of a schema and unconcerned with the link directions, testing for proper weights and making estimates for convergence speed and scalability are necessary for a specific new domain. The reason is that the type and the size of a weight matrix seem to have an effect on the computation performance. As a result, our algorithm is more suitable for a domain-specific controlled environment. Nevertheless, general users do not have to mind the weights or the weight-setting approaches. They have only to use the web pages as they normally did when there were no weights in the schema.

Possible areas for future research are as follows. First, commonly consented property weights and a framework for weight assignment may be needed for a socially important domain. This paper focused on the development of a ranking framework that can process various combinations of property weights and did not examine a way of determining the weights objectively. Various techniques, including factor analysis and regression, could be applied to this topic. Weights can be adjusted in accordance with the purpose of the application in which the ranking algorithm is embedded. Second, more studies about other real domains using the new algorithm are needed and an efficient implementation strategy for significantly huge amounts of data should be considered. Even though our proposed method to undergo similar matrix multiplications such as PageRank does not seem to pose any scalability problem, it will be necessary to collect more data about scalability, because the convergence speed is also affected by the specific type of weight matrix. Third, a method for considering the data-type property together will be useful. In this study, all the links corresponding to the data-type property 'owl:DatatypeProperty' were removed before calculating the importance score and only the object property 'owl:ObjectProperty' was considered, as in the previous studies. When there is a data-type property to have some positive weight, the normalized data-type property score may be added to the normalized resource importance score obtained from the link analysis with the predetermined weights. The normalized data-type property score could be acquired from comparing all the values of class instances. Fourth, more research on ontology, which has more than one layer, is also worth studying as we assumed only one layer in the hierarchy of class and property for simplicity. For this issue, the treatment procedure shown in this paper can be applied for the lowest layer of class and property.

ACKNOWLEDGMENT

This research was supported by research grants from the Institute of Management Research at the Seoul National University and the algorithm developed in this work has been applied for a patent in Korea.

REFERENCES

Aleman-Meza, B., Halaschek-Wiener, C., Arpinar, I. B., Ramakrishnan, C., & Sheth, A. (2005). Ranking complex relationships on the Semantic Web. *IEEE Internet Computing*, *9*(3), 37–44. doi:10.1109/MIC.2005.63

Aleman-Meza, B., Halaschek-Wiener, C., Arpinar, I. B., & Sheth, A. (2003). Context-aware semantic association ranking. In *Proceedings of the Semantic Web and Database Workshop,* Berlin (pp. 33-50).

Anyanwu, K., Maduko, A., & Sheth, A. (2005). SemRank: Ranking complex relationship search results on the Semantic Web. In *Proceedings of the International World Wide Web Conference Committee (IW3C2),* Chiba, Japan (pp. 117-127).

Bamba, B., & Mukherjea, S. (2004). Utilizing resource importance for ranking Semantic Web query results. In C. Bussler et al. (Eds.), *Proceedings of the Second Toronto International Workshop on Semantic Web Databases (SWDB)*, Toronto, ON, Canada (pp. 185-198). Berlin: Springer-Verlag.

Berners-Lee, T. (2005). *Semantic Web stack*. Retrieved October 13, 2008, from http://www.w3.org/2005/Talks/0511-keynote-tbl/#[17]

Berners-Lee, T., Hendler, J., & Lassila, O. (2001). The Semantic Web. *Scientific American Magazine*. Retrieved March 26, 2008, from http://www.sciam.com/article.cfm?id=the-semantic-web&print=true

Brickley, D., & Guha, R. V. (Eds.). (2004). *RDF vocabulary description language 1.0: RDF schema*. Retrieved October 15, 2008, from http://www.w3.org/TR/rdf-schema/

Brin, S., Motwani, R., Page, L., & Winograd, T. (1998). What can you do with a Web in your pocket. *Bulletin of the IEEE Computer Society Technical Committee on Data Engineering*, *21*(2), 37–47.

Brin, S., & Page, L. (1998). The anatomy of a large-scale hypertextual Web search engine. *Special Issue of the 7th International World Wide Web Conference on Computer Networks and ISDN Systems, 30*(1-7), 107-117.

Burden, R. L., & Faires, J. D. (2001). *Numerical Analysis*. Pacific Grove, CA: Brooks/Cole.

Ding, L., Finin, T., Joshi, A., Pan, R., Cost, R. S., Peng, Y., et al. (2004). Swoogle: A semantic Web search and metadata engine. In *Proceedings of the 13th ACM Conference on Information and Knowledge Management* (pp. 652-659).

Ding, L., Finin, T., Joshi, A., Peng, Y., Pan, R., & Reddivari, P. (2005). Search on the Semantic Web. *Computer*, *38*(10), 62–69. doi:10.1109/MC.2005.350

Ding, L., Pan, R., Finin, T., Joshi, A., Peng, Y., & Kolari, P. (2005). Finding and ranking knowledge on the Semantic Web. In *Proceedings of the 4th Galway IE International Semantic Web Conference,* Galway, Ireland (pp. 156-170). Berlin: Springer-Verlag.

Ehrlich, L. W. (1969). *Rate of Convergence Proofs of the Method for Finding Roots of Polynomials (or Eigenvalues of Matrices) by the Power and Inverse Power Methods* (Tech. Rep. No. AD707331). Alexandria, VA: National Technical Information Service.

Finin, T., & Ding, L. (2006). Search engines for Semantic Web knowledge. In *Proceedings of XTech 2006: Building Web 2.0*, Amsterdam, The Netherlands.

Franz, T., Schultz, A., Sizov, S., & Staab, S. (2009). TripleRank: Ranking Semantic Web Data By Tensor Decomposition. In *Proceedings of the 8th International Semantic Web Conference* (pp. 213-228). Berlin: Springer-Verlag.

Golub, G., & Van Loan, C. F. (1989). *Matrix Computations*. Baltimore, MD: Johns Hopkins University Press.

Graves, A., Adali, S., & Hendler, J. (2008). A method to rank nodes in an RDF graph. In *Proceedings of the 7th International Semantic Web Conference (ISWC2008)* (Vol. 401). CEUR-WS.

Halaschek, C., Aleman-Meza, B., Arpinar, I. B., & Sheth, A. (2004). Discovering and ranking semantic associations over a large RDF metabase. In *Proceedings of the 30th VLDB Conference,* Toronto, ON, Canada (pp. 1317-1320). VLDB Endowment.

Haveliwala, T. H. (1999). *Efficient Computation of PageRank (Tech. Rep.)*. Stanford, CA: Stanford University.

Hurtado, C. A., Poulovassilis, A., & Wood, P. T. (2009). Ranking Approximate Answers to Semantic Web Queries. In *Proceedings of the 6th European Semantic Web Conference* (pp. 263-277). Berlin: Springer-Verlag.

Kleinberg, J. (1999). Authoritative sources in a hyperlinked environment. *Journal of the ACM, 46*(5), 604–632. doi:10.1145/324133.324140

Klyne, G., & Carroll, J. (Eds.). (2004). *Resource description framework (RDF): Concepts and abstract syntax.* Retrieved October 15, 2008, from http://www.w3.org/TR/rdf-concepts/

Maedche, A., & Staab, S. (2002). Measuring similarity between ontologies. In *Proceedings of the European Conference of Knowledge Acquisition and Management (EKAW2002),* Madrid, Spain (LNCS 2473, pp. 15-21).

Maedche, A., Staab, S., Stojanovic, N., Studer, R., & Sure, Y. (2001). SEAL-A Framework for Developing SEmantic Web PortALs. In *Advances in Databases* (LNCS 2097, pp. 1-22).

Manola, F., & Miller, E. (Eds.). (2004). *RDF primer.* Retrieved October 15, 2008, from http://www.w3.org/TR/rdf-primer/

Marchiori, M. (1997). The quest for correct information on the Web: Hyper Search Engines. In *Proceedings of the 6th International WWW Conference,* Santa Clara, CA (pp. 1225-1235). Amsterdam, The Netherlands: Elsevier Science Publishers Ltd.

Mendenhall, W., Wackerly, D. D., & Scheaffer, R. L. (1990). *Mathematical Statistics with Applications.* Boston: PWS Publishers.

Mukherjea, S., & Bamba, B. (2004). BioPatentMiner: An information retrieval system for biomedical patents. In *Proceedings of the 30th Toronto Conference on Very Large Databases (VLDB)* (pp. 1066-1077).

Mukherjea, S., Bamba, B., & Kankar, P. (2005). Information retrieval and knowledge discovery utilizing a biomedical patent Semantic Web. *IEEE Transactions on Knowledge and Data Engineering, 17*(8), 1099–1110. doi:10.1109/TKDE.2005.130

National Research Council. (2003). *Assessing research-doctorate programs: A methodology study.* Retrieved October 15, 2008, from http://www7.nationalacademies.org/resdoc/ranking_and_ratings.html

Page, L., Brin, S., Motwani, R., & Winograd, T. (1998). *The PageRank Citation Ranking: Bringing Order to the Web* (Tech. Rep. No. SIDL-WP-1999-0120). Stanford, CA: Stanford University.

Perron & Frobenius. (2003). *Perron-frobenius theory.* Retrieved October 15, 2008, from http://www.win.tue.nl/~aeb/srgbk/node4.html

Prud'hommeaux, E., & Seaborne, A. (Eds.). (2007). *SPARQL query language for RDF.* Retrieved October 15, 2008, from http://www.w3.org/TR/rdf-sparql-query/

Ren, J., & Taylor, R. N. (2007). Automatic and versatile publications ranking for research institutions and scholars. *Communications of the ACM, 50*(6), 81–85. doi:10.1145/1247001.1247010

Schneider, P., Hayes, P., & Horrocks, I. (Eds.). (2004). *OWL Web ontology language semantics and abstract syntax.* Retrieved October 15, 2008, from http://www.w3.org/TR/owl-semantics/

Sheth, A., Aleman-Meza, B., Arpinar, I. B., Halaschek, C., & Ramakrishnan, C. (2005). Semantic association identification and knowledge discovery for national security applications. *Journal of Database Management, 16*(1), 33–53.

Wu, G., & Li, J. (2007). SWRank: An Approach for Ranking Semantic Web Reversely and Consistently. In *Proceedings of the Third International Conference on Semantics, Knowledge and Grid (SKG 2007)* (pp. 116-121).

APPENDIX

Example of Class-Oriented Weight Assignment

Figure 19. Class-one: class-oriented weight assignment (class view)

1. RESEARCHER		
published	0.6	PAPER
invented	0.2	PATENT
wrote	0.1	BOOK
graduated_from	0.095	UNIVERSITY
has_nationality	0.005	COUNTRY
joins	0	CLUB
has_homepage	0	HOMEPAGE
annual_salary	0	
birth_date	0	
cell_phone	0	

2. PAPER		
printed_by	0.5	JOURNAL
referenced_by	0.3	PAPER
(obj)published	0.1	(dom)RESEARCHER
(obj)published	0.1	(dom)PROFESSOR
has_keyword	0.05	KEYWORD
(obj)referenced_by	0.05	(dom)PAPER
(obj)links_to	0	(dom)HOMEPAGE
:		:

3. KEYWORD		
(obj)has_keyword	0.6	(dom)PAPER
classified_as	0.2	FIELD
(obj)has_keyword	0.2	(dom)PATENT
:		:

4. FIELD		
(obj)classified_as	0.5	(dom)KEYWORD
(obj)deals_with	0.3	(dom)JOURNAL
(obj)has_topic	0.2	(dom)BOOK
:		:

5. JOURNAL		
(obj)printed_by	0.8	(dom)PAPER
deals_with	0.2	FIELD
(obj)links_to	0	(dom)HOMEPAGE
evaluation_score	0	
journal_name	0	
:		:

6. UNIVERSITY		
employs	0.6	PROFESSOR
(obj)graduated_from	0.2	(dom)PROFESSOR
(obj)graduated_from	0.15	(dom)RESEARCHER
located_in	0.05	COUNTRY
has_homepage	0	HOMEPAGE
evaluation_score	0	
number_of_undergraduates	0	
:		:

7. COUNTRY		
(obj)has_nationality	0.3	(dom)RESEARCHER
(obj)has_nationality	0.3	(dom)PROFESSOR
(obj)belongs_to	0.3	(dom)PATENT
(obj)located_in	0.1	(dom)UNIVERSITY
personal_income	0	
telecom_infra	0	
:		:

8. PUBLISHING_COM.		
published	0.8	BOOK
has_homepage	0.2	HOMEPAGE
net_income	0	
total_sales	0	
number_of_staffs	0	
address	0	
telephone_num.	0	
:		:

9. BOOK		
(obj)published	0.6	(dom)PUBLISHING_COM.
has_topic	0.2	FIELD
(obj)wrote	0.2	(dom)RESEARCHER
(obj)wrote	0.2	(dom)PROFESSOR
number_of_copies_sold	0	
:		:

10. PATENT		
(obj)invented	0.5	(dom)RESEARCHER
(obj)invented	0.5	(dom)PROFESSOR
belongs_to	0.3	COUNTRY
keyword	0.2	KEYWORD
tech_value_evaluation	0	
:		:

11. PROFESSOR		
published	0.5	PAPER
invented	0.15	PATENT
wrote	0.15	BOOK
(obj)employs	0.1	(dom)UNIVERSITY
graduated_from	0.095	UNIVERSITY
has_nationality	0.005	COUNTRY
has_homepage	0	HOMEPAGE
cell_phone	0	
:		:

12. CLUB		
(obj)joins	0.5	(dom)RESEARCHER
connected_with	0.3	CLUB
has_homepage	0.2	HOMEPAGE
:		:

13. HOMEPAGE		
(obj)links_to	0.4	(dom)HOMEPAGE
(obj)has_homepage	0.2	(dom)PUBLISHING_COM.
(obj)has_homepage	0.2	(dom)RESEARCHER
(obj)has_homepage	0.2	(dom)UNIVERSITY
links_to	0.15	PAPER
links_to	0.15	JOURNAL
links_to	0.1	HOMEPAGE
:		:

This work was previously published in the Journal of Database Management, Volume 22, Issue 1, edited by Keng Siau, pp. 1-25, copyright 2011 by IGI Publishing (an imprint of IGI Global).

Chapter 2
A Study of Open Source Software Development from Control Perspective

Bo Xu
Fudan University, China

Zhangxi Lin
Texas Tech University, USA

Yan Xu
Del Mar College, USA

ABSTRACT

Open source software (OSS) has achieved great success and exerted significant impact on the software industry. OSS development takes online community as its organizational form, and developers voluntarily work for the project. In the project execution process, control aligns individual behaviors toward the organizational goals via the Internet and becomes critical to the success of OSS projects. This paper investigates the control modes in OSS project communities, and their effects on project performance. Based on a web survey and archival data from OSS projects, it is revealed that three types of control modes, that is, outcome, clanship, and self-control, are effective in an OSS project community. The study contributes to a better understanding of OSS project organizations and processes, and provides advice for OSS development.

INTRODUCTION

The past decade has seen a marked expansion in the open source software (OSS) movement. The open source initiative sprung from the idea that software should be free and open. OSS contrasts with the traditional software distribution model, in which computer software is sold only with a license to use precompiled binary code without giving users the access to the source code. OSS, on the other hand, is licensed to guarantee free access to the source code, often under a license that sets conditions for modification, reuse, and re-distribution (Bretthauer, 2002). The concept

DOI: 10.4018/978-1-4666-2044-5.ch002

of copyleft is the core to OSS. To copyleft a program, the programmer, besides copyrighting the program to himself, also signs a General Public License (GPL) granting everyone the right to use, modify, and distribute the program on the condition that the license also grants similar rights over the modifications he or she has made. Under this arrangement, everyone has free access to the program but it is protected from becoming someone's private intellectual property (Lerner & Tirole, 2002).

Open source software is the result of Web-based collaboration. Once started, an OSS project is usually accomplished by a community of participants that are geographically dispersed and communicate through the Internet (Lee & Cole, 2003), which makes OSS different from traditional software development in both organizing and process (Feller & Fitzgerald, 2002). Today, numerous open source projects are categorized into three types: (1) community projects, which are completely online community based, involving voluntary software developers; (2) non-profit organization projects that have matured to the level where they can get funding towards a more formal organization but still maintain some features of community projects (e.g. Apache Software Foundation), in which developers can be either paid workers or volunteers; and, (3) commercial projects sponsored by companies like IBM, HP, SUN, etc., in which major contributors are paid developers from the companies (Fitzgerald, 2006). Currently, most of the open source projects belong to the community projects category, and most of the successful software products (e.g. Linux, Apache) used to be community projects in their initial stages, although some of them took on the non-profit organization or commercial project model after they became very popular. Thus, in this paper we choose community projects as the target for research, and refer open source software to those developed by online communities of volunteers.

Open source project participation is developers' voluntary actions. The motivations for project participation include reputation gaining, job prospects, enjoyment, learning purpose, cooperation needs, open source ideology, and personal software needs (Hars & Ou, 2002; Roberts, Hann, & Slaughter, 2006; von Hippel, & von Krogh, 2003). And each member in an open source project community may have different motivations for participation (Wu, Gerlach, & Young, 2007). However, it has been demonstrated that although OSS development is a process of voluntary activities, the developers' behaviors can be affected by the project environment, such as the values, beliefs, and norms in project community (Stewart & Gosain, 2006), interpersonal relationship between developers (Xu, Jones, & Shao, 2009), and satisfaction of developers' psychological needs (Agerfalk & Fitzgerald, 2008). Thus, the development activities of an OSS project can be regulated to some extent although the project takes online community as its organizational form.

In traditional software development teams, how to control members' behaviors to align them with the goals of the project is critical to project success (Henderson & Lee, 1992; Kirsch, 1996, 1997). It has been demonstrated that control mechanisms play an important role in the governance and management of software development internally within an organization (Nidumolu & Subramani, 2003) and externally between alliances (Choudhury & Sabherwal, 2003). Both formal and informal control modes are used in traditional organizations and software development teams (Kirsch, 1996; Ouchi, 1980). The formal controls depend on the formal rules, procedures and evaluations, while informal controls depend on the factors like cultures, values, beliefs and members' self-regulation. OSS development is significantly different from traditional software development in both organizational form and process. Previous research indicated that in OSS project communities there exists some types of governance that take effects as controls in traditional organizations, and they are necessary to project success (Hagan, Watson, & Barron, 2007). For example, Demil and Lecocq (2006) defined the governance structure in open source projects as neither market nor hierarchy, and termed it as "bazaar governance". However, to provide guidance for OSS development it is essential to understand the controls in open source community in more depth. For this purpose, this paper investigates the control mechanisms common in open source projects, and empirically tests how they affect the outcome of projects.

The rest of the paper is organized as follows: First, the theories and literature of management controls are reviewed; Second, the control modes in open source projects are discussed based on the theories; Third, an empirical test is conducted to demonstrate the effects of the control modes on open source project performance; Finally, a discussion on the findings and implications concludes the paper.

THEORETICAL BACKGROUND AND LITERATURE REVIEW

Control in organizations has long been a topic of interests for researchers and practitioners alike, who generally recognize that control mechanisms are needed to help and ensure organizations achieve their goals. In project management, controls are conducted for various purposes, like the control processes for scope, schedule, cost, risk, and quality. While control can be viewed from various perspectives, it is studied here in a behavioral sense, i.e. to ensure that individuals working on organizational projects act in accordance with an agreed-upon strategy to achieve desired objectives (Jaworski, 1988; Merchant, 1988). From this angle, software development is not only a technical process, but also a social process with multiple stakeholders whose behaviors are influential to the performance of software development projects (Guinan, Cooprider, & Faraj, 1998). Exercising control is a powerful approach to ensuring project progress by fusing together the complementary roles and capabilities of project participants and motivating them to work in accordance with organizational goals and objectives (Henderson & Lee, 1992).

The control mechanisms have been studied in either organizational or software development context. In the organizational context, Ouchi (1977, 1978, 1980) categorized the organizational control mechanisms into market, bureaucratic, and clan, and found that the adoption of control mechanisms is related to the organizational structure and task situation. Market mechanism is efficient when performance evaluation is not ambiguous, but the goals are incongruent; Bureaucratic mechanism is efficient when both evaluation ambiguity and goals incongruence are moderately high; Clan mechanism is the most effective if evaluation is ambiguous, but goal congruity is high (Ouchi, 1980).

Henderson and Lee (1992) indicated that control is important to the management of software development. According to Kirsch (1996, 1997), both formal and informal modes of controls are used in software development projects. The formal controls include behavior and outcome controls. In behavior control, specific rules and procedures are articulated, and controllers observe the behaviors of the controllees, who are rewarded based on the degree to which they follow the procedures (Eisenhardt, 1985; Mahmood, 1987). To implement outcome control, controllees are rewarded for meeting the desired outcomes or goals (Eisenhardt, 1985; Snell, 1992). Informal control is rooted in social and people strategies, and mainly includes clan and self controls. Clan control is implemented by promulgating common values, beliefs, and philosophy within a clan, which is defined as a group of individuals who are dependent on one another and who share a set of common goals (Ouchi, 1980). For self control, an individual sets his own goals for a particular task, and then proceeds to self monitor, self reward, and self sanction. Thus, it is a function of individual objectives, standards, and intrinsic motivations (Manz, Mossholder, & Luthans, 1987).

According to Kirsch (1996, 1997), different portfolios of control modes are used in different situations in traditional software development. Behavior and outcome controls are implemented if the appropriate procedures are known, outcomes are measurable, and the project manager is able to assess whether the target has been reached; clan and self controls are often implemented, when the task is complex, there is lack of rules and procedures for completing the task, and the performance evaluation is ambiguous (Kirsch, Sambamurthy, Ko, & Purvis, 2002). Choudhury and Sabherwal (2003) investigated the control mechanisms in alliance-based software development like outsourcing, and found that both formal and informal modes are used in outsourced software development projects. There are also some studies on the dynamics of control modes to know how control evolves with the maturity of an organization (Cardinal, Sitkin, & Long, 2004) or in the different phases of a development project (Kirsch, 2004).

As described above, multiple control modes are exerted in traditional organizations, which are termed as "Cathedral" in Raymond (2001). These controls are performed by the leaders (formal controls), by the members themselves (self control), or by the collectives (clan control). OSS development takes a totally new online community-based organizational form, which is described as "Bazaar". How controls apply to the open source context still remains unclear.

CONTROLS IN OPEN SOURCE SOFTWARE DEVELOPMENT

Open source software development is significantly different from traditional software development in both organization and process (Ljungberg, 2000). An open source project begins when an individual or a group of individuals contribute to an initial functional prototype of the software (Raymond, 2001). Then a project community grows as more and more persons are attracted into the project as developers. They work collaboratively to continue developing the software (Crowston & Howison, 2005; Long & Siau, 2007).

The software evolves incrementally through rapid development iterations produced by the community. In the development process, developers offer most of the contributions and fulfill most of the development tasks. After they submit a code patch, the source code is tested and reviewed by the peripheral users, who may request for bug fixes, patches, supports, and new features. The requests are usually treated by developers as recognized work tasks (Stewart & Gosain, 2006). Thus, the participation of developers is critical to the success of open source projects. The controls in open source projects are mainly related to the controls over the activities of developers.

Since the success of an OSS project depends on the voluntary contribution from developers, how to align the developers with the objectives of the project is critical to the final outcome of the project. In this section, the existence and effects of various control modes are discussed for the context of open source project.

Formal Controls

There are two types of formal controls: behavior control and outcome control. Behavior control, or process control, is exercised when managers attempt to influence the process of a given job. It therefore centers on evaluating an individual in terms of the means or procedures that are thought to lead to a given outcome (Ouchi, 1980). For example, on an assembly line the manager closely monitors whether the workers are following the established procedure. Outcome control, in contrast, is exercised when a given individual is evaluated in terms of the results relative to set standards of performance (Ouchi, 1980). University professors are evaluated based on their teaching evaluation and the number and quality of their academic publications. This is a typical outcome control, because the university may only monitor their results of teaching and research, and they have much autonomy on how to reach the results.

Behavior Control

Among the four major types of controls (behavior, outcome, clan, self), behavior control is infeasible in OSS development since OSS development is an incremental innovation process which is based on participants' autonomy and initiatives, and there is no pre-defined procedures in the process. In addition, because a typical OSS project community is composed of geographically dispersed developers communicating through the Internet, it is impossible to closely monitor the developers' behaviors. Behavior control may also have negative impact on technological innovation (Cardinal, 2001). Nidumolu and Subramani (2003) empirically demonstrated that centralized behavior controls would decrease the software development performance for the innovative projects that depend more on the developers' initiatives and improvisation. In open source context, the project leaders may assign tasks to developers, but do not regulate how they perform the tasks. In addition, many volunteers participate in OSS projects because they enjoy the sense of freedom and autonomy, control on their behaviors may have negative impacts on their motivations and initiatives. Therefore, we can conclude that behavior control is not appropriate for OSS development.

Outcome Control

Outcome control is a control model in which controllees are rewarded for meeting the desired goals or performance standards (Eisenhardt, 1985). Cardinal (2001) indicated that outcome control may increase the likelihood of enhancement innovation by encouraging participants to put more efforts into the innovative project. In OSS development, a developer's performance can be reviewed based on the volume and quality of his contributions. And there is still rewarding or punishing on the developers' performance through some mechanism, for example, voting by the project members. In a matured open source community, some relatively formal authority could be developed, and project leaders may conduct the control or governance based on the shared conception of the community (O'Mahony & Ferraro, 2007). Fielding (1999) indicated that there is a hierarchy of ranks in some successful open source projects. For example, the Apache project community has a ranking system that is composed of the levels of developer, committer, project management committee member, and Apache Software Foundation member, in order of increasing status; and good performance of a developer can be recognized by promotion to higher rank in the project community. In many less popular open source projects, there exists a similar mechanism, in which developers are periodically evaluated and better performance are recognized by advancement within the ranking system. Thus, in an OSS project, outcome control is enacted to some extent. The level of outcome control is expected to impact the project performance.

Hypothesis 1: Outcome control is positively related to the performance of open source software development.

Informal Controls

Informal controls differ from formal controls in that they are based on social or people strategies (Eisenhardt, 1985; Jaworski, 1988). Informal controls include the modes of clan control and self-control. They are often used when the formal controls are infeasible or insufficient (Kirsch, 1996).

Clan Control

Clan control is a mode of informal control that relies on values, beliefs, organizational culture, shared norms, or interpersonal relationships, to regulate human behaviors and facilitate the reaching of organizational goals (Eisenhardt, 1985). Ouchi (1980) described a clan as a group of individuals who are dependent on one another. OSS development is a collective innovative process, and clanship control is considered effective in such a context. Prior studies found that common values, norms, and beliefs do exist among developers in open source projects, and they have great influences on developers' participative activities (Xu et al., 2009).

Stewart and Gosain (2006) defined open source ideology as a set of shared values, norms, and beliefs that are recognized by the open source communities, and found that the shared values, norms, and beliefs have significant impact on the developers' efforts, and consequently have influence on the project effectiveness. In addition, trusting relationships are developed among members in many open source projects (Bergquist & Ljungberg, 2001; Gallivan, 2001), and have significant influence on developers' involvement and participative behaviors (Xu et al., 2009). Clanship is characterized by the shared values and beliefs, and collegial relationships among members in a collective (Jaworski, Stathakopoulos, & Krishnan, 1993). OSS developers are volunteers, they are not formally affiliated, and do not have legal or contractual relationship to the project. There is no much formal control over the voluntary developers. Thus, to make the project community a clanship is critical to the project performance. In open source projects, common values and beliefs can be recognized and promulgated through communications among developers; and relationships can be developed among developers in the process of collaboration. The level of clan control is expected to have significant effects on the project performance.

Hypothesis 2: Clan control is positively related to the performance of open source software development.

Self-Control

Self-control is a mode of informal control in which an individual sets his own goals, self-monitors goal achievement, and rewards or sanctions himself accordingly (Manz et al., 1987). Whereas clan control is a function of organizational culture and peer influence in a group, self-control stems from individual objectives and standards (Jaworski, 1988). The community-based nature of OSS development predetermines that external force or intervention is limited. Although there is some outcome control and clanship control in open source projects as discussed above, the success of software development still relies on developers' self control or self management. In addition, many developers put efforts into software development because they enjoy the way of open source coding, from which they obtain the sense of autonomy, competence and freedom (Roberts et al., 2006). Over-regulation may have negative impact on developers' motivations (Nidumolu & Subramani, 2003). Thus, to promote developers' initiatives and inspire their creativity, OSS development highly depends on developers' self control. To conduct effective and successful self control, it is essential to have individual goals aligned with the project goals. In OSS development, self control can be realized by involving developers in setting project goals. If the project goals are determined through the developers' consensus, then the developers may self-regulate their activities against the agreed goals consciously. The level of self control is expected to significantly influence the project performance.

The relationship between self and clan control is subtle as described by Kirsch (1996). They complement each other. Self-control leads to more active participation and creativity, while clan control is important to safeguard and promote cooperation in the project.

Hypothesis 3: Self-control is positively related to the performance of open source software development.

Therefore, based on the control theories, three control modes are expected to take effects in OSS development. The portfolios of outcome, clan and self controls may be diversified in different projects and in different stages of a project, but they are important to project success.

CONTROL MODES AND OPEN SOURCE PROJECT PERFORMANCE

To test the relationships between the control modes and open source project performance, an empirical study was conducted with data collected from open source projects. The methods and findings are described in the following parts of this section.

Sampling Procedure

Many studies of OSS have focused on case studies of the largest, most well-known projects such as Linux and Apache. These projects are interesting and important, but they may not be representative of the majority of OSS projects, which are in the "initial" stage, and attain much lower levels of participation and prominence. In addition, this study is to investigate the control aspects of open source project communities. Thus, only those projects that are purely community-based are included in the study. Corporate-related products, like Red Hat Linux, are not targets for the study. Data of open source projects were collected from Sourceforge.net, one of the world's largest websites with free virtual community hosting services for OSS projects. By February 2009, there were more than 230,000 registered projects, and more than 2 million registered users on it. Sourceforge provides these projects with a standard technology toolset, thereby reducing the variance in project effectiveness that may be due to differences in technology used to support workflow, code distribution and versioning. We chose the category of communications on Sourceforge to control the differences across different product categories. We selected those projects that had some activities in the prior month before data collection in terms of the contributions of participants to the code repository, changes in mailing list or discussion forum, or requests for bug fixes, supports, patches or features. This was done to ensure the sample include ongoing projects that had not been abandoned by developers. Since the research is related to the social control factors in virtual communities, only the OSS projects with at least four members (including project managers and other developers) were eligible for the study.

472 projects met the criteria and were selected as the subjects for study. These projects covered a wide range of topics, such as BBS, chat, and ICQ. They were in various development phases, including planning, pre-alpha, alpha, beta, production, and maturity.

Measurements

Meeting budgets and requirements may not be relevant in OSS (Scacchi, 2002). Thus, the more appropriate measurement for OSS project success may be through the ongoing productivity of the project. The Sourceforge site tracks the number of requests for bug fixes, patches, supports, and new features on each project as well as the number of such requests that have an uncompleted status. The requests are treated as identified work tasks in the OSS project. The extent to which identified work tasks are completed (task completion) reflects the effectiveness of the project in feature addition, code modification, and bug fixing. It was used in prior studies of OSS development such as Stewart and Gosain (2006) to measure the project effectiveness. In this study, we used task completion as the measurement for project performance, and calculate task completion as the percentage of tasks completed: task completion = (total requests – requests open)/total requests x 100.

The control modes are assessed using multiple item measures through the perception of project members. They are measured based on well-established scales from information systems, management science, and organization science. Minor modifications are made to the scales to fit the research context better. The measurements use a 1-7 likert scale. The measurement for outcome control is adapted from Kirsch et al. (2002) and Jaworski et al. (1993). The scale asks several questions about how much the developers' positions or status in the project community are based on their merits or performance. It is difficult for project members to directly perceive and report the level of common goals, values, and norms that characterize clan control in the project. Thus, in this study we use the measurement for clan control adapted from Jaworski and MacInnis (1989) and Jaworski et al. (1993). The scale includes several questions about interactions, communications, and cooperation among project members, which is more perceivable and critical to the reaching of clanship. For self control, the controllee sets the goals, self-monitors, and self-evaluates accordingly. Thus, self control is characterized by controllee as the source of project goals. In OSS development, self control occurs when the project goals are set by the developers rather than totally decided by the project manager. Then the developers may act consciously to meet the goals without external interference. In this study, the measurement for self-control is adapted from Kirsch (1996) and Kirsch et al. (2002). The scale includes questions about the developers' role in setting of project goals and procedures. The questionnaire is shown in the Appendix.

The form and level of control modes, and developers' motivations seem to vary with the age and stage of open source projects. In addition, project community size may also have influence on project performance, which is measured with task completion. Thus, project tenure (number of days from project registration), development stage (planning, pre-alpha, alpha, beta, production, and maturity), and community size (number of developers in the project) are treated as control variables when we study the effects of the control modes on project performance.

Data Collection

The study is at the community or project level. To measure the community-level constructs, we used the project members as informants, and the level of controls in the projects were measured through their perception. There were totally 3,214 members in the selected projects on Sourceforge. Among them 826 were project managers. Data were collected using the web survey. The questionnaire was posted on the researcher's website. Members of the selected projects were contacted through emails. The email address of every member was obtained from the project web pages on Sourceforge, and email was sent to each of the 3,214 members. The content of the email was to explain the purpose of the research and invite them participating in the survey. In order to get a higher response rate, one week later, a reminder email was sent to request that they answer the survey if they had not done so. 253 emails were bounced back, and remaining 2,961 emails were believed to have reached the project members. 423 responses to the survey were received by the end of data collection. Considering the fact that project managers and other developers may have different perception or feelings toward the projects, only projects with at least one response from managers and one response from other developers were kept in the sample, which resulted in the final data set of 265 responses from 93 different projects. The responses covered OSS projects with various development phases, topics, intended audiences, and license types.

The response rate was 14.3%. Non-response bias was estimated using the extrapolation method (Armstrong & Overton, 1977). The extrapolation method is based on the assumption that subjects who respond less readily are more likely non-respondents. There were two waves of responses in this study, the first wave followed the first round of invitation emails, and the second wave followed the reminder emails. Responses from the two different waves were compared, and no significant difference was found between the early and late responses. This indicates that the respondents in the study can represent the whole sample, and the conclusions from the responses can be generalized to the population.

To measure project performance, numbers of total and open requests for each project in the sample were obtained from Sourceforge website; and the control variables, such as value for project tenure, development stage, and community size, were also collected from the website.

The statistical characteristics of the sample projects are shown in Table 1.

Table 1. Project sample characteristics

Development Status	Number (N=93)	Percentage
Planning	2	2.2%
Pre-alpha	3	3.2%
Alpha	8	8.6%
Beta	33	35.5%
Production/Stable	45	48.4%
Maturity	2	2.2%
Project Age	**Number (N=93)**	**Percentage**
<1 year	8	8.8%
1-2 years	26	28.1%
2-3 years	19	20.2%
3-4 years	12	13.2%
4-5 years	14	14.9%
5-6 years	11	11.4%
>6 years	3	3.5%
License Type	**Number (N=93)**	**Percentage**
Apache Software License	2	2.2%
Artistic License	2	2.2%
BSD License	8	8.6%
GNU General Public License (GPL)	49	52.7%
GNU Library or Lesser General Public License	16	17.2%
MIT License	3	3.2%
Common Public License	6	6.5%
Others	7	7.5%
Community Size	**Number (N=93)**	**Percentage**
<=10	28	30.1%
11-20	51	54.8%
21-30	11	11.8%
31-40	3	3.2%

Data Analysis and Results

An exploratory factor analysis was conducted first. Four items with low loadings were dropped based on the results of the exploratory factor analysis.

Reliability and Validity

The constructs were assessed for reliability using Cronbach's α (Cronbach, 1951). Nunnally (1978) suggested that a value of at least 0.70 indicate the adequate reliability. The Cronbach's α of constructs are shown in Table 2.

The questions were tested for validity using confirmatory factor analysis with principal component analysis and varimax rotation. Convergent validity was assessed by checking loadings to see if terms within the same construct correlate highly amongst themselves. The results of confirmatory factor analysis are shown in Table 2.

The Cronbach's α values here range from 0.81 to 0.89, which is above the cut-off value of 0.70. Thus the reliability of constructs is confirmed. Item loadings should be greater than 0.70 for convergent validity (Chin, 1998). The item loadings range from 0.75 to 0.87, which suggests that the factor loadings are sufficiently large and the items loaded as intended for every construct. In addition, the cross-loading matrix in Table 3

Table 2. Item loadings and construct reliability

Construct	Item	Mean	Standard Deviation	Standard Loading	Cronbach's α
Outcome Control	Outcome1	5.18	1.31	0.80	0.89
	Outcome2	5.21	1.23	0.84	
	Outcome3	5.34	1.17	0.87	
Clan Control	Clan1	4.87	1.52	0.75	0.81
	Clan2	4.93	1.42	0.75	
	Clan3	4.63	1.32	0.81	
	Clan4	4.94	1.41	0.77	
Self Control	Self1	5.41	1.14	0.80	0.85
	Self2	5.18	1.18	0.81	
	Self3	5.49	1.04	0.81	

shows that each indicator loads much higher on the construct of interest than on any other factors. Thus, the convergent and discriminant validity of constructs is suggested.

The final constructs and items are shown in the Appendix.

Hypotheses Tests

Four factors were studied, project performance, outcome control, clan control, and self control. Three factors, project tenure, development stage, and community size, are included as control variables. The unit of analysis for this study is the project (n=93). The hypotheses are concerned with the relationship between control variables and performance for open source projects. Measures for the controls of each project are computed by averaging the scores of respondents from the project and computing the project scores. Equal weight is given for each respondent and each role. Prior to averaging respondents' scores, interrater agreement was assessed using the multiple-item estimator for within-group interrater reliability as proposed by James, Demaree, and Wolf (1984). The results indicate generally a strong agreement of ratings referring to the same project, which means there is no discrepancy between the managers and developers for rating the controls in the open source projects.

The descriptive statistics of the project level factors are shown in Table 4.

To test the relationship between control modes and open source project performance, multiple linear regression analysis was performed, with project performance as dependent variable, the control modes as independent variables, and project tenure, development stage, and community size as control variables. The results are reported in Table 5.

Table 3. Cross-loadings of constructs

Question	Factor 1	2	3
Outcome1	**0.80**	0.21	0.25
Outcome2	**0.84**	0.17	0.36
Outcome3	**0.87**	0.15	0.30
Clan1	0.17	**0.75**	0.22
Clan2	0.19	**0.75**	0.26
Clan3	0.05	**0.81**	0.07
Clan4	0.14	**0.77**	0.09
Self1	0.26	0.11	**0.80**
Self2	0.23	0.12	**0.81**
Self3	0.20	0.16	**0.81**

Table 4. Descriptive statistics of project factors

Factor	Mean	Standard Deviation	Median	Max. Value	Min. Value
Outcome Control	5.36	0.76	5.34	6.84	3.5
Clan Control	4.35	0.86	4.38	6	2
Self Control	5.39	0.62	5.5	6.5	3.5
Project Performance	79.21	10.09	81.18	96.73	43.93
Project Tenure	1730	590	1812	2578	533
Development Stage	4.31	0.94	5	6	1
Community Size	18.8	8.72	19.7	73	4

Table 5. Regression analysis results

Factor	DF	Parameter Estimate	Standard Error	T Value	Pr > |t|
Outcome Control	1	3.95	1.52	2.60	0.011*
Clan Control	1	2.59	1.06	2.44	0.017*
Self Control	1	4.60	1.80	2.56	0.012*
Project Tenure	1	0.0006	0.0014	0.42	0.679
Development Stage	1	0.16	0.89	0.18	0.854
Community Size	1	0.015	0.018	0.83	0.411

* $P < 5\%$, $R^2 = 0.43$

The regression results demonstrate that three types of control (outcome, clan and self control) have positive effects on the performance of open source project. And they account for 43% of the total variance in project performance, which is assessed through the percentage of task completion in the project. The effects of outcome control, clan control, and self control are significant at ($P \leq 0.05$) level.

DISCUSSION

OSS development takes the online community as the organizational form, and developers are volunteers who are not formally affiliated to the project. How to control the activities of developers in such a loosely-structured organization is important to software development and concerned by the leaders and managers of open source projects. By analyzing the data from OSS projects, this study finds that the portfolios of outcome control, clan control, and self control play a critical role in the performance of OSS projects. The levels of outcome control, clan control, and self control have significant impact on the OSS project performance.

This study contributes to research of OSS by providing an in-depth understanding of OSS development from the control perspective. Previously, there have been some studies to investigate factors related to open source project success. For example, Stewart, Ammeter, and Maruping (2006) indicated that license restrictiveness and organizational sponsorship have impacts on success of open source projects. Similarly, Subramaniam, Sen, and Nelson (2009) found that restrictive licenses have an adverse impact on OSS project success. Grewal, Lilien, and Mallapragada (2006) indicated that network embeddedness, which is the linkages of project managers and developers with other projects, is important to open source project success. Open source is adopted by some companies as a new software development organization form (Fitzgerald, 2006). Agerfalk and Fitzgerald (2008) discussed outsourcing to open source community from a psychological contract perspective. Each of these studies tried to understand the influential factors for open source project success from certain perspectives. However, they did not provide a comprehensive view on how to regulate developer activities for project management. Among the factors related to OSS development success, how to manage volunteers' participation behaviors is essential. Currently, research has been focused on the motivations of open source developers' participation, and found that participation is motivated and influenced by multiple factors, including extrinsic and intrinsic motives (Roberts et al., 2006), and social relational factors in the community (Bagozzi & Dholakia, 2006; Oh & Jeon, 2007). These studies made progresses in understanding the motivational factors. However, they did not reveal how to enhance or promote developers' motivations from the project management perspective. This paper, for the first time, incorporates the control concept and theory into OSS research, and indicates that the developers' activities can be controlled or "managed" to some extent to fit into the project goals, although OSS development is based on online communities. This provides implications for OSS researchers to conduct more study from management perspectives to better know how to regulate participants' activities for the success of OSS development.

This study shows that the controls in OSS development are different from those in traditional software development teams. In traditional software development, both formal and informal controls are incurred, and managers may choose to apply the formal controls, including process and outcome controls, when they have enough knowledge and skills, there is established procedure, and the results are measurable. Informal controls, like clan control and self control, are used mainly as complements for the formal controls in case the formal controls are infeasible or inefficient. However, in OSS development controls take effects mainly in informal way. Regulation of developer behaviors mainly depends on the clanship and developers' self control. Although there is outcome control to some extent, it is not as formal as in traditional teams, and just based on some common agreement among developers. In addition, in traditional teams the controls are mainly exerted by the leaders. However, in OSS projects the leadership of project managers is not so formal and the authority is quite limited. The controls are exerted mainly by the collective of developers through the means of voting, discussion, and peer influence.

The results have practical implications for project management in open source context. The role of outcome control implies that ranking mechanism is still important. OSS development requires initiatives and investment of time and energy. Ranking based on performance may stimulate participation and reduce the chance of free riding. In open source projects, monetary rewards may not be a concern of developers. Therefore, ranking may be an important factor to promote contribution since developers need to accomplish the sense of achievement through higher status in the projects. The role of clan control implies that the clanship or community quality is critical for project success. An effective OSS project leader is expected to be a good facilitator to build a high-quality community by promulgating the common values and norms among developers, facilitating communications and relationships building among developers, so as to promote clanship control in the project. The role of self-control implies the importance of developers' self-regulation. For self-control to be effective, it is necessary for project managers to set goals for the project collectively with other developers, or to socialize developers to the project goals, thus, the developers will behave according to the goals consciously.

Open source software is typically of the open content model, which refers to the online collaborative knowledge creation by volunteers. Today, the open content model has been applied to many other contexts in addition to software, such as open source music composition (e.g. jMusic), online encyclopedia (e.g. Wikipedia), and eR&D (e.g. Procter & Gamble's "Connect & Develop" R&D model). Thus, findings from this research may not only provide advice for open source software development, but also have implications for other open content systems as mentioned above.

The study has some limitations. First, as stated at the beginning of the paper, this research is conducted for community projects, which are online community-based with volunteers as developers. Thus, the research findings may not be appropriate for the non-profit organization and commercial projects. Second, the dataset is based on projects from Sourceforge.net. Currently, some large projects have their own websites and are not included. Thus the results may not be applicable to those projects not listed on Sourceforge.net. In addition, only projects that had activity within the month prior to data collection are considered for study in the research. This may cause certain biases since completed projects are not included in the study. However, the projects selected in this study are believed to be representative of community OSS projects, since they cover a wide range of topics, license types, and development phases. Third, this study demonstrates that the three modes of control are important in open source software development. However, it does not explain how they can affect the performance of open source software projects. Previous studies indicated that volunteers' participation and contribution in open source software development are motivated by their enjoyment (Hars & Ou, 2002; Xu et al., 2009), sense of achievement (Roberts et al., 2006), identification (Hars and Ou, 2002; Xu and Jones, 2010), and obligation (Xu & Jones, 2010). To further understand how and why the control modes affect open source software development, it is necessary to study the linkage between the control modes and the motivational factors, for example, how the control modes satisfy developers' sense of achievement, enhance their enjoyment, and promote their identification and obligation with the projects, and consequently affect the performance of open source software projects.

CONCLUSION

In this paper we investigate the control modes in OSS projects, and study their effects on OSS project performance. The research findings show that outcome control, clan control, and self control play important roles in OSS development. The research enriches the theory and literature of OSS development. It also has practical implications for OSS development and project management. According to prior studies of control mechanisms, control modes may change dynamically in the lifecycle of software development. The dynamics or evolution of control modes in open source context has not been studied, and it is expected to be investigated in the follow-up research. The current research is based on community open source projects. It could be extended to projects supported by non-profit organizations and conducted by commercial firms in future research, to see what control mechanisms are effective in other types of open source projects. Finally, some motivational factors can be included as mediators in future study to provide a better understanding on how the control modes affect open source project performance. The potential mediators may be the motivational factors such as sense of achievement, enjoyment, identification, and obligation. Relationship between the control modes and motivational factors will be studied in future research to know the paths that control modes influence the performance of open source software development.

ACKNOWLEDGMENT

This research was supported by the National Social Science Foundation of China (No. 09CTQ023).

REFERENCES

Agerfalk, P. J., & Fitzgerald, B. (2008). Outsourcing to an unknown workforce: Exploring opensourcing as a global sourcing strategy. *Management Information Systems Quarterly*, *32*(2), 385–409.

Armstrong, J. S., & Overton, T. S. (1977). Estimating nonresponse bias in mail surveys. *Journal of Marketing Research*, *14*, 396–402. doi:10.2307/3150783

Bagozzi, R. P., & Dholakia, U. M. (2006). Open source software user communities: a study of participation in Linux user groups. *Management Science*, *52*(7), 1099–1115. doi:10.1287/mnsc.1060.0545

Bergquist, M., & Ljungberg, J. (2001). The power of gifts: organizing social relationships in open source communities. *Information Systems Journal*, *11*, 305–320. doi:10.1046/j.1365-2575.2001.00111.x

Bretthauer, D. (2002). Open source software: A history. *Information Technology and Libraries*, *21*(1), 3–10.

Cardinal, L. B. (2001). Technological innovation in the pharmaceutical industry: The use of organizational control in managing research and development. *Organization Science*, *12*(1), 19–36. doi:10.1287/orsc.12.1.19.10119

Cardinal, L. B., Sitkin, S. B., & Long, C. P. (2004). Balancing and rebalancing in the creation and evolution of organizational control. *Organization Science*, *15*(4), 411–431. doi:10.1287/orsc.1040.0084

Chin, W. W. (1998). Issues and options on structural equation modeling. *Management Information Systems Quarterly*, *1*, 7–16.

Choudhury, V., & Sabherwal, R. (2003). Portfolios of control in outsourced software development projects. *Information Systems Research*, *14*(3), 291–314. doi:10.1287/isre.14.3.291.16563

Cronbach, L. J. (1951). Coefficient alpha and the internal structure of tests. *Psychometrika*, *16*, 297–334. doi:10.1007/BF02310555

Crowston, K., & Howison, J. (2005). The social structure of free and open source software development. *First Monday*, *10*(2).

Demil, B., & Lecocq, X. (2006). Neither market nor hierarchy nor network: The emergence of bazaar governance. *Organization Studies*, *27*(10), 1447–1466. doi:10.1177/0170840606067250

Eisenhardt, K. M. (1985). Control: organizational and economic approaches. *Management Science*, *31*(2), 134–149. doi:10.1287/mnsc.31.2.134

Feller, J., & Fitzgerald, B. (2002). *Understanding Open Source Software Development*. Reading, MA: Addison-Wesley.

Fielding, R. (1999). Shared leadership in the apache project. *Communications of the ACM*, *42*(4), 42–43. doi:10.1145/299157.299167

Fitzgerald, B. (2006). The transformation of open source software. *Management Information Systems Quarterly*, *30*(3), 587–598.

Gallivan, M. J. (2001). Striking a balance between trust and control in a virtual organization: a content analysis of open source software case studies. *Information Systems Journal*, *11*, 277–304. doi:10.1046/j.1365-2575.2001.00108.x

Grewal, R., Lilien, G. L., & Mallapragada, G. (2006). Location, location, location: How network embeddedness affects project success in open source systems. *Management Science*, *52*(7), 1043–1056. doi:10.1287/mnsc.1060.0550

Guinan, P. J., Cooprider, J. G., & Faraj, S. (1998). Enabling software development team performance during requirements definition: A behavioral versus technical approach. *Information Systems Research*, *9*(2), 101–125. doi:10.1287/isre.9.2.101

Hagan, D., Watson, O., & Barron, K. (2007). Ascending into order: A reflective analysis from a small open source development team. *International Journal of Information Management*, *27*(6), 397–405. doi:10.1016/j.ijinfomgt.2007.08.011

Hars, A., & Ou, S. (2002). Working for free? Motivations for participation in open source projects. *International Journal of Electronic Commerce*, *6*(3), 25–39.

Henderson, J. C., & Lee, S. (1992). Managing IS design teams: A control theories perspective. *Management Science*, *38*(6), 757–777. doi:10.1287/mnsc.38.6.757

Hertel, G., Niednerand, S., & Herrmann, S. (2003). Motivations of software developers in open source projects: an internet-based survey of contributors to the Linux kernel. *Research Policy*, *32*(7), 1159–1177. doi:10.1016/S0048-7333(03)00047-7

James, L., Demaree, R., & Wolf, G. (1984). Estimating within-group interrater reliability with and without response bias. *The Journal of Applied Psychology*, *69*(1), 85–98. doi:10.1037/0021-9010.69.1.85

Jaworski, B. J. (1988). Toward a theory of marketing control: Environmental context, control types, and consequences. *Journal of Marketing*, *52*(3), 23–39. doi:10.2307/1251447

Jaworski, B. J., & MacInnis, D. J. (1989). Marketing jobs and management controls: Toward a framework. *JMR, Journal of Marketing Research*, *26*(4), 406–419. doi:10.2307/3172761

Jaworski, B. J., Stathakopoulos, V., & Krishnan, H. S. (1993). Control combinations in marketing: Conceptual framework and empirical evidence. *Journal of Marketing*, *57*, 57–69. doi:10.2307/1252057

Kirsch, L. J. (1996). The management of complex tasks in organizations: controlling the systems development process. *Organization Science*, *7*(1), 1–21. doi:10.1287/orsc.7.1.1

Kirsch, L. J. (1997). Portfolios of control modes and IS project management. *Information Systems Research*, *8*(3), 215–239. doi:10.1287/isre.8.3.215

Kirsch, L. J. (2004). Deploying Common Systems Globally: The Dynamics of Control. *Information Systems Research*, *15*(4), 374–395. doi:10.1287/isre.1040.0036

Kirsch, L. J., Sambamurthy, V., Ko, D., & Purvis, R. L. (2002). Controlling information systems development projects: The view from the client. *Management Science*, *48*(4), 484–498. doi:10.1287/mnsc.48.4.484.204

Krogh, G., Spaeth, S., & Lakhani, K. R. (2003). Community, joining, and specialization in open source software innovation: a case study. *Research Policy*, *32*(7), 1217–1241. doi:10.1016/S0048-7333(03)00050-7

Lee, G. K., & Cole, R. E. (2003). From a firm-based to a community-based model of knowledge creation: the case of the Linux kernel development. *Organization Science*, *14*(6), 633–649. doi:10.1287/orsc.14.6.633.24866

Lerner, J., & Tirole, J. (2002). Some Simple Economics of Open Source. *The Journal of Industrial Economics*, *5*, 197–234.

Ljungberg, J. (2000). Open source movements as a model for organizing. *European Journal of Information Systems*, *9*, 208–216. doi:10.1057/palgrave/ejis/3000373

Long, Y., & Siau, K. (2007). Social network structures in open source software development teams. *Journal of Database Management*, *18*(2), 25–40.

Mahmood, M. A. (1987). System development methods – A comparative investigation. *Management Information Systems Quarterly*, *11*(3), 292–311. doi:10.2307/248674

Manz, C. C., Mossholder, K. W., & Luthans, F. (1987). An integrated perspective of self-control in organizations. *Administration & Society*, *19*(1). doi:10.1177/009539978701900101

Markus, M. L., Manville, B., & Agres, C. E. (2000). What makes a virtual organization work? *Sloan Management Review*, *42*(1), 13–26.

Merchant, K. A. (1988). Progressing toward a theory of marketing control: A comment. *Journal of Marketing*, *52*, 40–44. doi:10.2307/1251448

Nidumolu, S. R., & Subramani, M. R. (2003). The matrix of control: Combining process and structure approaches to managing software development. *Journal of Management Information Systems*, *20*(3), 159–196.

Nunally, J. C. (1978). *Psychometric Theory*. New York: McGraw-Hill.

O'Mahony, S., & Ferraro, F. (2007). The emergence of governance in an open source community. *Academy of Management Journal*, *50*(5), 1079–1105.

Oh, W., & Jeon, S. (2007). Membership herding and network stability in the open source community: The ising perspective. *Management Science*, *53*(7), 1086–1101. doi:10.1287/mnsc.1060.0623

Ouchi, W. G. (1977). The relationship between organizational structure and organizational control. *Administrative Science Quarterly*, *22*, 95–113. doi:10.2307/2391748

Ouchi, W. G. (1978). The transmission of control through organizational hierarchy. *Academy of Management Journal*, *21*(2), 173–192. doi:10.2307/255753

Ouchi, W. G. (1980). Markets, bureaucracies, and clans. *Administrative Science Quarterly*, *25*(1), 129–141. doi:10.2307/2392231

Raymond, E. (2001). *The Cathedral and the Bazaar: Musings on Linux and Open Source by an Accidental Revolutionary*. Cambridge, MA: O'Reilly & Associates.

Roberts, J., Hann, I., & Slaughter, S. (2006). Understanding the motivations, participation, and performance of open source software developers: A longitudinal study of the Apache Projects. *Management Science*, *52*(7), 984–999. doi:10.1287/mnsc.1060.0554

Scacchi, W. (2002). Understanding the requirements for developing open source software systems. *IEEE Proceedings on Software*, *149*(1), 24–39. doi:10.1049/ip-sen:20020202

Snell, S. A. (1992). Control theory in strategic human resource management: The mediating effect of administrative information. *Academy of Management Journal*, *35*(2), 292–327. doi:10.2307/256375

Stewart, K. J., Ammeter, A. P., & Maruping, L. M. (2006). Impacts of license choice and organizational sponsorship on user interest and development activity in open source software projects. *Information Systems Research*, *17*(2), 126–144. doi:10.1287/isre.1060.0082

Stewart, K. J., & Gosain, S. (2006). The impact of ideology on effectiveness in open source software development teams. *Management Information Systems Quarterly*, *30*(2), 291–314.

Subramaniam, C., Sen, R., & Nelson, M. (2009). Determinants of open source software project success: A longitudinal study. *Decision Support Systems*, *46*(2). doi:10.1016/j.dss.2008.10.005

von Hippel, E., & von Krogh, G. (2003). Open source software and the "private-collective" innovation model: issues for organization science. *Organization Science*, *14*(2), 209–223. doi:10.1287/orsc.14.2.209.14992

Wu, C. G., Gerlach, J. H., & Young, C. E. (2007). An empirical analysis of open source software developers' motivations and continuance intentions. *Information & Management*, *44*(3), 231–352. doi:10.1016/j.im.2006.12.006

Xu, B., & Jones, D. R. (2010). Volunteers' Participation in Open Source Software Development: A Study from the Social-Relational Perspective. *The Data Base for Advances in Information Systems*, *41*(3), 69–84.

Xu, B., Jones, D. R., & Shao, B. (2009). Volunteers' involvement in online community based software development. *Information & Management*, *46*(3), 151–158. doi:10.1016/j.im.2008.12.005

APPENDIX: MEASURES AND SCALES

Outcome Control

Outcome 1: To what extent developers are awarded higher level positions dependent on their performance in the project.
Outcome 2: To what degree developers' positions in the project are tied to their performance.
Outcome 3: To what extent developers' status in the project depends on the amount and quality of their contribution.

Clan Control

Clan 1: The project encourages cooperation between developers.
Clan 2: Developers in the project are familiar with each other.
Clan 3: The project fosters an environment where developers respect each other's work.
Clan 4: The project encourages discussions between developers.

Self Control

Self 1: The setting of the project goals is pretty much under developers' control.
Self 2: For this project, to what extent the developers are allowed a high degree of influence in determination of project goals.
Self 3: Developers have significant influence in setting specific procedures for project activities.

This work was previously published in the Journal of Database Management, Volume 22, Issue 1, edited by Keng Siau, pp. 26-42, copyright 2011 by IGI Publishing (an imprint of IGI Global).

Chapter 3
An MDA Approach and QVT Transformations for the Integrated Development of Goal-Oriented Data Warehouses and Data Marts

Jesús Pardillo
University of Alicante, Spain

Jose-Norberto Mazón
University of Alicante, Spain

Juan Trujillo
University of Alicante, Spain

ABSTRACT

To customize a data warehouse, many organizations develop concrete data marts focused on a particular department or business process. However, the integrated development of these data marts is an open problem for many organizations due to the technical and organizational challenges involved during the design of these repositories as a complete solution. In this article, the authors present a design approach that employs user requirements to build both corporate data warehouses and data marts in an integrated manner. The approach links information requirements to specific data marts elicited by using goal-oriented requirement engineering, which are automatically translated into the implementation of corresponding data repositories by means of model-driven engineering techniques. The authors provide two UML profiles that integrate the design of both data warehouses and data marts and a set of QVT transformations with which to automate this process. The advantage of this approach is that user requirements are captured from the early development stages of a data-warehousing project to automatically translate them into the entire data-warehousing platform, considering the different data marts. Finally, the authors provide screenshots of the CASE tools that support the approach, and a case study to show its benefits.

DOI: 10.4018/978-1-4666-2044-5.ch003

INTRODUCTION

A *corporate data warehouse* is a repository that provides decision makers with a large amount of historical data concerning the overall enterprise strategy. A data-warehousing architecture defines a set of data repositories and their relationships to support the decision-making process in a given organization. Several architectural options (Cabibbo & Torlone, 2001; Jarke et al., 1999; Jukic, 2006; Samos et al., 1998 ; Watson et al., 2001) and methodologies (Bonifati et al., 2001; Giorgini et al., 2008; Luján-Mora & Trujillo, 2006a; Mazón et al., 2007a; Sen & Sinha, 2005) have been proposed to develop these repositories. Specifically, two foundational data-warehousing alternatives have been broadly discussed (Breslin, 2004): the *top-down* approach originally stated by Inmon (2005) and the *bottom-up* approach stated by Kimball and Ross (2002). The basis of these approaches consists of which data repositories should be developed first: a *corporate data warehouse* in which an organization's data are stored and integrated in a single repository (top-down) or *departmental data marts* in which data are aggregated and customized for particular information needs (bottom-up). Although the former is considered to be the most elegant solution from a theoretical point of view, it is usually hard to implement since the project scope involves the whole organization (Watson et al, 2001), and the second approach is thus more suitable for agile developments despite the problems that arise during data-mart integration (Watson et al., 2001; Chaudhuri & Dayal, 1997). Both approaches fail when they attempt to derive the second data repositories (*i.e.*, data marts or corporate data warehouse, respectively) due to the inherent high cost associated to the integration of huge amongs of data (top-down) and to the duplicated integration tasks done by data marts (bottom-up). In order to overcome these limitations, Kimball and Ross (2002) have also proposed a bus architecture articulated by *conformed dimensions*. These dimensions account for 90 percent of the integration efforts made in order to tie data marts together (Kimball & Ross, 2002). They are obtained through the agreement of the entire organization, thus supporting truly cross-departmental decision-making processes. Despite all this, this solution is designed at the logical level (*i.e.*, by using relational schemata), and does not therefore provide suitable mechanisms to drive complex developments such as methodologies (Bonifati et al., 2001; Giorgini et al., 2008; Luján-Mora & Trujillo, 2006; Mazón et al., 2006; Mazón & Trujillo, 2008) based on conceptual modeling (Abelló et al., 2006; Golfarelli et al., 1998; Hüsemann et al., 2000; Luján-Mora et al., 2006). Furthermore, existing matching methods do not cover the particular problems of integrating data warehouse and data mart schemas (Evermann, 2008).

However, we believe that the surrounding architectural debate (Breslin, 2004) has been overlooked by the current development approaches which are mainly based on conceptual modelling. These approaches have focused on capturing information requirements by means of *multidimensional modelling* (Kimball & Ross, 2002; Chaudhuri & Dayal, 1997) which organizes data in terms of *facts* and *dimensions* of analysis, but does not specify how data repositories (*i.e.*, corporate data warehouse and their dependent data marts) are built from them. For instance, departmental data marts may be built by different development teams in isolation. They therefore lack incorporated conformity issues to solve the integrated development of data marts and corporate data warehouses, in order to assure cross-departmental information needs such as those answered by *drill-across* operations during "on-line analytical processing" (OLAP) (Chaudhuri & Dayal, 1997).

In this article, we present an approach based on *goal-oriented requirement engineering* (Yu & Mylopoulos, 1994) and *model-driven engineering* (Bézivin, 2006) technologies to solve the architectural debate (Breslin, 2004) by supporting Kimball's insights (Kimball & Ross, 2002) at the conceptual level. Goal elicitation was identified by Ang et al (1995) as the third most critical success factor in enterprise projects, being mandatory to begin any project with a conceptualisation of its goals and the ways to achieve them (Slevin & Pinto, 1987). This solution is based on our previous works (Luján-Mora et al., 2006; Luján-Mora & Trujillo, 2006b; Mazón et al., 2007a; Mazón & Trujillo, 2008; Pardillo et al., 2008) which propose: a modelling framework in terms of the goals that the data warehouse should achieve together with the information required to conform to analysis dimensions; and also, a transformation architecture based on the "model-driven architecture" (MDA) (OMG, 2008; Siau & Cao, 2001) approach through which to automatically derive both the corporate data warehouse and its dependent data marts in an integrated manner. We thus enable decision makers to respond to their cross-departmental information needs. It is worth noting that this modelling framework is not associated to any particular data-warehousing development method, thus, the proposed diagramming techniques and model transformations can be applied whenever a data-warehousing architecture should be designed.

Extended Material

This article is an extended version of the short paper (Pardillo & Trujillo, 2008) presented at the ER'08 conference[1]. In this version the short paper has been extended and improved by: (i) introducing a methodology based on MDA according to the proposed novel UML extensions, (ii) describing each of the design artefacts involved in greater detail and presenting more UML modelling diagrams in order to clarify their application, (iii) introducing two new UML profiles which provide a modelling language for data-mart requirements and data-warehousing repository modelling, (iv) introducing a set of QVT relations/transformations in order to be able to deal with automatic transformations for the novel UML profiles presented in this article, and finally (v), enlarging the case study throughout the entire article in order to clarify how to apply our method in real world projects. This extended version therefore constitutes a natural and significant evolution of the approach presented in (Pardillo & Trujillo, 2008).

The remainder of this article is organized as follows: the following section introduces a motivating example in order to illustrate common conformity problems. The section "Integrated Development of Model-Driven Goal-Oriented Corporate Data Warehouses and Data Marts" presents our goal-oriented model-driven approach for the integrated development of data warehouses. The section "Conceptual Modelling Mapping: From Goals to Data Structures" describes the mappings involved in the automatic development of data marts and corporate data warehouses. The related development platform and our example-scenario implementation are outlined in "Development Platform and Implementation". "Related Work" then discusses the related work. The final section expounds conclusions and outlines future work.

MOTIVATING EXAMPLE

Current development approaches (Bonifati et al., 2001; Giorgini et al., 2008; Luján-Mora & Trujillo, 2006a; Mazón et al., 2007a; Sen & Sinha, 2005) do not specify organizational data warehousing concerns with regard to the architectural debate (Breslin, 2004). Their practitioners design several schemata for each data mart which are not aligned by any criteria, *i.e.*, they are developed in isolation. As a result, developers obtain schemata in which data structures are ill-defined due to non-unified data representations such as that shown in the example scenario of Figure 1. These schemata show the multidimensional models of two independent data marts to support decision making in inventory and sales business processes. They have been modelled by using the UML profile for multidimensional modelling presented in (Luján et al., 2006). Figure 1 illustrates a common situation that occurs when developers do not deal with integration issues.

Multidimensional modelling is the foundation of data warehouses (Kimball & Ross, 2002; Chaudhuri & Dayal, 1997) in which data under analysis are arranged into facts (represented as in Figure 1) and dimensions ( ), so that analysts can describe them, and resemble the well-known star-like structures (Kimball & Ross, 2002). Both facts and dimensions are also represented by means of measures (FA) and aggregation hierarchies ( ) based on different aggregation levels ( ), respectively. Although both facts are described by similar dimensions (*i.e.*, by date, product, and store), decision makers cannot drill across them to fulfill their cross-departmental information needs since they are not integrated.

With regard to the dimensions involved (see Figure 1), several problems arise from an isolated data-mart development process:

- **Store dimension:** Stores are described at different granularities (Kimball & Ross, 2002) in each data mart (*i.e.*, a ZIP aggregation level in the inventory and the city level in the sales fact). Cities are aggregated into different levels in each model (*i.e.*, countries for retail stores and states for sales stores).
- **Date dimension:** The concept of date is described by different formats (*i.e.*, day *vs.* dates). Years in the inventory data mart are fiscal years whereas years in the sales data mart are calendar years (although they are given the same name). Dates are aggregated by months or weeks depending on the data mart.
- **Product dimension:** Products are managed at different granularities (*i.e.*, pieces *vs.* the products themselves). Products have different semantics (*i.e.*, assembled products). Aggregation levels depend on the actual semantics of products (*i.e.*, brand grouping pieces *vs.* products). Product types may be related to their sizes (and should therefore be correctly related).
- **Promotion dimension:** This dimension is required by only one of the data marts.

These facts signify that, in the current approaches, drilling across these dimensions is not possible (Kimball & Ross, 2002; Abelló et al., 2002) and data marts remain isolated.

Kimball and Ross (2002) propose the conformity of dimensions through an agreement between every data-mart development team, later providing a foundational definition of conformed dimensions: "two dimensions are *conformed* if the fields that are used as common row headers have the same domain" (Kimball, 2003). However, this definition is oriented towards the logical level (Hüsemann et al., 2000), in which the name matching of logical structures (*i.e.*, tables, columns, and rows) is necessary to enable drill-across operations to take place by sorting and merging relational database structures. Some authors (Abelló et al., 2002; Cabibbo & Torlone, 2004) therefore generalize the conformity constraints at the conceptual level. For example, (Abelló et al., 2002) supports conformity by finding functional dependencies between dimension instances. On the other hand, other authors (Hurtado et al., 1999) in literature establish more general schema equivalences in terms of their information capacity.

We assume an adaptation of the definition stated in (Kimball, 2003) for the conceptual level: sharing dimensions between conceptual multidimensional models implies that they can be reused through data marts in order to permit cross-departmental decision-making processes. Therefore, our approach is based on using agreement to discover information needs through data marts and combining them in a master conformed template that fulfills all these needs.

Moreover, our approach can also be used to provide the integrated development of the corporate data-warehouse that populates the data marts,

Figure 1. Data models of two independent data marts: retail inventory and sales analysis

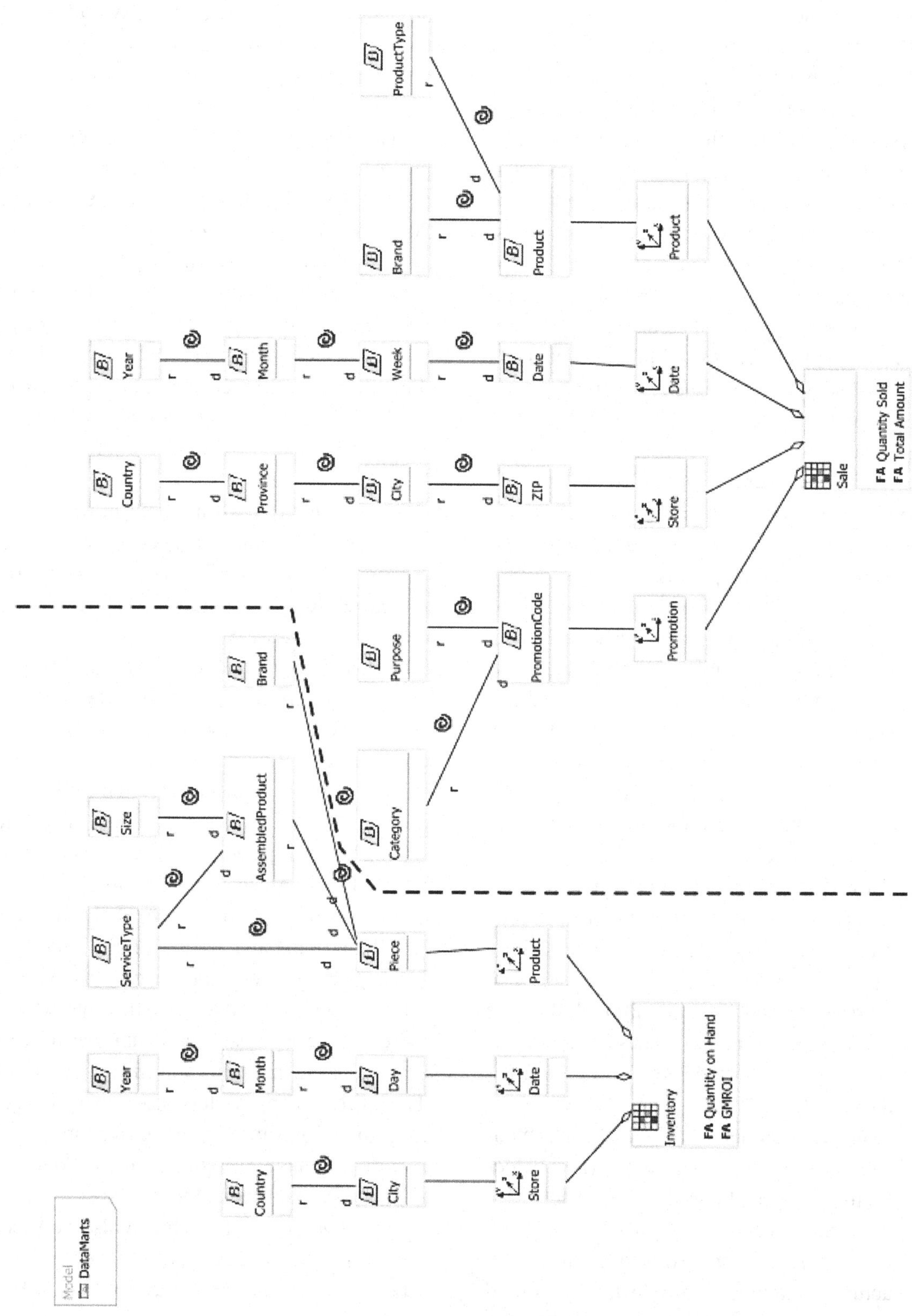

thus reducing the expensive efforts involved in data integration (Vassiliadis, 2000).

INTEGRATED DEVELOPMENT OF MODEL-DRIVEN GOAL-ORIENTED CORPORATE DATA WAREHOUSES AND DATA MARTS

In this section, we present a development approach for data warehouses based on: (i) discovering information needs for each data mart by applying goal-oriented requirement engineering techniques (Yu & Mylopoulos, 1994), (ii) permitting the dimension-related requirements obtained to conform by using a conformity authority that assures agreement and commitment between every data-mart stakeholder, (iii) providing a conceptual framework to model the underlying data repositories, and (iv) automatically translating the information requirements obtained from the very early stages of development to the final implementation by using a model-driven engineering approach (Bézivin, 2006), specifically the well-known MDA proposal (OMG, 2008; Siau & Cao, 2001) which has been successfully employed in our previous works (Luján-Mora et al., 2006; Luján-Mora & Trujillo, 2006b; Mazón et al., 2006; Mazón et al., 2007a; Mazón & Trujillo, 2008; Pardillo et al., 2008).

Goal-Oriented Reasoning to Permit Data Marts to Conform

Kimball and Ross (2002) advocate a "dimension authority" such as the stakeholder responsible for managing conformed dimensions by defining, maintaining and publishing them for each data mart; hence, conformity implies organizational commitment rather than simply a technical decision. Nevertheless, this author does not provide any mechanisms to support this.

Therefore, we propose to enrich the organizational modelling in goal-oriented approaches (Bonifati et al., 2001; Giorgini et al., 2008; Mazón et al., 2007a) by also taking into account conformity issues by explicitly establishing a dimension authority. It is worth mentioning that we can not only respond to data-mart needs, but can also integrate them into the strategic policies of the whole organization.

Figure 2 shows the general overview of the stakeholders involved in a data-mart development after including a dimension authority with the *i* notation* (Yu & Mylopoulos, 1994). The process starts with the elicitation of the information requirements for a particular decision maker in the department (*e.g.*, a sales or inventory manager in Figure 2). By using goal-modelling terminology (Yu & Mylopoulos, 1994), a data-mart developer *intentionally depends* (represented as -D-) on other organizational *actors* (◯), *i.e.*, decision makers, in order to obtain the *resource* (▭) of his/her particular information requirements. These dependencies are modelled by means of strategic-dependency diagrams like that shown in Figure 2. A data-mart developer therefore depends on the dimension authority to make dimensions conform as a result of the corporate agreement. On the other hand, for this aim, the dimension authority needs the dimensions to conform for the different data-mart teams. Hence, data marts can deploy already conformed data structures which enable decision makers to fulfil their information needs. The conformity achieved signifies that data-mart coalescing queries (Cabibbo & Torlone, 2004) can be employed during cross-departmental decision-making processes. It is worth noting that each data mart is designed from a set of predefined queries that are derived from the decision-maker's goals. This fact does not mean that decision makers cannot evolve their analyses by smoothly getting into completely new and unknown queries as usual in the OLAP technology.

In order to design an integrated modelling framework for this kind of requirements, we have defined a UML profile with which to model the conformity of multidimensional requirements

Figure 2. Stakeholders and their resource dependencies in a data-mart development

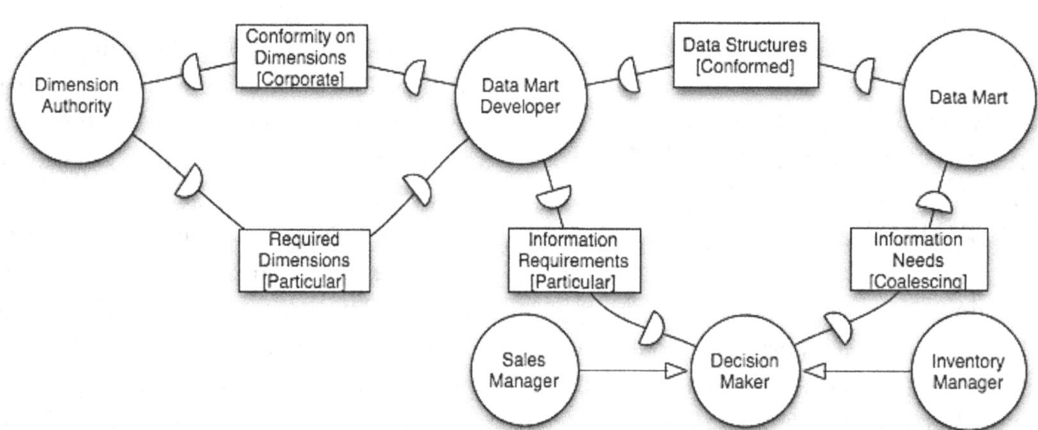

(called *Conformity@MultidimensionalRequirements*)[2]. The UML profile *Conformity@MultidimensionalRequirements* defines the modelling architecture that is shown in Figure 3. This is articulated by means of two additional profiling layers, namely, the UML profile for modelling multidimensional requirements in the framework of *i** (*MultidimensionalRequirements@iStar*) and the UML profile for modelling *i** by using UML based on the previous work (*iStar@UML*). The UML (OMG, 2008; Siau & Cao, 2001) thus enables us to articulate a coherent modelling architecture with which to incrementally extend UML, thus providing goal-oriented modelling, followed by data-warehousing requirements, and finally conformity. UML profiles are thus an easy mechanism with which to extend a modelling language. These profiles contain *stereotypes* of the modelling element to be extended (*metaclasses* of the language) which manage the tag definitions used to describe the extension attributes and the constraints used to specify well-formedness rules over the models. The designed extensions are explained, from the bottom to the upper layer, as follows.

iStar@UML Profile

The *i** modelling framework (Yu & Mylopoulos, 1994) provides mechanisms with which to represent actors, their dependencies, and the structuring of the business goals that an organization wishes to attain. This framework establishes two models: the *strategic dependency* (*SD*) model with which to describe the dependency relationships among various actors in an organizational context, and the *strategic rationale* (*SR*) model, used to describe actors' interests and concerns, and how they might be addressed. From here on, we shall focus on describing the SR models used to model decision makers' goals and information requirements.

The SR model (modelled with the *SR* stereotype and represented as) provides a detailed means of modelling the internal intentional elements and relationships of each actor (*iActor*,). We use intentional elements such as goals (*Goal*,), tasks (*Task*,), resources (*Resource*,); and intentional relationships such as means-end (*MeansEnds*,) to represent alternative means of fulfilling goals, or task-decomposition (*Decomposition*,) representing the necessary elements that a task should perform.

MultidimensionalRequirements@ iStar Profile

In order to define SR models, goals, tasks, and resources are represented as intentional elements for each decision maker. Decision makers' goals are defined by using the *Strategic*, *Decision*, and *Information* stereotypes are defined by using the inheritance white-head arrow to specialize the previously defined *Goal* stereotype, and the intentional means-end relationships (*MeansEnds*, —▷-) between them. Information requirements (*Requirement*) are derived from information goals and are represented as tasks.

Furthermore, the requirements analysis of data warehouses necessitates the addition of certain multidimensional concepts (in the sense of (Giorgini et al., 2008)). This extension is achieved by using the UML profile for modelling multidimensional requirements by using *i** (*MultidimensionalRequirements@iStar*, see Figure 3). The following concepts are therefore added as resources: business processes related to decision makers' goals (*BusinessProcess* stereotype), relevant measures related to decision makers' information requirements (*Measure*), and contexts needed for analyzing these measures (*Context*). Any foreseen relations between the context of analysis are also modelled. For instance, the city context and the country context are related because cities can be aggregated in countries. These relationships were modelled by using the UML (shared) aggregation relationship (*Association* UML metaclass, represented as —◇).

Conformity@ MultidimensionalRequirements Profile

As previously stated, conformity issues require mechanisms to manage the involved rationale with which decisions are made in order to obtain conformed dimensions. Given the previous UML profiles, every stakeholder has a rationale which is necessary to accomplish his/her strategic dependencies in the organization. Thus, we can apply the same principles in order to additionally model the rationale of the dimension authority by means of *SR* diagrams. The extension achieved by the *Conformity@MultidimensionalRequirements* profile is defined through the use of the following stereotypes:

- *DataMartUser* is the decision maker that defines a set of information requirements that should be made to conform in order to design a data mart in the context of an integrated data-warehousing architecture.
- *DimensionAuthority* is the project's stakeholder that plays the role of obtaining the agreement for conformed dimensions of the data marts involved.
- *ConformableContext* is the information items that must be made to conform. They may be *conformed* (modelled as a tag definition of this stereotype) if and only if they have been agreed on by means of the dimension authority.
- *ConformityAgreement* is the dependency that links the dimension authority to the context to be conformed.

Designers can use these stereotypes to model the problematic elements of the conformed dimensions, as is shown next. Interestingly, this modeling extension enables us to define a set of model-to-model transformations (see "Conceptual Modeling Mapping: from Goals to Data Structures") which automate the design of the database structures that implement both data marts and the corporate data warehouses.

Application of the Modeling Framework

Figure 4 illustrates the rationale for our case study (see Figure 1). This figure shows a data mart user (*sales manager)* whose rationale concerning data analysis is modelled. This model is created by first

Figure 3. Profiling architecture to permit the conformation of multidimensional requirements with UML

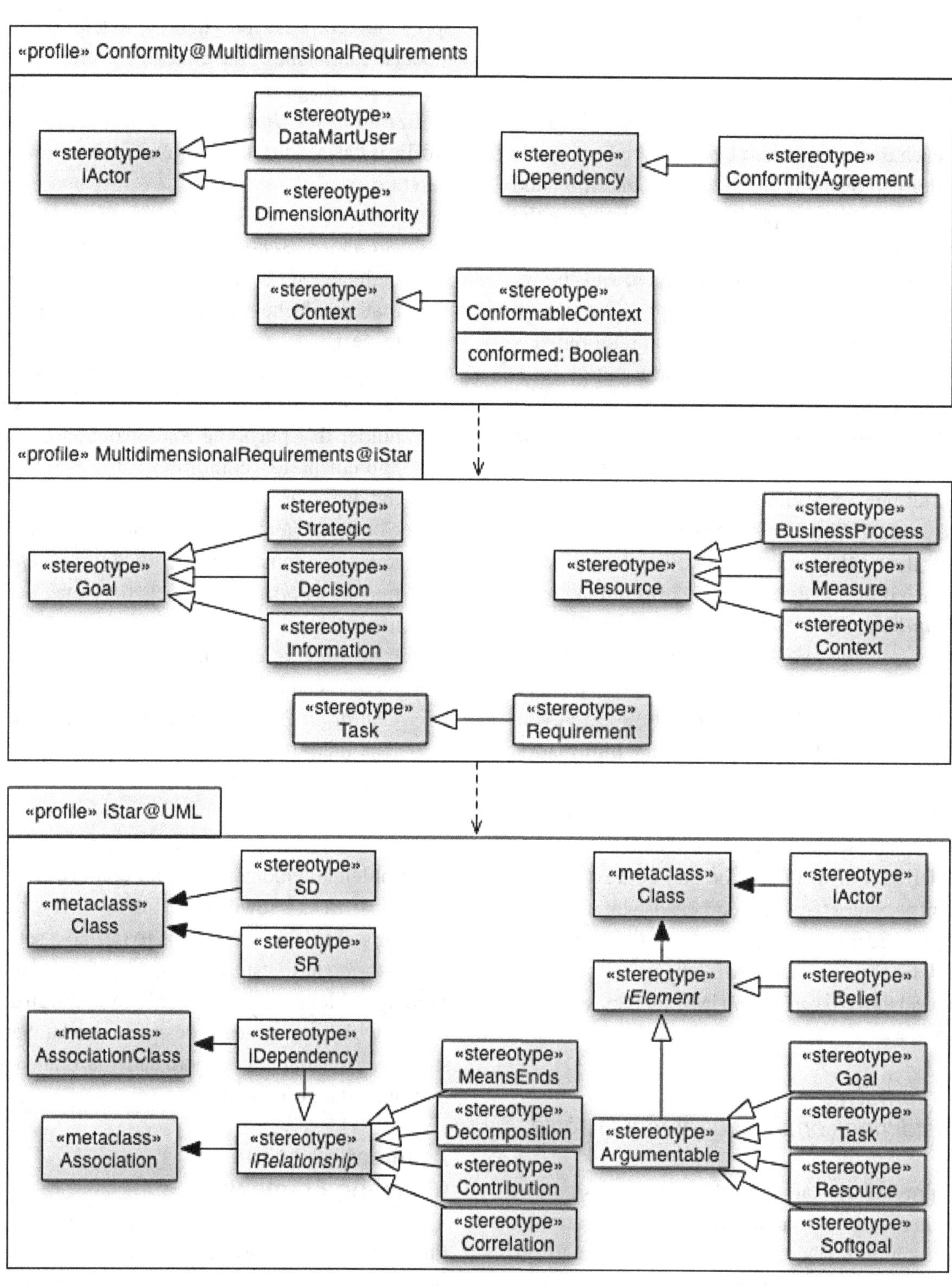

considering the business process *sales* which s/he has to manage. Given this, this user has a strategic goal to *increase sales* that may be refined into two decisional goals *decrease price* and *determine promotion*. In decisions, other informational goals are involved which have associated information requirements, respectively: *analyze price,* which implies *aggregate total amount by product and brand* and *analyze sales,* which implies *aggregate quantity sold by product type and promotion code*. After the goal refinement, information requirements are discovered in the form of the measures *total amount* and *quantity sold* and the contexts that must be made to conform (*brand, product*, and so on). Moreover, the contexts are aggregated to each other (*e.g.*, products into brands or product types).

A dimension authority should manage each conformable context discovered. Figure 5 shows this management for the contexts related to products. First, the most granular context is identified (*product* for the sales manager and *pieces* for the inventory manager). They are then made to conform to the project's dimension authority. To do this, the *conformity on product dimension* conformity agreements are modelled in the strategic-dependency diagram. The dimension authority's rationale (*sales & inventory authority*) is then employed to make the context of analysis of both data marts conform. They are related to the same strategic goal *conform product dimension.*

Figure 4. Discovering information requirements in products to be conformed

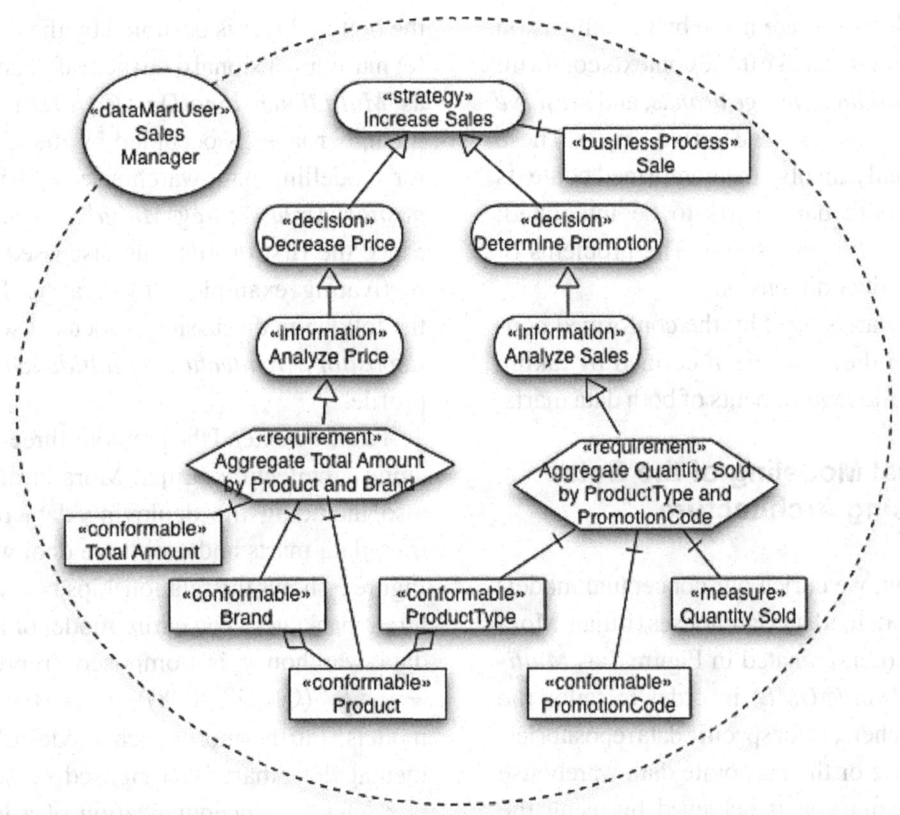

Figure 5. Making product dimension conform by means of the dimension authority

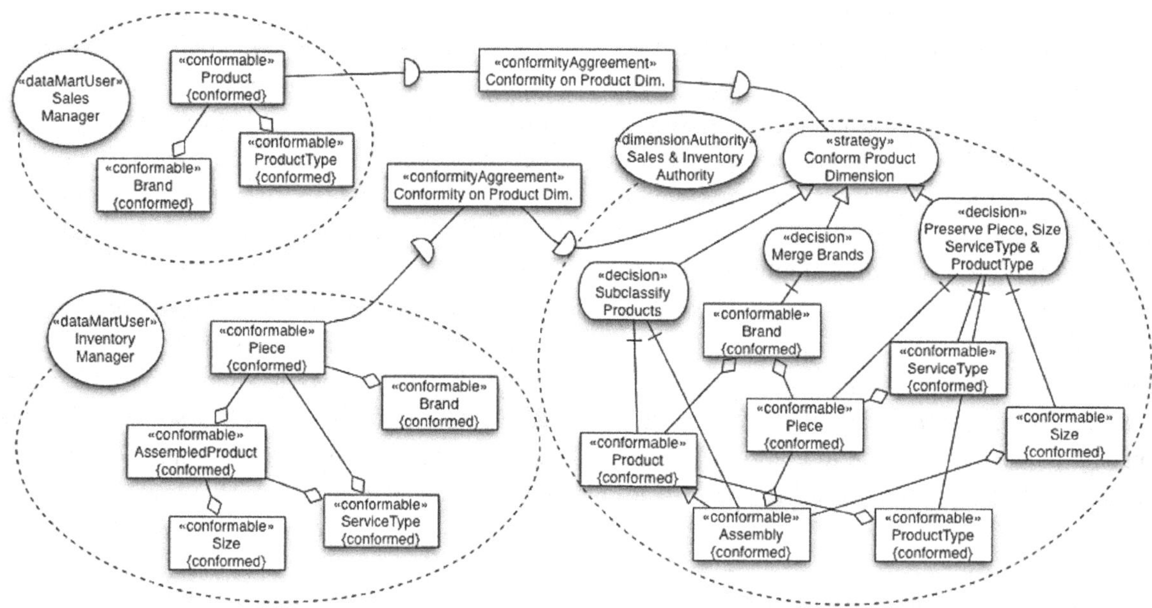

So, several decisions are made by the dimension authority in order to make these contexts conform: *subclassify products*, *merge brands*, and *preserve pieces, sizes, service types & product types*. These decisions finally involve the conformed contexts that enable both data marts to be integrated: *product*, *assembly*, and so on. The problems of the initial product dimension

(Figure 1) are solved by the conformed contexts because they have been defined by taking into account the requirements of both data marts.

Conceptual Modeling of the Data-Warehousing Architecture

In this section, we enrich our conceptual modelling framework for data warehouses (Luján-Mora et al., 2006) (denominated in Figure 7 as *MultidimensionalData@UML*) in order to tailor the represented schemata for specific data repositories, *i.e.*, data marts or the corporate data warehouse itself. This extension is achieved by using the modelling architecture shown in Figure 7. This is a two layer architecture of UML profiles in which the bottom layer is occupied by the UML profile for multidimensional data (here after denominated as *MultidimensionalData@UML* profile) and the upper layer is occupied by the UML profile for modelling data-warehouse repositories (*RepositoryArchitecture@MultidimensionalData*). Since the first profile was discussed during the motivating example ("Motivating Example"), the following discussion is focused solely on the *RepositoryArchitecture@MultidimensionalData* profile.

First, we extend the previous three-layer packaging architecture (Luján-Mora et al, 2006) by also including the deploying data repositories (*i.e.*, data marts and corporate data warehouse). Figure 6 shows the relationships between the different packages. The entire model of a corporate data warehouse is composed (represented as ——◆ (OMG, 2008)) of all the data-mart models. Furthermore, each model of a departmental data mart is composed of several *star packages* (a conceptualization of a logical *star schema* (Kimball & Ross, 2002; Moody & Kortink, 2000)), and each one is additionally composed of

Figure 6. Packaging architecture to model an integrated data-warehousing solution

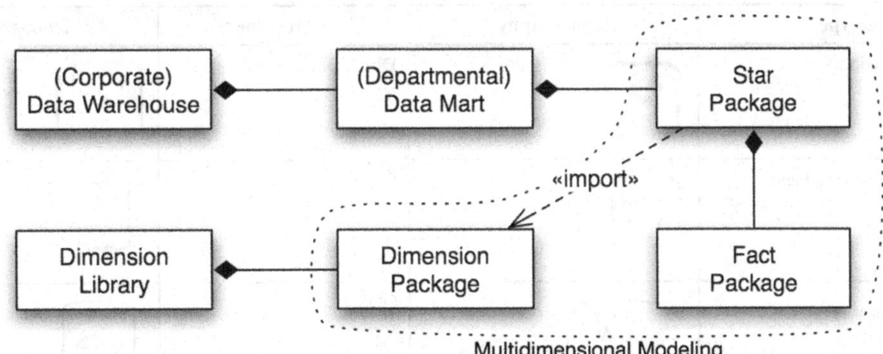

several *fact packages*. Moreover, we define a *dimension library* as a catalogue with which to publish master conformed dimensions that can be obtained from the dimension authority's rationale (explained in the following section) and reused in each data-mart model. Hence, the model is composed of several *dimension packages* containing the project's conformed dimensions which are (<<import>> dependency relationships (OMG, 2008)) imported by the star packages in order to describe the contained facts.

In Figure 7, we show the *RepositoryArchitecture@MultidimensionalData* profile containing several stereotype and tag definitions by extending some of the UML metaclasses, *i.e.*, its modeling elements. In this case, we only need to extend UML *packages* and *models*. In addition, this profile imports the definition of the *MultidimensionalData@UML* profile, as has previously been explained. Hence, we also extend raw dimensions from (Luján-Mora et al., 2006) by enriching their semantics in order to additionally include conformity issues. For each stereotype, we provide a representative icon that allows developers to easily understand and recognize the proposed modelling elements (see Table 1). The semantics of the provided stereotypes and tag definitions is the following:

- *ConformedDimension* defines the dimensions that may be conformed depending on the *conformed* tag value (it is true by default).
- *ConformedDimensionPackage* defines the package that contains a conformed dimension. It is made to conform depending on the *conformed* tag value (it is true by default).
- *DataArchitecture* defines an entire architectural model, which, technically speaking, acts as a container of the remaining modelling elements.
- *DimensionLibrary* defines the catalogue of conformed dimensions which data marts use in order to define an integrated data-warehousing solution.
- *DataRepository* (abstract) represents general data repositories in the architecture. It is additionally specialized by the other stereotypes.
- *DataWarehouse* represents a repository of historical data with the properties stated by Inmon (2005). It can be specialized by using their scope or type of analysis.
- *CorporateDW* is a data warehouse for an overall organization. It can be *integrated* if it has dependent data marts.
- *DataMart* is a departmental data repository that contains aggregated and customized data for responding to specific information needs. It can be *dependent* of a corporate data warehouse.

Table 1. Iconography for the defined stereotypes at the conceptual level

Stereotype	Iconography	Stereotype	Iconography
ConformedDimension		DimensionLibrary	
ConformedDimensionPackage		FlatFile	
CorporateDW	CDW	ODS	ODS
DataMart	DM	OLAP	OLAP
DataWarehouse	DW	OLTP	OLTP

- *OLAP* is a data warehouse, which is oriented towards OLAP analysis. It is therefore designed by using the multidimensional-modeling paradigm. In addition, the *technology* used can also be specified.
- *FlatFile* is a data store for analysis applications without any special information needs as regards data structures.
- *OLTP* is a data repository, which is oriented towards the "on-line transaction processing" which is typically used for populating data warehouses.
- *ODS* is an *operational data store* that serves as a staging area for the population of a data warehouse.

Application of the Modeling Framework

Specifically, Figure 8 shows the library of master conformed dimensions obtained from the dimension authority's rationale of our case study. It is worth noting that the dimension library is the foundation through which to later automatically derive the dependent data-mart schemata in an integrated manner. For instance, the required product dimensions are combined in the conformed product dimension which allows inventory and sales facts to be described through the commitment of every particular information requirement.

The proposed packaging architecture is applied to our example scenario and is shown in Figure 9. Inventory and sales data marts are modelled as packages (correctly stereotyped) which depend (<<import>> dependencies) on the corresponding {*conformed*} dimensions (correctly tagged) that are contained in the retail dimension library. Moreover, the retail corporate data warehouse is modelled as a package which contains every data mart (with relationships) in the data-warehousing architecture. The conceptual modelling framework provided can be used to translate the previously exposed goal reasoning into multidimensional models. These conceptualize required data structures in order to deploy not

Figure 7. A UML profile for data-warehousing repository modeling

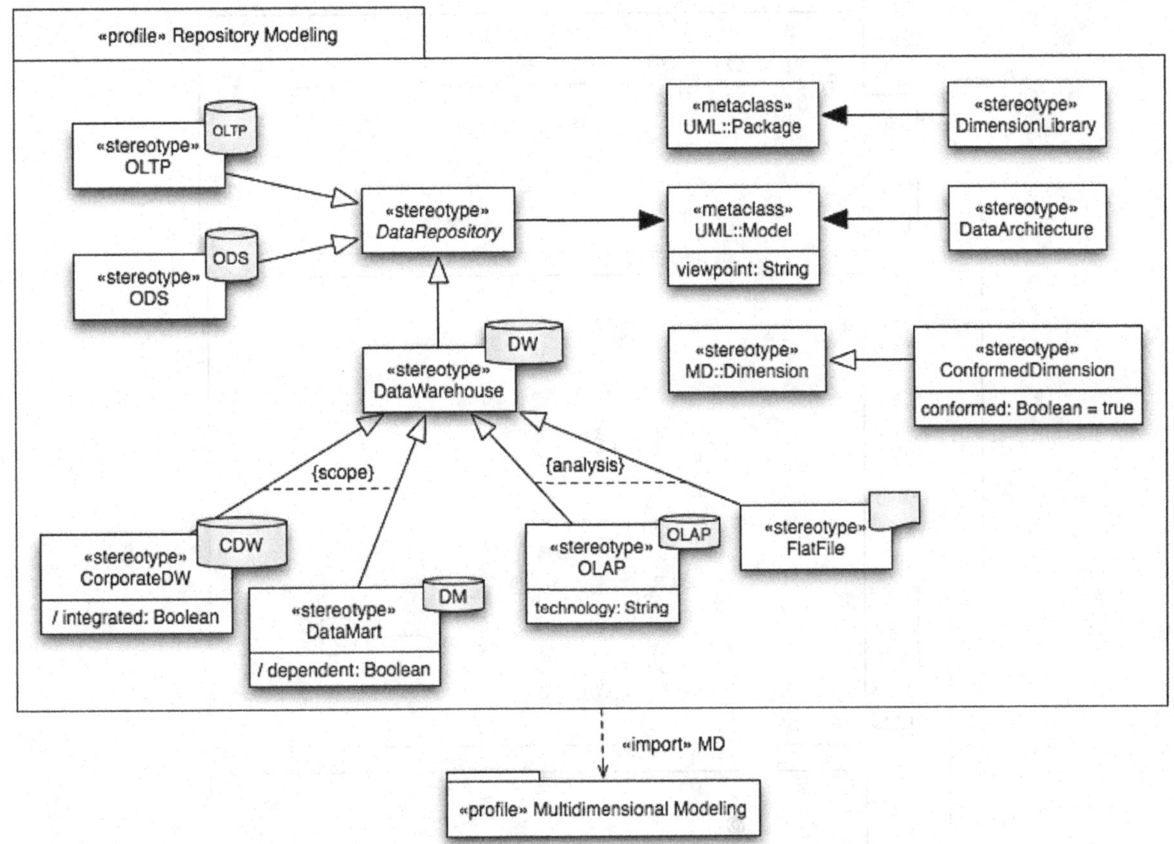

only data marts but also the entire corporate repository.

CONCEPTUAL MODELLING MAPPING: FROM GOALS TO DATA STRUCTURES

Any of the presented models (*i.e.*, goal-based or multidimensional) can be mapped in order to automatically derive data structures for both a corporate data warehouse and its dependent data marts.

Our solution is based on the best-known initiative for model-driven engineering (Bézivin, 2006), namely the "model-driven architecture" (MDA) (OMG, 2008). This proposal enables us to specify model-to-model transformations by means of "query/view/transformation'' (QVT) (OMG, 2008) language. It contains a declarative element which enables us to easily design the required model mappings in a visual form. Our transformation chain, as it is called in QVT terminology, is divided into three stages concerning each modelling framework: the "computer-independent model" (CIM), the "platform-independent model" (PIM), and the "platform-specific model" (PSM). These therefore allow us to smoothly isolate the deployment platform by means of different abstraction levels, thus tackling complex projects such as data warehousing.

Figure 10 shows the QVT relations designed to map the requirements models based on *i** into the discussed multidimensional models. Each relation has a source modelling element (marked as *checkonly* by QVT) which is translated into a

Figure 8. Dimension library for modelling conformed dimensions of the retail data marts

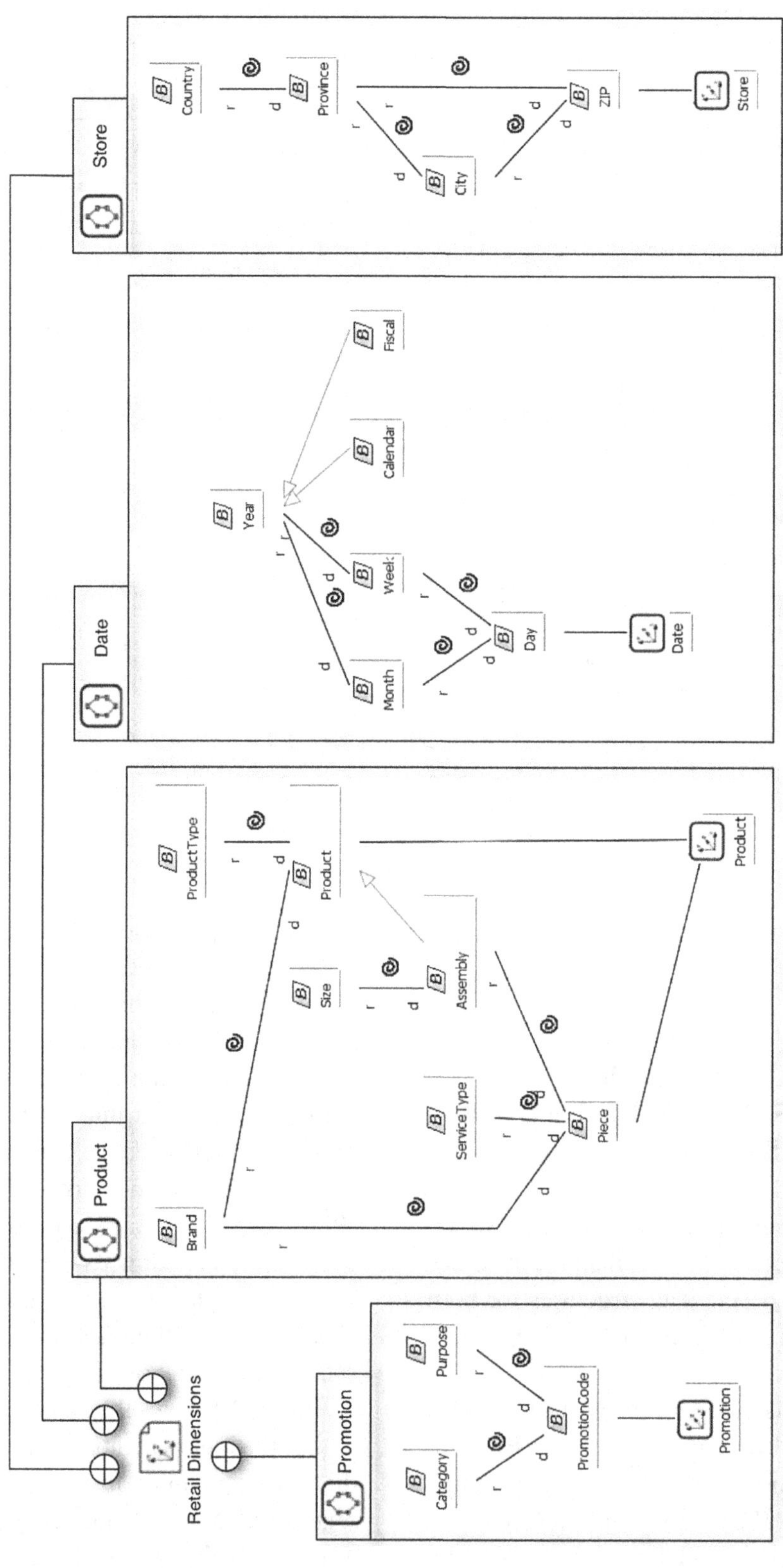

Figure 9. Integrated data-warehousing model for retail inventory and sales analysis

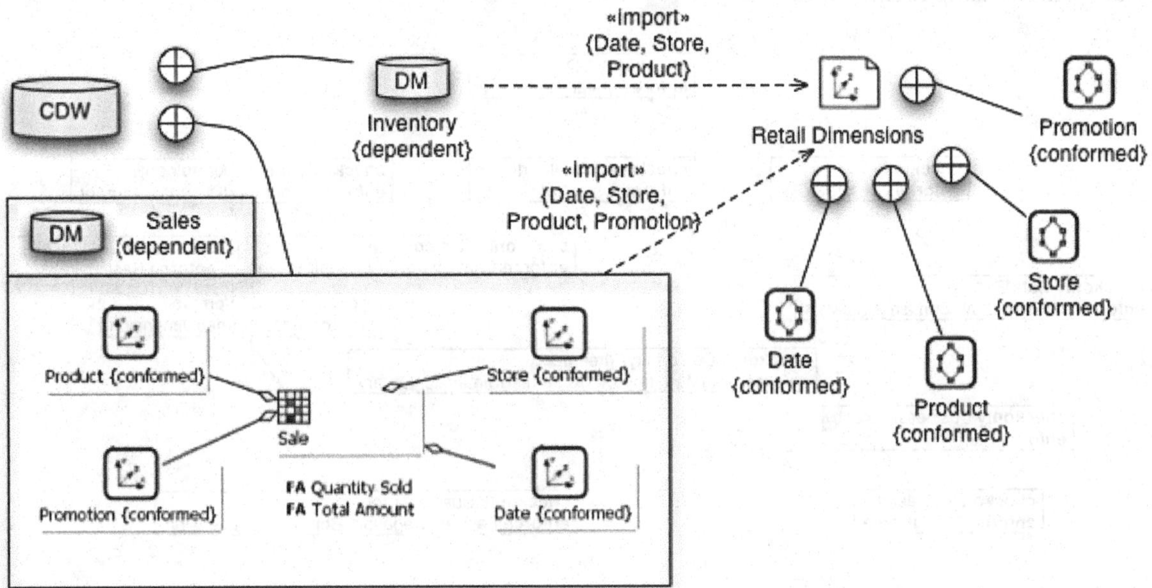

modelling element on the target metamodel (marked as *enforce*). For instance, data-mart users in our *i** extension are translated into data-mart packages at the conceptual level (by means of a *DataMartUser2DataMart* relation). Moreover, in order to translate a given modelling element, a relation may require others. These dependencies are also represented in Figure 10. The dependency graph roots the entire model mapping, *i.e.*, strategic dependency diagrams (*SD*) into data architectures (*DataArchitecture*). Packaging-related mapping can then be performed. For example, the dimension authority in *i** can be mapped into the conformed dimension library in multidimensional modelling. There are thus several mappings that translate the relationships and modelling elements contained in the previously mapped packages. In this layer, for example, dimensions are translated from a conformable context in *i**, and relationships between data marts and a conformed dimension library are translated from conformity agreements. These relations are rendered in QVT by means of a visual notation such as that presented in Figures 11 to 13.

A QVT relation (see Figure 11 as example) has two modelling languages (named *istar* and *md*) over which two modelling elements are labeled as the relation *domain*. These are used to specify certain modelling elements in order to define a pattern through which the source modelling will be checked in order to match or generate (since the target model is marked as enforced) the target modelling elements. For instance, Figure 11 shows the mapping from data-mart users into data marts. Data-mart users are represented by means of two primitives: a domain *class* (*dm_c*) and the *stereotype* which extends it (*dm_s*). In addition, this class is related to a given strategic dependency diagram which is also represented in a dual form due to the usage of UML profiles (package *sd_p* and stereotype *sd_s*). By means of pattern matching, the source structure is related to the target source in which domains are first matched by their *names* (value *n*). Moreover, due to its dependencies, this QVT relation has a *when* clause that acts as a mapping precondition. In this case, the precondition establishes that *sd_p* and *da_m* are related by means of the QVT relation *SD2DataArchitecture*. A QVT

Figure 10. Dependency graph of the designed mappings from conformed information requirements to a data-warehousing architecture

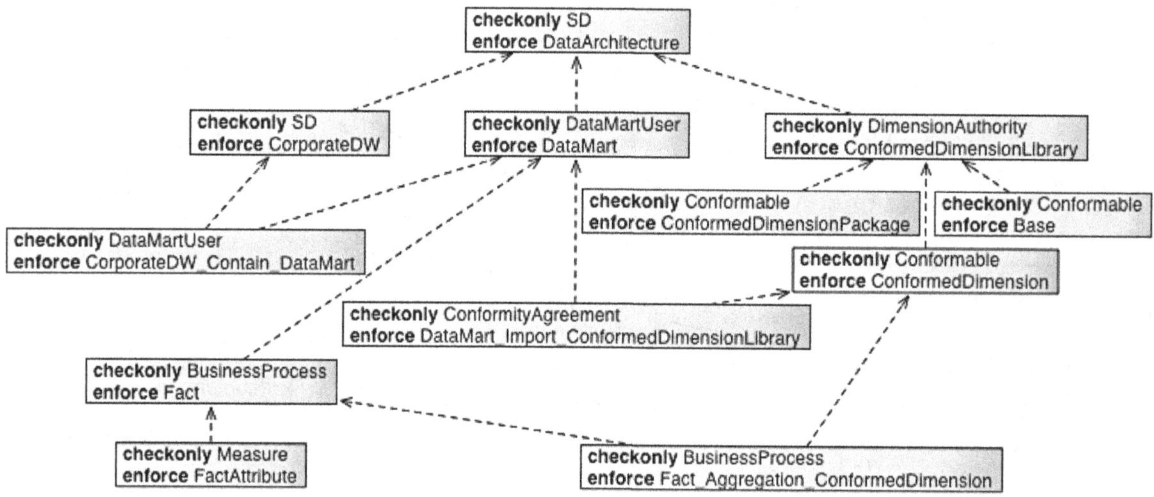

Figure 11. QVT relation for mapping data-mart users over i diagrams into data marts at the conceptual level*

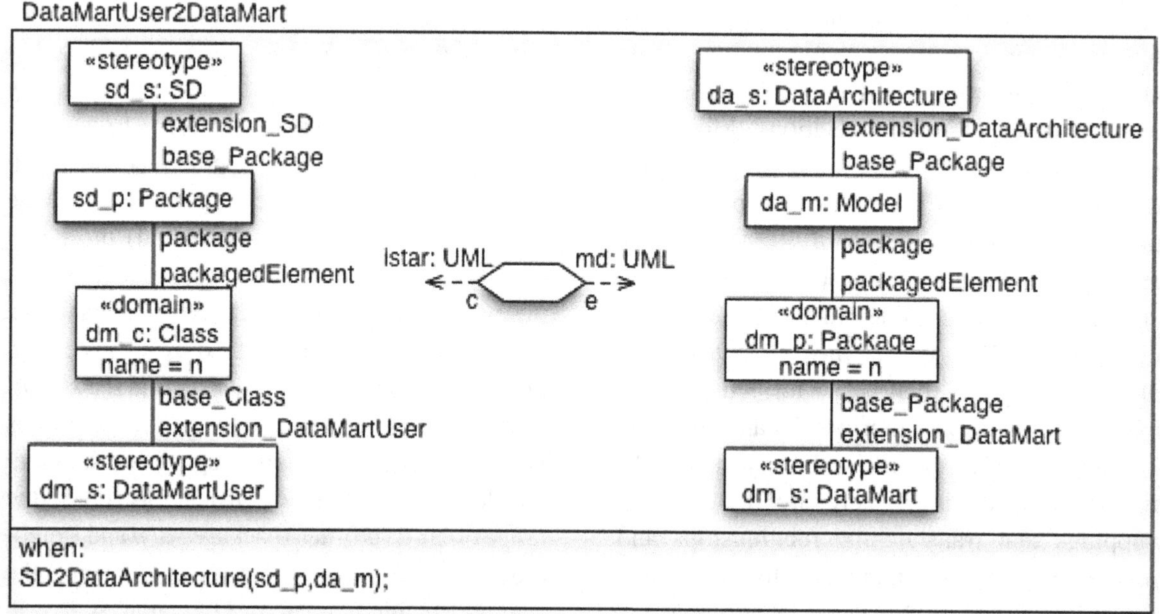

engine thus takes these declarative definitions and executes them in a particular order given the *when* and *where* clauses.

Figure 12 also shows the QVT relation for mapping conformable contexts into conformed dimensions. In this mapping, the *when* clause defines the condition on the context to be translated, which should be the most granular context in the aggregation hierarchy of context. Thus, its counterpart in the multidimensional model is a

Figure 12. QVT relation for mapping conformable contexts over i diagrams into conformed dimensions at the conceptual level*

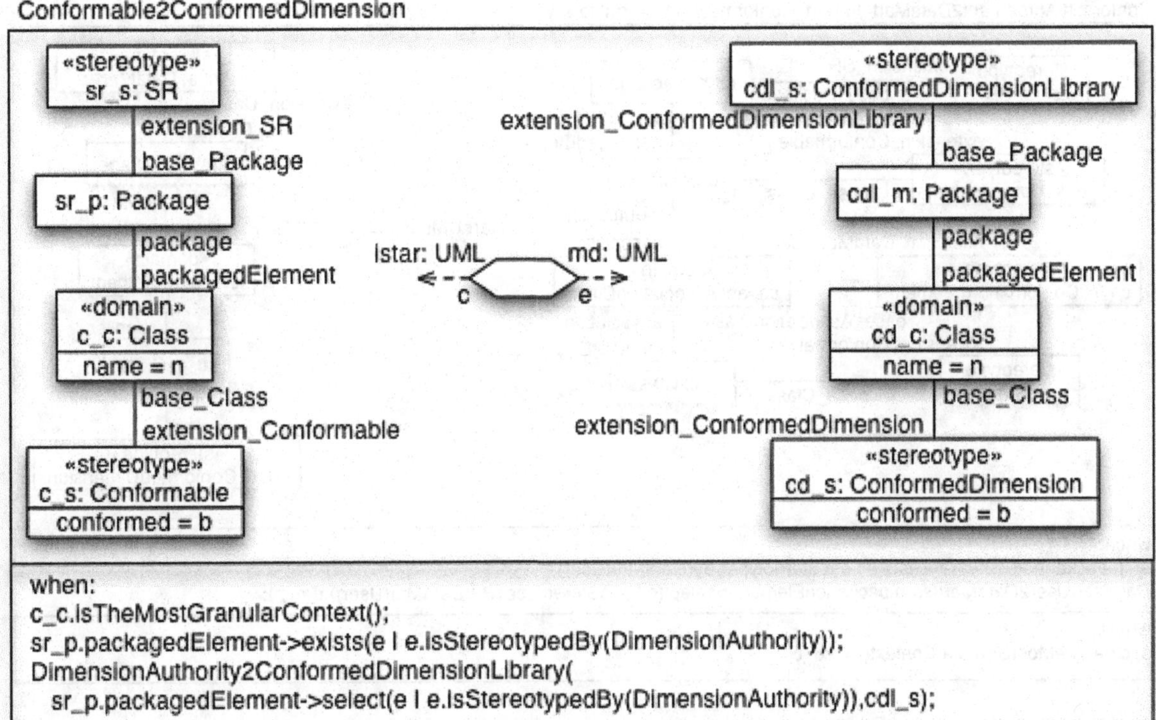

conformed dimension (which shares the same value as its *conformed* property). Conversely, if it is not the most granular context, this rule will not be executed. The *Conformable2Base* will be executed instead. The *when* clause also defines a condition for the related strategic rationale (*SR*), which should be the rationale of the dimension authority. The utility function *isStereotypedBy* is used for this purpose.

As a final example of the QVT relations designed, Figure 13 shows the relation between conformity agreements (which are represented by means of stereotype *ca_s* and association class *ca_ac*) and import relationships (*import element* metaclass) between data marts and conformed dimensions. In this case, a *where* clause is also specified to identify the most granular context which is, in fact, the context used for the conformity agreement.

Dealing With Existing Data Marts

It is worth noting that our approach is focused on a scenario in which the data warehouse project is in early stages of development, so data marts are not deployed yet. However, there is a different scenario in which our approach can be useful: in later stages of the development, when some of the data marts are already deployed. This scenario can be easily considered if we applying reverse engineering techniques to the existing data marts in order to obtain their corresponding conceptual multidimensional models. In our previous work (Mazón & Trujillo, 2007), an approach for the development of a data warehouse as a modernization process addressed the analysis of the available data sources to discover multidimensional structures with which to derive a conceptual multidimensional model. Therefore, this modernization

Figure 13. QVT relation for mapping conformity agreements over i diagrams into data-mart dependencies at the conceptual level*

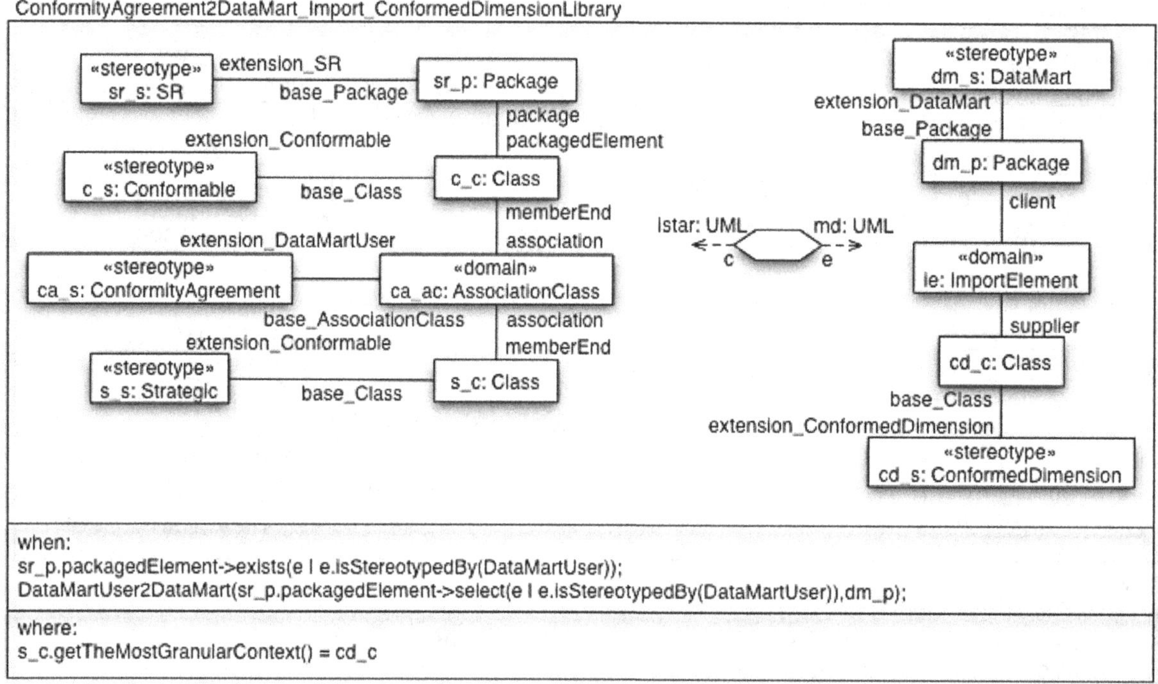

process can also be applied to an existing data mart before starting the design process defined in this paper in order to obtain the corresponding conceptual multidimensional model.

Application of the QVT Mappings

Figure 14 shows the model-transformation chain for our case study. The transformation chain begins from *i** diagrams (Yu & Mylopoulos, 1994) in our conceptual modelling framework.

We decompose the transformation process into *measure-fact* and *context-dimension* mappings. Whereas the mappings presented in (Mazón et al., 2007a) are oriented towards the generation of a single data repository in isolation, the information requirements to be translated herein are spread over: (i) rationales of data-mart decision makers for measure-fact mappings, and (ii) dimension authority's rationale for context-dimension mappings. Thus, we translate the dimension authority's rationale, which holds contexts of analysis, to the conceptual library which contains the translated conformed dimensions. However, together with each obtained dimension, we also map it into the required package structure (see Figure 6).

The mapping of decision maker's rationales, such as those of the inventory manager, implies a model merging with the dimension library (shared by data marts across every department). As Figure 9 shows, since conformed dimensions are already mapped into the dimension library, each context discovered in these rationales (conformed by the dimension authority) is translated into an <<import>> dependency from the related fact to the conformed dimension. We thus ensure that the facts in each data mart can be drilled across the conformed dimensions. Moreover, the model of the entire (corporate) data warehouse that contains every data mart is also

Figure 14. Model-driven architecture for data warehousing based on conformed dimensions

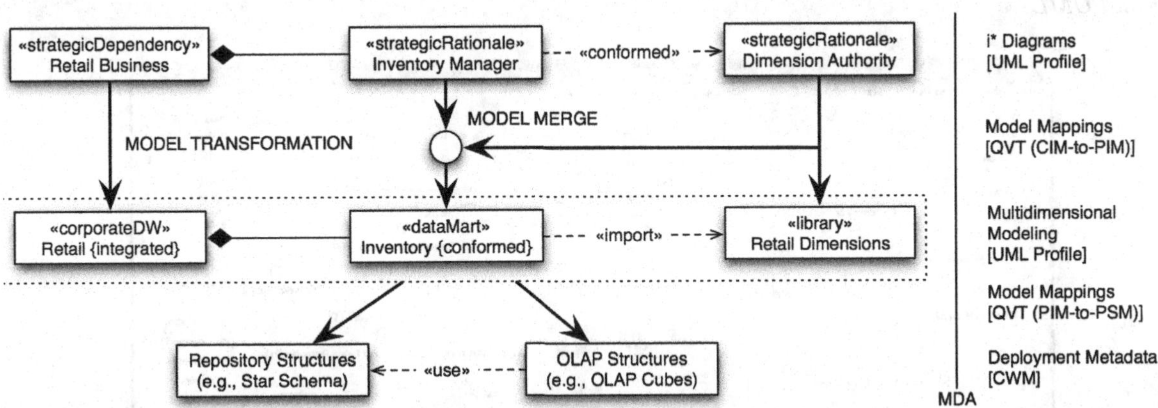

automatically derived from the whole strategic-dependency model (see Figure 2). Once again, the packaging scaffolding (see Figure 6) is also taken into account for deriving the models of data marts and the corporate data warehouse.

The conceptual modelling of data repositories can also be used to automatically derive the deployment metadata that implement them. These transformations are carried out by model mappings adapted from (Mazón et al., 2006; Mazón & Trujillo, 2008; Pardillo et al., 2008). Essentially, the mappings involved match each multidimensional concept with both the data structures of the data repository and the client metadata to query them by following a multidimensional view. Specifically, facts and dimensions, together with their measures and aggregation hierarchies, are mapped at the logical level (Hüsemann et al., 2000) into the corresponding tables and columns of a star schema (Kimball & Ross, 2002; Moody & Kortink, 2000) with regard to the relational model. Given the model of the corporate data warehouse that collects all the dependent data marts, by applying the mappings in (Mazón et al., 2006; Mazón & Trujillo, 2008), we obtain the data structures which the corporate repository implements. Given a data-mart model, we obtain the corresponding aggregated and customized version of the entire repository. It is worth noting that these data structures are conformed by their dimensions. We can therefore automatically obtain their deployment counterparts in an integrated manner. Moreover, using our previous work (Pardillo et al., 2008) as a basis, we also automatically generate the required metadata in order to query them by using OLAP applications (Chaudhuri & Dayal, 1997), thus amiliorating the tedious work of their manual definition. Concerning platform-specific design decisions such as indexing or partitioning, continue being able to be managed by similiar QVT transformations (in latter design phases) to which the article presents.

DEVELOPMENT PLATFORM AND IMPLEMENTATION

The related standards that we employ are also shown in Figure 14. On the one hand, for goal-oriented requirement engineering, we employ $i*$ diagrams (Yu & Mylopoulos, 1994) supported by our UML profile presented in (Mazón et al., 2007a). With regard to the multidimensional modelling of data warehouses, we use the UML profile presented in (Luján-Mora et al., 2006), which is enriched for their architectural modelling as has previously been described. In addition, the "common warehouse metamodel" (CWM) (OMG, 2008), which is widely used to deal with the interoperability of applications (Zhao & Siau,

Figure 15. Implementation of the modelling framework with which to make requirements conform with i and UML*

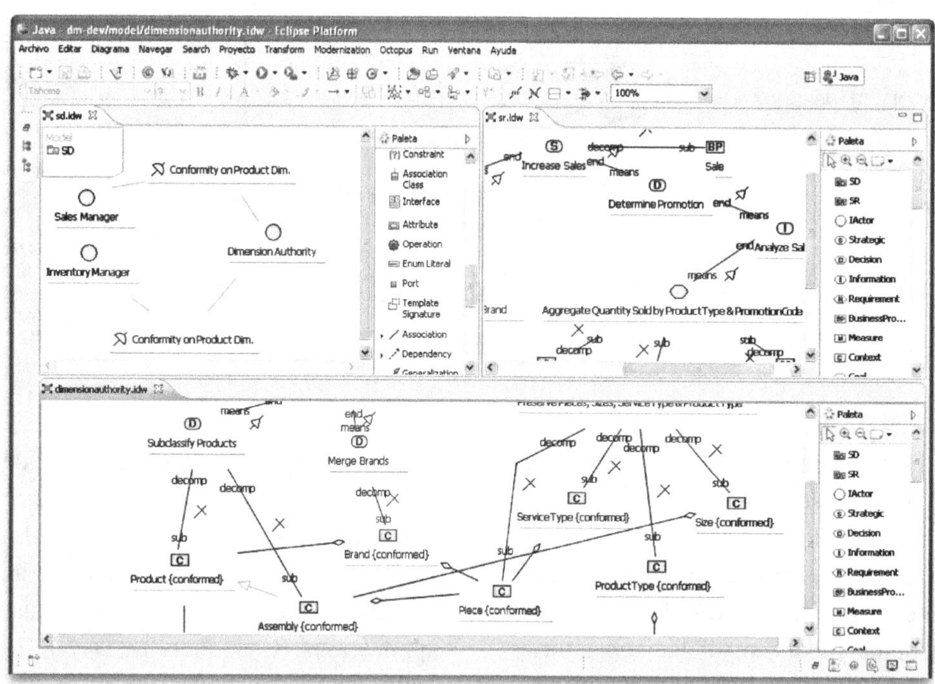

2007), is employed to represent the deployed data structures for both the underlying databases and OLAP applications (Chaudhuri & Dayal, 1997) in a vendor-independent manner.

All the modelling frameworks and model transformations with regard to our solution have been implemented in the Eclipse[3] development platform, since a key factor for the success of any MDE or MDA approach is an appropriate tool support (Saraiva & Silva, 2008).

Specifically, we employ several of its plugins that implement the MDA standards: for instance, "model development tools" (MDT) to support UML and UML profiles, the "eclipse modelling framework" (EMF) to specify CWM metadata representations in a vendor-independent manner, medini QVT and SmartQVT in order to specify and launch model-to-model QVT mappings with its declarative or imperative part, respectively, or MOFScript to design model-to-code Mof2Text (OMG, 2008) mappings in order to automatically implement the final data-warehousing solution. These have been combined to provide an "integrated development environment" (IDE) to manage data-warehousing projects based on model-driven engineering. This tool has been used to implement our case study as a proof of concept of our approach. It is shown in Figures 15 and 16. The first figure shows the modelling of conformed requirements by using *i**. Both an outline of the strategy dependency diagram (left-hand side) and strategic rationales are represented (for the sales manager on the right-hand side and for the dimension authority at the bottom). With regard to the second figure, in this case the inventory data mart is modelled on the left-hand side in order to automatically transform it into the deployment OLAP metadata (shown on the right-hand side), by applying the QVT mapping at the centre of Figure 16.

Figure 16. Model-driven data warehousing. Details of the conceptual modelling and model-to-model transformations

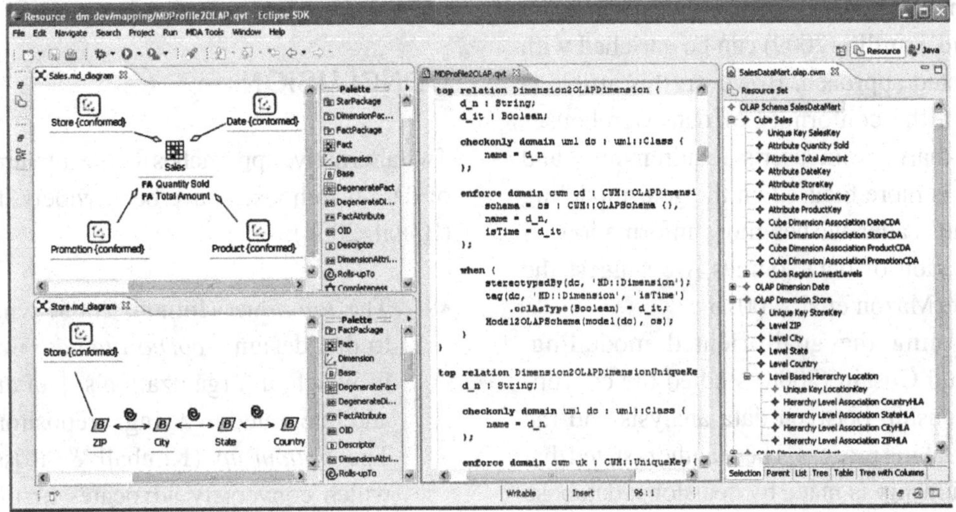

RELATED WORK

The development approaches for data warehouses that appear in literature can be divided into those that present methods or guidelines to capture information requirements such as (Bonifati et al., 2001; Giorgini et al., 2008; Luján-Mora & Trujillo, 2006a; Mazón et al., 2007a) and those that present modelling frameworks for data structures that respond to these requirements (Abelló et al., 2006; Golfarelli et al., 1998; Hüsemann et al., 2000; Luján-Mora et al., 2006).

Specifically, very few authors(Bonifati et al., 2001; Giorgini et al., 2008; Mazón et al., 2007a) have investigated goal-oriented approaches such as that presented here, and none of them have attempted to capture conformity issues between decision maker's requirements or to derive multidimensional data models for the every data repository involved in an entire data-warehousing architecture. Thus, those researchers that have investigated the conceptual modelling of data warehouses have mainly focused on *intraschema* properties such as additivity (Horner et al., 2004) and aggregation hierarchies (Malinowski & Zimanyi, 2006).

However, the research community has made great efforts in the related issues of data integration and view materialization, as can be observed by the number of research papers published in the field (Vassiliadis, 2000). For instance, Moody and Kortink (2000) recognize three kinds of multi-star data models (*i.e.*, constellation, galaxy, and star cluster). These are, however, focused on the logical structures. Thus, real conformity mechanisms or data-repository deployments are not established. At the conceptual level, the best efforts for modeling *interschema* properties have been made by (Abelló et al., 2002; Abelló et al., 2006; Cabibbo & Torlone, 2004). In Abelló et al. (2002), several kinds of relationships between facts and dimensions to drill across different schemata are discussed. Nevertheless, this model is oriented towards complex data relationships that decision makers do not usually require (Pedersen, 2004). Once again, there are no mechanisms with which to achieve agreement and commitment between data-mart stakeholders. In addition, Cabibbo & Torlone (2004) propose the "dimension compatibility" notion to drill across data marts; nevertheless, this is not oriented towards the integrated development of the data repositories involved. It is also worth noting that data-warehouse design can never avoid the analysis of data sources. For this purpose, hybrid methods such as the presented by Mazón and Trujillo (2009) can be enriched with the presented approach. However, this article is focused on the conformity of data warehouses and data marts from user's requirements, and therefore, is more focused on the goal-modeling part. If the reader wishes more information on the integration of data sources, we suggest the reading of (Mazón et al., 2007b).

Concerning the goal-oriented modelling, Prakash and Gosain (2008) studied the conceptual relationship between data analysis and the decision-making process. These authors stated that such relationship is made by decisions: database queries answer information needs, that support some decision, that in addition is taken in order to achieve some goal. Paim and Castro (2002) also proposed a goal-oriented framework for modelling data warehousing requirements. They studied many of the non-functional requirements that are involved in such technology and their interrelationship. In particular, these authors classify the issues dealt with by our proposal as part of the 'multidimensionality' non-functional requirement ("Ability to represent decision-support requirements as and provide access to dimensional and factual data."), being actually identified as 'conformance' ("Ability to represent common data warehouse aspects in identically the same way across the entire data warehouse specification").

Finally, the proposed library of conformed dimensions is a similar concept to the design pattern approach that has been investigated by Jones and Song (2008) in order to propose dimensional patterns for data warehouses. However, these patterns act as design guidelines, and they do not signify suitable conformity mechanisms which enable integrated architectural deployments. It is worth noting that other authors such as Niemi et al. (2001) also propose automatic mechanisms to generate OLAP schemata. However these mechanisms are not conceived to solve the conformity among dimensions or to drive an entire data-warehousing architecture.

CONCLUSION

Two alternative approaches for the implementation of data-warehouses have been widely discussed (Bresil, 2004):

- The *top-down* (Inmon, 2005) which aims to first design a *corporate data warehouse* in which an organization's data are stored and integrated in a single repository.
- The *bottom-up* (Kimball & Ross, 2002) which conversely advocates first developing *departmental data marts* in which data are aggregated and customized for particular information needs.

The *top-down* approach is usually difficult to implement since the project scope involves the whole organization (Watson et al., 2001), and thus, the *bottom-up* approach is preferred in most cases (Chaudhuri & Dayal, 1997; Watson et al., 2001). However, this second approach fails when data marts are conformed to support cross-departamental decision making processes. To overcome this drawback, in this work we present an approach for the integrated design of an entire architecture for data warehousing from the very-early stages of development.

The cornerstones of our approach are as follows:

1. A goal-oriented requirements engineering approach based on *i** (Yu & Mylopoulos, 1994) is used to capture information requirements at the early development stages, thus allowing us to anticipate risks at the very beginning of every project. A goal-oriented approach also allows developers to align particular information needs with the strategic policies of the whole organization. Finally,

the agreement and commitment between distributed data-mart stakeholders to make their multidimensional models conform is coordinated by using this goal-oriented approach, and also provides artefacts with which to document these conformity agreements.
2. The usage of a model-driven approach is useful for complex developments (Bézivin, 2006) such as data-warehousing architectures from their inception to their final deployment. The use of a model-driven approach has the following advantages:
    a. The data warehouse architecture is developed in an implementation independent manner, without concentrating on the underlying software platforms, this knowledge being delegated to the scaffolding model-transformation architecture based on QVT.
    b. It provides reusable assets for multidimensional models by means of a catalogue of conformed dimensions, thus permitting the design of modular systems.
    c. The automatic and integrated deployment of both corporate data warehouse and dependent data marts by using QVT signifies a practical solution to the architectural debate (Breslin, 2004).
    d. It enables cross-departmental queries by automatically generating the OLAP metadata supported by conformed dimensions for each data mart involved.

Further investigations can be carried out in order to enrich the proposed approach and could, for instance, provide semantics-aware frameworks for conformity reasoning and information-requirement discovery, suitability metrics to compare the ideal dimensions obtained from the data-mart requirements with the master conformed dimensions that we have designed, or recommendation capabilities over existing architectures. Importantly, our ongoing research is focused on assessing the suitability of the presented diagramming techniques, e.g., providing more concise visual primitives or richer mechanisms to decompose diagrams in manageable logical units. Importantly, our short-term future work consists of formalizing the specification of the underlying methodology in a process-oriented modelling language, accompanied by the appropriate empirical validation to assess the benefits of the presented framework and study its expressivity and completeness in real-world scenarios. It will be done by means of a collection of experiments in which the approach will be evaluated by first considering computer science students and then practitioners from a company in the sense of our previous experimental works (Serrano et al. 2004, 2007).

ACKNOWLEDGMENT

This work has been partially supported by the MESOLAP project (TIN2010-14860) from the Spanish Ministry of Education and Science, and by the QUASIMODO project (PAC08-0157-0668) from the Castilla-La Mancha Ministry of Education and Science (Spain). Jesús Pardillo is funded by the Spanish Ministry of Education and Science under FPU grant AP2006-00332.

REFERENCES

Abelló, A., Samos, J., & Saltor, F. (2002, November 8). On relationships offering new drill-across possibilities. In *Proceedings of the ACM Fifth International Workshop on Data Warehousing and OLAP,* McLean, VA (pp. 7-13).

Abelló, A., Samos, J., & Saltor, F. (2006). YAM2: a multidimensional conceptual model extending UML. *Information Systems, 31*(6), 541–567. doi:10.1016/j.is.2004.12.002

Ang, J. S. K., Sum, C. C., & Chung, W. F. (1995). Critical Success Factors in Implementing MRP and Government Asistance: A Singapore Context. *Information & Management*, *29*(2), 63–70. doi:10.1016/0378-7206(95)00017-Q

Bézivin, J. (2006, July 4-8). Model Driven Engineering: An Emerging Technical Space. In *Proceedings of the Generative and Transformational Techniques in Software Engineering, International Summer School*, Braga, Portugal (LNCS 4143, pp. 36-64).

Bonifati, A., Cattaneo, F., Ceri, S., Fuggetta, A., & Paraboschi, S. (2001). Designing Data Marts for Data Warehouses. *ACM Transactions on Software Engineering and Methodology*, *10*(4), 452–483. doi:10.1145/384189.384190

Breslin, M. (2004). Data Warehousing Battle of the Giants: Comparing the Basics of the Kimball and Inmon Models. *Business Intelligence Journal*, *9*(1), 6–20.

Cabibbo, L., & Torlone, R. (2001). An Architecture for Data Warehousing Supporting Data Independence and Interoperability. *International Journal of Cooperative Information Systems*, *10*(3), 377–397. doi:10.1142/S0218843001000394

Cabibbo, L., & Torlone, R. (2004, June 21-23). On the Integration of Autonomous Data Marts. In *Proceedings of the 16th International Conference on Scientific and Statistical Database Management,* Santorini Island, Greece (pp. 223-231). Washington, DC: IEEE Computer Society.

Chaudhuri, S., & Dayal, U. (1997). An Overview of Data Warehousing and OLAP Technology. *SIGMOD Record*, *26*(1), 65–74. doi:10.1145/248603.248616

De Sousa Saraiva, J., & da Silva, A. R. (2008). Evaluation of mde tools from a metamodeling perspective. *Journal of Database Management*, *19*(4), 21–46.

Evermann, J. (2008). Theories of meaning in schema matching: A review. *Journal of Database Management*, *19*(3), 55–82.

Giorgini, P., Rizzi, S., & Garzetti, M. (2005). GRAnD: A goal-oriented approach to requirement analysis in data warehouses. *Decision Support Systems*, *45*(1), 4–21. doi:10.1016/j.dss.2006.12.001

Golfarelli, M., Maio, D., & Rizzi, S. (1998). The Dimensional Fact Model: A Conceptual Model for Data Warehouses. *International Journal of Cooperative Information Systems*, *7*(2-3), 215–247. doi:10.1142/S0218843098000118

Horner, J., Song, I. Y., & Chen, P. P. (2004, November 12-13). An analysis of additivity in OLAP systems. In *Proceedings of the ACM Seventh International Workshop on Data Warehousing and OLAP,* Washington, DC (pp. 83-91).

Hurtado, C. A., Mendelzon, A. O., & Vaisman, A. A. (1999, November 6). Updating OLAP Dimensions. In *Proceedings of the ACM Second International Workshop on Data Warehousing and OLAP,* Kansas City, MO (pp. 60-66).

Hüsemann, B., Lechtenbörger, J., & Vossen, G. (2000). Conceptual Data Warehouse Modeling. In *Proceedings of the 2nd International Workshop on Design and Management of Data Warehouses (DMDW'00),* Stockholm, Sweden (pp. 6.1-6.11).

Inmon, W. H. (2005). *Building the Data Warehouse*. New York: Wiley.

Jarke, M., Jeusfeld, M. A., Quix, C., & Vassiliadis, P. (1999). Architecture and Quality in Data Warehouses: An Extended Repository Approach. *Information Systems*, *24*(3), 229–253. doi:10.1016/S0306-4379(99)00017-4

Jones, M. E., & Song, I. Y. (2008). Dimensional modeling: Identification, classification, and evaluation of patterns. *Decision Support Systems*, *45*(1), 59–76. doi:10.1016/j.dss.2006.12.004

Jukic, N. (2006). Modeling Strategies and Alternatives for Data Warehousing Projects. *Communications of the ACM, 49*(4), 83–88. doi:10.1145/1121949.1121952

Kimball, R. (2003). *The Soul of the Data Warehouse, Part Two: Drilling Across*. Intelligent Enterprise Magazine.

Kimball, R., & Ross, M. (2002). *The Data Warehouse Toolkit: The Complete Guide to Dimensional Modeling*. New York: Wiley.

Luján-Mora, S., & Trujillo, J. (2006a). Applying the UML and the Unified Process to the design of Data Warehouses. *Journal of Computer Information Systems, 17*(2), 12–42.

Luján-Mora, S., & Trujillo, J. (2006b). Physical modeling of data warehouses using uml component and deployment diagrams: Design and implementation issues. *Journal of Database Management, 17*(2), 12–42.

Luján-Mora, S., Trujillo, J., & Song, I. Y. (2006). A UML profile for multidimensional modeling in data warehouses. *Data & Knowledge Engineering, 59*(3), 725–769. doi:10.1016/j.datak.2005.11.004

Malinowski, E., & Zimányi, E. (2006). Hierarchies in a multidimensional model: From conceptual modeling to logical representation. *Data & Knowledge Engineering, 59*(2), 348–377. doi:10.1016/j.datak.2005.08.003

Mazón, J. N., Pardillo, J., & Trujillo, J. (2006, September 4-8). Applying Transformations to Model Driven Data Warehouses. In *Proceedings of the 8th International Conference on Data Warehousing and Knowledge Discovery*, Krakow, Poland (LNCS 4081, pp. 13-22).

Mazón, J. N., Pardillo, J., & Trujillo, J. (2007, November 5-9). A Model-Driven Goal-Oriented Requirement Engineering Approach for Data Warehouses. In *Proceedings of the International Workshop on Requirements, Intentions and Goals in Conceptual Modelling*, Auckland, New Zealand (LNCS 4802, pp. 255-264).

Mazón, J. N., & Trujillo, J. (2007, November 5-9). A Model Driven Modernization Approach for Automatically Deriving Multidimensional Models in Data Warehouses. In *Proceedings of the 26th International Conference on Conceptual Modeling (ER 2007)*, Auckland, New Zealand (LNCS 4801, pp. 56-71).

Mazón, J. N., & Trujillo, J. (2008). An MDA approach for the development of data warehouses. *Decision Support Systems, 45*(1), 41–58. doi:10.1016/j.dss.2006.12.003

Mazón, J.-N., & Trujillo, J. (2009). A Hybrid Model Driven Development Framework for the Multidimensional Modeling of Data Warehouses. *SIGMOD Record, 28*(2), 12–17. doi:10.1145/1815918.1815920

Mazón, J. N., Trujillo, J., & Lechtenbörger, J. (2007). Reconciling requirement-driven data warehouses with data sources via multidimensional normal forms. *Data & Knowledge Engineering, 63*(3), 725–751. doi:10.1016/j.datak.2007.04.004

Moody, D. L., & Kortink, M. A. R. (2000). From enterprise models to dimensional models: a methodology for data warehouse and data mart design. In *Proceedings of the 2nd International Workshop on Design and Management of Data Warehouses (DMDW'00)*, Stockholm, Sweden (pp. 5.1-5.11).

Niemi, T., Nummenmaa, J., & Thanisch, P. (2001, November 9). Constructing OLAP Cubes Based on Queries. In *Proceedings of the Fourth International Workshop on Data Warehousing and OLAP*, Atlanta, GA (pp. 9-11).

Object Management Group (OMG). (2008). *Model Driven Architecture (MDA), Unified Modeling Language (UML), Common Warehouse Metamodel (CWM), Query/View/Transformation Language (QVT), MOF Model to Text Transformation Language (Mof2Text)*. Retrieved from http://www.omg.org

Paim, F. R. S., & Castro, J. (2002). Enhancing Data Warehouse Design with the NFR Framework. In *Proceedings of the Workshop em Engenharia de Requisitos (WER)*, Valencia, Spain (pp. 40-57).

Pardillo, J., Mazón, J. N., & Trujillo, J. (2008, July 7-10). Model-driven OLAP Metadata for Data Warehouses. In *Proceedings of the 25th British National Conference on Databases, BNCOD 25*, Cardiff, UK (LNCS 5071, pp. 203-206).

Pardillo, J., & Trujillo, J. (2008, October 20-24). Integrated Model-Driven Development of Goal-Oriented Data Warehouses and Data Marts. In *Proceedings of the 27th International Conference on Conceptual Modeling (ER 2008)*, Barcelona, Spain (LNCS 52I31, pp. 426-439).

Pedersen, T. B. (2004, September 1-3). How Is BI Used in Industry?: Report from a Knowledge Exchange Network. In *Proceedings of the 6th International Conference on Data Warehousing and Knowledge Discovery*, Zaragoza, Spain (LNCS 3181, pp. 179-188).

Prakash, N., & Gosain, A. (2008). An approach to engineering the requirements of data warehouses. *Requirements Engineering, 13*(1), 49–72. doi:10.1007/s00766-007-0057-x

Samos, J., Saltor, F., Sistac, J., & Bardés, A. (1998, August 24-28). Database Architecture for Data Warehousing: An Evolutionary Approach. In *Proceedings of the 9th International Conference on Database and Expert Systems Applications (DEXA)*, Vienna, Austria (LNCS 1460, pp. 746-756).

Sen, A., & Sinha, A. P. (2005). A Comparison of Data Warehousing Methodologies. *Communications of the ACM, 48*(3), 79–84. doi:10.1145/1047671.1047673

Serrano, M., Trujillo, J., Calero, C., Luján, S., & Piattini, M. (2004, June 7-11). Empirical Validation of Metrics for Conceptual Models of Data Warehouses. In *Proceedings of the 16th International Conference on Advanced Information Systems Engineering (CAiSE 2004)*, Riga, Latvia (LNCS 3084, pp. 506-520).

Serrano, M., Trujillo, J., Calero, C., & Piattini, M. (2007). Metrics for data warehouse conceptual models understandability. *Information and Software Technology, 49*(8), 851–870. doi:10.1016/j.infsof.2006.09.008

Siau, K., & Cao, Q. (2001). Unified modeling language: A complexity analysis. *Journal of Database Management, 12*(1), 26–34.

Slevin, D. P., & Pinto, J. K. (1987). Balancing Strategy and Tactics in Project Implementation. *Sloan Management Review, 29*(1), 33–41.

Vassiliadis, P. (2000). Gulliver in the land of data warehousing: practical experiences and observations of a researcher. In *Proceedings of the 2nd International Workshop on Design and Management of Data Warehouses (DMDW'00)*, Stockholm, Sweden (pp. 12.1-12.11).

Watson, H. J., Annino, D. A., Wixom, B. H., Avery, K. L., & Rutherford, M. (2001). Current Practices in Data Warehousing. *Information Systems Management, 18*(1), 1–9. doi:10.1201/1078/43194.18.1.20010101/31264.6

Yu, E. S. K., & Mylopoulos, J. (1994, May 16-21). Understanding "Why" in Software Process Modelling, Analysis, and Design. In *Proceedings of the 16th International Conference on Software Engineering (ICSE)*, Sorrento, Italy (pp. 159-168).

Zhao, L., & Siau, K. (2007). Information mediation using metamodels: An approach using XML and Common Warehouse Metamodel. *Journal of Database Management*, *18*(3), 69–82.

ENDNOTES

1. 28th International Conference on Conceptual Modeling (ER'08)
2. UML profiles are herein denominated as *guest@host* where *guest* is the modelling language to be hosted, and the *host* is the modelling language that allocates the previous one.
3. http://www.eclipse.org (March 2008)

This work was previously published in the Journal of Database Management, Volume 22, Issue 1, edited by Keng Siau, pp. 43-68, copyright 2011 by IGI Publishing (an imprint of IGI Global).

Chapter 4

Understanding Business Domain Models:
The Effect of Recognizing Resource-Event-Agent Conceptual Modeling Structures

Geert Poels
Faculty of Economics & Business Administration, Ghent University, Belgium

ABSTRACT

In this paper, the author investigates the effect on understanding of using business domain models that are constructed with Resource-Event-Agent (REA) modeling patterns. First, the author analyzes REA modeling structures to identify the enabling factors and the mechanisms by means of which users recognize these structures in a conceptual model and description of an information retrieval and interpretation task. Based on this understanding, the author hypothesizes positive effects on model understanding for situations where REA patterns can be recognized in both task and model. An experiment is then conducted to demonstrate a better understanding of models with REA patterns compared to information equivalent models without REA patterns. The results of this experiment indicate that REA patterns can be recognized with minimal prior patterns training and that the use of REA patterns leads to models that are easier to understand for novice model users.

INTRODUCTION

The Resource-Event-Agent (REA) enterprise information architecture (Geerts & McCarthy, 2002) is a consensually agreed and theoretically-founded ontology for enterprises that is used as a conceptual modeling framework for enterprise information systems (Dunn, Cherrington, & Hollander, 2005; Hruby, Kiehn, & Scheller, 2006). An ontology is an explicit specification of a conceptualization: the objects, concepts and other entities that are assumed to exist in some area of interest and the relationships that hold among them (Gruber, 1993). Whereas general-purpose

DOI: 10.4018/978-1-4666-2044-5.ch004

conceptual modeling languages (e.g., UML) do not prescribe which objects, relationships, and properties to include in models of some domain, a domain ontology identifies the objects of interest in the domain and offers rules to connect these objects into information structures.

The concepts and structures of the REA ontology are presented as a collection of modeling patterns. Analysts can use the templates that document these patterns as a base solution when creating models. Model users can use the patterns as a reference when reading models and trying to understand them. In this study, we examine the structuring capabilities offered by the REA patterns and their effect on the conceptual modeling outcome. Prior research indicates that the use of REA patterns helps in creating more accurate conceptual models (Gerard, 2005), which is important given that information systems are developed based on such models (Olivé, 2007). Conceptual models are, however, also used to help understand phenomena of interest within a domain and to support the communication between users, analysts and developers (Wand & Weber, 2002). The benefits of using patterns for understanding models have not been thoroughly explored. Therefore, we investigate whether recognizing REA conceptual modeling structures improves model understanding.

The second section of the paper provides an introduction to the REA ontology, presents its core structuring principle, i.e., the resource-event-agent pattern, and explains its use in constructing domain models of business processes, thereby defining the type and scope of the conceptual models to which this research applies. The third section reviews prior research and further refines the research question. The fourth section proposes a research model that is based on the premise that users who interact with REA-based conceptual models recognize the resource-event-agent structures. Accordingly, hypotheses are developed based on pattern recognition theories from cognitive psychology. The fifth and sixth sections present the design and conduct of an experiment to test these hypotheses and the analysis of the collected data. Finally, the seventh section presents conclusions, discusses the study limitations and the implications of the research findings, and outlines further research directions.

THE RESOURCE-EVENT-AGENT ONTOLOGY

The REA ontology has been accepted in August 2007 as the international ISO/IEC standard 15944-4, referred to as the Open-edi Business Transaction Ontology (OeBTO). Different reference models and methodologies for designing business services in e-collaboration contexts (e.g., the UN/CEFACT's Modeling Methodology (UMM), the E-Commerce Integration Meta-Framework (ECIMF), the ISO/IEC 14662:1997 reference model for electronic data interchange) use REA as underlying business ontology for grounding the constructs of their modeling formalisms.

Alternative ontologies for the same domain may differ because of the lens through which they look at reality and that determines their domain conceptualization (i.e., the domain concepts that they consider relevant). The basis of REA is the semantic data model for accounting proposed by McCarthy (1982). REA thus focuses heavily on those enterprise concepts that are required to implement accountability and control principles. The conceptualization of an enterprise specified by REA is that of a chain of interconnected transaction cycles that all contribute to the generation of 'value' for the enterprise. Each transaction cycle is an aggregate of (usually two) business processes that effectuate either market exchange transactions or internal conversion operations. An example of the former is the revenues cycle, which integrates sales and collection processes (i.e., the order taking and delivery of a product or service and the collection of the payment make up a 'cycle'). An example of the latter is the production cycle, where the use or consumption of resources like raw materials, labor, machinery, energy, etc. leads to the production of finished goods.

REA describes in a generic way the concepts and relationships that can be identified in the transactional/transformational core of any transaction cycle: the value-affecting events that occur and which are bound by the principle of economic reciprocity (i.e., 'give and take'), the resources whose value is affected by these events and the agents involved in these events. The conceptual modeling structure shown in Figure 1(a) is an ER diagram encoding of this core pattern of concepts and relationships that recurs in every transaction cycle. Figure 1(b) illustrates how this pattern is used to model a retail company's expenditures cycle, which integrates acquisition and payment processes. Economically valuable resources of the company (e.g., *Inventory*, *Cash*) are related to the events occurring in the cycle that cause resource inflows or outflows (e.g., *Purchase*, *Cash Disbursement*). Events that result in resource inflows (e.g., *Purchase*) are related via duality relationships (reflecting economic reciprocity) to events that result in resource outflows (e.g., *Cash Disbursement*). Participation relationships relate events with agents representing the inside parties (e.g., *Purchase Agent*, *Cashier*) and outside parties (e.g., *Vendor*) to the economic exchange that is modeled.

The REA transactional/transformational core pattern shown in Figure 1(a) and additional REA patterns for describing non-core elements of transaction cycles such as claims, policies, schedules, contracts and commitments (see Geerts & McCarthy, 2006; Hruby et al., 2006) constitute a comprehensive and coherent set of patterns for describing enterprise reality. All these patterns are variations of resource-event-agent conceptual modeling structures, meaning constellations of entities in which an agent does something (i.e., performing the event related to the resource) for the benefit of another agent, who does something in return. For instance, in a commitment variation of the core pattern, the events are replaced by commitments, which are promises to execute events in the foreseeable future. In a typification variation, one or more of the resources, events and agents are replaced by an abstract type image (e.g., a particular type of sales like sales with a 10% discount is made to a particular type of customers like 'gold' customers). In an internal conversion context (e.g., production), there typically is only one agent present in the resource-event-agent constellations as there are no outside parties to be represented. This rich set of business patterns has been used as a conceptual modeling framework in the development of various types of enterprise systems, including both accounting information systems (Batra & Sin, 2008; Rosli, Ahmi, & Mohamad, 2009) and non-accounting applications like enterprise planning systems (Church & Smith, 2008), supply chain collaboration systems (Haugen & McCarthy, 2000) and systems supporting production processes (Hruby et al., 2006).

Note that the view of a transaction cycle that is inherent in the REA core pattern (see Figure 1(a)) is a structural view rather than a behavioral view. A structural view on some relevant part of the real world is the view commonly taken in *conceptual data modeling*, which emphasizes the concepts (relevant things and their properties) that constitute that part of the real world (also referred to as the Universe of Discourse (UoD)) and the relationships that provide structure to these concepts. A behavioral view on a transaction cycle and its composing business processes would emphasize more the sequencing of the different process steps or transformations of process states and the (temporal) constraints that determine which execution sequences are valid. To distinguish with the behavioral view, common in *business process and workflow modeling*, we refer to a conceptual model of a transaction cycle according to the structural view as a *domain model* whereas we reserve the term *process model* for the behavioral view.

Figure 1. ER diagram encodings of resource-event-agent conceptual modeling structures (a) The REA core pattern (b) The REA core pattern applied to the expenditures cycle in a retail company

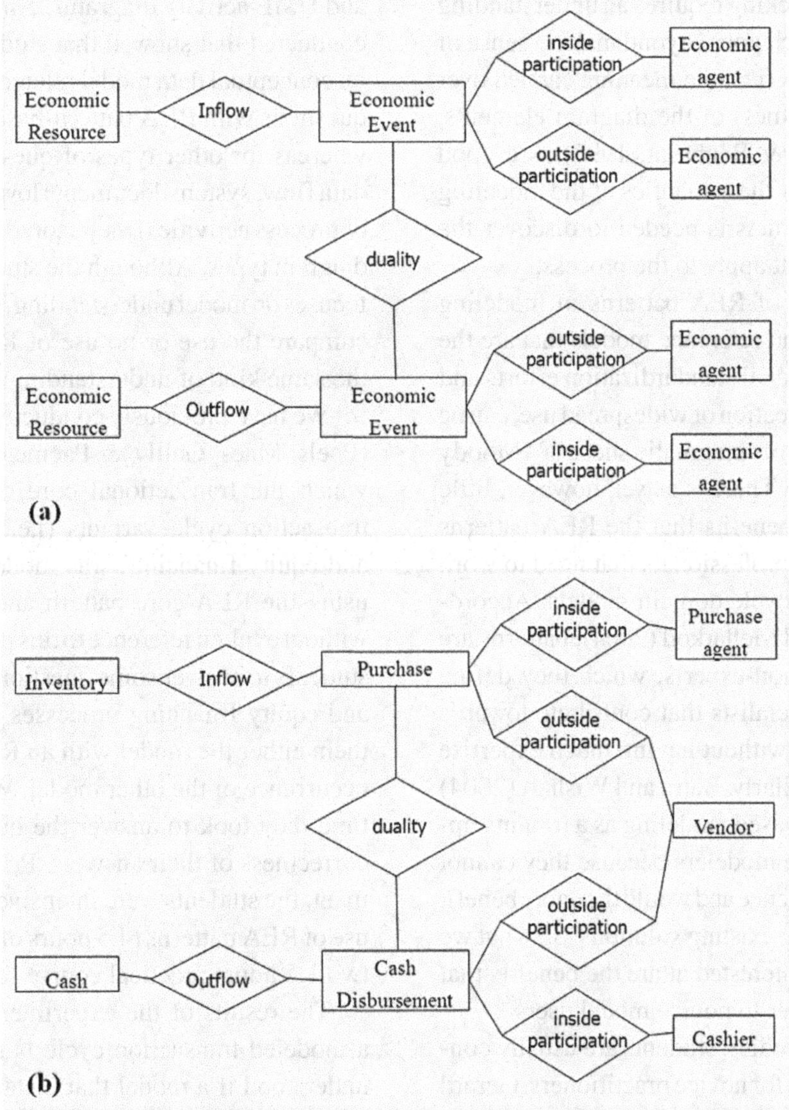

PRIOR RESEARCH

Transaction cycles are modeled by analysts and transaction cycle information is communicated (via the models) to various kinds of business professionals, including business process workers and managers, and external business consultants. Many of these stakeholders have previously provided input to the modeling process (i.e., during requirements elicitation) and are later asked to validate the models that the analyst has developed based upon this (and possibly other) input (Maes and Poels, 2007). There are other types of business professionals that have not participated in the modeling process, but still must be able to use domain models for retrieving relevant information and correctly interpreting it. Auditors, for instance, check the conformance of business process executions (also called 'cases') by comparing 'audit trails' stored in a log to the domain model. Model-based conformance checking requires an understanding of the model which goes beyond making sense of surface semantics (i.e., the meaning carried over by the labels (names) of the diagram elements, see Siau, Wand, & Benbasat, 1997) as a good comprehension of the semantics of the modeling grammar's constructs is needed to discover the business rules that apply to the process.

The adoption of REA patterns in modeling methodologies and reference models that are the result of international standardization efforts and the possible implication of widespread use, can be seen as measures of 'pragmatic success' (Moody & Shanks, 2003). There is as yet, however, little evidence of the benefits that the REA patterns offer to business professionals that need to work with transaction cycle domain models. According to Antony and Mellarkod (2004), patterns are most useful for non-experts, which they define as functional specialists that contribute towards systems analysis without having much expertise in modeling. Similarly, Batra and Wishart (2004) propose pattern-based modeling as a training approach for novice modelers because they cannot rely on past experience and would therefore benefit most from reusing existing solutions. So what we are particularly interested at are the benefits that REA patterns offer to novice model users.

In scientific studies, students are usually considered as proxies for novice practitioners. Gerard (2005) showed that students possessing knowledge structures consistent with the REA core pattern (as a result of learning) were more accurate in the conceptual design of accounting databases than students with less consistent knowledge structures. The study of Gerard demonstrated the positive effect of the structuring capabilities of the REA core pattern on modeling performance, but did not investigate whether REA patterns also help in understanding models developed by others. Jones, Tsay, and Griggs (2005) compared the task-specific relative strength of five types of diagrams: ER diagrams constructed with REA patterns, process maps, flowcharts, data flow diagrams and UML activity diagrams. An experiment was conducted that showed that students scored best on conceptual data model related comprehension questions with REA pattern-based ER diagrams, whereas for other types of questions (related to data flow, system document flow and sequencing of process activities) they scored better with other diagram types. Although the study of Jones et al. focuses on model understanding, it did not directly compare the use or no use of REA patterns for the same kind of understanding task.

We have previously conducted an experiment (Poels, Maes, Gailly, & Paemeleire, in press) in which the transactional core of two financial transaction cycle variants (i.e., debt financing and equity financing) was modeled a first time using the REA core pattern and a second time without explicit reference to this pattern. We asked students to answer some questions about the debt and equity financing processes modeled giving them either the model with an REA core pattern occurrence or the other model. We measured the time they took to answer the questions and the correctness of their answers. Prior to the experiment, the students were intensively trained in the use of REA patterns (4.5 hours of instruction plus two 1.5 hours practical course sessions).

The results of the experiment indicated that a modeled transaction cycle is more accurately understood if a model that instantiates the REA core pattern is used, however, no statistical significant difference in the time taken to perform the experimental task was observed. As noted in (Poels et al., in press), the absence of a demonstrable efficiency effect might be the result of a too low statistical power level for the hypotheses tests, because of the small scale of our experiment (only 30 participants). Another explanation offered is that we should have used also perception-based measures (e.g., ease of use, user information satisfaction) to investigate whether the correct answers to the questions asked can be inferred easier and quicker from the information provided by the model with the REA pattern occurrence.

Although the results of this first study indicate that an experimental investigation of the benefits that REA patterns offer to novice model users is feasible, a larger scale study that employs a wider variety of measures (both performance- and perception-based) is needed to provide a more conclusive answer to the following research question:

Is an ER diagram that is used as a conceptual model of a transaction cycle better understood by novice business users if it contains REA pattern occurrences?

It is important to note that an ER diagram showing transaction cycle related information can be developed without using the REA patterns. Such an ER diagram may also contain other pattern occurrences than REA patterns. Batra (2005) provides a synthesis of conceptual data modeling patterns, some of which can be used to model transactions. These patterns describe conceptual modeling structures that frequently occur in real-world conceptual data models. From a scientific point of view it could be worthwhile to compare the effect on model understanding of using the ontology-based REA patterns with that of using alternative, empirically-derived transaction patterns. Instead, the research question formulated here is motivated by a pragmatic consideration. Given that several international standards for modeling collaborative business processes (i.e., ISO/IEC 15944, ISO/IEC 14662:1997, UMM and ECIMF) have based their modeling methodologies and reference models on REA patterns, an answer to the research question would help practitioners deciding whether or not to adopt an REA-based modeling standard. We believe that such a decision is a more realistic practical motive for our research than the question which collection of patterns to use, even if from a scientific standpoint such a study may provide valuable insights into the relative merits of ontology-derived and empirically-derived patterns.

RESEARCH MODEL

To derive testable hypotheses from our research question we looked at theories that explain the mental process called pattern recognition. Pattern recognition research in psychology has identified enabling factors and the cognitive and perceptual mechanisms that trigger pattern recognition. Batra (2005) and Antony and Mellarkod (2004) have suggested a number of theories used in the fields of analogical reasoning and similarity finding that might be useful for explaining how conceptual data modeling patterns are recognized. An example is the Structure-Mapping Theory (Gentner & Medina, 1998), which proposes three mechanisms (i.e., literal similarity, abstraction and analogy) by means of which pattern recognition works (Antony & Mellarkod, 2004).

Considering enabling factors for pattern recognition, the REA core pattern and its representation as a template (i.e., the generic pattern, as in Figure 1(a), or as an ER diagram fragment, see the pattern occurrence in Figure 1(b)) exhibit two specific features that facilitate pattern recognition processes and mechanisms. The first feature is called *localization* (Dunn & Grabski, 2001) and relates to the ontological structuring of information elements offered by a modeling pattern. Localization means that a modeling pattern acts as a conceptual topological structure in which information elements can easily be localized because of their predetermined position relative to each other. This feature holds also for the other patterns that are part of the REA ontology.

The second feature, not shared by the other REA patterns, is *secondary notation* (Petre, 1995) which refers to the visual structuring capabilities offered by a fixed format modeling template, which ensures that the REA core pattern's topological structure of information elements becomes a spatial topological structure (instead of a purely conceptual topological structure). The fixed format of the REA core pattern template (see Figure 1(a)) is formed by a diagram layout where the entities representing resources, events and agents are placed in respectively a left, middle, and right column of the diagram. By instantiating the REA core pattern template of Figure 1(a), the position of information elements in a model is not only fixed relative to each other, but also fixed relative to the page containing the model (i.e., a fixed absolute positioning). The use of spatial relations and location in the plane when drawing system design diagrams has been investigated by Nickerson, Corter, Tversky, Zahner, and Rho (2008) who show that such 'affordances of the page' help making designs clearer. For instance, the physical separation of clusters facilitates grouping and abstraction processes that reduce memory load by reducing the number of units to keep in mind. The grouping of resources, events and agents in separate diagram columns can be seen as an example of such a physical clustering process.

Localization, and for the REA core pattern also secondary notation, ensure that the REA patterns behave like patterns according to the notion assumed in the pattern recognition theories discussed, i.e., as recurring structures of information elements that can be recognized because of their unique clues for discrimination. For instance, if a user familiar with the REA patterns sees an ER diagram with entities arranged in three columns and she can interpret one of the entities in the middle column as an event, then she can quickly follow one or a few links to the left, right or to other entities in the middle column and check whether the entities found match her expectations (i.e., being resources, agents or other events). If so, she will likely conclude that the diagram is built around an REA core pattern occurrence, i.e., she has recognized the pattern. After this recognition, the other elements of the pattern can easily be found (because the user knows where to look for them) and interpreted in terms of REA ontological semantics.

With respect to pattern recognition in the description of an information retrieval and interpretation task, it is possible that users familiar with the REA patterns will structure their mental representation of the required information according to these patterns for tasks that fit the purpose of REA pattern-based modeling. A task requiring the retrieval and interpretation of transaction cycle information from a business domain model would fit that purpose. For instance, if somebody (e.g., an internal auditor) needs to find out which function in the enterprise is responsible for accepting deliveries of goods, and this person is familiar with the REA patterns, then she is likely to interpret the question as "which internal agent participates in accept delivery of goods events?".

The research question and the reviewed pattern recognition theories suggest a research model for this study. The research model shown in Figure 2 includes the relevant constructs and relationships that are used as variables and hypotheses in this study. Note that the model is already operationalized for the experiment conducted. However, the discussion of the operational details like treatments and measures is deferred to the next section.

The main factor under investigation is the *Representation Method* for domain models of transaction cycles and its effect on the user understanding of the models. Given that for the conceptual modeling of a single transaction cycle, the use of the REA pattern-based modeling approach results in an ER diagram (hereafter called an *REA diagram*) with REA pattern occurrences that can be recognized by users familiar with the REA patterns, we hypothesize that such a diagram is better understood than an ER diagram that was not obtained using the REA approach (hereafter called a *Non-REA diagram*). The argumentation for this hypothesis is that users confronted with a task requiring transaction cycle information to be retrieved from an ER diagram (i.e., a model comprehension task), will create a mental repre-

Figure 2. Research model

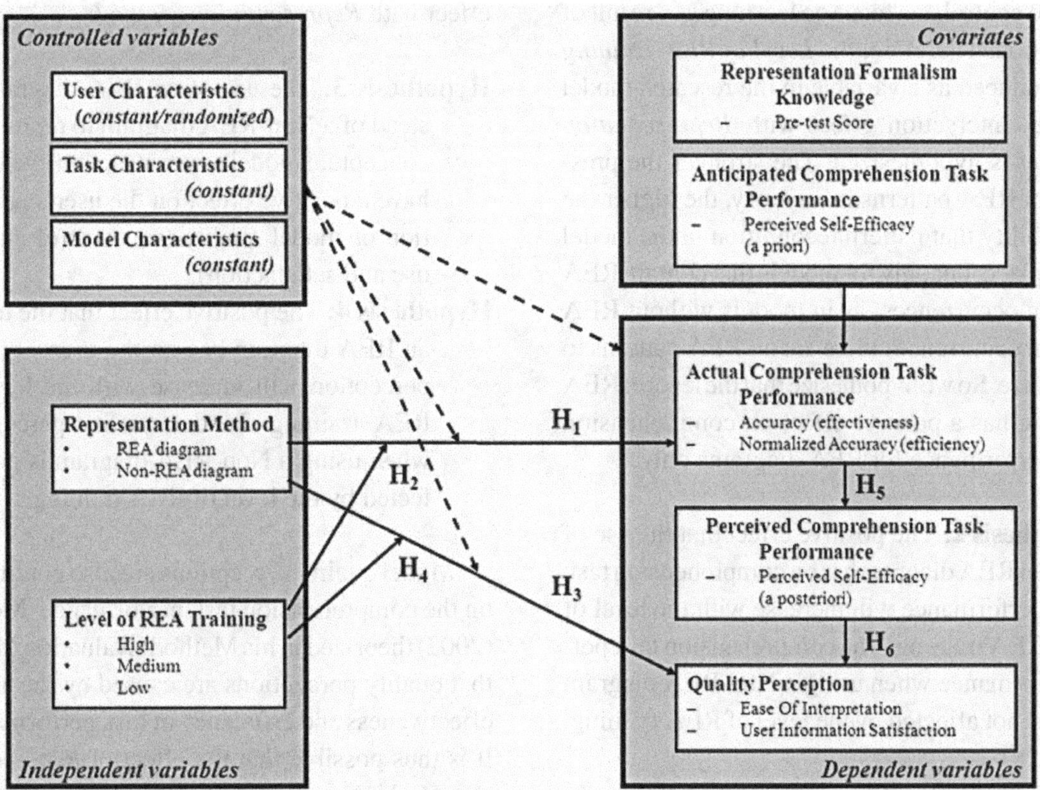

sentation in which the required information is structured according to the familiar REA patterns (i.e., pattern recognition in the task). If the ER diagram is an REA diagram, then it is likely that the users will recognize these structures of information in the model. Therefore we hypothesize that *Actual Comprehension Task Performance* will be *effective* (i.e., successful retrieval and interpretation of the required information) and *efficient* (i.e., with low cognitive effort involved, thus fast). If on the other hand the ER diagram is a Non-REA diagram, then no REA patterns can be recognized in the model. Consequently, a less effective and efficient task performance is expected.

Hypothesis 1: The use of an REA diagram instead of a Non-REA diagram to represent a conceptual model of a transaction cycle will have a positive effect on comprehension task performance (in terms of effectiveness and efficiency).

The pattern recognition theories reviewed stress that to recognize a pattern it must be present in one's memory. This presence is achieved through learning, which is a mental process that can involve instruction, training and experience. Without this learning, pattern recognition cannot occur, so to investigate our research question, we need to consider both processes. Hypothesis 1 assumes the presence of REA patterns in memory so that the REA pattern occurrences in the REA diagram can be recognized, but abstracts from the strength of their presence. The probability that patterns are recognized when a user sees an REA diagram increases with the strength of their presence in memory, which we assume to be related to the amount of learning. As experience is hard to control, we focus on learning as a result of education. Therefore, the *Level of REA Training* is introduced as a variable in the research model and an interaction effect with *Representation Method* is hypothesized. The stronger the presence of REA patterns in memory, the higher the probability that pattern recognition in the model takes place, but only for models that contain REA pattern occurrences, as in models without REA pattern occurrences there are no REA patterns to recognize. So we hypothesize that the level of REA training has a positive effect on comprehension task performance for REA diagrams only.

Hypothesis 2: The positive effect that the use of an REA diagram has on comprehension task performance will increase with the level of REA training. The comprehension task performance when using a Non-REA diagram is not affected by the level of REA training.

The usability of conceptual modeling techniques should not only be measured in terms of objective performance, but also in terms of users' attitudes towards the techniques, the tasks performed using the techniques, and their own performance (Topi & Ramesh, 2002). It is probable that users that can recognize REA patterns will be less satisfied when they have to solve the problem posed by the task using a diagram that does not contain REA pattern occurrences. It is also likely that such users will perceive non-REA diagrams as more difficult to use than REA diagrams. In line with our previous hypotheses, we hypothesize that in situations where pattern recognition in the model is likely to occur, users will have a more favorable perception of ease of use and will be more satisfied. Similar to the hypothesized effect on performance, we formulate two hypotheses related to *Quality Perception*. Hypothesis 3 assumes that REA patterns have been learned but abstracts from the amount of learning. On the other hand, Hypothesis 4 takes the *Level of REA Training* into account and states an interaction effect with *Representation Method*.

Hypothesis 3: The use of an REA diagram instead of a Non-REA diagram to represent a conceptual model of a transaction cycle will have a positive effect on the user's perception of model quality (in terms of ease of use and satisfaction).

Hypothesis 4: The positive effect that the use of an REA diagram has on the user's quality perception will increase with the level of REA training. Model quality perception when using a Non-REA diagram is not affected by the level of REA training.

Model quality perceptions are also contingent on the comprehension task performance. Moody (2002) theorized in his Method Evaluation Model that quality perceptions are caused by the actual effectiveness and efficiency of task performance. It is thus possible that the effect of *Representation Method* on *Quality Perception* (as well as the interaction effect with training) is only indirect, via *Actual Comprehension Task Performance*. This would mean that quality perception is high because the comprehension task was performed effectively and efficiently, which we hypothesized to be the case when using REA diagrams (Hypothesis 1) and especially when REA diagrams are used by users with a high level of REA training (Hypothesis 2). To test this alternative explanation, a link from comprehension task performance to quality perception is introduced in the research model. If users have not received feedback on their task performance (as in the experiment conducted; see the next section), this link must be implemented using another user attitude, *Perceived Comprehension Task Performance* (Goodhue & Thompson, 1995). This variable captures the user's perception of task performance. This perception might be different from the actual outcome (unknown to the user). Burton-Jones and Meso (2008) showed that measures of perceived understanding are less effective in assessing real understanding than measures of actual understanding. Nevertheless, we cannot preclude that when users perform bad (or good), they are aware of this (even if not knowing the actual results) and perceive their task performance accordingly.

Hypothesis 5: Actual comprehension task performance is related to perceived comprehension task performance.

Hypothesis 6: Perceived comprehension task performance is related to perceived model quality (in terms of ease of use and satisfaction).

The research model shows a number of other variables that will be controlled in the experiment to increase the internal validity of the study. They include *User Characteristics* other than level of REA training (e.g., demographic and personality characteristics, domain familiarity, working experience), *Task Characteristics* (e.g., task fit with purpose of REA ontology, task difficulty, nature of the task), and *Model* (or *Representation*) *Characteristics* other than representation method (e.g., size and complexity of the diagram, modeling language and notational system used). For instance, if users are intimately familiar with the domain that is modeled, they might perform the comprehension task based on their previous knowledge of the domain instead of the information conveyed by the diagram (Burton-Jones & Weber, 1999). So, the domain familiarity of the study participants must be controlled by presenting them with models of not too familiar domains and by ensuring that, if still some level of domain familiarity is expected, that this level is the same for all treatment groups.

Two further variables will be controlled in the study by including them as covariates in the data analysis. The first variable is *Representation Formalism Knowledge*, a user characteristic. Knowing how information elements and structures are represented using the constructs of the ER Model is a prerequisite for being able to derive domain information from ER diagrams. Research has shown that data modeling experience and knowledge of modeling techniques impact model comprehension (Kim & March, 1995; Parsons, 2003; Khatri, Vessey, Ramesh, Clay, & Park, 2006). As we cannot preclude that higher levels of REA training are associated with better knowledge of the ER formalism, this variable must be controlled and its effect cancelled out using appropriate data analysis techniques. The second variable, also a user characteristic, is the user's belief in her ability to successfully perform the task. This belief has been described using the concept of perceived self-efficacy (Bandura, 1997; Ajzen, 2002), which has been shown to be related to actual task performance outcomes (Smith, Change, & Moores, 2003). As users having received more REA training might have higher levels of self-efficacy, the impact of this variable on actual comprehension task performance can be controlled by using it as a covariate. To distinguish this variable from *Actual Comprehension Task Performance* (i.e., observed task performance) and *Perceived Comprehension Task Performance* (i.e., user perception of the task performance), the self-efficacy of users *before* the task is referred to as *Anticipated Comprehension Task Performance*.

RESEARCH METHOD

Topi and Ramesh (2002) assume in their generic research model for human factors related research in conceptual modeling, complex moderating effects of the user and task variables on the relationship between representation formalism/method and user performance and attitudes. Parsons and Cole (2005) state, however, that because of the relative small amount of theory-based experimental work in the area of conceptual modeling, a focus on simple, theoretically causal relationships involving one or a few independent variables is needed. To demonstrate the basic causal effects of representation mechanisms and control other variables, a laboratory experiment is preferred because the complexity and lack of control in real settings would make such study nearly impossible (Parsons, 2005; Siau & Rossi, in press). We therefore designed a 2 × 3 between-subjects experiment. The two levels of the first factor, *Representation Method*, are the experimental treatments (i.e., REA diagram and Non-REA diagram). The second factor, *Level of REA Training*, has three levels (i.e., Low, Medium, and High). This design allows assessing the representation method's impact on task performance and user quality perceptions (Hypotheses 1 and 3) as well as the interaction effect of representation method and level of REA training (Hypotheses 2 and 4).

Participants and Allocation to Experimental Groups

The participants were a group of business students enrolled in a junior-level Management Information Systems (MIS) course at a European university. This group of students approximates a representative sample of the target population, i.e., business professionals that are novices with respect to the use of transaction cycle domain models. The advantage of student participants instead of using 'real' novice model users is that controlling the *User Characteristics* variable becomes easier. In particular, a student's familiarity with the REA patterns is relatively easy to assess, compared to people working in business, which might have diverse (educational) backgrounds. The learning of REA patterns can be explicit (i.e., education) or implicit (e.g., experience), but implicit learning is much harder to observe and measure. The students participating in the experiment formed a more homogeneous group with respect to their educational background and working experience, which would not be the case if business professionals were used, even if only novices were selected to participate. With this students group, the possibility of REA ontology patterns present in memory because of working experience can practically be ruled out, which facilitates the operationalization of the *Level of REA Training* independent variable and the control over a possible confound posed by working experience.

During the course module that focused on conceptual data modeling, students were first taught the constructs and grammatical rules of the ER model. The notation used for ER diagrams was based on UML. Apart from studying the ER model, students were shown examples of and learned to read ER diagrams of various domains (e.g., university personnel management, hospital operations). The subsequent course module exercises required students to retrieve and interpret information conveyed by ER diagrams (e.g., answering questions like 'Can a research assistant be a PhD student?' and 'Can a patient be treated by a doctor from another hospital?').

After the course sessions on ER modeling, the students were given a 1-hour lecture on business domain reference models in which they were introduced to the main patterns of the REA enterprise ontology. Four reference models (order-to-cash, purchase-to-pay, payroll, and production) were explained in this lecture. Following the lecture, students could engage in one or two parts of practical course work similar to the previous ER diagram exercises, but now performed on REA diagrams (i.e., conceptual models instantiating the REA ontology-based reference models seen in class). Students had to register for these optional parts of the course, so the identity of the students participating was known to us. These two 1.5 hours exercise sessions were run in small groups (maximum 6 students), each under the supervision of a teaching assistant. Although attendance was strictly controlled and student participation was intense, the teaching assistant did not actually test the learning outcome at the end of each session. Hence we can only assume that the additional exposure to REA conceptual modeling structures strengthened their presence in memory for those students attending the exercise sessions.

Apart from the lecture on reference models and the subsequent practical course work, no other lecture, practice session or course assignment was devoted to REA patterns. We thus observe three levels of REA training differing in their extent of exposure to the REA patterns:

- **Low:** Students not participating in the practical course work on REA modeling;
- **Medium:** Students participating in only the first part of REA practice;
- **High:** Students participating in both the first and second part.

An assumption underlying the construction of the *Level of REA Training* variable is that the differences in the extent of exposure to REA patterns between the Low, Medium and High levels reflect differences in the amount of learning and thus differences in the strength of presence of REA patterns in memory. Note that apart from differences in the amount of exposure, the additional exposure to REA patterns was also more recent (at the time of the experiment) for the Medium and High groups, which may also strengthen their presence in memory.

The experiment was conducted after finishing the conceptual modeling module of the course. A total of 124 students from the course participated in the experiment, of which 22 were classified as Low, 69 as Medium, and 33 as High with respect to their level of REA training. This uneven distribution of participants across the three levels of REA training implies that this factor is a measured, rather than a manipulated variable. Both participation in the REA exercises and in the experiment was voluntary making it impossible to ensure that each level of REA training was equally well covered. On the other hand, the allocation of the participants to the REA diagram and Non-REA diagram treatments was random, so representation method is a manipulated variable. The randomization of the *User Characteristics* variable per treatment controls for possible differential influences on the dependent variables. Table 1 summarizes the experimental design and participant allocation.

Instrumentation

The REA and Non-REA diagrams used as experimental objects are included in the Appendix (see Figures 7 and 8). These diagrams had to be representations of the same domain to control the possible confounding effects of domain complexity and familiarity. The example chosen for the experiment was the hiring, employing and paying of external consulting services which is a cycle of transactions that the experiment participants had not looked at during the course (neither during the optional exercises with REA diagrams).

Another requirement for the experimental objects is their informational equivalence (Siau, 2004). Otherwise, differences in information content may confound attempts to measure the impact of the independent variables on the dependent variables (Parsons & Cole, 2005). To ensure the informational equivalence of the REA and Non-REA diagrams, the different treatment diagrams were constructed by applying diagram transformations that are information-preserving, meaning that they do not change the information content of the diagrams. Two kinds of transformations were applied:

1. Changing the diagram layout by repositioning diagram elements: this transformation changes the look but not the information content of the diagram. Hence, informational equivalence is ensured by definition.
2. Direct representation or objectification of many-to-many relationships: A many-to-many relationship between two entities can be directly represented by means of an UML association or can be objectified, i.e., replaced by a new entity and two one-to-many relationships between this new entity and the existing entities. The informational

Table 1. Experimental design and participant allocation

Number of participants in each condition		Representation Method		Total
		Non-REA diagram	REA diagram	
Level of REA Training	*Low*	11	11	22
	Medium	34	35	69
	High	17	16	33
Total		62	62	124

equivalence between both types of representation has been demonstrated (Dedene & Snoeck, 1995; Wand, Storey, & Weber, 1999). In the conceptual data modeling module of the MIS course from which our study participants were drawn, both types of relationship representation were taught. Figure 3 provides an example of objectification. The many-to-many relationship *ProductSold* in Figure 3(a) is replaced in Figure 3(b) by the entity *ProductSold*, the one-to-many relationship between *Sale* and *ProductSold* and the one-to-many relationship between *Product* and *ProductSold*. The primary key of *ProductSold* is a concatenation of the primary keys of *Sale* and *Product*, which avoids the existence of multiple links between a particular sale and a particular product.

Related to the second transformation (objectification), we also considered modeling events as relationships instead of entities (Allen & March, 2006). If events are modeled as relationships then their attributes will be contained in an UML association class attached to the UML association that represents the relationship. The number of entities related to the event determines the degree of the relationship that would be used to model the event. Although the transformation of events modeled as entities into events modeled as relationships seems an obvious choice, it does not result in informationally equivalent models as often a particular resource and a particular agent can be linked more than once via events (of the same type). Modeling events as relationships would not allow showing these multiple links.

To create the Non-REA diagram, objectification was applied to the *IsPaymentFor* duality relationship in the REA diagram (see Figure 4). The explicit modeling of the duality of 'give' and 'take' events is the most distinctive structuring idea of the REA ontology. Also the *Orders* relationship was objectified (see Figure 5). The explicit modeling of relationships between commitments and resources is another essential modeling structure, widely used in REA ontology-based reference models, including those shown in the one hour lecture on business domain reference models given to experimental participants. Objectifying the duality and reservation relationships helps in hiding the conceptual topological structure that REA-trained users expect to find when looking at a diagrammatic representation of a business process. For instance, if a REA-trained user interprets the *Get Consulting Services* entity as an event, then she knows that its dual event (*Pay Consulting Services*) can be found by navigating a single (duality) relationship. The introduction of a connecting entity *Consulting Services Paid* in the Non-REA diagram reduces this localization and thus makes the matching of diagram fragments to the pattern templates stored in memory more difficult.

By repositioning diagram elements we strived for a layout design for the Non-REA diagram that is different from the REA modeling conventions. In the layout for the Non-REA diagram that we

Figure 3. Objectification (a) The relationship ProductSold between Sale and Product represented as an UML association (b) The relationship ProductSold represented as an UML class

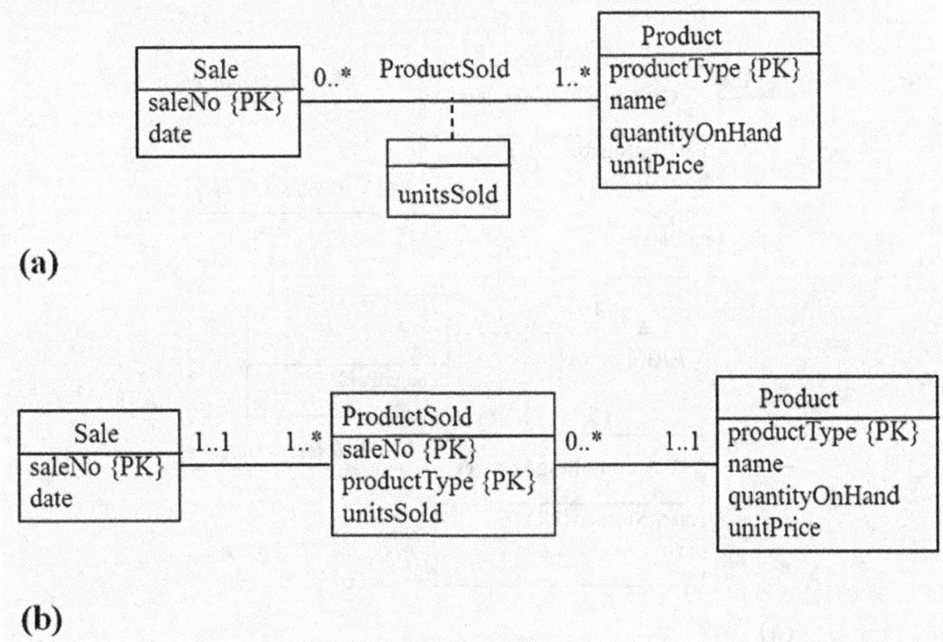

created (see Figure 8 in the Appendix), the entity representing the outside party (*Consulting Firm*) was selected as the central diagram element. Further, the sequence of event occurrences (*Order Consulting Services – Get Consulting Services – Pay Consulting Services*) was positioned around this central element (in counterclockwise order) such that there is a logical path that can be followed when reading the diagram. Hence, the logic of the Non-REA diagram layout can equally well be justified as that of the REA diagram. The main difference with the REA diagram is that the usual three-column R-E-A arrangement is no longer present. The physical repositioning of diagram elements removes this secondary notation clue and thus hinders the analogy mapping process.

Experimental Tasks

There were two tasks: a pre-test for measuring knowledge of the ER representation formalism (a covariate in the study) and the experimental task proper, which was a comprehension task.

The pre-test (included in the Appendix) was the same for all participants and comprised 15 questions either literally taken from or derived from a similar test presented in Parsons and Cole (2005). The purpose of this test is to assess the user's understanding of the semantics conveyed by ER diagram structural elements (i.e., entities, relationships and structural constraints). The test evaluates how well users can apply their knowledge of the domain-independent semantics of the ER model constructs when interpreting ER diagrams.

The experimental task proper was performed using the diagram given (either the REA or the Non-REA diagram). The task consisted of answer-

Figure 4. Objectifying the IsPaymentFor duality relationship (a) fragment of the REA diagram (confer Figure 7) (b) fragment of the non-REA diagram (confer Figure 8)

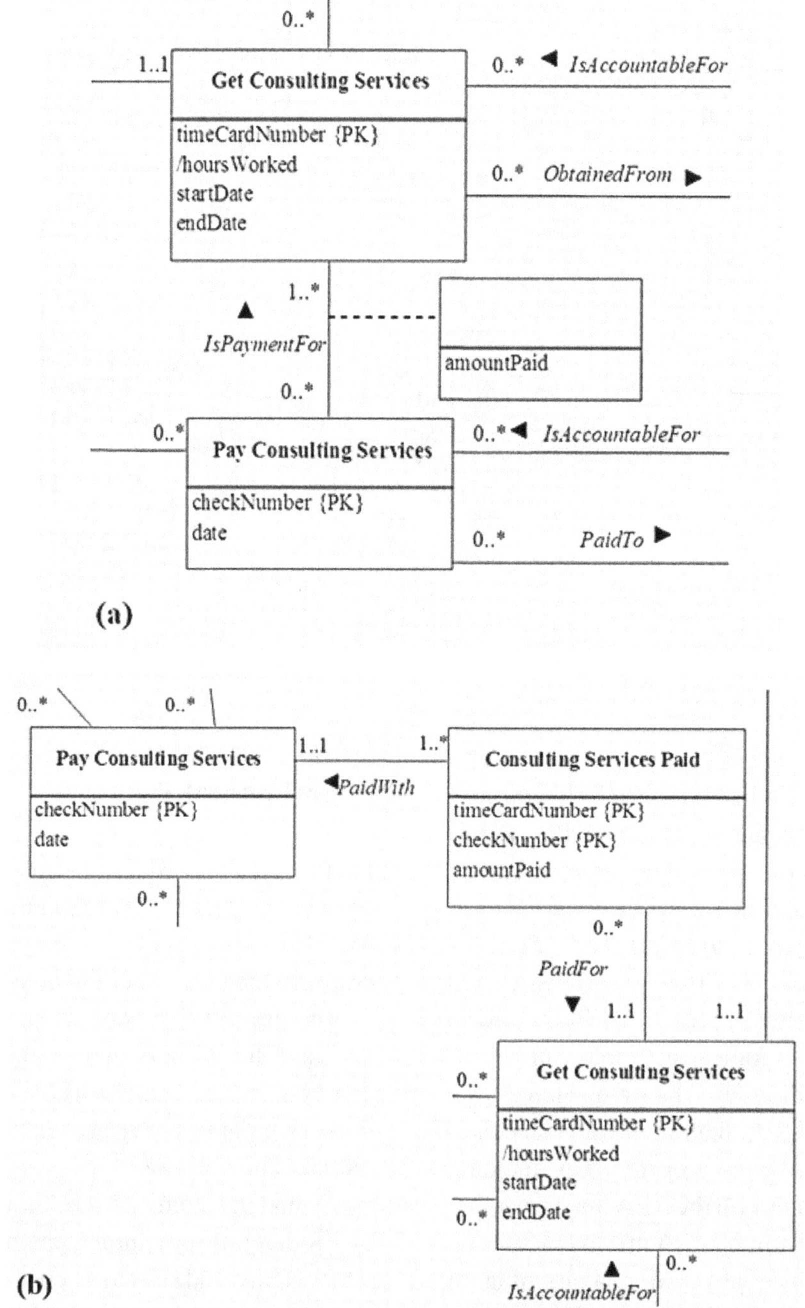

Figure 5. Objectifying the Orders reservation relationship (a) fragment of the REA diagram (confer Figure 7) (b) fragment of the non-REA diagram (confer Figure 8)

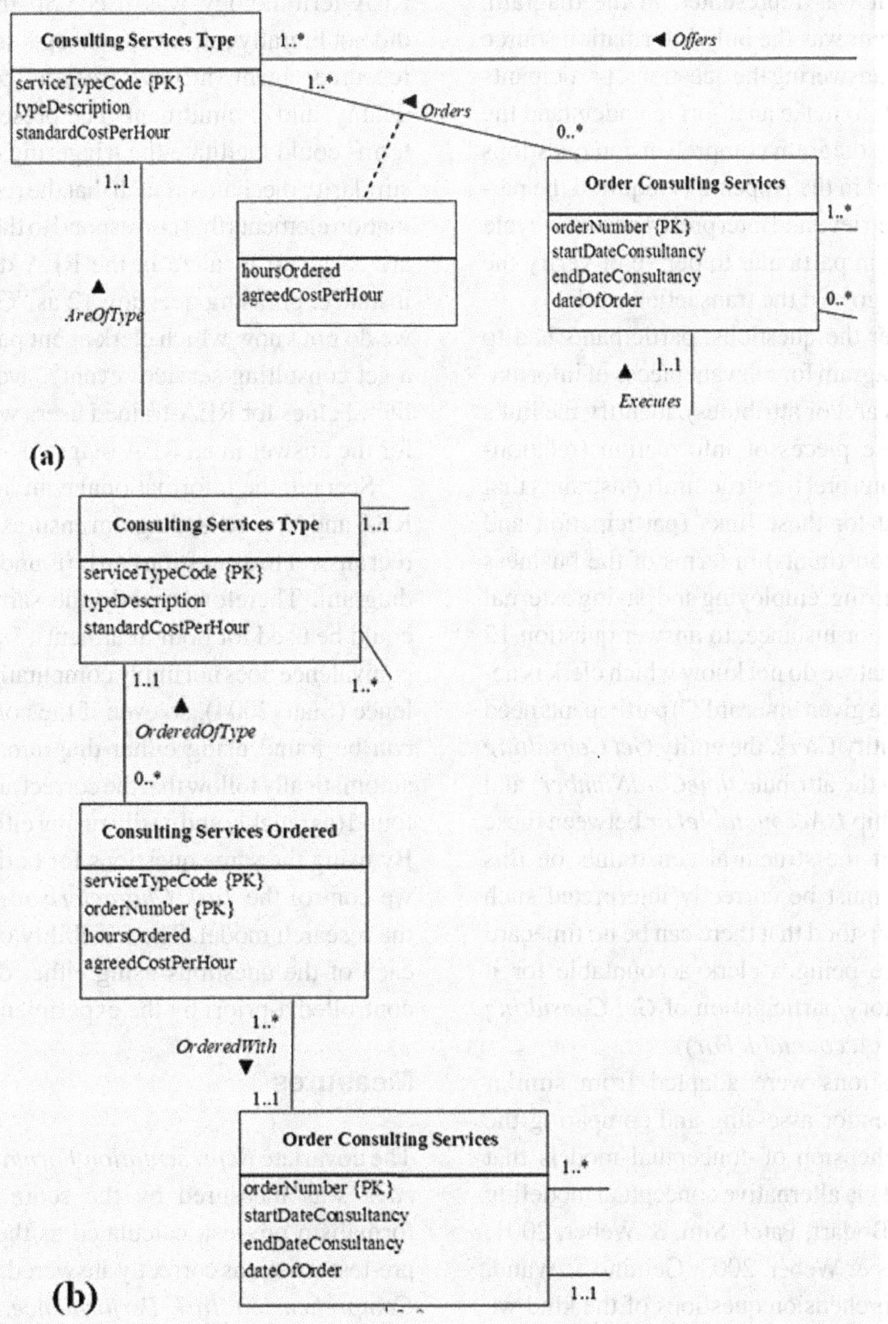

ing 15 questions about the transaction cycle that deals with the engagement of external consulting services as it was represented in the diagram. As the diagram was the only information source available for answering the questions, participants were 'forced' to make an effort to understand the diagram. The diagram comprehension questions (also included in the Appendix) required the participants to retrieve and interpret transaction cycle information, in particular to derive or verify the policies that govern the transaction cycle.

To answer the questions, participants had to search the diagram for relevant pieces of information (entities and/or attributes), identify the links between these pieces of information (relationships), and interpret the structural constraints that are specified for these links (participation and cardinality constraints) in terms of the business rules set for hiring, employing and paying external consultants. For instance, to answer question 12 ("Can it be that we do not know which clerk is accountable for a given timecard?") participants need to find the entity *Clerk*, the entity *Get Consulting Services* (via the attribute *timeCardNumber*) and the relationship *IsAccountableFor* between these entities. Next the structural constraints on this relationship must be correctly interpreted such that it is understood that there can be no timecard without there being a clerk accountable for it (i.e., mandatory participation of *Get Consulting Services* in *IsAccountableFor*)).

The questions were adapted from similar questionnaires for assessing and comparing the user comprehension of conceptual models that are produced via alternative conceptual modeling techniques (Bodart, Patel, Sim, & Weber, 2001; Burton-Jones & Weber, 2003; Gemino & Wand, 2005). Comprehension questions of the kind we used are the conventional instrument for measuring how well users understand the information that is conveyed by a conceptual model (Gemino & Wand, 2003; Parsons & Cole, 2005).

In order to make sure that the comprehension questions were not biased towards the REA treatment two design controls were implemented. First, the questions were phrased such that no specific REA terminology was used. So the questions did not literally reference concepts such as event, resource, agent, inflow, outflow, participation, duality, and commitment. The presence of these terms could facilitate the triggering of the literal similarity mechanism such that the required information elements that correspond to these concepts are easier to localize in the REA diagram. For instance, phrasing question 12 as "Can it be that we do not know which clerk agent participates in a get consulting services event?" would provide literal clues for REA-trained users where to look for the answer in an REA diagram.

Second, the informational equivalence of the REA and Non-REA diagram ensures that the correct answer to a question can be found using either diagram. Therefore exactly the same questions could be used for both treatments. Informational equivalence does not imply computational equivalence (Siau, 2004), so even if the correct answer *can* be found using either diagram, it does not automatically follow that the correct answer *will* be found (as quickly and easily) using either diagram. By using the same questions for both treatments we control the *Task Characteristics* variable of the research model. The feasibility of answering each of the questions using either diagram was controlled a-priori by the experimenters.

Measures

The covariate *Representation Formalism Knowledge* was measured by the score on the ER formalism pre-test, calculated as the number of pre-test questions correctly answered. *Anticipated Comprehension Task Performance*, the second covariate, was measured via the Perceived Self-Efficacy (PSE) construct. Since PSE is a task-specific construct, its measurement should also be specific to the particular task under investigation (Bandura, 1997). Previous studies employing PSE were mainly concerned with end-user training and basic computer use rather than information systems development tasks. The PSE measure that we developed is based on the PSE measures used in (Ryan, Bordoloi, & Harrison, 2000; Smith et al., 2003) who investigated PSE in a conceptual modeling research context. The measure is referred to as the PSE_before measure, to distinguish it from the PSE_after measure used for *Perceived Comprehension Task Performance* (confer infra). The items of the PSE_before instrument (included in the Appendix) were administered as a pre-experiment questionnaire.

To measure the effectiveness dimension of *Actual Comprehension Task Performance*, comprehension task accuracy was defined as the number of correctly answered comprehension questions. To measure the efficiency of a diagram in communicating domain information to the user, the Normalized Accuracy measure of Bodart et al. (2001) was used. This measure relates a participant's comprehension task accuracy and task completion time. It is calculated as the number of comprehension questions correctly answered divided by the time taken to complete the comprehension task. Other research (see Genero, Poels, & Piattini, 2008; Parsons, 2003) has used task completion time as an alternative, but completion time measures efficiency reliably only if a certain level of accuracy is reached. In practice, a better comprehension may be compromised by a faster comprehension, and vice versa (Bodart et al., 2001). Normalized accuracy should in this context be understood as a productivity measure, i.e., relating an output variable (accuracy of comprehension) to an input variable (comprehension time).

The *Perceived Comprehension Task Performance* was again measured via the PSE items that we defined, but now formulated in the past tense, and referred to as the PSE_after items (see the Appendix). We believed that, when formulated in the past tense, the items would capture the participants' perception of how well they accomplished the task (on condition that the instrument is administered directly after the experimental task).

Finally, the *Quality Perception* construct, and more specifically, the dependent variables Perceived Ease Of Interpretation (PEOI) and User Information Satisfaction (UIS), were assessed using existing measures that have been validated before in empirical studies on conceptual modeling (Dunn & Grabski, 2001; Gemino & Wand, 2005). The items of the PEOI and UIS instruments can also be found in the Appendix. Together with the PSE_after items they constituted the post-experiment questionnaire.

Operational Procedures

The experiment was organized as a class room exercise. The students were informed beforehand that this exercise was also part of a research study and that additional data in the form of questionnaires would be collected. However, no information was given with respect to the research questions that would be tested (to avoid experimenter bias). Participation was strictly voluntary and no course credits could be earned.

Students were motivated to participate in two ways. First, we promised feedback on their performance, suggesting that a similar exercise could be part of the final course exam. Second, four prizes (iPod Shuffles and Nanos) were distributed to the best performers. Students were informed that the ranking would be determined based on their scores, and, in case of equal scores, on the time spent. To avoid a ceiling effect, no time limit was set.

When participants entered the class room, they were randomly distributed by a teaching assistant across the two treatment groups and assigned a seat such that neighbors belonged to different treatment groups. The exercise/experiment consisted of four parts, to be executed in the order given (only when a previous part was handed in, the participant received the next part):

1. A sheet containing instructions, asking for the participant's name and student number, and containing the pre-experiment questionnaire with the PSE_before items;
2. The ER formalism pre-test (15 questions);
3. The comprehension task (15 questions) – at this moment the REA or Non-REA diagram was given to the participant and the time was written down by a teaching assistant; when finished, the participant wrote down the time again (projected on a screen in front of the class room) and notified the teaching assistant (who collected the solutions and checked the times);
4. The post-experiment questionnaire with the PSE_after items, and the PEOI and UIS items (intermingled on the questionnaire).

DATA ANALYSIS AND INTERPRETATION

Effect on Comprehension Task Performance (Hypotheses 1-2)

First, the hypothesized effect of *Representation Method* on *Comprehension Task Performance* (Hypothesis 1) and the interaction effect with *Level of REA Training* (Hypothesis 2) are tested. Table 2 presents descriptive statistics for comprehension task Accuracy and Normalized Accuracy.

To test the hypotheses, a MANCOVA was performed with Accuracy and Normalized Accuracy as dependent variables, *Representation Method* and *Level of REA Training* as factors, *Representation Method* × *Level of REA Training* as interaction term, and Pre-test Score (measuring *Representation Formalism Knowledge*) and a priori Perceived Self-Efficacy (PSE_before; measuring *Anticipated Comprehension Task Performance*) as covariates. Results are shown in Table 3.

The model with Normalized Accuracy as dependent variable is not significant ($p = 0.325$), so no effect on the efficiency of comprehension task performance can be demonstrated. The model with Accuracy as dependent variable is significant ($p = 0.001$) with significant effects observed for the factors *Representation Method* ($p = 0.003$) and *Level of REA Training* ($p = 0.019$), and the covariate Pre-test Score ($p = 0.007$). No significant effects are found for the interaction term ($p = 0.447$) and the covariate PSE_before ($p = 0.250$).

These results provide partial support for Hypothesis 1: REA diagram users scored significantly higher on the comprehension task than Non-REA diagram users (mean Accuracy score of 11.4 for REA (maximum = 15) versus 10.5 for Non-REA with an observed effect size of 0.39 which represents a medium effect size). In other words, the use of REA patterns in the ER diagram had a positive effect on the effectiveness dimension of user comprehension, meaning that REA diagram users showed a more accurate understanding of the business process as modeled.

The absence of an interaction effect between *Representation Method* and *Level of REA Training* means that there is no support for Hypothesis 2, which stated that comprehension task performance when using an REA diagram increases with the level of REA training, whereas comprehension task performance when using a Non-REA diagram would not be affected by the level of REA training. The profile plot in Figure 6 shows that the *Level of REA Training* affects the accuracy of user comprehension, but that this effect is not essentially different for REA and Non-REA diagram users. Post-hoc tests showed a significant difference in Accuracy score between the Low and High training groups ($p = 0.005$) and a marginally significant difference between the Low and Medium groups ($p = 0.058$). Hence, regardless of the representation method used for the ER diagram, users with medium to high levels of REA training gave more correct answers to the comprehension questions than users with a low level of REA training. The increase in accuracy when going from Low over

Table 2. Descriptive statistics of Comprehension Task Performance for each experimental condition

	Representation Method	Level of REA Training	Mean	Std. Deviation	N
Accuracy	REA	Low	11.0909	2.16585	11
		Medium	11.2857	1.84026	35
		High	11.9375	1.38894	16
		Total	11.4194	1.79752	62
	Non-REA	Low	9.3636	1.96330	11
		Medium	10.5000	1.74512	34
		High	11.1765	1.38000	17
		Total	10.4839	1.77174	62
	Total	Low	10.2273	2.20242	22
		Medium	10.8986	1.82422	69
		High	11.5455	1.41622	33
		Total	10.9516	1.83841	124
Normalized Accuracy	REA	Low	0.93645	0.383526	11
		Medium	0.76267	0.285855	35
		High	0.79778	0.264155	16
		Total	0.80256	0.301610	62
	Non-REA	Low	0.62115	0.248058	22
		Medium	0.74898	0.301293	69
		High	0.76573	0.238924	33
		Total	0.73089	0.277240	124
	Total	Low	0.77880	0.354095	22
		Medium	0.75593	0.291475	69
		High	0.78127	0.248023	33
		Total	0.76673	0.290736	124

Table 3. MANCOVA comprehension task performance

Source	Dependent Variable	Type III Sum of Squares	Df	Mean Square	F	Sig.	Partial Eta Squared
Corrected Model	Accuracy	80.020[a]	7	11.431	3.950	0.001	0.192
	Normalized Accuracy	0.686[b]	7	0.098	1.170	0.325	0.066
Intercept	Accuracy	57.791	1	57.791	19.970	<0.001	0.147
	Normalized Accuracy	0.333	1	0.333	3.983	0.048	0.033
Pre-test score	Accuracy	22.144	1	22.144	7.652	0.007	0.062
	Normalized Accuracy	0.004	1	0.004	0.045	0.833	<0.001
PSE_before	Accuracy	3.876	1	3.876	1.339	0.250	0.011
	Normalized Accuracy	0.108	1	0.108	1.287	0.259	0.011
Representation Method	Accuracy	27.268	1	27.268	9.422	0.003	0.075
	Normalized Accuracy	0.367	1	0.367	4.387	0.038	0.036
Level of REA Training	Accuracy	23.890	2	11.945	4.128	0.019	0.066
	Normalized Accuracy	0.007	2	0.004	0.044	0.957	0.001
Representation Method X level of REA Training	Accuracy	4.692	2	2.346	0.811	0.447	0.014
	Normalized Accuracy	0.367	2	0.183	2.192	0.116	0.036
Error	Accuracy	335.690	116	2.894			
	Normalized Accuracy	9.711	116	0.084			
Total	Accuracy	15288.000	124				
	Normalized Accuracy	83.293	124				
Corrected Total	Accuracy	415.710	123				
	Normalized Accuracy	10.397	123				

a. R Squared =0.192 (Adjusted R Squared=0.144)

b. R Squared =0.066 (Adjusted R Squared =0.010)

Medium to High levels of REA training is stronger for Non-REA diagram users than for REA diagram users, and accordingly the differences between the REA and Non-REA treatments are not as big as at the Low level of training. It seems that additional REA training is beneficial for understanding REA diagrams, but that the benefits gained in terms of better understanding need to be balanced against the cost of this additional training.

As expected, participants that demonstrated a better understanding of ER modeling concepts (*Representation Formalism Knowledge*, measured in the pre-test), were also more accurate in the subsequent comprehension task. This result is not surprising given that knowledge of the representation formalism is a prerequisite for the correct interpretation of models. The inclusion of *Representation Formalism Knowledge* as a covariate in the research model allows controlling this user characteristic and eliminating its effect when testing the main and interaction effects. As a Post-Hoc test we verified that the mean Pre-test Score was not different between the 2 × 3 experimental groups. An ANOVA revealed no significant differences, which is especially relevant for the 'measured' *Level of REA Training* variable. The lack of correlation between the Pre-test Score and the *Level of REA Training* confirms that the additional exposure to REA for the medium and high *Level of REA Training* groups did not deepen the students' ER formalism knowledge.

The performance on the comprehension task anticipated by the participants (as measured by PSE_before; Cronbach's alpha 0.848) was not related to their actual performance. In fact, this variable was not significantly correlated to any of the other variables used in the MANCOVA, indicating that the self-efficacy of the participants *prior to the experiment* was effectively controlled in the experiment and that this user characteristic plays no role of interest in the study.

Effect on Quality Perception (Hypotheses 3-6)

The post-experiment questionnaire included the items of the Perceived Ease Of Interpretation (PEOI), User Information Satisfaction (UIS), and Perceived Self-Efficacy (in the a posteriori version, i.e., PSE_after) measures. Whereas PEOI and UIS are existing measures, PSE_after was newly developed for this study. Therefore, and because all three measures capture perceptions about the use of a conceptual model, a reliability and validity analysis was conducted before testing hypotheses 3 – 6.

Initial Cronbach alpha's were 0.722 for PEOI, 0.826 for UIS, and 0.837 for PSE_after. A factor analysis revealed a problem of low discriminant validity for PEOI item 2 ("Using the conceptual schema was seldom frustrating"), so it was not further considered in the rest of the analysis (i.e., the average PEOI scores were calculated without item 2 scores). The removal of PEOI item 2 increased the Cronbach alpha value for PEOI to 0.791, well above the usual reliability threshold

Figure 6. Profile plot accuracy

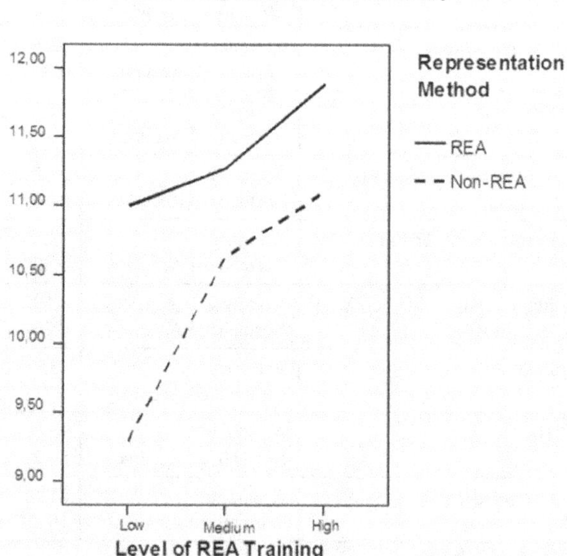

value of 0.70. It was further verified that all items of the new PSE_after measure loaded on a single factor, separate from the PEOI and UIS items.

Next, the hypothesized effect of *Representation Method* on *Quality Perception* (Hypothesis 3) and the interaction effect with *Level of REA Training* (Hypothesis 4) were tested. Table 4 presents descriptive statistics for the perception-based variables PEOI and UIS.

The hypotheses were tested by means of a MANCOVA with PEOI and UIS as dependent variables, *Representation Method* and *Level of REA Training* as factors, *Representation Method* × *Level of REA Training* as interaction term, and a posteriori Perceived Self-Efficacy (PSE_after; measuring *Perceived Comprehension Task Performance*) as covariate. The inclusion of PSE_after as a covariate in the analysis is legitimate as covariates can be (continuous) independent variables in their own right (and given that the other independent variables are categorical). The MANCOVA is thus also used to test the hypothesized relationship between *Perceived Comprehension Task Performance* and *Quality Perception* (Hypothesis 6). The results of the MANCOVA are shown in Table 5.

Both models are significant ($p < 0.001$) with a strongly significant effect observed for PSE_after ($p < 0.001$). The MANCOVA results allow accepting Hypothesis 6 stating that the perception of model quality is related to the perception of comprehension task performance.

Empirical evidence of an effect of *Representation Method* on the quality perceptions (Hypothesis 3) is found in the marginally significant effect that this factor has on PEOI ($p = 0.083$). The inclusion of PSE_after as a covariate in the analysis adjusts the means on the PEOI dependent variable to what it would be if all participants scored identically on PSE_after. So, independent of the effect that PSE_after has on PEOI, using an REA diagram instead of a non-REA diagram has

Table 4. Descriptive statistics of Quality Perception for each experimental condition

	Representation Method	Level of REA Training	Mean	Std. Deviation	N
UIS	REA	Low	5.022	0.5528	11
		Medium	4.335	1.1261	35
		High	4.843	0.9911	16
		Total	4.588	1.0422	62
	Non-REA	Low	4.454	0.8277	11
		Medium	4.360	0.9578	34
		High	4.485	0.9456	17
		Total	4.411	0.9200	62
	Total	Low	4.738	0.7459	22
		Medium	4.347	1.0389	69
		High	4.659	0.9698	33
		Total	4.500	0.9830	124
PEOI	REA	Low	4.545	1.2496	11
		Medium	3.619	1.0668	35
		High	4.041	1.2224	16
		Total	3.892	1.1762	62
	Non-REA	Low	3.242	1.0337	11
		Medium	3.607	1.1502	34
		High	3.843	1.2862	17
		Total	3.607	1.1680	62
	Total	Low	3.893	1.3027	22
		Medium	3.613	1.1005	69
		High	3.939	1.2401	33
		Total	3.750	1.1761	124

Table 5. MANCOVA quality perception

Source	Dependent Variable	Type III Sum of Squares	Df	Mean Square	F	Sig.	Partial Eta Squared
Corrected Model	UIS PEOI	34.65[a] 64.14[b]	6 6	5.775 10.69	8.023 11.80	<0.001 <0.001	0.291 0.377
Intercept	UIS PEOI	29.91 3.479	1 1	29.91 3.479	41.56 3.841	<0.001 0.052	0.262 0.032
PSE_after	UIS PEOI	28.12 51.55	1 1	28.12 51.55	39.06 56.90	<0.001 <0.001	0.250 0.327
Representation Method	UIS PEOI	0.765 2.776	1 1	0.765 2.776	1.063 3.064	0.305 0.083	0.009 0.026
Level of REA Training	UIS PEOI	3.144 1.971	2 2	1.572 0.985	2.183 1.088	0.117 0.340	0.036 0.018
Representation Method x Level of REA Training	UIS PEOI	0.866 0.450	2 2	0.433 0.225	0.601 0.248	0.550 0.781	0.010 0.004
Error	UIS PEOI	84.22 105.99	117 117	0.720 0.906			
Total	UIS PEOI	2629.87 1913.88	124 124				
Corrected Total	UIS PEOI	118.87 170.13	123 123				

a. R Squared=0.291 (Adjusted R Squared =0.255)
b. R Squared=0.377 (Adjusted R Squared =0.345)

a (slight) positive effect on the user's perceived ease of interpreting the model. This effect found provides weak support for Hypothesis 3. As an effect of *Representation Method* on UIS was not shown (p = 0.305), the support for Hypothesis 3 is only partial (i.e., only with respect to PEOI).

Apart from the effect of PSE_after on PEOI and UIS and the effect of *Representation Method* on PEOI, no other effects of the factors and interaction term on the dependent variables are observed. There is no support for Hypothesis 4 as no interaction effect is present in the data collected. Contrary to what we observed for Accuracy, the Level of REA Training has no direct effect on model quality perception.

To test the hypothesized relationship between actual and perceived task performance (Hypothesis 5), two separate regressions were performed (given the significant correlation between the Accuracy and Normalized Accuracy scores). ANOVA results showed significant correlations between Accuracy and PSE_after (p = 0.015) and between Normalized Accuracy and PSE_after (p < 0.001), leading to the acceptance of Hypothesis 5. Hence, the hypothesized relationship between actual and perceived comprehension task performance was corroborated.

Given that both hypotheses 5 and 6 were accepted, it is plausible that diagram users that performed well on the comprehension task (both in terms of effectiveness and efficiency) developed a favorable perception of their task performance (i.e., they realized that they correctly understood the diagram without spending much effort) and accordingly perceived the diagram as easy to interpret, and were satisfied with the information provided for answering the comprehension questions. Note that by itself, the acceptance of hypotheses 5 and 6 does not imply that REA diagram users perceived the diagram as easier to interpret and were more satisfied with it than Non-REA diagram users. Also Non-REA diagram users with good comprehension task performance (both actual and perceived) are likely to form high-quality perceptions of the diagram. On the other hand, as demonstrated in the previous subsection, comprehension task performance measured as accuracy was higher with REA diagram users. Furthermore, the partial support found for Hypothesis 3 evidences a direct effect of REA diagram use on the perceived ease of interpretation.

DISCUSSION AND CONCLUSION

In our experiment, REA diagram users were more accurate than Non-REA diagram users in solving the model comprehension task. This observed effect is only an effectiveness effect as no significant differences were found when relating the number of correct answers to the time taken to perform the task. This result confirms the findings of our previous study (Poels et al., in press), which suffered from low statistical power because of its small scale. A difference with this previous study is that the experiment also showed that the actual comprehension task performance was related to perceptual and satisfaction outcomes (perceived performance, ease of use and user satisfaction). These relationships indicate that participants who performed well on the comprehension task also perceived the diagram as easy to interpret and were satisfied with using the diagram for retrieving the information required by the task. However, apart from these relationships, also a (weak) direct effect of representation method (REA or Non-REA diagram) on perceived ease of interpretation was found. Because comprehension task performance was used as a covariate in the statistical data analysis, the observed effect on quality perception stands besides the performance effect that was demonstrated. Hence, our study provides further evidence of the computational nonequivalence of informational equivalent REA and Non-REA diagrams. Based on the results we can conclude that users that have learned the REA patterns perceive diagrams with REA pattern occurrences as easier to interpret than diagrams without, so their perception is that they can draw easier and quicker inferences from the information present in REA diagrams. Given that all the participants received minimal REA education (though some of them were trained more intensively) and were to some extent familiar with the REA patterns' semantics and representation conventions, the more accurate model understanding and the more favorable perception of ease of understanding with REA diagrams provide evidence of pattern recognition taking place.

It was also noted that participants who received additional training in REA were significantly more accurate in the comprehension task than participants with minimal REA training. But this effect was observed for both REA and Non-REA diagram users, so there is no direct evidence that pattern recognition is stronger or more frequent when users are (assumingly) more familiar with the patterns. It is possible that the extra REA training (in the form of exercises) provided to (some of) the students helped them understand the conceptual model better because of the additional and more recent exposure to solving comprehension tasks of the type required in the experiment. The higher or more recent experience with model comprehension tasks might explain the positive effect of REA training on comprehension accuracy, regardless of the representation method used. Our study thus demonstrates the intuitive relationship between training and performance. Training novice model users in understanding conceptual data models helps them to better understand models. However, based on the results of this experiment, we cannot conclude that novice model users should be intensively trained in the use of REA conceptual modeling structures as maybe training with other kinds of conceptual data models would also improve model understanding.

The results of this study have implications for practice. Our experiment with business students indicates that transaction cycle domain models constructed with REA patterns are better understood than models without. This finding is significant given that resource-event-agent structures frequently occur in conceptual data models of enterprise information systems. For instance, McCarthy (2004) estimates that 60% of the ER diagrams that make up SAP's ERP reference model consist of resource-event-agent structures. Also O'Leary (2004) found SAP data models to be consistent with resource-event-agent structures and concludes that REA is robust in its ability to represent SAP data models. The practical significance of our finding is further strengthened by the use of the REA patterns in various international standards, methodologies and reference models for modeling collaborative business processes (i.e., ISO/IEC 15944, ISO/IEC 14662:1997, UMM and ECIMF).

Our study also shows that the use of REA patterns can be beneficial even at a limited level of REA education. Whereas in the previous study (Poels et al., in press) an effect on the accuracy of model understanding was shown for users extensively trained in REA patterns (4.5 hours of instruction plus 3 hours of training in working with REA diagrams), we now observe differential effects for participants that received between 1 and 4 hours of REA education. For the group of students that only received a 1 hour lecture on business domain reference models constructed using REA patterns, the improvement in mean Accuracy score by using an REA diagram instead of a Non-REA diagram is 18.45%. While it is hard to evaluate whether this improvement is practically meaningful (in terms of improved communication between analysts and business professionals), the cost of one hour of instruction is probably not excessive given the improvement in model understanding that can be expected. The use of REA conceptual modeling structures will of course also require training for the analysts and thus present an additional cost, but on the other hand, as indicated by the study of Gerard (2005), also positive effects on modeling performance may result from the use of REA patterns.

At higher levels of training, model understanding further improves. Companies that adopt the use of REA conceptual modeling structures may expect further increases in model understanding when they provide more REA training to their novice model users. However, based on our study alone it is difficult to tell whether more intensive levels of REA training really pay off as this also depends on the cost of training. Compared to the improvement of 18.45% in mean Accuracy score by using an REA diagram instead of a Non-REA diagram (at a limited level of REA education), the marginal gains in the accuracy in understanding REA diagrams observed at higher levels of training seem limited. In the experiment, the improvements in mean Accuracy score for REA diagram users go up with 1.76% and 5.78% when moving from the Low to Medium and from the Medium to the High levels of training. The statistically significant difference in Accuracy score between the Low and High training groups is mainly due to the improvement observed for the Non-REA diagram users, where the mean score has increased with 19.36%.

Apart from evaluating REA patterns-based conceptual modeling, our study also contributes to the research on conceptual (data) modeling patterns. The focus of the research to date is on performance effects of pattern use by (novice) designers or analysts and the pattern matching (or retrieval) techniques that are used in this process (Batra & Wishart, 2004; Irwin, 2002; Purao, Storey, & Hahn, 2003). Whereas previous research has emphasized pattern recognition in the information requirements put forward by a modeling task, our study also pays attention to pattern recognition in the conceptual model itself and provides first indications that the use of patterns can also be beneficial for model users. Although our study identified two features of REA patterns, localization and secondary notation, as enabling factors for pattern recognition, the data collected does not allow isolating their effects and studying how these pattern characteristics trigger pattern recognition mechanisms like analogy, abstraction or literal similarity. Further explorative research is required to generalize the findings of this study to other modeling patterns that exhibit the same characteristics. Such research could use verbal techniques of protocol analysis to get deeper insights into the mental process of pattern recognition, i.e., to find out how patterns really help in understanding conceptual models.

Most of the conceptual modeling patterns research done focuses on patterns that have been empirically derived (i.e., through discovery of recurrent structures in real models). Our study suggests that patterns derived from an ontology may be especially useful for helping users to better understand models. Because of their level of comprehensiveness, abstraction and structuredness, enterprise ontologies are valuable educational instruments for teaching the conceptual modeling of enterprise systems, something which is clearly demonstrated for the REA ontology (Gailly, Laurier, & Poels, 2008). Patterns derived from ontologies all share the same level of abstraction and granularity, and their occurrences can easily be integrated because the patterns are positioned in an overarching structure. So, another implication of our study results is that it could be worthwhile further investigating ontology-derived patterns and not focusing solely on empirically-derived patterns. It logically follows that, as suggested earlier in the paper, a comparative study of ontology-derived and empirically-derived patterns may provide valuable insights into the relative merits of both types of patterns.

The limitations of this study are the degree to which the results can be generalized and the degree of confidence we can have in causation conclusions from a single laboratory experiment. Task characteristics were held constant by having the same task to be performed under all treatments. This task was realistic in the sense that it reflects typical use of business domain models by business professionals. Moreover, the task was tailored to the purpose of the type of models that can be constructed with REA patterns as it involved the retrieval and interpretation of transaction cycle information that is relevant from an accountability and control perspective. A consequence of this intended task-technology fit is that we do not and cannot demonstrate better performance for other purposes than those for which REA patterns-based conceptual modeling is intended. Apart from the use or no use of REA pattern occurrences, all other model and representational characteristics were held constant. Further, only one case was used in the experiment. These experimental design choices helped increasing internal validity by controlling variables such as informational equivalence, domain familiarity, model size, and notational system used. With respect to domain familiarity, Khatri et al. (2006) showed that domain knowledge has little effect on comprehension task performance if the task involves extracting knowledge directly represented in the model, which was the case in our study. Nevertheless, future research may wish to replicate this study using other examples of transaction cycles, with different model sizes and/or other modeling notations to confirm our results and hence increase the generalizability of the conclusions drawn.

Another limitation is the construction of the *Level of REA Training* variable. We realize that our operationalization of this variable only considers the amount of exposure to REA patterns and not the participants' knowledge of REA conceptual modeling structures. The required assumption that the amount of exposure (i.e., low, medium, high) is related to the amount of learning could have been avoided by conducting a pre- or post-test of the participants' REA knowledge (i.e., by measuring the outcome of REA patterns learning).

We are also aware that, independent from the role that pattern recognition plays, the applied diagram transformations might cause the diagrams to be non computationally equivalent. Therefore, ideally, the isolated and combined effects of the applied transformations (i.e., objectification and repositioning diagram elements) should also have been investigated outside a REA patterns recognition context, in order to compare the results. To date, almost no such studies have been conducted. We are aware of only one study that empirically investigated user performance effects of objectification, and this study by Poels, Gailly, Maes, and Paemeleire (2005) concludes that it is plausible that users perform better with the representation (i.e., directly represented or objectified relationships) they are more familiar with (recall that our study participants received training in both ways of representing relationships). The empirical study of diagram layout effectiveness is another excellent opportunity for future research (Moody, 2009).

Finally, we are aware that the use of business student participants as surrogates of real business professionals reduces external validity. Given that there is consensus in the research literature that pattern-based approaches to conceptual modeling are most useful for novice users, we have deliberately defined the target population of our study as novice business professionals in the role of model user. Although strictly spoken, the study participants are not a sample from this population, they do approximate such a sample which alleviates this threat to external validity.

REFERENCES

Ajzen, I. (2002). Perceived Behavioral Control, Self-Efficacy, Locus of Control, and the Theory of Planned Behavior. *Journal of Applied Social Psychology*, *32*(4), 665–683. doi:10.1111/j.1559-1816.2002.tb00236.x

Allen, G. N., & March, S. T. (2006). The Effects of State-Based and Event-Based Data Representation on User Performance in Query Formulation Tasks. *Management Information Systems Quarterly*, *30*(2), 269–290.

Antony, S., & Mellarkod, V. (2004). A Methodology for using Data-modeling Patterns. In D. Batra, J. Parsons, & V. Ramesh (Eds.), *Proceedings of the 3rd Symposium on research in Systems Analysis and Design*. St. John's, NL, Canada.

Bandura, A. (1997). *Self-Efficacy: The Excercise of Control*. New York: W.H. Freeman.

Batra, D. (2005). Conceptual Data Modeling Patterns: Representation and Validation. *Journal of Database Management*, *16*(2), 84–106.

Batra, D., & Sin, T. (2008). The READY Model: Patterns of Dynamic Behavior in REA-Based Accounting Applications. *Information Systems Management*, *25*, 200–210. doi:10.1080/10580530802151103

Batra, D., & Wishart, N. A. (2004). Comparing a rule-based approach with a pattern-based approach at different levels of complexity of conceptual data modelling tasks. *International Journal of Human-Computer Studies*, *61*, 397–419. doi:10.1016/j.ijhcs.2003.12.019

Bodart, F., Patel, A., Sim, M., & Weber, R. (2001). Should Optional Properties Be Used in Conceptual Modelling? A Theory and Three Empirical Tests. *Information Systems Research*, *12*, 384–405. doi:10.1287/isre.12.4.384.9702

Burton-Jones, A., & Meso, P. N. (2008). The Effects of Decomposition Quality and Multiple Forms of Information on Novices' Understanding of a Domain from a Conceptual Model. *Journal of the Association for Information Systems*, *9*(12), 748–802.

Burton-Jones, A., & Weber, R. (1999). Understanding Relationships with Attributes in Entity-Relationship Diagrams. In *Proceedings of the Twentieth International Conference on Information Systems* (pp. 214-228).

Burton-Jones, A., & Weber, R. (2003). Properties do not have properties: Investigating a questionable conceptual modelling practice. In D. Batra, J. Parsons, & V. Ramesh (Eds.), *Proceedings of the 2nd Annual Symposium on Research in Systems Analysis and Design*.

Church, K., & Smith, R. (2008). REA Ontology-Based Simulation Models for Enterprise Strategic Planning. *Journal of Information Systems*, *22*(2), 301–329. doi:10.2308/jis.2008.22.2.301

Connolly, T. M., & Begg, C. E. (2005). *Database Systems: a Practical Approach to Design, Implementation, and Management* (4th ed.). New York: Addison-Wesley.

Dedene, G., & Snoeck, M. (1995). Formal Deadlock Elimination in an Object-Oriented Conceptual Schema. *Data & Knowledge Engineering*, *15*(1), 1–30. doi:10.1016/0169-023X(94)00031-9

Dunn, C., & Grabski, S. (2001). An Investigation of Localization as an Element of Cognitive Fit in Accounting Model Representations. *Decision Sciences*, *32*(1), 55–94. doi:10.1111/j.1540-5915.2001.tb00953.x

Dunn, C. L., Cherrington, J. O., & Hollander, A. S. (2005). *Enterprise Information Systems: A Pattern Based Approach*. New York: McGraw-Hill.

Gailly, F., Laurier, W., & Poels, G. (2008). Positioning and Formalizing the REA enterprise ontology. *Journal of Information Systems*, *22*(2), 219–248. doi:10.2308/jis.2008.22.2.219

Geerts, G., & McCarthy, W. E. (2002). An Ontological Analysis of the Economic Primitives of the Extended-REA Enterprise Information Architecture. *International Journal of Accounting Information Systems*, *3*(1), 1–16. doi:10.1016/S1467-0895(01)00020-3

Geerts, G., & McCarthy, W. E. (2006). Policy-Level Specification in REA Enterprise Information Systems. *Journal of Information Systems*, *20*(2), 37–63. doi:10.2308/jis.2006.20.2.37

Gemino, A., & Wand, Y. (2003). Foundations for Empirical Comparisons of Conceptual Modelling Techniques. In D. Batra, J. Parsons, & V. Ramesh (Eds.), *Proceedings of the 2nd Symposium on Research in Systems Analysis and Design*.

Gemino, A., & Wand, Y. (2005). Complexity and clarity in conceptual modeling: Comparison of mandatory and optional properties. *Data & Knowledge Engineering*, *55*(3), 301–326. doi:10.1016/j.datak.2004.12.009

Genero, M., Poels, G., & Piattini, M. (2008). Defining and Validating Metrics for Assessing the Understandability of Entity-Relationship Diagrams. *Data & Knowledge Engineering*, *64*(3), 534–557. doi:10.1016/j.datak.2007.09.011

Gentner, D., & Medina, J. (1998). Similarity and the development of rules. *Cognition*, *65*, 263–297. doi:10.1016/S0010-0277(98)00002-X

Gerard, G. J. (2005). The REA Pattern, Knowledge Structures and Conceptual Modeling Performance. *Journal of Information Systems*, *19*(1), 57–77. doi:10.2308/jis.2005.19.2.57

Goodhue, D. L., & Thompson, R. L. (1995). Task-Technology Fit and Individual-Performance. *Management Information Systems Quarterly*, *19*(2), 213–236. doi:10.2307/249689

Gruber, T. R. (1993). A Translation Approach to Portable Ontology Specifications. *Knowledge Acquisition*, *5*, 199–220. doi:10.1006/knac.1993.1008

Haugen, R., & McCarthy, W. E. (2000). *REA, a semantic model for Internet supply chain collaboration.* Retrieved from https://www.msu.edu/user/mccarth4/paplist1.html

Hruby, P., Kiehn, J., & Scheller, C. V. (2006). *Model-Driven Design Using Business Patterns*. New York: Springer.

Irwin, G. (2002). The Role of Similarity in the Reuse of Object-Oriented Analysis Models. *Journal of Management Information Systems*, *19*(2), 219–248.

Jones, R. A., Tsay, J. E., & Griggs, K. (2005). An Empirical Investigation of the Task Specific Relative Strengths of Selected Accounting and Information Systems Diagramming Techniques. *Journal of Computer Information Systems*, *46*, 99–114.

Khatri, V., Vessey, I., Ramesh, V., Clay, P., & Park, S.-J. (2006). Understanding Conceptual Schemas: Exploring the Role of Application and IS Domain Knowledge. *Information Systems Research*, *17*, 81–99. doi:10.1287/isre.1060.0081

Kim, Y. G., & March, S. T. (1995). Comparing Data Modeling Formalisms. *Communications of the ACM*, *38*(6), 103–115. doi:10.1145/203241.203265

Maes, A., & Poels, G. (2007). Evaluating Quality of Conceptual Modelling Scripts Based on User Perceptions. *Data & Knowledge Engineering*, *63*(3), 701–724. doi:10.1016/j.datak.2007.04.008

McCarthy, W. E. (1982). The REA Accounting Model: A Generalized Framework for Accounting Systems in A Shared Data Environment. *Accounting Review*, *57*, 554–578.

McCarthy, W. E. (2004). The Evolution toward REA Accountability Infrastructures for Enterprise Systems. In *Proceedings of the First International Conference on Enterprise Systems and Accounting,* Thesaloniki, Greece (pp. 1-2).

Moody, D. (2002). Comparative Evaluation of Large Data Representation Methods: The Analyst's Perspective. In *Conceptual Modeling* (LNCS 2503, pp. 214-231).

Moody, D. (2009). The "Physics" of Notations: Towards a Scientific Basis for Constructing Visual Notations in Software Engineering. *IEEE Transactions on Software Engineering*, *35*(6), 756–779. doi:10.1109/TSE.2009.67

Moody, D., & Shanks, G. (2003). Improving the quality of data models: empirical validation of a quality management framework. *Information Systems*, *28*, 619–650. doi:10.1016/S0306-4379(02)00043-1

Nickerson, J. V., Corter, J. E., Tversky, B., Zahner, D., & Rho, Y. J. (2008). *The Spatial Nature of Thought: Understanding Systems Design Through Diagrams.* Paper presented at the 2008 International Conference on Information Systems.

O'Leary, D. E. (2004). On the relationship between REA and SAP. *International Journal of Accounting Information Systems*, *5*, 65–81. doi:10.1016/j.accinf.2004.02.004

Olivé, A. (2007). *Conceptual Modeling of Information Systems*. New York: Springer.

Parsons, J. (2003). Effects of Local versus Global Schema Diagrams on Verification and Communication in Conceptual Data Modelling. *Journal of Management Information Systems*, *19*(3), 155–183.

Parsons, J. (2005). Empirical Research in Conceptual Modeling - Using Experiments to Understand Semantic Expression. *Wirtschaftsinformatik*, *47*(2), 155–156.

Parsons, J., & Cole, L. (2005). What do the pictures mean? Guidelines for experimental evaluation of representation fidelity in diagrammatical conceptual modeling techniques. *Data & Knowledge Engineering*, *55*(3), 327–342. doi:10.1016/j.datak.2004.12.008

Petre, M. (1995). Why Looking Isn't Always Seeing - Readership Skills and Graphical Programming. *Communications of the ACM, 38*(6), 33–44. doi:10.1145/203241.203251

Poels, G., Gailly, F., Maes, A., & Paemeleire, R. (2005). Object Class or Association class? Testing the User Effect on Cardinality Interpretation. In *Perspectives in Conceptual Modeling* (LNCS 3770, pp. 33-42).

Poels, G., Maes, A., Gailly, F., & Paemeleire, R. (in press). The pragmatic quality of Resources-Events-Agents diagrams: an experimental evaluation. *Information Systems Journal, 21*(1).

Purao, S., Storey, V. C., & Han, T. D. (2003). Improving analysis pattern reuse in conceptual design: Augmenting automated processes with supervised learning. *Information Systems Research, 14*(3), 269–290. doi:10.1287/isre.14.3.269.16559

Rosli, K., Ahmi, A., & Mohamad, L. (2009). Resource-Event-Agent (REA) Modelling in Revenue Information System (RiS) Development: Smart Application for Direct-Selling Dealers and SMEs. *Journal for the Advancement of Science & Arts, 1*(1), 43–62.

Ryan, S. D., Bordoloi, B., & Harrison, D. A. (2000). Acquiring Conceptual Data Modeling Skills: The Effect of Cooperative Learning and Self-Efficacy on Learning Outcomes. *The Data Base for Advances in Information Systems, 31*, 9–24.

Siau, K. (2004). Informational and Computational Equivalence in Comparing Information Methods. *Journal of Database Management, 15*(1), 73–86.

Siau, K., & Rossi, M. (in press). Evaluation techniques for systems analysis and design modelling methods – a review and comparative analysis. *Information Systems Journal, 21*(1).

Siau, K., Wand, Y., & Benbasat, I. (1997). The relative importance of structural constraints and surface semantics in information modeling. *Information Systems, 22*(2-3), 155–170. doi:10.1016/S0306-4379(97)00009-4

Smith, D. K., Chang, J., & Moores, T. T. (2003). *Comparing Self-Efficacy and Meta-Cognition as Indicators of Learning*. Paper presented at the 9th Americas Conference on Information Systems.

Topi, H., & Ramesh, V. (2002). Human Factors research on Data Modeling: A review of Prior Research, An extended Framework and Future Research Directions. *Journal of Database Management, 13*(2), 3–19.

Wand, Y., Storey, V. C., & Weber, R. (1999). An Ontological Analysis of the Relationship Construct in Conceptual Modeling. *ACM Transactions on Database Systems, 24*, 494–528. doi:10.1145/331983.331989

Wand, Y., & Weber, R. (2002). Research Commentary: Information Systems and Conceptual Modeling - A Research Agenda. *Information Systems Research, 13*(4), 363–377. doi:10.1287/isre.13.4.363.69

APPENDIX

Figure 7. REA diagram

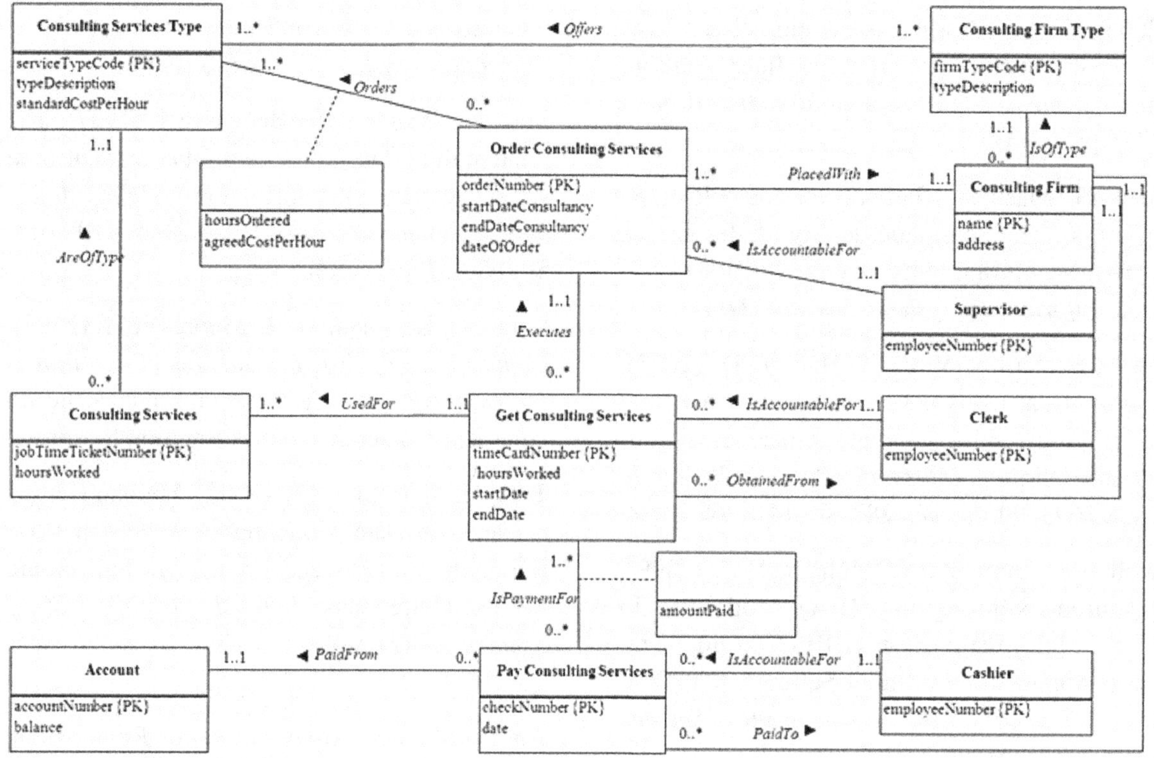

Figure 8. Non-REA diagram

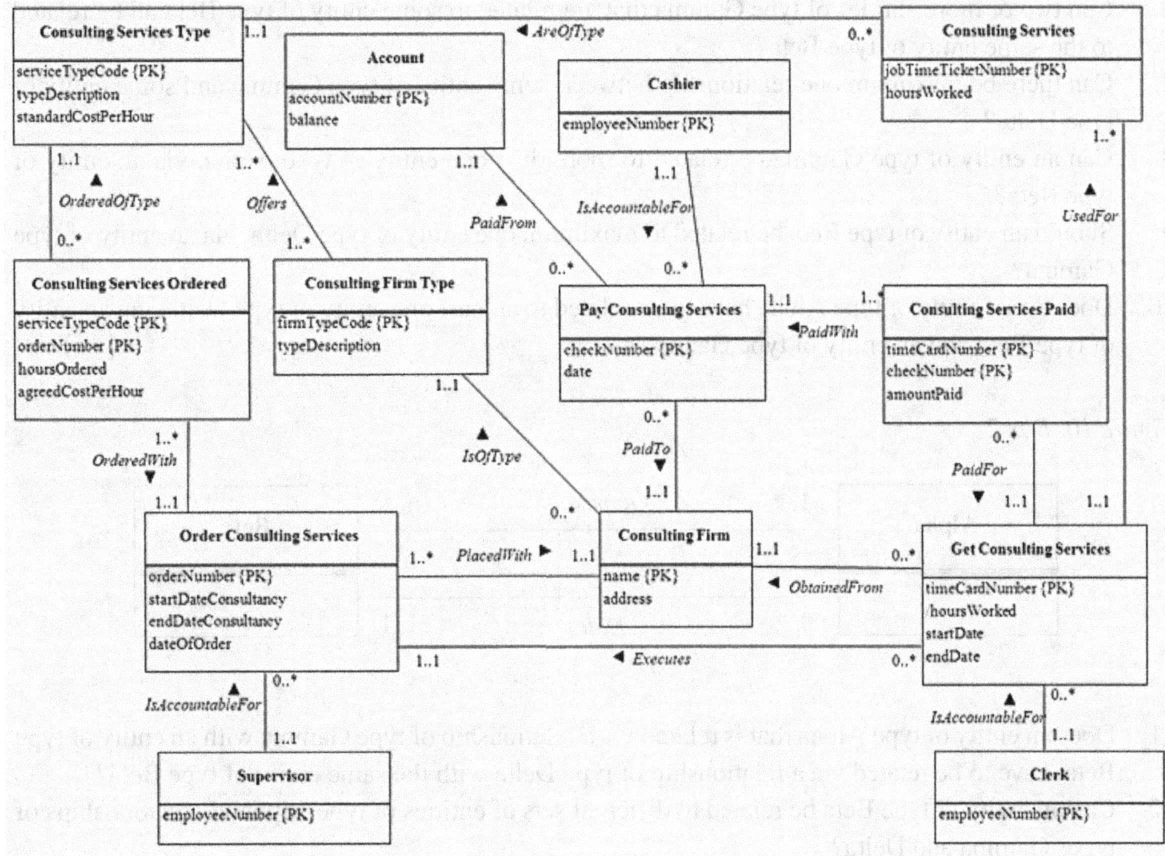

ER Formalism Knowledge Pre-test Questions

Figure 9. Box 1

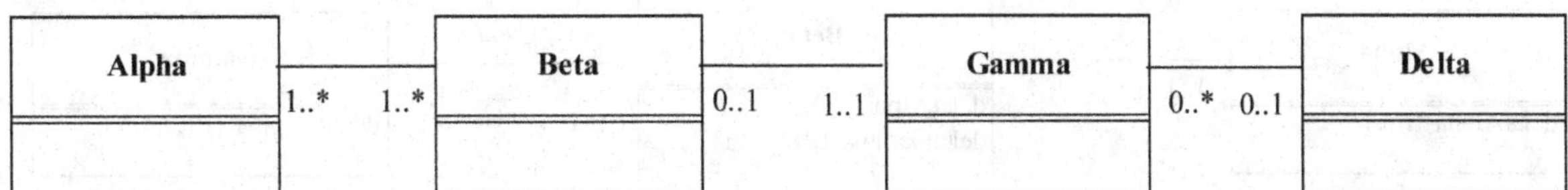

1. Can an entity of type Alpha be related to an entity of type Beta that is not related to an entity of type Gamma?
2. Does the diagram specify an upper limit on the number of entities of type Gamma that are related to the same entity of type Delta?
3. Does every entity of type Gamma have to be related to an entity of type Beta?
4. Can an entity of type Gamma be related to only one entity of type Delta?

5. Should each entity of type Alpha be related to each entity of type Beta and vice versa?
6. Can two or more entities of type Gamma that are related to some entity of type Beta all be related to the same entity of type Beta?
7. Can there be maximum one relationship between some entity of type Gamma and some entity of type Delta?
8. Can an entity of type Gamma be related to more than one entity of type Alpha, via an entity of type Beta?
9. Should an entity of type Beta be related to maximum one entity of type Delta, via an entity of type Gamma?
10. Does every entity of type Alpha have to be related to at least one entity of type Delta, via an entity of type Beta and an entity of type Gamma?

Figure 10. Box 2

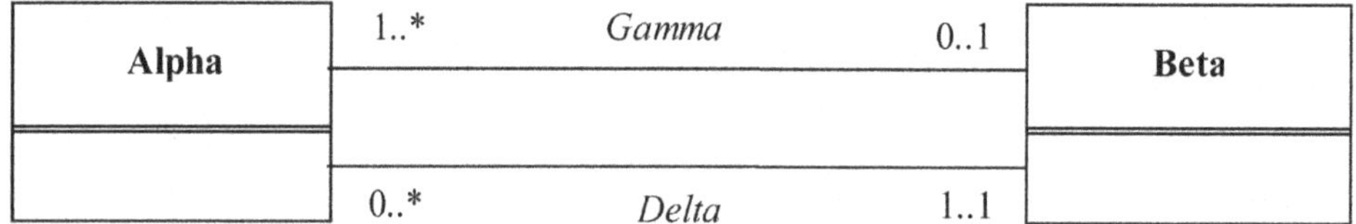

11. Does an entity of type Alpha that is related via a relationship of type Gamma with an entity of type Beta, have to be related via a relationship of type Delta with the same entity of type Beta?
12. Can an entity of type Beta be related to different sets of entities of type Alpha via relationships of types Gamma and Delta?
13. Assume that an entity of type Alpha is related via a relationship of type Delta to some entity of type Beta. Does this entity of type Beta have to be related to the same entity of type Alpha via a relationship of type Gamma?

Figure 11. Box 3

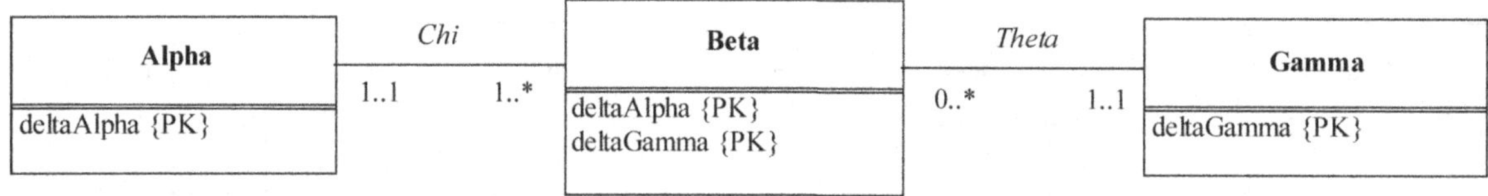

14. Does there exist a many-to-many entity connection between the types Alpha and Gamma via relationships of the types Chi and Theta with entities of type Beta?
15. Can the entity of type Alpha that has the value “1” for the attribute deltaAlpha and the entity of type Gamma that has the value “x” for the attribute deltaGamma be connected to each other more than once via relationships of the types Chi and Theta with entities of type Beta?

Model Comprehension Questions

1. Can consulting services only be obtained from a consulting firm where a supervisor has placed an order?
2. Can a cashier make payments for consulting services which have not been charged to a timecard?
3. Can consulting services with working hours registered on several time cards, be paid for with one single payment transaction?
4. Do all working hours, for jointly obtained and charged consulting services, have to be registered on at least one job-time ticket?
5. Can a supervisor order different types of consulting services with one single order?
6. Can a cashier make a payment to a consulting firm with money drawn from more than one account?
7. Can the consulting working hours that are registered on one and the same job-time ticket, have been obtained on different occasions?
8. Must jointly obtained and charged consulting services belong to a single consulting services type?
9. Must jointly obtained and charged consulting services, be paid with a single payment transaction?
10. Can a cashier make payments for consulting services that have been charged to a timecard, but were not ordered?
11. Must all consulting services obtained from the same consulting firm, be ordered by the same supervisor?
12. Can it be that we do not know which clerk is accountable for a given timecard?
13. Can a type of consulting services be described and be assigned a standard cost per hour without there being any order of this type of services?
14. Must a consulting firm be paid immediately for consulting services charged to a timecard?
15. Can consulting working hours registered on the same job-time ticket be related to more than one order?

Measurement Scales

All items are seven-point Likert scales, anchored at "Strongly disagree" and "Strongly agree".

Perceived Self-Efficacy

PSE_before: present tense ("I am able to …")
PSE_after: past tense ("I was able to …")
PSE_1: I am/was able to correctly interpret the meaning of ER Model constructs.
PSE_2: I am/was able to interpret the meaning of ER Model constructs without much effort.
PSE_3: I am/was able to understand the structure of a business process modelled in an ER diagram (i.e. which activities?, who is involved?, …).
PSE_4: I am/was able to quickly see in an ER diagram the structure of a business process (i.e. which activities?, who is involved?, …).
PSE_5: I am/was able to derive the business policies that govern a business process using an ER diagram.
PSE_6: I am/was able to quickly see in an ER diagram the business policies that govern a business process.

Perceived Ease of Interpretation

$PEOI_1$: It was easy for me to understand what the conceptual schema was trying to model.
$PEOI_2$: Using the conceptual schema was seldom frustrating.
$PEOI_3$: Overall, the conceptual schema was easy to use.
$PEOI_4$: Learning how to read the conceptual schema was easy.

User Information Satisfaction

UIS_1: The conceptual schema adequately met the information needs that I was asked to support.
UIS_2: The conceptual schema was efficient in providing the information I needed.
UIS_3: The conceptual schema was effective in providing the information I needed.
UIS_4: Overall, I am satisfied with the conceptual schema for providing the information I needed.

This work was previously published in the Journal of Database Management, Volume 22, Issue 1, edited by Keng Siau, pp. 69-101, copyright 2011 by IGI Publishing (an imprint of IGI Global).

Chapter 5
A Survey of Approaches to Web Service Discovery in Service-Oriented Architectures

Marco Crasso
ISISTAN - UNICEN, Argentina

Alejandro Zunino
ISISTAN - UNICEN, Argentina

Marcelo Campo
ISISTAN - UNICEN, Argentina

ABSTRACT

Discovering services acquires importance as Service-Oriented Computing (SOC) becomes an adopted paradigm. SOC's most popular materializations, namely Web Services technologies, have different challenges related to service discovery and, in turn, many approaches have been proposed. As these approaches are different, one solution may be better than another according to certain requirements. In consequence, choosing a service discovery system is a hard task. To alleviate this task, this paper proposes eight criteria, based on the requirements for discovering services within common service-oriented environments, allowing the characterization of discovery systems. These criteria cover functional and non-functional aspects of approaches to service discovery. The results of the characterization of 22 contemporary approaches and potential research directions for the area are also shown.

INTRODUCTION

Service-Oriented Computing (SOC) is an emerging computing paradigm whose main goal is to support the development of distributed applications in heterogeneous environments (Erickson & Siau, 2008). SOC enables composing or assembling together distributed functionality to build software systems. This functionality comes in the form of basic building blocks called *services*. A service can be defined as a piece of functionality done by an external provider who is specialized in the management of this operation. Besides, a service is wrapped with a network-addressable

DOI: 10.4018/978-1-4666-2044-5.ch005

interface that exposes its capabilities to the outer world while hiding implementation details that may constraint interoperability.

The most widespread process for building applications according to the SOC paradigm comprises replacing the development of specific software components with a combination of service discovery, selection and engagement. Providers publish their services in a service registry establishing: the terms of engagement, technical constraints, requirements and semantic information. On the other hand, service consumers discover published services through a registry, and in turn select and contract them.

SOC is mostly implemented by using *Web Services technologies*, because they are designed to support interoperable *provider-to-consumer* interaction over the Internet (Li et al., 2007). Broadband and ubiquitous connections enable accessing the Internet from everywhere and at every time. This has enabled global registries of services that have been deliberately designed as reusable components (Crasso et al., 2009b). Such registries, besides heavily encouraging software reuse, promote *outsourcing* of third-party components, which results in lower ongoing investments in the entire software engineering process (McConnell, 2006).

Because of the significance of service discovery for the SOC paradigm, both researchers and industry practitioners have been developing service discovery systems. Up to now, common materializations in the software industry for service inventories supply developers with keyword-based search engines and category browsing for services as Universal Description, Discovery and Integration (UDDI)[1] does. UDDI is an open specification of a registry to publish and discover Web Services sponsored by the Organization for the Advancement of Structured Information Standards (OASIS). Similarly, the Common Object Request Broker Architecture (CORBA)[2] offers the Naming Service, which allows developers to find services, or "objects" in CORBA terminology, based on alphanumeric identifiers, and the Trading Service, which lets programmers find services based on one or more <key, value> pairs. Recently, Web-based search engines (e.g., Google) have become a new source for finding Web Services (Song et al., 2007), because service descriptions usually reside on Web servers that are crawled and indexed by search engines.

On the other hand, by adapting existing Information Retrieval (IR) techniques, some researchers have proposed to treat descriptions of Web Services as documents, thus reducing the problem of discovering relevant services to the well-known problem of finding relevant documents (Garofalakis et al., 2006). Other academical approaches propose to annotate the service descriptions with meta-data, such as non-ambiguous concept definitions from shared ontologies –or sometimes simply referred as *semantics*–, which gave origin to the notion of Semantic Web Services (Paolucci & Sycara, 2003).

There are essential differences between the approaches to service discovery mentioned in last paragraphs. One of the main differences is what such approaches consider/require as service descriptions. For example, semantic approaches depend on shared ontologies and annotated resources, whereas IR-based ones depend on textual descriptions. Scalability, fault tolerance and standard conformance are important aspects of service registries, and of databases in general (Bouguettaya et al., 2004), in which service discovery approaches present differences as well. Therefore, though service discovery systems strive to solve the same problem, they may be very different from each other and one alternative may be appropriate in a particular environment but not in others. The variety of alternatives for discovering Web Services motivates the need for sound criteria to characterize them.

Toma et al. (2005) present a characterization of service discovery systems along an analysis of five alternatives. Afterward, the authors propose a combination of the most relevant features from different approaches as aspects that should be considered when developing a discovery mechanism. Garofalakis et al. (2006) present a comprehensive survey of methods, architectures and models related to Web Service discovery. The authors have thoroughly analyzed over 30 approaches for discovering Web Services (including industrial and academic ones). They have developed a taxonomy for organizing these approaches, based on four main categories: Architecture, Standards, Data model and QoS-aware.

In this paper, we present eight criteria, covering functional and non-functional characteristics of service discovery systems. We have designed these criteria taking into account the requirements for discovering services within common service-oriented environments, in order to allow designers of service-oriented systems to analyze whether an evaluated registry fits these requirements or not. In opposition to previous related works, accompanying each criterion definition we present a fixed range of values that the criterion accepts. This, besides allowing evaluators to compare and rank the evaluated approaches, facilitates the characterization of forthcoming approaches. We have employed the proposed criteria for characterizing approaches for discovering Web Services and Semantic Web Services, because of their popularity and related future research possibilities. To sum up, the main contributions of this paper are:

- A reusable set of criteria for the characterization of service discovery systems,
- A survey of Web Services and Semantic Web Services discovery system alternatives,
- A detailed analysis of the surveyed alternatives, and
- A list of future research opportunities in service discovery.

The rest of the paper is organized as follows. The next section takes a deeper look at service discovery, reviewing the evolution of the requirements for discovering services at the different environments in which the SOC paradigm has been implemented. The most relevant service discovery approaches are presented. We describe our criteria and discuss the results of the characterization of the alternatives described in the section "Approaches to discover Web Services". The section "Future research possibilities on service discovery" highlights future research possibilities and recommendations.

EVOLUTION OF SERVICE DISCOVERY REQUIREMENTS

Under the SOC model depicted in Figure 1, the service discovery system represents a crossroad in the path of providers and consumers. Providers can use the discovery system to advertise their services, while consumers can use it to discover services that match their needs.

The evolution of service-oriented systems is associated with the advances in distributed system technologies, but driven by the adoption of the SOC paradigm across application, company and community boundaries and the level of automatism that can be achieved. For instance, when local area network (LAN) technologies were widely adopted, some companies used SOC for manually connecting their own applications. After the popularization of the World Wide Web, some companies use the SOC paradigm for manually connecting applications from external companies. In the future, it is expected that software agents will be able to automatically discover, contract and consume external services without human intervention.

The requirements for discovering services evolve according to each environment in which the SOC paradigm has been adopted. We refer as an environment to a combination of the scale and levels of automatism in which a discovery system is planned to be implemented. Graphically, in Figure 2 we present a summary of these

Figure 1. The SOC model

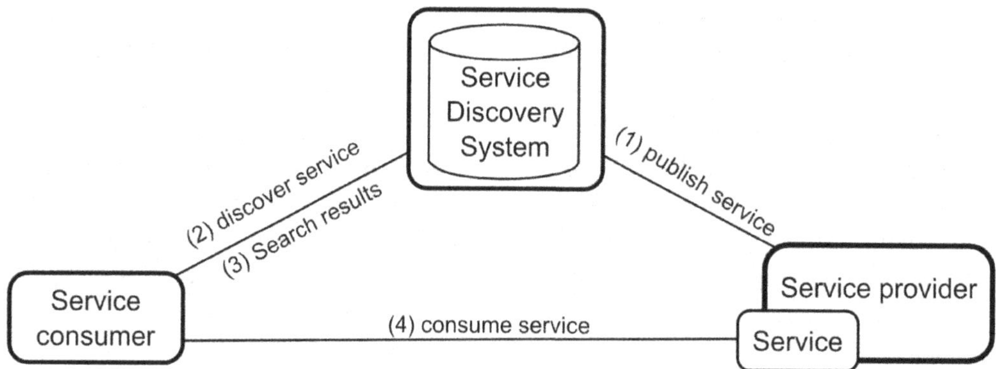

environments and their requirements. Below, we review this evolution, considering the following aspects introduced at each environment: (1) the more important concepts, (2) the requirements of discovery systems and (3) the more relevant technologies.

Service Discovery Requirements in Homogeneous Environments

The first stage of the evolution of the requirements for discovering services, which is depicted as the top layer in Figure 2, began when companies re-utilized their own products by manually combining isolated applications over LANs. Basically, a minimal service-oriented architecture for this environment comprised a proprietary application exposing some functionality as a service to another proprietary application. Here, service discovery systems had lightweight requirements, because usually the number of services of a company was small, different applications were managed by the same people and these applications had a common technological foundation. Moreover, service provider technical details such as location, interface, communication protocols, quality of service (QoS), etc., were communicated and tailored between the project leaders of the application that offers services and those applications that consume them. Here, the discovery and

Figure 2. Requirements for discovering services in different environments

Scale	Concepts	Technologies	Requirements
Intra-company	Service, provider, consumer, proxy	DCOM, RMI	(1) Few services (2) Homogeneity (3) Manual
Past	Service Broker, functional description, automatic proxy generation	CORBA	(3)(4) Abstract language (5) Heterogeneity
Inter-company	Global scale registry, Web-based standards, Non-functional description,	SOAP, UDDI, WSDL, XML, P2P	(3)(4)(5)(6) Large number of services (7) Contact information (8) Decentralized (9) QoS information
Present			
Inter-company	Semantic description, Service level information, Contract negotiation, Automatic	OWL-S, WSDL-S, WSMO	(4, 5, 6, 7, 8,9) (10) Machine-interpretable descriptions (11) Contract information (12) Automatic (13) Trust & reputation
Future			

engagement of services were manually done by a group of developers. In this way, providing and consuming services among software systems of the same company is, metaphorically, like connecting people who share a common language and culture. In fact, in many cases a special development group played the roles of provider and discoverer at the same time.

Many technologies have been used for connecting intra-company services, including Microsoft Distributed Component Object Model (DCOM)[3] and Sun Remote Method Invocation (RMI)[4]. DCOM allows applications distributed across multiple Microsoft Windows systems to communicate to each other. On the other hand, RMI allows Java developers to invoke object methods remotely. The discovery approach of these technologies requires that a provider publishes a service on a centralized registry, which assigns a unique id, or key, to the service. Finally, a consumer must know this key before accessing the service.

Service Discovery Requirements in Heterogeneous Environments

Recently, due to the advances in distributed system technologies, the trend in SOC has been converging towards doing inter-company computing. Graphically, this trend is depicted as a sub-layer between "Intra-company" and "Inter-company" layers in Figure 2. One of the main requirements for this stage is implementation heterogeneity, in contrast to the tight technological dependencies of the previous stage. The goal is to hide service implementation details from service consumers, because service implementation abstraction enables a distributed and heterogeneous collection of services to interoperate. For example, a service consumer software written in Python should be able to invoke a service implemented in C++, C#, Java or any other programming language.

Following the aforementioned metaphor, suppose that a group of people speaks Spanish, another speaks German and another speaks Greek. One possible solution to connect both groups would be to employ interpreters for mediating between speakers of different languages. A more flexible approach would be to agree on a common language, e.g., English, and employ interpreters for translating from this common language to the others. This context motivates the necessity of a common language for describing services.

An example of such a common service description language is Interface Description Language (IDL). CORBA uses IDL as an abstract language for describing services. IDL allows providers to explicitly describe service arguments and expected results or invariants, independently of the underlying implementation of the service. This common language, besides hiding technological characteristics –a.k.a. virtualization– of external services, allows consumers to generate proxies by using their preferred programming language. A proxy is a local object working as an interface to a remote service, which shields service consumers from all non-functional activities of service consumption. The concept of proxy was firstly introduced in the earliest SOC environment, since provider's processes usually run on a different computer than the computer that executes consumer's processes. Returning to IDL, many programming languages incorporate built-in capabilities for generating proxies automatically by *interpreting* an IDL contract (Hauck et al., 2005).

Other concept introduced in this stage was provider transparency. In this sense, a broker or middle man component allows better decoupling of consumers and services. Providers use the broker to announce their services. Then, consumers access the functionality of providers by sending requests via the broker. Once a discoverer has selected a service, a broker is responsible for locating the appropriate service provider, forwarding the request to the server and transmitting results and exceptions back to the service consumer. As a result, consumer applications are unaware of providers' existence. In "Discussion" we will discuss about the implications of using brokers when eliciting trustworthy information about providers.

Service Discovery Requirements in Web-Based Environments

The Internet allows a global scale marketplace of software services. In such a marketplace, providers may offer their services and consumers may contract them. This vision shares some aspects with the concept of *outsourcing* in globalized business practices. During the 1980s, *outsourcing* became part of the business lexicon. It refers to the delegation of operations from internal production to an external entity, which is specialized in the management of these operations. This stage is represented as the middle layer in Figure 2.

Conceptually, this stage of the evolution of discovery system requirements introduces the notion of "registry". A registry is a repository of service descriptions, which is analogous to telephone yellow pages. Here, a provider publishes a description of her/his service in a registry, along with personal contact information and meta-data for indexing services. At the same time, a consumer browses this registry until she/he finds a description that matches her/his expectations. One of the main requirements of a discovery system is to allow consumers to look up services by exploiting the aforementioned pieces of information.

Discovering services over the Internet requires to adopt Web-based technologies. The term "Web Services" is used for referring to a stack of technology standards for modular applications that can be published, located, and invoked across the Web (Erickson & Siau, 2008). Basically, this stack comprises four levels: (1) communication, (2) serialization, (3) description and (4) discovery. A comprehensive description of the stack can be found in (Yu et al., 2008). From the lowest level to the highest, the first level defines the protocols that a service provider may use for sending and receiving data. The second level is in charge of serializing data over a communication channel. The next level defines how to describe a service, its operations and arguments. Finally, the top level specifies how to publish and discover services. A forthcoming section describes the levels associated with describing and discovering services.

Two more requirements for service discovery systems in this environment are high scalability and availability. The idea of doing SOC on "a global scale" suggests that a discovery system should be able to manage a huge number of service, and such a system must be available 24x7. Decentralized architectures are suitable alternatives to achieve proper levels of scalability, robustness and failure resistance. In particular, with Peer-To-Peer (P2P) (Gotthelf et al., 2008) distributed architectures, all participating nodes assume client and server tasks, share their capabilities and exploit the cumulative capabilities of network participants. In theory, an ideal P2P supports an infinite number of peers, then the cumulative capabilities are also infinite, and a peer failure does not affect the whole network. The UDDI specification[5] defines a federated registry as one or more decentralized UDDI nodes. Due to the decentralized nature of distributed architectures, effectively querying such distributed registries implies more challenges (Firat et al., 2009).

Finally, another requirement of service discovery systems in this environment is eliciting, managing and exploiting QoS descriptions. This stage of the SOC evolution encourages competition among providers to gain customers. Therefore, when there are, at least, two services designed for performing the same task, describing the offered QoS becomes a significant factor in distinguishing service providers.

Service Discovery Requirements in Environments With High Levels of Automatism

The future vision of SOC suggests that software agents will be able to *outsource* a proper service on behalf of their users. Finding suitable services automatically depends on the available facilities for allowing: (1) providers to describe the capabilities of their services, and (2) consumers to describe their requirements in an unambiguous and machine-interpretable form. Conceptually, this means to expand the idea of the Semantic Web to include services. The vision of the Semantic Web suggests a new kind of Web content that is meaningful to software applications (Shadbolt et al., 2006).

During the past few years, some research has been undertaken to add meaningful data to Web Services, which has originated the Semantic Web Services (Paolucci & Sycara, 2003). This requires ordinary content to be linked with a definition of its organization and content (a.k.a. meta-data). Semantic Web Services have originated four main lines of research: defining, generating, managing and exploiting service meta-data. First, automatically contracting services depends on the definition of a model for describing service level characteristics, providers' reputation and payment information required for invoking a service. Second, service descriptions must be annotated with meta-data according to such a model. In the third place, the aforementioned annotations must be stored and efficiently retrieved in semantics-aware registries. Fourth, these registries must provide discovery mechanisms that take advantage from semantic descriptions. Therefore, the last two lines present requirements for discovering services in this environment.

Automatic discovery of services requires that discoverers' can trust on providers' descriptions. Wang et al. (2008) state that just because the Internet is a very open heterogeneous environment, the SOC paradigm must face a major challenge, namely, the trust between service consumers and providers. This is an interesting problem that presents many opportunities for research, which not only comprise how to ensure classic non-functional QoS requirements such as response time or availability, but also functional aspects –determine services functionality– and legal ones such as licenses and copyrights. Wang and Vassileva (2007) discuss current trust and reputation mechanisms that have been applied to Web Services.

Having presented the requirements of service discovery systems according to the environments in which they may be used, we are interested in reviewing the existing approaches that are focused on discovering Web Services as well as Semantic Web Services. The next section describes and discusses the most relevant approaches to the purpose of this article.

APPROACHES TO DISCOVER WEB SERVICES

The data within a discovery system include two major categories: documents and queries, or the expressions of information need. The key problems are how to state a query and how to identify documents that match that need. The implementation of a discovery system will depend on the documents that must be retrieved. In this way, a good starting point to conveniently understand the challenges associated with discovery systems is the Web Service approach for representing "documents", i.e., service descriptions.

Web Service Description Language (WSDL)[6] is an XML format for describing a service as a set of operations, whose invocation is based on message exchange. In object-oriented terms, a WSDL document describes a service as an interface, an operation as a method, and a message as a method argument (inputs or outputs, indistinctly). Moreover, WSDL allows providers to describe exceptions as messages also. Optionally, each part of a WSDL document may contain documentation in the form of comments. Figure 3 depicts a conceptual overview of a WSDL document along with a concrete definition of a service.

UDDI is a specification of a registry for publishing and discovering Web Services. Central to UDDI purpose is the representation of meta-data about businesses and their offered services. Con-

Figure 3. Standard Web Service description

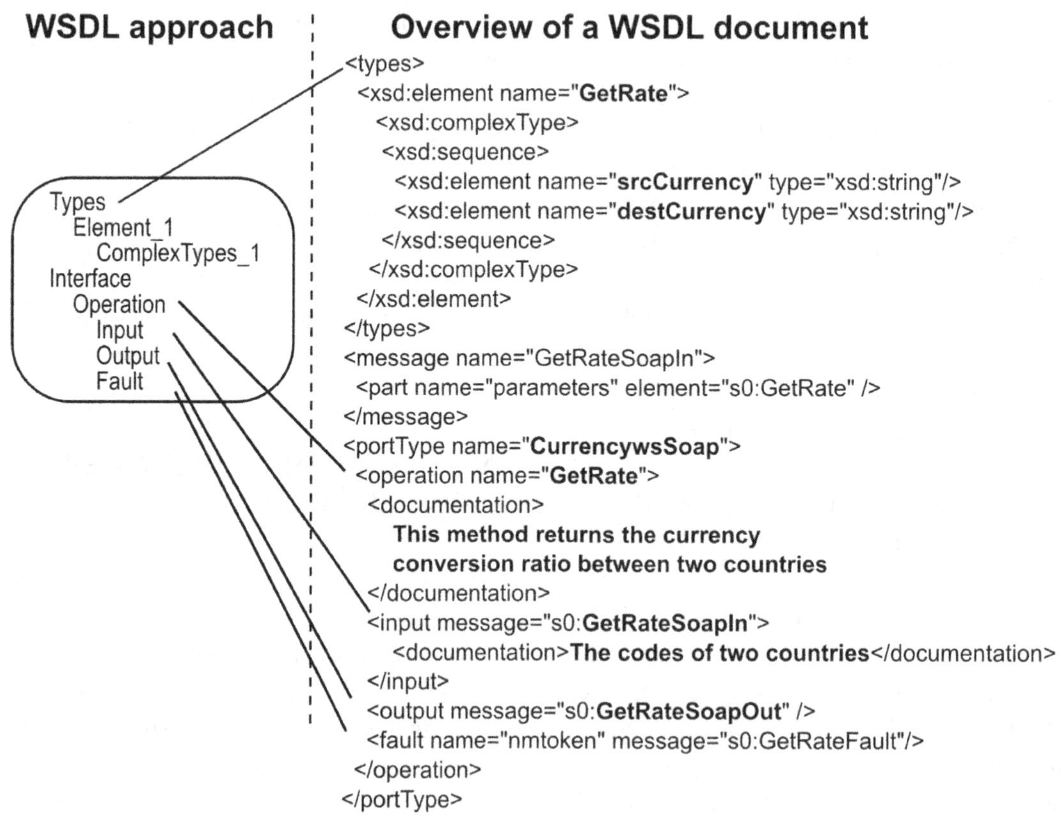

ceptually, the UDDI specification arranges three groups of meta-data: White, Green and Yellow pages. White pages stand for business information (e.g., address, contact, and known identifiers). Yellow pages associate a service with industrial categorizations based on standard taxonomies, such as the United Nations Standard Products and Services Code (UNSPSC)[7], the Standard Industrial Classification (SIC)[8] or the North American Industry Classification System (NAICS)[9]. Finally, Green Pages store technical information about services exposed by one or more businesses, for example a WSDL document. In concrete terms, this specification consists of four core data-types, namely businessEntity, businessService, bindingTemplate and tModel (Technical Model), which are defined in XML.

In Figure 4 we present the UDDI data model, associate it with a concrete example, and map the example onto the idea of White, Green and Yellow pages. In the end, a "document" consists of a service description using WSDL and an entry in an UDDI registry.

UDDI represents a baseline for other approaches to Web Service discovery. UDDI is not designed to provide powerful capabilities for discovering services, but it is designed to provide standardized formats for programmatic business and service discovery, so that search engines could be built on top of it. UDDI provides only a category-based browsing and keyword-based matching discovery service (Jian & Zhaohui, 2005). To the best of our knowledge, there are many commercial implementations of UDDI and only one open source. The Apache Software Foundation maintains jUDDI[10], the open source alternative. For an updated list of UDDI implementations, the reader should refer to the UDDI Web site[11].

Figure 4. UDDI data model

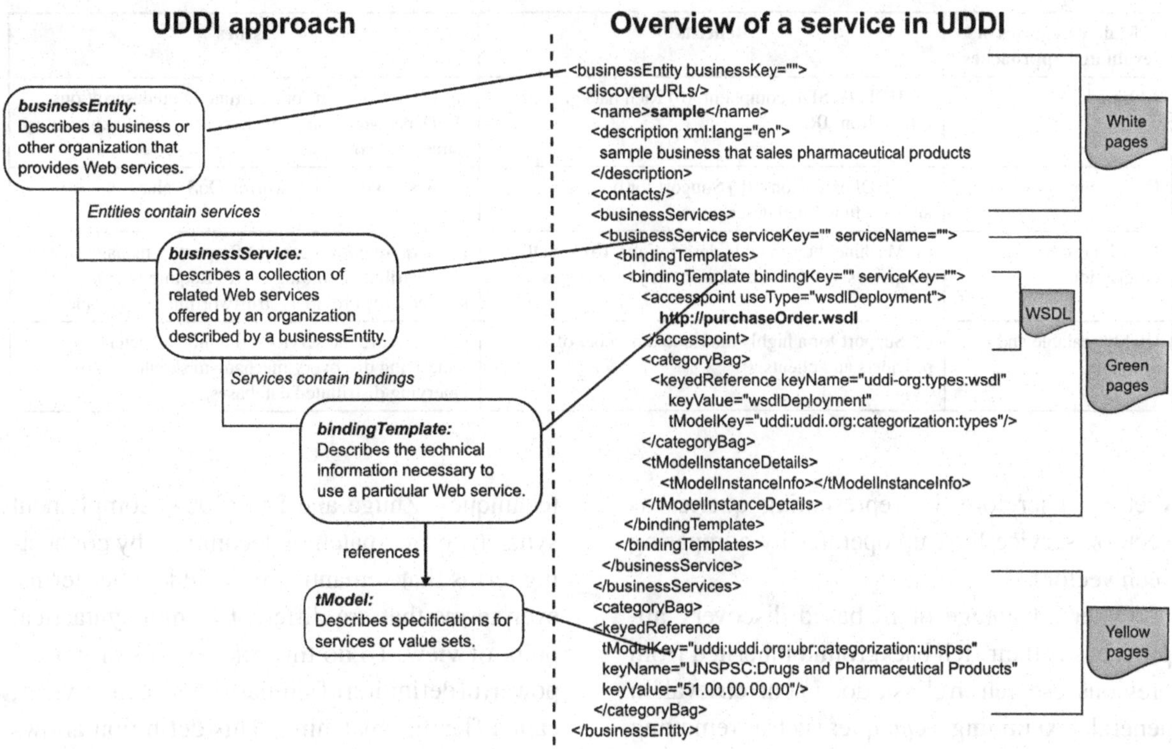

We reviewed current literature and then we identified four main approaches to supply discoverers with more powerful discovery capabilities than those supplied by UDDI. Table 1 highlights their benefits and issues, while the rest of this section presents the revised approaches.

Information Retrieval-Based Approaches for Discovering Web Services

Recently, some approaches have exploited classic Information Retrieval (IR) techniques, to reduce the problem of discovering relevant services to the well-known problem of finding relevant documents. In this way, textual descriptions available in UDDI and WSDL files, stand for documents. One of the main contributions of these approaches is that discoverers may look up services by providing a natural language description, or a handful set of keywords. This additional capability for declaring queries, supplies discoverers with a "Google-like" inquiry interface, which most developers are familiar with. On the other hand, it depends on publishers' use of best practices for documenting services, operations and arguments (Rodriguez et al., 2009), because these techniques compare strings of characters syntactically.

The cornerstone of most IR-based approaches is to use a vectorial representation for documents and queries and then to find out those with the most similar vectors. With the Vector Space Model (VSM) (Salton et al., 1975), a vector $\vec{v} = (e_0, \ldots, e_n)$ stands for a document, whose elements e_i represent the importance of each distinct word w_i for that document. Then similar documents will have similar vector representations. Some researchers (Stroulia & Wang, 2005; Jian & Zhaohui, 2005; Platzer & Dustdar, 2005; Kokash et al., 2006; Lee et al., 2007) adapt the VSM to translate Web Service descriptions onto

Table 1. Main approaches to service discovery

Main categories of evaluated approaches	Benefits	Issues
IR-based	(a) UDDI/WSDL complaint. (b) Rich background inherit from IR.	(a) Do not support for non-functional descriptions. (b) Dependency on publishers use of self-explanatory names and comments.
QoS-aware	(a) UDDI extensions. (b) Support for both functional and non-functional descriptions.	(a) Assurance of trustworthy QoS values.
Based on semantic descriptions	(a) Machine interpretable descriptions. (b) WSDL extensions. (c) Automatic discovery of services.	(a) Require ontologies. (b) Require to manage shared and distributed ontologies. (c) Require to annotate services. (d) Providers' trustworthiness assurance.
Highly scalable and available	(a) Support for a highly distributed number of providers and clients.	(a) The more the services, the more efficient the underlying discovery mechanism should be. (b) Querying distributed databases.

vectors. Therefore, by representing queries as vectors, service look up operates by comparing such vectors.

Other advantage of IR-based discovery approaches is their rich background inherited from previous research on classic document retrieval. In general, text mining techniques such as removing non relevant words (a.k.a. *stop-words*), bridging synonyms and removing the commoner morphological and inflectional endings from words (a.k.a. *stemming*), have been identified as being very appropriate to enhance the performance of these approaches (Korfhage, 1997). Some researchers have adapted the aforementioned techniques for dealing with syntactic differences at Web Service descriptions. For example, Dong et al. (2004); Kokash et al. (2006) have suggested to remove stop-words and pull out stems from Web Service documentation. Stroulia and Wang (2005) have suggested to use WordNet Lexical Database (Fellbaum, 1989) for dealing with synonyms. Other researchers have introduced new text mining techniques, for example Platzer and Dustdar (2005); Crasso et al. (2008) proposed heuristics for bridging different WSDL message styles by mining relevant terms from data-type definitions.

Before analyzing other radically different approaches for service discovery, it is worth describing five approaches that have enhanced the classic IR approach with some additional techniques. Zhuge and Liu (2004) complement syntactic exact matching techniques by connecting terms that semantically include other terms, even terms that are different from a syntactical point of view. To do this, the authors propose a powerful definition of similarity between services, called flexible matching. This definition allows discoverers to look for services that are identical, more specific or more general than their queries. For example, flexible matching takes into account the distance between two categories in a taxonomy (e.g., an available operation belongs to a category that is a subcategory of requested category), or if a requested set of keywords, which stands for operation inputs, is completely or partially met. Another contribution of this discovery approach is that developers should find its query language straightforward to learn, because it borrows the syntax and semantics from SQL. This approach uses a relational model of Web Service data based on the standard Web Service schema information present in UDDI.

Wang and Stroulia (2003) propose to combine a VSM based method with a structural-matching heuristic. This approach consists of two filtering stages and two kinds of queries. The first kind of query is a textual description of the expected service, which is translated into a vector and then used for retrieving relevant services from a VSM. The second stage, receives the WSDL documents most similar to the first query and compares their structure against a, possibly partial, WSDL specification of the desired service (second kind of query). The basis of this structural-matching heuristic is the comparison of the XML syntax of the data-types present in WSDL documents. Well structured documents, like WSDL ones, are formed according to a definition, i.e., an schema. A structural-matching technique deals with finding documents with similar constructions, which are valid according to the schema of a particular kind of documents (Evermann, 2008).

Birukou et al. (2007) combine a VSM with information of past Web Services usage within a community of developers. The authors collect community members' query descriptions, the retrieved list of candidates for each query, and successfully invoked services as well. During discovery, this approach proposes to match new queries, requiring certain functionality, against past requests. The description of a query comprises a textual description of the goal, the operation and its arguments. Subsequently, these descriptions are compared using a VSM, and expanding queries based on lexical relations from WordNet. Central to this approach is the idea of *implicit culture*, a concept that leads to encourage newcomers to behave similarly to more experienced members of a community.

Woogle (Dong et al., 2004) is an approach that combines multiple vector spaces with clustering techniques. Broadly, the authors propose to assess the similarity between two Web Service descriptions by separately assessing the similarity between each part of these descriptions, and then relating the individual results. To do this, they build separate vector spaces, each one for representing the documentation associated with a particular element of a WSDL document. The goal is to consider the structure of WSDL documents. Furthermore, they adapt a clustering technique for assessing the conceptual similarity between a pair of operation arguments. Clustering deals with partitioning a data-set into subsets or clusters, according to a feature that, ideally, the samples of a particular cluster share. In this sense, Woogle generates clusters for operation parameters that share the same meaning, by assuming that a pair of parameters tends to express the same concept if both co-occur within operations (Dong et al., 2004).

(Crasso et al., 2008) propose to combine a Query-by-Example (QBE) approach with a VSM along with a classification system (Sebastiani, 2002). This QBE-based approach, allows developers to state a query using their preferred programming language, by specifying the potential functional interface of the service that they want to discover. Then, some novel text mining techniques pull out relevant keywords about the desired service from the commented source code of the client-side software. Based on this information, WSQBE generates a vector and then looks for relevant third-party services within a sub-space of the VSM. Concretely, by exploiting relevant information from service descriptions that have been previously published and categorized in UDDI registries, WSQBE builds a classification system and a VSM composed of one sub-space per service category. Given an example, or query, this classifier deduces a sequence of categories that maximizes the similarity between their center of mass and the example. As a result, WSQBE looks for services relevant to the example only within the sub-spaces suggested by the classifier, which is more efficient than comparing an example against the whole vector space, like other approaches do (Wang & Stroulia, 2003; Dong et al., 2004; Platzer & Dustdar, 2005).

Although there is not a benchmark for evaluating Web Service discovery systems, at least to the best of our knowledge, many of the aforementioned approaches have been evaluated and compared showing promising results. These evaluations assess the retrieval effectiveness of the approaches, by using classic IR measures, such as Recall, Precision and R-Precision (Korfhage, 1997).

Kokash (2006) summarizes and compares the most relevant algorithms for assessing the similarity between two Web Service descriptions. The paper reports an evaluation of different algorithms with the same corpus of Web Services, concluding that algorithms based on the classic statistical measure used to evaluate how important a word is to a document, namely TF-IDF (Korfhage, 1997), over performed other approaches in most cases. Oldham et al. (2004) show that an IR-inspired technique for finding similar services surpassed a technique based on graph matching, which was described in (Patil et al., 2004). Stroulia and Wang (2005) show a comparison between the two filtering stages of their previous work (Wang & Stroulia, 2003). Similarly to (Oldham et al., 2004), their results have empirically shown that "the IR method performs better than the structure-matching method" (Stroulia & Wang, 2005).

The precision of Woogle was evaluated with a public data-set of 411 Web Services, in which 25 Web Service operations represented queries (Dong et al., 2004). On the other hand, Recall was evaluated with 8 queries, i.e., operations. In terms of retrieval effectiveness, the approach has shown promising results under these test conditions –*R-precision* was 78% and *Recall* was 88%–.

WSQBE was evaluated using a publicly available data-set that comprises 391 Web Services and 30 queries written in Java (Crasso et al., 2008). The evaluations have shown that WSQBE alleviates discoverers by narrowing down the number of candidate services from 40 to only 1 in 83% of the experiments. Concretely, the average R-precision was 72% and the average Recall was 91% under these test conditions. Third and finally, the processing time and scalability of the approach with the number of registered services were evaluated, showing encouraging results as well (Crasso et al., 2008).

Birukou et al. (2007) report empirical evaluations using 20 services crawled from a public repository and 100 queries with 4 and 20 community members. These experiments have shown that the overall precision was below 80%, but precision was below 60% until, at least, 40 past evidences had been collected.

QoS-Aware Approaches for Discovering Web Services

One shortcoming of the UDDI model, and of those approaches based on it, is that it is limited to discovery of functional requirements only. However, though two or more services may be similar from a functional point of view, they may offer different QoS characteristics. Having only functional descriptions about services makes impossible to differentiate them by other attributes. This section presents approaches to allow discoverers to find services basing on non-functional properties, such as availability, cost and reliability.

First, we will describe two approaches to describe QoS characteristics. Ran (2003) illustrates many aspects of QoS important to Web Services, discusses the current UDDI model and proposes an extension. The author proposes to augment the businessService data-type, to incorporate non-functional attributes for a particular service, which are organized in 5 categories, namely run-time, transaction support, configuration management, cost and security. Then, under this new model discoverers may ask for Web Services using QoS constraints. For instance, a discoverer may look up services with a desired 0.9 availability.

Figure 5 shows a service discovery request example using Ran's model, where the attributes relevant to QoS are in bold.

Overhage and Thomas (2003) revise the UDDI data model and assert that such model lacks of information referring to the conditions of purchase. Moreover, the authors claim that such information must be understandable for both human discoverers and software agents, which discover proper services on behalf of their users. This leads to the "UDDI Blue pages" concept (Overhage & Thomas, 2003). In this way, some semantics-aware approaches, which we will discuss in the section

Figure 5. UDDI plus QoS request

```
<?xml version="1.0" encoding="UTF-8" ?>
  <envelope xmlns="http://schemas.xmlsoap.org/soap/envelope/">
    <body>
      <find_service businessKey="*" generic="1.0"
                xmlns="urn:uddi-org:api" maxRows="100">
        <findQualifiers></findQualifiers>
        <name>Stock quote</name>
        <qualityInformation>
          <availability> 0.9 </availability>
        </qualityInformation>
      </find_service>
    </body>
  </envelope>
```

"Semantic-aware approaches for discovering Web Services", support non-functional descriptions of service operations.

There are different approaches to fill the aforementioned models with data that reflect actual QoS characteristics of published services. The simplest way assume that features such as response time, throughput and availability are supplied by providers. Unfortunately, that scheme raises several concerns such as integrity and reliability (Al-Masri & Mahmoud, 2007). In other words, the aforementioned features might be manipulated. To overcome this, (Makris et al., 2006) propose to recollect the duration that a service took to process a request under specific load conditions, and then deduce the performance of an immediate invocation based on gathered and current load conditions. To do this, every host that offers a service must implement an API for retrieving its current system state. Then, services with similar functionality are ranked according to the deduced performance and predictions based on gathered past information.

Ran (2003) affirms that a QoS-based extension must be complemented with a trusted certifier component, which verifies the claims of QoS for a Web Service before its registration. Alternatively, Zhou et al. (2004) present a different way to combine UDDI with QoS measurements, called UX (UDDI eXtension). UX instead of asking service providers about their QoS characteristics, proposes to ask consumers. If consumers share their experiences when invoking a service, then UX will predict the future performance of a service that has been previously consumed. In this context, shared experiences are like sellers' reputation in an e-market context. Unfortunately, irresponsible consumers can lead to manipulated measures as well. Al-Masri and Mahmoud (2007) suggest that an ideal trusted broker allows publishers to provide only QoS information that cannot be inferred (e.g., cost per invocation), whereas other QoS features should be automatically computed. To do this, a broker monitors service invocations and, in turn, collects QoS information about Web Services.

Now, we describe two approaches for exploiting collected QoS information. Kozlenkov et al. (2007) propose a novel query language, which allows discoverers to state QoS requirements. Basically, this work derives queries from behavioral and structural Unified Modeling Language (UML) design models of service-oriented systems. These models must be specified by using an UML extension, a.k.a. profile. This profile allows designers to indicate whether an operation must be either implemented or delegated to a third-party service. Moreover, by using this profile designers can specify desired QoS requirements about the services and operations that should be discovered. To assess the similarity between an UML-based query and available services, a two step process is used. In the first step, services with operations that satisfy the non-functional requirements of the query are retrieved. The second step uses a similarity heuristic, based on graph-matching, for finding the operations that best match the query.

Al-Masri and Mahmoud (2007) present a function for ranking Web Services according to their QoS characteristics, which had been gathered by a broker. The function computes a matrix that represents a Web Service in a row and each single QoS parameter in a column. Due to the fact that QoS parameters vary in units and magnitude, values are normalized. A second matrix is computed by dividing each column by the maximum normalized value that occurs within it. In other words, for each Web Service, any QoS parameter is divided by the maximum value for that parameter that has been collected from other services. Then, a discoverer defines a vector of weights indicating the importance level assigned to each QoS parameter. The larger the weight the more important its associated QoS parameter is to the client. The values of these weights range from 0 to 1 and all weights must add up to 1. Finally, these weights are introduced into the matrix as factors and all values are re-calculated. The row that maximizes the sum of its weighted parameters represents the first ranked Web Service, and so on.

Semantics-Aware Approaches for Discovering Web Services

Another feature that UDDI and those approaches based on it do not support, is a machine-interpretable description of Web Services (Martin et al., 2007). By annotating services with ontologies, discoverers can access to an unambiguous shared definition of each part of a Web Service (e.g., input, output, operation, etc.). For example, suppose that the output message of an operation is named "temp", then a discoverer might not be able to accurately deduce what it means. Instead, if this output is associated with a concept that defines the current temperature of a certain region, the discoverer may understand its meaning. Moreover, ontologies support semantic matching algorithms (Euzenat & Shvaiko, 2007; Chen et al., 2006). Contrary to syntactic matching, semantic matching allows differentiating between syntactically equivalent terms, but semantically different, e.g., "temp" can stand for a temporal value or can be related to temperature. This is essential for software agents that attempt to discover services automatically, i.e., without a human discoverer's intervention. However, the promised high levels of automatism can only be achieved at the expenses of placing effort on correctly specifying ontologies, managing them and annotating services.

There are three main efforts for defining the meta model, or type of semantic information, for describing a Web Service, namely OWL-S (Martin et al., 2007), WSMO (Roman et al., 2005) and WSDL-S (Sivashanmugam et al., 2003). OWL-S (Martin et al., 2007), which was accepted as a W3C submission in November 2004, provides a framework for describing both the functions and advertisements for Web Services by using OWL (Ontology Web Language)[12]. OWL is a W3C recommendation for describing the semantic relationships of a domain. Although OWL-S includes three sub-ontologies, namely *Service Profile*, *Process Model* and *Grounding*, the *Service Profile* sub-ontology is directly related to service discovery, because it describes *what* a service does. Broadly, this sub-ontology not only allows publishers to annotate preconditions, inputs, outputs and effects of Web Service operations, but also some non-functional attributes.

OWL is designed to represent machine interpretable content on the Web. OWL is based on RDF-S, a structured language based on XML. RDF-S extends the Resource Definition Framework (RDF)[13] with a set of predefined types, high level constructors (e.g., *class*, *subClassOf*, *property*) and range and domain constraints over properties. Above RDF-S, OWL defines more facilities (e.g., *inverseOf, equivalentClass, sameAs, symmetry*) for expressing meaning and semantics than XML, RDF, and RDF-S.

WSMO (Roman et al., 2005) is a conceptual model for Web Services, which was incorporated as a W3C submission in April 2005. It comprises *Ontologies*, *Web Services*, *Goals* and *Mediators*. The *Web Services* model allows publishers to annotate the interfaces, non-functional attributes, preconditions, post-conditions, effects and assumptions of service operations. On the other hand, the *Goals* model allows discoverers to annotate functional and non-functional requirements. In addition, the *Mediators* model can be used to define mediators responsible for aligning different ontologies. Broadly, ontology alignment, a.k.a. ontology mapping, deals with mapping one ontology onto another. This means that for each concept in one ontology, an alignment algorithm finds a corresponding entity that has the same intended meaning, but belongs to other ontology. Similarly to the OWL-S *Service Profile* ontology, these two WSMO models are relevant to discovery systems. WSMO defines these models by means of a language specially designed to express semantic descriptions according to the WSMO meta model, called Web Service Modeling Language (WSML) (de Bruijn et al., 2006). The main components of the language are concepts, attributes, binary relations and instances, as well as concept and relation hierarchies and support for data-types.

One of the main contributions of OWL-S and WSMO is the possibility of reasoning and mediating over service descriptions, which is supported by their underlying languages, i.e., OWL and WSML. Complementary to OWL-S and WSML, WSDL-S (Sivashanmugam et al., 2003) incorporates semantic descriptions into current Web Service standards. This approach uses standard extensibility elements to refer from WSDL documents to external ontologies. The semantic information specified in WSDL-S comprises definitions of the preconditions, inputs, outputs and effects of Web Service operations. Graphically, Figure 6 shows this approach from a conceptual point of view along with a concrete example. This approach is loosely coupled with ontology representation languages, thus annotations in WSDL-S may be defined by using OWL, RDF, WSML or UML. WSDL-S is part of the METEOR-S project[14].

Upon the aforementioned models, different discovery systems have been developed. Paolucci et al. (2002) describe a matchmaking algorithm for Web Service descriptions written in OWL-S, which takes advantage of the underlying OWL logic to infer the logical relations between the inputs and outputs of a request, with the inputs and outputs of published semantic services. This algorithm is based on an heuristic for determining the structural similarity of a pair of concepts. Ontologically, two concepts in OWL can be equivalent (e.g., *x equivalentClass y*) or a concept can be a specialization of a super-concept (e.g., *x subClassOf y*). As a consequence, two services would be equivalent if their inputs and outputs are equivalent, or one would be a specialization of the another if its parameters are more specific.

Matchmaker (Kawamura et al., 2005) is a discovery system developed by Toshiba and Carnegie Mellon University, which is a further improved version of (Paolucci et al., 2002). Conceptually, this approach proposes to incorporate IR-based techniques, semantic annotations and constraint declarations into UDDI. Then, the authors propose four filtering stages for incrementally reducing the search space, namely *Namespace*, *Text*, *I/O type* and *Constraint* filter. These filters are sequentially connected. Each filter outputs 10 percent of the services received from the previous filter. The first stage of the filtering process determines whether the requested service and the registered services share, at least, one namespace. The second stage compares human-readable service documentation elements against a textual description of the desired service. At the third stage, the matching algorithm introduced in (Paolucci et al., 2002),

Figure 6. Overview of the WSDL-S approach

WSDL-S approach

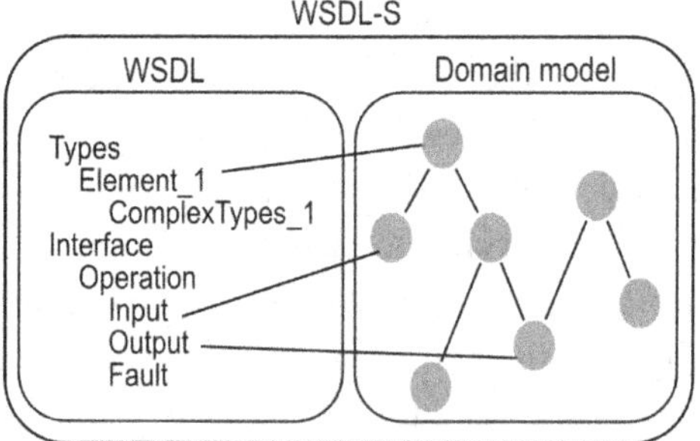

Overview of a WSDL-S document

```
<types>
 <xs:element name="GetRate">
   <xs:complexType>
    <xs:sequence>
     <xs:element name="srcCurrency" type="xs:string"
       wssem:modelReference=
         "ConversionsOntology#Currency"/>
     <xs:element name="destCurrency" type="xs:string"
       wssem:modelReference=
         "ConversionsOntology#Currency"/>
    </xs:sequence>
   </xs:complexType>
 </xs:element>
</types>
<message name="GetRateSoapIn">
 <part name="parameters" element="s0:GetRate" />
</message>
<portType name="CurrencywsSoap">
 <operation name="GetRate">
  <documentation>
    This method returns the currency
    conversion ratio between two countries
  </documentation>
  <input message="s0:GetRateSoapIn" />
  <output message="s0:GetRateSoapOut" />
  </operation>
</portType>
```

checks whether the ontological definitions of the inputs and outputs match. Finally, the constraint filter determines whether the registered services satisfy a user's requested constraints or not.

Cardoso and Sheth (2003) also propose an algorithm to exploit syntactic and semantic information. This algorithm augments syntactic descriptions present at WSDL documents with semantic descriptions, and in turn uses both descriptions to increase matching precision. This algorithm supports Web Services described with WSMO and OWL-S, or annotated with WSDL-S. In addition, this algorithm aims at dealing with mediation between different ontologies. Here, the discovery system is part of an approach for easing work-flow instantiation based on discovering and composing Web Services.

Sivashanmugam et al. (2003) describe a semantic discovery system that follows WSDL-S for annotating and OWL for defining concepts. Broadly, the authors present a three stages algorithm that allows discoverers to search for services by specifying partially annotated services. During the first stage, a semantic matching algorithm matches Web Service operations based on the concepts that annotate their functionality. In the second stage, the result set is ranked according to the semantic similarity between input and output concepts. Optionally, the third stage ranks the result set based on the semantic similarity of precondition and effect concepts. A further improved implementation of (Sivashanmugam et al., 2003) was proposed in (Li et al., 2006).

Highly Scalable and Available Approaches for Discovering Web Services

The scalability of a service discovery systems is a crucial issue for highly distributed environments. In order to scale in the number of published services, the UDDI v3 specification proposes a federated environment, with a registry as a collection of one or more nodes. As such a federated architecture suffers from a single point of access and failure also (Schmidt and Parashar, 2004), the current trend consists of adapting existing discovery approaches to execute over P2P networks. These approaches must face the challenge of performing distributed queries to retrieve accurate results efficiently. Below we describe the most relevant approaches in this direction.

Schmidt and Parashar (2004) combine a VSM-based discovery system with a P2P overlay network. Conceptually, this paper proposes a novel indexing scheme that allows distribution of similar service descriptions on a single peer or its neighbors. In this way, a sequence of keywords that characterizes a Web Service, is mapped onto a number corresponding to the index of a physical peer. Contrary to mapping the identifier or key of a service onto the index of a peer, the cornerstone of this approach is preserving the locality of similar service descriptions, so that similar content is mapped onto the same peer. The peers of this network contain the WSDL documents of the services. As a result, this indexing scheme allows discoverers to find out which peer contains similar service descriptions given a keyword-based query.

As we explained in "Information Retrieval-based approaches for discovering Web Services", a WSDL document can be described as a sequence of n keywords representing the spatial coordinates of an n -dimensional space. Mapping a sequence of keywords onto an index, or number, is a dimension reduction problem. The implementation described in (Schmidt & Parashar, 2004), uses Hilbert's space filling curves (Sagan, 1994) for such mapping. On the other hand, it uses Chord (Stoica et al., 2003) for the overlay P2P network topology.

MWSDI (Verma et al., 2005), a part of the METEOR-S project, is an hybrid P2P-based approach for discovering Semantic Web Services. MWSDI acts as a middle-ware for inter-connecting isolated registries, in which each one offers the discovery capabilities described in (Sivashanmugam et al., 2003). The authors propose to organize distributed registries based on the domain of their published Web Services, classify a request (publication or discovery), and then redirect this request to a registry that belongs to the same domain. One or more ontologies stand for a domain, and then a Web Service registry is associated with a domain by connecting it to these ontologies, named registry ontologies. MWSDI uses a P2P approach with three types of peers. One type is in charge of managing registry ontologies. One centralized peer is responsible for coordinating new registries joining the network. Having this single point of failure makes this approach an hybrid P2P (Yang & Garcia-Molina, 2001). The third type of peer acts as the glue between a concrete registry and the infrastructure.

Sapkota et al. (2005) present another approach for combining a Semantic Web Service discovery system with a P2P. They use WSMO for describing services and matchmaking users' requests. This approach builds clusters of registries that contain similar services. A cluster consists of, at least, one super-peer, which indexes the Web Services registered within its cluster and facilitates communication between other clusters. A super-peer is dynamically selected among the members of a cluster, based on its computational capabilities and load factors. When a peer receives a discoverer's request, it attempts to resolve the query locally. When no local matching services can be found, the peer forwards the request to its super-peer. Unless the super-peer can found similar services, the request is forwarded to other clusters.

Paolucci et al. (2003) enhance their previous work (Paolucci et al., 2002) by interconnecting a collection of distributed OWL-S Matchmakers over a P2P network. Broadly, the authors propose to organize a collection of Matchmakers, broadcast a query, and then collect different results. This work proposes an architecture based on Gnutella (Steinmetz & Wehrle, 2005), an unstructured P2P approach that uses a restricted flooding method (a message has a *time to live*, which limits the number of hops before it is removed from the network) for spreading messages out to the peers.

The next section evaluates the described approaches with regard to their functional and non-functional characteristics and introduces eight criteria that may be used to characterize other approaches as well.

CHARACTERIZATION AND SURVEY OF DISCOVERY MECHANISMS

A previous section described the requirements of service discovery systems and how they evolved to support from homogeneous environments to heterogeneous and automatic ones. There are different problems related to service discovery, which range from how to describe services, to how to manage these descriptions. As discussed, service discovery approaches may be very different from each other, therefore there is a clear need for a criteria to characterize them.

We have identified and defined eight criteria that should be taken under consideration when evaluating discovery systems. Table 2 divides these criteria in two groups. The first group is intended to evaluate functional features of discovery systems, whereas the second focuses on non-functional ones. The next section describes the group of functional criteria, while the following presents the non-functional one. Accompanying the presentation of each group of criteria, the results of using them to evaluate the discovery approaches described in the section "Approaches to discover Web Services" are shown. This section concludes discussing the overall results.

Functional Characterization

From a discoverer's perspective, the functional characterization of a discovery system focuses on answering: what may a discoverer expect as outputs from such a system? and what does such a system require as inputs? Below, we present a set of functional criteria and, accompanying each criterion definition, we present a fixed range of values that the criterion accepts. By default, these values are mutually exclusive, unless we explicitly define when they may appear together.

Recoverable Information

This criterion identifies which types of information a discovery system supports for describing services. The values that this criterion accepts are: *business*, *functional*, *non-functional* and *meta-model*. The *business* value indicates that a system supports provider's descriptions, such as location, contact details, etc. The *functional* value is intended to evaluate if a system supplies consumers with a description of *what* a service does. Instead, the *non-functional* value concentrates upon *how*, i.e., this value indicates that a discovery system supports non-functional descriptions of available services. It is worth noting that the non-functional value is not associated with the quality attributes of the discovery system under characterization. As we will explain, the second group of criteria refers to these attributes. Finally, the *meta-model* value describes whether an approach supplies the definition of the semantics of service descriptions. These values are not exclusive, e.g. the recoverable information of UDDI is "business" and "functional".

Functional descriptions are necessary for communicating what a service does. Non-functional characteristics become important when there are, at least, two services designed for performing the same task. Indeed, having a description of how this task is carried out allows discoverers to select the service that best fits their QoS requirements. On the other hand, meta-model descriptions are essential in automatic environments. However, these require to place extra effort on building domain ontologies and annotations.

Table 2. Summary of characterization criteria

Criterion group	Criterion name	Accepted Values	Mutually exclusive
Functional	Recoverable information	business, functional, non-functional, meta-model	no
	Query language	keyword, natural language, constraint, template, meta-model	no
	Mediation support	syntactic mediation, semantic matching, ontology alignment, none	yes
	Results granularity	service, operation	no
Non-functional	Scalability	a growth in the number of "*x*"	no
	Availability	centralized, federated, hybrid, P2P	yes
	Provider abstraction	brokering, matchmaking	yes
	Standards conformance	name of the adopted standard/s, none	no

Query Language

This criterion deals with how easy is to formulate a query and how expressive a query language is. The values that we propose for this criterion are: *keyword*, *natural language*, *constraint*, *template* and *meta-model*. The *keyword* and *natural language* values are intended to describe syntactical keyword-based and textual querying approaches, respectively. We use the *constraint* value for referring to languages that accept assertions, like *"availability greater than 0.9"*. The *template* value is intended to describe languages that accept service descriptions as queries. For example, Woogle (Dong et al., 2004) expects a WSDL document as a query, so that we evaluate its query language as being "template". Finally, the *meta-model* value focuses on languages that allow discoverers to query based on the definition of service descriptions. Also, these values are not exclusive, for example we evaluate the query language of Matchmaker (Kawamura et al., 2005) as being "keyword", "natural language", "constraint", "template" and "meta-model".

The implication of the type of query language supported is twofold. In the first place, different query languages enable achieving different degrees of accuracy in search results. Qualitatively, the search results achieved by using annotations are better than the results achieved by keyword-based approaches, because semantic-based query languages allow discoverers to precisely state their needs. In the second place, in the case of constraint-based and semantics-based queries, modeling a need may require developers to learn a new query language.

Mediation Support

This criterion evaluates if a discoverer system supports mediation. Conceptually, mediation attempts to bridge different representations of the same concept. In the context of Web Service discovery, mediation occurs between the representations of service descriptions and queries. We propose four possible values for this criterion: *none, syntactic mediation, concept alignment* and *ontology alignment*. The second value is intended to describe when syntactic exact matching is complemented with mediation. Examples of syntactic mediation are: bridging synonyms –words that represent the same idea but are syntactically different from each other–, bridging different WSDL styles for specifying data-types, clustering parameter names that usually co-occur, and partially matching a bag of keywords.

The semantic matching value refers to mediation between two concepts from an ontology. We define this value for identifying those approaches exploiting semantic relations (e.g., "same as", "sub-class of", "inverse of") among concepts, such as the semantic matching algorithm presented in (Paolucci et al., 2002). The ontology alignment value represents those approaches that mediate between two or more ontologies.

The mediation support characteristic carries several implications. If a discovery system does not supply discoverers and publishers with mediation (the *none* value), both must strive to accurately describe their needs and advertisements respectively, to produce unambiguous representations. Consequently, connecting services to consumers becomes harder. Although the *concept alignment* and *ontology alignment* values seem similar, the difference is that the former value requires providers and consumers to agree on a shared ontology. Instead, the second value allows users to bridge different conceptualizations of the same domain.

Results Granularity

The results granularity criterion differentiates between approaches returning a service description and those returning an operation description. Here, a service description consists of a set of operation descriptions. Accepted values for this criterion are: *service* and *operation*. It is worth noting that the *service* value does not subsume the *operation* value, thus these values are not mutually exclusive.

The granularity of the results is important for invoking discovered services. An operation is defined as the smallest piece of software that a discoverer may invoke by using Web Services. Let us consider a Web Service that provides classic e-mail operations, such as validate addresses, filter spam and send anonymous messages. If this service is retrieved when looking for a spam filter, a discoverer must analyze the Web Service description to obtain the proper operation. Ideally, discovering operations allows consumers to directly invoke them. Conversely, if the granularity of the results is service, then the discoverer must crumble the description of the retrieved service to analyze its operations. However, some services present order dependencies between their operations. For example, non-free of charge Web Services often require to invoke an operation for checking account permissions, e.g., "log-in", before invoking any other offered operation. In this context, it is essential for the discoverer to obtain the whole service description as well.

Table 3 shows the results, after using the aforementioned criteria for analyzing the approaches described in the section "Approaches to discover Web Services". In the section "Discussion" we will discuss these results.

Non-Functional Characterization

When looking for a Web Service discovery system for production environments, it is worth evaluating its non-functional attributes such as scalability, availability, provider abstraction and standards conformance. This kind of attributes allows publishers to select a discovery system for advertising their services. For instance, suppose a publisher wants to advertise in a highly available registry, to avoid compromising the discovery of her/his services. From a discovery system administrator's point of view, a non-functional characterization points out the challenges involved in setting up and managing the different alternatives. In this sense, a centralized approach may be rather easier to set up than a decentralized one. Below, we define a set of non-functional criteria.

Scalability

This criterion evaluates whether a system is designed for dealing with a growth of the number of published services, categories, nodes or not. Accepted values are: *number of nodes*, *number of services*, *number of categories* and *none*. A "number of *x*" value tells that an approach has been designed for managing a growth in *x*. In this context, we use the term "node" according to the UDDI specification, and the terms "categories"

Table 3. Functional characterization of Web Service discovery systems

Evaluated approach	Recoverable Information	Query language	Mediation support	Mediation support
UDDI	business, functional	keyword	none	service
(Zhuge & Liu, 2004; Schmidt & Parashar, 2004)	business, functional	keyword	syntactic mediation	service
(Wang & Stroulia, 2003; Jian & Zhaohui, 2005; Platzer & Dustdar, 2005; Kokash et al., 2006; Lee et al., 2007)	functional	keyword, natural language	none	service
(Dong et al., 2004)	functional	template	syntactic mediation	service, operation
(Crasso et al., 2008)	business, functional	keyword, natural language, template	syntactic mediation	service, operation
(Birukou et al., 2007)	functional	keyword, natural language	syntactic mediation	operation
(Ran, 2003; Al-Masri & Mahmoud, 2007)	business, functional, non-functional	keyword, constraint	none	service
(Zhou et al., 2004)	business, functional, non-functional	keyword	none	service
(Makris et al., 2006)	business, functional, non-functional	template	none	operation
(Kozlenkov et al., 2007)	functional, non-functional	template, constraint	none	operation
(Kawamura et al., 2005; Paolucci et al., 2003)	business, functional, non-functional, meta-model	keyword, natural language, constraint, template, meta-model	semantic matching	operation
(Cardoso & Sheth, 2003)	functional, meta-model	natural language, template, meta-model	ontology alignment	operation
(Sivashanmugam et al., 2003; Verma et al., 2005)	functional, meta-model	template, meta-model	semantic matching	operation
(Sapkota et al., 2005)	meta-model	meta-model	ontology alignment	service

and "domains" as being indistinct. In addition, these values are not exclusive.

Scalability determines for which environments a discovery systems is appropriate. Achieving high levels of scalability is more appropriate for environments where the number of services changes frequently and there are no clear boundaries on the expected scalability. For instance, P2P systems are more appropriate in dynamic environments, e.g., in ubiquitous computing where nodes leave or join a network in unpredictable manners. However, an scalable infrastructure may be challenging from several points of views (manageability, uncertainty, deployability, etc.) (Gotthelf et al., 2008). Instead, if the number of services is known beforehand, a non-scalable infrastructure may be a good choice. Centralized registries are more appropriate when service publications occur sporadically.

Availability

This criterion evaluates how robust a system is. The possible values this criterion can take are: *centralized*, *federated*, *hybrid* or *P2P*. From an architectural point of view, the first value refers to centralized approaches with a single point of failure. The *federated* value refers to a collection of distributed nodes governed by a master registry, which, in fact, acts as a single point of access and failure. On the contrary, the *P2P* value focuses on decentralized approaches, like distributed connected peers. The *hybrid* value refers to an architectural approach that is between the aforementioned two, for example a P2P network with a centralized super-peer, but with mechanisms for recovering when the super-peer fails. Similarly to the scalability criterion, achieving respectable levels of availability with centralized approaches may be rather hard. In addition, availability may even be not crucial in scenarios where discovery occurs sporadically.

Provider Abstraction

This criterion deals with differentiating discovery systems that interfere in the interaction between requested and matched services, from those that merely match requested and published services. The valid values for this criterion are: *brokering* and *matchmaking*.

This criterion has several implications related to the availability criterion. A *brokering* approach allows better decoupling of consumers and services. A broker governs both discovery and invocation, because the broker is responsible for locating an appropriate service, forwarding the request to its provider and transmitting results and exceptions back to the service consumer. This approach imposes stronger availability requirements than matchmaking systems. Instead, when a *matchmaking* approach is used, once a service has been discovered, it may be consumed even if the discovery system is unavailable.

Table 4 shows the results, in terms of non-functional aspects, after characterizing the discovery approaches described in the section "Approaches to discover Web Services".

Standards Conformance

We propose this criterion to evaluate whether a discovery system follows standards. The accepted values for this criterion are the names of the standards that have been adopted by the system under review. For example, accepted non-exclusive values are: *UDDI*, *WSDL*, *WSDL-S*, *OWL-S* and *WSMO*. In general, these standards are well-founded and documented. One of the main implications of following well-founded and documented practices, is that complaint discovery systems may be potentially easier to implement and adopt than ad-hoc solutions.

Table 4. Non-functional characterization of Web Service discovery systems

Evaluated approach	Scalability	Availability	Provider abstraction
(Sivashanmugam et al., 2003; Ran, 2003; Zhou et al., 2004; Zhuge & Liu, 2004)	number of nodes	federated	matchmaking
(Al-Masri & Mahmoud, 2007)	number of nodes	federated	brokering
(Wang & Stroulia, 2003; Cardoso & Sheth, 2003; Dong et al., 2004; Platzer & Dustdar, 2005; Jian & Zhaohui, 2005; Kawamura et al., 2005; Makris et al., 2006; Kokash et al., 2006; Lee et al., 2007; Kozlenkov et al., 2007)	none	centralized	matchmaking
(Crasso et al., 2008)	number of nodes, number of domains	centralized	matchmaking
(Schmidt & Parashar, 2004)	number of services	P2P	matchmaking
(Verma et al., 2005)	number of domains	hybrid	matchmaking
(Sapkota et al., 2005)	number of nodes	hybrid	matchmaking
(Paolucci et al., 2003)	number of nodes	P2P	matchmaking

Table 5 summarizes most relevant approaches to service discovery with regard to standard conformance. The approaches that adhere to WSDL-S also adhere to WSDL, because the WSDL-S specification extends WSDL by means of WSDL supported extensibility elements, thus a WSDL-S document is also a valid WSDL document. The approaches that do not explicit adhere to any standard have been omitted from the table. For instance, the approach described in (Birukou et al., 2007) matches a request against past requests made by experienced community members. However, despite it can be theoretically integrated with UDDI registries or any other IR-based approaches, it does not explicitly adopt any standard. It is worth noting that the query language presented in (Kozlenkov et al., 2007) follows UML.

Discussion

We employed eight criteria for analyzing relevant and contemporary discovery systems throughout this section. The analysis results allow identifying:

1. Some characteristics that are more popular than others within discovery approaches,
2. Four dependencies among the evaluated aspects,
3. Lessons learned from analyzed approaches, and
4. Major research possibilities in the field.

Popularity of Analyzed Characteristics

The characterization results show that some characteristics are more popular than others. For instance, most of the discovery systems follow the UDDI and WSDL specifications (see Table 5), support queries based on keywords and natural language descriptions (see Table 3), manage functional and business data, and follow a centralized matchmaking approach (see Table 4).

The popularity of these characteristics may be probably related to three facts. First, the design of many discovery systems might be influenced by the conception of a registry that was proposed with UDDI. Second, probably because that Web Service standards are text-oriented, many discovery systems adapt IR techniques, which are based on a centralized VSM and enable natural language queries. Third, IR-based approaches can be transparently adopted. The implication of the popularity of these characteristics is that the designers of service-oriented systems find more alternatives having these popular characteristics, when they look for a discovery system.

Identified Dependencies Among Characteristics

The characterization results show also allow the identification of four dependencies among the proposed criteria by overlapping the functional and non-functional characterizations. First, the scalability and availability of many approaches are limited to the number of nodes and federated values, respectively. Commonly, these approaches depend on the UDDI specification. For example, Zhuge and Liu (2004) employ a three layers architecture, wherein the lowest layer is an UDDI registry. Likewise, (Ran, 2003) and (Al-Masri & Mahmoud, 2007) extend the UDDI specification, whereas the former employs decentralized "certifiers" and the latter a brokering system.

Second, there is a correspondence among the foundations of IR-based approaches and the non-functional characterization results, which is shown in the column Scalability of Table 4. The reason behind this fact is that IR-inspired approaches, such as (Wang & Stroulia, 2003; Platzer & Dustdar, 2005; Birukou et al., 2007), employ a weighting technique –named TF-IDF– that has to be recomputed when new services are published in these systems. Intuitively, this characteristic may harm the performance of these approaches on dynamic and massively distributed

Table 5. Discovery approaches with respect to standard conformance

Evaluated approach	UDDI	WSDL	WSDL-S	WSMO	OWL-S
(Ran, 2003)	X				
(Makris et al., 2006)	X				
(Zhou et al., 2004)	X				
UDDI	X				
(Wang & Stroulia, 2003)		X			
(Schmidt & Parashar, 2004)		X			
(Dong et al., 2004)		X			
(Sivashanmugam et al., 2003)		X	X		
(Verma et al., 2005)		X	X		
(Cardoso & Sheth, 2003)		X	X	X	X
(Jian & Zhaohui, 2005)	X	X			
(Kokash et al., 2006)	X	X			
(Lee et al., 2007)	X	X			
(Crasso et al., 2008)	X	X			
(Zhuge & Liu, 2004)	X	X			
(Platzer & Dustdar, 2005)	X	X			
(Sapkota et al., 2005)				X	
(Paolucci et al., 2003)					X
(Kawamura et al., 2005)					X

environments, in which updates occur frequently and the VSM is shared among several distributed peers. Moreover, most of the analyzed IR-based approaches operate by matching a query against the vector representations of all available services, which requires more matching operations as the number of published services grows.

Third, it would be rational to expect that approaches supporting non-functional descriptions of services rely on brokers, because they are essential to collect reliable QoS information about providers. In spite of this, most of the alternatives that support non-functional information adopt a matchmaker approach. Instead, (Al-Masri & Mahmoud, 2007) employs a broking system.

The fourth dependency found appears by analyzing the results shown in Table 3 and Table 5 together. There is a clear correspondence between UDDI and WSDL standards and IR-based approaches. IR-based approaches have shown that they can be perfectly adapted to deal with Web Services, mainly because both UDDI and WSDL are text-oriented. Migrating from an UDDI-based platform to an IR-based counterpart, which should grant more query language facilities to discoverers, may not demand severe modifications. A fact that supports this claim is the large number of publicly available WSDL documents that have been used for evaluating IR-based approaches. On the other hand, if an approach follows WSDL then it should be easy to adopt the WSDL-S and, in turn, to incorporate annotations.

Lessons Learned

The presented characterization allows bringing together four lessons learned from the surveyed discovery systems that can be usefully applied on future service registries. Namely, these lessons are:

- **Retrieval effectiveness versus cost of adoption trade-off:** There is a correlation between discoverers/publishers' effort and the benefit they may obtain from a discovery system. Semantics-based approaches, for example, achieve high levels of retrieval effectiveness, which surpass the effectiveness achieved by syntactic-based ones. However, as the backbone of semantic approaches is describing each detail of publicly available services using machine interpretable languages, publishers must put extra effort into describing services by means of semantic meta-data. With search systems in general, the more effort we put into accurately describing our goods, the better retrieval effectiveness we get. This situation involves gaining retrieval effectiveness, at the expense of making service publication rather hard.
- **Incorrect usage of the meta-data that support Web Services discovery:** Many problems related to the efficiency of standard-compliant approaches to service discovery, may stem from the fact that current Web Service standards to describe services are incorrectly or not fully employed by publishers. These standards provide means for describing offered services from a functional perspective using text-oriented descritions. Accordingly, poorly documenting WSDL documents or using unintelligible naming conventions, may hinder the efficiency of approaches based on Web Service standards.
- **Limited support to describe what a discoverer is looking for:** Similarly to the aforementioned trade-off, there is a lack of powerful means to describe information needs without requiring heavy query descriptions or all the specifications of full semantic techniques. Web Service standards and IR-based approaches to service discovery provide merely keyword-based query support. Due to the heterogeneity of the Internet, and massively distributed environments in general, different keywords are commonly used for advertising services that offer the same functionality. In practice, this occurs because different services are built by different development teams, who might share neither the same programming conventions nor the same first language. The inconsistency between keywords in interfaces of publicly available services and queries, along with the intuitive limitations of this kind of queries to describe users' intentions, may be the cause of many problems related to the retrieval effectiveness of lightweight approaches to service discovery.
- **Missing plans to face the "curse of success":** As Web Service technologies become massively adopted, the number of published services is expected to grow. The success of Web Services and SOC in becoming the next big thing in the software industry, lies on the ability of service discovery systems to manage an ever increasing number of publicly available services. Recently, some researchers have striven to explore the ability of different service registries to deal with a growth of the number of advertised services. Obviously, studying the scalability of the infrastructure that supports the discovery process is a very important concern in this direction, however it is not the only direction worth exploring. Discoverers' frustration with search results, often increases with the space of published services. Therefore, more effort should be put into improving the scalability of discovery systems, without neglecting their retrieval effectiveness.

Future Research Possibilities on Service Discovery

The survey of ongoing approaches to service discovery allows us to identify major research possibilities in the field, which we will describe through next the subsections.

- **Opportunities to improve service descriptions with QoS data and semantics:** Regarding service descriptions, there is still more that can be accomplished. This review points out the need of a model for incorporate QoS service descriptions into Web Service standards. As Web Services proliferate, a larger number of them will compete in providing similar functionalities, therefore standard methods concerned with describing the degree to which services can achieve the required functionality should spring. Discovery systems based on semantics present two research challenges, at least. These approaches lack their vital inputs, namely ontologies and semantically annotated Web Services. To make Semantic Web Services a reality, it is necessary to define standard domain ontologies for describing services. In parallel, more effort should be placed on developing semi-automatic tools for annotating Web Services, such as the work of Crasso et al. (2009a), to make publishers' tasks easier. We believe that the proliferation of semantically annotated services will promote more research in automatic discovery and composition of Web Services. Alternatively, annotated Web Service descriptions may be influenced by the recent Web 2.0 and Social Web successes (McCool, 2006). For instance, Seedka![15] is a repository of "tagged" services that announces 27.388 annotated services at the moment of writing this paper. Tags are keyword-based annotations without the notion of synonyms or disambiguation, but these are easy to create, share and use. As semantic descriptions are intended to automatize the discovery and invocation process, another line of research involves the ensure the trust between service consumers and providers. Besides ensuring classic non-functional QoS requirements, this problem comprises vetting the services to determine their functionality, safety –lack of malware– and legal aspects, such as licenses and copyright violations (Wang & Vassileva, 2007).
- **Opportunities for IR-based Web Services discovery systems:** There are three main research challenges for IR-based approaches to service discovery. From an architectural perspective, the scalability of those approaches that use TF-IDF should be improved to handle high scalability requirements of ubiquitous service-oriented environments. To the best of our knowledge, term distributions (Lertnattee & Theeramunkong, 2004) and TF-ICF (Reed et al., 2006) are two weighting schemes that are not dependent on the entire collection of services and have shown promissory results, but they have not been used in the context of Web Services yet. Second, though IR-based approaches rely on the descriptiveness of service specifications, more effort should be placed to define algorithms and heuristics for identifying poorly documented WSDL documents, and correcting them. Alternatively, natural language processing, a major area of artificial intelligence research, may be adapted to analyze the representativeness of comments present in service descriptions. In this direction, Rodriguez et al. (2010) propose a catalog of frequent practices when building WSDL documents that should be avoided to improve the discoverability of the associated services. The authors also

explain how to correct the problems that the identified practices cause, and empirically show that the retrieval performance of an IR-based approach to service discovery experienced an important improvement after manually applying the proposed solutions. All in all, automatically improving Web Service descriptions for discovery is still an open issue (Rodriguez et al., 2010). Third, and finally, there are many research challenges related to generating effective queries, i.e., a description of users' needs that allows a discovery system to retrieve proper services. With IR-based approaches, a query is a collection of keywords. We believe that many software documentation elements may represent additional sources of relevant keywords for enhancing the description of users' requests. For instance, recently Crasso et al. (2009b) have explored the idea of gathering keywords from client-side software that is intended to consume external Web Services. The authors define approaches to query expansion, conduct a comparative analysis of the retrieval effectiveness of three discovery systems, and discuss the implications of using the original queries versus the ones that resulted after expanding them. More work can be done to analyze the impact of gathering terms from other sources of information.

- **Opportunities for benchmarking:** Comparing the retrieval effectiveness of two, or more, discovery systems is still an open problem. Although the identified criteria allow users to compare some essential aspects of discovery systems, it does not enable a fair quantitative comparison in terms of retrieval effectiveness. Recently, Oh and Lee (2009) have presented an effort in this direction called WSBen. WSBen is a toolkit for testing syntactic Web Services discovery and composition algorithms. This toolkit comprises a set of functions to simplify the benchmarking process, such as generating a collection of synthetically generated WSDL documents and queries, automatically. WSBen is an important contribution to the field and represents a starting line to build a benchmark that should comprise: (1) a publicly available train data-set of real world Web Services, (2) a publicly available test data-set, (3) a list of all services in the train data-set relevant to each query of the test data-set, and (4) a reproducible evaluation methodology. We believe that such a benchmark will promote more and better research in the field, specially for IR-based discovery systems. This, besides allowing evaluators to make trustworthy judgments about an approach, when using real world Web Services, will add the chance that other scientists observe experimental errors and possibly cooperate to rectify them. A benchmark for semantic discovery systems, on the other hand, presents even more challenges. First of all, annotating train and test data-sets may be a cumbersome process. Even worse, because of the diversity of models and languages for describing Semantic Web Services, different data-sets should be built for each variant, e.g., a benchmark for OWL-based discovery systems and another for WSMO-based ones.
- **Opportunities to measure the cost of adopting approaches to service discovery:** Finally, though intuitively the lightweightness of IR-inspired approaches –compared with semantic-based counterparts– and their full compliance with Web Service standards, make IR-inspired approaches easier to adopt, no research has been formally done regarding measuring the costs associated with adopting different service discovery approaches (Erickson and Siau, 2008). Therefore, more effort should be placed on the formal definition

of metrics to asses the impact of adopting different approaches to service discovery, which is a central part of any service-oriented system.

CONCLUSION

The key concept behind the SOC paradigm is to replace the development of specific software components with a combination of service discovery, selection and engagement. As this paradigm may be implemented according to different scales, which range from intra-application to inter-company, and different levels of automatism, service discovery presents many challenges. These challenges originate many alternatives for discovering services. Then, the need for criteria to characterize these alternatives arises.

In this paper we analyzed service discovery requirements in the context of past, present and future stages of SOC. As a result, we have developed eight criteria for pointing out how do Web Service and Semantic Web Service discovery systems satisfy these requirements. We have used these criteria for the characterization of 22 recent approaches related to connect consumers to services. Accordingly, we have presented and discussed the results of the evaluation. Moreover, we have identified and presented open problems and future research directions related to service discovery.

We will extend this work in one direction. As mentioned in "Future research possibilities on service discovery", these criteria allow users to compare some essential aspects of discovery systems, however these criteria do not enable a fair comparison in terms of retrieval effectiveness. Therefore, we will develop an evaluation benchmark for Web Service discovery systems. To do this, we are extending the data-sets employed in (Crasso et al., 2008). First, we will add more queries to the test data-set, which currently consists of 30 queries. Second, we will manually revise the train corpus, i.e., 391 public services, to detect and eradicate frequent bad practices in the development of Web Services that may attempt against their discoverability (Rodriguez et al., 2010). In parallel, we will determine the relevant services for each new query of the test data-set, by manually revising the functionalities of the Web Services in the corpus. This benchmark will allow researchers to conduct a comparative analysis of the retrieval effectiveness of their discovery systems, by using the original corpus of Web Services versus the one that resulted after correcting observed problems. We believe that this work will not only allow evaluators to make trustworthy judgments about discovery approaches, but will also motivate resarch on methods to produce more discoverable Web Services.

ACKNOWLEDGMENT

We thank the anonymous reviewers for their helpful comments and suggestions to improve the quality of the paper. We acknowledge the financial support provided by ANPCyT through grants PAE-PICT 2007-02311 and PAE-PICT 2007-02312.

REFERENCES

Al-Masri, E., & Mahmoud, Q. H. (2007). Qos-based discovery and ranking of Web Services. In *Proceedings of the International Conference on Computer Communications and Networks* (pp. 529–534). Los Alamitos, CA: IEEE Computer Society.

Birukou, A., Blanzieri, E., D'Andrea, V., Giorgini, P., & Kokash, N. (2007). Improving Web Service discovery with usage data. *IEEE Software*, *24*(6), 47–54. doi:10.1109/MS.2007.169

Bouguettaya, A., Malik, Z., Rezgui, A., & Korff, L. (2004). A scalable middleware for web databases. *Journal of Database Management, 17*, 20–46.

Cardoso, J., & Sheth, A. (2003). Semantic e-workflow composition. *Journal of Intelligent Information Systems, 21*(3), 191–225. doi:10.1023/A:1025542915514

Chen, Y., Zhou, L., & Zhang, D. (2006). Ontology-supported Web Service composition: An approach to service-oriented knowledge management in corporate services. *Journal of Database Management, 17*(1), 67–84.

Crasso, M., Zunino, A., & Campo, M. (2008). Easy Web Service discovery: a Query-by-Example approach. *Science of Computer Programming, 71*(2), 144–164. doi:10.1016/j.scico.2008.02.002

Crasso, M., Zunino, A., & Campo, M. (2009a). Semantic Web: Standards, Tools and Ontologies. In *An Approach to Assist Developers to Annotate Web Services with Ontologies* (pp. 195-229). Hauppauge, NY: Nova Science Publishers.

Crasso, M., Zunino, A., & Campo, M. (2009b). Combining query-by-example and query expansion for simplifying Web Service discovery. In *Information Systems Frontiers*.

de Bruijn, J., Lausen, H., Polleres, A., & Fensel, D. (2006). The Web Service modeling language WSML: An overview. In *ESWC* (LNCS 4011, pp. 590–604).

Dong, Z., Halevy, A. Y., Madhavan, J., Nemes, E., & Zhang, J. (2004). Similarity search for Web Services. In *Proceedings of the Thirtieth International Conference on Very Large Data Bases*, Toronto, ON, Canada (pp. 372–383). San Francisco: Morgan Kaufmann.

Erickson, J., & Siau, K. (2008). Web Service, Service-Oriented Computing, and Service-Oriented Architecture: Separating hype from reality. *Journal of Database Management, 19*(3), 42–54.

Euzenat, J., & Shvaiko, P. (2007). *Ontology Matching*. New York: Springer-Verlag.

Evermann, J. (2008). Theories of meaning in schema matching: A review. *Journal of Database Management, 19*, 55–82.

Fellbaum, C. (Ed.). (1989). *WordNet: An Electronic Lexical Database*. Cambridge, MA: MIT Press.

Firat, A., Wu, L., & Madnick, S. (2009). General strategy for querying web sources in a data federation environment. *Journal of Database Management, 20*, 1–18.

Garofalakis, J. D., Panagis, Y., Sakkopoulos, E., & Tsakalidis, A. K. (2006). Contemporary Web Service Discovery Mechanisms. *Journal of Web Engineering, 5*(3), 265–290.

Gotthelf, P., Zunino, A., & Campo, M. A. (2008). Peer-To-Peer communication infrastructure for groupware applications. *International Journal of Cooperative Information Systems, 17*(4), 523–554. doi:10.1142/S0218843008001920

Hauck, F. J., Kapitza, R., Reiser, H. P., & Schmied, A. I. (2005). A flexible and extensible object middleware: Corba and beyond. In *SEM '05: Proceedings of the 5th International Workshop on Software Engineering and Middleware* (pp. 69–75). New York: ACM.

Kawamura, T., Hasegawa, T., Ohsuga, A., Paolucci, M., & Sycara, K. (2005). Web Services lookup: A matchmaker experiment. *IT Professional, 7*(2), 36–41. doi:10.1109/MITP.2005.45

Kokash, N. (2006, August 28-29). A comparison of Web Service interface similarity measures. In *Proceedings of the 3rd European Starting AI Researcher Symposium*, Riva del Garda, Italy (pp. 220–231). IOS Press.

Kokash, N., van den Heuvel, W.-J., & D'Andrea, V. (2006, December 4-7). Leveraging Web Services discovery with customizable hybrid matching. In *Proceedings of the International Conference on Service-Oriented Computing*, Chicago (LNCS 4294, pp. 522–528).

Korfhage, R. R. (1997). *Information Storage and Retrieval*. New York: John Wiley & Sons.

Kozlenkov, A., Spanoudakis, G., Zisman, A., Fasoulas, V., & Sanchez Cid, F. (2007). Architecture-driven service discovery for service centric systems. *International Journal of Web Services Research*, *4*(2), 82–113.

Lee, K.-H., Lee, M.-Y., Hwang, Y.-Y., & Lee, K.-C. (2007, April 26-28). A framework for XML Web Services retrieval with ranking. In *Proceedings of the International Conference on Multimedia and Ubiquitous Engineering*, Seoul, Korea (pp. 773–778). Washington, DC: IEEE Computer Society.

Lertnattee, V., & Theeramunkong, T. (2004). Effect of term distributions on centroid-based text categorization. *Information Sciences*, *158*, 89–115. doi:10.1016/j.ins.2003.07.007

Li, K., Verma, K., Mulye, R., Rabbani, R., Miller, J., & Sheth, A. P. (2006). Designing semantic web processes: The WSDL-S approach. In *Semantic Web Services* (pp. 161–193). Processes and Applications.

Li, S.-H., Huang, S.-M., Yen, D. C., & Chang, C.-C. (2007). Migrating legacy information systems to Web Services architecture. *Journal of Database Management*, *18*(4), 1–25.

Makris, C., Panagis, Y., Sakkopoulos, E., & Tsakalidis, A. (2006). Efficient and adaptive discovery techniques of Web Services handling large data sets. *Journal of Systems and Software*, *79*(4), 480–495. doi:10.1016/j.jss.2005.06.002

Martin, D., Burstein, M., Mcdermott, D., Mcilraith, S., Paolucci, M., & Sycara, K. (2007). Bringing semantics to Web Services with owl-s. *World Wide Web (Bussum)*, *10*(3), 243–277. doi:10.1007/s11280-007-0033-x

McConnell, S. (2006). *Software Estimation: Demystifying the Black Art*. Redmond, CA: Microsoft Corporation.

McCool, R. (2006). Rethinking the Semantic Web, part II. *IEEE Internet Computing*, *10*(1), 93–96. doi:10.1109/MIC.2006.18

Oh, S.-C., & Lee, D. (2009). Wsben: A Web Services discovery and composition benchmark toolkit. *International Journal of Web Services Research*, *6*(1), 1–19.

Oldham, N., Thomas, C., Sheth, A. P., & Verma, K. (2004). METEOR-S Web Service annotation framework with machine learning classification. In *Proceedings of SWSWPC* (LNCS 3387, pp. 137–146).

Overhage, S., & Thomas, P. (2003). Ws-specification: Specifying Web Services using uddi improvements. In *Revised Papers from the NODe 2002 Web and Database-Related Workshops on Web, Web-Services, and Database Systems*, London (LNCS 2593, pp. 100–119).

Paolucci, M., Kawamura, T., Payne, T. R., & Sycara, K. P. (2002). Semantic matching of Web Services capabilities. In *ISWC '02: Proceedings of the First International Semantic Web Conference on The Semantic Web,* London (pp. 333–347). Berlin: Springer-Verlag.

Paolucci, M., & Sycara, K. (2003). Autonomous semantic Web Services. *IEEE Internet Computing*, *7*(5), 34–41. doi:10.1109/MIC.2003.1232516

Paolucci, M., Sycara, K. P., Nishimura, T., & Srinivasan, N. (2003). Using DAML-S for P2P discovery. In *Proceedings of IWCS* (pp. 203–207). CSREA Press.

Patil, A. A., Oundhakar, S. A., Sheth, A. P., & Verma, K. (2004). METEOR-S Web Service annotation framework. In *WWW '04: Proceedings of the 13th International Conference on World Wide Web*, New York (pp. 553–562). New York: ACM Press.

Platzer, C., & Dustdar, S. A. (2005, November). vector space search engine for Web Services. In *Proceedings of the 3rd European Conference on Web Services* (pp. 62–71). Washington, DC: IEEE Computer Society.

Ran, S. (2003). A model for Web Service discovery with QoS. *SIGecom Exchanges, 4*(1), 1–10. doi:10.1145/844357.844360

Reed, J. W., Jiao, Y., Potok, T. E., Klump, B., Elmore, M. T., & Hurson, A. R. (2006). TF-ICF: A new term weighting scheme for clustering dynamic data streams. In *ICMLA '06: Proceedings of the 5th International Conference on Machine Learning and Applications*, (pp. 258–263). Washington, DC: IEEE Computer Society.

Rodriguez, J. M., Crasso, M., Zunino, A., & Campo, M. (2009). Discoverability anti-patterns: frequent ways of making undiscoverable Web Service descriptions. In *Proceedings of the 10th Argentine Symposium on Software Engineering (ASSE2009) - 38th JAIIO* (pp. 1–15).

Rodriguez, J. M., Crasso, M., Zunino, A., & Campo, M. (2010). Improving Web Service descriptions for effective service discovery. *Science of Computer Programming*.

Roman, D., Keller, U., Lausen, H., de Bruijn, J., Lara, R., & Stollberg, M. (2005). Web Service Modeling Ontology. *Applied Ontology, 1*(1), 77–106.

Sagan, H. (1994). *Space-Filling Curves*. New York: Springer-Verlag.

Salton, G., Wong, A., & Yang, C. S. (1975). A vector space model for automatic indexing. *Communications of the ACM, 18*(11), 613–620. doi:10.1145/361219.361220

Sapkota, B., Vasiliu, L., Toma, I., Roman, D., & Bussler, C. (2005). Peer-to-Peer technology usage in Web Service discovery and matchmaking. In *Proceedings of the 6th International Conference on Web Information Systems Engineering (WISE)* (pp. 418–425).

Schmidt, C., & Parashar, M. A. (2004). Peer-to-Peer approach to Web Service discovery. *World Wide Web (Bussum), 7*(2), 211–229. doi:10.1023/B:WWWJ.0000017210.55153.3d

Sebastiani, F. (2002). Machine learning in automated text categorization. *ACM Computing Surveys, 34*(1), 1–47. doi:10.1145/505282.505283

Shadbolt, N., Berners-Lee, T., & Hall, W. (2006). The Semantic Web revisited. *IEEE Intelligent Systems, 21*(3), 96–101. doi:10.1109/MIS.2006.62

Sivashanmugam, K., Verma, K., Sheth, A. P., & Miller, J. A. (2003). Adding semantics to Web Services standards. In *Proceedings of the 2003 International Conference on Web Services*, Las Vegas, NV (pp. 395–401). CSREA Press.

Song, H., Cheng, D., Messer, A., & Kalasapur, S. (2007, July). Web Service discovery using general-purpose search engines. In *Proceedings of the IEEE International Conference on Web Services (ICWS)* (pp. 265–271).

Steinmetz, R., & Wehrle, K. (2005). *Peer-to-Peer Systems and Applications*. New York: Springer-Verlag. doi:10.1007/11530657

Stoica, I., Morris, R., Liben-Nowell, D., Karger, D. R., Kaashoek, M. F., & Dabek, F. (2003). Chord: A scalable Peer-to-Peer lookup service for internet applications. *IEEE/ACM Transactions on Networking, 11*(1), 17–32. doi:10.1109/TNET.2002.808407

Stroulia, E., & Wang, Y. (2005). Structural and semantic matching for assessing Web Service similarity. *International Journal of Cooperative Information Systems, 14*(4), 407–438. doi:10.1142/S0218843005001213

Toma, I., Iqbal, K., Moran, M., Roman, D., Strang, T., & Fensel, D. (2005, September 19-22). An evaluation of discovery approaches in Grid and Web Services environments. In *Proceedings of the 2nd International Conference on Grid Services Engineering and Management*, Erfurt, Germany (LNI 69, pp. 233–247). Bonner Köllen Verlag.

Verma, K., Sivashanmugam, K., Sheth, A., Patil, A., Oundhakar, S., & Miller, J. (2005). METEOR-S WSDI: A scalable Peer-to-Peer infrastructure of registries for semantic publication and discovery of Web Services. *Information Technology Management*, *6*(1), 17–39. doi:10.1007/s10799-004-7773-4

Wang, S., Zhang, L., & Ma, N. (2008). A quantitative measurement for reputation of Web Service and providers based on cloud model. In *Proceedings of the International Conference on Computational Intelligence for Modelling, Control and Automation* (pp. 500–505). Los Alamitos, CA: IEEE Computer Society.

Wang, Y., & Stroulia, E. (2003). Flexible interface matching for Web Service discovery. In *WISE '03: Proceedings of the Fourth International Conference on Web Information Systems Engineering* (p. 147). Washington, DC: IEEE Computer Society.

Wang, Y., & Vassileva, J. (2007). A review on trust and reputation for Web Service selection. *International Transactions on Systems Science and Applications*, *3*(2), 118–132.

Wu, J., & Wu, Z. (2005. July 11-15). Similarity-based Web Service matchmaking. In *Proceedings of the IEEE International Conference on Services Computing,* Orlando, FL (Vol. 1, pp. 287–294). Washington, DC: IEEE Computer Society.

Yang, B., & Garcia-Molina, H. (2001). Comparing hybrid Peer-to-Peer systems. In *VLDB '01: Proceedings of the 27th International Conference on Very Large Data Bases* (pp. 561–570). San Francisco: Morgan Kaufmann Publishers.

Yu, Q., Liu, X., Bouguettaya, A., & Medjahed, B. (2008). Deploying and managing Web Services: issues, solutions, and directions. *The International Journal on Very Large Data Bases*, *17*(3), 537–572. doi:10.1007/s00778-006-0020-3

Zhou, C., Chia, L.-T., & Lee, B.-S. (2004). QoS-aware and federated enhancement for UDDI. *International Journal of Web Services Research*, *1*(2), 58–85.

Zhuge, H., & Liu, J. (2004). Flexible retrieval of Web Services. *Journal of Systems and Software*, *70*(1-2), 107–116. doi:10.1016/S0164-1212(03)00003-7

ENDNOTES

1 UDDI, http://uddi.xml.org/
2 CORBA, http://www.corba.org/
3 DCOM, http://msdn.microsoft.com/en-us/library/cc201989.aspx
4 RMI, http://java.sun.com/j2se/1.5.0/docs/guide/rmi/index.html
5 UDDI, http://uddi.xml.org/
6 WSDL, http://www.w3.org/TR/wsdl
7 UNSPSC, http://www.unspsc.org/
8 SIC, http://www.osha.gov/pls/imis/sic-search.html
9 NAICS, http://www.naics.com
10 jUDDI, http://ws.apache.org/juddi/
11 UDDI products, http://uddi.xml.org/products
12 OWL, http://www.w3.org/TR/owl-features/
13 RDF, www.w3.org/RDF/
14 METEOR-S Project, http://lsdis.cs.uga.edu/projects/meteor-s/
15 Seedka!, http://seekda.com/

This work was previously published in the Journal of Database Management, Volume 22, Issue 1, edited by Keng Siau, pp. 102-132, copyright 2011 by IGI Publishing (an imprint of IGI Global).

Chapter 6
Multi-Level Modeling of Web Service Compositions with Transactional Properties

K. Vidyasankar
Memorial University, Canada

Gottfried Vossen
University of Muenster, Germany

ABSTRACT

Web services have become popular as a vehicle for the design, integration, composition, reuse, and deployment of distributed and heterogeneous software. However, although industry standards for the description, composition, and orchestration of Web services have been under development, their conceptual underpinnings are not fully understood. Conceptual models for service specification are rare, as are investigations based on them. This paper presents and studies a multi-level service composition model that perceives service specification as going through several levels of abstraction. It starts from transactional operations at the lowest level and abstracts into activities at higher levels that are close to the service provider or end user. The authors treat service composition from a specification and execution point of view, where the former is about composition logic and the latter about transactional guarantees. Consequently, the model allows for the specification of a number of transactional properties, such as atomicity and guaranteed termination, at all levels. Different ways of achieving the composition properties and implications of the model are presented. The authors also discuss how the model subsumes practical proposals like the OASIS Business Transaction Protocol, Sun's WS-TXM, and execution aspects of the BPEL4WS standard.

DOI: 10.4018/978-1-4666-2044-5.ch006

INTRODUCTION

Web services (Alonso et al., 2004; Casati & Dayal, 2002) have become popular as a vehicle for the design, integration, composition, reuse, and deployment of distributed and heterogeneous software, based on the premise that distributed computing can be made a reality easier than with previous approaches such as RPC, object-orientation, or static middleware. However, while industry standards for the description, composition, and orchestration of Web services have been under development for quite some time already, their conceptual underpinnings are still not fully understood. Indeed, conceptual models for service specification are rare, as are investigations based on them. This paper tries to make a contribution in this direction. In particular, it presents a *multi-level service composition model* that perceives service specification as a process that goes through several levels of abstraction: It starts from transactional concepts at the lowest level, and then gradually abstracts into activities at higher levels that are close to the service provider or even the end user. Importantly, the model allows for a specification of desirable composition properties such as *atomicity* and *guaranteed termination* at all levels, thereby encompassing a number of real-world approaches such as the OASIS BTP or Sun's WS-TXM.

Web services are currently seen by software vendors and application developers as an appropriate way of handling both application and data integration problems. The general vision is that services can be described in an implementation-independent fashion, and that users or clients can compose such descriptions into new services and execute the results by referring back to the respective service providers. To achieve these goals, a variety of industry standards have become available, most notably SOAP (*Simple Object Access Protocol*) for transportation purposes (Newcomer, 2002), WSDL (*Web Services Description Language*) for service descriptions (Newcomer, 2002), and BPEL4WS *Business Process Execution Language for Web Services* (IBM, 2007) for the description of service compositions in the form of graph-based process models.

Second, Web services represent an important way of realizing a so-called *service-oriented architecture* (SOA) (Huhns & Singh, 2005; Singh & Huhns, 2005). An SOA tries to answer the question of which services are available within a given enterprise or application context, which ones need to be newly implemented, and which ones need to be obtained from an external provider. To this end, it is reasonable to assume that, from a top-down development perspective, it makes sense to come up with one or more process models that clarify and fix the goals and procedures clients want to support by appropriately chosen services. Such models will typically be tied to a particular application domain, such as commerce, banking, the travel industry, etc. and their components will ultimately be mapped to services. The result will then be an architecture fixing the composition and integration details at a conceptual level (Vossen, 2006).

As has been noted, for example, by Hull et al. (2003), the conceptual underpinnings of Web services are still not fully understood. For example, in BPEL4WS it is possible to define choreographies (or service compositions) by defining a flow of control using guarded links between the respective activities (which appear in <flow> tags); yet this is entirely syntactic, and there is no way to argue about the properties of the resulting flow. On the other hand, studies such as Hull et al. (2003) indicate that service composition may be more intricate than what the standardization committees assume. Using models such as Mealy automata, Hull and others have been able to show that undesirable side effects may occur when certain types of services are composed (e.g., the result of composing "regular" services may all of a sudden be a "context-sensitive" service).

The model we are proposing and studying in this paper is based on the perception that service composition is not adequately described as long as flat models are used; indeed, in a *flat* model, be it classical transactions, finite-state automata, or Petri nets, the composition designer has to fix a particular level of abstraction and then will run into difficulties when trying to argue about properties that relate to (lower-level) components or to (higher-level) aggregations and that hence actually span several logical levels of the composition. Opposed to this, our intention is to construct a "bridge" between a low-level model that is based on classical transactions (Weikum & Vossen, 2002), a model that generalizes transactional guarantees to an (intermediate) process level (Schuldt et al., 2002), and a high-level model such as the ones used in PARIDE (Mecella et al., 2002) that orchestrates e-services via Petri nets.

A Service Composition Example

As a motivating example, we consider an electronic shopping scenario, where a customer is hunting for some specific goods (such as a musical instrument). To this end, the various services he or she plans to compose are the following (in the order given):

1. Initially, the customer starts a *price comparison* by turning to a service such as dealtime.com. Individual actions are the inspection of various offers made for the product in question, and comparing them based on price, delivery charge, availability, delivery time, etc. Once the customer decides on the shop he wants to buy from, he can turn to the next service.
2. The second service is provided by the *shop*. We assume that the product (e.g., a digital piano) is available in various versions (e.g., dark or light wood), and that the customer can pick one of these. If availability is not granted, he may change his decision. Once committed, the transaction is handed over to a broker (e.g., PayPal) for collecting the payment.
3. The *payment broker* is actually a subservice of the previous service. If payment is transferred successfully, the supplier of the goods enters terminating actions, in this case packaging and delivery. However, if payment transfer is not successful, a different stream of terminating actions is entered: the customer may pay cash or cancel the order.
4. The final service in this case, to be activated within the sequence of termination actions that follow successful payment, is the *delivery service*, which can be an ordinary furniture mover (who might take up to 10 days until delivery, yet is cheap), an express service delivering within 3 to 4 days, or the customer may decide to pick up the piece himself, so that delivery time is minimized.

An illustration of this service composition appears in Figure 1. What can be seen from this figure are some of the main ingredients of a Web service.

Various individually described and implemented services get combined into a new service. This combination can involve sequencing (price comparison, purchase and delivery in this example), concurrency (getting details from various shops in price comparison), nesting (payment nested within purchase) and, in fact, any complex arrangement that needs to be described using a more sophisticated specification language; we will later assume that a user is capable of providing service compositions at the highest level of abstraction.

The various activities that get composed and combined are different in nature: Some are as simple as a database ACID transaction (Weikum & Vossen, 2002) and can hence be easily *undone* (e.g., the result of a price comparison) or *compensated* for (e.g., overpayment), while others (in our case the payment for the piano in Step 3) mark a decisive point in a service execution which cannot be gone back beyond (at least not easily); following Schuldt et al. (2002) we call such activities *pivotal*. The occurrence of a pivotal

Figure 1. Shopping service composition

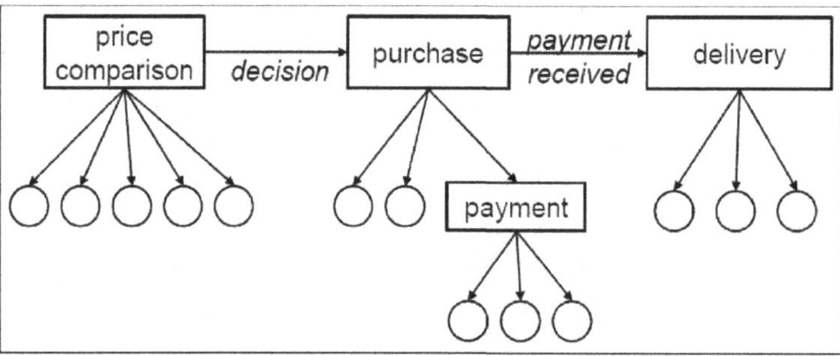

activity has implications for whatever follows in the service composition, since once the pivot has been executed, there should be a guarantee that the "remainder" of the service is also executed and terminated successfully; below we will call this the *guaranteed termination property*. In particular, if a customer has decided on goods to purchase, he or she wants to finish the deal.

Contributions and Organization

The points which extend those made by Vidyasankar and Vossen (2004) in this paper are the following:

1. An issue such as service composition should be treated from a specification *and* an execution point of view at the same time, where the former is about the composition logic and the latter about transactional guarantees.
2. To remedy the current situation that all activities composed into a service are treated at the same level of abstraction, we present a *multi-level* approach to service composition in this paper: It starts from underlying transactions (in the context of which activities ultimately get executed), and ends at a high level where processes can be abstractly described.

Notice that the latter is in line with previous studies within a variety of contexts; for example, multi-level transaction models (Weikum & Vossen, 2002) have been devised for being able to tolerate non-serializable executions, given the availability of (higher-level) semantic information.

The organization of the remainder of this paper is as follows: In the next section, we review related work, in particular work on which our approach is built. Next, our service composition and execution model are presented and different ways of achieving the relevant composition properties are discussed. We point out several service issues that can be captured nicely in our model, among which are the *sharing of responsibilities* and *added value*. We then generalize our basic path model to trees of services, and then present our multi-level model. The last section puts our model framework in perspective and concludes the paper.

RELATED WORK

In this section, we review related work; we restrict our attention to approaches on which we build or which we target for extension. Our emphasis is in showing that most *conceptual* models discussed up to now in the literature have been flat models which are limited in their ability to properly describe service compositions. We mention that industry standards such as WSFL can easily establish complex models, by providing the possibility to deliver highly nested XML documents. However, such a form of nesting is purely syntactic, and is unable to associate distinct properties with individual levels of nesting.

An excellent survey of work on modeling individual as well as composite services has been delivered by Hull et al. (2003). As far as individual services are concerned, formal models that have been employed include *method signatures* as known from object-oriented programming and *finite-state automata*, mostly in the form of *Mealy* machines. The former approach typically considers a service as a black-box from which only input and output can be seen, whereas the Mealy machine approach considers a service as a "white-box" whose inner structure is visible.

It turns out that such models are not too far from what is happening in industry consortia at the moment. For example, WSDL, the *Web Service Definition Language*, knows I/O signatures and in particular has two categories of message types, *reactive* (where a message is input to a service and can be one-way or of type "request-response") and *proactive* (where a message is output from a service and can be notification or of type "solicit-response"). On the other hand, simple Mealy machines, although capable of reading input and producing output, are hardly suited for handling data as well. To this end, they have been enhanced, for example, by storage capabilities in the style of relational transducers (Abiteboul et al., 2000).

A major emphasis has recently been put on the specification of service *conversations*, which denote single enactments of a global process. Standards such as WSCL (the *Web Service Conversation Language*) use automata to this end, which from a conceptual perspective are compositions of the Mealy-type of automata mentioned earlier. Indeed, such a composition can proceed in the style common for finite state machines, i.e., they can be composed serially or in parallel, and they can be composed to form loops (corresponding to concatenation, alternatives, and Kleene star in regular expressions, resp.). Compositions are presently formed as peer-to-peer systems with distributed control (Fauvet et al., 2001; Bultan et al., 2003), as hub-and-spoke systems that employ publish-and-subscribe techniques (Schuler et al., 2001), or as systems using mediators like in the WebTransact Architecture (Pires et al., 2002) or in BPEL4WS.

Our interest is in service compositions and conversations for which certain properties can be specified at design time and verified at run time. Work in this direction is gradually evolving, for example in the verification technique described by Fu et al., (2002) which can check for deadlock avoidance or response times. More promising from our perspective are approaches that relate the service composition task to workflow specification, in particular to the specification of workflows and processes that cross organizational boundaries (since individual services typically have distinct providers). Work in this direction has been reported by Colombo et al. (2002) as well as in the service orchestration approach used in PARIDE (Mecella et al., 2002) which is based on Petri nets. Finally, Schuldt et al. (2002) extend concurrency control and recovery techniques from ordinary transactions to processes and their composition; since this work is the most relevant to ours, we review it in more detail next.

In the model of Schuldt et al. (2002), an *activity* corresponds to a conventional (database) transaction or a *transaction program* executed in a transactional application. A *transactional process* is specified in a *process program* which is a set of partially ordered activities. All activities have the atomicity (all-or-nothing) property, that is, every execution will either *commit*, with the intended non-null effect, or *abort*, with the null effect. Next, three important properties of activities are defined by Schuldt et al. (2002):

1. An activity a is *compensatable* if there exists a compensating activity (that can be executed after a) which semantically undoes the effects of a.

2. An activity a is *assured* or *retriable* if its commit is guaranteed, perhaps after repeated trials (i.e., aborts and restarts).
3. An activity is a *pivot* if it is not compensatable.

Note that compensatability and retriability are orthogonal properties: a compensatable transaction may or may not be retriable, and vice versa. The following is a brief description of a process program:

- A process program is a (rooted) directed tree whose nodes may be of one of the following two types: *singleton* nodes, each corresponding to one activity, or *multi-activity* nodes, each corresponding to a partially ordered set of activities. Two different order constraints may be associated with the activities of a multi-activity node: a partial *strong order* and a partial *weak order*. Activities related by weak order can be executed concurrently but the result of the execution must be equivalent to one where the order is preserved. Those related by strong order must be executed in the given order.
- The edges of the tree correspond to the strong order constraints between the activities of the end nodes.
- Each pivot must be a singleton node. This captures the fact that no other activity of a process may be executed in parallel to a pivotal activity.
- A total order, called *preference order,* is defined on the children of a pivot. The last child must be the root of an *assured termination tree*, consisting only of retriable activities.
- The execution of the program starts at the root. A (possibly empty) sequence of nodes with compensatable activities is executed. If any of these activities abort, then all activities executed thus far are compensated. Then a pivot will be executed. If it aborts, again all the activities executed thus far will be compensated and the execution terminates.
- If the pivot commits, the subtree rooted at the first child of the pivot is executed. If that execution terminates with abort, the subtree rooted at the second child will be executed, and so on. As a last resort, the assured termination tree, rooted at the last child of the pivot, will be executed.
- Finally, a process program may not have any pivot. In that case, it has the same properties as a regular transaction, that is, it can be aborted any time prior to its commit.

We illustrate the model just described in the following figures, where we use circles to indicate compensatable activities, squares for pivots, and triangles for retriable activities, resp., as shown in Figure 2(a). A process program conforming to the properties listed above will in the sequel be said to have the *guaranteed termination property*. Figure 2(b) shows four distinct guaranteed terminations. A *process* is an execution of a process program. The execution may contain aborted activities, compensated and compensating activities, aborted activities of sub-processes, etc. However, the actual (net) *effects* of a process are represented by a path in the tree; this path will contain zero or more pivots. Notice that the guaranteed termination property of processes is a generalization of the atomicity property of the traditional transactions.

The emphasis in Schuldt et al. (2002) is put on defining a unified model for process concurrency control and recovery, which essentially extends earlier work by Schek et al. (1993) and Alonso et al. (1994); beyond this, they present a dynamic scheduling protocol for the execution of transactional processes that achieves correct executions in the sense defined. Opposed to this, our work considers a model of Web services where processes have services or activities and components, yet we preserve the distinction

Figure 2. Model illustration

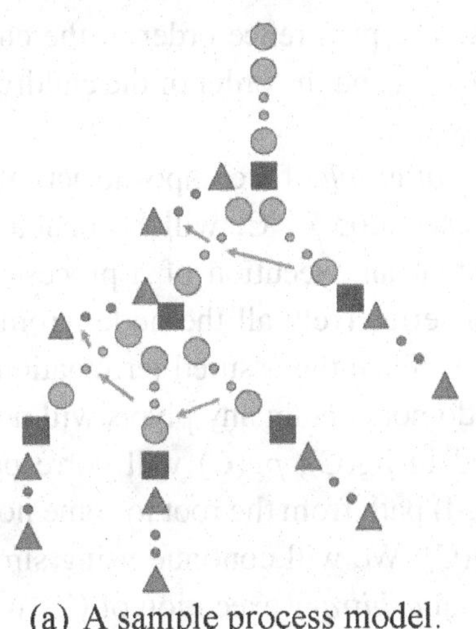

(a) A sample process model.

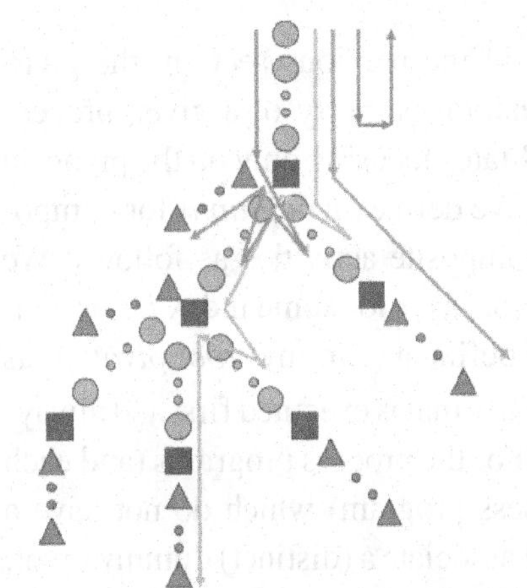

(b) The various guaranteed terminations.

between compensatable, pivot, and retriable ones. This extension of the model just described is the subject of the next section.

A MULTI-LEVEL COMPOSITION MODEL

In this section, we present our multi-level model of service composition; in particular, we consider the properties defined for activities by Schuldt et al. (2002), which we have reviewed in the previous section, and extend them to composite activities.

We will consider a process program as a *composition*, denoted (in bold) **C** and an execution of the program, that is, a process, as a *composite activity*, denoted (in italic) *C*. We will refer to the activities of the process (that is, the transactions) as *basic activities*. In the following, we extend the transactional properties of the basic activities to composite activities; in other words, we will extend what is illustrated in Figures 2(b) to multiple levels of abstraction. We have considered atomicity, and compensatability, pivotal, and retriability properties; we will use the abbreviation *c, p, r* to denote the last three properties, resp.

Atomicity of Basic Activities

As stated in the previous section, every execution of a basic activity will either *commit*, with the intended non-null effect, or *abort*, with the null effect. In the sequel, we will call the former case the *non-null* termination and the latter case the *null* termination of the activity; we will also denote the two cases as the *successful termination*, called *s-termination*, and the *failed termination*, called *f-termination*, resp. We use the following definition for atomicity.

Definition 3.1 (Atomicity of a basic activity): A basic activity is *atomic* if its execution is guaranteed to result in either the null termination or the *s*-termination.

We also assume that the termination properties and hence the atomicity, and the *c, p, r* properties are relative to the composition (and therefore every execution of that composition). Hence, if *a* is a basic activity of a composite activity *C*, then the last three properties are denoted *c*[*C*], *p*[*C*] and *r*[*C*].

Pivot Graphs

As indicated in the previous section, the guaranteed termination property of a given process program facilitates focusing only on the pivots in the program. We define *pivot graphs* for compositions and composite activities as follows. We denote the pivots as p_i for some index *i*. For convenience, we define a (dummy) *root pivot* $p_\perp$ as an empty activity that is executed first and always successfully. For the process programs (and each such subprocess program) which do not have a pivot, we will associate a (distinct) dummy pivot; this is different from the root pivot.

Definition 3.2 (Pivot graph): A *pivot graph* of a composition C, denoted *pg*(C), is a directed tree rooted at $p_\perp$ such that

1. It has at least one node in addition to the root,
2. Its non-root nodes correspond to the pivots in C,
3. The edges correspond to the precedence relation among the pivots in C, and
4. The children of each pivot are totally ordered according to the preference order of the subtrees containing them in C.

Essentially, each node p_i in *pg*(C) represents the corresponding (real or dummy) pivot p_i in C together with the compensatable activities preceding p_i in C; the retriable activities in the assured termination path of p_i are ignored. Note that, technically, a different notation should be used in the pivot graph to distinguish this node from p_i in C; but, for easy readability, we will use p_i itself.

Example 3.1: Figure 3 shows the pivot graph of a composition.

We use this as the running example in this section. The preference order of the children of p_1 is (p_2, p_3), and the order of the children of p_3 is (p_4, p_5, p_6).

A *pivot graph* of a composite activity *C*, that is, an execution of C, will be denoted *pg*(*C*). Recall that an execution of a process program contains effectively all the nodes from the root to a leaf. Since the assured termination trees of C that do not contain any pivots will not be represented in *pg*(C), *pg*(*C*) will correspond to a (directed) path from the root to some node in the tree *pg*(C). We will continue using simply *C* to denote an *arbitrary* execution of C. To denote a *particular* execution, we will use the sequence of pivots that have been executed in C as a subscript of *C*: if $(p_\perp, p_i, p_j, p_k)$ is the sequence, then we will denote *C* as C_{ijk} omitting ⊥; if $(p_\perp)$ is the sequence, then we will use $C_\perp$. We will also use the notation $C_{[\perp, m]}$ to denote an execution where all the pivots from the root to p_m in *pg*(C) have been executed. In this notation, the above two cases will be represented as $C_{[\perp, k]}$ and $C_{[\perp,\perp]}$. As a concrete example, the execution of Figure 3 where only $p_\perp$, p_1 and p_3 have been successfully executed will be denoted as C_{13} and as $C_{[\perp, 3]}$.

Figure 3. Pivot graph of a composition

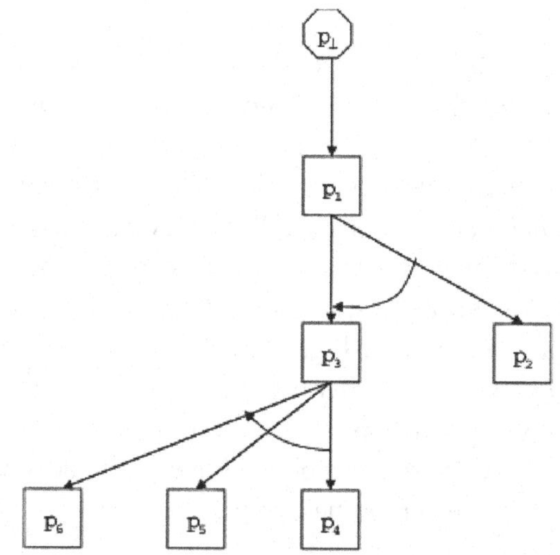

We note that, by our convention, *pg*(*C*) will always contain $p_\perp$. If it contains *only* $p_\perp$, then *C* has the null effect and we will call *C* the *null* termination of C. In all other cases, *pg*(*C*) will contain one or more pivots in addition to $p_\perp$, and *C* will be called a *non-null* termination of C.

Termination Properties of Composite Activities

Given a composition C, we next consider a higher-level composition U that contains C, and let *U* be an execution of U that contains *C*. We will associate the transactional properties, namely, atomicity as well as the *c, p, r* properties, to *C relative to* (U and) *U*. Since we have categorized the termination possibilities of *C* as null and non-null, we will assume that the application semantics of the composition U will determine whether a non-null termination of *C* is a successful termination or a failed termination relative to U. That is, we assume that, based on the application semantics, each non-null termination of *C* can be mapped to either an *f*-termination or an *s*-termination relative to the composition U; and each null termination of *C* will be an *f*-termination relative to U.

Example 3.2: Let us consider the example of Figure 3 again (cf. Example 3.1). We will first associate semantics to the activities. We assume that this composition is for planning a trip from St. John's (Newfoundland) to London (England) to attend a conference. We assume the following details:

1. Air Canada is the only carrier offering direct service between these two cities. (Pivot p_1 is for the purchase of flight tickets with Air Canada.)
2. The conference has arranged special rates with (a hypothetical) Ideal Hotel.
3. The hotel has two locations, called Ideal-A and Ideal-B.
4. The conference will be held in Ideal-A. A small number of rooms in Ideal-A and a substantially large number of rooms in Ideal-B are available at a special conference rate. (Pivot p_2 corresponds to making a reservation in Ideal-A, and pivot p_3 to making one in Ideal-B.)
5. Ideal-B is quite far from Ideal-A.
    a. The conference organizers have arranged a shuttle bus from Ideal-B to Ideal-A, but the capacity of the bus is limited and so reservation is absolutely essential. (Pivot p_4 is for shuttle bus reservation.)
    b. Those who could not get a reservation for the shuttle bus can rent a car to go from Ideal-B to Ideal-A. (Pivot p_5 is for car rental.)
    c. Public transportation can also be used, but it is time-consuming. A special pass can be purchased to use the public transportation. (Pivot p_6 is for the purchase of a pass.)

An execution of this process program will first try to get the flight tickets (p_1), then try hotel reservation in Ideal-A (p_2), and, if unsuccessful, try reservation in Ideal-B (p_3). If successful in the latter case, it will first try for reservation in the shuttle bus (p_4). If that fails, then a car rental will be tried (p_5). If that also fails, then a pass for the public transportation will be purchased (*p*6). Thus different executions may have different outcomes. For example, C_{12} refers to (successful) flight ticket purchase and reservation in Ideal-A, whereas C_{135} refers to flight ticket purchase, reservation in Ideal-B and a car rental.

Notice in the previous example that different users may have different requirements and therefore accept different sets of outcomes as *s*-terminated executions. For instance:

- User_1 may not accept anything other than C_{12};

- $User_2$ may accept C_{12}, C_{134}, C_{135}, but not C_{136}; (We ignore preferences in this paper;)
- $User_3$ may accept C_{12}, C_{134}, C_{135}, and C_{136}; and
- $User_4$ may accept successful execution of p_1 (flight tickets purchase) and any outcome of the remaining activities (namely, C_1, C_{12}, C_{13}, C_{134}, C_{135}, C_{136}), that is, every non-null execution.

It is reasonable to assume that a given composition C can be "tailored" to various user requirements. Indeed, consider the users just mentioned: For $User_1$, option p_3 (and the subtree rooted at p_3) should not be provided and *pg*(C) should contain only $p_\perp$, p_1 and p_2; for $User_2$, option p_6 should not be provided.

The requirement for $User_3$ suggests the following notion for *s*-termination: Any execution of C where *all* the pivots in *some* path from the root to a leaf of *pg*(C) have been executed successfully is an *s*-termination relative to U. With $User_4$ in mind, we will generalize this notion as follows:

Definition 3.3 (s-termination): An *s-termination* of a composition C is an execution where, for some path from the root to a leaf, the pivots of some specified prefix of that path have been executed successfully.

For example, execution C_1 in the previous example is an *f*-termination for $User_3$, but it is an *s*-termination for $User_4$. Thus, depending on given user requirements, a non-null execution will be mapped to either an *s*-termination or an *f*-termination.

Transactional Properties of Composite Activities

We consider the transactional properties next. First we note that the *c, p, r* properties of *C* relative to *U* are independent of the properties of the basic activities of *C* relative to *C*. We illustrate this with the following examples.

Example 3.3: In the composition of Figure 3, the purchase of the flight tickets p_1 may be a pivot to the travel agency in the sense that the airlines will not refund the money. However, the travel agency may not treat it as a pivot for the customer for whom the ticket is intended, if the agency is able to use the ticket for another customer. (Sometimes travel agencies buy seats in bulk from airlines and then sell them to customers on their own.) That is, C_1 may be compensatable for the customer.

Example 3.4: Suppose that, in a composition **U** like the one shown in Figure 1, *C* refers to the composite activity *purchase* of an article and has (among others) an activity *payment* denoted as *a*. Then *C* may be compensatable relative to *U*, *c*[*U*], (with the compensating composite activity being the *refund*) if the purchased item is returnable; otherwise (for example, if the store policy is "no exchange, no return") it will be pivotal, *p*[*U*]. Also, even if the refund policy dictates some penalty (for example, 10% of the cost), if the penalty is acceptable for the composition **U** then, in that case also, the *purchase* activity may be considered to be compensatable relative to *U*. Note that in the composition level **C**, the *payment* activity may always be pivotal relative to *C*, *p*[*C*], and similarly the *refund* activity *C*' may contain a *refund-payment* activity *a*' which is also pivotal relative to *C*', *p*[*C*'].

We now define the atomicity and the *c, p, r* properties for a composition C, that is, for any execution *C* of C. Again, all these properties are relative to the composition U. For brevity, we will not state this in the following definitions. The atomicity definition is similar to that for a basic activity:

Definition 3.4 (Atomicity of a composition): A composition is *atomic* if its execution is guaranteed to result in either the null termination or an *s*-termination.

The *c, p, r* properties can be extended to atomic compositions in a straight-forward manner.

Definition 3.5:

1. A composite activity *C* is *compensatable* if a compensating activity exists (relative to U) which semantically undoes the effects of *C*. An atomic composition C is *compensatable* if each of its *s*-terminations is compensatable.
2. An atomic composition C is *retriable* if one of its *s*-terminations can be guaranteed perhaps after a few attempts.
3. A composite activity *C* is a *pivot* if it is not compensatable. An atomic composition C is *pivot* if some of its *s*-terminations are pivots.

The underlying assumption is that we would like the composition U to consist of (basic or composite) atomic activities. The above definitions state the requirements for the *c, p, r* properties in addition to atomicity. Atomicity itself can be described in terms of compensatability and retriability. We first introduce some terminology needed below. For a pivot p_i in C, we define *the suffix of* C *from* p_i, denoted $C_{[i]}$, as the subtree of C rooted at p_i, with p_i replaced by $p_\perp$. Clearly, $C_{[i]}$ is a (sub) process program. Note that $C_{[\perp]}$ is the same as C. For example, for the pivot graph *pg*(C) of Figure 3, $pg(C_{[1]})$ and $pg(C_{[3]})$ are given in Figure 4. For various reasons, a suffix $C_{[i]}$ of C may not be executable (independent of C). In the following, any property stated for $C_{[i]}$ is applicable only when $C_{[i]}$ is executable.

Definition 3.6 (Recoverability): An *f*-termination $C_{[\perp, i]}$ of C is:

- *Backward-recoverable* if $C_{[\perp, i]}$ is compensatable;
- *Forward-recoverable* if $C_{[i]}$ or a (sub) composition $C_{[i]'}$ semantically equivalent to $C_{[i]}$ is retriable; and
- *Recoverable* if it is either backward-recoverable or forward-recoverable.

We are now able to state a sufficient condition for the atomicity of a composition:

Theorem 3.1: *A composition* C *is atomic if each of its f-terminations is recoverable.*

Proof: Suppose an execution of C results in an *f*-termination $C_{[\perp, i]}$. If $C_{[\perp, i]}$ is backward-recoverable, the execution can be compensated to get the null termination; if it is forward-recoverable, then $C_{[i]}$ or an equivalent $C_{[i]'}$ can be retried to get an *s*-termination. Thus an atomic execution of C can be guaranteed.

Figure 4. $C_{[1]}$ (left) and $C_{[3]}$ (right) suffixes for pivot graph from Figure 3

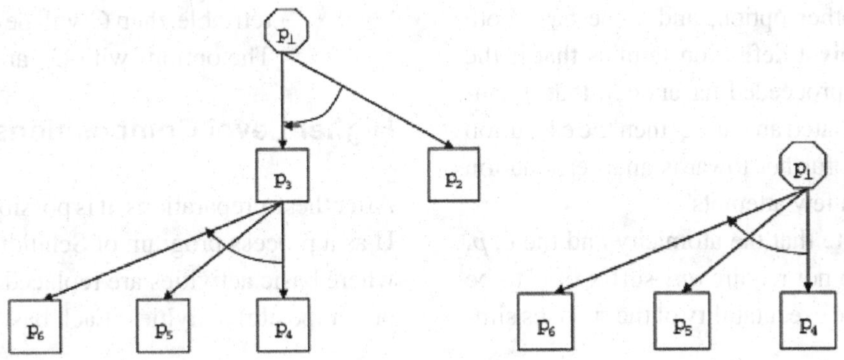

We can now derive the requirements for the *c*, *p*, *r* properties for an arbitrary composition, incorporating those required for atomicity explicitly. By doing so, we get additional flexibility in obtaining these properties in an execution.

Corollary 2: Let C be an arbitrary composition.

1. If C has only one non-root pivot, then
   a. C is compensatable if its *s*-termination can be compensated;
   b. C is retriable if its *s*-termination can be guaranteed (possibly after several attempts); and
   c. C is pivot if it is not compensatable.
2. If C has more than one non-root pivot, then
   a. C is compensatable if all its non-null (*f*- and *s*-) terminations are compensatable;
   b. C is retriable if one of its *s*-terminations can be guaranteed (possibly after several attempts) and each of its *f*-terminations is recoverable; and
   c. C is pivot if some of its *s*-terminations are not compensatable and each of its *f*-terminations is recoverable.

Compensatability is straight-forward. Retriability allows for an *f*-termination to be compensated and the entire composite activity to be restarted, or the suffix following the *f*-termination having the retriable property. It is possible that some *f*-terminations have one option, some others have the other option, and some have both options. The pivot definition implies that if the execution has proceeded far enough that it cannot be compensated any more, then the execution can be carried further towards an *s*-termination perhaps after a few attempts.

We also note that the atomicity and the *c*, *p*, *r* properties do not require *any* suffix of *C* to be executable. The executability of the suffixes simply adds flexibility to the execution of the entire composite activity.

Example 3.5: Let us consider these properties for the composition C in our running Example 3.1 for $User_3$. Recall that the *s*-terminations are C_{12}, C_{134}, C_{135}, and C_{136}.

1. As mentioned, the compensatability notion is straightforward.
2. For retriability, first we need the property that an *s*-termination of C can be guaranteed in a finite number of attempts. Next, C_1 and C_{13} are two *f*-terminations. For C_1, we need the property that C_1 is compensatable, or $C_{[1]}$ is retriable, or both. Similarly, for C_{13} we need the property that C_{13} is compensatable, or $C_{[3]}$ is retriable, or both. As stated earlier, it is possible that different options are available for the two *f*-terminations. For example, (a) C_1 may be compensatable and $C_{[1]}$ may not be retriable (or even executable), and (b) C_{13} may not be compensatable but $C_{[3]}$ is retriable. This would mean that every execution of C resulting in C_1 must be compensated and retried, and if C_{13} is obtained in some attempt then $C_{[3]}$ is executed a few times until an *s*-termination is obtained.
3. Similarly, for a pivot, if C_1 is not compensatable, then $C_{[1]}$ must be retriable. If C_1 is compensatable and $C_{[1]}$ is retriable, then $C_{[1]}$ can be tried. If C_1 is compensatable and $C_{[1]}$ is not retriable, then C_1 will be compensated. The options with C_{13} are similar.

Higher Level Compositions

After these preparations, it is possible to compose U as a process program of Schuldt et al. (2002), where basic activities are replaced by any (basic or composite) activities. Each basic activity will be executed by its transaction program and each composite activity will be executed by its own process program; these programs are independent of the process program U. With the atomicity and the *c*, *p*, *r* properties established for each of the constituent activities, null and non-null terminations can be established for U. Now U can be an end-user level composition or can be used in a higher level composition. In either case, denoting the composition as G, depending on the application semantics, the terminations of U can be mapped into *f*-terminations and *s*-terminations relative to G, and the atomicity and the *c*, *p*, *r* properties can be defined for U relative to G, exactly as they were defined for C relative to U. Thus, atomicity and the *c*, *p*, *r* properties can be carried to any activity in any level of the composition. As will be seen below, this allows for an adequate description of a variety of service issues that has not been possible before.

SERVICE ISSUES

In this section, we consider various issues in connection with Web services that can be made precise in our framework. To this end, we first look at different ways of achieving the atomicity and the *c*, *p*, *r* properties for composite activities, in the context of Web services. Then we consider the "added value" aspect in service composition.

As before, we consider a composition U consisting of (basic or composite) atomic activities. Let U contain a composition C whose execution yields a composite activity *C*. As stated earlier, *f*-termination, *s*-termination, atomicity and the *c*, *p*, *r* properties of C are relative to U. Since we have assumed the process program model of Schuldt et al. (2002) for U, the intended (*c*, *p* or *r*) property of C is known to U.

Sharing of Responsibilities

We now assume that each (basic or composite) activity will be executed by a Web service. (We will simply use the term "service" to also mean "service provider.") Thus, let a service SU execute process program U, and let a service SC execute composition C. We do not exclude the possibility that service SC is using some other (sub) services to execute some of its activities, nor the possibility that SC is SU itself. Also, SC may execute some other compositions of U in addition to C. Our premise is the following:

- Basic activities correspond to atomic transactions, and their atomicity is guaranteed by the database management systems executing them.
- For composite activities, we have distinguished two properties, namely, guaranteed termination and atomicity.
- We expect that a service provider executing a composite activity assures at least its guaranteed termination.
- Atomicity of composite activities is assumed in higher level compositions. Here, atomicity of C is assumed in U.
- If the provider does not assure atomicity of the composite activity, then the service requestor must be responsible for its atomicity. Thus, if SC does not assure atomic execution of C, then SU takes the responsibility.
- Whether backward- or forward-recovery is done to achieve atomicity of C may depend upon the *c*, *p*, *r* properties of C (relative to U).
- We assume that compensation of both *f*-terminations and *s*-terminations of C is the responsibility of SU. In some cases, SC may also do these. We allow for this possibility in the following.

In the following, we look into different ways of SU and SC sharing the responsibilities for achieving the atomicity and the *c*, *p*, *r* properties of C. By *executability* of a composition, we mean the availability of a service provider to execute that composition.

1. SC *guarantees atomicity of C.* In this case, SC returns the null termination or an s-termination. For compensatability, any *s*-termination of C must be compensatable by SC or SU (perhaps by delegating the compensation to some other service provider). For retriability, if SC returns the null termination, then SU must delegate C to another service provider, and keep doing so until an *s*-termination is obtained. For pivot, SU may simply accept the outcome of SC and proceed appropriately.
2. SC *does not guarantee atomicity of C.* In this case, SC may return non-null *f*-terminations. With such an *f*-termination $C_{[\perp,\ i]}$, (i) for obtaining the null termination SU must execute an appropriate compensating activity, and (ii) for getting an *s*-termination, when it is possible and desirable, either $C_{[\perp,\ i]}$ can be compensated and C retried, or $C_{[i]}$ or an equivalent $C_{[i]'}$ retried by SU, perhaps by delegating the task to another service provider.

We illustrate some options with our running example (trip planning from Newfoundland to England) from the previous section.

Example 4.1: Consider an *f*-termination C_1, i.e., only the flight tickets have been purchased, but hotel accommodation has not been reserved.

1. C_1 is compensatable and $C_{[1]}$ is not retriable. The travel agency is willing to treat the flight tickets purchase as compensatable for a customer. In addition, that travel agency might only be allowed to sell the entire package, not a part of it. There may be several travel agencies delegated to this conference each given a quota of reservations. If one does not succeed, another may succeed. Then C_1 may be compensated and C tried with another travel agent (another service provider).
2. C_1 is not compensatable and $C_{[1]}$ is retriable. That particular travel agency might not succeed in hotel reservation (due to a limited quota it has been given), but the conference organizers (another service provider) may step in and guarantee the reservation to the customer directly.

There may exist other sophisticated ways too, for achieving an atomic execution of C. We illustrate two possibilities next.

a. Partial forward-recovery: $C_{[i]}$ may be retried by SC or another provider even if its *s*-termination cannot be guaranteed, but the effective execution can be 'extended' from $C_{[\perp,\ i]}$ to $C_{[\perp,\ j]}$, for a node p_j which is a descendant of p_i in *pg*(C), in case another service provider can take over from $C_{[\perp,\ j]}$ but not from $C_{[\perp,\ i]}$.
   Example 4.2: After C_1, SC may try and guarantee up to C_{13}. The customer may decide to buy a public transportation pass by himself.
b. Partial backward-recovery and retry: It may be possible to do partial compensation in some cases (irrespective of whether full compensation is possible or not). In other words, with a termination $C_{[\perp,i]}$, a compensating activity may yield effectively $C_{[\perp,\ i']}$ for some node $p_{i'}$ which is an ancestor of p_i in the path $pg(C_{[\perp,\ i]})$. Then $C_{[i']}$ may be retried. This will help in the situation where $C_{[i']}$ is retriable but $C_{[i]}$ is not, for example, if a service provider is available for the first but not the second, etc. Partial compensation may also result when a compensating

activity is also a composite activity and its execution results in an *f*-termination.

Example 4.3: Suppose $C_{[1]}$ is retriable, but $C_{[3]}$ is not. Then, after the *f*-termination C_{13}, the hotel reservation part p_3 might be compensated and $C_{[1]}$ tried again.

We can summarize the characteristics as follows.

1. The atomicity and the *c*, *p*, *r* properties are those of the activity C, and not necessarily of a service provider of C. SU is ultimately responsible for achieving these properties.
2. The *c*, *p*, *r* properties of C need not be known to SC. Of course, the retriability requirement of C should be known to SC when it is capable, and is required, to guarantee retriability. Also, SC needs to know which terminations are *s*-terminations relative to U, whenever it is expected to yield an *s*-termination.
3. When SC does not guarantee atomicity, SU has to perform the forward or backward recovery of *f*-terminations, perhaps using other service providers. Thus SC may not know which *f*-terminations are recoverable. Therefore, it can only specify the *f*-terminations it can provide, and it is up to SU to figure out whether they all are recoverable.

There are two issues which are related to the above. The first is that there may exist distinct *views* in a service composition. While a service provider SC needs to have the complete process program C, the "view" of C known to SU may be limited to the pivot graph *pg*(C). In fact, depending on the guarantee provided by SC, some of the pivots may be combined into 'higher level' pivots and a more abstract view may be given to SU. In our running example, if atomicity of $C_{[3]}$ is guaranteed by the travel agent, then the subtree rooted at p_3 may be represented as a single pivot p'_3 to SU.

The second related issue is the role of subservices. Indeed, service provider SC may employ subservices to execute some of the activities of C. As mentioned before, SC is expected, at the very least, to provide (to SU) a guaranteed termination of C. SC may delegate part of this responsibility to its subservices. For example, the execution of activities related to the atomicity of one or more pivots of C can be delegated to a subservice.

Framework for Sharing Responsibilities

In this subsection, we propose a framework for SU and SC to share responsibilities for achieving the transactional properties for C. Our framework is different from the mechanisms proposed in BPEL4WS for the transactional properties. We first describe our framework below and then compare with that of BPEL4WS. We take C as a composite activity consisting of some basic or composite activities.

1. **Fault handlers:** We have assumed so far that guaranteed termination of C is the responsibility of SC. In this section, we allow for SU taking that responsibility, if SC does not provide guaranteed termination. To achieve guaranteed termination, some backward- or forward-recovery may be needed, as per our process program model. We recall the recovery procedure below for the simple case where C has only one pivot. Note that, in this case, guaranteed termination property is the same as atomicity.

   An execution of C can be denoted as $x_1, x_2, \ldots, x_p, y, z_1, z_2, \ldots, z_m$, where each x_i is compensatable, y is pivot, and each z_j is retriable.
   - When some x_i fails, then the backward-recovery, namely, the compensation of the part $x_1 \ldots x_{i-1}$ will be done. The recovery may consist of compensating x_j, for each j between 1 and $i-1$, starting from x_{i-1} in the re-

verse order, or by some other means, for example, compensating some x_j's together. The important point is that the recovery may depend on the extent of the compensatable activities that have been executed before the failure occurred.

- When the pivot y fails, the compensation has to be performed for x_1, x_2, ..., x_l.
- When some z_i fails, then the forward-recovery will be done. This might typically involve retrying z_i and then continuing the execution of the rest of the retriable activities of C.

To coordinate such recovery and obtain a guaranteed termination, we assign a *fault handler* fh_C(C) to C. We also assign a *fault handler for* C *in* U, fh_U(C). If fh_C(C) is unable to get a guaranteed termination of C, then fh_U(C) will try. If that also fails, then it is taken as an unguaranteed termination of U, and fh_U(U) tries for guaranteed termination of U. If that also fails, then the responsibility falls on the fault handlers associated with the parent G of U, and so on.

2. *Recovery handlers.* Next, we consider achieving atomicity from guaranteed termination. This amounts to getting the null termination or an *s*-termination from an *f*-termination. As we argued above, this can be done by SC or SU. For this, we associate two *recovery handlers*: rh_C (C) associated with SC and rh_U(C) associated with SU. On a (guaranteed) *f*-termination of C, rh_C(C) will do backward-recovery consisting of compensating the activities executed thus far to get the null termination, or attempt forward-recovery trying to execute the appropriate suffix. Both backward- and forward-recovery may even be partial, as illustrated in the last subsection. Either SC completes the recovery, or it forwards the resulting *f*-termination to SU and then rh_U(C) will take over the recovery. By the assumption in our model that C is atomic relative to U, if rh_C(C) does not succeed, then rh_U(C) will definitely succeed in getting an atomic execution of C.
3. *Compensating activity.* An *s*-termination of C may have to be compensated due to an *f*-termination of an activity subsequent to C in U. The compensation might be done by SC or SU. Compensation will be triggered by SU. Since compensation can be considered as a backward recovery, we delegate it to rh_C(C), and if it fails then to rh_U(C). The compensation might involve executing an activity C'. Then SU will execute this, perhaps by delegating it to a service provider SC' (which could be the same as SC). Again, SC' may assure atomicity or just guaranteed termination. The fault handlers $fh_{C'}$(C') and fh_U(C') will be responsible for the guaranteed termination. Any non-null (guaranteed) *f*-termination will be handled by $rh_{C'}$ (C') and then, if needed, by rh_U(C').

To summarize:

- Fault handlers fh_C(C) and fh_U(C) are responsible for achieving a guaranteed termination of C;
- Recovery handler rh_C(C) in C tries to achieve the atomicity of C; and
- Recovery handler rh_U(C) in U achieves the atomicity of C in case rh_C (C) does not.

We note that fh_C(C) and fh_U(C) deal with compensation at the "lower" level, that is, compensation of the constituent activities of C, whereas rh_C(C) and rh_U(C) deal with compensation of the "pivotal components" of C.

In the next higher level, assuming G to be the parent composition of U, the fault handlers fh_U(U) and fh_G(U) will be responsible for obtaining a guaranteed termination of U, and the recovery handlers rh_U(U) and rh_G(U) will be responsible for obtaining the atomicity of U relative to G.

We now compare our proposal with the BPEL4WS proposal. The BPEL4WS mechanisms are described below briefly.

- Two kinds of activities, *basic* and *structured*, are defined. A structured activity is a partially ordered set of activities. It corresponds to a composite activity in our model.
- Each activity implicitly defines a *scope*.
- The activities of a structured activity in a scope either all complete or are all compensated. An execution of the structured activity that does not accomplish this, that is, a non-null *f*-termination, in our terminology, is taken as a *fault*.
- Scopes can be nested.
- *Fault handlers* and *compensation handlers* are associated with a scope.
- Fault handlers "catch" the faults, that is, *f*-terminations of the structured activity, and take care of their compensation, either within that scope or by "throwing" them to the enclosing scope.
- Compensation handlers undo already completed activities, that is, *s*-terminations. Compensation handlers are defined within the scope.
- A compensating activity may also fail, in which case the fault handler will compensate this compensating activity. When compensation is not possible within a scope, the fault is thrown to the enclosing scope.

Thus, identifying a scope for C and treating U as its enclosing scope, fault handlers and compensation handlers can be used to define the responsibility for atomicity of C. We can observe the following main differences between our approach and the BPEL4WS proposal.

1. Fault handlers are used in BPEL4WS for achieving atomicity. They are used in our model to get guaranteed termination. We use recovery handlers additionally to achieve atomicity.
2. The fault handler associated with a scope is expected to handle *any* fault: (i) that may occur in the execution of the normal activities in that scope; (ii) that may be thrown from the compensation handler of that scope; or (iii) that may be thrown from the fault handlers of the enclosed (children) scopes. In our model, fault handlers are used only for the first category above.
3. A fault in a scope can be thrown to any ancestral scope, one scope at a time, in BPEL4WS. In our model, unsuccessful recovery (to atomicity) in one level is thrown to its parent level only where the recovery is expected to be completed.

We note that our framework is simple, modular, and applicable to compositions of any number of levels.

Added Value

As observed above, we have defined a composition U as consisting of atomic activities. Consider a composition C in U having several pivots. It may be possible to replace C by a set of (appropriately ordered) subcompositions each consisting of a subset of those pivots, and each such subcomposition executed by a (perhaps different) service. We will call the resulting composition U'. Then, with respect to functionality, U and U' will be equivalent. However, U may have some added value compared to U'. That is, an atomic execution of C by a single service may be more desirable than the atomic executions of the individual subcompositions of C by different services. We explain this in the following.

For simple exposition, we will confine our attention to the case of C decomposed into a sequence $C_1;C_2$.

1. **Reduction in the total cost:** It may be cheaper to execute C by the same service compared to executing C_1 and C_2 by different services. Some examples are:
   a. If printing and binding of a document are done in the same place, the cost of transporting the printed material for binding can be avoided.
   b. With electronic documents, the two activities executed at two different sites may necessitate preparing an XML document from the output of one activity, sending that XML file to the second site, and extracting the information from that document for input to the second activity in that site. This intermediate XML document preparation and transportation can be avoided if both activities are executed at the same site.
   c. A furniture store might be able to deliver the purchased items cheaply through a company contracted for all its deliveries.
   d. It may be that certain common resources are needed to both activities, and so it will be cheaper for a service provider to do them together.
2. **Quality of service:** There may be implicit dependencies between the activities affecting the quality of the end product. For example, in an e-learning environment, an intermediate test on the materials of a learning session might be easier and better prepared, and administered, by the same service provider who designs and supervises that session, than a different service provider.
3. **Atomicity guarantee:** It is possible that an *s*-termination of C_1 cannot be compensated (and C_2 is not retriable), but a service provider (only if executing both C_1 and C_2) can keep C_1 in a prepared-to-commit state until the execution of C_2 reaches the commit stage and then commit both C_1 and C_2 together.

We note that the facility of keeping an execution of an activity in a prepared-to-commit or "pending" state, and later committing or aborting based on the execution of subsequent activities is called *virtual compensatability* in Pires et al. (2002). We do not distinguish virtual compensatability from real compensatability, where a committed activity can be undone by executing a compensating activity, in our model.

4. **Increased security and autonomy:** For service providers, this may amount to, for example, not letting out trade, contract, or service secrets.

Note that in many such examples, a non-null *f*-termination (which necessitates the execution of a suffix of the composition) might imply "loosing" the added value. This, in practice, may prompt some penalty to the service provider who is expected to deliver an *s*-termination. The penalty may be determined depending on the *f*-terminations.

FROM PATH TO GRAPH COMPOSITION MODELS

We will call the process model introduced the *path model*, for the obvious reason that completion of a process execution always follows a path through the underlying process model. As will be shown in this section, we can generalize this model, still retaining the properties we have established so far.

In order to clearly state the generalizations, we briefly review the path model and highlight some of its main characteristics in the following. We refer only to pivot graphs in this section, and use C to refer to *pg*(C) also, and similarly *C* to refer to *pg*(*C*) also.

Path Model

A. Composition

- Composition C is a tree, as described previously. C is part of a higher level composition U.
- In C, the children of each non-leaf node are totally ordered. Exactly one child needs to be executed in an execution of C. The order indicates execution preference among the children. We will call this *children execution logic*, abbreviated as *ce-logic*, at that node. We take the ce-logic at the leaves of C as null.

B. Execution

- A composite activity *C* is a path in C, from the root to a leaf node. C contains all possible composite activities and only those. That is, any path in C from the root to a leaf refers to a composite activity. (Note that, in Definition 3.3, we allowed for some of the paths from the root to some non-leaf nodes also to be *s*-terminations and hence to be composite activities. For simplicity, we ignore this generalization in this section.)
- Partial execution is represented by a path from the root to some node p_i in the tree, denoted $C_{[\perp,\ i]}$. The part that is yet to be executed (for an *s*-termination) is the subcomposition of C from p_i, called the suffix of C from p_i, denoted $C_{[i]}$. The subcomposition will contain the subtree of C rooted at p_i, all nodes in the subtree will have the same ce-logic as in C, and the node label of p_i will be replaced by $\perp$.

C. Transactional Properties

- First, a guaranteed termination of C is desired. Then, the entire composition C is intended to be atomic in U. In addition, C is compensatable, pivot or retriable relative to U.
- For atomicity, every *f*-termination of C should be forward- or backward-recoverable.
- Backward-recovery of an *f*-termination $C_{[\perp,\ i]}$ amounts to rolling back the entire execution to a null execution. Partial backward-recovery refers to rolling back some pivots in $C_{[\perp,\ i]}$, in reverse order.
- All roll backs are logical. To roll back from p_i to p_j, a *compensating* subcomposition, denoted $C^{-1}_{[j,\ i]}$, rooted at p_i is to be executed. This will facilitate different compensation options. (Again, the compensation may be delegated to some provider.) After the compensating subcomposition has been executed successfully, normal processing can continue with $C_{[j]}$. The pivots in the compensating part need not correspond to those in the compensated part.
- For forward-recovery from p_i, the suffix $C_{[i]}$, or an equivalent $C_{[i]'}$, is to be executed from p_i.
- Whether forward- and/or backward-recovery is possible depends on the *c*, *p*, *r* properties of C relative to U.

D. Service Issues

- SC and SU are service providers for C and U, respectively.
- Two fault handlers $fh_C(C)$ and $fh_U(C)$ are associated with SC and SU respectively, for obtaining a guaranteed termination of C. On an unguaranteed termination of C, first, $fh_C(C)$ tries for guaranteed termination of C, and if it fails, then $fh_U(C)$ tries. If that also fails, it is taken as an unguaranteed termination of U.
- Two recovery handlers $rh_C(C)$ and $rh_U(C)$ are associated with SC and SU respectively, for obtaining an atomic execution of C relative to U. For atomicity, as stated

earlier, every (guaranteed) *f*-termination of C should be forward- or backward-recoverable. Such recovery is first attempted by rh_C(C), and if that is not successful, then by rh_U(C).

- Compensation of an *s*-termination is also delegated to rh_C(C) first, and to rh_U(C) later.

Tree Model

First, we present an extension, called the *tree model*, that allows for getting a tree as a pivot graph of a composite activity. All the features of the path model are applicable here also. We describe the additional features in the following.

A. Composition

- Here also, a composition C is a tree and it is a part of a higher level composition U.
- Again, a ce-logic is associated with each node, and the ce-logic is null for all leaves of C. However, the ce-logic at non-leaf nodes may be sophisticated:
- More than one child may be required to be executed.
- In general, several sets of children may be specified with the requirement that one of those sets be executed.
- These sets may be prioritized in an arbitrary way.
- Execution of children within a set may also be prioritized in an arbitrary way.

Example 5.1: We consider an elaborate electronic shopping example, Shopping for Bedroom set, denoted SB. We use this as a running example in this subsection. It consists of the purchase followed by the delivery of a set of furniture from among the following: bed, dresser (D), night table (N), and armoire (A). For bed, a bed frame and a mattress (M) need to be purchased. Two types of bed frames are available, called F1 and F2. For F1, a box spring (B) is also needed.

Denoting the purchase of item I as PI, the preferred purchase options are described by the following ce-logic: For the bed, the preference order is {PF1,PB,PM}, {PF2,PM}; for the bedroom set, any bed and dresser and night table, or any bed and armoire, in that order, that is, ({PF1,PB,PM},{PF2,PM}), and ({PD,PN},PA).

Each of the purchased items has to be shipped. Some items need to be packed for shipping whereas some others are already in a packed form. We denote the packaging and delivery of an item I as XI and DI, respectively. When there are several options for delivery, they are denoted as DI1,

Figure 5. Activities involved in SB shopping

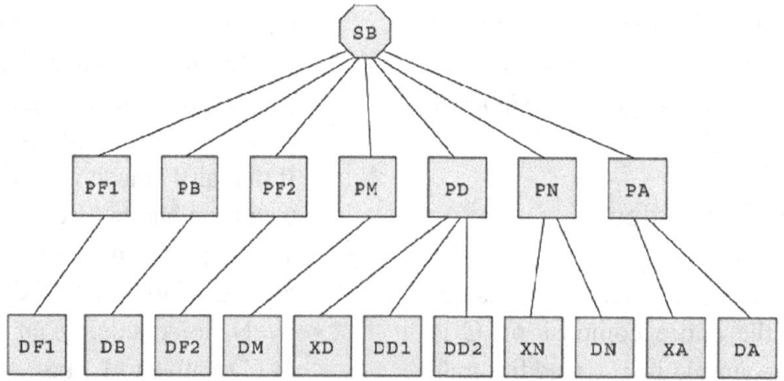

DI2, etc. For shipping, we use a simple ce-logic of packaging where needed and choosing any delivery option. The activities involved in SB are shown in Figure 5.

B. Execution

- A composite activity *C* is a subtree of C such that
- It includes the root, some leaves of C, and all nodes and edges in the paths from the root to those leaves in C, and
- The children of each non-leaf node of the subtree satisfy the ce-logic specified in C for that node. Then, C is the union of trees corresponding to the composite activities, and any composite activity *C* is a subtree of C. However, not every subtree of C would correspond to a composite activity.
- A partial execution *E* of C will be represented by a subtree of C, called *execution-tree*, consisting of all the nodes of C that have been executed and edges between them. If *L* is the set of leaves in this subtree, then the execution is denoted as $C_{[\perp, L]}$. (We use the following notation. For a given *C*, $C_{[\perp, Lk]}$ will denote the subtree of *C* from node p_k to the set of descendants L_k of p_k in *C*. For a set of nodes *X*, $C_{[X, Y]}$ will refer to the forest which is the union of $C_{[k, Lk]}$ for p_k in *X* and *Y* is the union of L_k for p_k in *X*.)
- In general, the ce-logic would have been completely satisfied for some of the nodes in *E*. That is, a set of children corresponding to an execution choice of the ce-logic at their nodes would have been executed (successfully). These nodes are called *finished* nodes. Others are called *unfinished* nodes. For some unfinished nodes, *one* execution choice of the ce-logic would have been satisfied partially; we call them *partially unfinished* nodes. Other unfinished nodes are *totally unfinished* ones. 'Finishing' is with respect to the current execution *E*. We also note that since the ce-logic is null for the leaves of C, all these nodes, if any, in the execution-tree are trivially finished nodes.
- We define the *adjusted ce-logic* for (the nodes in) *E* as follows:
- Null for the finished nodes;
- Same as in C for totally unfinished nodes; and
- For each partially unfinished node, the part of the ce-logic of the set of yet-to-be-executed children in the execution choice chosen for that node in *E*.
- For p_i in *E*, the suffix of C from p_i, denoted again as $C_{[i]}$, is defined as the subcomposition that contains the subtree of C with (i) root p_i, (ii) all the children of p_i which have not been executed, and the subtrees rooted at them, and (iii) all nodes in the subtree having the ce-logic adjusted for *E*.
- The suffix of the execution *E* is the set of suffixes $C_{[i]}$ for each unfinished node p_i in *E*.

Example 5.2: Figure 6(a) shows a partial execution of the composition in Example 5.1. Here, the root node, PN, XN, DN and XD are finished nodes, PF2 and PM are totally unfinished nodes, and PD is a partially unfinished node. Figure 6(b) shows another partial execution where all nodes except XD are unfinished. PF2 and PM are totally unfinished. The others are partially unfinished. The adjusted ce-logics at SB and PD are {PN} and one of DD1 and DD2, respectively. The adjusted ce-logics at all other nodes are the same as the original ones. Figure 7 shows the suffixes of the execution in Figure 6(b).

Figure 6. Partial executions

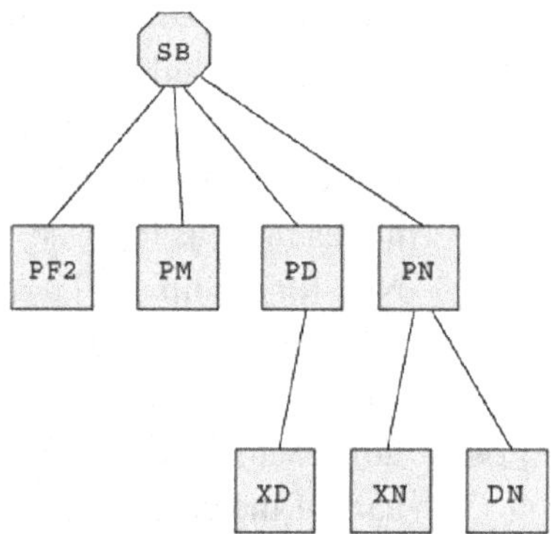

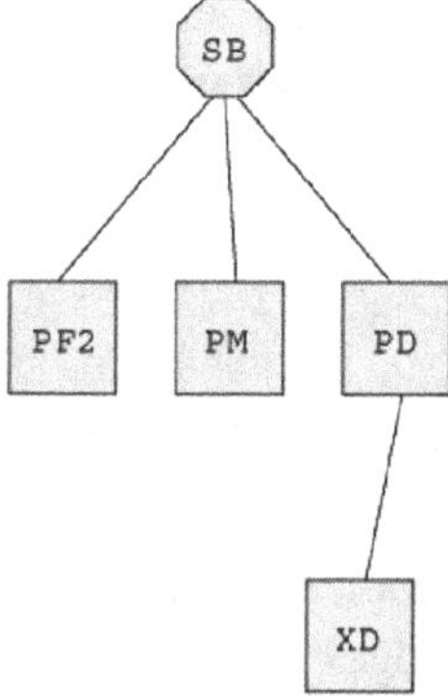

C. Transactional Properties

- Forward-recovery of an *f*-termination *E* will consist of execution of the suffix of *E*. Again, either SU or some other provider(s) may execute the subcompositions. There could be several subcompositions, each being a tree, and different providers might be delegated for execution of different subcompositions. The subcompositions used in a forward-recovery may even be different from, but equivalent to, those in the original composition.
- Partial backward-recovery of *E* will consist of (logically) rolling back some of the pivots of the execution-tree. Let *L'* denote the set of leaves of the tree obtained after a partial backward-recovery. Clearly, *L'* will contain nodes in *L* or their ancestors. Then the *recovered part* can be expressed as $C^{-1}_{[L', L]}$, meaning that the part between *L'* and *L* has been rolled back. The compensating subcomposition that does this roll back will be denoted as $C^{-1}_{[L', L]}$. Full backward-recovery should roll back all the pivots in the execution-tree and yield the null execution. Thus the recovered part will be $C^{-1}_{[\perp, L]}$.
- Backward-recovery can also be done as follows. For a given *f*-termination *E*, the part intended to be recovered, in terms of the set *L'* can be determined first. Again, the nodes in *L'* are the ancestors of those in *L*. (We use the convention that a node is an ancestor of itself.) Then the recovery $C^{-1}_{[L', L]}$ can be carried out by means of executing compensating subcompositions $C^{-1}_{[j, Lj]}$ at nodes p_j in *L'*. Here, L_j is the subset of *L* which are descendants of p_j. This will roll back the descendants of p_j in *E*. (Note that the execution of the compensating subcomposition is also according to the tree model.)

Example 5.3: In Example 5.1, starting with the partial execution in Figure 6(a), suppose that none of the delivery options {DD1, DD2} are feasible. Then, forward recovery would consist of finding some other option for delivering dresser D. A backward recovery of *E* would essentially involve compensating all the activities in the subtrees of PD and PN. Then, the next choice in the ce-logic of the root node (purchasing F2, M, and A) can be tried. If this is successful, we will obtain the tree shown in Figure 8.

Note that a compensating subtree, consisting of edges shown in thick lines, has been added to the root node. Compensating the delivery DN is

Figure 7. Suffixes of the execution in Figure 6(b)

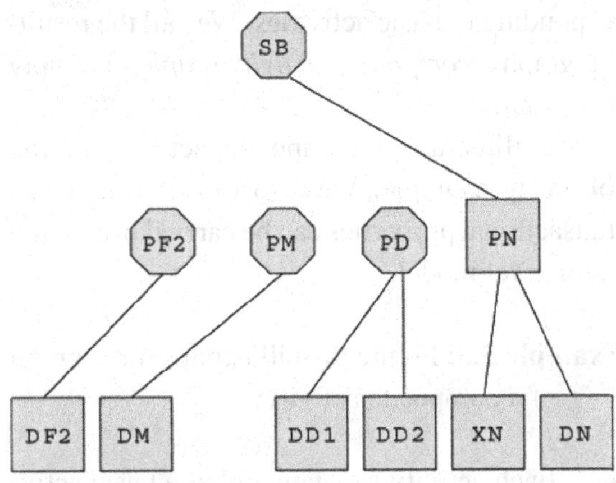

implemented by "return" RN, and XD and XN are compensated by the null activities, meaning that the packagings are untouched. The purchases PD and PN are compensated by -PD and -PN.

Example 5.4: As another example, consider the electronic shopping scenario from Figure 1 once more, where we assume that a tree root called *buying process* has been added. In the resulting tree, the non-leaf nodes include *price comparison*, *purchase*, *payment* and *delivery*, and for each we may assume that more than one child need to be executed. For example, the buyer might decide to buy an expensive piece, and the money needed for that may have to come from several sources (e.g., a bank account, an investment fund, stocks, etc.) in an order specified by the buyer. Thus, the ce-logic for the payment activity may consist of (a) collecting the money from various sources and (b) making the payment. Alternatively, it might consist of getting a loan first and then have the seller agree to a number of, say, monthly payments.

D. Service Issues

- Fault handlers fh_C(C) and fh_U(C), and recovery handlers rh_C(C) and rh_U(C) are assigned, and have the same role, as in the path model. The fault handlers will be responsible for obtaining a guaranteed termination of an *f*-termination (exactly as in the path model), and the recovery handlers will do the forward- and backward-recoveries, and also compensation of *s*-terminations.

Multi-Level Model

So far, we have dealt with compositions at a single level. We described a composition C in terms of a graph *pg*(C) containing the pivots of C. (Again, each node in *pg*(C) represents the corresponding (real or dummy) pivot in C together with the compensatable activities preceding that pivot in C. We continue keeping this distinction implicit.) An execution of C yields a composite activity *C* which is also described by means of a pivot graph *pg*(*C*). This has the pivots of C which have been executed. It is a path in the path model, and a tree in the tree model: we call this a *composite activity sequence* (*c-seq* in short), and *composite activity tree* (*c-tree* in short), respectively, in the following. We note that a c-seq is a c-tree also.

Figure 8. SB shopping execution along alternate routes

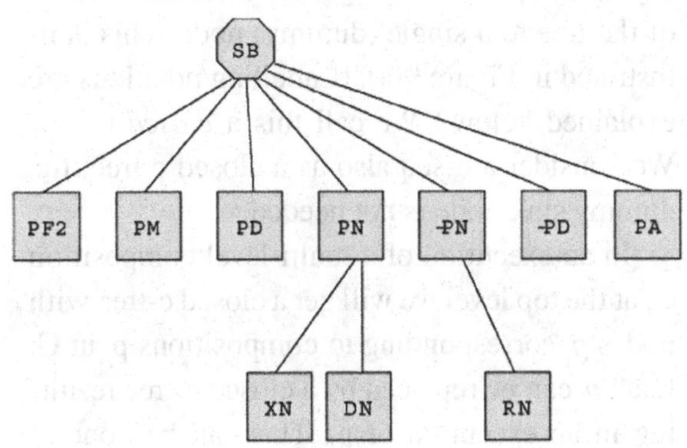

So far, for ease of exposition, a node in $pg(C)$ was represented the same way as in $pg(\mathrm{C})$. To describe the multi-level model unambiguously, in the following, we will use different representations in these graphs. Nodes in $pg(C)$ will be represented as p_1, p_2, p_3, etc. as before. However, nodes in $pg(\mathrm{C})$ will be represented as p_1, p_2, p_3 etc. As we have mentioned, each node p_i in the $pg(C)$ is a basic or composite activity. For a basic activity, p_i refers to p_i itself. However, for a composite activity, p_i can be taken as the composition whose execution yields p_i.

Now, our multi-level model is the following:

A. Composition

- A composition C is a tree as in the tree model where activities p_i are replaced by compositions p_i.
- p_i is the same as p_i for a basic activity.
- For a composite activity, p_i is a composition C_i which is, again, a tree in the tree model.

We now describe a composite activity. As observed in the previous section, a composition in the tree model yields a composite activity which is a tree, that is, a c-tree. Thus, a node p_i in C that represents a composition C_i yields a tree. In C, after p_i, some other node(s) may have to be executed. They may also yield trees. To be able to put these trees together, we use the following notation.

A c-tree is converted to a one source one sink acyclic graph, by adding edges from the leaves of the tree to a single (dummy) node. This is illustrated in Figure 9(a). (Labelling notations are explained below.) We call this a *closed* c-tree. We consider a c-seq also as a closed c-tree; the dummy sink node is not needed.

In an execution of a multi-level composition C, at the top level we will get a closed c-tree with nodes p_i corresponding to compositions p_i in C. Each p_i can be replaced by a closed c-tree resulting in an execution of p_i. This can be done at every level, until all c-trees are single nodes corresponding to basic activities. We call the resulting graph a *component activity graph*, or simply a *c-graph*.

We illustrate a composite activity in the following example. We also illustrate how the transactional properties can be carried over to the multi-level model.

Example 5.5: Figure 9(b) illustrates the c-graph of a composite activity:

- Each activity is, again, either a basic activity or a composite activity. An activity is represented, as before, as *p*, with appropriate subscript.
- We use C_α, where α is a string, to denote a (closed) c-tree of activities, $p_{\alpha.1}$, $p_{\alpha.2}$, etc. In $p_{\alpha.i}$, α is a *c-tree id*, and *i* is the *id* of a node in that c-tree. At the outermost level, we represent the composite activity as a c-tree C_ϕ or simply *C*, where ϕ is the empty string. Therefore, the activities will be $p_{\Phi.1}$, $p_{\Phi.2}$, etc., or simply, p_1, p_2, etc.
- A composite activity $p_{\alpha.i}$ will consist of a set of one or more closed c-trees, denoted $C_{\alpha.i.1}$, $C_{\alpha.i.2}$, etc. In the following, we consider c-seq's in detail, for simplicity. Treatment of c-trees is similar.
- A particular c-seq $C_{\alpha.i.q}$ will have activities $p_{\alpha.i.q.1}$, $p_{\alpha.i.q.2}$, etc. If we denote $\alpha.i.q$ as α', then the c-seq is $C_{\alpha'}$, and the activities in the sequence are $p_{\alpha'.1}$, $p_{\alpha'.2}$, etc.

In Figure 9(b), we have the following.

- The nodes of C_ϕ are $p_{\Phi.\perp}$, $p_{\Phi.1}$, $p_{\Phi.2}$ and $p_{\Phi.3.}$
- $p_{\phi.2}$ consists of two c-seq's, $C_{\phi.2.1}$ and $C_{\phi.2.3}$, and a closed c-tree $C_{\phi.2.2}$ shown in Figure 9(a).
- $C_{\phi.2.1}$ consists of activities $p_{\phi.2.1.1}$ and $p_{\phi.2.1.2}$.
- $p_{\phi.2.1.2}$ consists of two c-seq's $C_{\phi.2.1.2.1}$ and $C_{\phi.2.1.2.2}$.

Figure 9. The multi-level model

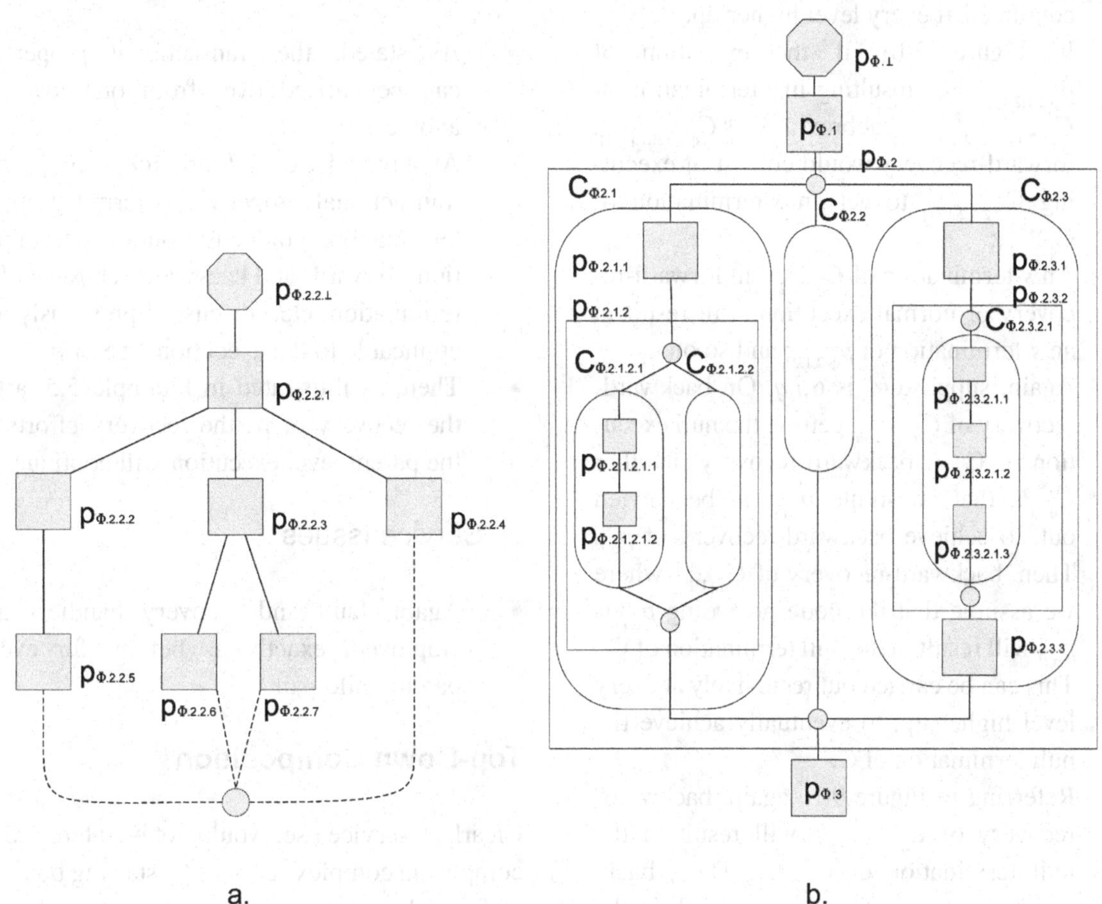

- An example where a node consists of just one c-seq is $p_{\phi.2.3.2}$.
- The composition for a c-seq C_α will be denoted C_α. The composition will be described as in the path model, the first, the process model. We use the same notation as in the previous section to denote an execution of a c-seq and its suffix composition. We assume, as before, that each c-seq starts with a dummy root pivot. An execution of the c-seq $C_{\alpha'}$ from the root to some pivot $p_{\alpha.m}$ will be denoted as $C_{\alpha.[\perp,m]}$, and its suffix will be the composition $C_{\alpha.[m]}$.
- We specify *multi-level* atomicity of C: Each activity *p*, at any level, must be executed atomically, and each c-seq, again at any level, must be executed atomically. For atomicity of $C_{\alpha'}$, any *f*-termination $C_{\alpha'.[\perp,m]}$ must be either forward-recoverable or backward-recoverable. For forward-recoverability, $C_{\alpha'.[m]}$ must be executed, to achieve an *s*-termination of $C_{\alpha'}$. For backward-recoverability, $C^{-1}_{\alpha'.[\perp,m]}$ is to be executed, at $p_{\alpha'.m'}$, to achieve the null termination of $C_{\alpha'}$. Partial forward- and backward-recovery executions can also be specified as stated previously.
- Suppose α' is *α.i.q*. Then, on *s*-termination of $C_{\alpha'.i.q'}$, and on *s*-terminations of other $C_{\alpha'.i.r}$'s that constitute $p_{\alpha.i'}$, we get an *s*-termination of $p_{\alpha.i}$. Then, further forward-recovery would consist of execution of $C_{\alpha.[i]}$,

to get an *s*-termination of C_α. This has to be continued at every level higher up.

- In Figure 9(b), if the execution of $p_{\phi.2.1.2.1.2}$. fails resulting in *f*-termination of $C_{[\phi.2.1.2.1.\perp,\phi.2.1.2.1.1]}$, abbreviated as $C_{\phi.2.1.2.1.[\perp,1]}$, forward-recovery would consist of executing $C_{\phi.2.1.2.1.[1]}$ to get an *s*-termination of $C_{\phi.2.1.2.1}$;
- An *s*-termination of $C_{\phi.2.1.2.2}$, in forward-recovery or normal execution, will result in an *s*-termination of $p_{\phi.2.1.2}$; and so on.
- Again, suppose α' is α.*i*.*q*. On backward-recovery of $C_{\alpha.i.q.[\perp,m]}$ getting the null execution of $C_{\alpha'i.q}$, backward-recovery of other $C_{\alpha.i.r}$'s that constitute $p_{\alpha.i}$ can be carried out, to achieve backward-recovery of $p_{\alpha.i}$. Then, backward-recovery of $C_{\alpha.[\perp,i']}$, where we assume that the node preceding $p_{\alpha.i}$ is $p_{\alpha.i'}$, will result in the null termination of C_α. This can be carried out recursively at every level higher up, to eventually achieve the null termination of C.
- Referring to Figure 9(b) again, backward-recovery of $C_{\phi.2.1.2.1.[\perp,1]}$ will result in the null termination of $C_{\phi.2.1.2.1}$. Then, backward-recovery of $C_{\phi.2.1.2.2}$ will result in the null termination of $p_{\phi.2.1.2}$, and so on.

B. Execution

- A composite activity *C* of a multi-level composition C is a c-graph such that at the outermost level, it is a closed c-tree, with nodes p_i corresponding to compositions p_i in C, and each composite activity p_i is replaced by a closed c-tree resulting in an execution of p_i, and this process carried out until all activities are basic.
- Partial execution is considered as in the tree model, level by level, in nested fashion (as illustrated in the Example 5.5).

C. Transactional Properties

- As stated, the transactional properties can be carried over from one level to another.
- At any individual level, for each p_i, the transactional properties (*s*-termination, *f*-termination, compensation of *s*-termination, forward- and backward-recovery of *f*-termination, etc.) discussed previously are applicable to the execution-tree of p_i.
- Then, as illustrated in Example 5.5, after the recovery of p_i, the recovery efforts at the parent level execution will continue.

D. Service Issues

- Again, fault and recovery handlers are employed, exactly as before, for every parent-child pair.

Top-Down Composition

Clearly, a service user would not be interested in composing complex services by starting bottom-up from elementary ones, as we have done so far. Instead, a user would be interested in obtaining a high-level description of each service he or she may need, and then start composing at that level. We imagine that, typically, graphical interfaces will be used to that end, for example an interface where the individual service can be described as a *Petri net* (Reisig, 1985). What would then be needed is a way to map each task represented by an activity or a process in a Petri net to a service appropriately, taking availability, user preferences, timing, costs, etc. into account.

In this section, we show that our model facilitates top-down compositions also. Recall that in the tree model we have:

- A composition C is a tree;

- At each node p_i, several children may need to be executed, and the execution preferences are described by ce-logic at p_i; and
- After the execution of a set of children satisfying the ce-logic, execution continues with the children of those children.

We now define *descendent execution logic*, abbreviated as *de-logic*, at p_i, as the union of the ce-logic of p_i and all its descendants. Note that the de-logic describes not just the individual children nodes but also (transitively) their subtrees which need to be executed. The execution preferences in the ce-logics at various nodes become collectively the execution preferences in the de-logic.

Then, the execution preferences at each node can be described by the more general de-logic, instead of ce-logic. In fact, we can carry this idea further. If we take a choice of children in the ce-logic at p_i, for each child in that choice, select a choice in the ce-logic of that child, and continue this recursively, we will get a c-graph that reflects the choices made at every level. Different combinations will give rise to different c-graphs. Then, execution preferences at p_i can be stated, in a higher level, in terms of such c-graphs.

Though we defined de-logic from ce-logic, we can also start with de-logic or even (perhaps an abstract description of) the desired c-graphs, and then derive the ce-logic at various nodes. This would amount to a top-down approach.

DISCUSSION

In this paper, we have extended the model for Web service composition originally proposed by Schuldt et al. (2002) to a multi-level model that enables a description of desirable transactional properties at each level of the composition. It has been widely accepted that the traditional ACID properties need to be relaxed for transactions in the Web service environment. A few relaxations have appeared in the literature. We discuss some of them in the following and show that the relaxations can be explained neatly in our model.

1. The requirement of atomicity of a composition (with multiple pivots) has been stated in the literature, for example, by Mikalsen et al. (2002), Pires et al. (2002), or Casati et al. (2000).
   a. Mikalsen et al. (2002) introduce *transactional attitudes* "to explicitly describe the otherwise implicit transactional semantic, capabilities, and requirements of individual applications". They consider *Client Transactional Attitudes* (CTAs) and *Provider Transactional Attitudes* (PTAs). One CTA, called *flexible atom* (FA), is given. Here, "a set of client actions (provider transactions) are grouped into an atomic group that can have one out of a set of defined group outcomes; that is to say, some actions are declared *critical* to the success of the transaction, whereas others are part of the transaction though not pivotal to its success. The client specifies the acceptable outcomes as an *outcome condition*, described in terms of the success or failure of the individual actions, and when ready (i.e., after executing the forward operations of these actions), requests the completion of the flexible atom according to that condition". We note that this CTA resembles the specification in our model, by SU to SC, of the *s*-terminations of **C** relative to **U** and the requirement of atomicity. We can specify, in addition, the retriability requirement also as a CTA. Three PTAs, *pending-commit, group-pending-commit,* and *commit-compensate*, are described by Mikalsen et al. (2002). The first two

relate to providing the prepared-to-commit states for single activity or a group of activities, resp., and the last describes the facility for compensation after the commitment of an activity. Compensatability of *f*-terminations and *s*-terminations, atomicity and retriability are some possible additional PTAs. In fact, even the guaranteed termination property is a PTA.

b. The *s*-termination set concept appears in Pires et al. (2002) as follows. Here also a composite task consists of several tasks each of which could be atomic or composite. Different successful executions of a composite task are specified in terms of successful executions of a set of (component) *mandatory* tasks and a set of *desirable* tasks.

c. In Casati et al. (2000), a set of activities that need to be executed atomically is grouped into a *transactional region*.

2. The OASIS Business Transaction Protocol (BTP) (OASIS, n.d.) allows a type of composite activity called *cohesion*. It contains a set of activities that can be performed autonomously by different service providers. An *s*-termination of the composite activity is determined, eventually, by the outcomes of the individual activities. As a result, some of the activities done successfully may have to be undone. It is also possible that some participants "leave", that is, some activities are eliminated from the cohesion. Thus the composition is very dynamic. A coordinated termination, involving commit of certain activities and abort of some activities, is facilitated.

The multi-activity node in our model can depict cohesion effectively. Potential concurrent execution can be described by weak order among the activities. The relaxed atomicity of the cohesion can be translated to *s*-terminations and the atomicity of the multi-activity composite node.

3. We conclude our discussion by mentioning the connection of our model to Sun's *Web Services Transaction Management* (WS-TXM) (Silicon.com, n.d.). WS-TXM talks about models and properties for Web Services transactions, stating that "Web Services-based transactions differ from traditional transactions in that they execute over long periods, they require commitments to the transaction to be "negotiated" at runtime, and isolation levels have to be relaxed."

WS-TXM defines three types of transactions: Atomic Transaction (AT), Long Running Action (LRA) and Business Process (BP) transaction. Atomicity is strived for in each type, very strictly in ATs by way of 2PC protocols, somewhat loosely with LRAs allowing use of compensation, and even more liberally with BPs by being flexible with the anticipated outcome of an execution. In LRAs and BPS, the term "compensation" is used to denote the more general backward and/or forward recovery that may include retrys and substitution of new transactions to achieve the business goals.

WS-TXM also emphasizes that "In the world of Web Services transactions, it is less likely that automatic recovery will be possible in as many cases as in a more tightly controlled environment, and more likely that human intervention will need to play a bigger part in restoring the system to normalcy." Thus, failures and hence partial, non-atomic, executions of transactions are anticipated. They are designated as *heuristic* (*rollback, commit, mixed* and *hazard*) outcomes in ATs. These are intended to be resolved "manually" by user or system administrator according to the application environment. Similarly, non-atomic executions of LRAs and BPs are meant to be handled non-automatically. Failures in execution of compensating actions are also considered.

Our model accommodates the features of WS-TXM. We elaborate some of them in the following.

1. Determining whether a termination of an activity is an s-termination or an f-termination is left to the application semantics, in terms of st-predicates and the acceptability criteria for subtrees of the composition (as execution-trees) for composite activities.
2. The ce-predicates and the recovery procedures allow for specifying, in a generalized way, compensating transactions and substitution of new transactions accomplishing the business goals.
3. The recovery procedures take into account non-atomic executions of transactions, using failure and recovery handlers.

Our model can deal with all the issues dealt with in WS-TXM, yet in a much more structured way. The multi-level approach delineates the atomicity and other transactional issues arising in each level and identifies explicitly the issues (to be) resolved in that level and those passed on to be resolved in higher levels. Our model also, as WS-TXM, supports heterogeneity and interoperability requirements of Web Service executions.

As illustrated above, our model accommodates and unifies many proposals previously made in the literature. Furthermore, our model can explain the context, for example, the purpose of compensation across levels, for the transactional activities. We also note that whereas compensatability and compensation have been considered at some length in the literature, the concept of retriability has not been discussed, at least explicitly. In our model, both compensatability and retriability are complementary towards achieving the atomicity of a composite activity. A related issue, namely, suffix executability has also not been discussed in the literature.

We conclude by mentioning that a number of issues are related to what has been discussed above, and that these issues can now be made precise in the framework of our model: (1) Atomicity of an activity will serve as a non-functional trait of a service provider. Atomicity and suffix executability may be taken into account while dealing with compatability and substitutability of services (De Antonellis et al., 2003). (2) In the design of business processes, responsibilities for the execution of business activities (roles) must be specified (Papazoglou & Yang, 2002). Responsibility for atomicity or guaranteed termination will also be a part of the specification. (3) It is possible that a service provider offers different levels of atomicity to different customers, and at different costs. (4) As stated earlier, SU does not need to know **C**, but does need *pg*(**C**) (especially when SU takes responsibility for executing suffixes of *f*-terminations). Here, *pg*(**C**) can be considered as containing information about *what* are done in **C**, without exposing *how* they are done. Thus, *pg*(**C**) represents a *glass box* view of **C**, according to the distinction suggested by (Battle, 2003).

Future work along the lines established in this paper may stem from the fact that we have here decided to associate compensatability and retriability with composite activities instead of just individual transactions; what new consequences can be derived from this? Guaranteed termination is implied by our model, but what about termination within predefined bounds (e.g., meeting a deadline, not exceeding a given budget, etc.)? Another question is whether it is possible to quantify the “added value” that is supposed to be brought along by a service composition.

Finally, we need to mention that a model like ours, which is based on conceptual considerations rather than a programming paradigm or a practical tool for service, deserves, if not requires, an evaluation. This is especially due to the fact that our model accommodates a number of other models and transactional proposals; as a consequence, we are currently performing an evaluation among a group of selected practitioners who have agreed to apply the model in their daily work. The results of this study will be reported in a future paper.

The model presented in this paper constitutes a big leap from the process model presented in Schuldt et al. (2002) in the sense that it enables studying transactional properties across multiple levels of a hierarchy in contrast to just within one level in Schuldt et al. (2002). This model for Web services has been extended to activities in e-contracts in Vidyasankar et al. (2007). We believe that the Web services composition model will serve as a stepping stone for studying transactional properties in other complex application environments also.

ACKNOWLEDGMENT

A preliminary version of this paper appeared in *Proceedings of the 3rd IEEE International Conference on Web Services (ICWS) 2004,* San Diego, USA (pp. 462-469). The work of K. Vidyasankar was partially done while visiting the University of Muenster in 2006 and is supported in part by the Natural Sciences and Engineering Research Council of Canada Discovery Grant 3182.

REFERENCES

Abiteboul, S., Vianu, V., Fordham, B. S., & Yesha, Y. (2000). Relational Transducers for Electronic Commerce. *Journal of Computer and System Sciences, 61,* 236–269. doi:10.1006/jcss.2000.1708

Alonso, G., Casati, F., Kuno, H., & Machiraju, V. (2004). *Web Services - Concepts, Architectures and Applications.* Berlin, Germany: Springer-Verlag.

Alonso, G., Vingralek, R., Agrawal, D., Breitbart, Y., El Abbadi, A., Schek, H.-J., & Weikum, G. (1994). Unifying Concurrency Control and Recovery of Transactions. *Information Systems, 19,* 101–115. doi:10.1016/0306-4379(94)90029-9

Battle, S. (2003). *Boxes: black, white, grey and glass box view of web-services* (Tech. Rep. No. HPL-2003-30). Bristol, UK: HP Laboratories Bristol.

Bultan, T., Fu, X., Hull, R., & Su, J. (2003). Conversation Specification: A New Approach to Design and Analysis of E-Service Composition. In *Proceedings of the International World Wide Web Conference 2003 (WWW2003)* (pp. 403-410).

Casati, F., & Dayal, U. (Eds.). (2002). Special Issue on Web Services. *IEEE Bulletin of the Technical Committee on Data Engineering, 25*(4).

Casati, F., Ilnicki, S., Jin, L., Krishnamoorthy, V., & Shan, M.-C. (2000). Adaptive and Dynamic Service Composition in eFlow, HP Labs Report HPL-2000-39.

Christophides, V., Hull, R., Karvounarakis, G., Kumar, A., Tong, G., & Xiong, M. (2001). Beyond Discrete E-Services: Composing Session-Oriented Services in Telecommunications. In *Proceedings of the 2nd International Workshop on Technologies for E-Services (TES) 2001* (LNCS 2193, pp. 58-73).

Colombo, E., Francalanci, C., & Pernici, B. (2002). Modeling Coordination and Control in Cross-Organizational Workflows. In *Proceedings of the CoopIS-DOA-ODBASE 2002 Conference* (LNCS 2519, pp. 91-106).

De Antonellis, V., Melchiori, M., Pernici, B., & Plebani, P. (2003). A Methodology for e-Service Substitutability in a Virtual District Environment. In *Advanced Information Systems Engineering: Proceedings of CAiSE '03,* Klagenfurt, Austria (LNCS 2681, pp. 552-567).

Fauvet, M.-C., Dumas, M., Benatallah, B., & Paik, H.-Y. (2001). Peer-to-Peer Traced Execution of Composite Services. In *Proceedings of the 2nd International Workshop on Technologies for E-Services (TES) 2001* (LNCS 2193, pp. 103-117).

Fu, X., Bultan, T., & Su, J. (2002). Formal Verification of e-Services and Workflows. In *Proceedings of the International Workshop on Web Services, E-Business, and the Semantic Web (WES) 2002* (LNCS 2512, pp. 188-202).

Huhns, M. N., & Singh, M. P. (2005). Service-Oriented Computing: Key Concepts and Principles. *IEEE Internet Computing*, *9*(1), 75–81. doi:10.1109/MIC.2005.21

Hull, R., Benedikt, M., Christophides, V., & Su, J. (2003). E-Services: A Look Behind the Curtain. In *Proceedings of the 22nd ACM Symposium on Principles of Database Systems (PODS) 2003*, San Diego, CA.

IBM. (2007). *Business Process Execution Language for Web Services version 1.1.* Retrieved from http://www-106.ibm.com/developerworks/library/ws-bpel/

Mecella, M., Presicce, F. P., & Pernici, B. (2002). Modeling E-Service Orchestration through Petri Nets. In *Proceedings of the 3rd International Workshop on Technologies for E-Services (TES) 2002* (LNCS 2444, pp. 38-47).

Mikalsen, T., Tai, S., & Rouvellou, I. (2002). *Transactional Attitudes: Reliable Composition of Autonomous Web Services.* Paper presented at the Workshop on Dependable Middleware-based Systems (WDMS '02), Washington, DC.

Newcomer, E. (2002). *Understanding Web Services: XML, WSDL, SOAP, and UDDI.* Harlow, MA: Addison-Wesley.

OASIS. (n.d.). *OASIS Business Transaction Protocol.* Retrieved from http://www.oasis-open.org/committees/business-transactions/documents/primer/Primerhtml/

Papazoglou, P., & Yang, J. (2002). Design Methodology for Web Services and Business Processes. In *Proceedings of the 3rd International Workshop on Technologies for E-Services (TES) 2002* (LNCS 2444, pp. 54-64).

Pires, P. F., Benevides, M. R. F., & Mattoso, M. (2002). Building Reliable Web Services Compositions. In *Proceedings of the Workshop on the Web, Web-Services, and Database Systems 2002* (LNCS 2593, pp. 59-72).

Reisig, W. (1985). *Petri Nets, an Introduction.* Berlin, Germany: Springer Verlag.

Schek, H.-J., Weikum, G., & Ye, H. (1993). Towards a Unified Theory of Concurrency Control and Recovery. In *Proceedings of the 12th ACM SIGACT-SIGMOD-SIGART Symposium on Principles of Database Systems* (pp. 300-311).

Schuldt, H., Alonso, G., Beeri, C., & Schek, H. J. (2002). Atomicity and Isolation for Transactional Processes. *ACM Transactions on Database Systems*, *27*, 63–116. doi:10.1145/507234.507236

Schuler, C., Schuldt, H., & Schek, H. J. (2001). Supporting Reliable Transactional Business Processes by Publish-Subscribe Techniques. In *Proceedings of the 2nd International Workshop on Technologies for E-Services (TES) 2001* (LNCS 2193, pp. 118-131).

Silicon.com. (n.d.). *Latest white papers.* Retrieved from http://whitepapers.silicon.com

Singh, M. P., & Huhns, M. N. (2005). *Service-Oriented Computing — Semantics, Processes, Agents.* London, UK: John Wiley & Sons.

Vidyasankar, K., Radha Krishna, P., & Karlapalem, K. (2007). A Multi-Level Model for Activity Commitments in E-contracts. In *Proceedings of CoopIS 2007* (LNCS 4803, pp. 300-317).

Vidyasankar, K., & Vossen, G. (2004). A Multi-Level Model for Web Service Composition. In *Proceedings of the 3rd IEEE International Conference on Web Services 2004*, San Diego, CA (pp. 462-469).

Vossen, G. (2006). Have Service-Oriented Architectures Taken a Wrong Turn Already? In A. Min Tjoa, L. Xu, & S. Chaudhry (Eds.), *Research and Practical Issues of Enterprise Information Systems: Proceedings of the IFIP TC 8 International Conference on Research and Practical Issues of Enterprise Information Systems (CONFENIS) 2006,* Vienna, Austria (Vol. 205, pp. xxiii-xxix). International Federation for Information Processing.

Weikum, G., & Vossen, G. (2002). *Transactional Information Systems: Theory, Algorithms, and the Practice of Concurrency Control and Recovery*. San Francisco, CA: Morgan-Kaufmann Publishers.

This work was previously published in the Journal of Database Management, Volume 22, Issue 2, edited by Keng Siau, pp. 1-31, copyright 2011 by IGI Publishing (an imprint of IGI Global).

Chapter 7
Service Composition and Interaction in a SOC Middleware Supporting Separation of Concerns with Flows and Views

Dickson K. W. Chiu
Dickson Computer Systems, Hong Kong

Qing Li
City University of Hong Kong, Hong Kong

Patrick C. K. Hung
University of Ontario, Canada

Zhe Shan
City University of Hong Kong, Hong Kong

S. C. Cheung
Hong Kong University of Science & Technology, Hong Kong

Yu Yang
City University of Hong Kong, Hong Kong

Matthias Farwick
University of Innsbruck, Austria

ABSTRACT

Service-Oriented Computing (SOC) has recently gained attention both within industry and academia; however, its characteristics cannot be easily solved using existing distributed computing technologies. Composition and interaction issues have been the central concerns, because SOC applications are composed of heterogeneous and distributed processes. To tackle the complexity of inter-organizational service integration, the authors propose a methodology to decompose complex process requirements into different types of flows, such as control, data, exception, and security. The subset of each type of flow necessary for the interactions with each partner can be determined in each service. These subsets collectively constitute a process view, based on which interactions can be systematically designed and managed for system integration through service composition. The authors illustrate how the proposed SOC middleware, named FlowEngine, implements and manages these flows with contemporary Web services technologies. An experimental case study in an e-governmental environment further demonstrates how the methodology can facilitate the design of complex inter-organizational processes.

DOI: 10.4018/978-1-4666-2044-5.ch007

INTRODUCTION

Recently, Service-Oriented Computing (SOC) (Papazoglou & Georgakopoulos, 2003) has gained a lot of attention within both the industry and academy. SOC is a computing paradigm that utilizes services as fundamental elements, which relies on Service-Oriented Architecture (SOA) (Francisco et al., 2003) to build inter-relating service models. Services-oriented applications share specific characteristics that are distinguishable from traditional distributed applications (Papazoglou & van den Heuvel, 2007). Firstly, they are technology neutral: they interact through standardized protocols in a highly heterogeneous environment, thus offering a broader choice for integration and are loosely coupled. Also, they declaratively define their functionalities, capabilities, and quality-of-service (QoS) requirements in a repository (Curbera et al., 2005) in order to enable dynamic and automated service discovery. Finally, service-oriented applications are created as compositions of services, which benefit from features like abstract modeling and adaptable monitoring.

However, the SOC characteristics stated above cannot be easily solved by using existing distributed computing technologies. Middleware technology provides a common interface for applications to interact with each other as well as their runtime environments (Britton & Bye, 2004). Through such an interface, applications are relieved from handling tedious tasks of resource management, event monitoring, distributed transaction services, and so on. Typically, middleware is implemented to adapt to environmental fluctuations (such as network connections, memory availability, thread pools) and to provide a standard for interoperation. As a result, the applications such developed are less system dependent and therefore more interoperable. This is a particularly essential feature for the composition of service-centric applications as well as the integration of the emerging SOA standards and legacy services. Based on this, the main challenge in service composition reduces to the interaction of services and the associated requirement elicitation. Interaction refers to the interoperation and the integration with applications both internal and external to the systems. This has been a central concern because these applications are composed of heterogeneous and distributed processes. The problem is prominent in service composition, where interactions are complex and can vary across different types of organizations. Business process modeling languages like BPMN (White, 2008) try to capture all relevant aspect of composed applications in one view, leading to complex models that are hard to understand. To tackle this problem, first of all, we need a sophisticated middleware to implement such interactions and to facilitate their management. In addition, because of the complexity, ad hoc use of the middleware is inadequate to solve the problem. A comprehensive methodology is required to make good use of the middleware for a systematic design of service composition and the management of interactions among services.

In this paper, we propose to use both the paradigm of *views* and *flows* to tackle the complexity of service composition and interaction in a SOC middleware. Our approach is based on the principle of separation of concerns, which is often considered as one of the key principles in software engineering. Process (workflow) view (Chiu, Karlapalem, & Li, 2001; Liu & Shen, 2003) has been proposed as a novel approach to address business-to-business interoperation. A process view is a structurally correct subset of a process (Chiu et al., 2004). The use of process views facilitates sophisticated interactions among services and allows these interactions to interoperate in a gray-box mode (that is, they can access each other's internal information to some pre-defined extent). Each view can be regarded as a separate concern based on some specific client requirements of a service scenario. Therefore, the artifact of process views is a handy mechanism to enact and enforce cross-organizational process interoperability for service composition.

However, like the design of a process itself, the design of the process views is far from obvious in the context of service composition. To tackle this problem, we propose the concept of flows for service composition requirements elicitation. The interactions in a process are partitioned into different flows according to different types of requirements. Some typical examples of flow that are the most concerned include control, data, security, and exception. Consequently, a key benefit of adopting flows is that composition requirement analysis and design could be streamlined through another level of separation of concern. After partitioning the flows, we can determine for each type of flows the subset necessary for the interactions with a specific kind of composite services. These resultant subsets are therefore, control flow view, data flow view, exception flow view, and security flow view, respectively. These flow views collectively constitute a process view, based on which compositions and interactions of services can be systematically designed and managed. Figure 1 provides a class diagram in the Unified Modeling Language (UML) (Larman, 1997) summarizing the conceptual model of our approach.

In order to support such a model in the SOC middleware, a companion 2-phased methodology is also necessary and thus introduced. In the first phase, the SOC middleware should reengineer the interaction interface offered by service providers into different categories such as control ports, data ports, security ports, and exception ports. Based on this new interface, different subsets of ports can be selected for different requirements. In the next phase, the SOC middleware can compose various advanced services by grouping appropriate ports into flows, and then flows into processes.

Figure 1. Conceptual model of process views and flows

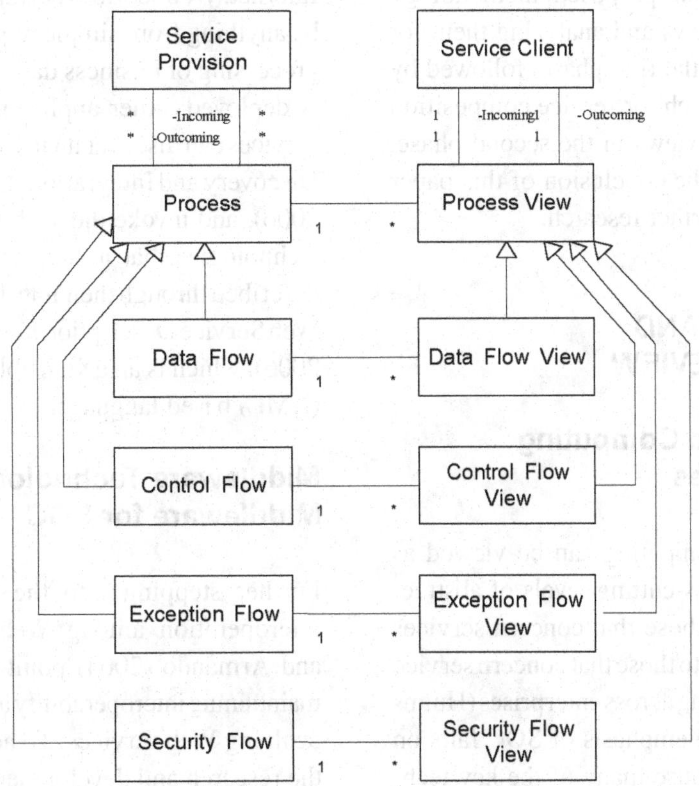

As a highlight of the conceptual model based on flows and views, which constitutes the basis of our methodology for service composition and interaction management, we present a middleware, named *FlowEngine* to demonstrate the feasibility and advantages of our flow-view solution. It is implemented based on Web services technologies in line with the current trends of information and communication technology (ICT) accelerating the widespread use of Web services.

The rest of the paper is organized as follows. We first review related and background work. Then, we introduce a motivating case study of e-Government service middleware, to illustrate the complexity of the composition and interaction in a real-life service-oriented computing case; we also present the definition of flows via the example of this case study. Next, we highlight the architecture of FlowEngine and describe our implementation framework based on various Web services technologies. To demonstrate the applicability of FlowEngine through our case study, we present our proposed methodology for eliciting these flows and analyzing them for view formulation in the first phase, followed by a composition approach for service composition based on flows and views in the second phase. Finally, we discuss the conclusion of this paper with our plans for further research.

BACKGROUND AND LITERATURE REVIEW

Service-Oriented Computing and Web Services

Service-Oriented Computing can be viewed as several different cross-cutting levels of abstractions, ranging from those that concern services within an application to those that concern service applications interacting across enterprises (Huhns & Singh, 2005). The emphasis of SOC falls on the architecture, because many of the key techniques for its component - databases, transactions, software design - are already well understood in isolation. Service-Oriented Architecture (SOA) is essentially a collection of services which communicate with each other (Erl, 2006). SOA is a logical way of designing software systems to provide services to either end-user applications or other services distributed in a network through published and discoverable interfaces (Papazoglou & Georgakopoulos, 2003). The basic SOA is not merely an architecture about services, but also describes the relationship of three kinds of participants: the service provider, the service discovery agency, and the service requestor (client). Other than Web services, the paradigm of SOA also applies in other areas such as mobile services (van Thanh & Jorstad, 2005).

The adoption of Web Services on SOA is mainly driven by its interoperability for Internet applications. Web Services typically offer self-contained and self-describing services that can be published, located, and invoked across the Internet. Web services perform functions that can be anything from simple requests to complicated processing of business data. Once a Web service is deployed, other applications as well as Web services can discover it via Universal Description, Discovery and Integration (UDDI) registries (Erl, 2006), and invoke the Web service based on the technologies that it supports. Web services are described through their interface definitions in the Web Service Description Language (WSDL) (Erl, 2006), which is an eXtensible Markup Language (XML) based language.

Middleware Technology and Middleware for SOC

Further stepping into the problem about the interoperation among Web services, Shankar and Armando (2004) point out the problem on maintaining interoperability among independently evolving Web services. To address this problem, the research and development of middleware for

SOA has been started. For example, Yu, Taleb-Bendiab, and Reilly (2004) present a runtime service adaptation mechanism that supports end-users to dynamically adapt to variations in the execution environment, without altering their original design, crossing multiple standards, and middleware architectures. Colombo (Curbera et al., 2005) is a middleware platform for service-oriented computing, providing transactional, reliable, and secured interactions among services. However, these researches in middleware have not reached the stage of offering comprehensive methodology for systematic design and management of service composition.

Although, commercially available middleware like Oracles Fusion Middleware (Oracle, 2008) and SAPs NetWeaver middleware (SAP, n.d.) provide a wide range of functionality like monitoring, security management, and process modeling, none of the two market leaders provide a clean process view separation for complex workflows. It has to be mentioned that the concepts presented in this paper could be incorporated into these systems with ease.

Services Composition

In the context of SOA, a service is usually a business function implemented in software, wrapped with a formally defined interface (Michael, 2003). Service composition creates new services by assembling existing ones and can potentially add more value beyond merely a nicer interface to a single old service (Singh & Huhns, 2005). When referring to the approaches of service composition, it is often said that the general process of service composition has several steps. For example, Yang, Papazoglou, and van den Heuvel (2002) approach service composition in three steps: planning, definition, and implementation; while Kiwata et al. (2007) suggest two steps: provisioning and collaboration, instead of enumerating concrete methods. Generally, services can be composed in two modes, static and dynamic. In a static composition, the services to be composed are chosen at design time by the designer, while in a dynamic composition, the services to be composed are chosen at run-time.

However, when referring to Web service composition, numerous concrete approaches are proposed. Milanovic and Malek (2004) survey many existing proposals for Web service composition including Business Process Execution Language (BPEL), Semantic Web, Web components, algebraic process, Petri nets, model checking, and finite-state machines. Liu et al. (2010) also survey some more recent work on Web Service provision. Hull and Su (2005) present a three-dimension measurement of Web service description and composition models and provide a brief tour of composition models including Semantic Web services, the "Roman" model, and the Mealy conversation model. Brogi, Corfini and Popescu (2008) present a novel approach for service discovery based on Semantic Web technologies. Furthermore, Li et al. (2009) describe in a very recent contribution how context heterogeneity can be overcome in service composition. BPEL is an XML language that supports process-oriented service composition. Details about it can be found in Alves et al. (2007). In addition, we stress on the importance of enforcement (exception detection and handling) and relationship management during service composition and propose a methodology from such requirements to their event driven realization (Chiu et al., 2010). This motivates the inclusion of exception flows in our approach.

Another related area is the field of service interaction patterns. Barros, Dumas, and ter Hofstede (2005) give an overview of the service interaction patterns that need to be considered in contemporary web service middleware. Wohed et al. (2003) present an excellent comparison between BPEL and other composition languages, which use workflow patterns and communication patterns as the evaluating criteria. Other works on BPEL include transformation algorithms between it and other languages (Moon et al., 2005);

intensive analysis of its features, such as dead-path elimination (van Breugel & Koshkina, 2005) and exception handling (Curbera et al., 2003). From the composition of data service also results the problem of securing the data flows between all workflow participants. This problem of data flow security is tackled by the recent publication of by the use of digital certificates (She et al., 2009).

On Separation of Concerns

To the best of our knowledge, there is little work containing the idea of "separation of concerns" in service composition. There are also few reports on the pre-treatment of component services before composition. Papazoglou and van den Heuvel (2007) give a comprehensive overview of the current research issues in SOC, stating that research on abstraction and separation between different aspects is needed in research on service composition. Orriens, Yang, and Papazoglou (2003) divide the life cycle of service composition into four phases and analyze some elements and rules required in each phase. The elements involve activities, control flows, conditions, events, messages, providers, and roles. The business rules are classified into five kinds: structure rules, data rules, constraint rules, resource rules, and exception rules. Schmit and Dustdar (2005) discuss the separation between structural, transactional, security, and workflow issues.

Recently, the research community has recognized the complexity in the design and management of service composition and therefore started to examine methodologies for its design and management. Our earlier work using flows (Hung & Chiu, 2004) as the basic metaphor for the analysis has been motivated by the principle of "separation of concerns" in software engineering. Among various definitions of concern, most are very broad and general. For example, Robillard (2003) describes a concern as "any consideration ... about the implementation of a program." Similarly, Ossher and Tarr (2000) define a concern to be a part of a software system that is relevant to a specific concept or purpose. They also note that there can be many different kinds of concerns at the different stages of the software life cycle. Sutton and Rouvellou (2005) add their own general characterization of a concern as "any matter of interest in a software system." While there is nothing inherently wrong with these definitions because they are so flexible, their generality leaves the meaning of "concern" unclear. Lai and Murphy (1999) as well as Turner et al. (1998) have a more specific definition in which concerns are considered to be features: a functional property of a system that is visible to the user. However, it is clear that there are important non-feature concerns, such as performance. Aspect-oriented programming (AOP) (Kiczales et al., 1997) is a specific instance of separation of concerns that modularizes concerns that cross-cut a system's functionality, such as memory access patterns. AOP terms these units that are not a part of the system's functional decomposition aspects. Clearly, there is no consensus on the definition of a concern since researchers' definitions range from the vague "any consideration" to functional properties such as features to crosscutting aspects. As such, our model does not limit the different types of flows although in this paper we do focus on the most commonly used ones. Any other special concerns such as QoS flow or semantic flow could be added and fit in our framework.

Workflow Views

There have been some earlier works in the area of process (workflow) views and related notions of a partial workflow. The work of Eshuis and Grefen (2008) presents a formal model for creating process views and proposes a two step methodology for view elicitation. However, this approach only focuses on the process engine on one side of the communication, rather than a middleware that handles views and flows on both the client and provider sides. Tran, Zdun, and Dustdar (2007) present an approach for process views of BPEL processes to reduce the complexity and to foster integration of domain experts. This approach does not provide the sophisticated methodology for service elicitation presented as part of this contribution. Liu and Shen (2003) present an algorithm for constructing a process view from a given workflow, but do not discuss its correctness with respect to inter-organizational workflows.

Van der Aalst and Kumar (2003) present an approach to workflow schema exchange in an XML dialect called Exchangeable Routing Language (XRL), but it does not include the support for workflow views. Besides, van der Aalst (1999) models inter-organizational workflows and their communication structures by means of Petri Nets and message sequence charts (MSCs), respectively. Since the model does not consider data and external triggers, the proposed communication protocol is less precise than the inter-operation protocol presented in the workflow view approach (Chiu et al., 2004). To address the derivation of private workflows from inter-organizational workflows, van der Aalst and Weske use the concept of workflow projection inheritance (van der Aalst & Weske, 2001; Basten & van der Aalst, 2001). A couple of derivation rules are proposed so that a derived workflow is behaviorally bi-similar to the original workflow based on branching semantics, in contrast to the trace semantics adopted in the workflow view model. Schulz and Orlowska (2004) propose to tightly couple private workflow and workflow view with state dependencies, whilst to loosely couple workflow views with control flow dependencies. They also develop cross-organizational workflow architecture for view-based cross-organizational workflow execution.

Our previous work on workflow views has been presented in (Chiu et al., 2002). From then, workflow views have been utilized as a beneficial approach to support the interactions of business processes in E-service environments (Chiu et al., 2002, 2004). We have also adopted the object deputy model (Kambayashi & Peng, 1996) to support the realization of workflow views (Shan et al., 2005). On the other hand, we have extended our process view mechanism into three-tier views for mobile service adaptation (Chiu et al., 2003). We have also introduced the notion of flows for process based information integration and how exception handling could be facilitated (Hung & Chiu, 2004). However, there have been no comprehensive studies on how the requirements of workflow (process) views can be elicited.

In summary, the development of solutions for service composition and interaction is promising and challenging. To our knowledge, none of the prior research studies have used process (workflow) technologies to materialize service interaction from different types of flows in a unified approach. Also, no methodology for systematic partial or restricted process formulation, especially for the context of service computing, has been discussed.

SOC MIDDLEWARE FOR SERVICE COMPOSITION

Following the basic architecture of SOA, the SOC middleware stands between service client and the other two parties, namely the service provider and the service registry. Firstly, it searches the service registries for information of available services. Then, according to requirements from clients, it derives advanced services via the composition of services. In the running stage, it takes charge of the communication and interaction between service providers and service clients.

Motivating Example – E-Government Service Middleware

To illustrate our approach, we present a case study of an e-Government service middleware that involves personal record information investigation in the Hong Kong Special Administrative Region governmental context.

Figure 2. Application Scenario of SOC Middleware

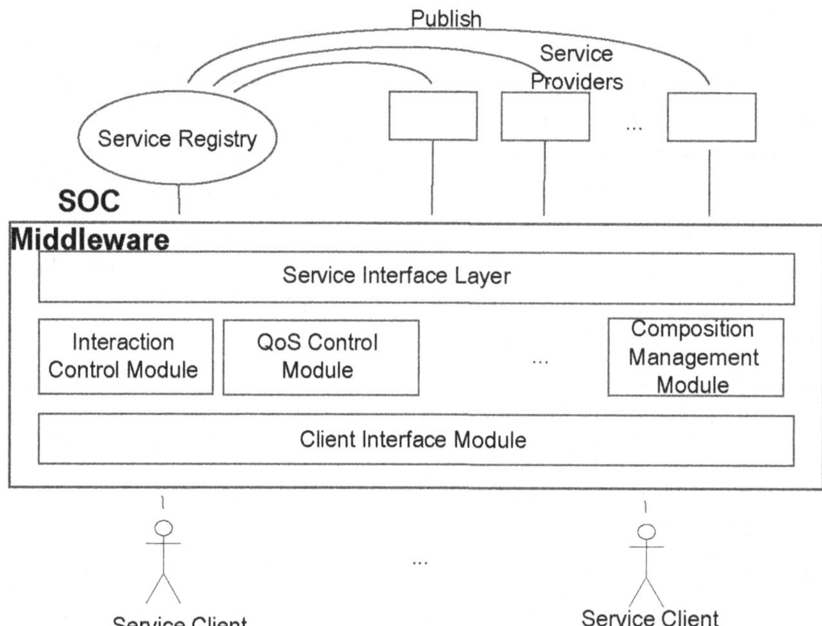

In this case study, through the e-Government service middleware, an internal (government official) or external user (detective) investigates a suspect by inspecting an integrated view of records (e.g., ID information, criminal records, border control, and bank transactions) sourced from different government departments and commercial organizations such as Immigration Department, Police Office, Customs Department, and Monetary Authority. For example, bank transactions within one month before and after a trip above a certain threshold amount are retrieved. As an illustration, a sample information integration schema (see Figure 3) is designed with the following relations and attributes (in parentheses):

- IDrecord (id-no, tax-file-no, name, sex, date-of-birth, area-code, phone-no, address, postal-code) is held by the Immigration Department (as in the case for Hong Kong).
- BorderRecord (id-no, entry-or-exit, place, vehicle, day-of-event) is held by the Customs Department.
- CrimeRecord (id-no, crime-description, sentence, day-of-event) is held by the Police Force.
- BankRecord (tax-file-no, bank-no, account-no, transaction, amount, balance, day-of-event) is held by individual banks under the control of the Monetary Authority.

In order to access the relevant records, the e-Government service middleware has to interact with underlying services both via control and data ports. Also, it needs to take care of the security and exception aspects of the process. Even with information retrieval only (i.e., without update), the scenario is complicated enough to show the complexity of the composition design and interaction management by the SOC middleware. Adding update scenarios to this example will require the rigorous implementation of transaction mechanisms, which is out of the scope of this contribution and left for future work.

Figure 3. Motivating case study: e-government service middleware

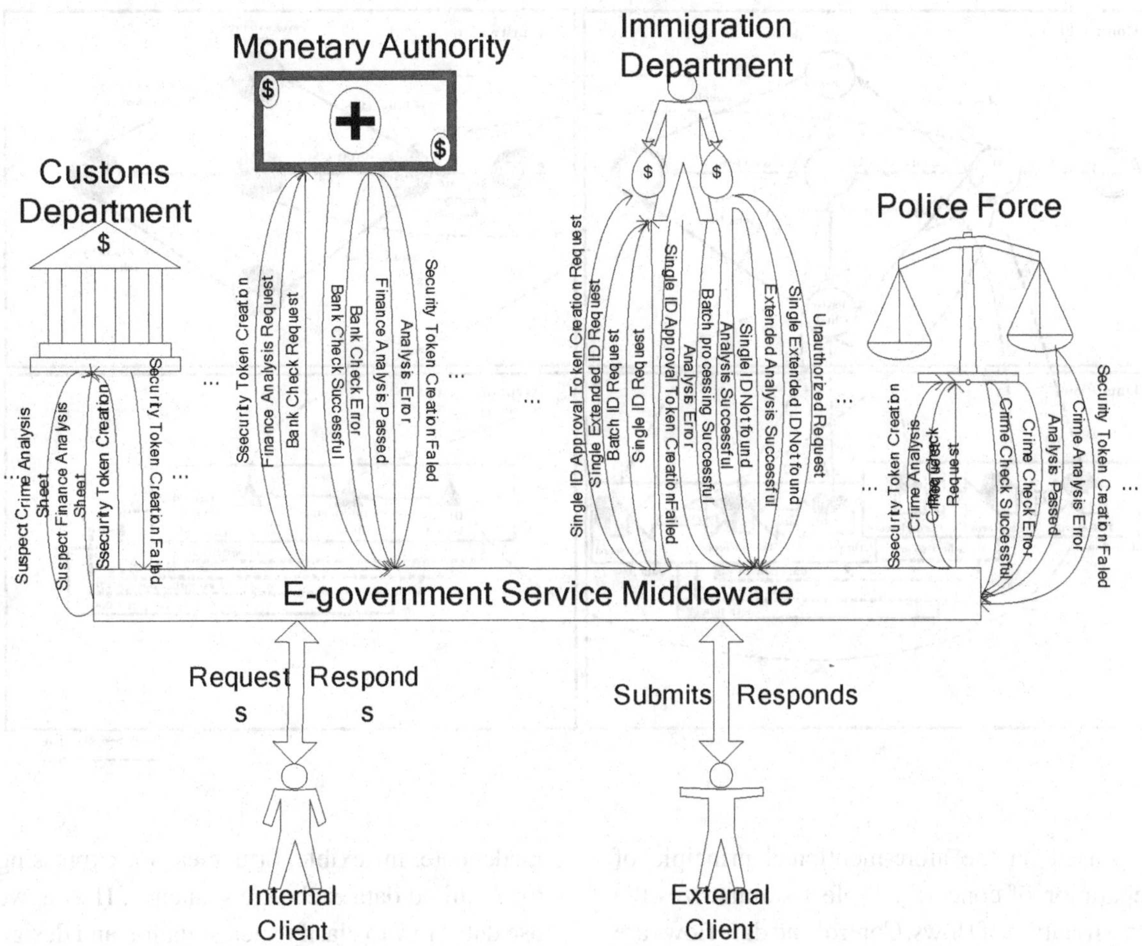

Flows in Service Composition

To manage and monitor different types of flows (control flows, data flows, security flows, and exception flows) for the e-Government service middleware, each flow is separated and depicted in Figure 4 as a distinct flow. This is also called flow independency. The separation of flows results in the increased flexibility of information services for cross-organizational processes integration. Furthermore, because of the separation of concerns, the process model designers can easily add or change the information integration plans for different situations of service composition.

Typically, each organization publishes services from their individual (mostly existing) activities and processes, while the flows and process views orchestrate them together for various integration purposes. Figure 4 describes the processes in which all the activities (in circle) are performed for retrieving the datasets from various databases (labeled by the activity's name), and are coordinated by a set of flows (in single arrow lines). In particular, some activities for some requestors have to first obtain a read-access approval from each data custodian and data service provider. This further justifies a process-based integration as human users may be involved in the approval procedures.

Figure 4. Example of different types of flows

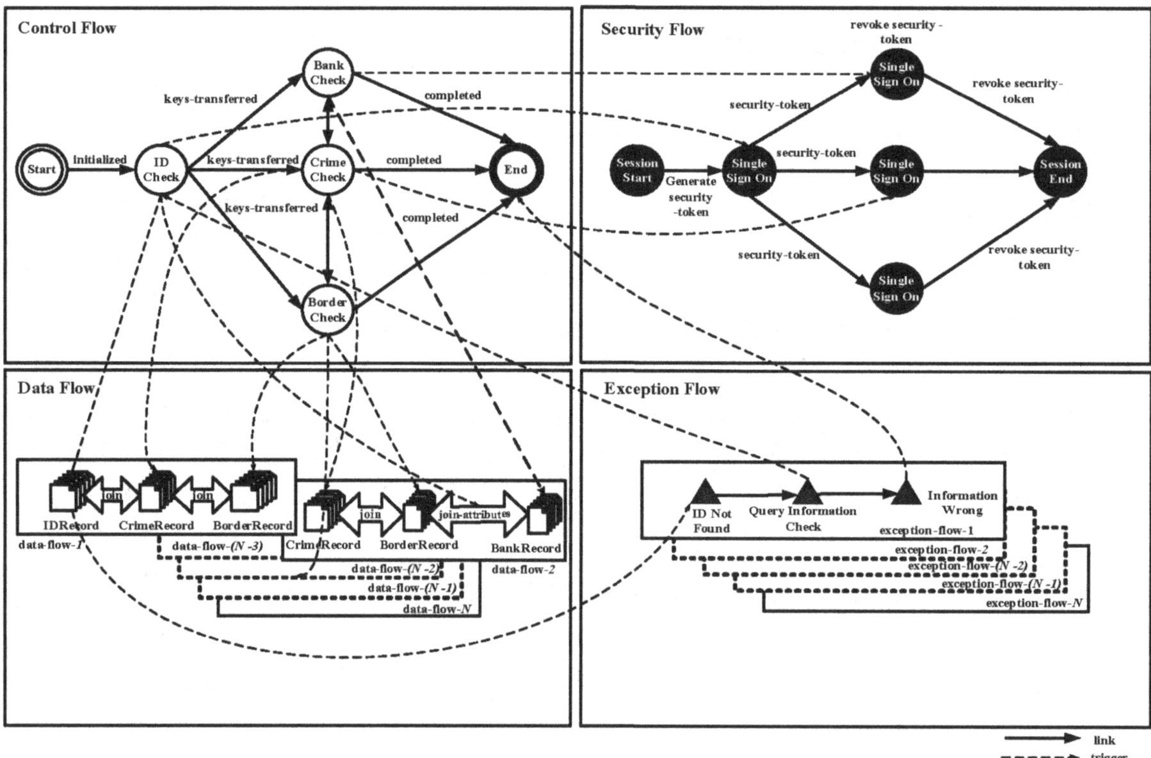

Based on the afore-mentioned principle of separation of concerns, Table 1 summarizes the classification of flows. Control and data flows are the main concern, while security and exception flow are special concerns that could be added afterwards to enhance the system. Note that if the system requires more special concerns, more types of flows, such as QoS flow and semantic flow, those could be added and fit into the framework.

Control flows specify the conducting order of activities which are allowed in a process. In this way, control flows depict the execution picture of the process logic in that (cross-organizational) process.

Data flows define the flow of specific data or a dataset required by a process. In processes that involve only simple data exchange, the data flows may often be the same as the control flows. However, for service composition that deals with more data in parallel, control flows are often inadequate, inflexible, or unclear for expressing the required data exchange sequence. Hence, we use data flow to clarify such situation and design in order to separate the concern from the control flows.

Security flows define the flow of security control information (such as authentication) required by a process. This involves the creation, exchange, and revocation of security tokens to implement security policies. A security policy is the set of laws, rules, and practices that regulates how a flow prevents information and resources from being misused against the security requirements. Thus, security tokens represent a collection of claims (i.e., personal information) like name, identity, privilege, and capability for the security services of authentication and authorization. As security tokens are often passed along the process based on the principle of single-sign-on, the delega-

Table 1. Classification of flows

Property Flow	Main Stakeholder (Who)	Artifact (What)	Circumstance (When)	Behavior (How)
Control Flow	Users	Service requests	Request calls	Activity execution
Data Flow	Users	Data items	Data processing	Data collection or analysis
Security Flow	Users	Security tokens	Authentication and authorization	Security verification
Exception Flow	Internal activity	Exception messages	Service abnormity	Exception handling

tion or propagation should be well designed and described in the security flow.

Exception flows are pervasively required by anything that has an algorithmic flow (Perry, Romanovsky, & Tripathi, 2000). In general, there are two types of exceptions in our proposed conceptual workflow model: expected and unexpected exceptions (Casati et al., 1999; Chiu & Karlaparlem, 2000). Unexpected exceptions mainly correspond to mismatches between an activity specification and its execution, and other unanticipated situations. These situations usually require human attention and handling. Suitable alerts should be sent to the appropriate personnel (Kafeza et al., 2004). Expected exceptions are predictable deviations from the normal behavior of the workflow. Usually, information systems can only deal with expected exceptions automatically. This means exception flows will trigger the corresponding exception handler processes pre-defined by the system designers. How the exceptions are handled belongs to the logic of the affected requestor process and should be specified in the flow. In our proposed process model, there are five categories of expected exceptions. Control exceptions are raised in correspondence to control flows such as start or completion of activities (e.g., access approval request is rejected). Data exceptions are raised in correspondence to data flows such as data integration processes (e.g., record of an ID is not found). Temporal exceptions are raised in correspondence to both control flows and data flows such as the occurrence of a given timestamp or a pre-defined interval elapsed (e.g., excessive access to ID records in a period of time without approval). External exceptions are raised in correspondence to control flows and data flows explicitly notified by external services such as system failures. Security exceptions are raised in correspondence to access control or security violations (e.g., access of border records from departments other than the Police or the Customs without approval). External and temporal exceptions are in general asynchronous, but control, data, and security exceptions often occur synchronously with activity executions.

The interactions among different types of flows are triggered by external messages (in dashed arrow lines) which represent the corresponding service requests. Referring to Figure 4, there is a set of data flows that are performed along with the control flows. Each data flow is also assigned to a service for execution by a matchmaking process if necessary. In general, the process will terminate once all the control flows and data flows are completed successfully.

IMPLEMENTATION OF FLOWS AND VIEWS WITH FLOWENGINE

In this section, we illustrate how flows and views can be effectively implemented with contemporary Web services technologies on our SOC middleware, FlowEngine.

Deployment Architecture

The FlowEngine Deployment Architecture is illustrated in Figure 5. Here, the flow and view editor helps design the flows and process views for services. The flows and views thus defined are published in a public UDDI directory so that partner organizations can access such meta-information effectively. Various back-end storage spaces are required for storing the process view definitions, process view instances, flow definitions, flow instances, and interaction logs.

Based on flows, the interaction manager is in charge of all the flows with partner organizations. It has the following sub-modules. The View Runtime Manager (VRM) deals with the instantiation of new process view instances and the necessary section management. It also maps between process views and internal processes. Here, one can think of the mapping between the distinct process views of Figure 4 and the actually executed process that is managed by the VRM. The interaction monitor maintains the interaction log and offers monitoring functions for system administrators and business partners. The Flow Manager (FM) is responsible for maintaining the flows for all process view instances. It maps the interaction messages between the local processes and business partners with transformation if necessary.

When a service client invokes the Web service corresponding to the first activity of a process view, the FM usually expects a security flow with a valid and appropriate security token for authentication. Only after such security flow has passed (i.e., the security token successfully verified), the VRM creates a process view instance (i.e., a session starts in the implementation layer). This security token will be used in subsequent requests to identify the process view instance throughout its lifecycle. So, both the VRM and the requestor should keep track of this token. With all the Web services invocation and flows recorded in the interaction log, the FM can determine which flow an incoming Web service call belongs to and whether it conforms to a valid calling sequence of the process view definition by checking the pre-condition of the flow.

Figure 5. FlowEngine deployment architecture

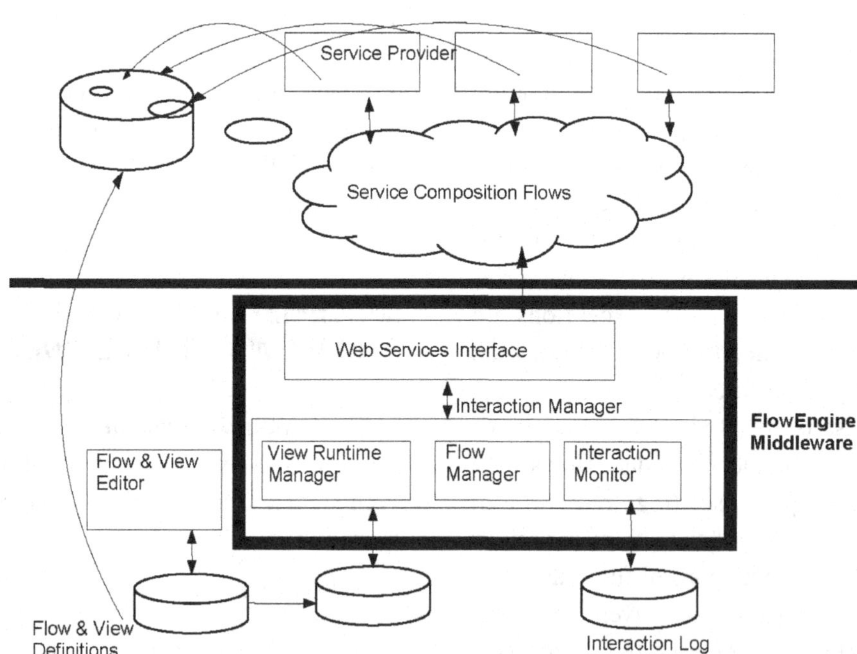

The FM can then look up the internal activity of the process corresponding to the validated Web service request from the process view definition for execution. However, as the external message format might be different from that of the existing activity, translation may be required. In our current implementation, we make use of the convenience of the XML stylesheet (XSL) technology for this purpose. In general, a user defined function could be used instead. Similarly, before sending back the output of a process as a response of the Web service, the FM may need to perform another translation.

Implementation Issues

Figure 6 summarizes the conceptual implementation model that provides a context for the subsequent discussions in this section.

Basic Web Service Implementation Interfaces

Figure 7 shows how Web service definitions can be systematically generated from process view definitions in our implementation based on standard Web Service Definition Language (WSDL). We map a process view to a "service" in the WSDL. We further map each activity (sub-service) of a process view to a WSDL "port". As a sub-service may have more than one incoming flow, we have to map each of them into a WSDL "operation". The request and response messages can then be mapped to those in the binding definitions (see the next section for our detailed generation and verification methodology). Such definitions can then be posted to UDDI directories for integration with different partners. In this way, we can easily limit partner access to only the intended process views (now implemented with Web services). Furthermore, existing processes and their access points are thus shielded from being exposed to uncontrolled access with the view runtime manager discussed in the previous sub-section. In addition, this implementation allows interactions with partners without fully incorporating a process view engine: they only need to understand the view mechanism and invoke the permitted services in the UDDI directory according to the calling conventions. Figure 8 depicts a summary of the WSDL for the process view of the ID Check service to the Customs.

Figure 6. Conceptual implementation model

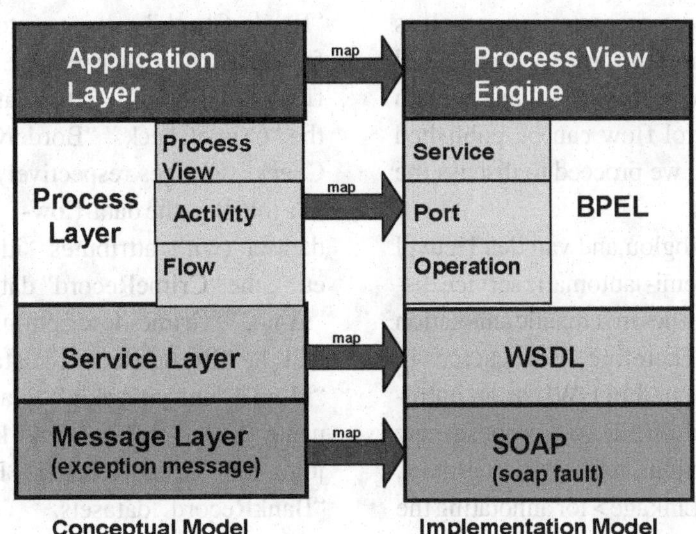

Figure 7. WSDL Code Generated for Process Views

```
<definitions>
  <types>  <!-- XML Schema --> </types>
  <message name="ViewNFlowFRequest" />
<message name="ViewNFlowFResponse" />
...
  <portType name="ViewNActivityMInterface">
    <operation name="ViewNFlowF">
      <input message="ViewNFlowFRequest" />
      <output message="ViewNFlowFResponse" />
    </operation>
   ...
</portType>
...
<binding name="ViewNActivityMBinding"
type="ViewNActivityMInterface">
    <soap:binding transport="http://schemas.xmlsoap.org/soap/http" />
    ...
</binding>
...
<service name="WfviewN">
 <port name="WfviewNActivityMPort"
binding="WfviewNActivityMBinding">
<soap:address
location="http://dept.gov.hk/ServicesS/ViewN" />
    </port>
...
  </service>
</definitions>
```

Extended Web Service Orchestration Interfaces

For the automatic service orchestration as well as the full comprehension of the process views, a full implementation of the process view mechanism is required. The control flow can be published in the BPEL standard; we proceed to discuss the flows in the following.

As stated by Papazoglou and van den Heuvel (2007), the future of (semi-)automatic service discovery and composition lies in semantic annotation of service interfaces. Therefore, data schemas in our system are represented in OWL as an ontology. In the context of BPEL, we propose new data-integration assertions named <integrate>, <dataset>, and <dataLinkage> for annotating the data flows. Referring to Figure 9, the data-flow-1 is used to join (in double arrows) the datasets returned from the "IDCheck," "CrimeCheck," and "BorderCheck" services into an integrated view for a particular user request. Similarly, the data-flow-2 is used to join the datasets returned from the "CrimeCheck," "BorderCheck," and "BankCheck" services respectively. Using the "id-no" as a join key, the data-flow-1 joins the "IDrecord" dataset (with attributes "id-no," "sex," "age," etc.), the "CrimeRecord" dataset (with attributes "id-no," "Crime-description," "sentence," etc.), and the "BorderRecord" dataset (with attributes "id-no," "entry-or-exit," "place," etc.). Similarly, using the "id-no" as a join key, the data-flow-2 joins the "CrimeRecord," "BorderRecord," and "BankRecord" datasets.

Figure 8. A summary for the basic WSDL for the process view of the ID service to the Customs

```
Name: ID Check Service
Location/Provider: Immigration Department
<!-- Control Flow --!>
+Port 1 - Input: Batch ID Approval Request
            * User Name
        * User Organization
            * Suspect Names
            * Request Reason
    - Output: Approval Message/Rejection Message
            * Request Status (Approved/Rejected)
            * Security Token (if approved)
<!-- Data Flow --!>
+ Port 2 - Input: Single ID Request
                * Suspect Name
                * Suspect Description
    - Output: Basic ID Information/Error Message
                * Suspect ID
                * Suspect Birthday
                * Suspect Phone Number
                * Suspect Address ...
+ Port3 - Input: Single Extended ID Request        ...
      - Output: Extended ID Information/Error Message...
+ Port 4  -  Input: Batch ID Request        ...
    + Output: Batch Suspect Analysis Report (with ID information)   ...
<!—Security Flow --!>
+ Port 5 - Input: Any Government Department Security Token
    - Output: Accept Message/Rejection Message
+ Port 6        - Output: Batch ID Token
+ Port 7        - Input: Batch ID Token
    - Output: Accept Message / Rejection Message...
<!—Exception Flow --!>
+ Port 8 - Output: ID Not Found Exception
+ Port 9     - Output: Analysis Error Exception
+ Port 10 - Output: Token Invalid Exception/Security Alert Exception
...
```

Extensions for Security

We employ the standard of WS-Security (Rosenberg & Remy, 2004) to implement a security token, as shown in Figure 10. Based on the security token defined in the SOAP header, we propose the following assertions for annotating a security flow in BPEL: <sessionStart/>, <clearance/>, <securityToken/>, <tokenType/>, and <sessionEnd/> (as shown in Figure 11). The <sessionStart/> assertion is used to identify the time when the user's security token is generated by the information system, and the <sessionEnd/> assertion is used to identify the time when the user's security token should be revoked.

The security flow is orchestrated with the control flow. As such, authentication is based not only on the "Username" and "Password", but also on other relevant information such as the "SubjectName" and "SubjectDepartment". Each activity of each service can define whether the security clearance assertion <clearance/> is required and the details such as the type of security token <securityToken/> and <tokenType/>. For the tokens, Security Assertions Markup Language (SAML) (Rosenberg & Remy, 2004) is used to define such authentication and authorization decisions. Briefly, SAML is an XML-based framework for exchanging security credentials in the form of assertions about subjects.

Exception Flows

Figure 12 describes our proposed exception-handling approach in the different levels of protocols (namely, BPEL and SOAP). Once an exception is raised towards a requestor, the corresponding Web service will make use of the SOAP fault to convey the exception in the exception flows. In the context of BPEL, new exception-handling assertions named <exceptionHandling>, <event> (corresponding to the exception message in our analysis methodology), <condition> (corresponding to the pre-condition), and <action> (corresponding to the activity) are proposed for annotating the exception flows (see Figure 13). Moreover, the conceptual process model requires a termination mechanism to prevent exceptions from triggering each other indefinitely. In the worst case, if the process designer cannot find any feasible exception-handling procedure, the problematic activity has to abort and therefore the request has to abort as well. In this case, a new exception-handling assertion named <exceptionHandlingDefault> is proposed for specifying the abort action if none of the rules can handle the exception.

SERVICE COMPOSITION METHODOLOGY

After understanding the architecture and the technologies employed in our approach, we proceed to present a methodology to make systematic use of it for service composition and interaction management based on our experience from this case study. We formulate our methodology mainly based on searching of flows with a graph model. This methodology is therefore in the category

Figure 9. New BPEL Assertions for Data Flows

```
<flow name="data-flows">
 <integrate name="data-flow-1">
  <dataset name="IDrecord">
   <attributes name="id-no" key="primary"/>
   <attributes name="sex"/>
   <attributes name="age"/>
     ...
  </dataset>
  <dataset name="CrimeRecord"
   <attributes name="id-no" key="primary"/>
   <attributes name="crime-description"/>
   <attributes name="sentence"/>
     ...
  </dataset>
  <dataset name="BorderRecord"
   <attributes name="id-no" key="primary"/>
   <attributes name="entry-or-exit"/>
   <attributes name="place"/>
   <attributes name="date"/>
     ...
  </dataset>
 </integrate>
<integrate name="data-flow-2">
  <dataset name="CrimeRecord"
   <attributes name="id-no" key="primary"/>
   <attributes name="crime-description"/>
   <attributes name="sentence"/> ...
  </dataset>
  <dataset name="BorderRecord"
   <attributes name="id-no" key="primary"/>
   <attributes name="entry-or-exit"/>
   <attributes name="place"/>
   <attributes name="date"/>     ...
  </dataset>
  <dataLinkage name="IDrecord">
   <attributes name="id-no" key="foreign"/>
   <attributes name="tax-file-no" key=foriegn"/>
  <dataLinkage/>
  <dataset name="BankRecord"
   <attributes name="tax-file-no" key="primary"/>
   <attributes name="bank-no"/>
   <attributes name="account-no"/>
   <attributes name="transaction"/>          ...
  </dataset>
 </integrate>
</flow>
```

Figure 10. An example security token

```
<S:Envelope xmlns:S="http://www.w3.org/2001/12/soap-envelope"
     xmlns:wsse=http://schemas.xmlsoap.org/ws/2002/04/secext
     xmlns:wii="http://schemas.workflow.org/wii/2003/12/authentication">
  <S:Header>          ...
    <wsse:Security>
      <wsse:UsernameToken>
        <wsse:Username>93856543</wsse:Username>
        <wsse:Password>3875</wsse:Password>
        <wii:SubjectName>Sherlock Holmes</wii:SubjectName>
        <wii:SubjectDepartment>Police</wii:SubjectLocation>
      </wsse:UsernameToken>
    </wsse:Security>   ...
  </S:Header>   ...
</S:Envelope>
```

"design as a search process," according to the framework of Hevner et al. (2004). In particular, our methodology searches for the desired services and then the desired flows among the available services, utilizing the input / output dependency relations (edges of the search graph) as the key constraints together with the requirements satisfying different concerns. The flows thus found are grouped into different views (i.e., the desired artifacts), targeting the requirements for different business partners. A key advantage of this graph-based search methodology is that such analysis is amenable to efficient searching techniques. Next, as we have developed a validation model on the flow consistency between a process view and its base process based on process algebra and automata theory in our earlier work (Chiu et al., 2003), the correctness and consistency of our methodology have solid formal foundations. This methodology further strengthens the completeness over our previous work because the formulation of the graph-search space first involves a complete enumeration of all the services required by different aspects and concerns.

It should be noted that the e-government service example discussed in the previous section is just one of the composite services that require composition. Instead of considering each of these compositions from scratch, we employ a two-phase approach. In the first phase, each provider publishes its services based on its existing processes and formulates service views to customize and restrict the access for different users. This forms a service infrastructure for the design and implementation of subsequent service composition.

Figure 11. A simplified BPEL code for illustrating security flows

```
<flow name="security-flow">
  <sessionStart>generateSecurityToken</sessionStart>
  <clearance activityName="IDCheck">
    <securityToken required="True">
      <tokenType>SAML</tokenType>
    <securityToken/>
  </clearance>
  <clearance activityName="BankCheck">
    <securityToken required="True">
      <tokenType>SAML</tokenType>
    <securityToken/>
  </clearance>
  <clearance activityName="CrimeCheck">
    <securityToken required="True">
      <tokenType>SAML</tokenType>
    <securityToken/>
  </clearance>
  <clearance activityName="BorderCheck"
    <securityToken required="True">
      <tokenType>SAML</tokenType>
    <securityToken/>
  </clearance>
<sessionEnd>revokeSecurityToken</sessionEnd>
</flow>
```

Figure 12. Proposed exception-handling approach

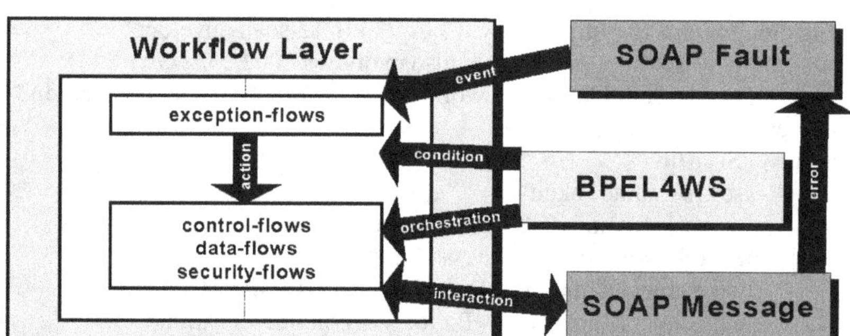

In the second phase, via a service composition approach, the SOC middleware can compose the advanced services by invoking such appropriate services to satisfy different client requirements.

Eliciting Flows for Service Provision

Based on various flows, process views can be formulated according to the policies toward different partner organizations. Consider, for example, some of the use cases of the Immigration Department in our e-government services case study. In particular, the Immigration Department provides controlled access to the ID records and border records, partly for the Police Force's Intelligence Information System. Because the basic ID record consists of basic personal information, the information systems of other government departments are, in principle, also allowed to retrieve a limited number of records for their services. For the *extended* ID records (which contain the photo and fingerprint images) as well as the border records which are more personal and sensitive, only the information systems of the Police and the Customs are allowed to access them. Except for the Police, those accesses to more than a threshold number of records within a period of time (e.g., for its own batch processing) may require approval similar to batch record access service, otherwise exceptions are raised. As the Customs quite often require batch access, an automatic approval procedure can grant such accesses, provided the requestor has an endorsement from an officer ranked superintendent or above. Similar batch restrictions apply to the access of the border records (say, used by the Inland Revenue Department for collecting tax).

1. To model and summarize the overall requirements of service provision, an organization can consider the different flows which constitute different process views for different partners. We present a methodology comprised of the following steps, with an illustration by the results obtained and shown in Appendix A for the ID service of the Immigration Department.
2. Determine the main processes (e.g., ID service process and border record service process) that are offered to middleware as services.
3. For each of the main service process, determine the sub-services[1], which includes different service options (e.g., single basic ID information, single extend ID information, and batch ID information) and supporting services (e.g., approvals).
4. For each service[2], determine the expected requestors and under which pre-conditions they are allowed to access. These are the incoming flows.
5. If any of the pre-conditions is related to security, formulate security services that deal with security flow for the checking. A successful security check will become the required pre-condition.

Figure 13. Proposed BPEL assertions for exception flow

```
<flow name="exception-flow">
 <exceptionHandling name="rule-1">
  <event>anyActivitySpecificException</event>
  <condition>affectDataIntegration</condition>
  <action>remedyOrforwardRecoveryProcedure</action>
 </exceptionHandling>
 <exceptionHandling name="rule-2">
  <event>anyCrossActivityException</event>
  <condition>affectDataLinkage</condition>
  <action>backwardRecoveryProcedure</action>
 </exceptionHandling>
 <exceptionHandlingDefault>
  <action>abortControlFlow</action>
 </exceptionHandlingDefault>
</flow>
```

6. Relate the pre-conditions with any other service constraints, such as limitations of the request parameters.
7. If any security check is related to pre-approval procedures, formulate control supporting services that deals with the control flow of the approval activity. A successful approval activity will initiate a security flow (via an internal token creation service) to grant a security token to the requestor.
8. For each service, determine the possible outcomes.
9. For each of the outcomes, specify the post-conditions and whether any messages should be sent back to the requestor, any other parties, and/or any internal services. These are the outgoing flows.
10. If an outcome message is targeted to any internal services, make sure that such a service exists, the message is appropriate, and the post-condition of the former service matches with the pre-condition of the latter service.
11. For each of the services, determine any possible abnormal outcome.
12. For each abnormal outcome, forward the exception to an exception services (such as an exception manager) that can initiate exception flow toward one or more internal or external targets.
13. Consider also the provision of exception handler services for handling internal and/or external exception flows.

Flow Analysis and View Formulation

The flows that are obtained with the methodology presented in the previous sections describe the overall service provision. Now we have to analyze the flows in order to check for missing ones as well as organize them into process views. The analysis in this sub-section has been actually motivated by our earlier research on data-driven analysis (Cheung, Chiu, & Till, 2003). When eliciting process views based on flows, the source of a message can be either an activity from which the message is published, or another flow item from which the message is derived. The sink of a message is an activity, which subscribes the message. For instance, the message "Single ID Request" is produced and published from a process in a government department. To facilitate flow requirement analysis, we define the following three relations:

1. Publish = {(p, m) | p is a party that publish message m in some activity}
2. Subscribe = {(p, m) | p is a party that subscribes message m in some activity}
3. Depend = {(d, m) | data item d is derived from message m}
4. For convenience, we write R(x, y) if and only if (x, y) is in a relation R. The following can be derived from the flow requirements in Appendix A.
5. Publish(Any Government User, Single ID Request)
6. Subscribe(Any Government User, Basic ID Information)
7. Depend(id-no, Single ID Request)
8. Depend(tax-file-no, Basic ID Information)

When an activity receives a data item from an external party due to a request message, the external party is also considered as the source of the data item. Our flow analysis is conducted through the following action items:

1. Identification of Incoming Messages - The existence of Publish(p,d) identifies an incoming message InMsg(p, d).
2. Identification of Outgoing Messages - The existence of Subscribe(p,d) identifies an outgoing message OutMsg(p,d).
3. Identification of Immediate Responses of Incoming Messages - Let G = (V, E) be a directed graph where V is the set of data items involved in the service process and E is given by the Depend relation. We say that an outgoing message OutMsg(p, e) is an immediate response of an incoming message InMsg(p, d), if d is reachable by e in G; and $\neg\exists$ InMsg(p, f) such that d is reachable by f and f is reachable by e in G.
4. Identification of Data and Flow Relevancy - Assume G as defined in Step 3. An incoming message InMsg(p, d) is said to be a root incoming message and d a root data item if $\neg\exists$ InMsg(p, e) such that e is reachable by d in G. The set of reachable nodes of each data item in a service process should contain at least one root flow item. This is useful for examining the relevancy of information contained in an outgoing message. For implementation, an incoming message and its immediate response can be supported through a Web Service interface where d and e are data items contained in the incoming and outgoing XML messages, respectively. Let us also denote them as OutMsg(s, e) and InMsg(s, d) where s is the service.
5. Identification of Independent Incoming or Outgoing Message Pairs - Assume G is defined in Step 3. Two incoming message InMsg(p, d) and InMsg(q, e) are independent if d is not reachable by e, and e is not reachable by d in G. The information helps workflow optimization and the design of web services interfaces.
6. View Tabulation - For the formulation of view based on flows, tabulate the incoming messages and their immediate responses identified for each of the partner party. Table 2 shows the process views of the ID service processes composed from the elicited flows and presented to different government departments.

Service Composition

After all the organizations have published their process views of their existing processes to other organizations in a common UDDI directory, the design of service composition can be facilitated through service composition. Following our earlier example case study, Appendix B summarizes the flow requirements for the composition of the (Police) Intelligence Information System. Based on this, our methodology of the flow design for service composition can be described through the following steps:

1. Determine the set of data items D required for the integration.
2. Based on the services registered in the common UDDI directory, determine the service and organization from which those data items can be obtained from. That is, for each item d $\in$D, find service s such that OutMsg(s, m) $\wedge$ Depend(d, m). Let S denote the set of required services thus found.
3. For each s$\in$S, consider InMsg(s, n), the request n required by service s. For each d' in Depend(d', n), if d'$\notin$D, add d' into D. Re-iterate from step 1 until no more items can be added to D, i.e., all the transitively dependent data requirements D as well as the set of services S providing them are found.

Table 2. Views of the ID service process to other departments

Department	View Composed of the Flows (numbered in Appendix A)
Police	i1->o1, i1->(o2->)o18, i1->o3, i5->o11, i5->(o12->i13->)o22, i8-> o16, i8-> (o17->i15)->o24, i15->o25
Customs	i3->o7, i3->(o8->i10->)o19, i6-> o13, i6->(o14->i14->)o23, i8->o16, i8->(o17->i15->)o24, i15->o25
Other Govt. Users	i4->o9, i4->(o10->)o19, i8->o16, i8->(o17->i15->)o24, i15->o25
Central IT Security Center	i8->(o17->i15->)o25, i7->(o15->i17->)o25, i19->o25,

4. For each s∈S, consider the pre-condition requirements of the flows. Determine the extra security flow (such as approved security token) and control flow (such as approval applications) required. Re-iterate from Step 1 if extra data items are required or from Step 4 if only extra control and security services are required.
5. Determine any relevant exception flows that could occur and design handler activities / services if necessary.
6. Implement the internal process for the integration of the control, data, security, and exception flows.
7. Design process views of this new service process for other organizations, according to the methodology discussed in previous sub-sections, as the new service process is now ready,.

The above explained algorithms present the methodology to create cleanly separated process views, operating on strictly defined service interfaces. This method can also be extended with semantic web service composition methodologies, which is one of the main directions of our future work.

DISCUSSION AND CONCLUSION

Middleware provides a common interface through which services may interact with one another via their runtime environments. It provides a uniform mechanism to decouple services from platform specific functions and to handle environmental fluctuation. Services constructed as such are highly interoperable and amenable to composition.

In this paper, we have detailed the design rationale and architecture of our FlowEngine middleware based on the concepts of flows and views, together with a prototypical implementation based on contemporary Web services technologies. Web services technologies provide a unified platform for effective synchronous process enactment as well as timely asynchronous communications of events and exceptions. Automatic generation of WSDL from process view definition greatly simplifies the deployment and management Web services for B2B interactions, and helps the mapping of messages at runtime. The additional message mapping of asynchronous communications further increases the flexibility. With our implementation of process views and flows in strict accordance with the basic Web service (WSDL and SOAP) standard, all participants can easily make use of the basic service provision even without employing a process view engine. Therefore, smooth migration is enabled with a gradual adoption of FlowEngine middleware for integration partners until they need advanced and automatic features of flows and views.

This paper has also presented a new perspective of process views through a subset of various flows of the original process. As such, process views are now enriched, in addition to basic control flow, with such typical flow types as data flow, exception flow, and security flow. This leads to a pragmatic methodology of requirements engineering for service composition, especially from a service provision viewpoint. The technical merits of our approach are discussed with respect to the system developers as well as the benefits to the management.

To tackle the complexity of the design and management of service composition, we have developed a pragmatic methodology for the elicitation of service composition and the required interactions with flows and process views. For service developers, the process view mechanism employed in the FlowEngine targets at systematic mapping between public services and private processes together with their definition, enactment, and management. It is most useful when service providers have existing processes or information systems and want to offer them as services for different partners with different access control or service variations. Our aim is to enable different types of interactions with different participants for the interaction, avoiding changes to existing systems and processes as far as possible. As a result, cross-organizational interactions can be adequately tested and incrementally deployed in a relatively short period of time. Not only does this save development cost, it is also essential to system stability in this increasingly competitive digital economy age.

Our two-phased methodology conceptually decomposes heterogeneous information systems into a unified collection of flows and views to facilitate their complex integration for different purposes and operations. In particular, each organization is most knowledgeable of its own processes and their potential to service provision. The first phase of our methodology (namely, the initial process view formulation) provides a solid service infrastructure for service composition. As the services are well defined, other partners are likely to be satisfied with them and work efficiently on their own in composing services for their required integrations, avoiding most of the tedious and often costly negotiations for service provision requests. In a case where new services are really required to be added, other partners may also make use of the new services (subjected to view-based control).

The second phase of our methodology presents a systematic method for composing the available component service endpoints that constitutes the different views of the advanced services in order to satisfy different client requirements. Should new requirements arise with new applications and new service endpoints are required, our methodology can be re-applied to support iterative development cycles. The investigation into such development cycle as well as managing development outsourcing (Chan et al., 2007) is one direction of our future research.

Our methodology is a viable solution for the systematic design of process views, leading to better process specification and management, especially in the context of service composition. The application of the "separation of concerns" principle enables better understanding of complex application semantics and is especially useful for large-scaled information systems. In addition, our approach is extensible because the methodology is still valid even when new types of flows (say, QoS, semantic, and privacy flow) are identified.

For the service providers, this approach is resilient to requirement changes, because new flows or modified flows (of different types) required can be easily identified. For example, in the e-Governmental case study environment, if some later access further requires a court warrant, we can just add the required control flow and security flow for "court warrant" without changing other unaffected flows of the existing processes. Therefore, our methodology facilitates better testability through independently testable flows and faster development of highly complex systems by hiding unnecessary details in each view. This also allows for easier changes for the same reason. Compared with other research efforts on this topic, our approach provides an improved environment for various types of process enactment, which can adapt to changing requirements, with extensive support for reuse in the context of service composition.

The major benefit of our middleware to the management is due to the convergence of disparate business functionalities into various services. Our FlowEngine provides tangible benefit for organizations by allowing systematic and managed information sharing between partners and participants. This facilitates cross-organization collaboration and therefore increases business opportunities. In particular, through standardized Web services technologies, the challenges in converging and interfacing different businesses across different organizations can be tackled in a proper approach. Our FlowEngine middleware facilitates synchronous and asynchronous message exchange and provides timely information to help (the right level of) the management to react and make decisions accordingly. Provision of monitoring facilities through the services is also possible for increasing the process transparency. This helps more flexible and timely exception handling as well as improves relationships with business partners.

In order to balance trust and security, the management of an organization would like to provide information on only the relevant part of its internal workflow to business partners. To achieve this, our approach organizes interactions with different business partners systematically into process views, so that customized interactions captured with flows. Overall, this new middleware helps capture and manage knowledge for business interactions across different types of business partners as well as to facilitate such related automation. These advantages in combination can also lead to cost savings as a major business advantage and can foster system stability.

As a continuing work, we are studying semantic flows and how they can help exception handling. An in-depth study of this topic is of paramount interest since it is one of the most useful applications of Semantic Web technologies to process management and integration. Semantic flow dealing with heterogeneous ontology and ontology integration problems is another topic for future research. Also, focus will be laid on the integration for updating scenarios with transaction management.

On the other hand, privacy flow relationships describe each service's data practices, what information they collect from individuals, and what (e.g., purposes) they do with it. In particular, security flows and privacy flows are conflicting but both are required according to laws and regulations. We further plan to work on alerts (Kafeza et al., 2004; Chiu et al., 2009), that is, process urgency requirements, which is also in line with the flow concept.

In addition, we are further working on details of formal definitions, security, construction and verification algorithms, view update mechanisms, and support for more operations and especially further confirmation of the efficiency and effectiveness of our approach. For interaction protocols, we plan to work on such details as process adaptation for interoperability, interaction protocol negotiation, multiple-party protocols and sub-protocols.

ACKNOWLEDGMENT

The work described in this paper was supported by grants from the CityU Strategic Research Grant (No. 7002212), the Research Grants Council of the Hong Kong Special Administrative Region, China, under Project No.s CityU 117608 and HKUST6170/03E.

REFERENCES

Alves, A., Arkin, A., Askary, S., Barreto, C., Bloch, B., & Curbera, F. (2007). *Web Services Business Process Execution Language Version 2.0*. Burlington, MA: OASIS.

Barros, A. P., Dumas, M., & ter Hofstede, A. H. M. (2005). Service Interaction Patterns. In *Proceedings of the 3rd International Conference on Business Process Management* (pp. 302-318). Berlin, Germany: Springer.

Basten, T., & van der Aalst, W. M. P. (2001). Inheritance of Behavior. *Journal of Logic and Algebraic Programming*, *47*(2), 47–145. doi:10.1016/S1567-8326(00)00004-7

Britton, C., & Bye, P. (2004). *IT Architectures and Middleware: Strategies for Building Large, Integrated Systems* (2nd ed.). Boston, MA: Addison-Wesley Professional.

Brogi, A., Corfini, S., & Popescu, R. (2008). Semantics-based composition-oriented discovery of Web services. *ACM Transactions on Internet Technology*, *8*, 1–39. doi:10.1145/1391949.1391953

Casati, F., Ceri, S., Paraboschi, S., & Pozzi, G. (1999). Specification and implementation of exceptions in workflow management systems. *ACM Transactions on Database Systems*, *24*(3), 405–451. doi:10.1145/328939.328996

Chan, V. C. T., Chiu, D. K. W., Chow, S., & Hung, P. C. K. (2007). e-Monitoring of Outsourcing IS Project in Financial Institutions: A Case Study on Mandatory Provident Fund Projects in Hong Kong. In *Proceedings of the 2007 IEEE International Conference on e-Business Engineering* (pp. 460-465). Washington, DC: IEEE Computer Society.

Cheung, S. C., Chiu, D. K. W., & Till, S. (2003). Data-driven methodology to extending workflows to e-services over the internet. In *Proceedings of the 36th Annual Hawaii International Conference on System Sciences (HICSS 2003),* Big Island, HI. Washington, DC: IEEE Computer Society.

Chiu, D. K. W., Cheung, S. C., Kafeza, E., & Ho-Fung, L. (2003). A three-tier view-based methodology for M-services adaptation. Systems. *IEEE Transactions on Man and Cybernetics. Part A*, *33*(6), 725–741.

Chiu, D. K. W., Cheung, S. C., Till, S., Karlapalem, K., Li, Q., & Kafeza, E. (2004). Workflow View Driven Cross-Organizational Interoperability in a Web Service Environment. *Information Technology Management*, *5*(3-4), 221–250. doi:10.1023/B:ITEM.0000031580.57966.d4

Chiu, D. K. W., Cheung, S. C., Till, S., Narupiyakul, L., & Hung, P. C. K. (2010). Enhancing E-service Collaboration with Enforcement and Relationship Management: a Methodology from Requirements to Event Driven Realization. *International Journal of Organizational and Collective Intelligence*, *1*(1), 15–43. doi:10.4018/joci.2010100802

Chiu, D. K. W., Kafeza, K., Cheung, S. C., Kafeza, E., & Hung, P. C. K. (2009). Alerts in Healthcare Applications: Process and Data Integration. *International Journal of Healthcare Information Systems and Informatics*, *4*(2), 36–56. doi:10.4018/jhisi.2009040103

Chiu, D. K. W., Karlapalem, K., & Li, Q. (2001). Views for Inter-organization Workflow in an E-commerce Environment. In *Semantic Issues in E-Commerce Systems: Proceedings of the IFIP TC2/WG2.6 9th Working Conference on Database Semantics,* Hong Kong (pp. 137-151). Dordrecht, The Netherlands: Kluwer.

Chiu, D. K. W., Karlapalem, K., Li, Q., & Kafeza, E. (2002). Workflow View Based E-Contracts in a Cross-Organizational E-Services Environment. *Distributed and Parallel Databases*, *12*(2-3), 193–216. doi:10.1023/A:1016503218569

Chiu, D. K. W., Li, Q., & Karlapalem, K. (2000). Web Interface-Driven Cooperative Exception Handling in ADOME Workflow Management System. *Information Systems*, *26*(2), 93–120. doi:10.1016/S0306-4379(01)00012-6

Curbera, F., Duftler, M. J., Khalaf, R., Nagy, W. A., Mukhi, N., & Weerawarana, S. (2005). Colombo: Lightweight middleware for service-oriented computing. *IBM Systems Journal, 44*(4), 799–820. doi:10.1147/sj.444.0799

Curbera, F., Khalaf, R., Leymann, F., & Weerawarana, S. (2003). Exception handling in the BPEL4WS language. In *Proceedings of the International Conference on Business Process Management (BPM 2003),* Eindhoven, The Netherlands (pp. 276-290). Berlin, Germany: Springer.

Erl, T. (2006). *Service-Oriented Architecture: Concepts, Technology, and Design*. Upper Saddle River, NJ: Prentice-Hall.

Eshuis, R., & Grefen, P. (2008). Constructing customized process views. *Data & Knowledge Engineering, 64*(2), 419–438. doi:10.1016/j.datak.2007.07.003

Francisco, C., Rania, K., Nirmal, M., Stefan, T., & Sanjiva, W. (2003). The Next Step in Web Services. *Communications of the ACM, 46*(10), 29–34. doi:10.1145/944217.944234

Hevner, A. R., March, S. T., Park, J., & Ram, S. (2004). Design Science in Information Systems Research. *Management Information Systems Quarterly, 28*(1), 75–105.

Huhns, M. N., & Singh, M. P. (2005). Service-oriented computing: key concepts and principles. *IEEE Internet Computing, 9*(1), 75–81. doi:10.1109/MIC.2005.21

Hull, R., & Su, J. (2005). Tools for Composite Web Services: A Short Overview. *SIGMOD Record, 34*(2), 86–95. doi:10.1145/1083784.1083807

Hung, P. C. K., & Chiu, D. K. W. (2004). Developing workflow-based information integration (WII) with exception support in a web services environment. In *Proceedings of the 37th Annual Hawaii International Conference on System Sciences (HICSS 2004),* Big Island, HI. Washington, DC: IEEE Computer Society.

Kafeza, E., Chiu, D. K. W., Cheung, S. C., & Kafeza, M. (2004). Alerts in mobile healthcare applications: requirements and pilot study. *IEEE Transactions on Information Technology in Biomedicine, 8*(2), 173–181. doi:10.1109/TITB.2004.828888

Kambayashi, Y., & Peng, Z. (1996). An Object Deputy Model for Realization of Flexible and Powerful Objectbases. *Journal of Systems Integration, 6*, 329–362. doi:10.1007/BF02265083

Kiczales, G., Lamping, J., Mendhekar, A., Maeda, C., Lopes, C., Loingtier, J.-M., & Irwin, J. (1997). Aspect-Oriented Programming. In *Proceedings of the 11th European Conference on Object-Oriented Programming (ECOOP97),* Jyväskylä, Finland (LNCS 1241, pp. 220-242).

Kiwata, K., Nakano, A., Yura, S., Uchihashi, T., & Kanai, A. (2007). Scenario-based service composition method in the open service environment. In *Proceedings of the 5th International Symposium on Autonomous Decentralized Systems* (pp. 135-140). Washington, DC: IEEE Computer Society.

Lai, A., & Murphy, G. C. (1999). *The Structure of Features in Java Code: An exploratory investigation.* Paper presented at the 1st International Workshop on Multi-dimensional Separation of Concerns (OOPSLA'99), Denver, CO.

Larman, C. (1997). *Applying UML and Patterns.* Upper Saddle River, NJ: Prentice-Hall.

Li, X., Madnick, S., Zhu, H., & Fan, Y. (2009). An Approach to Composing Web Services with Context Heterogeneity. In *Proceedings of the IEEE International Conference on Web Services* (pp. 695-702). Washington, DC: IEEE Computer Society.

Liu, A., Liu, H., Lin, B., Huang, L., Gu, N., & Li, Q. (2010). A Survey of Web Services Provision. *International Journal of Systems and Service-Oriented Engineering*, *1*(1), 26–45. doi:10.4018/jssoe.2010092102

Liu, D.-R., & Shen, M. (2003). Workflow modeling for virtual processes: an order-preserving process-view approach. *Information Systems*, *28*(6), 505–532. doi:10.1016/S0306-4379(02)00028-5

Michael, P. P. (2003). Web Services and Business Transactions. *World Wide Web (Bussum)*, *6*(1), 49–91. doi:10.1023/A:1022308532661

Milanovic, N., & Malek, M. (2004). Current Solutions for Web Service Composition. *IEEE Internet Computing*, *8*(6), 51–59. doi:10.1109/MIC.2004.58

Moon, J., Kim, R., Song, B., & Cho, H. (2005). Transformation algorithms between WSCI and BPEL4WS for the collaborative business process. In *Proceedings of the 7th International Conference on Advanced Communication Technology* (pp. 285-290). Washington, DC: IEEE Computer Society.

Moon, J., Lee, D., Park, C., & Cho, H. (2004). Transformation algorithms between BPEL4WS and BPML for the executable business process. In *Proceedings of the 13th IEEE International Workshops on Enabling Technologies: Infrastructure for Collaborative Enterprises* (pp. 135-140). Washington, DC: IEEE Computer Society.

Oracle. (2008). *Oracle Fusion Middleware*. Retrieved April 4, 2009, from http://www.oracle.com/technology/products/middleware/index.html

Orriens, B., Yang, J., & Papazoglou, M. P. (2003). A framework for business rule driven service composition. In *Proceedings of the 4th VLDB Workshop on Technologies for E-Services* (pp. 14-27). London, UK: Springer-Verlag.

Ossher, H., & Tarr, P. (2001). Using multidimensional separation of concerns to (re)shape evolving software. *Communications of the ACM*, *44*(10), 43–50. doi:10.1145/383845.383856

Papazoglou, M. P., & Georgakopoulos, D. (2003). Service-Oriented Computing: Introduction. *Communications of the ACM*, *46*(10), 24–28. doi:10.1145/944217.944233

Papazoglou, M. P., & van den Heuvel, W.-J. (2007). Service-oriented computing: concepts, characteristics and directions. *The VLDB Journal*, *16*(3), 389–415. doi:10.1007/s00778-007-0044-3

Perry, D. E., Romanovsky, A., & Tripathi, A. (2000). Current trends in exception handling. *IEEE Transactions on Software Engineering*, *26*(10), 921–922. doi:10.1109/TSE.2000.879816

Robillard, M. P., & Murphy, G. C. (2007). Representing Concerns in Source Code. *ACM Transactions on Software Engineering and Methodology*, *16*(1), 3. doi:10.1145/1189748.1189751

Rosenberg, J., & Remy, D. (2004). *Securing Web Services with WS-Security: Demystifying WS-Security, WS-Policy, SAML, XML Signature, and XML Encryption*. Sebastopol, CA: Sams.

SAP. (n.d.). *SAP NetWeaver Technology Platform*. Retrieved April 4, 2009, from http://www.sap.com/platform/netweaver/index.epx

Schmit, B. A., & Dustdar, S. (2005). Towards Transactional Web Services. In *Proceedings of the 7th IEEE International Conference on E-Commerce Technology Workshops* (pp. 12-20). Washington, DC: IEEE Computer Society.

Schulz, K. A., & Orlowska, M. E. (2004). Facilitating cross-organisational workflows with a workflow view approach. *Data & Knowledge Engineering*, *51*(1), 109–147. doi:10.1016/j.datak.2004.03.008

Shan, Z., Li, Q., Luo, Y., & Peng, Z. (2005). Deputy Mechanism for Workflow Views. In *Proceedings of the 10th International Conference on Database Systems for Advanced Applications (DASFAA 2005)* (pp. 816-827). Berlin, Heidelberg: Springer.

Shankar, R. P., & Armando, F. (2004). Interoperability among independently evolving web services. In *Proceedings of the 5th ACM/IFIP/USENIX International Conference on Middleware* (pp. 331-351). New York, NY: ACM.

She, W., Yen, I., Thuraisingham, B., & Bertino, E. (2009). The SCIFC Model for Information Flow Control in Web Service Composition. In *Proceedings of the IEEE International Conference on Web Services* (pp. 1-8). Washington, DC: IEEE Computer Society Press.

Singh, M. P., & Huhns, M. N. (2005). *Service-Oriented Computing: Semantics, Processes, Agents*. Hoboken, NJ: John Wiley & Sons.

Sutton, J. S. M., & Rouvellou, I. (2002). Modeling of software concerns in cosmos. In *Proceedings of the 1st International Conference on Aspect-oriented Software Development (AOSD'02)* (pp. 127-133). New York: ACM.

Tran, H., Zdun, U., & Dustdar, S. (2007). View-based and Model-driven Approach for Reducing the Development Complexity in Process-Driven SOA. In *Proceedings of the International Working Conference on Business Process and Services Computing (BPSC'07)* (LNI 116, pp. 105-124).

Turner, C. R., Fuggetta, A., Lavazza, L., & Wolf, A. L. (1998). Feature engineering software development. In *Proceedings of the 9th International Workshop on Software Specification and Design* (pp. 162-164). New York, NY: ACM.

van Breugel, F., & Koshkina, M. (2005). Dead-path-elimination in BPEL4WS. In *Proceedings of the 5th International Conference on Application of Concurrency to System Design* (pp. 192-201). Los Alamitos, CA: IEEE Computer Society.

van der Aalst, W. M. P. (1999). Interorganizational Workflows: An Approach based on Message Sequence Charts and Petri Nets. *Systems Analysis - Modelling - Simulation, 34*(3), 335-367.

van der Aalst, W. M. P., Dumas, M., & ter Hofstede, A. H. M. (2003). Web Service Composition Languages: Old Wine in New Bottles? In *Proceedings of the 29th Euromicro Conference* (pp. 298-305). Los Alamitos, CA: IEEE Computer Society.

van der Aalst, W. M. P., & Kumar, A. (2003). XML Based Schema Definition for Support of Inter-organizational Workflow. *Information Systems Research*, *14*(1), 23–46. doi:10.1287/isre.14.1.23.14768

van der Aalst, W. M. P., & Weske, M. (2001). The P2P Approach to Interorganizational Workflows. In *Proceedings of the 13th International Conference Advanced Information Systems Engineering* (pp. 140-156). Berlin, Germany: Springer.

van Thanh, D., & Jorstad, I. (2005). A Service-Oriented Architecture Framework for Mobile Services. In *Proceedings of the Advanced Industrial Conference on Telecommunications/Service Assurance with Partial and Intermittent Resources Conference/ E-Learning on Telecommunications Workshop* (pp. 65-70). Los Alamitos, CA: IEEE Computer Society Press.

White, S. A. (2008). *BPMN Modeling and Reference Guide*. Lighthouse Point, FL: Future Strategies.

Wohed, P., Van Der Aalst, W. M. P., Dumas, M., & ter Hofstede, A. H. M. (2003). Analysis of Web Services Composition Languages: The Case of BPEL4WS. In *Proceedings of the 22nd International Conference on Conceptual Modeling (ER 2003)* (pp. 200-215). Berlin, Germany: Springer.

Yang, J., Papazoglou, M. P., & van den Heuvel, W. J. (2002). Tackling the challenges of service composition in e-marketplaces. In *Proceedings of the 12th International Workshop on Research Issues in Data Engineering: Engineering E-Commerce/E-Business Systems* (pp. 125-133). Los Alamitos, CA: IEEE Computer Society Press.

Yu, M., Taleb-Bendiab, A., & Reilly, D. (2004). A polyarchical middleware for self-regenerative invocation of multi-standard ubiquitous services. In *Proceedings of the 2004 IEEE International Conference on Web Services* (pp. 410-417). Los Alamitos, CA: IEEE Computer Society Press.

ENDNOTES

1 To simplify subsequent discussion, we do not explicitly say "sub-service" unless such a term is necessary to distinguish with the overall service.

2 Data services provide information and deal with data flow; control services provide procedure automation and deal with control flow; security services deal with security checks; exceptions services deal with exception situations. Usually, data or control services are the main ones to be considered first.

APPENDIX A

Table A1. Flow requirements for the ID service

Flow	Incoming Flow			Pre-condition	Activity/ Sub-Service	Post-condition	Outgoing Flow		
	#	Expected Requestor	Incoming Item				Outgoing Item	Destination	#
CONTROL	I1	Any Govt User	Single Extended ID Approval Request		Single Extended ID Approval	Single Extended ID Approved	Approval Message	Requestor	O1
							Token Creation Request	Token Creation Task	O2
						Single Extended ID Rejected	Rejection Message	Requestor	O3
	I2	Any Govt User	Batch ID Approval Request		Batch ID Service Manual Approval	Batch ID Approved	Approval Message	Requestor	O4
							Token Creation Request	Token Creation Task	O5
						Batch ID Rejected	Rejection Message	Requestor	O6
	I3	Customs		Customs security token verified & superintendent endorsement supplied	Batch ID Service Automatic Approval	Batch ID Approved	Approval Message	Requestor	O7
							Token Creation Request	Token Creation Task	O8
			...						
DATA	I4	Any Government User	Single ID Request	Any Government Department security token verified	Single Basic ID Information	Analysis Successful	Basic ID information	Requestor	O9
						ID not found	Error Message	Exception Manager	O 10
	I5	Police/ Customs/ Approved Users	Single Extended ID Request	Police/ Customs/ Single Extended ID Security Token verified	Single Extended ID Information	Extended Analysis Successful	Extended ID information	Requestor	O 11
						ID not found	Error Message	Exception Manager	O 12
	I6	Police/ Approved Users	Batch ID Request	Batch ID/Police Security Token verified	Batch ID Information	Batch processing Successful	Batch Suspect Analysis Report (with ID Information)	Requestor	O 13
						Analysis Error	Error Message	Exception Manager	O 14
	I7	Any User	Any Request	No/Invalid Security Token	Any Service	Unauthorized Request	Rejection Message	Requestor	O 15
			...						

continued on following page

Table A1. Continued

SECURITY	I8	Any Govt User	Any Government Department Security Token		External Security Token Verification	External Security Token Verified	Accept Message	Requestor	O 16
						Invalid External Security Token	Rejection Message	Exception Manager	O 17
	I9	Single ID Approval Task	Token Creation Request	Single Extended ID Approved	Token Creation		Single Extended ID Token	Requestor	O 18
	I10	Batch ID Approval Task	Token Creation Request	Batch ID Approved	Token Creation		Batch ID Token	Requestor	O 19
	I11	Approved User	Single Extended ID Token		Internal Security Token Verification	Internal Security Token Verified	Accept Message	Requestor	O 20
	I12	Approved User	Batch ID Token			Invalid Internal Security Token	Rejection Message	Exception Manager	O 21
			...						
EXCEPTION	I13	Single Basic/ Extend ID Information Analysis Task	Internal Exception	ID not found	Exception Manager		ID Not Found Exception	Requestor	O 22
	I14	Batch ID Information Analysis Task	Internal Exception	Analysis Error	Exception Manager		Analysis Error Exception	Requestor	O 23
	I15	External Security Token Verification Task	Internal Exception	External Security Token Invalid	Exception Manager		Token Invalid Exception	Requestor	O 24
					Exception Manager		Security Alert Exception	Central IT Security Control	O 25
	I16	Internal Security Token Verification Task	Internal Exception	Internal Security Token Invalid	Exception Manager		Token Invalid Exception	Requestor	O 26
					Exception Manager		Security Alert Exception	Department IT Security Control	O 27
	I17	Any Data Service	Internal Exception	Unauthorized Request	Exception Manager		Unauthorized Request Exception	Requestor	O 28
					Exception Manager		Security Alert Exception	Central IT Security Control	O 29
	I18	Flow Monitor	Internal Exception	Request Limit Exceeded	Exception Manager		Request Limit Exception	Requestor	O 30
	I19	Flow Monitor	Internal Exception	Too many Request Limit Exceeded Exception Raised	Exception Manager		Service Abuse Exception	Central IT Security Control	O 31
	I20	Original Requestor	Investigation Abort Exception	Same security token as original requestor	Abort current analysis	Analysis aborted	Abortion successful message	Requestor	O 29
			...						

APPENDIX B

Table A2. Flow requirement for the composition of an intelligence information system

Flow	Incoming Flow		Pre-condition	Activity/Sub-Service	Post-condition	Outgoing Flow	
	Expected Requestor	Incoming Item				Outgoing Item	Destination
Control	End User	Query Request		ID Query Approval	Request Approved	Single Extended ID Approval Request	ID Information Service: Single Extended ID Approval
	ID Information Service	Approval Message		Bank/Crime Query Automatic Approval		General Bank Approval Request	Bank Information Service: General Bank Service Automatic Approval
						Crime Approval Request	Crime Information Service: Crime Service Manual Approval
	ID Information Service	Rejection Message		Rejection Analysis	Token Creation Requested		
					Request Rejected	Rejection Message	End User
			Security Token Created	ID Query Authorization		Single Extended ID Approval Request	ID Information Service: Single Extended ID Approval
	Bank Information Service	Approval Message		Border Query Automatic Approval		Border Approval Request	Border Information Service: Border Service Automatic Approval
	Crime Information Service	Approval Message					
	Border Information Service	Approval Message		Suspect Information Analysis Approval		Analysis Result Notification	End User

continued on following page

Table A2. Continued

Data Security	End UserID Information Service	Suspect General Information-Extended ID Information	Request Approved	Query Information CheckID Information Analysis		Single Extended ID Request-General Bank Service Request	ID Information Service: Single Extended ID Information AnalysisBank Information Service: General Bank Information Analysis
						Crime Service Request	Crime Information Service: Crime Information Analysis
	Bank Information Service	General Bank Information		Bank/Crime Information Analysis		Border Service Request	Border Information Service: Border Information Analysis
	Crime Information Service	Crime Information					
	Border Information Service	Border Information		Border Information Analysis		Suspect Analysis Report	End User
	End User	Any Government User Security Token		Security Token Verification	Security Token Verified	Any Government User Security Token	ID Information Service: External Security Token Verification
						Any Government User Security Token	Bank Information Service: Security Token Verification
						Any Government User Security Token	Crime Information Service: Security Token Verification
						Any Government User Security Token	Border Information Service: Security Token Verification
						Accept Message	End User
					Invalid Security Token	Rejection Message	End User
			Token Creation Requested	Token Creation	Security Token Created	Police Security Token	ID Information Service: External Security Token Verification
Exception	ID Information Service	ID Not Found		Query Information Check	Query Aborted	Information Wrong	End User

This work was previously published in the Journal of Database Management, Volume 22, Issue 2, edited by Keng Siau, pp. 32-63, copyright 2011 by IGI Publishing (an imprint of IGI Global).

Chapter 8
Ensuring Customised Transactional Reliability of Composite Services

Sami Bhiri
National University of Ireland, Galway, Ireland

Walid Gaaloul
Telecom & Management SudParis, France

Claude Godart
LORIA-INRIA, France

Olivier Perrin
LORIA-INRIA, France

Maciej Zaremba
National University of Ireland, Galway, Ireland

Wassim Derguech
National University of Ireland, Galway, Ireland

ABSTRACT

Web services are defined independently of any execution context. Due to their inherent autonomy and heterogeneity, it is difficult to examine the behaviour of composite services, especially in case of failures. This paper is interested in ensuring composite services reliability. Reliable composition is defined as a composition where all instance executions are correct from a transactional and business point of view. In this paper, the authors propose a transactional approach for ensuring reliable Web service compositions. The approach integrates the expressivity power of workflow models and the reliability of Advanced Transactional Models (ATM). This method offers flexibility for designers to specify their requirements in terms of control structure, using workflow patterns, and execution correctness. Contrary to ATM, the authors start from the designers' specifications to define the appropriate transactional mechanisms that ensure correct executions according to their requirements.

INTRODUCTION

The Web services approach (Erickson & Siau, 2008) has gained broad acceptance as a key technology to automate Business-to-Business (aka B2B) interactions. The Web services technology is an implementation of Service Oriented Architecture[1]. A Web service can be defined as an independent and auto descriptive software component that can be dynamically discovered and invoked through the Internet (or Intranet).

Companies can encapsulate their business processes and publish them as services; and

DOI: 10.4018/978-1-4666-2044-5.ch008

afterwards discover, share and aggregate them. One interesting feature is the possibility to create added value services by composing other services. It is worth noting that the term composite service is usually used to denote composition of operations offered by different services (Alonso, Casati, Kuno, & Machiraju, 2004; Jordan et al., 2007). Throughout this paper, and without loss of generality, we consider services offering only one operation.

Different from business process components, services are generally provided by different organisations independently of any execution context. Since each organisation has its own rules, Web services are treated like strictly autonomous entities. Due to their inherent heterogeneity and autonomy it is difficult to predict the behaviour of composite services especially in case of failures.

The problem we tackle in this paper is how to ensure composite services reliability. By reliable composition, we mean every composition where all its instances have correct execution. An execution is said to be correct if it performs and finishes as intended (from a business point of view). In other terms, an instance execution is correct if it reaches its objectives and completes successfully or it fails properly in a consistent state according to designers requirements.

Current Web service technologies are unable to solve this problem efficiently. These technologies rely mainly on two strong approaches: Workflow Systems (WfS for short) (Georgakopoulos, Hornick, & Sheth, 1995; Jablonski & Bussler, 1996; Leymann & Roller, 1999; van der Aalst & van Hee, 2002; Fischer, 2007) and Advanced Transactional Models (ATM for short) (Georgakopoulos, Hornick, Krychniak, & Manola, 1994; Elmagarmid, Leu, Litwin, & Rusinkiewicz, 1990; Elmagarmid, 1992; Garcia-Molina & Salem, 1987; Garcia-Molina et al., 1991; Moss, 1981; Weikum & Schek, 1992). Taken separately, these technologies are unable to resolve composite services reliability in an effective way.

Indeed, while Workflow management is the key technology for automating business processes enabling their modelling, enactment and analysis, they don't consider reliability problems in case of task failures. On the other hand, ATM ensures reliability of advanced transactions by extending the flat structure of the ACID transactional model and relaxing atomicity and isolation properties. Nevertheless, ATM remains limited for supporting workflow-like applications. First, their control structure still remain primitive compared to those of business processes and consequently to those of composite services. Secondly, they impose a set of constraints regarding the structure and transactional semantics that designers must comply to when modelling their applications.

In this paper, we propose a model for composite Web services that combines the expressivity power of workflow models and the reliability of transactional models. Based on this model, we present a set of techniques enabling to ensure reliability according to designers' requirements (in terms of control flow and failure atomicity). We use the Accepted Termination States (ATS for short) (Elmagarmid et al., 1990; Rusinkiewicz & Sheth, 1995) property as an execution correctness criterion to relax atomicity.

The originality of our approach is the flexibility offered to designers to specify their requirements in terms of control flow and correction (by specifying the set of ATS). Contrary to ATM, we start from designers' specifications to define transactional mechanisms allowing ensuring correct executions according to their requirements. To the best of our knowledge, and as stated in (Rusinkiewicz & Sheth, 1995), "defining a transaction with a particular set of properties" (ATS in our case) "and assuring", a priori, that every execution "will preserve these properties remains a difficult problem" (p. 3).

The remainder of the paper is organised as follows. We first motivate our work through an example which we use throughout the paper. Then we present our transactional Web service model which allows for capturing both the control and the transactional flow of composite services. Next, we propose a pattern based approach for modelling transactional composite services. Then we illustrate how we proceed to ensure reliability according to designers' requirements and describe some implementation issues. Finally we discuss some related work, conclude the paper and draw some perspectives.

MOTIVATING EXAMPLE

Let us consider an application for Online Travel Arrangement (OTA for short) showing enterprise interactions in a B2B context. The execution logic of the application is illustrated in Figure 1[2]. First, the customer specifies his requirements in terms of destination and hotels through the task Customer Requirements Specification (CRS for short). Then, the application launches two tasks in parallel: the Flight Reservation task (FR for short) and Hotel Reservation task (HR for short). Once these tasks completed, the task Online Payment (OP for short) is launched allowing the customer to pay his travel. Finally, the documents (flight coupons and hotel booking confirmation) are sent to the customer using one of the three available tasks: Send Document by FedEx, Send Document by DHL, and Send Document by TNT (SDF, SDD, and SDT for short respectively). The Web services approach enables to define the OTA application as a composite service while booking, online payment, and delivery tasks are provided by different organisations as services.

In order to handle failures, designers can specify, in addition to the control flow, recovery mechanisms enabling a composite service to recover to a consistent state in case of failures. Back to our example, designers can specify that: (i) OP, SDD, and SDT always complete successfully, (ii) in case of failure of the service HR, the service FR must be cancelled or compensated (depending on its current state, still running or completed), (iii) in case of failure of the service SDF, the service SDD must be activated as an alternative.

It is worth emphasizing that other designers in other contexts may choose other component services that have different properties and define other recovery rules. The problem we are interested in is how to check that the specified model ensures the transactional reliability expected by the designers. For instance, the composite service shown in Figure 1 may abort due to the failure of FR while the hotel reservation is still maintained which may be accepted by some designers and not accepted by others.

Current technologies are unable to ensure transactional reliability of applications having such a complex control structure. Their main shortcomings follow from the lack of integration of the following dimensions:

- **Business process adequacy:** Contrary to transactional models and similar to workflow systems, one should start from design-

Figure 1. Composite service: control flow enhanced with recovery mechanisms

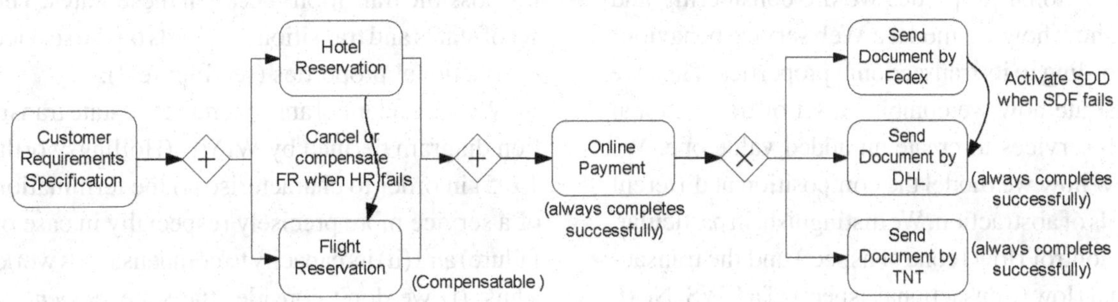

ers requirements in terms of control structure and reliability. This implies being able to support control structures more complex than those of ATM and allowing designers to specify their reliability requirements.

- **Transactional correctness:** Contrary to workflow systems and like ATM, one should ensure reliable compositions based on a correctness criterion, itself defined according to designers' specifications. This implies developing a set of techniques to validate composite service models with respect to the defined correctness criterion.

In other terms the required solution should combine the business process adequacy offered by workflow systems and transactional correctness ensured by ATM.

TRANSACTIONAL WEB SERVICES MODEL

In this section, we introduce our Web service composition model. We distinguish in particular between the control and the transactional aspects of a composite Web service (CWS for short). On one hand, a CWS can be seen as a flow of autonomous and heterogeneous services. On the other hand, it can be considered as a structured transaction where the component services are the sub-transactions and the interactions are the dependencies.

In the following we introduce the concept of transactional Web service. We present the transactional properties we are considering and we show how we model a Web service behaviour according to its transactional properties. Then we illustrate how we combine a set of transactional Web services to create an added value one. We show how we model the composition at different levels of abstraction. We distinguish, in particular, the control flow (control aspect) and the transactional flow (transactional aspect) of a CWS. Next, we detail the relation between the control flow and the transactional flow of a CWS.

Transactional Web Service: TWS

Transactional Properties

In this paper, by Web service we mean a self-contained modular program that can be discovered and invoked across the Internet. A transactional Web service is a Web service of which the behaviour manifests transactional properties.

The main transactional properties of a Web service we are considering are retriable, compensatable and pivot (Mehrotra, Rastogi, Korth, & Silberschatz, 1992). A service s is said to be retriable, s^r, if it is sure to complete after several finite activations. s is said to be compensatable, s^{cp}, if it offers compensation policies to semantically undo its effects. Then, s is said to be pivot, s^p, if once it completes successfully, its effects remain forever and cannot be semantically undone. Naturally, a service can combine properties, and the set of all possible combinations is $\{r; cp; p; (r; cp); (r; p)\}$.

The rationale behind using these properties is that they enable to characterise two properties relevant for reliability namely the failure possibility of a service and its compensation capacity.

Modelling Transactional Behaviour

Every service can be associated to a life cycle state chart that models the possible states which the executions of this service can go through, and the possible transitions between these states. The set of states and transitions depends on the service transactional properties (see Figure 2).

We have adapted and extended the state transition diagram defined by WfMC (Hollingsworth, 1995) in order to characterise (i) the termination of a service more precisely (especially in case of failure) and (ii) its capacity to compensate its work. Thus, (i) we don't consider the state *suspended*

Figure 2. State transition diagrams of transactional Web services according to their transactional properties

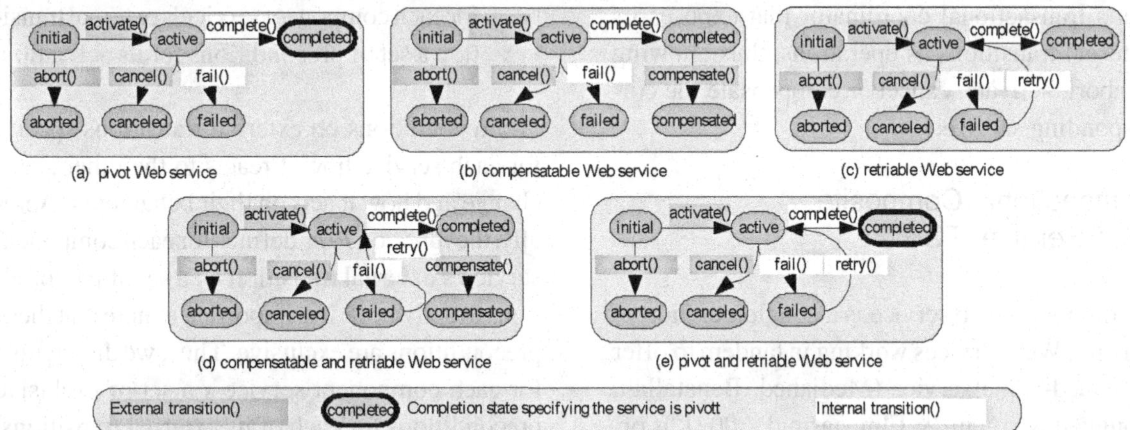

(which we integrate with the state *active*), (ii) we add a new state compensated to mark that the service has been compensated and (iii) we add a transition *retry()* to characterise that the service is retriable.

Figure 2 illustrates the state transition diagrams of transactional services according to their transactional properties. Each service has a minimal set of states (initial, aborted, active, cancelled, failed, completed) and a minimal set of transitions (*abort(), activate(), cancel(), fail(), complete()*). When a service is instantiated, the state of the instance is *initial*. Then this instance can either be aborted or activated. Once it is *active*, the instance can normally continue its execution or it can be *cancelled* during its execution. In the first case, it can achieve its objective and completes successfully or it can fail. A compensatable service has, in addition, a state *compensated* and a transition *compensate()*. A retriable service has, in addition to this minimal set, a transition *retry()* that changes the state of a service from *failed* to *active*.

Within a transactional service, we distinguish between external and internal transitions. External transitions are triggered by external entities. Typically they allow a service to interact with the outside and to specify composite services orchestration (see next section). The external transitions we consider are *activate()*, *abort()*, *cancel()*, and *compensate()*. Internal transitions are triggered by the service itself (the service agent). Internal transitions we consider are *complete()*, *fail()*, and *retry()*. We note TWS the set of all transactional Web services.

Specifying Transactional Properties

Thanks to semantic Web services description, it is possible to specify service transactional properties. WSMO (Roman, Lausen, & Keller, 2006) defines a set of non-functional properties of a semantic service. This initiative defines, among others, the attribute transactional for specifying transactional properties of semantic Web services. WSMO does not specify a model for non functional properties in general and for transactional properties in particular. Using WSML (Bruijn, 2005), it is possible to define transactional properties of a service as the value of the attribute transactional.

Compared to WSMO, OWL-S (Martin, 2004) defines a limited number of non-functional properties. However it enables defining new ones using the attribute *ServiceParameter* of the concept *ServiceProfile*. Thus, it is possible to add a new property to define transactional properties of a service.

In accordance with Web services coordination (Newcomer, Robinson, Feingold, & Jeyaraman,

2007), we suppose that each transactional service has a transactional coordinator that exposes its external transitions as operations, thus allowing to abort, activate, cancel or compensate the corresponding service.

Transactional Composite Web Service: TCS

A composite Web service is a conglomeration of existing Web services working in tandem to offer an added-value service (Medjahed, Benatallah, Bouguettaya, Ngu, & Elmagarmid, 2003). It orchestrates a set of services, as a workflow based composition, to achieve a specific goal.

A transactional composite (Web) service (TCS for short) is a composite Web service where its component services are TWS. Such a service takes advantage of component services' transactional properties to specify failure handling and recovery mechanisms.

Composition of Transactional Web Services

A TCS defines a set of preconditions on each component service's external transition in order to define how these component services are orchestrated. These preconditions specify for each component service when it will be aborted, activated, cancelled, or compensated.

For example, the OTA service in Figure 1 specifies that *OP* will be activated after the completion of *HR* and *FR*. That means the precondition of the transition *activate()* of *OP* is the completion of *HR* and the completion of *FR*.

Thus, a TCS can be defined as the set of its component services and the set of the preconditions defined on their external transitions. More formally we define a TCS as following.

Definition 1: A transactional composite Web service *tcs* is a couple $tcs = (ES \subset \text{TWS}, Prec)$ where *ES* is the set of its component Web services and *Prec* is a function that defines for each component service's external transition a set of preconditions for its activation.

Preconditions on external transitions specify for each service how it reacts to the other states change and how it acts on their behaviours. Actually, the function *Prec* defines for each component service's external transition *t()* a set of preconditions to activate it. It is important to note that these preconditions are exclusive. Thus, we distinguish for each component service *s* a set of exclusive preconditions for each of its external transitions, *activate()*, *abort()*, *cancel()*, and *compensate()*.

For instance, the OTA service specifies that *SDD* will be activated either after the completion of OP[3] or after the failure of *SDF*. That means *Prec(SDD.activate())* = {(*OP.completed* ∧ SDD chosen for delivery), (*SDF.failed* ∧ SDD can be used for delivery)}. We note TCS the set of all transactional composite Web services.

Dependencies Between a TCS's Component Services

Preconditions express at a higher abstract level relations (successions, alternatives, etc.) between component services in the form of dependencies. These dependencies express how services are coupled and how the behaviour of certain component service(s) influences the behaviour of other one(s). For example, the precondition on the external transition *activate()* of *SDD* expresses (i) a succession relation (or dependency) between *OP* and *SDD* and (ii) an alternative relation (or dependency) between *SDF* and *SDD*. More formally:

Definition 2: Let *cs* be a TCS, s_1 and s_2 two component services of *cs*, $s_1.t_1()$ a transition of s_1, and $s_2.t_2()$ an external transition of s_2, a dependency from $s_1.t_1()$ to $s_2.t_2()$, denoted $dep(s_1.t_1(), s_2.t_2())$, exists if the completion of $s_1.t_1()$ may trigger $s_2.t_2()$.

Dependencies express relations between services; however they do not describe interactions between services precisely. A dependency $dep(s_1.t_1(), s_2.t_2())$ does not specify when $s_2.t_2()$ will be activated (following $s_1.t_1()$ completion). $dep(s1.t1(), s2.t2())$ is defined according to $Prec(s_2.t_2())$. In our approach, we consider *activation*, *alternative*, *compensation* and *cancellation* dependencies which we detail in the following.

Activation Dependency and Activation Condition

An activation dependency expresses a succession relation between two services. An activation dependency from s_1 to s_2 exists *iff* the completion of s_1 may trigger the activation of s_2. More formally and according to definition 2:

$ActDep(s_1, s_2) = dep(s_1.complete(), s_2.activate())$.

An activation dependency from s_1 to s_2 expresses only a succession relation between them. However, it does not specify when s_2 will be activated (following the termination of s_1). Regarding its definition, an activation dependency $ActDep(s_1,s_2)$ is defined according to $Prec(s_2.activate())$ and more precisely according to the activation condition of s_2. The activation condition of a service *s* (as a successor) determines when it will be activated as a successor for other(s) service(s). We note the activation condition of a service *s* *ActCond(s)*.

For example, the composite service shown in Figure 1 defines an activation dependency from *OP* to *SDD* such that *SDD* will be activated when *OP* completes and *SDD* is chosen for delivery. That means *ActCond(SDD)* = {*OP.completed* $\wedge$ *SDD chosen for delivery*}.

Alternative Dependency and Alternative Condition

Alternative dependencies allow defining execution alternatives as forward recovery mechanisms. An alternative dependency from s_1 to s_2 exists *iff* the failure of s_1 may fire the activation of s_2. More formally and according to definition 2:

$AltDep(s_1, s_2) = dep(s_1.fail(), s_2.activate())$.

Regarding its definition, an alternative dependency $AltDep(s_1, s_2)$ is defined according to $Prec(s_2.activate())$ and more precisely according to the alternative condition of s_2. The alternative condition of a service s, *AltCond(s),* specifies when *s* will be activated as an alternative of other service(s).

For instance the OTA composite service shown in Figure 1 defines an alternative dependency from *SDF* to *SDD* such that *SDD* will be activated when *SDF* fails. That means *AltCond(SDD)* = *{SDF.failed Λ SDD can be used for delivery}*.

Note that the activation condition of the transition *activate()* of a service *s* is defined by *s* activation condition (as a successor), *ActCond(s)*, and by *s* alternative condition *AltCond(s)*: *Prec(s.activate())* = *ActCond(s)* $\cup$ *AltCond(s)*. For instance, *Prec(SDD.activate())* = *ActCond(SDD)* $\cup$ *AltCond(SDD)* = *{(OP.completed Λ SDD chosen f or delivery), (SDF.failed Λ SDD can be used f or delivery)}*.

Abortion Dependency and Abortion Condition

An abortion dependency enables to propagate failures (causing TCS abortion) from one service to its successor(s) by aborting them. An abortion dependency from s_1 to s_2 exists *iff* the failure, cancellation or the abortion of s_1 may fire the abortion of s2. More formally and according to definition 2:

$AbrDep(s_1, s_2) = dep(s_1.abort(), s_2.abort()) \vee dep(s_1.fail(), s_2.abort()) \vee dep(s_1.cancel(), s_2.abort())$.

An abortion dependency $AbrDep(s_1, s_2)$ is defined according to $Prec(s_2.abort())$. $Prec(s.abort())$ defines the abortion condition of *s*, *AbrCond(s)*, which determines when *s* will be aborted.

Compensation Dependency and Compensation Condition

A compensation dependency enables to define a backward recovery mechanism by compensation. A compensation dependency from s_1 to s_2 exists *iff* the failure or the compensation of s_1 may fire the compensation of s_2. More formally and according to definition 2:

$CpsDep(s_1, s_2) = dep(s_1.fail(), s_2.compensate()) \vee dep(s_1.compensate(), s_2.compensate())$.

A compensation dependency $CpsDep(s_1, s_2)$ is defined according to $Prec(s_2.compensate())$. *Prec(s.compensate())* defines the compensation condition of *s*, *CpsCond(s)*, which determines when *s* will be compensated.

The composite service illustrated in Figure 1 defines a compensation dependency from *HR* to *FR* such that *FR* will be compensated when *HR* fails. That means *CpsCond(FR) = Prec(FR.compensate()) = {HR.failed}*.

Cancellation Dependency and Cancellation Condition

A cancellation dependency enables to signal a service execution failure to other service(s) being carried out in parallel by cancelling their execution if necessary. A cancellation dependency from s_1 to s_2 exists *iff* the failure of s_1 may fire the cancellation of s_2. More formally and according to definition 2:

$CnlDep(s_1, s_2) = dep(s_1.fail(), s_2.cancel())$

A cancellation dependency $CnlDep(s_1, s_2)$ is defined according to $Prec(s_2.fail())$. *Prec(s.fail())* defines the cancellation condition of *s*, *CnlCond(s)*, which specifies when *s* will be cancelled.

Control and Transactional Flow of a TCS

We call activation and abortion dependencies control dependencies. We call compensation, cancellation and alternative dependencies transactional dependencies. Control and transactional dependencies express, at a higher abstract level, the control flow and the transactional flow of a TCS respectively.

Control Flow

The control flow of a TCS specifies partial ordering between component service activations. Intuitively the control flow of a TCS is defined by the set of its control dependencies. Formally, we define a control flow as a TCS where the only dependencies it defines are control dependencies.

Definition 3: A control flow is a *TCS*, $cf = (ES, Prec)$ such that $\forall s \in ES\ AltCond(s) = \perp$, $CpsCond(s) = \perp$ and $CnlCond(s) = \perp$.

We note *CFlow* the set of all control flows. We define the function *getCFlow* that returns the control flow of a given TCS.

Definition 4: We define the function *getCFlow* that returns the control flow of a TCS.

$getCFlow: TCS \rightarrow CFlow$

$cs = (ES,Prec) \rightarrow cf\ (ES';Prec')$

such that $ES' = ES$ and $\forall s \in ES$ $Prec'(s.activate()) = ActCond(s)$;

$Prec'(s.cancel()) = \perp$; $Prec'(s.compensate()) = \perp$.

Transactional Flow

The transactional flow of a TCS specifies the recovery mechanisms. Intuitively, a transactional flow of a TCS is defined by the transactional properties of its component services and its set of transactional dependencies. Formally we define a transactional flow as a TCS of which the only dependencies are transactional dependencies.

Definition 5: A transactional flow defined according to a control flow *cf* is a TCS, $tf_{cf} = (ES,Prec)$ such that $\forall s \in ES$ $ActCond(s) = \perp$ and $AbrCond(s) = \perp$.

We note *TFlow* the set of all transactional flows. We define the function *getTFlow* that returns the transactional flow of a given TCS.

Definition 6: We define the function *getTFlow* that returns the transactional flow of a TCS.

getTFlow: $TCS \rightarrow TFlow$

$sc = (ES,Prec) \rightarrow fc = (ES';Prec')$

such that $ES' = ES$ and $\forall s \in ES$ $Prec'(s.activate()) = AltCond(s)$ and $Prec'(s.abort()) = \perp$.

Union of Transactional Composite Services

A TCS, *cs*, can be seen as the union of its control flow, *getCFlow(cs)*, and its transactional flow *getTFlow(cs)*. In general, the union of two TCS cs_1 and cs_2 is a TCS where (i) the set of its component services is the union of cs_1's and cs_2's component services (ii) the precondition of an external transition of a component service *s* is the one defined by cs_1 if *s* belongs only to cs_1, the one defined by cs_2 if *s* belongs only to cs_2, or the union of the preconditions defined by cs_1 and cs_2 if *s* belongs to both of them.

Definition 7: Let cs_1 and cs_2 be two TCS: $cs_1 = (ES_1,Prec_1)$ and $cs_2 = (ES_2,Prec_2)$. The union of cs_1 and cs_2 is the TCS *cs* defined as follows:

$cs = cs1 \cup cs_2 = (ES,Prec)$ where

- $ES = ES_1 \cup ES_2$.
- $\forall s \in ES$

$Prec_1(s)$ if $s \in ES_1 \wedge s \notin ES_2$

$Prec(s) = Prec_2(s)$ if $s \in ES_2 \wedge s \notin ES_1$

$Prec_1(s) \cup Prec_1(s)$ if $s \in ES_1$ and $s \in ES_2$

Thus every TCS *cs* is the union of its control flow and transactional flow: $cs = getCFlow(cs) \cup getTFlow(cs)$.

Relation Between the Control Flow and the Transactional Flow of a TCS

The transactional flow is tightly related to the control flow. Indeed, the recovery mechanisms (defined by the transactional flow) depend on the execution process logic (defined by the control flow). For example, regarding the OTA composite service, it is possible to define SDD as an alternative to SDF because (according to the XOR-split control flow operator) they are defined on exclusive branches. Similarly, it is possible to define a compensation dependency from HR to FR because (according to the AND-join control flow operator) the failure of HR requires the compensation of the partial work already done which might be the flight booking. More generally, a control flow tailors all possible recovery mechanisms implicitly. We call a potential transactional flow of a given control flow *cf* the transactional flow including all possible transactional dependencies (i.e. recovery mechanisms) that can be defined with respect to to *cf*. More formally, each component service *s* has according to the TCS control flow:

- **ptCpsCond(*s*):** Its potential compensation condition that specifies when *s* may eventually be compensated.
- **ptAltCond(*s*):** Its potential alternative condition that specifies when *s* may eventually be activated as an alternative.
- **ptCnlCond(*s*):** Its potential cancellation condition that specifies when *s* may eventually be cancelled.

Back to our example, according to the OTA service control flow FR may be compensated either after the failure or the compensation of OP, or after the failure of HR. That means *ptCpsCond(FR) = {OP.failed, OP.compensated, HR.failed}.*

Given a control flow *cf*, several TCS can be defined according to it. Each of these TCS will adopt *cf* as its control flow and will extend it by a transactional flow included in its potential transactional flow. More formally, given a TCS *tcs* the following holds:

∀ *s* a component service of *tcs*, $CpsCond(s) \subseteq ptCpsCond(s)$,

$CpsCnl(s) \subseteq ptCnlCond(s)$ and $AltCond(s) \subseteq ptAltCond(s)$

For instance the compensation condition of FR is the failure of HR which is included in its potential compensation condition given above.

PATTERN BASED MODELLING

In the previous section, we presented our transactional Web service model which enables to capture both the control and the transactional flow of a TCS. In this section, we show how we model a TCS. We adopt an approach based on workflow patterns (van der Aalst, ter Hofstede, Kiepuszewski, & Barros, 2003). We extend them in order to specify, in addition to the control flow they consider by default, TCS' transactional flow.

Pattern based modeling is interesting for many reasons. Patterns are relatively simple (compared to workflow languages) thanks to the abstraction they ensure. Patterns are practical since they are deduced from available workflow languages. In addition they enhance reusability and comprehension between designers. Pattern based modeling also allows modular and local processing. In the following, we introduce the composition patterns and their transactional potential. Then we show how we use them in order to specify TCS.

Composition Patterns

In this section, we present the workflow patterns from the perspective of our model. Then we show how a given workflow pattern tailors a set of possible transactional flows.

Workflow Patterns

Riehle and Zullighoven (1996) define a pattern as "the abstraction from a concrete form which keeps recurring in specific non arbitrary contexts" (p. 1). A workflow pattern (van der Aalst et al., 2003) can be seen as an abstract description of a recurrent class of interactions. For example, the *AND-join* pattern (van der Aalst et al., 2003) (see Figure 3b) describes an abstract service interaction as follows: a service is activated after the completion of several other services.

According to our TCS model, the basic workflow patterns (van der Aalst et al., 2003) consider only the control flow side. Thus, they can be considered as control flow patterns. Formally, we define a control flow pattern as a function that returns a control flow given a set of services.

Definition 8: A control flow pattern, *pat*, is a function *pat*: P^4(TWS) → *CFlow*, that returns a control flow *pat(S)* given a set of transactional services *S*. *pat* defines for each service $s \in S$, its activation condition *ActCond(s)* and its abortion condition *AbrCond(s)*.

In our approach, we consider the following patterns: *sequence*, *AND-split*, *OR-split*, *XOR-split*, *AND-join*, *OR-join*, *XOR-join* and *m-out-of-n* (van der Aalst et al., 2003). Due to lack of space, we put emphasis on the patterns we are using in our illustrative example namely *AND-split*, *AND-join* and *XOR-split* patterns. The formal definition of these patterns and more details about the other patterns can be found in Bhiri (2005).

AND-Split Pattern

Van der Aalst et al. (2003) define an *AND-split* pattern as "a point in the workflow process where a single thread of control splits into multiple threads of control which can be executed in parallel, thus allowing activities to be executed simultaneously or in any order" (p. 6). According to our approach, an *AND-split* pattern is a function which specifies that a set of services, $\{s_1, \ldots, s_n\}$, are activated after the completion of another service s_0. Informally speaking, this function defines a control flow such that (i) its component services are $\{s_0, s_1, \ldots, s_n\}$, (ii) the activation and the abortion conditions of s_0 are events external to the defined control flow, (iii) and for each s_i ($1 \leq i \leq n$) the activation condition of s_i is the completion of s_0 and (iv) the abortion condition of s_i is the failure of s_0. Figure 3a illustrates the control flow *AND-split(CRS,HR, FR)*.

AND-Join Pattern

Van der Aalst et al. (2003) define an *AND-join* pattern as "a point in the workflow process where multiple parallel sub processes/activities converge into one single thread of control, thus synchronizing multiple threads" (p.7). According to our approach, an *AND-Join* pattern is a function which specifies that a service s_0 is activated after the completion of a set of other services $\{s_1, \ldots, s_n\}$. Informally put, this function defines a control flow such that (i) its component services are $\{s_0, s_1, \ldots, s_n\}$, (ii) the activation condition of s_0 is the completion of all services $\{s_1, \ldots, s_n\}$, (iii) the abortion condition of s_0 is the failure of one service among $\{s_1, \ldots, s_n\}$, (iv) and for each s_i ($1 \leq i \leq n$) the activation and abortion conditions of s_i are events external to the defined control flow. Figure 3b illustrates the control flow *AND-join(OP, HR, FR)*.

XOR-Split Pattern

Van der Aalst et al. (2003) define a *XOR-split* pattern as "a point in the workflow process where, based on a decision or workflow control data, one of several branches is chosen" (p. 7). According to our approach, a *XOR-split* pattern is a function which specifies that a service among a set of other services $\{s_1, \ldots, s_n\}$ is activated after the completion of another service s_0. Informally speaking, this function defines a control flow such that (i) its component services are $\{s_0, s_1, \ldots s_n\}$, (ii) the activation and the abortion conditions of s_0 are events external to the defined control flow, (iii) for each s_i ($1 \leq i \leq n$) the activation condition of s_i is the completion of s_0 and the satisfaction of a given condition c_i (c_i, $1 \leq i \leq n$ are exclusive conditions), and (iv) the abortion condition of s_i is the failure of s_0. Figure 3c illustrates the control flow *XOR-split(OP, SDF, SDD, SDT)*.

Patterns' Transactional Potential

A workflow pattern *pat* defines a control flow *pat(S)* given a set of services. Similar to any control flow, *pat(S)* possesses a potential transactional flow. We define for each workflow pattern, *pat*, a function $potential_{pat}$ that returns, given a set of services *S*, the potential transactional flow of *pat(S)*.

Figure 3. The OTA service control flow is defined as a consistent union of a set of pattern instances

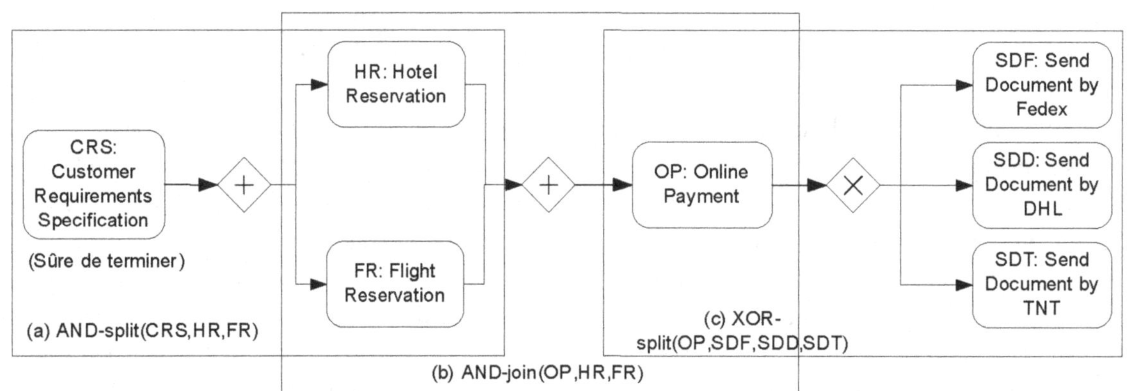

Definition 9: Let *pat* be a control flow pattern. The function $potential_{pat}: P(\mathrm{TWS}) \rightarrow TFlow$, returns given a set of services *S* the potential transactional flow of the control flow *pat(S)*.

$potential_{pat}$ defines for each service $s \in S$ its potential compensation condition, *ptCpsCond(s)*, its potential alternative condition, *ptAltCond(s)*, and its potential cancellation condition *ptCnlCond(s)*.

In the following, we detail the potential functions of the patterns *AND-split*, *AND-join*, and *XOR-split*. The formal definitions of these functions and the potential functions of additional patterns can be found in Bhiri (2005).

AND-Split Potential Function

The potential function of the pattern *AND-split*, denoted $potential_{AND\text{-}split}$, defines for a given set of services $\{s_0, s_1, \ldots, s_n\}$ the following transactional dependencies: s_0 is compensated when a service s_i $(1 \leq i \leq n)$ is compensated or cancelled, or when all services s_1, s_2 ... s_n fail. Figure 4a, illustrates $potential_{AND\text{-}split}(CRS, HR, FR)$, the potential transactional flow of the control flow *AND-split(CRS,HR, FR)*.

AND-Join Potential Function

The potential function of the pattern *AND-join*, denoted $potential_{AND\text{-}join}$, defines for a given set of services $\{s_0, s_1, \ldots, s_n\}$ the following transactional dependencies: each service s_i will be compensated or cancelled (according to its current state) when a service s_j fails (where $1 \leq i, j \leq n$ and $i \neq j$). Each service s_i $(1 \leq i \leq n)$ will be compensated when s_0 fails, is compensated or cancelled. Figure 4b illustrates $potential_{AND\text{-}join}(OP, HR, FR)$ the potential transactional flow of the control flow *AND-join(OP,HR,FR)*.

XOR-Split Potential Function

The potential function of the pattern *XOR-split*, denoted $potential_{XOR\text{-}split}$, defines for a given set of services $\{s_0, s_1, \ldots, s_n\}$ the following transactional dependencies: each service s_i is an alternative for s_j where $1 \leq i, j \leq n$ and $i \neq j$. s_0 will be compensated when (i) every service s_i $(1 \leq i \leq n)$ either has already failed or its control condition does not hold or (ii) it exists a service s_i $(1 \leq i \leq n)$ that has been compensated. Figure 4c illustrates $potential_{XOR\text{-}split}(OP, SDF, SDD, SDT)$ the potential transactional flow of the control flow *XOR-split(OP, SDF, SDD, SDT)*.

Figure 4. The potential transactional flow of the OTA service control flow

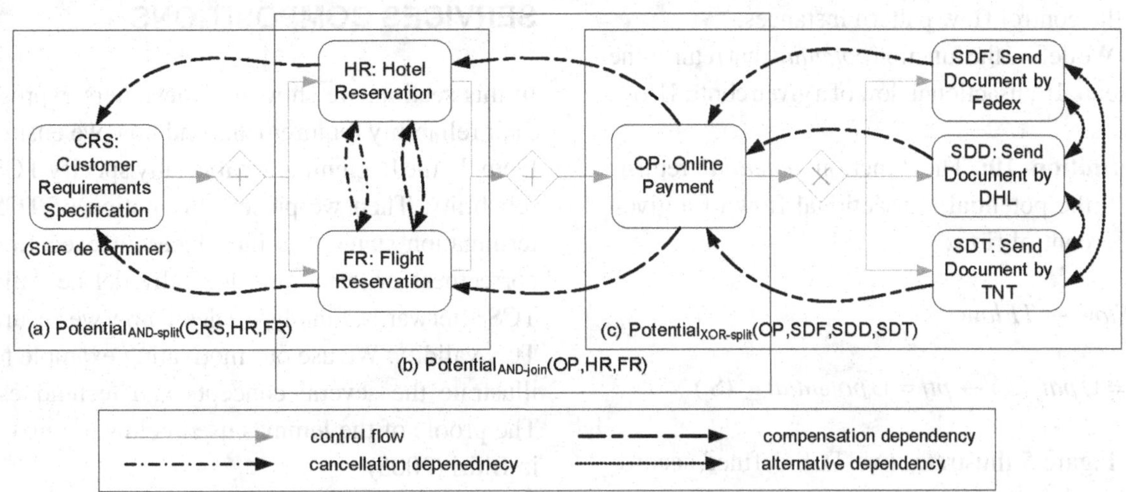

TCS Specification

Specifying a TCS returns to define its control and transactional flows. In the following we show how we use (i) workflow patterns for defining TCS' control flow and (ii) their transactional potential for defining TCS' transactional flow.

Control Flow Specification

We call pattern instance, the control flow resulting from the application of a pattern to a set of services. Let *pat* a pattern and *S* a set of services, *pat(S)* is an instance of *pat*. We use pattern instances as the basic brick for specifying TCS' control flows. Indeed, in our approach a control flow is defined as the union of pattern instances. Figure 3 shows how we define the control flow of the OTA service as a union of pattern instances. More formally:

∀ *TCS cs = (ES, Prec)* ∃ a set of patterns *{P1,..., Pn}* and a partition *S*

of ES: $S = \{S_1,\ldots, S_n\}$ (with ES = ∪1≤ i ≤ n(S$_i$)) |

getCFlow(cs) = ∪1≤ i ≤ n P_i (S_i)

To ensure the control flow consistency, we use a left contextual grammar (Bhiri, Perrin, & Godart, 2005) which defines the language of consistent control flows. It postulates that (i) a consistent control flow should start with either a sequence, or a split pattern, (ii) a *sequence* pattern can be followed by any split pattern, (iii) an *AND-split* pattern can be followed by any join pattern, (iv) an *OR-split* pattern can be followed by an *OR-join* or a *XOR-join* pattern, and (v) a *XOR-split* pattern can be followed only by a *XOR-join* pattern. In addition, a component service in a given TCS can be itself a composite service where its control flow is consistent (respects the same grammar); thus allowing to use patterns in a nested way inside a composition.

Transactional Flow Specification

As explained above, the transactional flow of a TCS is included in the potential transactional flow of its control flow. The potential transactional flow of a control flow is the union of the potential transactional flows of its pattern instances. Figure 4 displays the potential transactional flow of the control flow defined in Figure 3. It illustrates how it is the union of the potential transactional flows of the control flow pattern instances.

We define the function *potential* that returns the potential transactional flow of a given control flow.

Definition 10: The function *potential* returns the potential transactional flow of a given control flow:

$CFlow \rightarrow TFlow$

$cf = \cup_i pat_i\,(S_i) \rightarrow ptf = \cup_i potential_{pati}\,(S_i)$

Figure 5 illustrates two TCS defined according to the same control flow shown in Figure 3. Each of these services extends this control flow with a transactional flow included in its potential transactional flow shown in Figure 4.

ENSURING RELIABLE WEB SERVICES COMPOSITIONS

In this section, we show how designers express their reliability requirements and how we ensure them. In the beginning, we formally specify TCS reliability. Then we present the notion of TCS termination states. We introduce our execution correctness criterion and formally define valid TCS afterwards. Finally, we detail how we ensure TCS validity. We use our motivating example to illustrate the several concepts and techniques. The proofs of the lemmas used below are given in Bhiri (2005).

Valid TCS

TCS Termination States

Many executions can be instantiated according to the same TCS model. The state of a TCS instance

Figure 5. Two composite services defined according to the same control flow

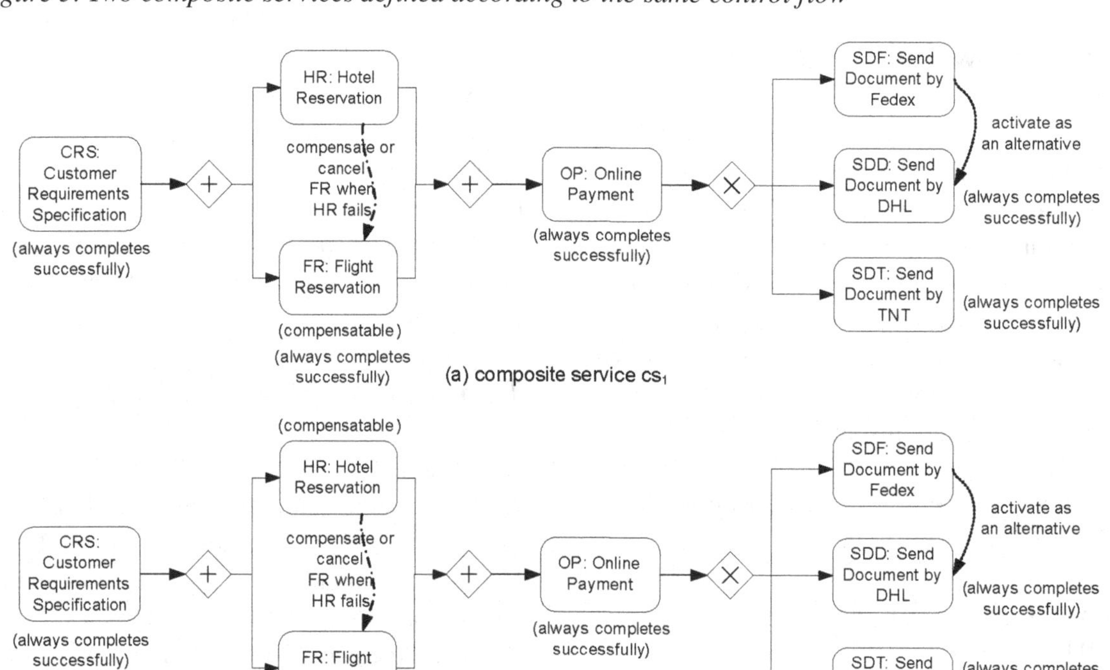

composed of n services can be represented by the tuple $(e_1, e_2, \ldots, e_n)$, where e_i is the state of the service instance s_i. The set of termination states (STS for short) of a TCS is the set of all possible termination states of its instances. We note *TS* the set of all TCS STS. Table 3 illustrates the STS of the composite service given in Figure 6.

Definition 11: (Set of Termination States) we define the function *STS*: *TCS* → *T S* that returns the set of termination states of a composite service *cs: STS(cs).*

Termination States Without Failures

We distinguish between two kinds of termination states. The first one corresponds to the termination states reached after normal executions (without failures unexpected by the control flow). We call such a termination state *a termination state without failures*. We note *TS*failures the domain of the STS without failures. Table 1 illustrates the STS without failures of both services cs_1 and cs_2 illustrated in Figure 5. The STS without failures of a TCS is defined by its control flow.

Definition 12: (Set of termination states without failures) We define the function

*STS*failures*: CFlow →TS*failures that returns the set of termination states (without failures) defined by a given control flow.

Termination States with Failures

The second kind of termination states corresponds to the ones reached in case of failure(s) of certain component service(s). We call a termination state of this second type a termination state with failures. We note $TS_{failures}$ the domain of the STS with failures. Tables 2a and 2b illustrate the STS with failures of the composite services cs_1 and cs_2 illustrated in Figure 5a and 5b respectively.

Definition 13: (Set of termination states with failures) we define the function $STS_{failures}$: $TFlow \rightarrow TS_{failures}$ that returns the set of termination states (with failures) defined by a given transactional flow.

The STS of a TCS *cs* is the union of the termination states defined by its control flow and those induced by its transactional flow. Formally *STS (cs)* = *STS*failures (*getCFlow* (*cs*)) ∪ $STS_{failures}$(*getTFlow* (*cs*))

ATS: Execution Correctness Criterion

Designers express their reliability requirements by specifying the set of Accepted Termination States (ATS for short). An accepted termination state is a state where designers accept an instance terminates (Elmagarmid et al., 1990; Rusinkiewicz & Sheth, 1995). Thus, ATS is our correctness criterion. It is important to note that an ATS, like a transactional flow, is defined according to a predefined control flow. Like any termination state, we distinguish two kinds of accepted termination states, with and

Table 1. The STS without failures of services cs_1 and cs_2 illustrated in Figure 5

Services ts	CRS	FR	HR	OP	SDF	SDD	SDT
ts_1	completed	completed	completed	completed	completed	initial	initial
ts_2	completed	completed	completed	completed	initial	completed	initial
ts_3	completed	completed	completed	completed	initial	initial	completed

Table 2. The set of termination states with failures of services cs_1 and cs_2 illustrated in Figure 5.

Services Ts	CRS	FR	HR	OP	SDF	SDD	SDT
$tsCS1_4$	completed	compensated	failed	aborted	aborted	aborted	aborted
$tsCS1_5$	completed	canceled	failed	aborted	aborted	aborted	aborted
$tsCS1_6$	completed	completed	completed	completed	failed	Completed	initial
(a) Set of termination states with failures of the service cs_1							
Services Ts	CRS	FR	HR	OP	SDF	SDD	SDT
$tsCS2_4$	completed	compensated	failed	aborted	aborted	aborted	aborted
$tsCS2_5$	completed	canceled	failed	aborted	aborted	aborted	aborted
$tsCS2_6$	completed	completed	completed	completed	failed	Completed	initial
$tsCS2_7$	completed	failed	completed	aborted	aborted	aborted	aborted
(b) Set of termination states with failures of the service cs_2							

without failures. We note *ATS*failures and $ATS_{failures}$ the set of accepted termination states without and with failures respectively. In the following, we suppose that designers specify the ATS given in Table 3 (required according to the control flow illustrated in Figure 3). The set $\{ats_1, ats_2, ats_3\}$ corresponds to *ATS*failures. It is worthy to note that ATSfailures is equal to the STS without failures (illustrated in Table 1) defined by the corresponding control flow. The set $\{ats_4, ats_5, ats_6, ats_7, ats_8, ats_9\}$ corresponds to $ATS_{failures}$.

Valid TCS Definition

By definition a composite service is valid *if and only if* all its instance executions are correct. That means their termination states are accepted by the designers.

Definition 14: (Valid TCS) A TCS *cs* is valid ⇔ $STS\ (cs) \subseteq ATS$.

This definition implies that a service *cs* is valid *if and only if* its STS with failures ($STS_{failures}$ $(getTFlow(cs))$) is included in $ATS_{failures}$.

Table 3. The set of accepted termination states required by the designers

Services ats	CRS	FR	HR	OP	SDF	SDD	SDT
ats_1	completed	completed	completed	completed	completed	Initial	initial
ats_2	completed	completed	completed	completed	initial	completed	initial
ats_3	completed	completed	completed	completed	initial	Initial	completed
ats_4	completed	compensated	failed	aborted	aborted	aborted	aborted
ats_5	completed	canceled	failed	aborted	aborted	aborted	aborted
ats_6	completed	failed	compensated	aborted	aborted	aborted	aborted
ats_7	completed	failed	failed	aborted	aborted	aborted	aborted
ats_8	completed	completed	completed	completed	failed	completed	initial
ats_9	completed	completed	completed	completed	failed	Failed	completed

Lemma 1: (Valid composite service) A composite service *cs* is valid ⇔

$STS_{failures}(getTFlow(cs)) \subseteq ATS_{failures}$.

Example: According to Definition 14, service cs_1 (see Figure 5a) is valid however service cs_2 (see Figure 5b) is not. Indeed, all the termination states of cs_1, especially those with failures, are acceptable states. However, the termination state $tsCS2_7$ of service cs_2 (see Table 2) is not acceptable.

Ensuring Valid TCS

In order to ensure valid compositions we generate a set of validation properties. A TCS is valid if and only if it respects these properties. We first present what validation properties are and explains why they ensure valid TCS. Then we detail how we compute them.

Validation Properties

In order to show what validation properties are and why they ensure valid TCS, we need to introduce two notions: *strong inclusion* of a transactional flow in another and *transactional flow induced by ATS*.

Strong Inclusion of a Transactional Flow in Another

A TCS transactional flow specifies the accepted failures (failures that may occur) and the corresponding recovery mechanisms. For instance, the transactional flow of service $cs_{induced}$ illustrated in Figure 6 accepts the following failures and specifies their recovery mechanisms as follows:

- $\mathbf{F_1}$**:** HR may fail. In such a case, we must cancel or compensate FR and abort the overall execution.
- $\mathbf{F_2}$**:** FR may fail. In such a case, we must cancel or compensate HR and abort the overall execution.
- $\mathbf{F_3}$**:** SDF may fail. In such a case, we must activate SDD as an alternative.
- $\mathbf{F_4}$**:** SDD may fail. In such a case, we must activate SDT as an alternative.

Given two transactional flows *tf1* and *tf2* defined according to the same control flow, we say that *tf2* is strongly included in *tf1*, denoted *tf2* ⊑ *tf1*, if and only if *tf2* accepts at most the failures accepted by *tf1* and manages them exactly as *tf1* does. *tf2* may not accept some failures accepted by *tf1*.

Definition 15: (Strong inclusion of a transactional flow in another)

Let *tf1* and *tf2* two transactional flows defined according to the control flow *cf*. *tf2* is strongly included in *tf1*, *tf2* ⊑ *tf1*, *if and only if* the following three conditions hold (*s* is a component service of *cf*. $\diamond_{tf2}$ *xxxCondtf1(s)* means that the xxx condition of *s* in *tf1* is eventually true in *tf2*.

- $\mathbf{C_1}$**:** ∀ *s* retriable in *tf1*, *s* is retriable in *tf2*
- $\mathbf{C_2}$**:** $\forall \diamond_{tf2}\, CpsCondtf1_i(s)$
  - *s* is compensatable in *tf2* and
  - $CpsCondtf1_i(s) \in CpsCondtf2(s)$
- $\mathbf{C_3}$**:** $\forall \diamond_{tf2} CnlCondtf1_i(s)$, $CnlCondtf1_i(s) \in CnlCondtf2(s)$
- **C4:** $\forall \diamond_{tf2} AltCondtf1_i(s)$, $AltCondtf1_i(s) \in AltCondtf2(s)$

Condition C_1 ensures that *tf2* accepts at most the failures accepted by *tf1*. Conditions C_2, C_3 and C_4 ensure that the failures accepted by *tf2* are exactly managed as they are in *tf1*. For instance, condition C_2 postulates that each compensation condition of *s* in *tf1* which is eventually true in *tf2* is also a compensation condition of *s* in *tf2* (obviously *s* will also be compensatable in *tf2*). Condition C_3 and C_4 postulate similar statements regarding cancellation and alternative conditions respectively.

Example: The transactional flow of service cs_1 (see Figure 5a) is strongly included in the transactional flow of service $cs_{induced}$ (see Figure 6). Indeed, service cs_1 accepts only failures F_1 and F_3 accepted by service $cs_{induced}$ and manages them as $cs_{induced}$ does. However the transactional flow of service cs_2 (see Figure 5b) is not strongly included in the one of $cs_{induced}$ because it does not manage the failure F_2 as it is specified in $cs_{induced}$.

Lemma 2: Let *tf1* and *tf2* be two transactional flows defined according to the same control flow $cf.tf2 \sqsubseteq tf1 \Leftrightarrow STS_{failures}(tf2) \subseteq STS_{failures}(tf1)$.

This lemma postulates that tf2 is strongly included in tf1 if and only if the STS of tf2 (with failures) is included in the STS (with failures) of tf1.

Transactional Flow Induced by ATS

A termination state with failures is reached following certain component service(s) failure(s). Such a kind of termination state keeps track of failure(s) that occurred during the execution and of the applied recovery mechanisms. For instance, the termination state with failures ats_4 (see Table 3) is reached following *HR* failure. In addition, the applied recovery mechanism consists in compensating *FR* and aborting the overall execution.

Let $STS_{withFailures}$ a STS with failures of a composite service *cs* (of which we know only its control flow *cf*). The transactional flow induced by $STS_{withFailures}$ is the transactional flow (defined according to *cf*) which leads to $STS_{withFailures}$ as a STS with failures. It is defined by the inverse function of $STS_{failures}$: $STS_{failures}^{-1}$.

Definition 16: (Induced transactional flow) The inverse function of $STS_{failures}$,

$STS_{failures}^{-1}: TS_{failures} \rightarrow TFlow$ defines the transactional flow (according to a predefined control flow) induced by a STS with failures $STS_{withFailures}$.

This function defines for each component service *s*: its transactional properties and its compensation, cancellation, and alternative conditions induced by $STS_{withFailures}$. These conditions specify respectively when *s* shall be compensated, cancelled, or activated as an alternative according to $STS_{withFailures}$.

We distinguish in particular the transactional flow induced by $ATS_{failures}$: $STS_{failures}^{-1}(ATS_{failures})$ (which we call transactional flow induced by *ATS*

Figure 6. Composite service $cs_{induced}$ showing the transactional flow induced by ATS

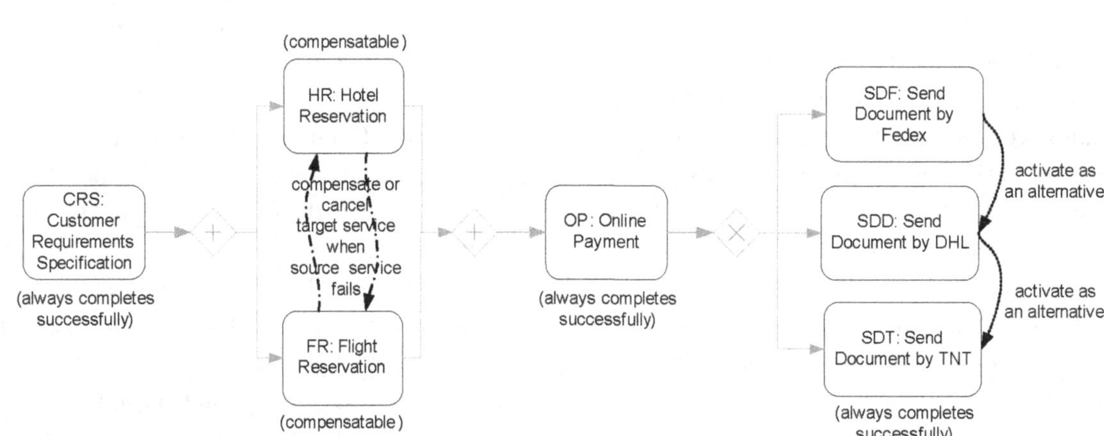

for short). The transactional flow of the service $cs_{induced}$ (see Figure 6) is the transactional flow induced by the *ATS* specified in Table 3.

Validation Properties: What and Why?

The transactional flow induced by *ATS*, $STS_{failures}^{-1}(ATS)$, specifies the accepted failures and their management according to designers' requirements. Thus, a TCS *cs* is valid if and only if its transactional flow is strongly included in the transactional flow induced by the specified *ATS*.

Lemma 3: A composite service *cs* is valid ⇔ $getTFlow\ (cs) \sqsubseteq STS_{failures}^{-1}(ATS_{failures})$.

Consequently, in order to guarantee that a composite service is valid, it returns to ensure that its transactional flow is strongly included in the transactional flow induced by ATS. And this is exactly what the validation properties allow ensuring. Each transactional flow that respects the validation properties is strongly included in the transactional flow induced by ATS and thereafter the corresponding service is valid.

Computing Validation Properties

We compute the validation properties in two steps. First we compute the transactional flow induced by *ATS*. Then we generate the validation properties from it.

Computing the Transactional Flow Induced by ATS

Computing the transactional flow induced by *ATS* returns to define for each component service *s*, its transactional properties, its compensation, cancellation and alternative conditions induced by *ATS*: *CpsCondATS(s)*, *CnlCondATS(s)* and *AltCondATS(s)*.

We can easily deduce the transactional properties of a component service *s* induced by ATS. We assume that *s* is retriable and not compensatable by default. Then, if *s* failed (respectively is compensated) in one of the acceptable termination states we deduce that it is considered not retriable (respectively compensatable). Figure 6 shows the computed transactional properties.

Algorithm 1 computes the compensation condition of *s* induced by ATS: *CpsCondATS(s)*. The principle is: a potential compensation condition of *s* becomes a compensation condition induced by *ATS* if it occurs in an acceptable termination state (with failures) where *s* is compensated. Thus, the algorithm will go through the set of termination states (line 4 to line 14). For each accepted termination state where *s* is compensated (line 5), the algorithm looks for the potential compensation condition of *s* that holds in this state (line 6 to line 13). Line 7 and line 13 enable to go through the potential compensation conditions of *s*. The boolean variable "*satisfied*" (line 6 and line 11) allows for marking if the current potential compensation condition holds or not in the current acceptable termination state (variable *ats*). A potential compensation condition that holds in *ats* is considered as a compensation condition of *s* induced by *ATS* (line 10). This condition is retrieved from the set of potential compensation condition of *s* in order to not to be examined again in the other termination states (line 12). We proceed similarly to extract the cancellation condition, *CnlCondATS(s)*, and the alternative condition, *AltCondATS(s)*, induced by ATS.

Example: The potential compensation condition of *FR*, *HR.failed*, becomes a compensation condition induced by *ATS* since it holds in ats_4 (in which the state of *FR* is *compensated*). Since ats_4 is the only state where *FR* is compensated we can deduce that the compensation condition of *FR* induced by *ATS* is the failure of *HR: CpsCondATS (FR) = {HR.failed}*. In the same way we can deduce that *CnlCondATS (FR) = {HR.failed}*, *CnlCondATS (HR) = {FR.failed}*, *AltCondATS (SDD) = {SDF.failed}* and *AltCondATS (SDT) = {SDD.failed}*.

Generating the Validation Properties

Once we calculate the transactional flow induced by *ATS*, we use a set of rules to generate the validation properties. In fact, these rules ensure through the generated properties the respect of conditions C_1, C_2, C_3 and C_4 of definition 15 such that the corresponding transactional flow, *tf*, is strongly included in the transactional flow induced by ATS.

Rule 1: ∀component service *s* ($\diamond_{tf} F$ denotes that *F* may be true in *tf*):

- R_1 if *s* is retriable in the transactional flow induced by *ATS*, then generate the validation property VP_r^s: *s* must be retriable.
- R_2 $\forall CpsCondATS_i(s) \in CpsCondATS(s)$, generate the validation property

VP_s^{cpi} : $(\diamond_{tf} (CpsCondATS_i(s))) \Rightarrow$

a. *s* must be compensatable and
b. $CpsCondATS_i(s) \in CpsCond(s)$

- R_3 $\forall CnlCondATS_i(s) \in CnlCondATS(s)$, generate the validation property

$VP_s^{cni}s$: $(\diamond_{tf} (CnlCondATS_i(s))) \Rightarrow CnlCondATS_i(s) \in CnlCond(s)$

- R_4 $\forall AltCondATS_i(s) \in AltCondATS(s)$, generate the validation property

$VP_s^{cti}s$: $(\diamond_{tf} (AltCondATS_i(s))) \Rightarrow AltCondATS_i(s) \in AltCond(s)$

The properties generated by rule R_1 ensure the respect of condition C_1. The properties generated by rule R_2 ensure the respect of condition C_2. This rule postulates that each compensation condition of *s* induced by *ATS* which is eventually true in *tf* must be a compensation condition of *s* (*s* is therefore also compensatable). Rule 3 and 4 postulate similar statements regarding cancellation and alternative conditions respectively.

Example: The application of these rules in our example enables generating the validation properties presented below {VP^r_{CRS}, VP^r_{SDT}, VP^{cp1}_{FR}, VP^{cp1}_{HR}, VP^{cn1}_{FR}, VP^{cn1}_{HR}, V^{at1}_{SDD}, V^{at1}_{SDT} }:

- By applying rule R_1, and since the services *CRS*, *OP* and *SDT* are retriable in the transactional flow induced by *ATS* then we obtain the validation properties VP^r_{CRS}, VP^r_{OP} and VP^r_{SDT} that postulates *CRS*, *OP* and *SDT* must respectively be retriable.
- By applying rule R_2, and since *CpsCondATS(FR) = {HR.failed}* (respectively *CpsCondATS(HR) = {FR.failed}*) we obtain the validation property VP^{cp1}_{FR} (respectively VP^{cp1}_{HR}):
  - VP^{cp1}_{FR} postulates that if *HR* may eventually fail (i.e is not retriable) then *FR* must be compensatable and it must be specified that *FR* will be compensated (if it has already terminated) when *HR* fails.
  - VP^{cp1}_{HR} postulates that if *FR* may eventually fail then *HR* must be compensatable and it must be specified that *HR* will be compensated (if it has already terminated) when *FR* fails.
- By applying rule R_3, and since *CnlCondATS(FR) = {HR.failed}* (respectively *CnlCondATS(HR) = {FR.failed}*), we obtain the validation property VP^{cn1}_{FR} (respectively VP^{cn1}_{HR}).
  - VP^{cn1}_{FR} postulates that if *HR* may eventually fail then it must

Algorithm 1. Extracting the compensation condition of a service s induced by ATS

```
Input: ATS: the set of acceptable termination states
ptCpsCond(s): The potential compensation condition of s defined by the control flow
Output: CpsCondATS(s): the compensation condition of s induced by ATS
Data: ats: the current acceptable termination state in ATS
ptCpsCond_i(s): a potential compensation condition of s
satisfied: a boolean variable set to true when ptCpsCond_i(s) is satisfied in ats
     begin
     CpsCondATS(s) ← ⊥
     ats ← the next ats in ATS
     while ats ≠ null do
            if the state of s in ats is compensated then
                  satisfied ← false
                  ptCpsCond_i(s) ← the next ptCpsCond_i(s) in ptCpsCond(s)
                  while none satisfied and ptCpsCond_i(s) ≠ null do
                        if ptCpsCond_i(s) is satisfied in ats then
                              CpsCondATS(s) ← CpsCondATS(s) ∪ ptCpsCond_i(s)
                              satisfied ← true
                              ptCpsCond(s) ← ptCpsCond(s) - ptCpsCond_i(s)
                  ptCpsCond_i(s) ← the next ptCpsCond_i(s) in ptCpsCond(s)
            ats ← the next ats in ATS
end
```

be specified that *FR* will be cancelled (if it is still running) when *HR* fails.

- VP^{cn1}_{HR} postulates that if *FR* may eventually fail then it must be specified that *HR* will be cancelled (if it is still running) when *FR* fails.

- By applying rule R_4, and since *AltCondATS (SDD) = {SDF.failed}* (respectively *AltCondATS (SDT) = {SDD.failed}*) we obtain the validation property V^{Pat1}_{SDD} (respectively V^{Pat1}_{SDT}).
  - V^{Pat1}_{SDD} postulates that if *SDF* may eventually fail then it must be specified that *SDD* must be activated (as an alternative) when *SDF* fails.
  - V^{Pat1}_{SDT} postulates that if *SDD* may eventually fail then it must be specified that *SDT* must be activated (as an alternative) when *SDD* fails.

Service cs_1 (illustrated in Figure 5a), which is valid, respects these validation properties in particular VP^{cp1}_{HR} (since *FR* is not retriable, its failure is no longer eventual and thereafter *HR* can be not compensatable). However, service cs_2 (illustrated in Figure 5b), which is not valid, does not respect the property VP^{cp1}_{HR}. As a consequence service cs_2 may terminate in the state $tsCS2_7$ which is not an acceptable state.

IMPLEMENTATION

In order to validate our approach, we developed a tool for composite services specification, validation and execution. Figure 7 illustrates the architecture of our prototype which we detail in the following. We also show how designers can use it to define a reliable composite service for our motivating example OTA.

- **Service Flow and ATS Specification:** The first part of our tool is a graphical user interface (see Figure 8) which enables to specify composite services and the required ATS. Designers can specify compositions by dragging and dropping the services, and by linking these services using different types of operators: *Sequence*, *AND-split*, *OR-split*, *XOR-split*, *AND-join*, *OR-join*, and *XOR-join* operators. Then they can express their reliability requirements by specifying the *ATS*. Designers can use this GUI in order to define, for instance, the TCS cs_2 illustrated in Figure 5b and specify the *ATS* shown in Table 3.
- **Composite services validation:** The second part of our tool is the validation component that implements the rules and algorithms we presented to check if a given composition is valid with respect to the specified *ATS*. The validation process can work in two modes. The first mode is called the deferred mode: the checking engine is activated once the composition, the services, and

ATS are defined. The second mode is the instant mode. This mode controls the validity of the composition as soon as it is designed. We can use this mode when we want to instantiate a service according to a model that was previously saved, with an *ATS* already specified. Thus, if a user selects a service which makes the composition not valid, s/he will be notified that the selected service is incompatible with respect to the *ATS* and that it is necessary to select another service with different transactional properties.

Back to our example, based on the control flow of cs_2 and the specified *ATS*, the validation component generates the set of validation properties just listed above. By checking the compliance of cs_2 to these validation properties, the validation component is able to detect that cs_2 is not reliable because it does not respect the validation property VP^{cp1}_{HR}. Based on the validation results; designers are supported to adjust their specifications and define thereafter a reliable composition.

Composite services execution: Once a reliable composition is reached, designers can deploy it on the execution engine and it thereafter becomes

Figure 7. Prototype architecture

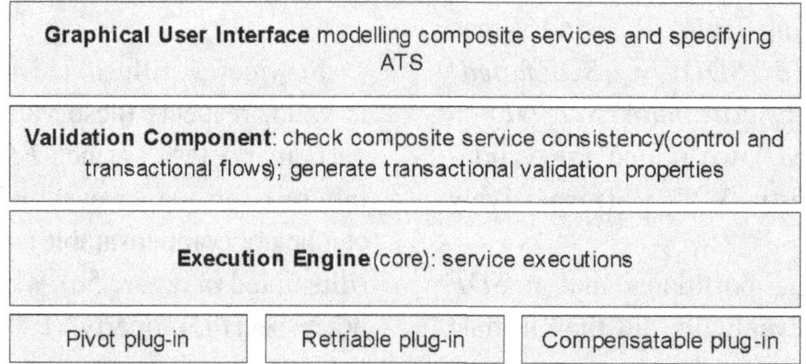

Figure 8. Graphical user interface for composite services and ATS specification

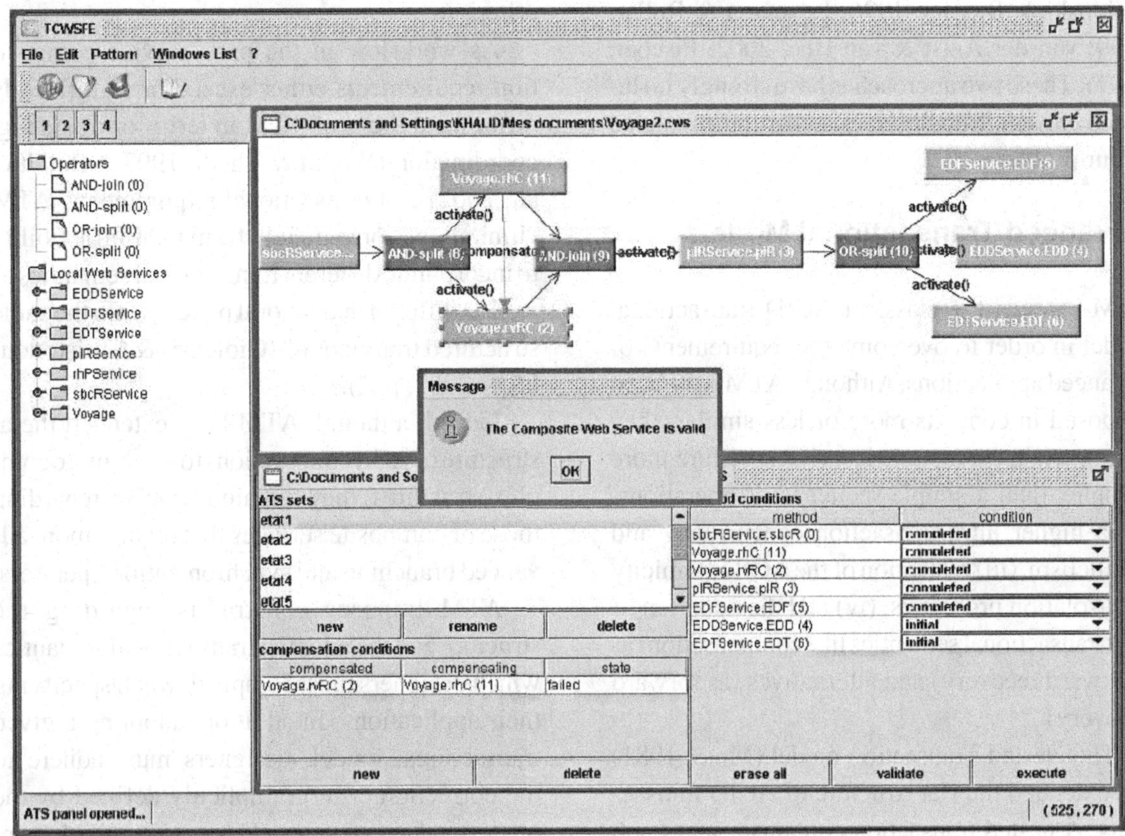

ready for enactment. Like many BPEL engines we adapted an existing workflow engine, Bonita (Miguel & Charoy, 2003), to support composite service executions. Bonita is a workflow engine built upon JonAS which is an implementation of J2EE. Bonita allows for invoking Web services via SOAP messages. In addition, its modular design enables us to implement our transactional properties easily.

The native version of Bonita manages classical transactional properties, i.e. commit/rollback. We modified Bonita in order to be easily able to add new transactional properties (pivot, compensatable, and retriable). To do so, we extracted from the engine the code that is in charge of the management of the transactional properties. A transactional property is managed by a plug-in which communicates with the execution engine according to some rules. This very flexible way for handling transactional properties enables to add, or modify a transactional behavior just by coding or modifying the corresponding plug-in.

RELATED WORK

The problem of reliable Web service compositions concerns two aspects that have to be integrated efficiently: the ability to express complex control structure and the ability to ensure correct executions. Within the literature, we recognize two main approaches that have addressed these two issues: Advanced Transactional Models (ATM for short) (Elmagarmid et al., 1990; El-magarmid, 1992; Garcia-Molina & Salem, 1987; Garcia-Molina et al., 1991; Moss, 1981; Weikum & Schek, 1992) and

Workflow Systems (Georgakopoulos et al., 1995; Jablonski & Bussler, 1996; Leymann & Roller, 1999; van der Aalst & van Hee, 2002; Fischer, 2007). These two approaches have strongly influenced current Web Services technologies related to our problem.

Advanced Transactional Models

ATM extends the classical ACID transactional model in order to overcome the requirements of advanced applications. Although ATM have been proposed in contexts more or less similar, they share certain characteristics: (i) a structure more complex than a simple sequence of operations, (ii) a higher intra transaction concurrency and parallelism, (iii) relaxation of the ACID atomicity and isolation properties, (iv) and the adoption of new transactional semantics like compensation (as backward recovery) and alternatives (as forward recovery).

The Nested Transaction model (Moss, 1981) has extended the flat structure of ACID transactions. A nested transaction contains a set of sub transactions that can recursively contain a set of other sub transactions, thus forming a tree of nested transactions. Open Nested Transaction model (Weikum & Schek, 1992) relaxes the isolation property by making visible the results of committed sub transactions (under certain conditions) to other nested transactions executing in parallel. SAGA (Garcia-Molina & Salem, 1987) introduced the notion of compensation as a backward recovery mechanism more adapted to long running transactions and to business processes. The flexible transactional model (Elmagarmid et al., 1990; Zhang, Nodine, Bhargava, & Bukhres, 1994; Ansari, Rusinkiewicz, & Sheth, 1992; Schuldt, Alonso, Beeri, & Schek, 2002) enables defining intra transaction dependencies, transaction typing (retriable, pivot, and compensatable transactions), alternatives management and set of accepted termination states as a correctness criterion.

As workflow in the past, service composition requirements either exceed or significantly differ from those of ATM in terms of modeling, coordination (Worah & Sheth, 1997; Schuldt et al., 2002) and transactional requirements. ATM "limitations come mainly from their inflexibility to incorporate different transactional semantics as well as different behavioral patterns into the same structured transaction" (Gioldasis & Christodoulakis, 2002, p. 2).

Indeed, although ATM have extended the at structure of ACID transactions towards more complex structures, they remain primitive regarding those of composite services that require more advanced branching and synchronization operators.

ATM imposes constraints regarding the structure and the adopted transactional semantics which designers must comply to when specifying their applications. In addition, adopting a given transactional model, designers must adhere to the correction criteria implicitly defined by the predefined set of rules. This makes ATM more appropriate for top-down approaches rather than for bottom-up ones. By top-down approach, we refer to approaches that start from a transactional model and try to design the application according to this model by respecting its rules and constraints. By bottom-up approach, we refer to approaches that start from an existing application (with a predefined control flow and a set of existing services) and try to ensure its reliability.

Contrary to ATM, our approach ensures reliability according to designers' requirements. Indeed, starting from designers' specifications in terms of composite service control flow and required reliability (specified as ATS), we generate a set properties that define the appropriate transactional mechanisms.

Transactional Workflow

Workflow systems (WfS for short) facilitate the modeling, the implementation, the execution, and the analysis of business processes. A process model specifies the activities and their dependencies, the resources and the program associated to each activity. A workflow management system is a system that transforms the explicit representation of a process model to an internal executable format and provides the operational environment for the execution, the administration, and the monitoring of the processes.

WfS have always been criticized for their lack of sound mechanisms for correction and reliability (Alonso, Agrawal, Abbadi, & Mohan, 1997). The term transactional workflow (Sheth & Rusinkiewicz, 1993) has been introduced to recognize the pertinence of transactions within workflow context for ensuring correction and reliability. Transactional workflows concern the coordination of a set of tasks and suggest the selective use of transactional properties for individual tasks or for the whole workflow. They provide the same functionalities as WfS in terms of automating business process execution. However, they also target ensuring correct executions.

Like WfS, the Contract model (Wätcher & Reuter, 1992) enables to specify the execution logic of an application. In addition, it integrates transactional semantics. So, it considers each step of the contract as an ACID transaction. It allows the explicit definition of forward recovery mechanisms by grouping certain steps within the same ACID transaction, and/or defining relations between steps. Compared to transactional models, the reliability of the contract model is limited. Indeed, recovery mechanisms are defined in ad-hoc way by designers. Contract model defines neither a correction criterion nor mechanisms to check the consistency and the correctness of designers' specifications.

The METEOR system (Rusinkiewicz & Sheth, 1995) defines the execution logic by specifying dependencies between the activities (based on their states). This allows defining both the control flow and recovery mechanisms. In addition, METEOR system defines the notion of Accepted Termination States as a correctness criterion. However, it does not provide mechanisms to check the correctness criterion a priori which makes it not adequate for long running and business applications.

Georgakopoulos, Hornick, and Manola (1996) propose a Transaction Specification and Management Environment which enables to support user-defined and application specific ATM. Hagen and Alonso (2000) defines the concept of sphere as a mean to specify, among others, process atomicity. Using transactional properties similar to ours it defines a set of rules to build a well formed sphere which is an extension of flexible transactions (Zhang et al., 1994) allowing parallel executions. Like ATM, these approaches follow a top down approach, however with more complex structure. In addition, our approach allows better characterization of parallelism by using workflow patterns.

Different from the above workflow initiatives, our approach explicitly integrates the transactional flow dimension as a first class citizen into composite service models. In addition, our approach relies on an execution correctness criterion, ATS, for ensuring reliability and does not perform in an ad-hoc way. Furthermore, our pattern based solution enables modular processing which enables to ensure reliability for local parts of the (and not necessarily for the entire) composite service.

Web Service Technologies

Regarding the current Web service technologies, we recognize two kinds of contributions, those workflow based like WSBPEL (Jordan et al., 2007) and WS-CDL (Kavantzas, Burdett, Ritzinger, & Lafon, 2004) and those transactional based like

WS-AtomicTransaction (Newcomer, Robinson, Little, & Wilkinson, 2007), WS-BusinessActivity (Newcomer, Robinson, Freund, & Little, 2007) and WS-TXM (Acid, BP, LRA) (Little, 2007).

WSBPEL is a process definition language allowing for orchestrating Web Services. WS-CDL is a choreography description language. It defines a choreography as a multi partner contract describing, from a global point of view, the common observable behavior of the collaborating services. WS-BPEL and WS-CDL define control flow operators using XML. Like workflow systems these two languages meet business processes needs in terms of complex control structure. However, they are unable to ensure reliability, especially, according to designers' specific needs. We believe that our approach can complement these efforts. It can be used on top of them to define reliable compositions. Then the defined model can be described either using WS-BPEL or WS-CDL. Obviously, we need to extend these two languages to support cancellation and alternative interactions.

WS-Transaction and WS-TXM define a set of transactional protocols based on WS-Coordination (Newcomer, Robinson, Feingold, & Jeyaraman, 2007) and WS-CF (Little, 2007) respectively. WS-Coordination and WS-CF are two similar approaches specifying basic mechanisms for the coordination of services according to a given protocol. WS-Transaction and WS-TXM distinguish between many kinds of protocols. They define transactional protocols for (i) supporting atomic transactions (WS-Atomic Transaction and TX-ACID), (ii) achieving long running transactions (TX-LRA), and (iii) accomplishing business process oriented interactions (WS-BusinessActivity and TX-BP). These protocols are variants of ATM adapted to a service oriented computing model. Like ATM these protocols are unable in most cases to model Business process due to their limited control structure. Our approach allows extending these protocols to support complex structure while preserving reliability. Indeed, a valid composition model can be considered as a transactional protocol that can be implemented over WS-Coordination or WS-CF.

RosettaNet[5] and ebXML[6] are two other propositions based on XML for conducting B2B interactions. They define common concepts (at the transport, data and process levels) to be shared and respected by partners. For instance, an enterprise willing publishing a service must respect the predefined process models "business process" for ebXML and PIP[7] for RosetaNet. The major inconvenience of these initiatives is that partners are constrained to comply to the predefined specifications.

Limthanmaphon and Zhang (2004) propose a model that integrates compensation and tentative hold approach. Schmit and Dustdar (2005) present a methodology for modeling composite services while distinguishing between different perspectives especially structural and transactional. Papazoglou (2003) gives a specification of business transactions along with standardization and research efforts. It identifies the principal components of a business transactions platform. According to the given classification, our approach enables to define transactional models for long running applications.

Other related work can be seen complementary to our approach. Robinson and Purao (2009) present an approach for (i) specifying agents' commitments within business processes, (ii) deriving interactions among these agents and (iii) monitoring their interactions and commitments. This approach complements our work. Indeed it enables to enforce and monitor the transactional properties and recovery mechanisms.

From another perspective, Haddad, Manouvrier, and Rukoz (2007) and Zhao et al. (2008) deal with concurrency between composite services while respecting such relaxed isolation (a composite service, considered as a transaction, may reveal partial results that can be used by other services). Haddad, Manouvrier, and Rukoz (2007) propose a concurrency control mechanism in order to eliminate inconsistencies caused by cascade and cycle dependency between services. Zhao et al. (2008) propose a hierarchical composition and use an optimistic protocol to ensure global concurrency control.

CONCLUSION AND PERSPECTIVES

In this paper, we have been interested in ensuring composite services (transactional) reliability. We have proposed a Transactional Composite Service (TCS for short) model that integrates the expressivity power and business adequacy of Workflow systems and the reliability of Advanced Transactional Models (ATM for short).

Based on our transactional model, we have proposed an approach where designers specify their requirements in terms of control flow and failure atomicity (as a set of accepted termination states). Then, we use a set of techniques for generating a set of validation properties. A TCS is valid (and consequently reliable) according to designers' specifications *if and only if* it respects the validation properties.

The originality of our approach is that it follows a bottom-up approach. Contrary to ATM, we start from designers' specifications (control structure and failure atomicity) to determine the transactional mechanisms, enabling reliable executions according to their requirements.

Perspectives: We expect two medium term perspectives to our work. The first one aims at extending our approach in order to support more complex control structure and manage dynamic transactional properties. Following our pattern based approach, this means considering advanced workflow patterns like loops, and multi instantiation patterns. The second perspective aims at studying the integration of our approach with current coordination technologies namely WS-Transaction and WS-TXM. The objective is allowing (i) coordination protocols with more complex structure and (ii) providing to BPEL and WS-CDL a set of techniques for ensuring a certain level of reliability.

As a short term perspective, we are currently working on alleviating the workload induced by specifying the set of accepted termination states. The main idea is to automatically generate a reference set of termination states based on the composite service control flow and component services reliability. Designers may adjust this reference set, by changing existing termination states or deriving new ones from them, in order to define their specific requirements.

ACKNOWLEDGMENT

Part of the work presented in this paper has been funded by Science Foundation Ireland under Grant No. SFI/08/CE/I1380 (DERI Lion-2).

REFERENCES

Alonso, G., Agrawal, D., Abbadi, A. E., & Mohan, C. (1997). Functionality and Limitations of Current Workflow Management Systems. *IEEE Expert, 12*(5), 68–74.

Alonso, G., Casati, F., Kuno, H., & Machiraju, V. (2004). *Web services concepts, architectures and applications*. Berlin, Germany: Springer-Verlag.

Ansari, N., Rusinkiewicz, L., & Sheth, A. (1992). Using flexible transaction to support multi-system telecommunication applications. In *Proceedings of the 18th VLDB Conference,* Vancouver, BC, Canada (pp. 65-76).

Bhiri, S. (2005). *Approche transactionnelle pour assurer des compositions fiables*. Nancy, France: University Henri Poincar - Nancy 1, LORIA.

Bhiri, S., Perrin, O., & Godart, C. (2005). Ensuring required failure atomicity of composite web services. In A. Ellis & T. Hagino (Eds.), *Proceedings of the 14th International Conference on World Wide Web* (pp. 138-147). New York, NY: ACM.

Bruijn, J. D. (2005). *D16.1v0.21 the web service modeling language wsml*. Retrieved from http://www.wsmo.org/TR/d16/d16.1/v0.21/.

Elmagarmid, A. (1992). *Transaction models for advanced database applications*. San Francisco, CA: Morgan-Kaufmann.

Elmagarmid, A., Leu, Y., Litwin, W., & Rusinkiewicz, M. (1990). A multi-database transaction model for interbase. In *Proceedings of the VLDB Conference* (pp. 507-518). San Francisco, CA: Morgan-Kaufmann.

Erickson, J., & Siau, K. (2008). Web services, service-oriented computing, and service-oriented architecture: separating hype from reality. *Journal of Database Management, 19*(3), 42–54. doi:10.4018/jdm.2008070103

Fischer, L. (Ed.). (2007). *Methods, concepts, case studies and standards in business process management and workflow*. Lighthouse Point, FL: Future Strategies.

Garcia-Molina, H., Gawlick, D., Klein, J., Kleissner, K., & Salem, K. (1991). Modeling long-running activities as nested sagas. *A Quarterly Bulletin of the Computer Society of the IEEE Technical Committee on Data Engineering, 14*(1), 14–18.

Garcia-Molina, H., & Salem, K. (1987, May 27-29). Sagas. In U. Dayal & I. L. Traiger (Eds.), *Proceedings of the ACM SIGMOD Conference,* San Francisco, CA (pp. 249-259). New York, NY: ACM.

Georgakopoulos, D., Hornick, M. F., Krychniak, P., & Manola, F. (1994, February 14-18). Specification and management of extended transactions in a programmable transaction environment. In *Proceedings of the ICDE Conference,* Houston, TX (pp. 462-473). Washington, DC: IEEE Computer Society.

Georgakopoulos, D., Hornick, M. F., & Manola, F. (1996). Customizing transaction models and mechanisms in a programmable environment supporting reliable workflow automation. *IEEE Transactions on Knowledge and Data Engineering, 8*(4), 630–649. doi:10.1109/69.536255

Georgakopoulos, D., Hornick, M. F., & Sheth, A. P. (1995). An overview of workflow management: From process modeling to workflow automation infrastructure. *Distributed and Parallel Databases, 3*(2), 119–153. doi:10.1007/BF01277643

Gioldasis, N., & Christodoulakis, S. (2002). UTML: Unified transaction modeling language. In *Proceedings of the 3rd International Conference on Web Information Systems Engineering* (pp. 115-126). Washington, DC: IEEE Computer Society.

Haddad, J. E., Manouvrier, M., & Rukoz, M. (2007). A hierarchical model for transactional web service composition in p2p networks. In *Proceedings of the ICWS Conference* (pp. 346-353). Washington, DC: IEEE Computer Society.

Hagen, C., & Alonso, G. (2000). Exception handling in workflow management systems. *IEEE Transactions on Software Engineering, 26*(10), 943–958. doi:10.1109/32.879818

Hollingsworth, D. (1995). *Workflow Management Coalition: The Workflow Reference Model.* Retrieved from http://www.wfmc.org/standards/docs/tc003v11.pdf

Jablonski, S., & Bussler, C. (1996). *Workflow Management: Modeling Concepts, Architecture, and Implementation*. Itp New Media.

Jordan, D., Evdemon, J., Alves, A., Arkin, A., Askary, S., Bareto, C., et al. (2007). *Business process execution language for web services version 2.0.* Retrieved from http://docs.oasis-open.org/wsbpel/2.0/OS/wsbpel-v2.0-OS.pdf

Kavantzas, N., Burdett, D., Ritzinger, G., & Lafon, Y. (2004). *Web services choreography description language version 1.0.* Retrieved from http://www.w3.org/TR/ws-cdl-10

Leymann, F., & Roller, D. (1999). *Production workflow: Concepts and techniques*. Upper Saddle River, NJ: Prentice Hall PTR.

Limthanmaphon, B., & Zhang, Y. (2004). Web service composition transaction management. In *Proceedings of the 15th Australasian Database Conference* (pp. 171-179).

Little, M. (2007). Ws-caf: Contexts, coordination and transactions for web services. In R. Meersman & Z. Tari (Eds.), *On the Move to Meaningful Internet Systems 2007: CoopIS, DOA, ODBASE, GADA, and IS Conferences* (LNCS 4803, pp. 439-453).

Martin, D. (2004). *Owl-s: Semantic markup for web services.* Retrieved from http://www.w3.org/Submission/OWL-S/

Medjahed, B., Benatallah, B., Bouguettaya, A., Ngu, A. H. H., & Elmagarmid, A. K. (2003). Business-to-business interactions: issues and enabling technologies. *The VLDB Journal, 12*(1), 59–85. doi:10.1007/s00778-003-0087-z

Mehrotra, S., Rastogi, R., Korth, H. F., & Silberschatz, A. (1992). A transaction model for multidatabase systems. In *Proceedings of the 12th International Conference on Distributed Computing Systems* (pp. 56-63).

Miguel, V., & Charoy, F. (2003). *Bonita: Workflow cooperative system.* Retrieved from http://bonita.objectweb.org

Moss, E. B. (1981). *Nested transactions: An approach to reliable distributed computing*. Cambridge, MA: MIT Press.

Newcomer, E., Robinson, I., Feingold, M., & Jeyaraman, R. (2007). *Web services coordination version 1.1.* Retrieved from http://docs.oasis-open.org/ws-tx/wstx-wscoor-1.1-spec-os.pdf

Newcomer, E., Robinson, I., Freund, T., & Little, M. (2007). *Web services business activity version 1.1.* Retrieved from http://docs.oasis-open.org/ws-tx/wstx-wsba-1.1-spec-errata-os.pdf

Newcomer, E., Robinson, I., Little, M., & Wilkinson, A. (2007). *Web services atomic transaction version 1.1.* Retrieved from http://docs.oasis-open.org/ws-tx/wstx-wsat-1.1-spec-os.pdf

Papazoglou, M. P. (2003). Web services and business transactions. *World Wide Web (Bussum), 6*(1), 49–91. doi:10.1023/A:1022308532661

Riehle, D., & Zullighoven, H. (1996). Understanding and using patterns in software development. *Theory and Practice of Object Systems, 2*(1), 3–13. doi:10.1002/(SICI)1096-9942(1996)2:1<3::AID-TAPO1>3.0.CO;2-#

Robinson, W. N., & Purao, S. (2009). Specifying and monitoring interactions and commitments in open business processes. *IEEE Software, 26*(2), 72–79. doi:10.1109/MS.2009.48

Roman, D., Lausen, H., & Keller, U. (2006). *D2v1.3. web service modeling ontology (WSMO).* Retrieved from http://www.wsmo.org/TR/d2/v1.3/

Rusinkiewicz, M., & Sheth, A. P. (1995). Specification and execution of transactional workflows. In Kim, W. (Ed.), *Modern database systems: the object model, interoperability, and beyond* (pp. 592–620).

Schmit, B. A., & Dustdar, S. (2005). Systematic design of web service transactions. In *Technologies for E-Services* (LNCS 3811, pp. 23-33).

Schuldt, H., Alonso, G., Beeri, C., & Schek, H. J. (2002). Atomicity and isolation for transactional processes. *ACM Transactions on Database Systems, 27*(1), 63–116. doi:10.1145/507234.507236

Sheth, A. P., & Rusinkiewicz, M. (1993). On transactional workflows. *Data Engineering Bulletin, 16*(2), 37–40.

van der Aalst, W. M. P., ter Hofstede, A. H. M., Kiepuszewski, B., & Barros, A. P. (2003). Workflow patterns. *Distributed and Parallel Databases, 14*(1), 5–51. doi:10.1023/A:1022883727209

van der Aalst, W. M. P., & van Hee, K. M. (2002). *Workflow management: models, methods and tools*. Cambridge, MA: MIT Press.

Wätcher, H., & Reuter, A. (1992). The contract model. In Elmagarmid, A. K. (Ed.), *Database transaction models for advanced applications* (pp. 219–263).

Weikum, G., & Schek, H. J. (1992). Concepts and applications of multilevel transactions and open nested transactions. In Elmagarmid, A. K. (Ed.), *Database transaction models for advanced applications* (pp. 515–553).

Worah, D., & Sheth, A. P. (1997). Transactions in transactional workflows. In Jajodia, S., & Kerschberg, L. (Eds.), *Advanced transaction models and architectures* (pp. 3–34).

Zhang, A., Nodine, M., Bhargava, B., & Bukhres, O. (1994). Ensuring relaxed atomicity for flexible transactions in multidatabase systems. In *Proceedings of the ACM SIGMOD Conference* (pp. 67-78). New York, NY: ACM.

Zhao, Z., Wei, J., Lin, L., & Ding, X. (2008). A concurrency control mechanism for composite service supporting user-defined relaxed atomicity. In *Proceedings of the COMPSAC Conference* (pp. 275-278). Washington, DC: IEEE Computer Society.

ENDNOTES

1. We use the terms service and Web service interchangeably throughout the paper.
2. We use BPMN (www.bpmn.org) to model the control flow of composite services.
3. When SDD is chosen for delivery
4. *P(S)* denotes the set of all subsets of S
5. www.rosettanet.org
6. www.ebxml.org
7. PIP stands for Partner Interface Process

This work was previously published in the Journal of Database Management, Volume 22, Issue 2, edited by Keng Siau, pp. 64-92, copyright 2011 by IGI Publishing (an imprint of IGI Global).

Chapter 9
Leveraging Early Aspects in End-to-End Model Driven Development for Non-Functional Properties in Service Oriented Architecture

Hiroshi Wada
National ICT Australia, Australia

Junichi Suzuki
University of Massachusetts, Boston, USA

Katsuya Oba
OGIS International, Inc., USA

ABSTRACT

In Service Oriented Architecture (SOA), each application is designed with a set of reusable services and a business process. To retain the reusability of services, non-functional properties of applications must be separated from their functional properties. This paper investigates a model-driven development framework that separates non-functional properties from functional properties and manages them. This framework proposes two components: (1) a programming language, called BALLAD, for a new per-process strategy to specify non-functional properties for business processes, and (2) a graphical modeling method, called FM-SNFPs, to define a series of constraints among non-functional properties. BALLAD leverages aspects in aspect oriented programming/modeling. Each aspect is used to specify a set of non-functional properties that crosscut multiple services in a business process. FM-SNFPs leverage the notion of feature modeling to define constraints among non-functional properties like dependency and mutual exclusion constraints. BALLAD and FM-SNFPs free application developers from manually specifying, maintaining and validating non-functional properties and constraints for services one by one, reducing the burdens/costs in development and maintenance of service-oriented applications. This

DOI: 10.4018/978-1-4666-2044-5.ch009

paper describes the design details of BALLAD and FM-SNFPs, and demonstrates how they are used in developing service-oriented applications. BALLAD significantly reduces the costs to implement and maintain non-functional properties in service-oriented applications.

INTRODUCTION

Service Oriented Architecture (SOA) is an emerging style of software architectures to build, integrate and maintain applications in a cost effective manner by improving their reusability (Bichler & Lin, 2006; Papazoglou & Heuvel, 2007; Erickson & Siau, 2008). In SOA, each application is often designed in an implementation independent manner with a set of reusable *services* and a *business process*. Each service encapsulates the function of an application component, and each business process defines how services interact to accomplish a certain business goal. Services are intended to be reusable (or sharable) for different applications to implement different business processes.

In order to retain the reusability of services, it is important to separate non-functional properties of applications (e.g., security and reliability) from their functional properties because different applications use each service in different non-functional contexts (e.g., different security policies) (Wada, Suzuki, & Oba, 2008; Bieberstein, Bose, Fiammante, Jones, & Shah, 2005). For example, an application may transmit signed and encrypted messages to a service when the messages travel to the service through third-party intermediaries in order to prevent the intermediaries from maliciously sniffing or altering messages. Another application may transmit plain messages to the service when it is deployed in-house. Separation of functional and non-functional properties improves the reusability of services in different non-functional contexts.

This paper investigates end-to-end model-driven development (MDD) that manages non-functional properties from high-level business process modeling to low-level configurations of implementation technologies such as transport protocols and remoting middleware. To this end, there exist two major research issues: (1) a lack of adequate strategies to specify non-functional properties in business processes and (2) a lack of adequate methods to manage constraints among non-functional properties.

The first issue is regarding the strategies to specify non-functional properties in business processes. In most of the current practice in separating functional and non-functional properties, non-functional properties are specified on a *per-service* basis (Wada et al., 2008; Amir & Zeid, 2004; Ortiz & Hernändez, 2006; Lodderstedt, Basin, & Doser, 2002; Jürjens, 2002; Nakamura, Tatsubori, Imamura, & Ono, 2005; Soler, Villarroel, Trujillo, Medina, & Piattini, 2006; Vokäc, 2005; Baligand & Monfort, 2004; Wang, Chen, Wang, Fung, & Uczekaj, 2004). However, with a per-service strategy, application developers need to manually ensure that each non-functional property is properly configured in a series of services in an ad-hoc manner because each non-functional property tends to scatter over multiple services simultaneously. For example, when a certain message encryption is consistently required throughout a purchasing business process, developers need to manually specify the encryption property for all services in the business process (e.g., retailers, suppliers, distributors and carriers) one by one. When a change occurs in the required encryption level, developers have to manually examine which services the change affects and carefully implement the change in the affected services. It is tedious, expensive and error-prone to consistently specify, maintain and validate non-functional properties on a per-service basis in a large-scale business process.

The second research issue this paper addresses is a lack of adequate methods to manage constraints among non-functional properties. In general, a series of constraints (e.g., dependency and mutual exclusion) exist among non-functional properties. For example, when messages are transmitted asynchronously between services, a timeout period should be specified as well to abort transmissions failures. Here, a dependency (or co-use) constraint exists between two non-functional properties: asynchronous message transmission and timeout. In order to maximize the reusability of services, non-functional constraints tend to be complicated and hard to maintain because their granularity becomes finer and their number grows. They are informally specified in natural languages in most of the current practice of separating functional and non-functional properties; it is tedious and error-prone for application developers to manually ensure that their applications satisfy required non-functional constraints (Wada et al., 2008; Amir & Zeid, 2004; Ortiz & Hernändez, 2006; Wang & Lee, 2005; Nakamura et al., 2005). Few methods exist to explicitly specify non-functional constraints and consistently validate and enforce them in applications.

In order to address the above two research issues, this paper proposes (1) a programming language for a new strategy to separate functional and non-functional properties in business processes and (2) a graphical modeling method to specify, validate and enforce non-functional constraints in service-oriented applications. The proposed language, BALLAD[1], facilitates a *per-process* strategy to specify non-functional properties for business processes rather than services. BALLAD leverages the notion of *aspects* in aspect oriented programming/modeling (Kiczales et al., 1997; Elrad, Aldawud, & Bader, 2002) or *early aspects*, which are crosscutting concerns that exist in early phases in application development process such as requirement analysis and business process design (Chitchyan et al., 2005). Each aspect is used to specify non-functional properties that crosscut multiple services in a business process. Given an aspect, a supporting tool, called Ark, identifies which services it is applied (or woven) to and automatically configures its corresponding non-functional properties to the identified services. This way, application developers do not need to manually specify and maintain non-functional properties for services one by one, thereby reducing the burdens/costs in development and maintenance of service-oriented applications.

The proposed modeling method, called FM-SNFPs, leverages the notion of feature modeling (Czarnecki & Eisenecker, 2000). Feature modeling is a simple yet powerful method to explicitly model a series of constraints among application's *features* (e.g., functionalities and configuration policies). By modeling a non-functional property as a feature, FM-SNFPs aids to graphically specify constraints among non-functional constraints and consistently validate the constraints in applications. Ark automatically enforces required non-functional constraints in applications by transforming their specification from business process models to application code (program code and deployment description) through intermediate models.

This paper overviews an end-to-end MDD framework that implements BALLAD and FM-SNFPs, and describes the design details of BALLAD and FM-SNFPs. It also demonstrates an application development with the proposed MDD framework. Empirical evaluation results show that BALLAD significantly reduces the burdens/costs to implement and maintain non-functional properties in service-oriented applications. BALLAD and FM-SNFPs are designed and implemented efficient and scalable.

THE PROPOSED END-TO-END MDD FRAMEWORK

Figure 1 overviews the proposed MDD framework that implements BALLAD and FM-SNFPs. The framework consists of (1) BALLAD, (2) FM-SNFPs, (3) a Unified Modeling Language (UML) profile to specify non-functional prop-

Figure 1. The Architecture of the proposed MDD framework

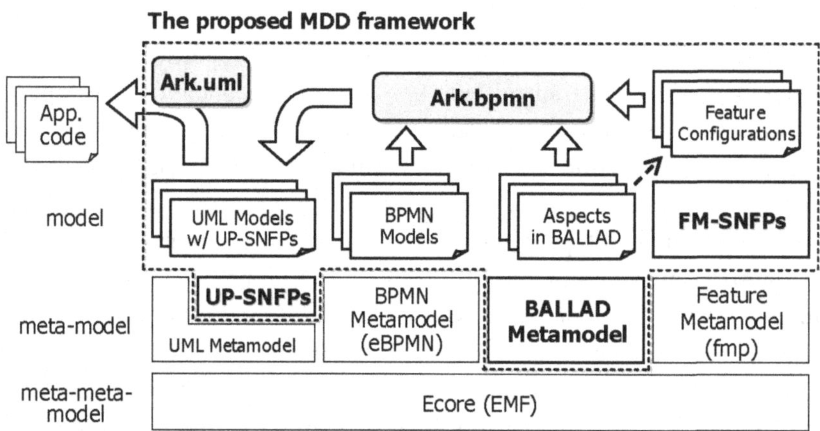

erties in SOA, called UP-SNFPs (Wada et al., 2008), and (4) a model transformation tool, called Ark. All artifacts in this framework are built and maintained with the metameta model (Ecore) in the Eclipse Modeling Framework (EMF[2]). The syntax of BALLAD is defined as a meta model on Ecore. FM-SNFPs are defined on the feature metamodel in fmp (Antkiewicz & Czarnecki, 2004)[3]. UP-SNFPs is defined as an extension (or profile) to the UML metamodel. Currently, Business Process Modeling Notation (BPMN) (BPM Initiative, 2004) is used as a language to graphically define business processes. BPMN models are defined with the BPMN metamodel in eBPMN[4]. Ark consists of two components, Ark.bpmn and Ark.uml, which transform BPMN models and UML models, respectively. Table 1 summarizes the artifacts and tools in the proposed MDD framework.

Figure 2 overviews the application development process using the proposed MDD framework. Application developers define a business process model in BPMN, an aspect in BALLAD, and a feature configuration(s) in FM-SNFPs. A feature configuration is an instance of FM-SNFPs, and it specifies a particular set of non-functional properties and their constraints that are used in a business process. A BALLAD aspect defines which feature configuration (i.e., a set of non-functional properties) is applied (or woven) to

Table 1. Artifacts and tools in the proposed MDD framework

Artifact/Tool	Description
BPMN	Business Process Modeling Language. A visual language to model business processes.
BALLAD	An aspect oriented language to define which non-functional properties are applied (or woven) to which model elements in a BPMN model.
FM-SNFPs	A feature model that defines a series of non-functional properties and constraints among them.
Feature configuration	An instance of FM-SNFPs. Each feature configuration specifies a particular set of non-functional properties and their constraints that are used in a business process.
UP-SNFPs	A UML profile that represents non-functional properties in UML.
Ark.bpmn	A model transformer that transforms a BPMN model into a UML model represented with UP-SNFPs according to a given BALLAD aspect and feature configuration(s).
Ark.uml	A model transformer that transforms a UML model represented with UP-SNFPs into application code (program code and deployment descriptor).

Figure 2. Application development process with the proposed MDD framework

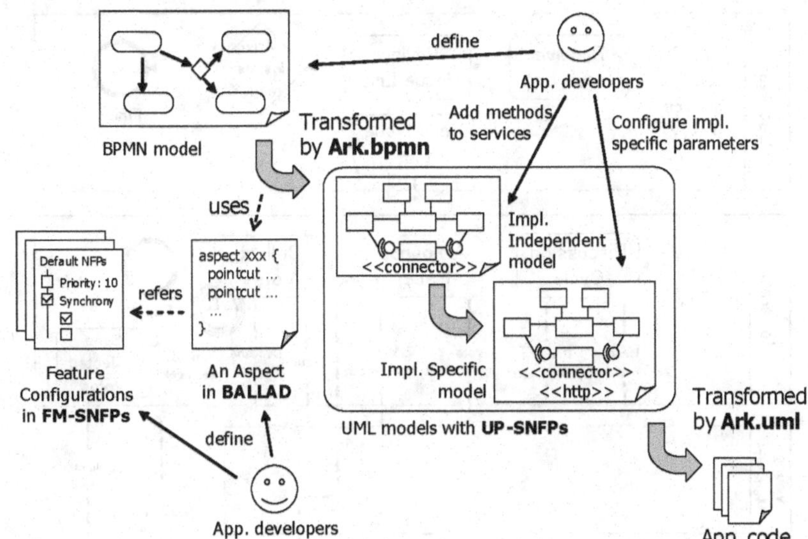

which model elements in a BPMN model. Ark. bpmn accepts a BPMN model, a BALLAD aspect and a feature configuration(s), and then transforms the BPMN model to a UML model represented with UP-SNFPs (an implementation-independent model in Figure 2) according to a given BALLAD aspect and feature configuration(s). During this transformation, Ark.bpmn automatically ensures that the generated UML model satisfies a set of constraints among non-functional properties defined in FM-SNFPs. Once an implementation-independent UML model is generated, application developers can add methods (or behaviors) to individual UML classes and map it to an implementation-specific UML model by specifying various parameters for implementation technologies such as transport protocols and Enterprise Service Buses (ESBs). Ark.uml transforms an implementation specific UML model into a skeleton of application code (program code and deployment descriptors).

Using BALLAD, non-functional properties can be specified for business processes in an implementation independent manner. They are portable and reusable across different implementation technologies. Throughout a chain of model transformations, they are separated from functional properties and gradually mapped from abstract implementation-independent models to application code through concrete implementation-specific models.

BACKGROUND: BUSINESS PROCESS MODELING NOTATION (BPMN)

This section briefly overviews BPMN. BPMN is a visual modeling language to define business processes. Figure 3 shows an electronic voting process in a certain online community. It involves four entities: Secretary, Moderator, Assistant Moderator and Voting Member[5]. A secretary examines, on every Friday, whether there exist any issues to discuss and decide. If there is not, the secretary sends an issue list to a moderator. The moderator initiates a discussion among voting members and waits for their votes for a week. An assistant moderator receives and reviews collected votes to examine whether if an issue in question is settled. If not, the issue is discussed for a revote.

Figure 3. A voting process model in BPMN

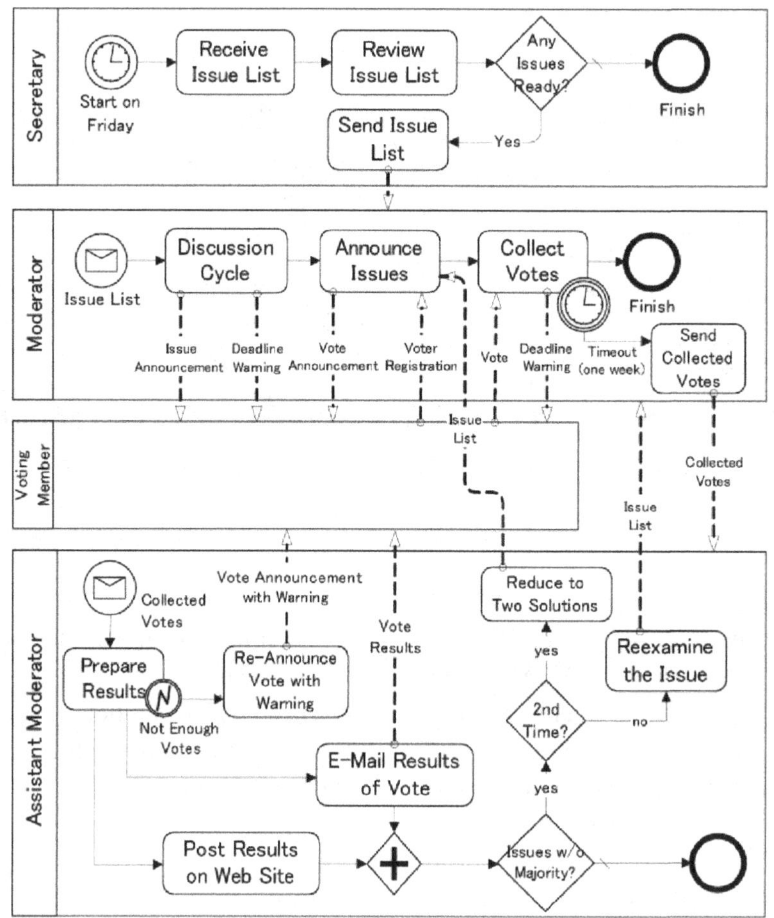

A BPMN model consists of *pools*, *tasks* and *sequence/message flows*. A pool, represented by a rectangle, denotes a participant in a business process; for example, Secretary in Figure 3. A task, represented as a rounded-corner rectangle, denotes a task performed by a participant; for example, Receive Issue List in Secretary. A *sequence flow*, represented as a solid line, denotes the order of tasks performed in a pool. A *message flow*, represented as a dashed line, denotes a flow of messages between two participants.

In addition to tasks, pools can contain *gateways* and *events*. A gateway, represented as a diamond shape, controls the divergence (forking) and convergence (merging) of sequence flows. For a divergence of sequence flows, a gateway can have the default sequence flow, represented as a sequence flow with a slash mark, which is chosen if other sequence flows are not selected. In Figure 3, a Secretary branches a flow depending on the existence of issues to discuss and vote. If issues exist, it performs Send Issue List; otherwise, it selects the default sequence flow and reaches Finish.

An event, represented as a circle, triggers a subsequent sequence flow. BPMN supports several types of events: *message*, *timer*, *rule*, *error*, *cancel* and *compensation*. A message, represented as a circle with an envelope icon inside, denotes a reception of a message from a participant. In Figure 3, a Moderator triggers its process when it receives an Issue List message. A timer, represented as a circle with a clock, denotes a specific time or interval. In Figure 3, a Moderator performs Send Collected Votes one week after it performs Collect Votes. An error, represented as a circle with a lightning inside, denotes a specific error condition. In Figure 3, an Assistant Moderator performs Re-Announce Vote with Warning when it does not receive enough votes in Prepare Result.

BALLAD: THE PROPOSED ASPECT ORIENTED LANGUAGE

In general, aspect oriented languages are designed to separate crosscutting concerns from other concerns and modularize crosscutting ones as an aspect (Kiczales et al., 1997; Elrad et al., 2002). Then, supporting tools (often called *aspect weavers*) weave aspects into the other parts of an application to complete it. An aspect consists of *advice*s and *pointcut*s. An advice defines or implements a concern that appears (or crosscuts) many places in an application. A pointcut specifies the places where advices appear.

As described in the Introduction section, non-functional properties are crosscutting concerns. Thus, BALLAD is designed to modularize a set of non-functional properties used in a business process as an aspect. In BALLAD, an advice is defined as a feature configuration, in FM-SNFPs, which specifies a set of non-functional properties. A pointcut specifies the places to which advices (i.e., non-functional properties) are woven in a BPMN model. Advices are visually defined, while pointcuts are defined in a textual form. Ark.bpmn serves as an aspect weaver for BALLAD; it weaves non-functional properties into a BPMN model according to the definition of pointcuts (see also Figures 1 and 2). This clear separation between functional and non-functional properties allows the two types of properties to evolve in parallel, thereby improving the maintainability of applications.

Listing 1 shows an example aspect in BALLAD. An aspect is defined with the keyword aspect, followed by its name. An aspect can define an arbitrary number of pointcuts and references to advices. A pointcut is defined with the keyword pointcut, followed by its name. Advices are defined separately from an aspect, and the aspect references them with their names.

In Listing 1, the pointcut discussion specifies paths between two model elements (task or message flow) in a BPMN model by using the within join point. (A join point is a place where advices can be woven, and a pointcut is a set of join points which actually used.) The within join point takes two names of model elements in regular expression as parameters. (:: represents a separator between model elements such as pools and tasks.) A set of model elements matched the first parameter and second parameter are interpreted as starting points and ending points of paths respectively. For example, the pointcut discussion specifies paths between Moderator::Discussion.* and Moderator::Finish. As Figure 3 shows, these two parameters match the tasks Discussion Cycle and Finish in Moderator respectively, and there are many paths between them. For example, the shortest path starts from Moderator::Discussion Cycle, passes through Moderator::Announce Issues and Moderator::Collect Votes, and reaches Moderator::Finish. Several paths go through the Timer event attached to Moderator::Collect Votes, pass tasks in Assistant Moderator and return to Moderator. This way, Ark.bpmn automatically finds a set of model elements that involved in (sub)processes according to pointcuts.

Ark.bpmn weaves advices into model elements in a BPMN model according to given references to advices, each of which consists of a pointcut name and advice name (discussion and DiscussionNFPs in Listing 1). When an aspect references multiple advices, Ark.bpmn weaves them to BPMN model elements following the order of their occurrence.

Listing 2 shows the syntax of BALLAD. As shown in the figure, BALLAD supports other join points than within: target, source, flow, trig-

Listing 1. An Example Aspect in BALLAD

```
aspectNFPsForVoting{
  //pointcuts
  pointcutdiscussion:
    within("Moderator::Discussion.*",
"Moderator::Finish");
  //referencestoadvices
  discussion:DiscussionNFPs;
}
```

ger, depth and default (see Table 2). Listing 3 shows an example aspect that uses these extra join points. In this example, DeliveryAssurance references an advice that represents a set of non-functional properties for assured/reliable message delivery. HighlevelSecurity references an advice regarding message encryption and access control enforcement.

target and source are simplified representations of within (".*", "PoolName::.*") and within ("PoolName::.*", ".*"), where PoolName serves as a parameter of target and source. They return all paths that arrive at and depart from certain pools, respectively. For example, in Listing 3, the pointcut fromVotingMember selects all paths departing from Voting Member (see also Figure 3) target and source aid in specifying non-functional properties that certain pools require for their incoming/outgoing message flows. In Listing 3, a set of message encryption properties is specified for all outgoing message flows from Voting Member.

flow is a simplified representation of within ("FlowName", "FlowName"), where FlowName serves as a parameter of flow. It directly specifies particular message flows. For example, in Listing 3, the pointcut vote selects the message flow Vote

Listing 2. The Syntax of BALLAD

```
<aspect>::= 'aspect' <aspectName> '{' (<pointcut>)+ (<adviceref>)+ '}'
<pointcut>::= 'pointcut' <pointcutName> ':' <joinpoint>* ';'
<adviceref>::= <pointcutName> ':' <adviceName> (',' <adviceName>)* ';'
<joinpoint>::= <mandatoryjp> ('&&' <mandatoryjp> | <optionaljp>)*
<mandatoryjp>::= <within>|<target>|<source>|<flow>|<trigger>
<optionaljp>::= <depth>|<default>
<within>::= 'within' '(' <elementName> ',' <elementName> ')'
<target>::= 'target' '(' <poolName> ')'
<source>::= 'source' '(' <poolName> ')'
<flow>::= 'flow' '(' <flowName> ')'
<trigger>::= 'trigger' '(' <eventType> ')'
<eventType>::='MESSAGE'|'TIMER'|'ERROR'|'CANCEL'|'COMPENSATION'|'RULE'
<depth>::= 'depth' '(' <integer> ')'
<default>::= 'default()' '(' ')'
<aspectName>::= <identifier>
<pointcutName>::= <identifier>
<adviceName>::= <identifier>
<elementName>::= '"' <regex> ('::' <regex>)* '"'
<poolName>::= '"' <regex> '"'
<flowName>::= '"' <regex> '"'
<regex>::= //regularexpression
```

Table 2. Join Points in BALLAD

Join Point	Description
within	Returns all paths between two model elements (tasks or message flows).
target	Returns all paths arriving at certain pools.
source	Returns all paths departing from certain pools.
flow	Specifies certain message flows.
trigger	Returns all paths departing from a certain type of event.
depth	Limits the number of unique pools in a path.
default	Follows only the default sequence flows at gateways.

in Figure 3. flow aids in defining non-functional properties that specific message flows require. In Listing 3, the Vote message flow requires higher security level than the other message flows do.

trigger returns all paths that start from a certain type of events (i.e., message, timer, rule, error, cancel or compensation). For example, in Listing 3, the pointcut error selects paths starting from error events in order to specify non-functional properties for error handling with message delivery assurance enabled.

depth is used with other join points. It limits the maximum number of unique pools to be included in a path (s) selected by other join points. For example, a selected path can contain up to three unique pools when a pointcut declares depth(2). In Listing 3, the pointcut secretary uses depth. Although its within joint point returns all paths in Figure 3, it returns the paths between Secretary and Moderator because of depth(1).

default is used with other join points. It selects the paths containing default sequence flows at gateways. For example, in Listing 3, the pointcut defaultProcess selects a default sequence flow at a gateway.

Join points can be used together. For example, Listing 3 defines the pointcut afterVoting, which uses trigger and target to select the paths starting from timer events and ending with the tasks in Assistant Moderator. When a pointcut uses multiple join points, Ark.bpmn returns the intersection of paths selected by them. For example, the pointcut afterVoting returns a set of paths contained in both trigger(TIMER) and target ("Assistant Moderator").

FM-SNFPS: A FEATURE MODEL FOR NON-FUNCTIONAL PROPERTIES IN SOA

A feature model describes a set of features and constraints among them through a hierarchical (or tree) structure. Application developers create an instance of a feature model, i.e., a feature configuration, by selecting features for their applications on a supporting tool. By not allowing users to create feature configurations that violate constraints, a supporting tool assures that feature configurations satisfy constraints among features defined in a feature model.

FM-SNFPs are a feature model that defines a set of non-functional properties in SOA and constraints among them, and aspects in BALLAD refer feature configurations of FM-SNFPs as their advices. FM-SNFPs cover the following four areas of non-functional properties.

- **Message Transmission Semantics:** Messaging synchrony, message delivery assurance, message queuing, multicast, manycast, anycast, message routing, message prioritization, messaging timeout, message logging, and message retention.

Listing 3. An Example Aspect in BALLAD

```
aspect NFPAspect{
  // pointcuts
 pointcut wholeProcess:
within("Secretary::Start.*", "Secretary::Finish");
 pointcut fromVotingMember: source("Voting Member");
 pointcut vote: flow("Vote");
 pointcut error: trigger(ERROR);
 pointcut secretary:
  within("Secretary::Start.*", "Secretary::Finish") && depth(1);
 pointcut defaultProcess:
  within("Secretary::Start.*","Secretary::Finish") && default();
 pointcut afterVoting:
  trigger(TIMER) && target("Assistant Moderator");
 // references to advices
 wholeProcess: DefaultSecurity, NoDeliveryAssurance;
 fromVotingMember: MessgeEncryption;
 vote: HighlevelSecurity;
 error: DeliveryAssurance;
 secretary: NoSecurity;
 defaultProcess: DeliveryAssurance;
 afterVoting: NoDeliveryAssurance;
}
```

- **Security Semantics:** Transport-level encryption, message-level encryption (entire/partial message encryption), message signature, message access control, service access control, and secure conversation.
- **Service Deployment Semantics:** Service redundancy.
- **Transport Protocols:** Properties in certain transport protocols.

Implementation Independent Non-Functional Properties in FM-SNFPs

Figure 4 shows the feature model in FM-SNFPs. There are several constraints and relationships among non-functional properties (see Table 3). White and black circle icons indicate optional and mandatory non-functional properties, respectively. For example, Message Priority, In Order Transmission (i.e., specifies whether the order of messages that a message destination receives is same as the order of messages that a message source sends out) and Message Integrity (i.e., checks whether messages are altered during their transmission) are optional. Retransmission is also optimal, however Number (the maximum number of retransmissions) is mandatory. Therefore, Number must be selected when Retransmission is selected. A feature may have its type. For example, the type of the Message Priority feature is Integer. When a typed feature is selected in a feature configuration, its value (e.g., integer value) must be specified at the same time.

A fork icon with a white sector denotes an *exclusive-OR* relationship among non-functional properties. In Figure 4, one of Sync, Async or

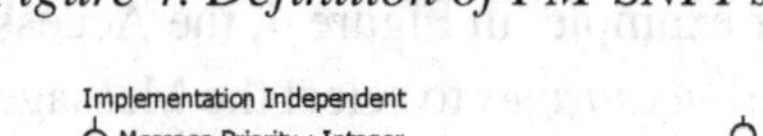

Figure 4. Definition of FM-SNFPs

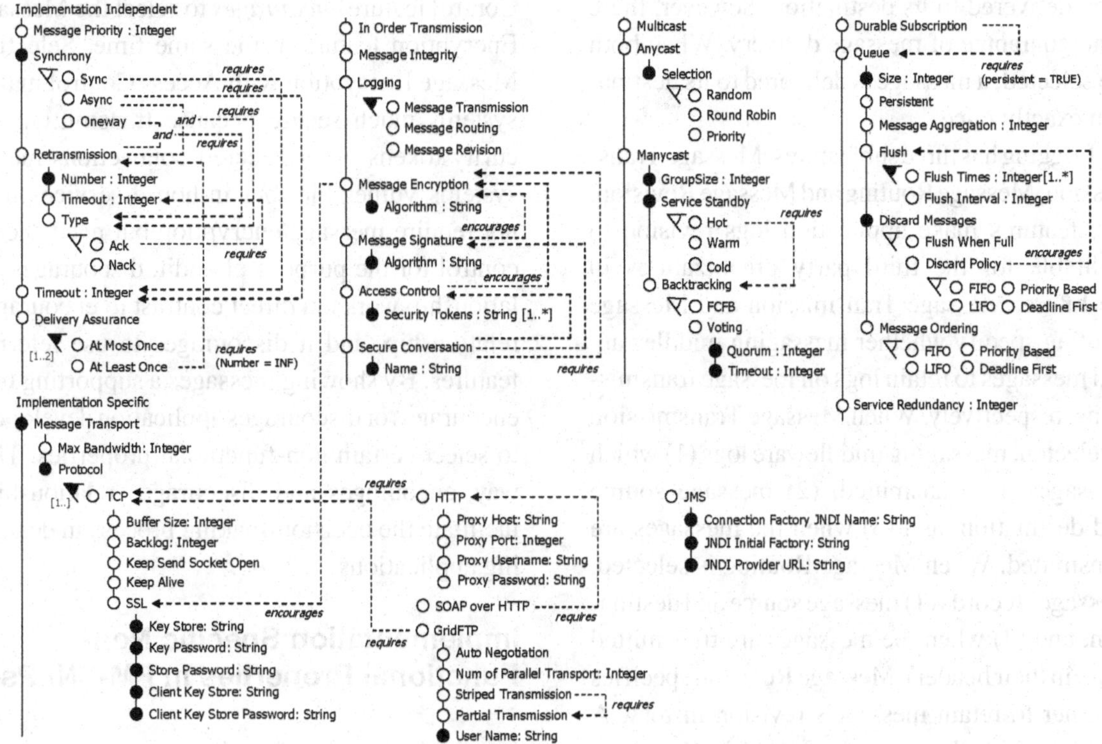

Oneway must be selected for Synchrony. A fork icon with a black sector denotes an *OR* relationship among non-functional properties. Cardinality indicates the number of subfeatures to be selected. Delivery Assurance feature has two subfeatures, and one or two of them should be selected when Delivery Assurance is selected. When cardinality is omitted, the default cardinality, i.e., one to the number of subfeatures, will be used (Czarnecki, Helsen, & Eisenecker, 2005). (Delivery Assurance shows the default cardinality explicitly.) At Least Once means that a connector retries delivering a message until its destination receives the message. However, the message may be delivered to its destination more than once. At Most Once means that a connector

Table 3. Constraints/relationships of features

Constraint/Relationship	Description
mandatory feature	A feature that must be selected.
optional feature	A feature that optionally be selected.
exclusive-Or	A mutual exclusion constraint among features. It enforces to select one of subfeatures.
OR	An inclusive relationship among features. It enforces to select one or more subfeatures.
requires	A dependency among features. It enforces to use the referred features at the same time.
encourages	A weak dependency among features. It endorses to use the referred features at the same time.
discourages	A weak mutual exclusion constraint among features. It discourages to use the referred features at the same time.

discards a message if the message has already been delivered to its destination; however, there is no guarantee of message delivery. When both are selected, a message is delivered to its destination exactly once.

Logging has three subfeatures: Message Transmission, Message Routing and Message Revision. The features make application logs revision to auditable for the third party organizations in the future. Message Transmission and Message Routing specify whether messaging middleware and messages to retain logs on message transmissions, respectively. When Message Transmission is selected, messaging middleware logs (1) which messages are transmitted, (2) message source and destination, and (3) when the messages are transmitted. When Message Routing is selected, messages records (1) message source and destination, and (2) when the messages are transmitted (e.g., in their header). Message Revision specifies whether to retain message's revision history. A message with this semantics records (1) which data fields are revised, (2) how they revised (i.e., newly created, replaced, or deleted), (3) when they revised, and (4) who revised them.

In addition to the hierarchical structure of features, three relationships among features are supported: requires, encourages and discourages (see Table 3). A requires relationship indicates a dependency among non-functional properties. For example, when Async and Retransmission are selected, Type of Retransmission (Ack-base or Nack-base) must be selected too. If the type of retransmission is Ack-base, Timeout must be selected too for configuring a timeout period of Ack messages. Secure Conversation requires Message Encryption, Message Signature and Access Control that used to establish secure connections shared with services.

encourages and discourages relationships are newly introduced in this research project. encourages is a relationship which is similar but weaker than requires. It has no mandatory power, but endorses to use the referred features at the same time. For example, in Figure 4, the Access Control feature *encourages* to select the Message Encryption feature at the same time. Selecting Message Encryption with Access Control makes systems much secure because transmitting security tokens via unsecured connections makes systems vulnerable, but in-house services may not require message encryption but need access control for the purpose of audit. discourages relationship works in direct contrast to encourages relationship, and it discourages to use referred features. By showing messages a supporting tool encourages or discourages application developers to select certain non-functional properties. This way, encourages and discourages relationships facilitate the decision-making process in designing applications.

Implementation Specific Non-Functional Properties in FM-SNFPs

In addition to non-functional properties independent from implementation technologies, FM-SNFPs defines non-functional properties specific to certain implementation technologies (see Figure 4). Protocol has five subfeatures: TCP, HTTP, SOAP over HTTP, GridFTP and JMS.

TCP represents TCP connections, and it has five subfeatures. Buffer Size specifies the buffer size (byte) used to read and write data. Backlog specifies the maximum queue length for incoming connections. Keep Send Socket Open specifies whether to reuse a single socket for multiple dispatches and keep it open until an application explicitly close it. Keep Alive specifies whether to send a packet via an unused open socket to a remote server every certain period. SSL is for configuring SSL (TSL) connection. Key Store and Client Key Store specify the location (a file path) of a server and client keystore used to create a secure socket respectively. Store Password and Client Key Store Password specifies the password used to access server and client key stores respectively. Key Password specifies a password used to check the integrity of keys. When a connector uses SSL, these five subfeatures must be selected and configured.

HTTP represents HTTP connections, and it has four subfeatures. When a connection uses a proxy host, proxyHost and proxyPort must be selected. Also, if a proxy host requires a user name and password, proxyUsername and proxyPassword must be selected. Since HTTP requires TCP, TCP must be selected with HTTP at the same time. SOAP over HTTP represents connections via SOAP over HTTP. Since it requires both TCP and HTTP, they must be selected with SOAP over HTTP at the same time.

Grid FTP represents connections via GridFTP,[1] and it has five subfeatures. Auto Negotiation enables an auto TCP buffer tuning that GridFTP supports. GridFTP allows for using multiple streams (connections) to transmit data, and Num of Parallel Streams specified the number of connections to use. GridFTP allows for a sink node to receive data from multiple source nodes at a time, and Striped Streams enables it. GridFTP allows for transmitting a fragment of data, and Partial Streams enables it. Also, User Name specifies the username to be used in a GridFTP server.

JMS represents connections via Java Messaging Service, and it has three subfeatures. JNDI Initial Factory specifies a class used to access to a Java Naming and Directory Interface (JNDI) server. JNDI Provider URL specifies a URL to access a JNDI server. Connection Factory JNDI Name specifies a name of a JNDI context to obtain a connection to JMS.

Figure 5 shows a feature configuration of FM-SNFPs. In this feature configuration, several features (e.g., Async subfeature and Retransmission feature) are selected. A supporting tool resolves the constraints between (sub)features. For example, the Sync and Oneway subfeatures are automatically deselected when the Async subfeature is selected. Also, it reports missing

Figure 5. An Example of a feature configuration

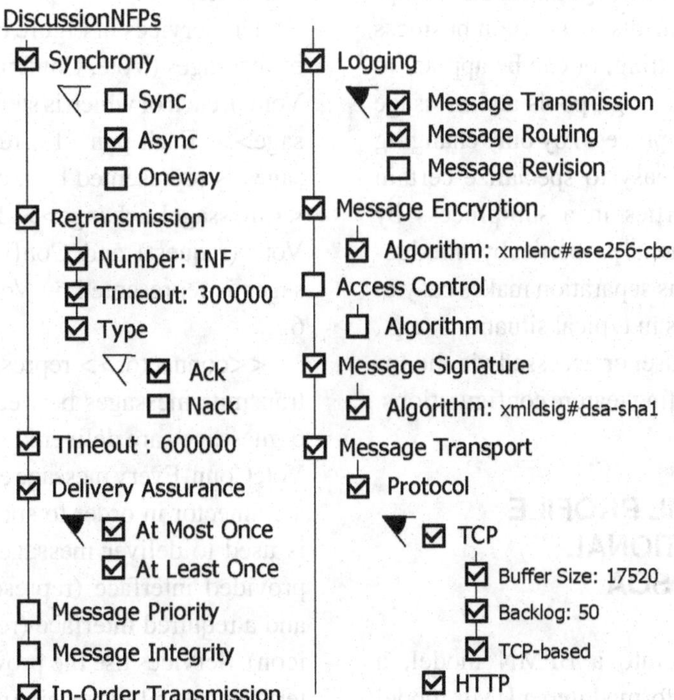

properties (e.g., an alert is shown when the value of the Timeout is not configured even though the feature is selected.) and existence of encouraged features (e.g., a message is shown to encourage to select Message Encryption when Access Control is selected.) to developers.

Ark.bpmn weaves feature configurations into a BPMN model in order of the references to advices. For example, Listing 3 weaves non-functional properties in DefaultSecurity and NoDeliveryAssurance into the pointcut wholeProcess. Since it is the first advice referred in an aspect, Ark.bpmn weaves the two sets of non-functional properties into a BPMN model first. Then, MessageEncryption is woven into fromVotingMember. When non-functional properties in DefaultSecurity and MessageEncryption are contradict with each other (e.g., they specify different security level), MessageEncryption overwrites DefaultSecurity since MessageEncryption appears after DefaultSecurity.

This way, BALLAD separates BPMN models and its non-functional properties well and improves the reusability of feature configurations. For example, a feature configuration can be applied to all model elements in a certain business process as a default setting, or can be applied to only specific elements (e.g., pools and message flows in a certain sub-process) by only changing pointcuts. Also, it is easy to specialize certain non-functional properties in a sub-process by overwriting non-functional properties by introducing new pointcuts. This separation makes easy to configure applications in typical situations (e.g., services hosted in-house, or accessed via the Internet) by reusing existing feature configurations.

UP-SNFPS: A UML PROFILE FOR NON-FUNCTIONAL PROPERTIES IN SOA

By weaving aspects into a BPMN model, a BPMN model is transformed into a UML model with non-functional properties (see Figure 2). Non-functional properties in a UML model are described through UP-SNFPs (Wada et al., 2008). UP-SNFPs is a UML profile to visually specify non-functional properties in UML's class and composite structure diagrams. It is designed around two major concepts: *services* and *connectors* between services. Each connector defines how services are connected with each other and how messages are exchanged through it. UP-SNFPs can be used to define implementation independent and implementation specific models with non-functional properties.

Implementation Independent Models with UP-SNFPs

Figure 6 shows an example model defined with UP-SNFPs. It illustrates a voting management application, which corresponds to a sub-process of the voting process in Figure 3. In this example, three services (Moderator, AssistantModerator and VotingMember) exchange messages. Each service is represented by a class stereotyped with <<service>>.

The services in Figure 6 exchange three types of messages (Vote, Confirmation and CollectedVotes), each of which is stereotyped with <<message>>. Each pair of a request and reply messages is represented by a class stereotyped with <<messageExchange>>. For example, a pair of Vote (request) and Confirmation (reply) messages is represented by VoteExchange in Figure 6.

<<connector>> represents a connection that transmits messages between services. In Figure 6, messages are delivered through the connector VoteConn. Every message exchange is bound with a connector in order to specify which connector is used to deliver messages. A connector has a provided interface (represented as a ball icon) and a required interface (represented as a socket icon). Services use the provided and required interfaces to send and receive messages, respectively.

Figure 6. An Example of a UML Model with UP-SNFPs

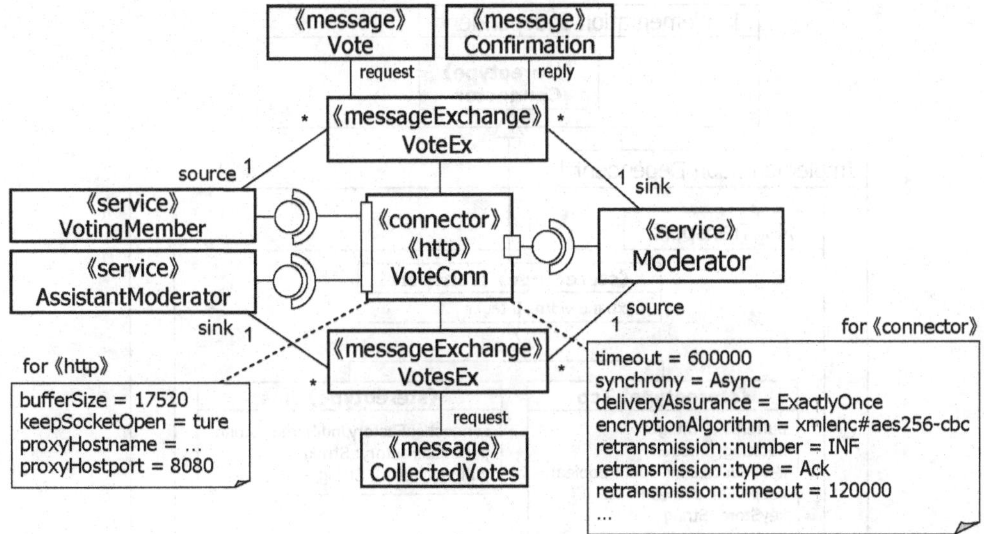

Each connector can have multiple tagged-values to specify a set of message transmission and processing semantics. In Figure 6, the connector VoteConn specifies the timeout of message transmissions (600,000 milliseconds), synchrony of message transmissions (asynchronous), assurance level of message delivery (exactly once), parameters of message retransmission (ack base and its timeout is 120,000 milliseconds), and an encryption algorithm for messages (Advanced Encryption Standard).

Implementation Specific Models with UP-SNFPs

In addition to stereotypes designed for implementation independent models, UP-SNFPs supports several stereotypes specific to implementation technologies such as transport protocols and middleware. They inherit the Connector stereotype (see Figure 7), and used to annotate connectors to specify to which implementation technologies the connectors are mapped. For example, services in Figure 6 exchange messages via HTTP since the connector VoteConn is stereotyped with <<http>>.

When a connector in an input UML model has a stereotype for a certain implementation technology, Ark.uml generates application code that uses the implementation technology. When a connector does not have stereotypes for certain implementation technologies, Ark.uml generates code but it is not bound with any implementation technology and developers are required to configure the generated code by hand to use certain implementation technologies.

APPLICATION DEVELOPMENT WITH ARK

Figure 2 shows the application development process with the proposed aspect oriented language. Ark.bpmn takes a BPMN model and an aspect in BALLAD, and transforms the BPMN model to a UML model defined with UP-SNFPs (see also Figure 1). Ark.uml transforms the generated UML model into a skeleton of application code.

Figure 7. Stereotypes for Implementation Technologies

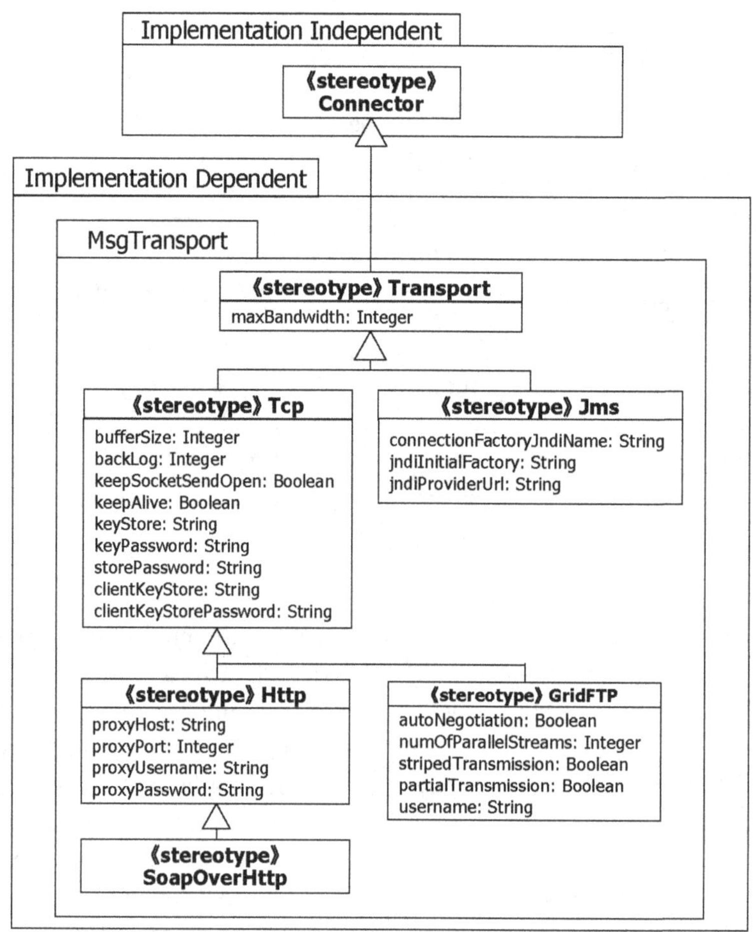

Defining an Aspect in BALLAD and FM-SNFPs

For defining aspects, Ark provides an editor for BALLAD and a modeling tool for FM-SNFPs running on Eclipse. Figure 8 illustrates the editor for BALLAD. As it shows, the editor shows built-in keywords in boldface, automatically performs a syntax check, and reports syntax errors while developers define aspects. The editor is implemented by leveraging openArchitectureware[7] (oAW). oAW allows developers to define the syntax of user-defined languages in EMF (BALLAD metamodel in Figure 1), and based on the syntax in EMF oAW generates editors for the languages (see Figure 8).

FM-SNFPs are defined on fmp (Antkiewicz & Czarnecki, 2004), which is a feature modeling tool implemented on EMF. This research project extends fmp to support encourages and discourages relationships. Figure 9 shows a feature configuration in a feature modeling tool. The editor does not allow users to create feature configurations that violate constraints defined in a feature model. For example users can select only one of features in mutual exclusion at a time. Also, the editor notifies users of missing information, encourages relationships and discourage relationships. In Figure 9, messages shown in the bottom notify the existence of a missing value in the Timeout feature and an encourages relationship.

Figure 8. A screenshot of an editor for BALLAD

```
voting.aspect
aspect NFPAspect{
  // pointcuts
  pointcut wholeProcess: within("Secretary::Start.*", "Secretary::Finish");
  pointcut fromVotingMember: source("Voting Member");
  pointcut vote: flow("Vote");
  pointcut error: trigger(ERROR);
  pointcut secretary: within("Secretary::Start.*", "Secretary::Finish") && depth(1);
  pointcut defaultProcess: within("Secretary::Start.*", "Secretary::Finish") && default();
  pointcut afterVoting: trigger(TIMER) && target("Assistant Moderator");

  // references to advices
  wholeProcess: DefaultSecurity, NoDeliveryAssurance;
  fromVotingMember: MessgeEncryption;
  vote: HighlevelSecurity;
  error: DeliveryAssurance;
  secretary: NoSecurity;
  defaultProcess: DeliveryAssurance;
  afterVoting: NoDeliveryAssurance;
}
```

Transformation from BPMN to UML

Ark.bpmn performs a model transformation from BPMN to UML in two steps: (1) transforming a BPMN model into a UML model without non-functional properties, and (2) configuring non-functional properties on the generated UML model based on the definition of an aspect in BALLAD.

The first step simply transforms a BPMN model into a UML model by following the transformation rules shown in Table 4. A generated UML model has several stereotypes defined in UP-SNFPs (e.g., <<service>> and <<connector>>), but does not have any non-functional properties yet. Figure 10 is a fragment of a UML model transformed from the BPMN model in Figure 3. (The UML model contains model elements corresponding to the Moderator and Voting Member pools, and the Issue Announcement and Vote message flows in Figure 3.) Ark.bpmn transforms a pool in a BPMN model into a class stereotyped with <<service>>. (e.g., the Moderator pool is mapped into the Moderator class.) Each task in a pool is transformed into a method in a class. (e.g., the Discussion Cycle task is mapped into the discussionCycle method.) Also, a message flow between pools is mapped into three classes: classes with <<connector>>, <<messageExchange>> and <<message>>. They represent a connector between services, a pair of a request and reply messages, and a request message respectively. (Since a message flow in BPMN represents an oneway message, only a request message is generated in a UML model.)

Configuring Non-Functional Properties in a UML model

Ark.bpmn parses an aspect in BALLAD and finds which feature configurations are applied to which model elements in a given BPMN model. When a feature configuration is applied to certain tasks and/or message flows in a BPMN model, the feature configuration is applied to services in a UML model that have methods corresponding to the tasks and/or connectors corresponding to the message flows. For example, the feature configuration DiscussionNFPs is applied to the pointcut moderator in Listing 1. Since the pointcut moderator returns paths that contain several tasks in Moderator and the Voting Member pool in a BPMN model (see Figure 3), non-functional properties in the feature configuration DiscussionNFPs is applied to Moderator and Voting Member services in a generated UML model (Figure 10).

Figure 9. A screenshot of a feature modeling tool

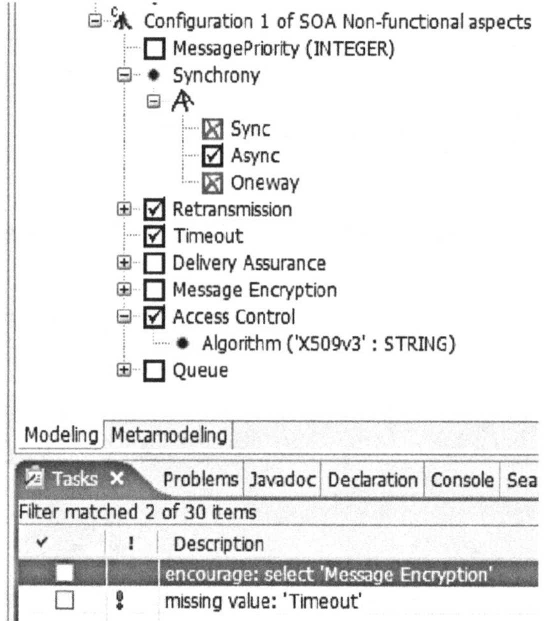

Also, since the paths contains several message flows between Moderator and Voting Member, the feature configuration DiscussionNFPs is applied to corresponding connectors in a generated UML model as well.

Then, Ark.bpmn saves the result in an XML file. Listing 4 is a fragment of the result obtained from NFPAspect in Listing 3. It lists pairs of the name of a feature configuration and a set of model elements where the feature configuration applies. As illustrated, the result contains a set of featureconfiguration tags. Each of them specifies which feature configuration is applied to which model elements using its name attribute and model tags respectively. A model tag has the attribute pattern specifying the name of a model element.

Ark.bpmn takes this XML file and configures tagged-values of model elements in a generated UML model. Listing 5 shows the process. Ark.bpmn traverses a generated UML and checks each model element (e in Listing 5) whether any feature configurations (featureConf in Listing 5) are applied. If yes, Ark.bpmn configures the model element's tagged-values according to feature configurations. Figure 11 is a UML model that Ark.bpmn generates by weaving the feature configuration in Figure 5 into the UML model in Figure 10.

Code Generation

Once Ark.bpmn completes its model transformation, Ark.uml transforms a UML model with UP-SNFPs to a skeleton of application code (program code and deployment descriptors) (see Figures 1 and 2). Currently, Ark.uml implements a transformation mapping for two major ESBs, Mule ESB[8] and ServiceMix ESB[9], and GridFTP.

When Mule ESB is selected as middleware to operate applications, Ark.uml transforms a UML class stereotyped with <<message>> to a

Table 4. Mapping rules from BPMN to UML

Model Element in BPMN	Model Element in UML
A pool	A class with <<service>> with the same name. (whitespace characters are removed.)
A task	A method with the same name. (whitespace characters are removed and the first character is decaptalized.)
A message flow	A class with <<connector>> with the name of *flowname*Conn. A class with messageExchange with the name of *flowname*Ex. A class with <<message>> with the name of *flowname*. (where *flowname* refers the name of a message flow.)
An outgoing message flow from a pool	An inclusive relationship among features. It enforces to select one or more subfeatures.
An incoming message flow to a pool	A dependency among features. It enforces to use the referred features at the same time.

Figure 10. A fragment of a generated UML model

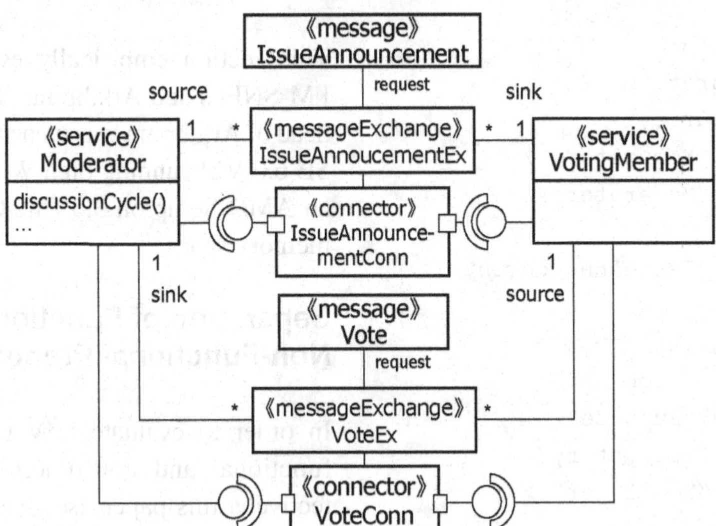

Java class that has the same class name. The Java class implements the interface Serializable. This is required to implement messages exchanged in Mule ESB. A UML class stereotyped with <<service>> is transformed to a Java class that has the same class name and the same methods. Also, Ark.uml inserts several methods to the Java class depending on whether its association role is source/sink against a message exchange.

Although UML classes stereotyped with <<messageExchange>> and <<connector>> are not transformed to particular Java classes, Ark.uml generates a corresponding deployment descriptor to configure connectors between services according to the message transmission/ processing semantics specified in a UML model. Listing 6 shows a fragment of a deployment descriptor generated from the UML model in Figure 11. <endpoint-identifier> specifies a name of an end point (name) and its URL (value), e.g., when a service is deployed to be accessed via HTTP, its value is http://.... <mule-descriptor> specifies the name (name) and implementation (implementation) of a service, <inbound-router> specifies the URL of a service by referencing an end point, and <connector> specifies a transport protocol to deliver messages. Since the VoteConn connector in Figure 11 is stereotyped with <<http>>, the generated deployment descriptor is configured to use org.mule.providers.http.HttpConnector, which is provided by Mule ESB, to access services via HTTP. Also, properties of a transport protocol are specified in <property>. See Wada et al. (2008) for full discussion on a transformation mapping for implementation independent stereotypes and tagged-values in UP-SNFPs.

Extensibility of the Proposed MDD Framework

Because of the huge diversity of non-functional properties, applications may require new non-functional properties and constraints that are not supported in the current proposed MDD framework. In order to introduce new non-functional properties and constraints, application developers are required to extend FM-SNFPs, UP-SNFPs and transformation rules. Since BALLAD does not depend on the definition of non-functional properties, any extensions have no affects on BALLAD.

Since the editor for FM-SNFPs (see Figure 9) allows for extending the FM-SNFPs'

Listing 4. A Result Saved in XML

```
<weaving>
 <featureconfiguration
name="DefaultSecurity">
 <model pattern="Securetary"/>
 <model pattern="Moderator"/>
 ...
 <model pattern="IssueAnnoucement"/>
 ...
 </featureconfiguration>
 <featureconfiguration
name="NoDeliveryAssurance">
 <model pattern="Securetary"/>
 <model pattern="Moderator"/>
 ...
 <model pattern="IssueAnnoucement"/>
 ...
 </featureconfiguration>
 <featureconfiguration
name="MessageEncryption">
 <model pattern="Moderator"/>
 <model pattern="VotingMember"/>
 <model pattern="Votes"/>
 ...
 </featureconfiguration>
 ...
</weaving>
```

model, application developers can easily add new non-functional properties and constraints to FM-SNFPs. UP-SNFPs is built on the UML standard metamodel with the standard extension mechanism, and application developers can add stereotypes and tagged-values representing new non-functional properties. In addition to the extension to FM-SNFPs and UP-SNFPs, extending transformation rules from FM-SNFPs to UP-SNFPs and rules from UP-SNFPs to application code completes the extension of the proposed MDD framework.

EMPIRICAL EVALUATION

This section empirically evaluates BALLAD, FM-SNFPs and Ark.bpmn. The execution overhead of Ark.bpmn was measured with a Sun Java SE 6.0 VM running on a Windows XP PC with an AMD Sempron 3.0 Ghz CPU and 1024 MB memory space.

Separation of Functional and Non-Functional Properties

In order to evaluate how BALLAD separates functional and non-functional properties effectively, this paper uses two metrics: Concern Diffusion over Components (CDC) (Sant'Anna, Garcia, Chavez, Lucena, & Staa, 2003) and Degree of Scattering (DOS) (Eaddy, Aho, & Murphy, 2007). Both are measured for a BPMN model with a BALLAD aspect and a UML model generated by Ark.bpmn. CDC counts the number of components (e.g., classes and aspects) that are intended to implement a crosscutting concern and the number of other components that access the concern. A higher CDC indicates higher degree of concern scattering. DOS is measured based on the variance of the lines of code (LOC) spent for a crosscutting concern. Figure 12 gives the DOS metric for a concern *c*. DOS ranges between 0 and 1. A higher DOS indicates a higher degree of concern scattering.

In this experiment, non-functional properties are considered as crosscutting concerns to measure CDC and DOS. DOS requires the LOC that implements a crosscutting concern because it was originally designed to evaluate textual aspect oriented languages. This experiment counts each feature of FM-SNFPs and each tagged-value of UP-SNFPs as one LOC. T in the above equation (a set of components) contains an aspect, a feature configuration and classes stereotyped with <<service>> and <<connector>>.

The voting process model in Figure 3 is used to measure CDC and DOC. Listing 7 defines an

Figure 11. A UML Model with non-functional properties

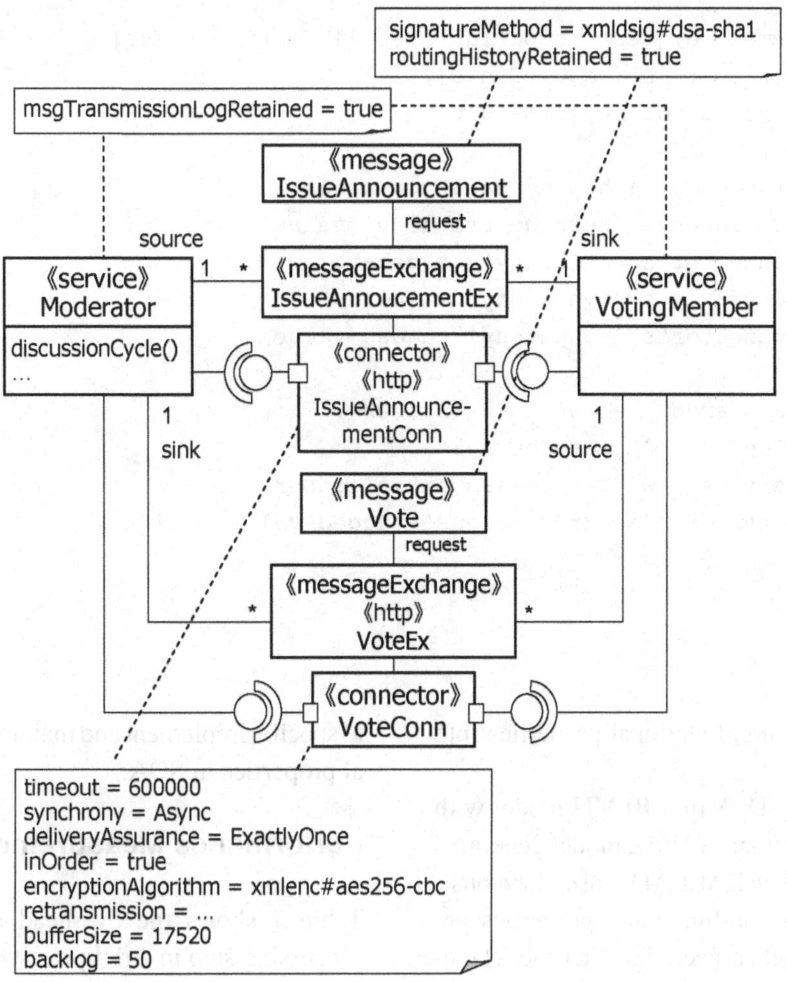

aspect that weaves four different feature configurations shown in Figure 13. Default specifies one-way and in-order message transmission. These non-functional properties are woven into all model elements throughput the voting process. LowLevelSecurity specifies message signature and logging. They are woven into the model elements that involve in a discussion that the Moderator moderates. HighLevelSecurity specifies extra security properties in addition to LowLevelSecurity. They are woven into the model elements that involves in message flows initiated by Voting Members. ReliableMessaging specifies retransmission, integrity, delivery assurance and queuing properties for message transmissions. They are woven into the model elements that involves in communication between Vote and Vote Announcement.

Table 5 shows CDC of a BPMN model with a BALLAD aspect and a UML model generated by Ark.bpmn. When a BALLAD aspect is used in a business process, CDC is always 2; an aspect and its corresponding feature configuration. In a UML model generated by Ark.bpmn, CDC counts the UML classes that specify non-functional properties and the classes stereotyped with <<service>> and <<connector>>. As Table 5 illustrates, BALLAD reduces CDC two to eight times

Listing 5. Pseudo Code for Weaving Process

```
weaving(UMLElement e, FeatureConfiguration[] featureConfs){
 foreach featureConf in featureConfs{
 if (featureConf is not applied to e)
  return;
 if (e is stereotyped with <<messageExchange>>)
  if (featureConf has a 'Message Priority' value)
  configure connector's 'priority' tagged-value
  if (featureConf has a 'Synchrony' value)
  configure connector's 'synchrony' tagged-value
  ...
 else if (e is stereotyped with <<service>>)
  if (featureConf has 'AccessControl')
  replace <<service>> with <<accessControlledService>>
  configure service's 'securityTokens' tagged-vale
  ...
 }
}
```

by encapsulating non-functional properties into a single aspect.

Table 6 shows DOS of a BPMN model with a BALLAD aspect and a UML model generated by Ark.bpmn. When BALLAD is used for a business process, all non-functional properties are specified in a single aspect. No other model elements specify non-functional properties. As a result, DOS remains low. In a UML model generated by Ark.bpmn, DOS is consistently higher with all of four feature configurations because non-functional properties scatter over UML classes. Eaddy et al. (2007) claim that DOC is 0.5 when crosscutting concerns are well modularized. DOS is close enough to 0.5 when using BALLAD; BALLAD better modularizes non-functional properties than UML models with UP-SNFPs.

As described in the Introduction section, higher degree of concern scattering increases the complexity of application development and maintenance. Figures 5 and 6 demonstrate that BALLAD can significantly reduce the burdens/costs to specify, implement and maintain non-functional properties in SOA.

Performance Measurement

Table 7 shows the overhead to execute each processing step in Ark.bpmn when it transforms the BPMN model in Figure 3 to a UML model by weaving the aspect in Listing 7. In this transformation process, Ark.bpmn (1) parses a given BALLAD aspect, (2) loads a BPMN model, (3)

Table 5. CDC Measurement

Feature Configuration	BPMN with BALLAD	UML with UP-SNFPs
Default	2	16 (4 services and 12 connectors)
LowLevelSecurity	2	14 (3 services and 11 connectors)
HighLevel Security	2	4 (2 services and 2 connectors)
Reliable Messaging	2	7 (3 services and 4 connectors)

Listing 6. An example of a deployment descriptor

```
<mule-configuration>
 <endpoint-identifiers>
 <endpoint-identifier
    name="Moderator_in_VoteEx" value="http://..."/>
 </endpoint-identifiers>
 <model>
 <mule-descriptor
    name="ModeratorService" implementation="Moderator">
  <inbound-router>
  <endpoint
      address="Moderator_in_VoteEx" connector="VoteConn"/>
  </inbound-router>
 </mule-descriptor>
 <mule-descriptor
name="VotingMemberService" implementation="VotingMember"/>
 </model>
 <connector
    name="VoteConn"
    className="org.mule.providers.http.HttpConnector">
 <properties>
  <property name="bufferSize" value="17520"/>
  <property name="backlog" value="50"/>
 </properties>
 </connector>
</mule-configuration>
```

finds paths in a BPMN model according to the aspect, (4) transforms the BPMN model into a UML model, and (5) configures non-functional properties in the generated UML model with FM-SNFPs. As Table 7 shows, the execution overhead of Ark.bpmn is small enough and acceptable even when it processes a fairly complex BPMN model.

In order to evaluate the scalability of Ark. bpmn, Figure 14 shows how its execution overhead changes as the size of an input BPMN model grows. Figure 15 illustrates an input BPMN

Figure 12. DOS metric for a concern c

$$DOS(c) = 1 - \frac{|T| \sum_t (Concentration(c,t) - 1/|T|)^2}{|T| - 1}$$

where

$$T = \{t : t \in all\ components\}$$

$$Concentration(c,t) = \frac{\text{LOC spent in component } t \text{ to implement a concern } c}{\text{Total LOC in all components that implement a concern c } c}$$

Figure 13. Feature configurations for a voting process model

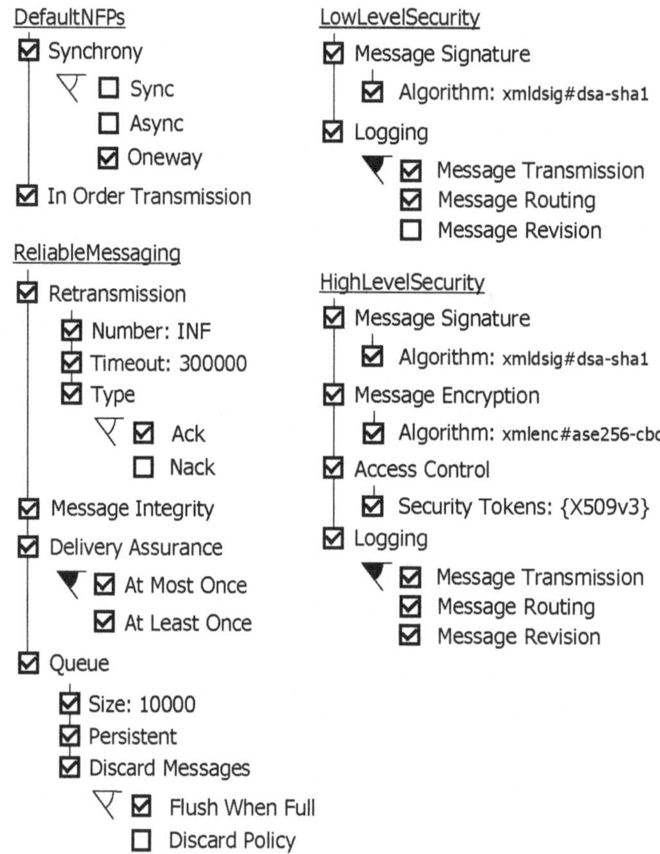

model. As shown, the model size grows by repeatedly adding participants (Server 01 to Server N). This experiment uses the pointcut within(".*", ".*"), which takes the longest time among all types of pointcuts, and weaves the Default feature configuration in Figure 13 into a input BPMN model. As Figure 14 shows, the total overhead increases at least linearly as the size of an input BPMN model grows. The increase in model size impacts the overhead of Step 3 and 4; however, the two steps remain reasonably lightweight. The increase has few or no impacts on the overhead of the other three steps. Figure 14 demonstrates that Ark.bpmn scales well against large-scale BPMN models.

Table 6. DOC Measurement

Feature Configuration	BPMN with BALLAD	UML with UP-SNFPs
Default	0.52	0.98
LowLevelSecurity	0.53	0.95
HighLevelSecurity	0.49	0.68
ReliableMessaging	0.43	0.85

In addition to the size of an input BPMN model, different types of pointcuts can impact the overhead of Step 3 differently. Figure 16 shows how the overhead of Step 3 changes with 8 different pointcuts. within(".*", ".*") and target("X") are the two slowest pointcuts; however, they are still lightweight enough. It takes only 1.2 and 0.4 seconds to execute the two pointcuts. The other six pointcuts are very fast, and their overhead can be even negligible. Figure 16 demonstrates that BALLAD is designed and implemented lightweight.

Listing 7. An aspect used for an empirical evaluation

```
aspect NFPsForVoting{
 // pointcuts
 pointcut wholeProcess:
  within("Secretary::Start.*", "Secretary::Finish");
 pointcut discussion:
  within("Moderator::Discussion.*", "Moderator::Finish");
 pointcut fromMembers: source("Voting Members") && depth(1);
 pointcut voting: within("Vote", "Vote Announcement.*");
 // references to advices
 wholeProcess: Default;
 discussion: LowLevelSecurity;
 fromMembers: HighLevelSecurity:
 voting: ReliableMessaging;
}
```

RELATED WORK

This paper focuses on a set of extensions to the authors' previous work (Wada et al., 2008; Wada, Suzuki, & Oba, 2007). The previous work studied non-functional properties in UML models on a per-service basis. In contrast, this paper considers non-functional properties in business processes and proposes an aspect oriented language for a new per-process strategy to separate functional and non-functional properties in service oriented applications. Moreover, this paper considers the transformation from implementation independent to implementation specific UML models, which were beyond of the scope of the previous work.

AspectViewpoint is an aspect oriented language to define aspects for BPMN models (Correal & Casallas, 2007). It uses aspects to define business processes, and extends an existing business process by weaving the new ones to it. For example, when a purchasing business process is defined as a BPMN model, a new business process (e.g., order cancellation process) can be defined as an aspect and woven to the purchasing process for considering order cancellation in purchasing. AOPML is an aspect oriented language to extend business processes by weaving new tasks into it (Leite, Cappelli, Batista, & Silva, 2009). Courbis and Finkelstein (2005) propose an aspect oriented language to specify aspects for business processes defined in Business Process Execution

Table 7. Execution overhead of each processing step in Ark.bpmn

Processing Step	Time (second)	Percentage (%)
(1) Parse an aspect	3.19	30.3
(2) Load a BPMN model	1.41	13.4
(3) Find paths in a BPMN model according to an aspect	0.02	0.2
(4) Transform a BPMN model into a UML model	4.44	42.3
(5) Configure a UML model based on FM-SNFPs	1.45	13.8
Total	10.50	100.

Figure 14. Execution overhead of Ark.bpmn with BPMN models of different sizes

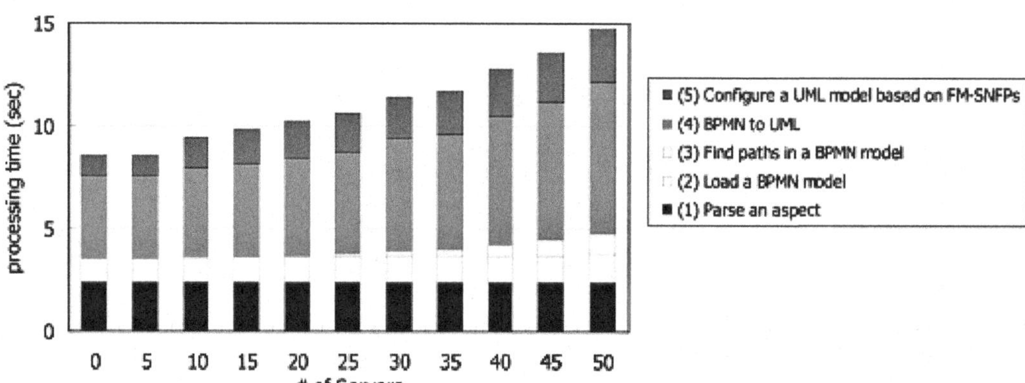

Language (BPEL) (OASIS, 2003). It uses aspects to define BPEL primitives (e.g., a branch of flows) and customize an existing business process by weaving the primitives to it. For example, an aspect may be defined to insert a <switch> block, which performs a branching operation in BPEL, right before <invoke> blocks, which are used to invoke services. This aspect modifies the semantics of service invocation by considering a certain condition(s). The above three languages are similar to BALLAD in that they study aspects for business processes. However, they focus on functional properties of business processes. Unlike them, BALLAD modularizes non-functional properties of business processes as aspects.

Figure 15. An example BPMN model for a scalability evaluation

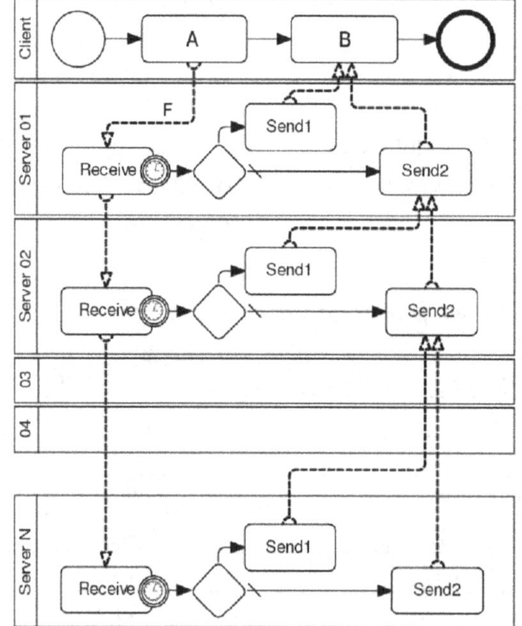

Figure 16. Execution overhead of finding paths

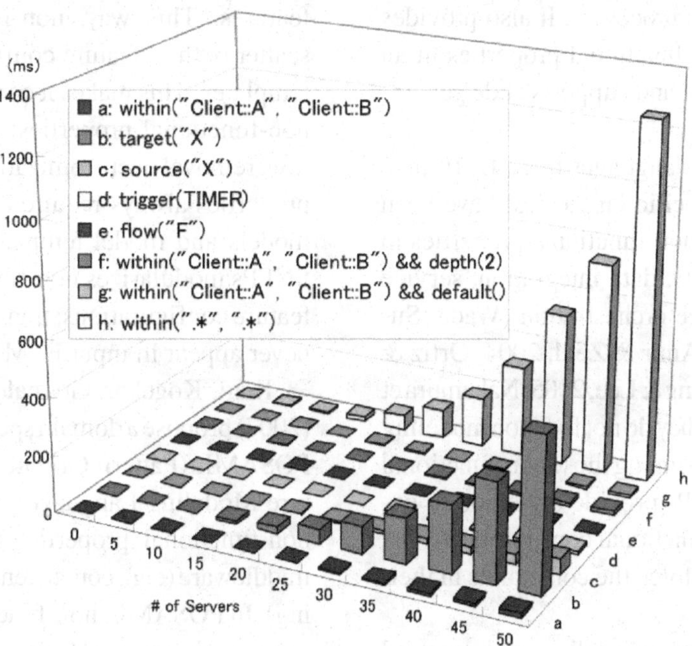

AO4BPEL is an aspect oriented language to extend BPEL business processes with non-functional properties such as reliable messaging, message encryption and transactions (Charfi, Schmeling, Heizenreder, & Mezini, 2006). Aspects can specify non-functional properties that are woven to services and their activities/tasks; however, a variety of pointcuts is limited in AO4BPEL. BALLAD offers higher expressiveness in defining aspects; it considers the pointcuts in control/message flows as well as tasks and pools. Also, it supports much more non-functional properties than AO4BPEL does.

Zou, Xiao, and Chan (2007) propose an aspect oriented language to weave non-functional properties to BPEL business processes. However, it does not provide specific non-functional properties and does not perform code generation. In contrast, BALLAD provides a specific set of non-functional properties in an unambiguous manner. BALLAD aspects are directly used for code generation.

Aburub, Odeh, and Beeson (2007) propose a method to model and analyze non-functional requirements in business processes (e.g., desirable response time and throughput). It examines whether each service has conflicting non-functional requirements by inspecting which services involve which business processes. However, Aburub et al. (2007) does not provide a language to explicitly declare non-functional requirements in business processes. As a result, the synthesis of functional and non-functional properties is manually performed. Code generation is not supported either. In contrast, BALLAD is intended to specify non-functional properties, which are adjustable parameters used for satisfying given non-functional requirements. BALLAD can explicitly express how to weave non-functional properties to business processes. Ark implements code generation for BALLAD aspects.

Xu, Ziv, Richardson, and Liu (2005) propose a method to define a set of non-functional requirements as an aspect and weave it to a UML class model. However, it does not provide specific non-functional properties and does not consider code generation. In contrast, BALLAD defines a set of non-functional properties as an aspect and weaves it to business processes. It also provides a specific set of non-functional properties in an unambiguous manner and supports code generation for them.

Several modeling languages (e.g., UML profiles and domain-specific languages) have been proposed to specify non-functional properties in SOA, such as security, data integration, service discovery and service orchestration (Wada, Suzuki, & Oba, 2006; Amir & Zeid, 2004; Ortiz & Hernändez, 2006; Wang & Lee, 2005; Nakamura et al., 2005). However, they do not focus on modeling a series of constraints among those non-functional properties. FM-SNFPs provide a method to explicitly model non-functional constraints in SOA and automatically enforce the constraints in their applications.

The notion of feature modeling has been used to, for example, configure the non-functional policies in embedded operating systems (e.g., concurrency and interruption policies) (Lohmann, Scheler, Preikschat, & Spinczyk, 2006), configure the functionalities of Eclipse plugins (e.g., multi-windows) (Antkiewicz & Czarnecki, 2006), configure underlying platform technologies (e.g., databases) used in applications (White et al., 2007) and select services in PBX systems (e.g., call request and call forwarding services) (Kang, Kim, Lee, & Lee, 1999). FM-SNFPs leverages feature modeling for managing non-functional constraints in SOA.

Czarnecki and Antkiewicz (2005) propose feature-based model templates designed to transform feature configurations to UML models. Each template is a UML class or activity diagram that defines a presence condition for each model element (e.g., class, association and action). A presence condition specifies when a corresponding model element appears in a UML diagram. For example, a class may have its presence condition Async & Ack in a class diagram template. The template generates the class in an output class diagram if the template accepts an input feature configuration that selects both Async and Ack features. This way, non-functional properties scatter both in feature configurations and model templates. This makes it complicated to maintain non-functional properties; a change (e.g., addition, removal or customization) in non-functional properties always require changing both feature models and model templates. In contrast, FM-SNFPs modularizes non-functional properties in feature configurations; non-functional properties never appear in input BPMN models.

Kaul, Kogekar, Gokhale, Gray, and Gokhale (2007) propose a domain specific language, called POSAML (Pattern Oriented Software Architecture Modeling Language), to visually configure non-functional properties in realtime CORBA middleware (e.g., concurrency and message queuing). In POSAML, non-functional constraints are specified in a textual form with Object Constraint Language (OCL) (Warmer & Kleppe, 2003). Although OCL provides higher expressiveness as a constraint specification language than feature models, FM-SNFPs employs feature models by trading visual intuitiveness for expressiveness.

Several methods exist to explicitly specify, examine and enforce non-functional requirements. Robinson and Purao (2009) propose an extension to OCL for defining functional and non-functional requirements in the interactions among services. For example, the language can specify, as a functional requirement, that a buyer receives a receipt within five minutes after a purchase. A monitoring tool examines whether given requirements are satisfied at runtime and notifies when a violation occurs. Chung, Nixon, Yu, and Mylopoulos (1999) propose a feature modeling method to define non-functional requirements and analyze the relationships among them. For example, the method can specify security and performance requirements and define their sub-requirements (e.g., integrity and confidentiality for the security requirement). It aids identifying and analyzing a potential conflict relationship between the integrity sub-requirement and performance requirement. The goals of these work and BALLAD are different. BALLAD focuses on generic non-functional properties and maps them to low-level implementation technologies such as transport protocols and remoting middleware, while Robinson and Purao (2009) and Chung et al. (1999) focus on application-specific non-functional requirements and does not consider their realization with implementation technologies. Moreover, they do not consider to modularize scattering non-functional requirements with the notion of aspects.

CONCLUSION

This paper investigates an end-to-end MDD framework that manages non-functional properties in SOA from high-level business processes to low-level configurations of implementation technologies such as transport protocols and remoting middleware. This framework proposes (1) an aspect oriented language, called BALLAD, for a new per-process strategy to specify non-functional properties in business processes, and (2) a graphical modeling method, called FM-SNFPs, to explicitly specify non-functional constraints and consistently validate and enforce them in applications. Empirical evaluation results show that BALLAD significantly reduces the costs to implement and maintain non-functional properties in SOA. BALLAD and FM-SNFPs are designed and implemented efficient and scalable.

REFERENCES

Aburub, F., Odeh, M., & Beeson, I. (2007). Modelling non-functional requirements of business processes. *Information and Software Technology*, *49*(11), 1162–1171. doi:10.1016/j.infsof.2006.12.002

Allcock, W., Bresnahan, J., Kettimuthu, R., Link, M., Dumitrescu, C., Raicu, I., & Foster, I. (2005, November). The globus striped gridFTP framework and server. In *Proceedings of the IEEE/ACM Conference on Supercomputing*.

Amir, R., & Zeid, A. (2004, October). A UML profile for service oriented architectures. In *Proceedings of the ACM SIGPLAN Conference on Object-Oriented Programming, Systems, Languages, and Applications.*

Antkiewicz, M., & Czarnecki, K. (2004, October). Featureplugin: Feature modeling plug-in for eclipse. In *Proceedings of the ACM SIGPLAN Conference on Object-Oriented Programming, Systems, Languages, and Applications, Workshop on Eclipse Technology Exchange.*

Antkiewicz, M., & Czarnecki, K. (2006, October). Framework-specific modeling languages with round-trip engineering. In *Proceedings of the ACM/IEEE International Conference on Model Driven Engineering Languages and Systems.*

Baligand, F., & Monfort, V. (2004, December). A concrete solution for web services adaptability using policies and aspects. In *Proceedings of the ACM SIGSOFT/ACM SIGWEB International Conference on Service Oriented Computing.*

Bichler, M., & Lin, K. (2006). Service-oriented computing. *IEEE Computer*, *39*(3), 99–101.

Bieberstein, N., Bose, S., Fiammante, M., Jones, K., & Shah, R. (2005). *Service-oriented architecture (soa) compass: Business value, planning, and enterprise roadmap.* Boston, MA: IBM Press.

BPM Initiative. (2004, May). *Business process modeling notation (bpmn) 1.0.* Needham, MA: Object Management Group.

Charfi, A., Schmeling, B., Heizenreder, A., & Mezini, M. (2006, December). Reliable, secure, and transacted web service compositions with ao4bpel. In *Proceedings of the IEEE European Conference on Web Services*.

Chitchyan, R., Rashid, A., Sawyer, P., Garcia, A., Alarcon, M. P., & Bakker, J. (2005). *Survey of aspect-oriented analysis and design approaches*. Lancaster, UK: AOSD-Europe.

Chung, L., Nixon, B., Yu, E., & Mylopoulos, J. (1999). *Non-functional requirements in software engineering*. Dordrecht, The Netherlands: Kluwer Academic Publishers.

Correal, D., & Casallas, R. (2007, October). Using domain specific languages for software process modeling. In *Proceedings of the ACM SIGPLAN Conference on Object-Oriented Programming, Systems, Languages, and Applications, Workshop on Domain-Specific Modeling*.

Courbis, C., & Finkelstein, A. (2005, October). Weaving aspects into web service orchestrations. In *Proceedings of the IEEE International Conference on Web Services*.

Czarnecki, K., & Antkiewicz, M. (2005, September). Mapping features to models: A template approach based on superimposed variants. In *Proceedings of the International Conference on Generative Programming and Component Engineering*.

Czarnecki, K., & Eisenecker, U. (2000). *Generative programming: Methods, tools and applications*. Reading, MA: Addison-Wesley.

Czarnecki, K., Helsen, S., & Eisenecker, U. (2005). Formalizing cardinality-based feature models and their specialization. *Software Process Improvement and Practice, 10*(1), 7–29. doi:10.1002/spip.213

Eaddy, M., Aho, A., & Murphy, G. C. (2007, May). *Identifying, assigning, and quantifying crosscutting concerns*. Paper presented at the AOSD-Europe International Workshop on Assessment of Contemporary Modularization Techniques.

Elrad, T., Aldawud, O., & Bader, A. (2002, October). Aspect-oriented modeling - bridging the gap between design and implementation. In *Proceedings of the ACM International Conference on Generative Programming and Component Engineering*.

Erickson, J., & Siau, K. (2008). Web services, service-oriented computing, and service-oriented architecture: Separating hype from reality. *Journal of Database Management, 19*(3), 42–54. doi:10.4018/jdm.2008070103

Jürjens, J. (2002, October). UMLsec: Extending UML for secure systems development. In *Proceedings of the ACM/IEEE International Conference on Unified Modeling Language*.

Kang, K., Kim, S., Lee, J., & Lee, K. (1999, December). Feature-oriented engineering of pbx software. In *Proceedings of the Asia-Pacific Software Engineering Conference*.

Kaul, D., Kogekar, A., Gokhale, A., Gray, J., & Gokhale, S. (2007, January). Posaml: A visual modeling framework for middleware provisioning. In *Proceedings of the Hawaiian International Conference on System Sciences*.

Kiczales, G., Lamping, J., Mendhekar, A., Maeda, C., Lopes, C., Loingtier, J. M., et al. (1997, June). Aspect-oriented programming. In *Proceedings of the European Conference on Object-Oriented Programming*.

Leite, J. C. S. P., Cappelli, C., Batista, T., & Silva, L. (2009, March). An aspect-oriented approach to business process modeling. In *Proceedings of the ACM International Conference on Aspect-Oriented Software Development, Workshop on Early Aspects*.

Lodderstedt, T., Basin, D., & Doser, J. (2002, October). Secureuml: A UML-based modeling language for model-driven security. In *Proceedings of the ACM/IEEE International Conference on Unified Modeling Language*.

Lohmann, D., Scheler, F., Preikschat, W. S., & Spinczyk, O. (2006, July). Pure embedded operating systems - ciao. In *Proceedings of the IEEE International Workshop on Operating System Platforms for Embedded Real-Time Applications*.

Nakamura, Y., Tatsubori, M., Imamura, T., & Ono, K. (2005, July). Model-driven security based on a web services security architecture. In *Proceedings of the IEEE International Conference on Services Computing*.

OASIS. (2003). *Web services business process execution language*.

Ortiz, G., & Hernändez, J. (2006, September). Toward UML profiles for web services and their extra-functional properties. In *Proceedings of the IEEE International Conference on Web Services*.

Papazoglou, M., & Heuvel, W. (2007). Service oriented architectures: Approaches, technologies and research issues. *International Journal on Very Large Data Bases*, *16*(3), 389–415. doi:10.1007/s00778-007-0044-3

Robinson, W. N., & Purao, S. (2009). Specifying and monitoring interactions and commitments in open business processes. *IEEE Software*, *26*(2), 72–79. doi:10.1109/MS.2009.48

Sant'Anna, C. N., Garcia, A. F., Chavez, C., Lucena, C. J. P., & Staa, A. (2003, October). *On the reuse and maintenance of aspect-oriented software: An assessment framework*. Paper presented at the Brazilian Symposium on Software Engineering.

Soler, E., Villarroel, R., Trujillo, J., Medina, E. F., & Piattini, M. (2006, April). Representing security and audit rules for data warehouses at the logical level by using the common warehouse metamodel. In *Proceedings of the International Conference on Availability, Reliability and Security*.

Vokäc, M. (2005, October). Using a domain-specific language and custom tools to model a multi-tier service-oriented application–experiences and challenges. In *Proceedings of the ACM/IEEE International Conference on Model Driven Engineering Languages and Systems*.

Wada, H., Suzuki, J., & Oba, K. (2006, September). Modeling non-functional aspects in service oriented architecture. In *Proceedings of the IEEE International Conference on Services Computing*.

Wada, H., Suzuki, J., & Oba, K. (2007, July). A feature modeling support for non-functional constraints in service oriented architecture. In *Proceedings of the IEEE International Conference on Services Computing*.

Wada, H., Suzuki, J., & Oba, K. (2008). A model-driven development framework for non-functional aspects in service oriented architecture. *Journal of Web Services Research*, *5*(4), 1–31. doi:10.4018/jwsr.2008100101

Wang, G., Chen, A., Wang, C., Fung, C., & Uczekaj, S. (2004). Integrated quality of service (QOS) management in service-oriented enterprise architectures. In *Proceedings of the IEEE Enterprise Distributed Object Computing Conference*.

Wang, L., & Lee, L. (2005). UML-based modeling of web services security. In *Proceedings of the IEEE European Conference on Web Services*.

Warmer, J., & Kleppe, A. (2003). *The object constraint language: Getting your models ready for mda* (2nd ed.). Reading, MA: Addison-Wesley.

White, J., Schmidt, D., Czarnecki, K., Wienands, C., Lenz, G., Wuchner, E., et al. (2007, October). Automated model-based configuration of enterprise java applications. In *Proceedings of the IEEE International Conference on Enterprise Distributed Object Computing*.

Xu, L., Ziv, H., Richardson, D., & Liu, Z. (2005, March). Towards modeling non-functional requirements in software architecture. In *Proceedings of the ACM International Conference on Aspect-Oriented Software Development, Early Aspects Workshop*.

Zou, Y., Xiao, H., & Chan, B. (2007, September). Weaving business requirements into model transformations. In *Proceedings of the ACM/IEEE International Conference on Model Driven Engineering Languages and Systems, Workshop on Aspect-Oriented Modeling*.

ENDNOTES

1 Business Process Aware Language for earLy Aspect Design. An extension to FTP for transmitting files of large size (Allcock et al., 2005).

2 http://www.eclipse.org/emf/

3 http://gp.uwaterloo.ca/fmp/

4 http://www.soyatec.com/ebpmn/

5 This model is made based on an example model included in the BPMN specification

6 An extension to FTP for transmitting files of large size (Allcock et al., 2005).

7 http://www.openarchitectureware.com/

8 http://mule.codehaus.org/

9 http://servicemix.apache.org/

This work was previously published in the Journal of Database Management, Volume 22, Issue 2, edited by Keng Siau, pp. 93-123, copyright 2011 by IGI Publishing (an imprint of IGI Global).

Chapter 10

Complementing Business Process Verification by Validity Analysis: A Theoretical and Empirical Evaluation

Pnina Soffer
University of Haifa, Israel

Maya Kaner
Ort Braude College, Israel

ABSTRACT

This paper investigates the need for complementing automated verification of business process models with a validity analysis performed by human analysts. As business processes become increasingly automated through process aware information systems, the quality of process design becomes crucial. Although verification of process models has gained much attention, their validation, relating to the reachability of the process goal, has hardly been addressed. The paper investigates the need for model validation both theoretically and empirically. The authors present a theoretical analysis, showing that process model verification and validation are complementary in nature, and an empirical evaluation of the effectiveness of validity criteria in validating a process model. The theoretical analysis, which relates to different aspects of process model quality, shows that process model verification and validation are complementary in nature. The empirical findings corroborate the effectiveness of validity criteria and indicate that a systematic criteria-supported validity analysis improves the identification of validity problems in process models.

DOI: 10.4018/978-1-4666-2044-5.ch010

INTRODUCTION

As business processes become increasingly automated through process aware information systems, the quality of process design becomes crucial. In the life-cycle of a business process, designed process models can be transformed into executable process models (Zur-Muhlen & Rosemann, 2004). As is the case with artifacts in various domains (e.g., software, product, service), problems are easier and cheaper to fix at the early development phases than afterwards (Bray, 2002). Furthermore, unattended design flaws will result in an execution model which preserves the same flaws.

In the area of software engineering, quality assurance entails validation and verification. Validation, often referred to as "building the right system", relates to whether the system meets the customer's requirements, while verification, often referred to as "building the system right", addresses the technical correctness of the system's operation (Sommerville, 2007).

In analogy between software functional requirements and the goal of a business process, validation of a business process can relate to its ability to achieve its goal. However, most process modeling languages do not entail a goal construct. Rather, they mainly focus on control-flow structures. As a consequence, the main focus of quality assurance in process modeling has been on verification of structural properties of process models.

The verified properties stand for the model's ability to be executed without reaching situations where the execution cannot complete (e.g., deadlocks, livelocks). Algorithms have been developed for verifying the existence of these properties in process models, usually related to specific modeling languages. Currently there is a variety of verification techniques which can automatically be applied to a designed process model. However, while these can be applied to a process model based solely on its structure, validation of the model requires the understanding of the business domain (van der Aalst, 2002; Sadiq et al., 2004). Typically, a process model can be validated by domain experts through simulation (Aguilar-Saven, 2004). However, this requires the process to already be implemented in some simulation tool and does not support the early phase of design. At that phase, validation can only be accomplished as a human based task. Since, as mentioned, most process modeling languages do not entail a goal construct, no structured validation procedure is practiced, thus the task remains to the intuition and common sense of the human analyst. In many cases validation per se is ignored, and verification of control-flow properties is considered as sufficient for determining whether the quality of a process model is satisfactory.

Goal-oriented approaches to process design (e.g., the Generic Process Model – GPM) (Soffer & Wand, 2004, 2005) entail criteria for goal reachability (also termed process validity) in a process model. However, these criteria are theoretical and abstract, and do not constitute a structured methodology to be followed. Furthermore, they are still not widely accepted in practice. The application of these criteria relates to the business logic of the process rather than to its structure. Currently, it is only based on human reasoning, not supported by automated algorithms.

This paper investigates the need for improving the current support to business process validation at design time. In particular, it investigates whether the commonly practiced verification needs to be complemented by validation based on goal reachability. As mentioned, validity criteria address goals, but can be applied by humans rather than in an automated manner. In contrast, verification methods can be performed automatically but without explicitly addressing goals. Hence, we propose to use the validity criteria while the process is being designed, and complement them with an automated verification of control flow properties.

We show that this combination is needed as follows. First, we theoretically analyze and compare the validity criteria and the verification-related properties, and show that they are complementary rather than equivalent. Second, we empirically test the effect of applying the validity criteria and their contribution to a designed process.

As mentioned, verification methods are language-specific. Hence, our investigation should relate to a specific modeling language. To this end, we decided to use Event-driven Process Chains (EPC) for two main reasons. First, it is a highly popular modeling language used for process design. Second, there is a body of literature dealing with its formalization and verification, thus there are a number of approaches for verifying EPC models. EPC has evolved as a semi-formal language, whose formalization has been the subject of ongoing efforts over the years. Its syntax allows the modeler some degree of freedom, e.g., in deciding whether to explicitly represent external events or to "hide" them. The rationale for hiding external events is twofold: first, representing external events may result in overloaded models, and second, some of the verification methods entail hiding external events (van der Aalst, 1999). These different representation options may affect the way validity is assessed. Hence, the empirical study reported addressed two research questions. The main research question relates to the applicability and contribution of validity criteria to process design, and the secondary question relates to the effect of explicit process model representation, particularly when using validity criteria. Therefore, this study examines not only the need for validity analysis, but also the settings in which this can be accomplished effectively.

The paper is organized as follows: The next section provides details about GPM and its validity criteria, and about EPC verification methods. These two are compared, and their complementary nature is assessed. Afterwards we present the setting and findings of the empirical study that evaluates the validity criteria, and discuss the findings. Finally, conclusions and future research are presented.

THEORETICAL BACKGROUND

This section reviews different approaches for business process quality assurance, concentrating on the goal oriented GPM's validity criteria and on a set of methods for verification of specific model properties. Note that while these properties relate to possible behavior of the modeled process, we refer to them as being structural properties. The properties (e.g., soundness) are derived from some token-based semantics, not anchored in the specific domain which the model depicts. As a result, verification methods can be applied to a model whose elements are not even labeled to denote the specific real world elements they represent (an "empty" model). This is in contrast to GPM's validity assessment, which can only be applied to a fully specified model, bearing the full information about the specific behavior of the modeled domain.

GPM and Its Validity Criteria

This section introduces the GPM framework and its derived criteria for analyzing process validity. The presentation here is mostly informal, and relates to the main concepts and principles of GPM, whose formal definitions are given in Soffer and Wand (2004, 2005).

GPM is a set of concepts which extends Bunge's ontology (Bunge, 1977, 1979), as adapted for information systems modeling (Wand & Weber, 1990, 1995; Weber, 2004), and for incorporating business process related issues. It looks at a process defined over a *domain*, which is a *composite thing*, a part of the world of which we have control. The *state* of the domain is the set of values assigned to its *properties* at a moment in time. These properties are expressed as *state variables*. The state of the domain can be *stable* or *unstable*. An unstable state is a state that must change by *law*, and these state changes are termed *events*. A stable state is a state that can only change as a result of an event external to the domain. A sub-domain is defined by a subset of the domain state variables. Its state is a projection of the state of the domain, and it can be stable while other parts of the domain are unstable.

A *process* is a sequence of unstable states, transformed by law until a stable state is reached. The definition of a process over a domain sets the boundaries of what is in a stable or an unstable state.

A process model in GPM is a three-tuple <L, I, G>, where L is the law, specified as mapping between subsets of states; I is a subset of unstable states, which are the possible initial states of the process after a triggering external event has occurred; G is a subset of stable states on which the process should terminate, namely, the goal of the process. Subsets of states are specified by conditions or predicates over values of the state variables of the domain. Hence, a process starts when a certain condition on the state of the domain holds, and ends when its goal is reached, i.e., when another condition specified on the state of the domain holds. As an example, a production process starts in a state where an order is given and all the resources are available, and ends in a state where the product is in finished goods inventory.

We briefly summarize this informal presentation by some formal notation.

Let $(x_1, x_2 \ldots x_n)$ be the state variables representing the process domain, $C_1(x_1, x_2 \ldots x_n)$ and $C_2(x_1, x_2 \ldots x_n)$ be predicates, and $S_1=\{s|C_1(x_1, x_2 \ldots x_n)=TRUE\}$, $S_2=\{s|C_2(x_1, x_2 \ldots x_n)=TRUE\}$ sets of states of the domain. Then the law $L:S_1 \rightarrow S_2$ is a mapping, which can also be specified as an operator $L(s_1)=s_2$, where $s_1 \in S_1$, and $s_2 \in S_2$. Given a predicate $C_G(x_1, x_2 \ldots x_n)$, which specifies the business condition for process termination, $G=\{s| C_G(x_1, x_2 \ldots x_n)=TRUE; L(s)=s\}$.

GPM's goal orientation is the basis for its validity analysis, presented in Soffer and Wand (2004, 2007), where validity is considered as goal reachability. A process model is termed valid if every process path leads to a goal state. Three types of problems are identified as sources of process invalidity, and establish the criteria for validity assessment:

1. **Incompleteness of the process definition:** A process definition is considered complete if the law is defined for every combination of state variable values that may be reached from process states by law or by external events.

Formally: Let S be the set of possible states in a process. The process definition is incomplete if $\exists s \in S$, such that $\neg \exists L(s)$.

An incomplete law definition might lead to a state where the process does not have a defined path by which to proceed and reach its goal. For example, consider a request that needs to be approved by two managers, and assume that the law is specified for the cases where both managers approve the request or reject it, but not for the case where one approves the request and the other rejects it. Completeness criteria are (a) completeness with respect to internal events, and (b) completeness with respect to external events. The analysis of completeness with respect to internal events should establish that the initial set of states at every step is reached as a final set of states at a previous step. Completeness analysis with respect to external events relates to a set of expected events (Soffer & Wand, 2007). The difficulty is that these events are not within the control of the process, and their outcome may be subject to uncertainty. Hence, whenever the process is affected by an external event, it must be verified that every possible outcome of that event is addressed by the law. When incompleteness of the definition is detected, it can be resolved by modifying the law so as to address the situations that were missing in its definition.

2. **Inconsistency between the law and the goal definition:** It is possible that as the process progresses, it reaches a state from which it cannot proceed further to reach a goal state.

Formally: Let S be the set of possible states and G the goal set of a process. The process law is inconsistent with the goal if $\exists s \in S$ and $\neg \exists n$ such that $L^n(s) \in G$.

Two possibilities exist here, resulting in two consistency criteria. First, the law may keep causing transitions without reaching a stable state. If the state space is finite, this would imply the process has entered an "infinite loop". Second, it is possible the process has reached a stable state not in the goal set for which there is no external event that can change it to an unstable state. The first case can be resolved by modifying the law to exit the loop under conditions that are certain to materialize. The second case may stand for a real exceptional situation. For example, in a sales process it may be found that the customer's credit card is not valid, nor does he have any other means for payment. Then the process must terminate without achieving its goal (sell the goods). Such stable states must be added to the goal set of the process (which denotes when the process terminates) as a special exception subset.

3. **Dependency of the process on external events:** The process might be in a stable state which is not in the goal set with respect to the domain law.

Formally: $\exists s \in S$ such that $s \notin G$ and $L(s)=s$.

As opposed to the case of inconsistency discussed above, where no conceivable external event can change that state, here the process can and is expected to be resumed when the state is changed to an unstable state. By definition, this can only be the outcome of an external event. In fact, the process is "waiting" for an external event to reactivate it. However, since external events are not within the control of the process, there is no guarantee the event will occur, and the process might remain "hanging". For example, a purchasing process waits for goods to arrive from a supplier. Goods arrival is expected, but is not certain to occur. A process which includes such stable state is termed *non-continuous*, and the stable state is termed a *discontinuity point* in the process. No modification of the law can gain control over external events. Nevertheless, the process model can become valid by (a) Modifying the law so that the occurrence of the external event is *monitored*, i.e., the state becomes unstable by a time-related event. (b) The law should be adjusted to map the new unstable state to a process path (e.g., reminding external actors to generate the expected event, or selecting a different path by which the goal can be reached). (c) Defining conditions under which the stable state is considered an exception state to be added to the goal set. These conditions specify when it is apparent that the external event will not occur and the process must terminate.

The GPM validity criteria are generic, so they can be applied even when the process is not specified in GPM terms. In our study they are applied with respect to EPC models.

EPC Formalization and Verification

This section presents formalization and verification approaches defined for EPC. EPC (Scheer, 1998) is a popular modeling language used for process design. It can refer to various views of the process: data view, organizational view, functional view, and control flow, or to combine them together. The control flow of EPC consists of three main constructs: function, event, and logical connector. Functions model the tasks or activities within the organization and focus on transformations from an initial state to a resulting state; events describe under what circumstances a function or a process works and in which state a function or a process results; logical connectors (AND, XOR, OR) make it possible to split the process from one flow to two or more flows and to join the process from two or more flows to one flow.

EPC's syntax has originally been semi-formal, hardly constraining the construction of models, and without precise semantics. Due to the popularity and intuitiveness of EPC as a process design language, much effort has been made to provide it with formal semantics, so mathematically proven verification procedures of EPC models can be developed. Nevertheless, while some restrictions were added to EPC syntax during the years, some degrees of modeling freedom still remain. For example, the modeler can decide whether to explicitly represent external events that occur during the process (as events without an incoming arc) or to hide them.

The commonly accepted formalization of EPC defines it as a five-tuple (E, F, C, T, A) where E, F, C are finite sets of events, functions and logical connectors respectively, T is a function which maps each connector onto connector type (AND, XOR, OR) and A is a set of arcs linking functions, events and connectors (van der Aalst, 1999; Kindler, 2004; van der Aalst, Desel, & Kindler, 2002). The syntax of EPC includes the following restrictions, as summarized in van der Aalst (1999):

- An arc cannot connect two functions or two events.
- There is at least one start event and at least one final event.
- For each event, the number of input and output arcs is no more than one; for each function, the number of input and output arcs is no more than one; for each connector, the number of input and output arcs is at least one.
- For each join connector, the number of input arcs is at least two and the number of output arcs is one; for each split connector, the number of input arcs is one and the number of output arcs is at least two.

As mentioned above, the formalization of EPC serves as a basis for model verification methods, where the main property addressed by EPC verification is *soundness*. Soundness was originally defined for Workflow-nets (WF-nets), which are a specific form of strongly connected Petri-nets, having one initial place and one final place (van der Aalst, 1998). Considering WF-nets, soundness satisfies three conditions that ensure the proper termination of the represented process, which should reach its final place and stop being active. The property of soundness is, in essence, applicable to various modelling languages, as demonstrated by Hee et al. (2008). However, it should rely on an accurate semantics assigned to these languages, usually depicting model behaviour in terms of token transitions and distribution.

The application of soundness to EPC had to solve several semantic difficulties. For example, soundness is based on a defined initial state and a defined final state in a model, whereas EPC may have multiple initial events (events that have no input arcs) and final events (events that have no output arcs). To resolve these difficulties, a number of approaches were proposed (Kindler, 2004, 2006; Verbeek & van der Aalst, 2006; Verbeek, van der Aalst, & Hofstede, 2007), relying on different semantic interpretations assigned to EPC. Most of the approaches require the EPC not to explicitly represent multiple initial and final events (namely, to "hide" them), before or during the verification procedure. Recently, a soundness definition was proposed, where multiple initial and final events are taken into account (Mendling & van der Aalst, 2007). Informally summarized, this definition of soundness requires the following three conditions: (1) The occurrence of every initial event is possible, (2) a final state is reachable from every state which is reachable from an initial state, and (3) every possible final state of the process is such that no other parts of the process are active when it is reached, and this does not hold for any EPC state that is not final. Based on this definition, a verification algorithm can be applied to EPC models which explicitly represent external events and do not "hide" them. Nevertheless, hiding these events is still commonly practiced, where the main motivation is to concentrate on the activities performed within the process and keep the representation from being overloaded. Hence, explicitly representing external events or hiding them remains a choice made by the process designer.

Note that there are other properties which are defined for EPC and related to soundness, such as relaxed soundness (Dehnert & Rittgen, 2001) and well-structuredness (van der Aalst, 1999). However, relaxed soundness is weaker than soundness, and well structuredness is not a sufficient condition for soundness, hence we do not address them in detail. Also note, that there are different methods for verification of soundness and of other properties (e.g., based on reachability graph (van der Aalst, 1999) or on reduction rules (Dongen, van der Aalst, & Verbeek, 2005). We address the verified property (namely, soundness) rather than the verification method.

A different property that can be verified regarding an EPC model is *robustness* (Dehnert & van der Aalst, 2004). While the soundness-related properties address the process as it should be executed by a workflow management system, robustness relates to the interaction between the process and its environment. An EPC is robust if its final event is reachable for every possible input from its environment, where the inputs can be results of external events or of evaluation of external information (i.e., decisions). In order to check an EPC for robustness, it should be transformed into a WF-net, and possible external events (or transitions controlled by the environment) should be identified. According to Dehnert and van der Aalst (2004), these can be identified when examining an EPC whose multiple initial events are explicitly represented.

Robustness may be comparable to the controllability property (Lohmann et al., 2008), which is defined for Open WF-nets (not for EPC). Open WF-nets are WF-nets that include an explicit specification of the interaction with the environment. Controllability verifies the absence of deadlocks in a model (including a lack of response from the environment). However, controllability does not address livelocks, hence it does not ensure the reachability of the final state. In that sense, it is weaker than robustness.

COMPARING VERIFICATION-RELATED PROPERTIES AND VALIDITY

The validity criteria are generic and not designed for a specific modeling language. Furthermore, they are not a technique that can be structurally or automatically applied. In this section, we start by relating the notion of goal to EPC models; then we examine the existing EPC verification techniques and show they cannot ensure a valid model.

Relating Process Goal to an EPC Model

As a first step towards identifying and evaluating the specification of the process goal in EPC, we provide an interpretation of a state in EPC, and distinguish stable from unstable states. We use the following notation taken from Mendling and van der Aalst (2007). The sets of incoming arcs and outgoing arcs of an event e are marked e_{in} and e_{out}, respectively. The set of events in an EPC includes three subsets: E_s the start events, E_{int} the intermediate events, and E_e the end events.

As mentioned, events in EPC describe pre- and post-conditions of functions. Hence, despite their name, they are not really "events" in the traditional meaning of the word (a momentary occurrence), but rather represent a state which might last for an unlimited period of time. In GPM terms, an event is equivalent to a set of states of a sub-domain, while arcs and functions reflect the law (note that functions, which are actions that lead to state transformation, are abstracted from in GPM). This interpretation is consistent with the GPM-based semantics of WF-nets (Soffer, Kaner, & Wand, 2008). The state of the entire domain is defined differently by different semantic interpretations of EPC. While all these interpretations are token-based, some address the state of an EPC as the token distribution among the nodes of the EPC (in correspondence to WF-nets, e.g., Dehnert & Rittgen, 2001), while others relate to the token distribution among the arcs (Kindler, 2004; Mendling & van der Aalst, 2007). Without going into the details of these different semantics, we extend our interpretation of an event, so the state of the entire domain at a moment in time is determined by all the events that are active ("holding tokens") at that moment.

Lemma 1 (state of sub-domain in an EPC): Let e be an event, and D_e be the sub-domain over which e is defined, then

1. If $e \in E_e$ then D_e is stable in e,
2. If $e \in E_s$ or $e \in E_{int}$ then D_e may be stable or unstable in e.

Proof: (a) For $e \in E_e$, $|e_{out}|=0$, so there is no law that maps e to a different state. Hence every state $s \in e$ is a stable state of D_e. (b) Proof by example: Figure 1(a) demonstrates that both are possible.

In Figure 1(a), E_s has three events. *Order received* denotes an unstable state for the sub-domain of the order, while *Item available* and *Item unavailable* include stable states with respect to the inventory sub-domain, and can transform only when an order is received (in the other sub-domain). E_{int} has two events, *Order confirmed* and *Payment received. Payment received* is an unstable state, which should transform to a state where the order has been delivered. In contrast, *Order confirmed* is a stable state, which can only transform when the customer pays for the order. Since this is an external event, the intermediate state of *Order confirmed* is a stable state where the process is "waiting" for an external event to proceed. As mentioned, EPC allows the modeler to decide whether to "hide" external events or to specify them, and Figure 1(a) demonstrates such "hiding". Figure 1(b) shows the same process without hiding the external event of the payment, and it is easier to see that the process cannot progress until the occurrence of the external event.

According to GPM, the process goal G is a set of states which are stable for the entire process domain.

For an EPC to be valid, its possible final states must be in the defined goal of the process. Assume an EPC has only one final event e, then it must satisfy $e \subseteq G$. In case an EPC has more than one final event, these can be the endings of alternative paths, or of paths that should be performed in parallel. In Figure 1(a) and (b), assume the goal is defined with respect to two state variables, the order status and the payment status, so $G=\{s|$ ((Order=delivered$\wedge$ (payment=completed)) $\vee$ (order=rejected)$\}$. The two final events, *Order rejected* and *Order delivered*, which can be denoted as $e_1=\{s|$ Order=rejected$\}$ and $e_2=\{s|$ Order=delivered; Payment=completed$\}$, satisfy $e_1 \subseteq G$ and $e_2 \subseteq G$. These events are on alternative paths, and only one of them should be reached by the process. As a second example, consider the process shown in Figure 1(c), and assume its goal is the same as the previous one. In that case the EPC has three final events, $e_1=\{s|$ Order=rejected$\}$, $e_2=\{s|$ Order=delivered$\}$, and $e_3=\{s|$ Payment=completed$\}$. The possible final states for the EPC to achieve its goal are e_1 or $e_2 \cap e_3$.

Summarizing this discussion, the combination of final events that form the goal of an EPC can be identified as follows.

Definition 1: Let G be the goal set of a process P, let P be the power set of E_e of an EPC that represents P, and let m be an element in P. m includes a *goal-fulfilling* final state of the EPC if $\cap(e_i \in m) \subseteq G$, and there is no $m' \in P$, such that m' is a goal-fulfilling final state and $m' \subseteq m$.

Note that we assume that every final event is well defined in terms of the state variables that define the goal.

Figure 1. Order delivery process examples

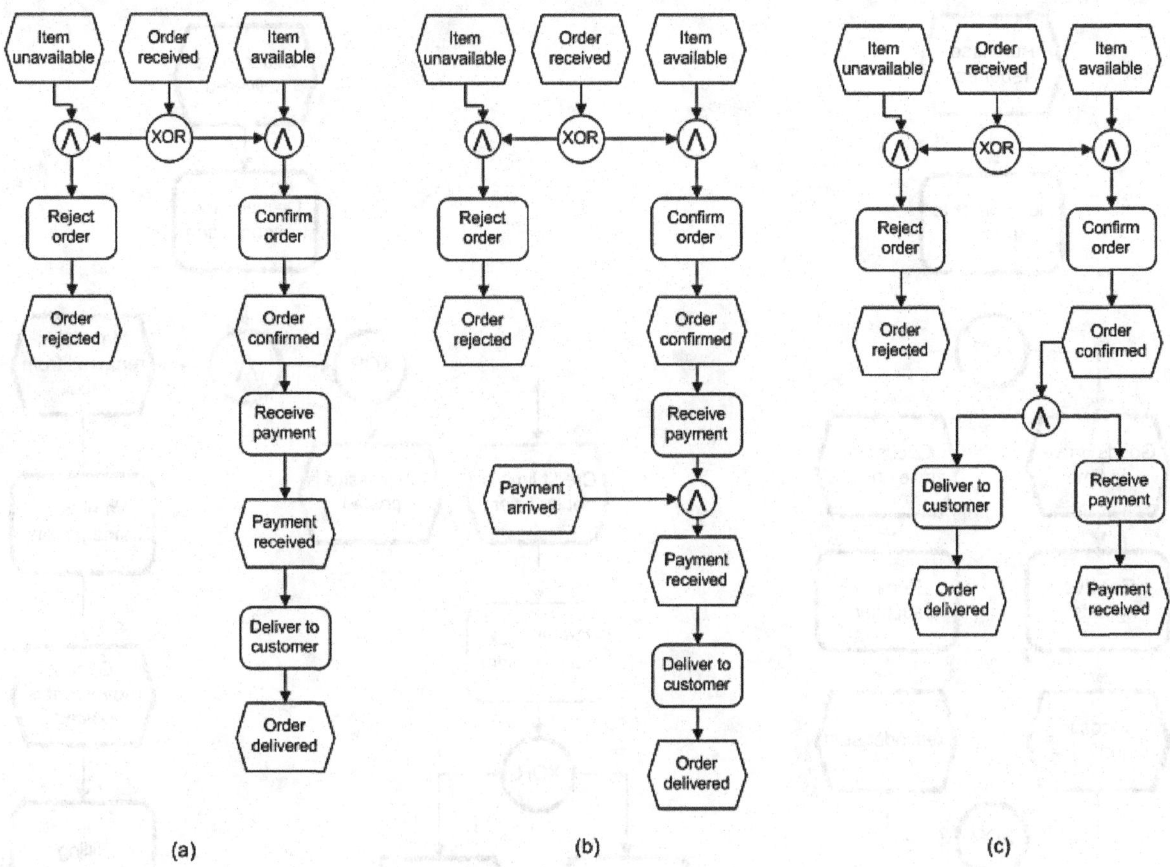

Validity Assessment

For a process model to be valid, we should make sure that every possible enactment of that process will reach a goal state (which meets the above condition). However, as mentioned above, the validity criteria provide a list of possible causes for invalidity rather than a structured technique for identifying them in a model. In what follows, we examine the verification techniques of soundness and robustness, to evaluate whether they can be used for assessing the validity of an EPC model.

Soundness relates to the internal structure of the process, while robustness relates to its interaction with the environment. Hence, the combination of soundness and robustness may suffice for validity assessment. However, examining these properties, we identified the following three shortcomings.

First, both soundness and robustness verification relate to the reachability of final events, without explicitly addressing the process goal. Figure 2 presents two example processes, which are both sound and robust. However, considering Figure 2(a), and assuming that the process goal should be $G=\{s \mid Goods=received \wedge Payment=completed\}$, the final event, $e=\{s \mid Payment=completed\}$, does not satisfy $e \subseteq G$. Clearly, the process model is not correct from a business view. Since it is possible to reach a state where payment is made although goods were not received, the process has a validity problem of inconsistency between the law and the goal. Figure 2(b) includes a simplified part of a process taken from the SAP

Figure 2. Process examples: sound, robust, and invalid

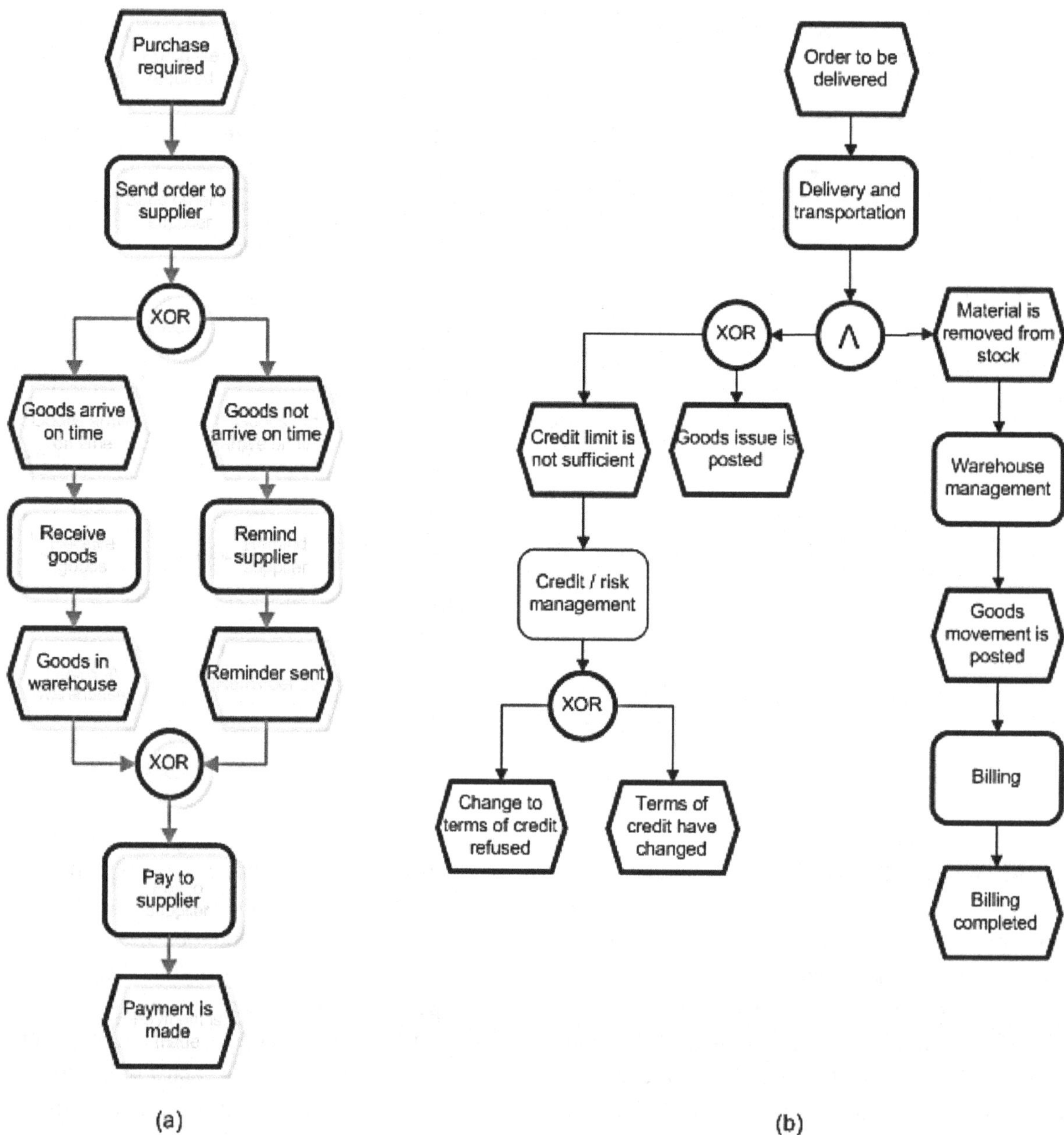

reference model. We assume that its goal should be G={s| (Billing document=completed ∧ Goods issue=posted) XOR Delivery=refused}. However, its possible final states are S_1={s| Billing document=completed ∧ Goods issue=posted}, S_2={s| Billing document=completed ∧ terms of credit=changed}, S_3={s| Billing document=completed ∧ terms of credit=change refusal}. Clearly, only S_1 is in the goal. Furthermore, S_3 is a state where billing was completed even though the customer is not credit worthy. Note that the SAP reference model, which was constructed as a "best practice" repository, has been subject to structural verification, which has revealed cases of unsound models (Mendling et al., 2007). Nevertheless, a structural verification which does not relate to the business logic of the process cannot detect this kind of modeling error, and indeed this validity problem was not revealed by it.

Second, assume the first shortcoming can be solved by (manually) verifying that the EPC includes a combination of final events that constitute a goal-fulfilling final state. Still, soundness as defined by Mendling and van der Aalst (2007) requires only the reachability of a final state where no other parts of the process are active. This may be any final state, not necessarily a final state which is in the goal. Note that other soundness definitions (van der Aalst, 1999) relate to an EPC that has only one final event, which can, in principle, be verified (manually) to be within the goal[1].

Third, robustness is a property of a process where, facing all possible inputs from the process environment, the final event can be reached. Robustness verification identifies environment-controlled transitions and analyzes the process reachability graph with respect to the possible external events generated by the actions of the environment. It does not take into account a possibility that the environment may not respond (as is highlighted when analyzing discontinuity points according to GPM's validity criteria). Such possibility should be identified prior to robustness verification and addressed (by monitoring), so that robustness verification may relate to the resulting process definition. Note that robustness relates to *the* final event, since it is based on a transformation to a WF-net, which has a single final place.

The robustness verification procedure operates under the assumption that the human modeler has identified all the possible environment behaviors and incorporated them into the process model. The validity criteria are aimed at supporting the modeler in performing these tasks.

Table 1 summarizes the relation of soundness and robustness verification to the different validity problems of GPM.

In summary, soundness and robustness verification address structural properties of the process, while the validity criteria relate to its business logic. While structural correctness can be established automatically and definitely by verification algorithms, validity in terms of the business logic and business goal requires human reasoning. The combination of human-based validity analysis with automated verification should be able to address both business logic and structural "correctness" of a process model. In proposing this combination, we assume that the validity criteria can affect the quality of models produced by humans even without a structured application method. However, this is an assertion that needs to be tested. To establish the need for using the validity criteria and their effectiveness in process design, we performed the empirical study reported in the following section.

Table 1. Summary of validity problems and verification techniques

Validity problem	Soundness verification	Robustness verification
Inconsistency between the law and the goal	Identifies structural problems (e.g., deadlocks), assuming every final event is in the goal	-
Incompleteness of the law (with respect to internal events)	Identifies structural problems (e.g., deadlocks), assuming every final event is in the goal	-
Incompleteness of the law (with respect to external events)	-	Identifies incompleteness if the process includes one final event and it is in the goal
Dependency on external events	-	-

EMPIRICAL STUDY

Aim and Model

As suggested in the previous section, we propose to use the validity criteria for supporting the human task of process design. The design of a process model is iterative in nature, where design alternatives are created, evaluated, and modified, until a final alternative is selected. We expect the validity criteria to guide the analysts when evaluating design alternatives and thus to contribute to the design of valid processes. Currently, no such support is available, and designing valid processes relies on the knowledge and expertise of the modeler. Furthermore, as discussed above, the validity criteria do not constitute a structured methodology. Hence, it may be questionable whether the mere awareness of these criteria can have any effect on the quality of models.

The aim of the empirical study reported here was to assess the applicability of the validity criteria and their contribution to model quality. Of the two tasks iteratively practiced at process design, namely, creating a model and evaluating it, validity criteria are expected to affect the latter. Hence, we addressed the evaluation task, where validity problems that exist in a model should be identified.

In addition, since EPC allows different forms of representation of a given process (as discussed in the previous section), the study aimed to find whether these representation possibilities influence differently the human ability to detect validity problems and the effectiveness of the validity criteria. In particular, we addressed the reduced or implicit representation where external events are "hidden", and compared it to an explicit representation of external events. Our expectation was that 1) the subjects' awareness of the generic problems (validity criteria) would better support the identification of these problems in the specific model; 2) an explicit representation of external events would better support the identification of validity problems that are associated with these events.

Considering this task, we asked the following three main research questions:

1. Does the guidance of GPM's validity criteria improve the human ability to identify process invalidity?
2. Does the explicit representation of external events improve the human ability to identify process invalidity?
3. Is there an interaction between the model evaluation approach (with and without validity criteria) and the model representation (explicit and implicit)?

Regarding these questions we used a two-factor factorial experimental design (Breyfogle, 2003; Shah & Madden, 2004). The first factor relates to the validity criteria. This factor has two levels: 1) validity criteria were provided; 2) validity criteria were not provided. The second factor relates to the model representation. This factor has two levels: 1) implicit representation of the external events; 2) explicit representation of the external events. Hence four groups of subjects participated in the experiment as illustrated in Figure 3.

We formulated the following sets of hypotheses respectively to the three research questions:

$H^1 0$: There is no effect of GPM's validity criteria on the identification of process validity problems (vs. a positive effect of GPM's validity criteria).

$H^2 0$: There is no effect of explicit representation of external events on the identification of process validity problems (vs. a positive effect of explicit representation).

$H^3 0$: There is no interaction between the model evaluation approach and the representation of external events (vs. there is an interaction between the two factors).

Figure 3. Four groups – two factors with two levels in the factorial design

<table>
<tr><td colspan="2"></td><td colspan="2">External event representation</td></tr>
<tr><td colspan="2"></td><td>Implicit</td><td>Explicit</td></tr>
<tr><td rowspan="2">Validity criteria</td><td>Provided</td><td>Group1</td><td>Group 2</td></tr>
<tr><td>Not provided</td><td>Group 3</td><td>Group 4</td></tr>
</table>

With respect to H^20, note that a positive effect is likely for validity problems that are related to external events. We assume that as a result, the overall performance will be affected.

Experimental Settings

The empirical study was conducted as a laboratory experiment whose subjects were students (novices). This choice of laboratory experiment is similar to the one made in other empirical studies addressing business process modeling (Sarshar & Loos, 2005; Recker, Rosemann, & van der Aalst, 2005; Vanderfeesten et al., 2008). The participants in the experiment were 80 MIS students in a Systems Analysis and Design course. Each of the participants was arbitrarily assigned to one of four groups as presented in Figure 2: 19 subjects in group 1; 20 subjects in group 2; 19 subjects in group 3; 22 subjects in group 4.

To guarantee that the arbitrary group assignment resulted in groups whose potential performance did not influence the experimental results, we took the following measure. At the end of the course we performed an ANOVA one way analysis of variance to the final grades achieved in the course. We compared means of grades of the students in these four groups. With respect to the hypothesis of no difference between the groups, we received a p-value =0.905 (Levene statistic equals 0.53), so we assume that all groups have the same mean of course final grades.

The students had all learnt and practiced the use of EPC as part of the course before the study was conducted. All subjects were given an EPC model of an order handling process, whose goal was stated as "ordered goods supplied to a customer whose credit card is approved". The students were instructed to identify all problems which may prevent the process from achieving its goal. The participants in group 1 and group 3 got the implicit representation of the process model as illustrated in Figure 4(a). The participants in group 2 and group 4 got the explicit representation of the model as illustrated in Figure 4(b). The validity criteria were given to the subjects in group 1 and group 2 as a list of possible problem categories (see Figure 5), and the students in these groups were instructed to classify each identified problem accordingly.

No information was given to the subjects regarding the number of problems they were expected to identify, and no time limitation was placed for performing the task. To increase the motivation of the students, a 5-point bonus in the course grade was promised to the four students whose task performance would be the best. The researchers were present in class at the time of the experiment and answered any question that was raised regarding the understanding of the modeled process.

Note that the list in Figure 5 is categorized differently than Table 1, where problems are associated with verification techniques. Problems 2.1 and 2.2 correspond to the first row in Table 1; problems 1.1 and 1.2 correspond to the second and third rows in the table; problem 3.1 corresponds to the fourth row.

Figure 4. EPCs in the experimental task

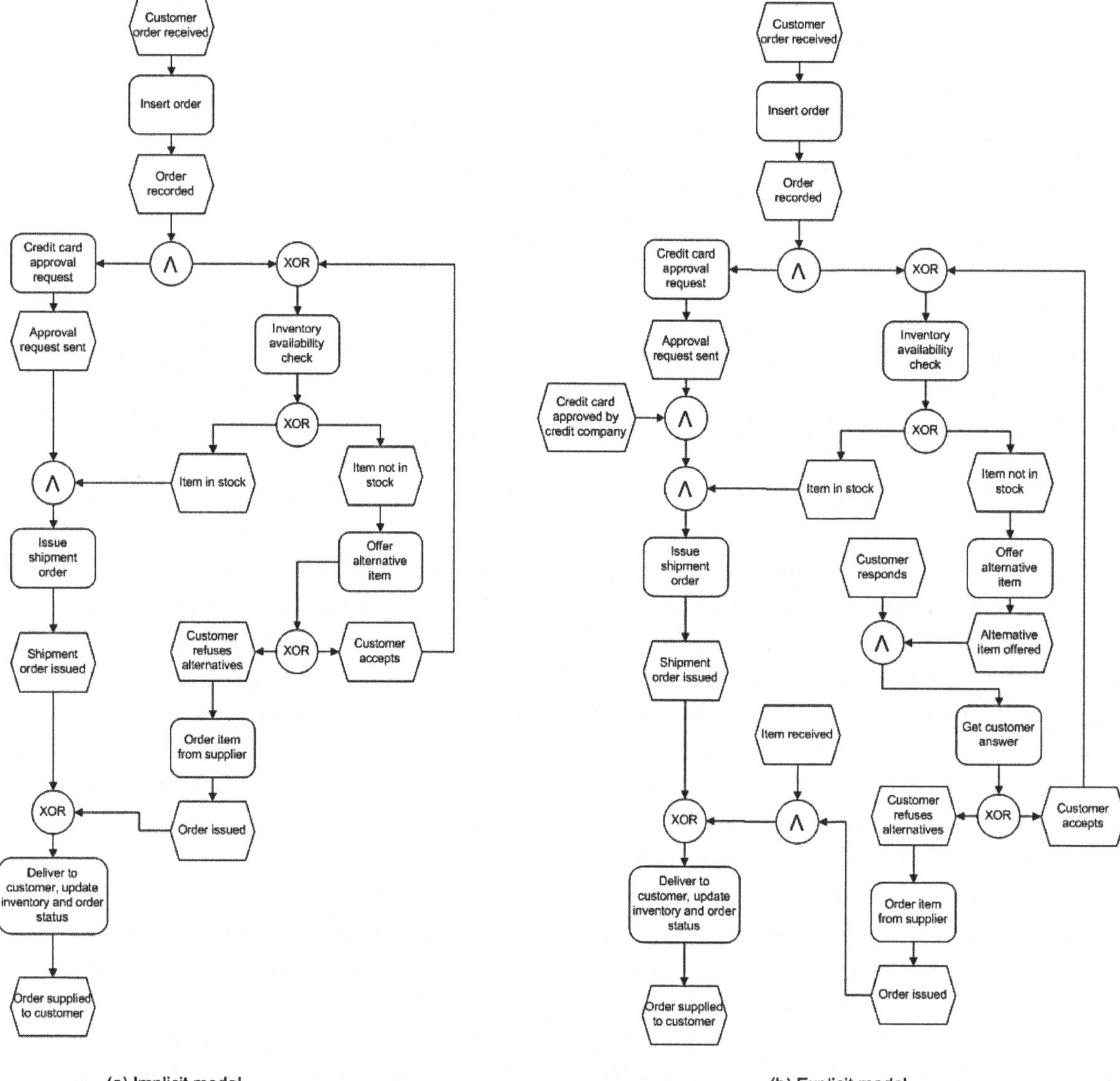

(a) Implicit model

(b) Explicit model

Data Analysis

The process model handed out to the students (see Figure 4) included the following five invalidity sources, where seven problems can be identified. These, according to Soffer and Wand (2004), represent all the possible problems categories (see Figure 5).

1. When a credit card approval request is issued, the process model does not address a possibility that
   a. The customer's credit card is not approved (incompleteness – problem 1.2), or
   b. That the credit company may not respond (discontinuity – problem 3.1).
2. An infinite loop is possible when alternative items, whose availability is not checked, are

Figure 5. List of invalidity categories derived from GPM, given to subjects in groups 1 and 2

Possible problem categories:

1. **Incompleteness of the process definition:**
   1.1 The process may reach a state for which no action is defined in the model.
   1.2 The process depends on the action of an external actor, whose outcome may not be as specified in the model.
2. **Inconsistency between the process progress and the goal definition:**
   2.1 The process may enter an "infinite loop".
   2.2 The process may stop or finish without achieving its goal.
3. **Dependency of the process on external events:**
   3.1 The process may be "waiting" for an external event to reactivate it. There is no guarantee the event will occur as expected, and the process might remain "hanging".

proposed to the customer (inconsistency – problem 2.1).

3. The process must wait for the customer's response to the alternative item offer. The model does not address a possibility that
   a. The customer may decide to cancel the order when the item ordered is out of stock (incompleteness – problem 1.1), or
   b. The customer may not respond to the offer (discontinuity – problem 3.1).
4. The process must wait for the supplier to provide the item, whereas the supplier may not do so (discontinuity point – problem 3.1).
5. There is a possibility for the customer order to be fulfilled even when the customer's credit card is not approved (inconsistency – problem 2.2).

Note that soundness verification would identify the process as being sound[2], and that robustness verification with respect to the external events specified in Figure 4(b) would find the process robust.

Based on these invalidity sources, the subjects' solutions were graded according to a scheme where identification of each problem scored one point out of seven possible.

To analyze this data according to the formulated hypotheses we used non-parametric tests, as the scores are not normally distributed. First, using the Kruskal-Wallis test we analyzed if there is a difference between the performance means of the four groups. The result of p-value<0.0001 indicates that there is a difference between the performance levels of the groups. In order to analyze the effect of GPM's validity criteria guidance on the identification of process validity problems (H^10) we compared the aggregate performance of groups 1 and 2 versus the aggregate performance of groups 3 and 4 using Mann Whitney test. In order to examine if there is a difference in the ability of students to identify problems belonging to different invalidity categories, we distinguished between problems 1 (1a and 1b), 3 (3a and 3b), and 4, which relate to the external environment, and problems 2 and 5 that relate to internal process inconsistency (see Figure 5).

In order to analyze the effect of the explicit representation of external events on the identification of process validity problems ($H^2 0$), we compared the aggregate performance (for different invalidity problems) of groups 1 and 3 versus the aggregate performance of groups 2 and 4 using Mann Whitney test.

In order to test the interaction between the model evaluation approach and the model representation ($H^3 0$), we analyzed the interaction graphs and used the Adjusted Transform test for analyzing interactions in nonparametric statistics (Sawilowsky, 1990).

Findings

This section presents the findings of the data analysis with respect to the research questions and hypotheses. Table 2 provides the means and standard deviations of the grades achieved in the four groups.

Research question 1 and the related hypothesis referred the effect of GPM's validity criteria on the identification of process validity problems. We tested whether the aggregate performance mean of the 39 subjects from groups 1 and 2, whose analysis was based on the validity criteria, is better than the aggregate performance mean of the 41 subjects from groups 3 and 4, whose analysis was without the use of validity criteria.

The comparison yielded a highly significant effect with respect to all problem categories (p-value (all)<0.001, p-value (1a, 1b, 3a, 3b, 4)<0.001, p-value (2, 5)=0.002). We can conclude that in general, $H^1 0$ can be rejected, thus our hypothesis that the validity criteria support better identification of process validity problems is corroborated.

Research question 2 and the related hypothesis addressed the effect of explicit representation of the external events on identification of process invalidity problems. In particular, we tested for a positive effect on the identification of problems related to external effects and hence on the overall performance.

We tested whether the aggregate performance mean of the 38 subjects from groups 1 and 3, whose models included an explicit representation of external events, is better than the aggregate performance mean of the 42 subjects from groups 2 and 4, whose models included an explicit representation of external events. This test showed that we can reject $H^2 0$ with respect to the external environment-related problems (p-value [1a, 1b, 3a, 3b, 4] = 0.0975) at a confidence level of 10%; however, we cannot reject $H^2 0$ with respect to all problems (p-value [all problems] =0.285). In other words, our hypothesis of a positive effect of

Table 2. Performance means and deviations

		Implicit representation			Explicit representation		
Validity criteria provided	**Group**	1			2		
	Number of subjects	19			20		
	Performance mean	2.16*	0.95**	3.11***	2.6	1.1	3.7
	Standard deviation	0.834	0.621	1.1	1.07	0.3	1.14
Validity criteria not provided	**Group**	3			4		
	Number of subjects	19			22		
	Performance mean	0.895	0.895	1.789	1.27	0.455	1.727
	Standard deviation	0.809	**0.567**	0.787	1.08	0.596	1.12

*- problems 1a, 1b, 3a, 3b, 4; ** - problems 2, 5; *** - all problems

explicit representation has been corroborated only with respect to external event-related problems.

To gain a better understanding, we tested the effect of model representation on the performance means of the groups, separating the different modes of evaluation – with and without the validity criteria (for the different problem categories).

Comparing groups 1 and 2 we found a positive effect of explicit representation on identification of problems 1a, 1b, 3a, 3b, 4 (p-value = 0.055) and, as a result, for all problems (p-value = 0.049). When comparing groups 3 and 4, no effect of explicit representation was found; however, the performance means (for problems 1a, 1b, 3a, 3b, 4) of students in group 4 (explicit representation) was higher than in group 3. We can conclude that when the validity criteria are used, an explicit representation supports better identification of validity problems.

Research question 3 and the related hypothesis addressed the interaction between the model evaluation approach (with or without validity criteria) and the representation of external events (implicit vs. explicit). The interaction graphs are shown in Figure 6 (for all problems), Figure 7 (problems 1a, 1b, 3a, 3b, 4), and Figure 8 (problems 2, 5).

The lines in Figure 6 (with respect to all problems) are not parallel, but without a statistical significance. Hence, H^30 cannot be rejected with respect to all problems. A separate analysis with respect to the different problem types yielded the following results. The parallel lines in Figure 7 show that there is no interaction between the factors; hence, H^30 cannot be rejected with respect to the external event-related problems. This result can be explained based on the findings mentioned above: for both evaluation modes an explicit representation supports a better identification of external event-related problems – significantly when validity criteria were used, and not significantly but with a higher performance mean when they have not been used.

The non-parallel lines in Figure 8 show the existence of an interaction (p-value =0.006) hence H^30 can be rejected with respect to the inconsistency problems. This result can be explained as follows: while no significant difference was found between the performance level of groups 1 and 2; a significant positive difference of implicit representation (p-value= 0.009) has been found between the performance means of group 3 and group 4. This may have two possible explanations: (1) an

Figure 6. Interaction graph: all problems

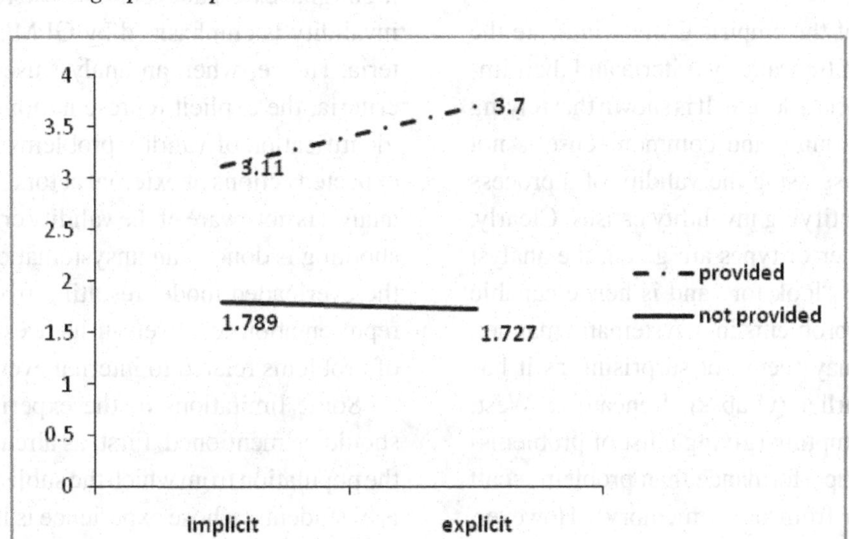

Figure 7. Interaction graph: problems 1a, 1b, 3a, 3b, 4

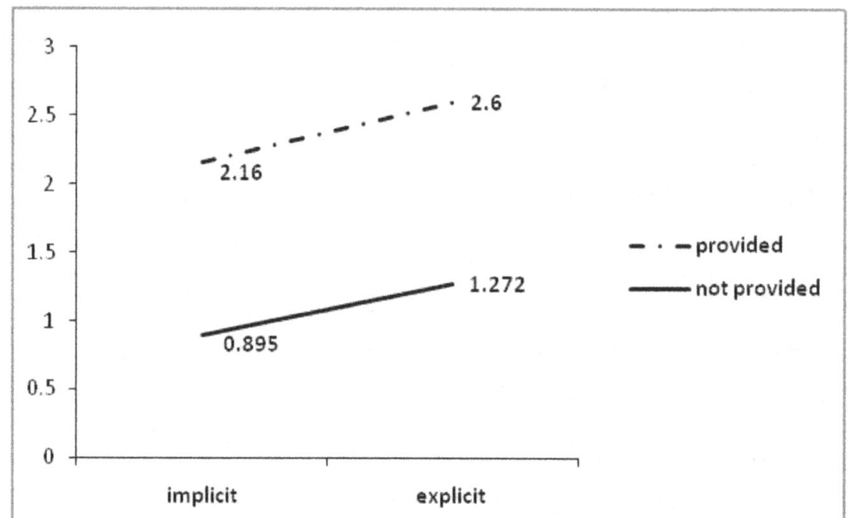

explicit representation of external events yields a more complicated model, which may even become too overloaded; (2) the subjects were not aware of the problems related to external events and hence concentrated on the process logic inconsistency manifested in problems 2 and 5.

DISCUSSION

The Empirical Findings

The findings of the empirical study indicate the applicability of the validity criteria and their importance in process design. It is shown that relying on human reasoning and common sense is not sufficient for assessing the validity of a process model and identifying invalidity causes. Clearly, when possible error types are given, the analyst knows what to "look for" and is hence capable of identifying problems in a systematic manner. This finding may seem not surprising as it has been found earlier (Grabski, Reneau, & West, 1987) that prompting (giving a list of problems) supports better performance than problem recall (determination from one's memory). However, the GPM validity criteria are at a rather abstract level, not directly related to the modeled domain or operationalized to EPC terms. Hence, their applicability, namely, the possibility of humans to effectively operationalize and apply them to a specific model, could not be taken for granted. In particular, the empirical findings indicate that even novices are able to benefit from the abstract validity criteria and apply them to a concrete situation.

Regarding the effect of explicit representation of external events, an explicit representation highlights external events, whose role in process invalidity is emphasized by GPM's validity criteria. Hence, when an analyst uses the validity criteria, the explicit representation assists in the identification of validity problems related to unexpected actions of external actors. Yet, when the analyst is not aware of the validity criteria, trouble shooting is done in an unsystematic manner, and the overloaded model resulting from an explicit representation negatively influences identification of problems related to internal events.

Some limitations of the experimental study should be mentioned. First, as already discussed, the population from which the subjects were taken is of students, whose experience is limited, as op-

Figure 8. Interaction graph: problems 2, 5

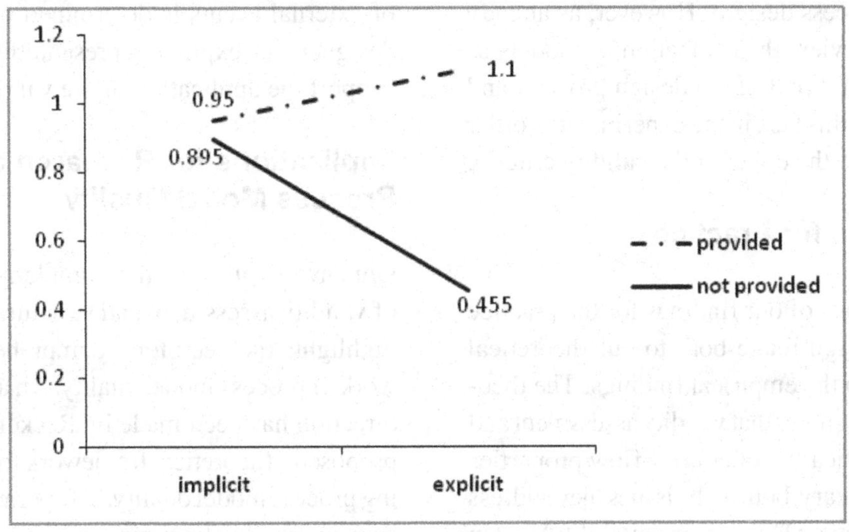

posed to professional analysts. However, the study deals with providing guidance and support to the design process, which seems to be particularly crucial when the analyst's experience is limited. It is possible that experienced analysts have developed reasoning skills which enable them to better identify validity problems in a process model. We believe it would be beneficial to conduct a similar study whose subjects are experienced analysts. Nevertheless, verification of models taken from the SAP reference model, which was constructed by experienced professionals, revealed cases of unsound and non-robust models (Verbeek, van der Aalst, & Hofstede, 2006; Mendling et al., 2008). The example given in Figure 2(b), taken from that reference model, shows that additional validity problems, undetected by verification algorithms, still exist there. Hence, while the findings of this study are at least applicable for analysts that have a relatively little experience, it is not unlikely that their applicability extends to experienced analysts too.

Second, the study included a model of a specific process in a single modeling language, EPC. The choice of EPC was made for the two main reasons explained before, namely, its popularity and its various verification capabilities. GPM's validity criteria, on the other hand, are notation independent and can be applied to processes modeled in other modeling languages as well. Hence it can be assumed that the findings that address the applicability of GPM's validity criteria are not specific to EPC models, while the findings related to explicit or implicit representations can be applicable only to languages where such different representations are possible. The process model itself was relatively simple and cannot indicate the scalability of the approach, which is yet to be tested. However, the following observations regarding scalability can be made. First, an explicit consideration of the process goal should not be affected by the size of the model. Second, the evaluation of possible results of external events is locally performed for each such event according to the validity criteria, independently of the size of the model.

Last, as opposed to the real-world situation, where the process designer is the one who designs and evaluates the validity of the process design, here the students were given a process model and were required only to evaluate its validity. It may also be argued that the students were not experienced in model evaluation (as their training was in process design). However, as already explained, we view the evaluation of models as being an integral part of the design process, and we focused on this task in the experiment in order to better isolate the effect of the validity criteria.

Implications for Practice

The implications of our findings for the practice of process design relate both to our theoretical analysis and to the empirical findings. The theoretical analysis shows that validity assessment and structural verification of control-flow properties are complementary, both in the issues they address (goals and business logic vs. executability) and in the ways by which they are achieved (human-based vs. automated algorithms). The importance of this finding lies in the fact that the validity criteria are not commonly used, and human intuition is usually relied upon for assessing the reachability of the process goal. Furthermore, while the use of verification techniques may give the impression that the process is "correct", we have shown that they do not consider the process goal and thus cannot replace validation. The empirical findings show that the application of validity criteria by humans is effective in detecting validity problems and that the need for such criteria to guide a systematic analysis of process validity is real. Moreover, most of the problems detected in our study are such that would not be identified by verification procedures. It is also shown that different possible representations may affect the human performance when applying the validity criteria.

The conclusion that follows the findings reported here is that process design should include a step of human-based validity assessment in which the validity criteria are applied and relate to the goal of the process. This step should be followed and complemented by an automated structural verification, which relates to the executability of the process after its business logic has been assessed. When the language used for process design is EPC, where explicit or implicit representation of external events is determined by the process designer, an explicit representation will better support the application of the validity criteria.

Implications for Research on Process Model Quality

Our investigation of the complementary nature of validity assessment and structural verification highlights the need for a comprehensive framework of process model quality. An attempt in that direction has been made by Recker (2007), who proposed a theoretical framework for understanding process model quality. To operationalize such framework, existing approaches and techniques should be mapped to it. Then it might be possible to identify sets of complementing techniques that together relate to all aspects of model quality.

The framework of Recker (2007) relates to a process model as a conceptual model, and follows notions developed for conceptual model quality. Most notably, it adapts the quality framework of Lindland, Sindre, and Solvberg (1994) to process models. Indeed, at the design phase in its life-cycle, a process model is a specific type of conceptual model, conceptualizing behavior of some part of the real world. Hence, we also use this framework as a basis for our discussion here. The framework distinguishes three dimensions of model quality: semantic quality, namely the correspondence between the model and the domain, syntactic quality, namely the correspondence between the model and the modeling language, and pragmatic quality, namely the correspondence between the model and its users.

Considering the properties addressed in this paper, namely, validity, soundness, and robustness, they are roughly classified by Recker (2007) as syntactic and semantic quality properties. Soundness is usually considered by the business process research community as standing for semantic quality (van der Aalst, 1999; Kindler, 2004; van der Aalst et al., 2009). However, the use of the term "semantic" in this context relates to the mathematical token-based semantics of the language rather than to the correspondence to the domain. Recker (2007) interprets executability as syntactic quality. However, we consider this interpretation as going beyond the meaning of "syntax". With respect to the essential syntactical rules of process modeling languages such as EPC, a model that follows the syntax rules is not necessarily executable.

The analysis in this paper leads to a different mapping of the properties under consideration to the quality dimensions. As indicated by Recker (2007), the application of the quality framework, and particularly the pragmatic quality dimension, should consider the intended use of the model under consideration. Traditionally, pragmatic quality has been considered as the interpretability of a model (Siau & Tan, 2005). However, this consideration is with respect to the intended use of conceptual models, which serve for purposes of communication and understanding (Mylopoulos, 1992). In contrast, the intended use of process models is not only to support communication, but to eventually be executed. Hence, the concept of pragmatic quality can be extended in this respect and include the executability of the modeled process. Considering this interpretation, we claim that the properties of soundness and robustness represent aspects of pragmatic quality. In addition, the verification of these properties ensures syntactic correctness of the model. Validity, on the other hand, relates both to semantic and to pragmatic quality. The semantic aspect of validity is in the assessment of whether the process model corresponds to the goal seeking nature of the real world process. A valid process model represents a real world process that has a defined goal which it is designed to achieve. The pragmatic aspect is in the assessment of the ability of the designed process to achieve its goal.

Based on this mapping, the complementary nature of validity assessment and structural verification is better understood. Yet, this does not mean that all the required quality aspects are covered by this combination. Other aspects of semantic quality, such as model expressiveness, and of pragmatic quality, such as model understandability, are not addressed here. Based on this discussion, we believe that a correct and consistent mapping of process model quality properties to the above discussed quality dimensions is a step towards the operationalization of the quality framework.

CONCLUSION

Validity of a process model should be achieved at the design phase, when errors can be easily corrected. Much effort has been made suggesting procedures for automated verification of specific structural properties. Currently, models that satisfy these properties are considered semantically correct. According to our analysis, such verification methods cannot be considered as validation, since they do not address the business logic of the process and its goal. Rather, they implicitly assume that the business logic of the process should be known and well addressed by the human designer. The validity criteria, proposed as part of the GPM framework, provide support to the human reasoning that should address the business logic to be expressed in the process model. As such, these criteria can be considered as complementary to verification.

The paper compares the properties of soundness and robustness, addressed by verification algorithms, to the property of validity, and shows that soundness and robustness, which relate to pragmatic quality of the model (with respect to the purpose of executing the model), do not ensure validity, which relates to both semantic and pragmatic quality. In addition, the paper reports an empirical study which investigated the need for a systematic support to the application of business logic in process design as provided by the validity criteria, and their applicability.

The empirical findings clearly indicate the need for a systematic analysis rather than relying on simple unguided human reasoning. They show that the validity criteria are applicable even at an abstract form, so even novices are able to benefit from them and apply them to a concrete situation. In addition, the empirical findings indicate that when using EPC as a modeling language, an explicit representation provides a better support to the application of GPM's validity criteria, thus to the identification of validity problems.

Future research of the validity criteria may take several directions. First, as discussed above, it would be interesting to perform a similar study whose subjects are experienced analysts. Second, we may experiment with models of different sizes to evaluate the scalability of the approach. Finally, major efforts should be devoted to the development of a structured methodology, possibly accompanied by tools, for supporting the application of the validity criteria.

REFERENCES

Aguilar-Saven, R. S. (2004). Business process modelling: Review and framework. *International Journal of Production Economics*, *90*, 129–149. doi:10.1016/S0925-5273(03)00102-6

Bray, K. (2002). *An introduction to requirements engineering*. Reading, MA: Addison-Wesley.

Breyfogle, F. W. (2003). *Implementing six sigma: Smarter solutions using statistical methods*. New York, NY: John Wiley & Sons.

Bunge, M. (1977). Treatise on basic philosophy: *Vol. 3. Ontology I: The furniture of the world*. Boston, MA: Reidel.

Bunge, M. (1979). Treatise on basic philosophy: *Vol. 4. Ontology II: A world of systems*. Boston, MA: Reidel.

Dehnert, J., & Rittgen, P. (2001). Relaxed soundness of business processes. In K. R. Dittrich, A. Geppert, & M. C. Norrie (Eds.), *Proceedings of the 13th International Conference on Advanced Information Systems Engineering* (LNCS 2068, pp. 157-170).

Dehnert, J., & van der Aalst, W. M. P. (2004). Bridging the gap between business models and workflow specifications. *International Journal of Cooperative Information Systems*, *13*(3), 289–332. doi:10.1142/S0218843004000973

Dongen, B. F., van der Aalst, W. M. P., & Verbeek, H. M. W. (2005). Verification of EPCs: Using reduction rules and petri nets. In A. Pastor & J. Falcao e Cunha (Eds.), *Proceedings of the 17th International Conference on Advanced Information Systems Engineering* (LNCS 3520, pp. 372-386).

Grabski, S. V., Reneau, J. H., & West, S. G. (1987). A comparison of judgment, skills, and prompting effects between auditors and systems analysts. *Management Information Systems Quarterly*, *11*(2), 151–162. doi:10.2307/249356

Hee, K., Oanea, O., Serebrenik, A., Sidorova, N., & Voorhoeve, M. (2008). History-based joins: Semantics, soundness and implementation. *Data & Knowledge Engineering*, *64*, 24–37. doi:10.1016/j.datak.2007.06.005

Kindler, E. (2004). On the semantics of EPCs: A framework for resolving the vicious circle. In J. Desel, B. Pernici, & M. Weske (Eds.), *Proceedings of the 2nd International Conference on Business Process Management* (LNCS 3080, pp. 82-97).

Kindler, E. (2006). On the semantics of EPCs: Resolving the vicious circle. *Data & Knowledge Engineering*, *56*, 23–40. doi:10.1016/j.datak.2005.02.005

Lindland, O. I., Sindre, G., & Solvberg, A. (1994). Understanding quality in conceptual modeling. *IEEE Software*, *11*(2), 42–49. doi:10.1109/52.268955

Lohmann, N., Massuthe, P., Stahl, C., & Weinberg, D. (2008). Analyzing interacting WS-BPEL processes using flexible model generation. *Data & Knowledge Engineering*, *64*, 38–54. doi:10.1016/j.datak.2007.06.006

Mendling, J., & van der Aalst, W. M. P. (2007). Formalization and verification of EPCs with OR-joins based on state and context. In J. Krogstie, A. L. Opdahl, & J. Sindre (Eds.), *Proceedings of the 19th International Conference on Advanced Information Systems Engineering* (LNCS 4495, pp. 439-453).

Mendling, J., Verbeek, H. M. W., van Dongen, B. F., van der Aalst, W. M. P., & Neumann, G. (2008). Detection and prediction of errors in EPCs of the SAP reference model. *Data & Knowledge Engineering*, *64*, 312–329. doi:10.1016/j.datak.2007.06.019

Mylopoulos, J. (1992). Conceptual modeling and telos. In Locoupoulos, P., & Zicari, R. (Eds.), *Conceptual modeling, databases, and cases*. New York, NY: John Wiley & Sons.

Recker, J. (2007). A socio-pragmatic constructionist framework for understanding quality in process modelling. *Australasian Journal of Information Systems*, *14*(2), 43–63.

Recker, J., Rosemann, M., & van der Aalst, W. M. P. (2005). On the user perception of configurable reference process models – Initial insights. In *Proceedings of the 16th Australian Conference on Information Systems*, Sydney, NSW, Australia.

Sadiq, S., Orlowska, M., Sadiq, W., & Cameron, F. (2004). Data flow and validation in workflow modelling. In *Proceedings of the 15th Australasian Database Conference*, Dunedin, New Zealand.

Sarshar, K., & Loos, P. (2005). Comparing the control-flow of EPC and petri net from the end-user perspective. In W. M. P. van der Aalst, B. Benatallah, F. Casati, & F. Curbera (Eds.), *Proceedings of the 3rd International Conference on Business Process Management* (LNCS 3649, pp. 434-439).

Sawilowsky, S. (1990). Nonparametric tests of interaction in experimental design. *Review of Educational Research*, *60*(1), 91–126.

Scheer, A. W. (1998). *ARIS-Business process modeling*. Berlin, Germany: Springer-Verlag.

Shah, D. A., & Madden, L. V. (2004). Nonparametric analysis of ordinal data in designed factorial experiments. *Phytopathology*, *94*(1), 33–43. doi:10.1094/PHYTO.2004.94.1.33

Siau, K., & Tan, X. (2005). Improving the quality of conceptual modeling using cognitive mapping techniques. *Data & Knowledge Engineering*, *55*, 343–365. doi:10.1016/j.datak.2004.12.006

Soffer, P., Kaner, M., & Wand, Y. (2008). Assigning ontology-based semantics to process models: The case of petri nets. In Z. Bellahsene & M. Leonard (Eds.), *Proceedings of the International Conference on Advanced Information Systems Engineering* (LNCS 5074, pp. 16-31).

Soffer, P., & Wand, Y. (2004). Goal-driven analysis of process model validity. In A. Pearsson & J. Stirna (Eds.), *Proceedings of the International Conference on Advanced Information Systems Engineering* (LNCS 3084, pp. 521-535).

Soffer, P., & Wand, Y. (2005). On the notion of soft goals in business process modeling. *Business Process Management Journal*, *11*(6), 663–679. doi:10.1108/14637150510630837

Soffer, P., & Wand, Y. (2007). Goal-driven multi-process analysis. *Journal of the Association for Information Systems*, *8*(3), 175–203.

Sommerville, I. (2007). *Software engineering* (8th ed.). Harlow, UK: Addison-Wesley.

van der Aalst, W. M. P. (1998). The application of petri nets to workflow management. *Journal of Circuits. Systems and Computers*, *8*(1), 21–66.

van der Aalst, W. M. P. (1999). Formalization and verification of event-driven process chains. *Information and Software Technology*, *41*(10), 639–650. doi:10.1016/S0950-5849(99)00016-6

van der Aalst, W. M. P. (2002). Making work flow: On the application of petri nets to business process management. In J. Esparza & C. Lakos (Eds.), *Proceedings of the 23rd International Conference on Application and Theory of Petri Nets* (LNCS 2360, pp. 1-22).

van der Aalst, W. M. P., Desel, J., & Kindler, E. (2002). On the semantics of EPCs: A vicious circle. In Nüttgens, M., & Rump, F. (Eds.), *Geschäftsprozessmanagement mit Ereignisgesteuerten Prozessketten* (pp. 71–79). Trier, Germany: Springer-Verlag.

van der Aalst, W. M. P., Dumas, M., Gottschalk, F., Hofstede, A. H. M., La Rosa, M., & Mendling, J. (2009). Preserving correctness during business process model configuration. *Formal Aspects of Computing*, *22*(3-4), 459–482.

Vanderfeesten, I., Reijers, H. A., Mendling, J., van der Aalst, W. M. P., & Cardoso, J. (2008). On a quest for good process models: The cross-connectivity metric. In Z. Bellahsene & M. Leonard (Eds.), *Proceedings of the International Conference on Advanced Information Systems Engineering* (LNCS 5074, pp. 480-494).

Verbeek, H. M. W., & van der Aalst, W. M. P. (2006). *On the verification of EPCs using T-invariants* (Tech. Rep. No. BPM-06-05). Eindhoven, The Netherlands: BPM Center.

Verbeek, H. M. W., van der Aalst, W. M. P., & Hofstede, A. H. M. (2007). Verifying workflows with cancellation regions and OR-joins: An approach based on relaxed soundness and invariants. *The Computer Journal*, *50*(3), 294–314. doi:10.1093/comjnl/bxl074

Wand, Y., & Weber, R. (1990). An ontological model of an information system. *IEEE Transactions on Software Engineering*, *16*(11), 1282–1292. doi:10.1109/32.60316

Wand, Y., & Weber, R. (1995). Towards a theory of deep structure of information systems. *Journal of Information Systems*, *5*(3), 203–223. doi:10.1111/j.1365-2575.1995.tb00108.x

Weber, R. (2004). Conceptual modelling and ontology: Possibilities and pitfalls. *Journal of Database Management*, *14*(3), 1–20. doi:10.4018/jdm.2003070101

Zur-Muehlen, M., & Rosemann, M. (2004). Multi-paradigm process management. In *Proceedings of the Workshop on Business Process Modeling, Development and Support* (pp. 169-175).

ENDNOTES

1. These soundness definitions correspond to the WF-nets soundness property. Soffer et al. (2008) proved that modeling rules derived from GPM's validity criteria yield sound WF-nets, and that in general, sound WF-nets are not necessarily valid.
2. According to the definition of Mendling and Aalst (2007). Note that the corresponding WF-net is not sound, and this verification can identify problem 5, but not the other problems.

This work was previously published in the Journal of Database Management, Volume 22, Issue 3, edited by Keng Siau, pp. 1-23, copyright 2011 by IGI Publishing (an imprint of IGI Global).

Chapter 11
Data Management and Data Administration:
Assessing 25 Years of Practice

Peter Aiken
Virginia Commonwealth University, USA

Mark L. Gillenson
University of Memphis, USA

Xihui Zhang
University of North Alabama, USA

David Rafner
Richmond Group Fund Co., Ltd., USA

ABSTRACT

Data management (DM) has existed in conjunction with software development and the management of the full set of information technology (IT)-related components. However, it has been more than two decades since research into DM as it is practiced has been published. In this paper, the authors compare aspects of DM across a quarter-century timeline, obtaining data using comparable sets of subject matter experts. Using this information to observe the profession's evolution, the authors have updated the understanding of DM as it is practiced, giving additional insight into DM, including its current responsibilities, reporting structures, and perceptions of success, among other factors. The analysis indicates that successfully investing in DM presents current, real challenges to IT and organizations. Although DM is evolving away from purely operational responsibilities toward higher-level responsibilities, perceptions of success have fallen. This paper details the quarter-century comparison of DM practices, analyzes them, and draws conclusions.

DOI: 10.4018/978-1-4666-2044-5.ch011

INTRODUCTION

Data management (DM) has long been practiced in conjunction with software development and the management of the full set of information technology (IT)-related components – often broadly categorized as: people, processes, hardware, software, and data. Today, the amount of data, and the information that organizations must derive from the data, is increasing precipitously, as are the requirements for successful application of information-based strategies (Swartz, 2007; "Data, data everywhere", 2010). This analysis resulted from an in-depth examination of organizational DM practices. Our results are centered on an opportunity to ask comparable subject matter experts, the same or similar questions – a quarter-century apart. Our goals are to provide insights into key aspects of how organizations are practicing DM as this crucial, shared business/IT responsibility continues to evolve across decades of computing.

The next section of this paper describes the research background and a brief description of the surveyed subject matter experts (SMEs). The third section summarizes analysis of comparable responses indicating statistical significance. After the incorporation of supplemental survey information, we summarize our findings.

RESEARCH BACKGROUND

A recent accepted definition of DM is "understanding the current and future data needs of an enterprise and making that data effective and efficient in supporting business activities" (Aiken, Allen, Parker, & Mattia, 2006, p. 49). Thus, DM's purpose to implement the coordinated set of practices required to marshal specific resources (organizational information assets) in support of strategy implementation. Successful achievement of organizational strategy would seem to be at least partially dependent on organizational DM practices.

This section describes previous research, the survey, and other incorporated sources. In 1981, IBM surveyed its data administration and database administration customers through its US offices (Gillenson, 1982). At the time, IBM's dominance of the mainframe environment provided a representative cross-section suitable for studying DM practices and this was the most comprehensive study of its kind at that time. While we will discuss this study in more detail later in this paper, we note here that in 1981, 71% of the organizations surveyed had some DM function. However, most DM activities focused on database administration as opposed to more strategically oriented DM goals.

Contemporaneous studies (Kahn, 1983; McCririck & Goldstein, 1980; Munzenberger, 1980; Weldon, 1979a, 1979b) reached conclusions similar to that of the 1981 survey. Data management activities were mostly limited to operational database administration functions and the movement towards strategic DM was in its nascent stage and but had achieved limited success at that point – in the eyes of DM practitioners.

A follow-up to the 1981 survey was conducted in 1983 by telephone with a subset of its respondents and was published as Gillenson (1985). Not surprisingly, it revealed that database management systems (DBMS) usage was increasing. A more important finding was that while database administration was stable, data administration was notably on the ascendance, only two years after the initial survey. This was significant because "data administration" was the first topic to incorporate activities described at the time as "liaison to systems analysts" and "long range planning." This constituted the start of managing data as a strategic corporate resource – the core of DM activities.

Several firms with "forward-thinking IS groups" were developing "subject area databases," "information databases" (which according to their descriptions, sounded like the beginnings of data warehouses), and "data architectures," and were engaging in "strategic data planning" (Goodhue, Kirsch, Quillard, & Wybo, 1992; Goodhue, Quillard, & Rockart, 1988). At this time, Trauth (1989) said that one facet of "information resource management" was to "maintain a global view of corporate data" (p. 257). Later, Gillenson (1991) found that a group of surveyed firms, "…expect data administration functions to have increasing visibility in the areas of data standards, data ownership, the understanding of the company's data, and the teaching of that understanding to others" (p. 10).

During 2007, we surveyed more than 1,000 data managers attending the annual Data Management Association (DAMA) Conference (now called Enterprise Data World) and many other regional events – partially listed at http://peteraiken.net (Aiken, 2010). Our results are based on approximately 100 responses or a respectable 10% return. (Note that not all respondents addressed all questions, as not all questions were relevant to all respondents.) We duplicated many of the 1981 survey questions in Gillenson (1982) – giving us the opportunity to ask identical questions and compare results from a quarter century apart – including: DM origins; DM group age (as a surrogate of maturity); DM centralization/de-centralization; DM career paths/shared experiences; relative placement of DM within IT and the organization; relative success of DM efforts; and overall progress managing organizational metadata – specifically care and feeding of the organizational data dictionary.

Demographics of the group we surveyed in 2007 are described by an internal publication of DAMA International (Perez, 2006) and well-describe the same population of DAMA Conference attendees. The typical DM professional was over 45 years old (43% were 45-54 and 22% were 55+) and had 20 years work experience (91% had over 10 years and 61% had over 20 years professional experience). They had spent over 12 years in DM and had begun a professional IT career in their mid-twenties, having had a career before IT. They moved voluntarily into DM after about 8 years in IT. 83% of DM professionals possessed an undergraduate degree and 36% had post-graduate education. Most attend DM conferences regularly and are otherwise well informed on the state of the practice. Based on their positions, longevity, sample size, and cross-section of organizations, they represent a comparable set of SMEs to those surveyed in 1981. We asked the 2007 group additional questions designed to probe more closely the nature of the increased responsibilities associated with the expanding practice areas.

Inclusion of other current DM survey results previously referenced as Aiken et al. (2006) permitted our collective studies to include roughly 1,000 organizational DM practice observations (see Figure 1).

COMPARING RESPONSES TO COMPARABLE 1981/2007 QUESTIONS

This section summarizes our analysis of response similarities and differences (between 1981 and 2007) in: DM origins; DM group age (as a surrogate of maturity); DM centralization/de-centralization; DM career paths/shared experiences; relative placement of DM within IT and the organization; relative success of DM efforts; and overall progress managing organizational metadata – specifically care and feeding of the organizational data dictionary. We will begin comparing responses, including evaluations of statistical significance using a standard two-sample test of proportions with the standard α of .05. Then we will address the remainder of the results. Throughout, we will incorporate our commentary about the meaning of these results to DM and to the IT profession in general. Each question from the survey is listed in the Appendix. The questions are referenced in the text as [QX] where X is the question number.

Figure 1. Distribution of approximately 1,000 surveyed DM practices

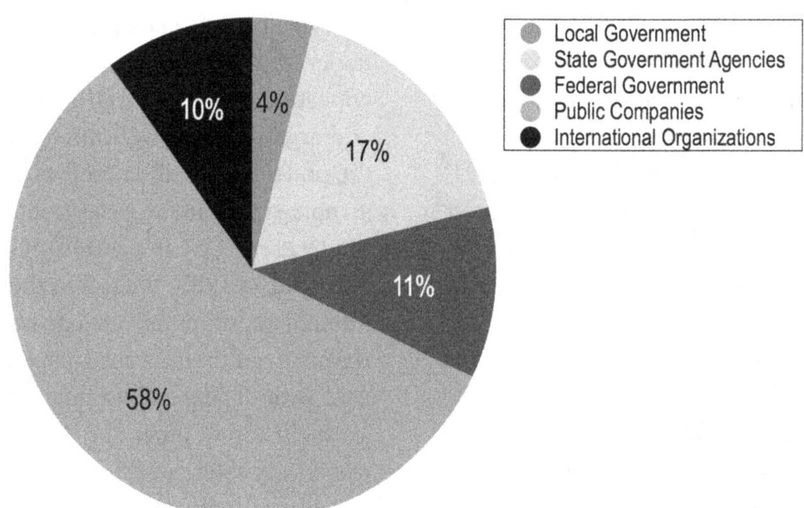

DM Organization Footprint

Organizations have moved away from the centralized DM model [Q1] and have increased in size [Q2]. In 1981, close to 90% had a centralized DM department. By 2007, only about half the organizations adhered to the centralized model. A little more than 17% had one DM practice per division. This was a significant difference with a z-value of 9.35 and a p-value < .002 indicating a valid comparison of these two populations is useful (other statistical differences are similarly favorable).

The rest of the organizations reported a mix of multiple DM departments in different divisions and other such corporate sub-structures (i.e., per project, per geographic unit, per BI unit). This is consistent with the increasing importance of DM being felt beyond corporate headquarters and into individual operating units. We note that distributed DM organizational groups (see Figure 2) face additional burdens involving coordination and accessing DM expertise.

DM Reporting Level

An interesting comparison can be made with the change in the number of managerial levels between the data management manager and the CIO. One might think that with the current increased emphasis on data management, these two roles would be drawn closer together. But, in 1981, about 74% of the data management managers either reported directly to the CIO or were one level of management removed, while the equivalent figure in 2007 dropped to 43% [Q3]. In 1981, 26% reported a separation of three or more levels of management while the equivalent number in 2007 jumped to 57% [Q4]. These differences were significant with z-values of +/- 5.37 and p-values < .002. The counterintuitive results are likely attributable to larger and much more complex IS organizations in which data management is but one of many specialized functions.

In terms of reporting path, the overall spread of who the data management manager reported to – the CIO, the head of application development, or other functions such as services or support – was similar then and now. We find it interesting that 22% of such managers reported into the application development function. Finally 40% reported

Figure 2. 2007 DM organization footprint

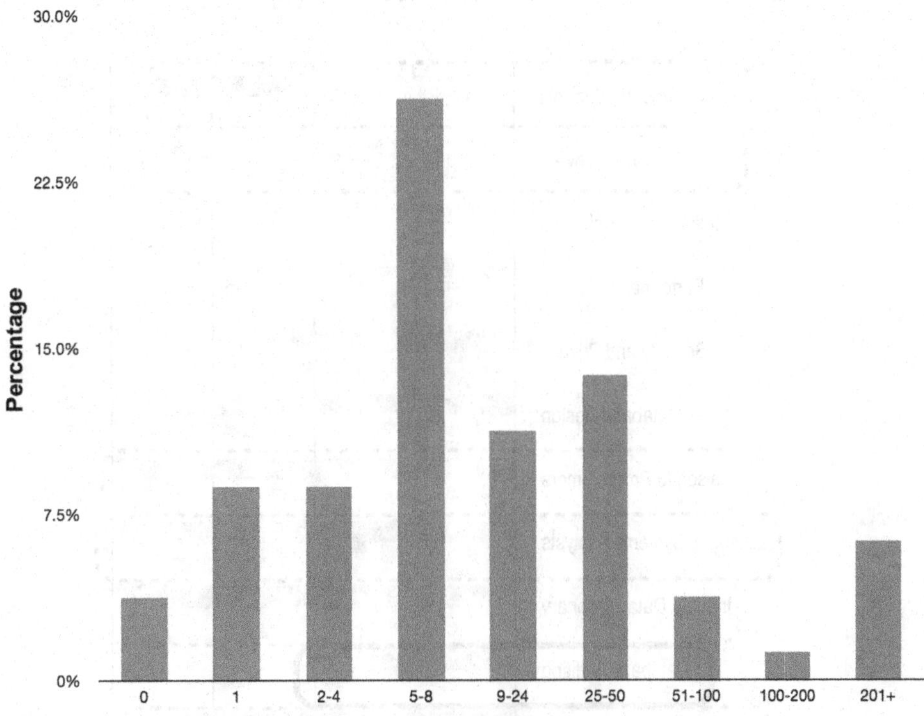

to a smattering of titles including: Director of Information Management, Chief Relationship Manager, Global Marketing Business Side, VP of CRM, and Head DBA.

An additional finding was that the approximately 1,000 data management professionals attending the *Enterprise Data World 2009* conference (see http://edw2009.wilshireconferences.com for details) registered using more that 300 job titles. We believe that the use of such a vast array of job titles by such a relatively homogeneous group of professionals leads to unnecessary confusion causing others in IT and in business to be uncertain what functions they perform.

Change in DM Responsibilities

The 2007 survey asked the respondents to check all of their DM organization's responsibilities from a provided list [Q5]. Responses were compared to the 1981 results. We checked the statistical significance in the differences. Figure 3 shows the comparative percentages (percent of respondents saying they did have the particular responsibility) for each survey. Seven of the categories showed statistically significant differences and of those, only one was an increase. The one that increased (circled with the darkest, solid lines) from 1981 to 2007 was database auditing, which is not surprising given the increasing pressures of laws such as Sarbanes-Oxley to have accurate financial data and the overall sense of the importance of accurate data to organizations. Statistically significant decreases (circled with lighter, dashed lines) were seen in environmental controls, backup and recovery, liaison to programmers, liaison to systems analysts, input to data dictionary, and managing the data dictionary. This indicates that the profession is evolving away from strictly low-level operations and towards managerial functions.

Figure 3. 1981 and 2007 responsibilities, compared – statistically significant decreases are circled with lighter, dashed lines and increases with the darkest, solid line

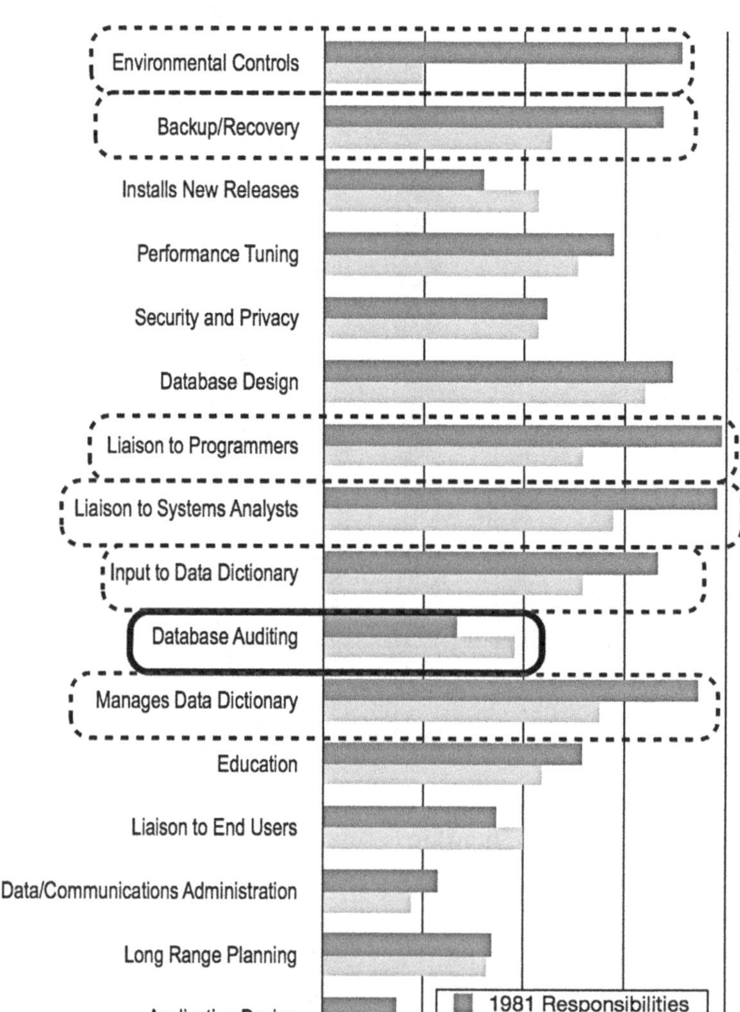

Perceived DM Success

With this question [Q6] we looked for any shifts in DM personnel's (all well qualified to provide such assessments) perceptions of the success of their own efforts. Figure 4 illustrates how, the percentage of DM organizations labeled "successful" fell from 43% to15% (z-value 4.37, p-value < .002); while the number labeled "partially successful" grew from 10% to 39% (z-value -6.58, p-value < .002); and the number labeled "unsuccessful" increased from 5% to 21% (z-value -4.95, p-value < .002). All of these differences are statistically significant.

Is this surprising? By now, shouldn't we have "gotten it right" with many more organizations considering their data management organization successful? The answer to this question is not simple, as a number of new factors have come into play. The volumes of data have grown tre-

Figure 4. Does DM organization feel that it has been successful?

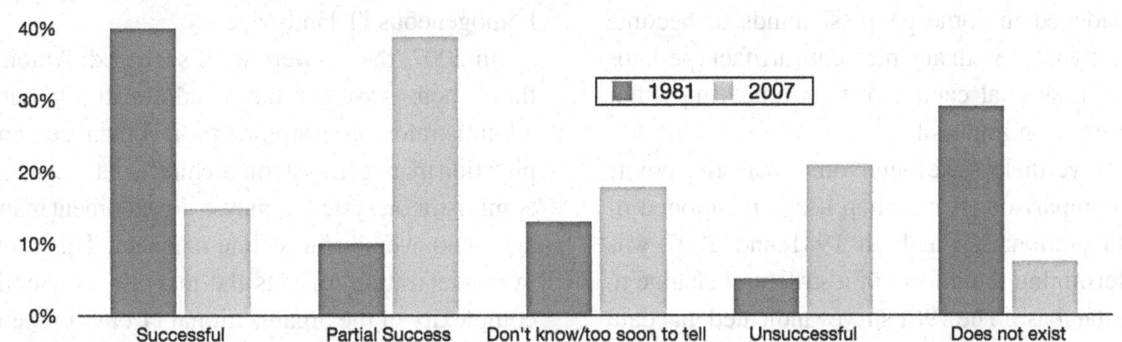

mendously, the sophistication and breadth of applications that use the data have mushroomed, the pitfalls of data management have increased, and the expectations for a successful DM group may have grown as well. Today's data management organizations may be much larger, may be doing much more than they used to, and may be doing many of these things much better, but with *increased expectations* they may be perceived to be only partially successful in greater numbers than before. For further discussion, see the analysis and conclusions sections of the paper.

Data Management Challenges

The 1981 survey listed a number of challenges or problems that the data management departments might have had and asked respondents to indicate all that applied to them. About 50% complained of too heavy a workload, responsibilities without the corresponding power, and resistance by others to changing job responsibilities. About 40% noted lack of strong enough management support, the data management department not being placed high enough in the organization, and resistance to data sharing.

In the 2007 survey, we focused on the respondents' number one challenge, while also allowing them to list others, sacrificing a statistical significance comparison between the two surveys on this point in favor of seeking their top challenge. In 2007, 16% reported that their number one challenge was too heavy of a workload and another 16% complained that their number one problem was lack of strong enough management support. Thus, two of the main complaints in 1981 were still with us in 2007 [Q7].

Interestingly, while responsibilities without the corresponding power and resistance by others to changing job responsibilities were two hot buttons in 1981, they were only reported as being the number one problem by, respectively, 8% and 2% of the respondents in 2007. It would appear that in the dynamic environment of 2007, distributed power and a culture of change are much more accepted. A result that is consistent with data reported elsewhere in this paper in 2007 is that 11% had as their number one problem that the data management group was not placed high enough in the organization.

Data Dictionary Usage

We sought to determine whether there was a significant difference in the penetration of data dictionaries in IT organizations from 1981 to 2007. The percentage of organizations using a data dictionary increased from 60% in 1981 to 70% in 2007, but statistically, this was only marginally significant with a z-value of -1.95 and a p-value of .05 [Q8-Q11]. Furthermore, we have a concern that in the 25-year spread between the two surveys, the term "data dictionary" may have broadened in some peoples' minds to become synonymous with any metadata artifact (perhaps even relational catalogs), thus rendering a fair comparison impossible.

Nevertheless, we found some interesting points of comparison. A common usage mentioned of data dictionaries in both 1981 and 2007 was determining the impact of a structural change to the database. The 1981 survey indicated that data management personnel were involved in dictionary input in 83% of the organizations; systems analysts in 30% of the organizations, application programmers 25%, and end-users 7%. These proportions hold true in 2007 as well.

While these consistent results may be impressive, on the other hand, we believe they contribute towards a rather stereotypical perspective that others have of DM. The care and feeding of the data dictionary is a widely understood DM function by IT personnel and it has been hard for outsiders to understand how data dictionaries are relevant to their particular job function. If DM is not understood to be adding value to projects, is it any wonder it has such a "low" strategic representation as an IT component, much less critical levels of understanding on the business side and at the executive level?

DM Professional's Last Position

The 1981 survey asked what the data manager's last position was before becoming involved in data management [Q12]. This question was designed to understand the background and likely previous experience that a typical data manager brought to the position. In 1981, the two most common answers were systems analyst, and programming or project manager or leader. In the 1980's IT personnel shared a common background that included COBOL, systems analysis, and some database. That, of course, was the IT world of the 1980s and the study group of DMs was cognizant of how their position supported this relatively homogeneous IT landscape.

In 2007, the answers were scattered. Among the responses were database administrator, data administrator, programmer, project manager, application manager, systems architect, data security administrator, systems analyst, development manager, and even business line manager. This drop in concentration reflects the increase in overall complexity of the organizational IT environment and presents a challenge to organizations seeking to improve their DM capabilities. DMs are being drawn to the profession from disciplines beyond the traditional programmer/analyst career tracks.

DM Origins

One of the survey questions asked whether the DM organization was established before the DBMS was acquired, or vice versa [Q13]. Best practices dictate that the DM group should first be established. Next should come an assessment, by the DM group, of organizational DM requirements. This should lead to evaluation of various DBMS technologies and only then, selection of one or more for implementation. Direct statistical comparison of the responses was infeasible. Yet, the differences are, to say the least, intriguing.

In 1981, 68% of DM professionals reported their organizations first acquired a DBMS and then established a DM group, only 26% establishing DM first and then determining which DBMS to procure. Figure 5 indicates these numbers worsen from 1981 to 2007 when only 9% of organizations established their DM prior to DBMS acquisition (Note that in 2007, 10% reported "not certain"). At first blush, we could say that this is disappointing because by 2007 most organizations should have been expected to be sophisticated enough in IT to recognize that the DM group should first be established and then carefully evaluate which DBMS to acquire. But the reality is that by 2007 the vast majority of companies already had a DBMS because of the general advance of IT technology or because of specific reasons such as a DBMS being required to run packaged software that the company has bought.

DM Group Longevity/Maturity

Perhaps technological advancements have misled executive management into thinking that many facets of DM have been subsumed into automated design, programming, management and integration tools. Thus those facets of DM are not seen as a core concern. Instead "compliance" and the like, take over as the DM expectation. Overlooked is the fact that success in compliance is a high level abstraction, built upon success in more concrete integration areas, etc.

DM shares the inherent complexities of all architecture-based disciplines including one key characteristic that is shared by all – it is impossible to create an organizationally relevant DM function overnight – instead goal achievement is measured in years. Thus, the age of the DM group can function as a limit to the overall DM practice maturity. The 2007 survey asked what year the DM groups were established and the response information was plotted as Figure 6 [Q14].

- 71% of organizations had DM organizations in 1981. At the time these averaged two-to-four years in age. A valid conclusion would be that approximately 30% of all organizations in 1981 were a half-decade away from achieving value from their DM investments.
- In 2007 about one-third of the companies reported that their data management organizations were established before 1990 and another 1/3 were reported established since 2000. We believe that this reflects a recent, increased focus on organizational DM.

If our interpretation is correct, DM experienced a drop in "popularity" beginning around 1983. It wasn't until 2003 that DM made up this apparent lost ground by surpassing the 1983 high mark. Additional evidence of this trend is that the change mirrored an industry trend towards decentralization that caused a temporary fragmentation of efforts (see also Gillenson, 1991). One of the

Figure 5. In which did the organization first invest?

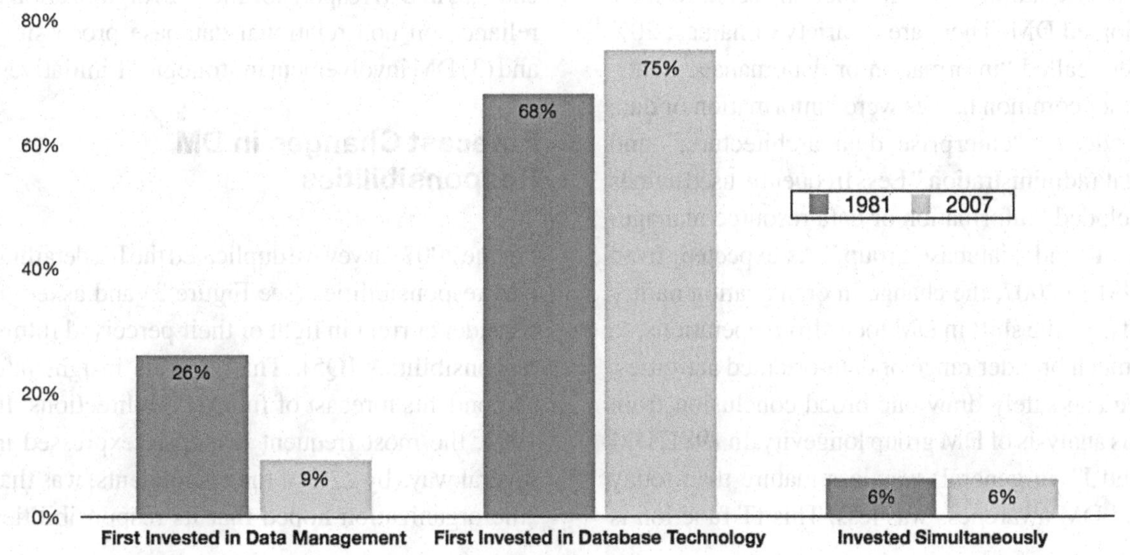

Figure 6. Inferred and representative percentages of organizational DM practices by year (Note: results are extrapolated for years 1978-1980 and 1984-1990)

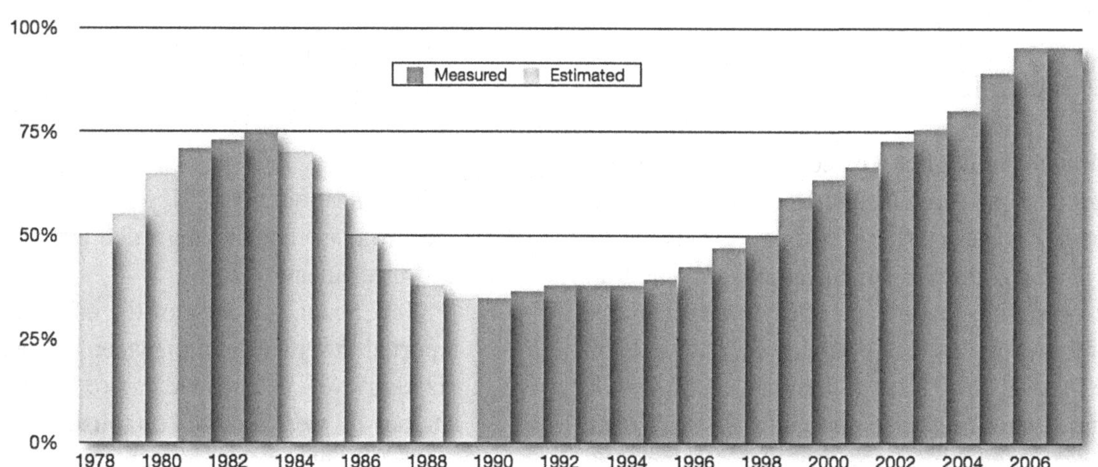

limitations of our analysis is that the various labels have evolved. In 1981, most DM organizations were oriented towards operations and so it was not surprising that 55% of them were called "database administration." Beyond that, 18% were called "data administration" and other popular labels included "data management" and "database groups."

By 2007, the landscape had changed considerably – fewer than 5% of organizations reported no DM function. Companies that may have only had database administration functions seem to have adopted DM. There are a variety of names: 20% were called "information or data management." Other common names were "information or data services," "enterprise data architecture," and "data administration." Less frequently used names included "information or data resource management" and "database group." As expected, from 1981 to 2007, the change in organization names reflects the shift in DM focus from operations, to a much broader range of data-oriented activities. We can safely draw one broad conclusion from this analysis of DM group longevity. In 1981, DM (and IT in general) was less mature than today and DM awareness was less. This IT function is seen as a mandatory capability as today virtually all organizations maintain DM groups – albeit in a variety of forms.

SUPPLEMENTAL RESPONSE ANALYSIS

Having discussed the directly comparable analysis results, we will now assess three areas surveyed in 2007 and not surveyed in 1981: (1) forecast changes in DM responsibilities; (2) organizational reliance on non-relational database processing; and (3) DM involvement in strategic IT initiatives.

Forecast Changes in DM Responsibilities

For the 2007 survey we duplicated the list detailing DM responsibilities (see Figure 3) and asked to consider current in light of their perceived future responsibilities [Q5]. This gave us insight into respondents forecast of future DM directions. In 1981, the most frequent response, expressed in several ways by 22% of the respondents, was that "the organization hoped that its responsibilities would be expanded in scope, so that the data processing organization would more fully embrace the concept of data administration" (Gillenson, 1982, p. 705). 15% hoped for more data dictionary usage. Other common responses included more applications in the database environment, more data integration or sharing, and moving from database administration to data administration.

The 2007 responses were more diverse and targeted toward contemporary topics. The most common included furthering data integration, master data management, and service oriented architecture. A panoply of other topics listed as either being introduced or improved included data governance (Khatri & Brown, 2010), data sharing, data quality (Even & Shankaranarayanan, 2009; Sun, Zhao, Nunamaker, & Sheng, 2006; Wang & Strong, 1996), alignment with the IT infrastructure, business intelligence, data services, data stewardship, and improved management support.

Figure 7 illustrates the 2007 figures using current (darker rows) versus future plan (lighter rows). These results forecast the continuation of the trends reported as Figure 3. The increase in the application design figures is significant (z-value -1.99, p-value .046). The increase in liaison to end-users is marginally significant (z-value -1.80, p-value .07) as is the increase in long-range planning (z-value -1.75, p-value .08). What these categories have in common and what makes these

Figure 7. Responses to the question: Please check all that apply what are the current (darker rows) and future (lighter rows) data management organization responsibilities? – statistically significant decreases are circled using lighter, dashed lines and increases are circled using the darkest line

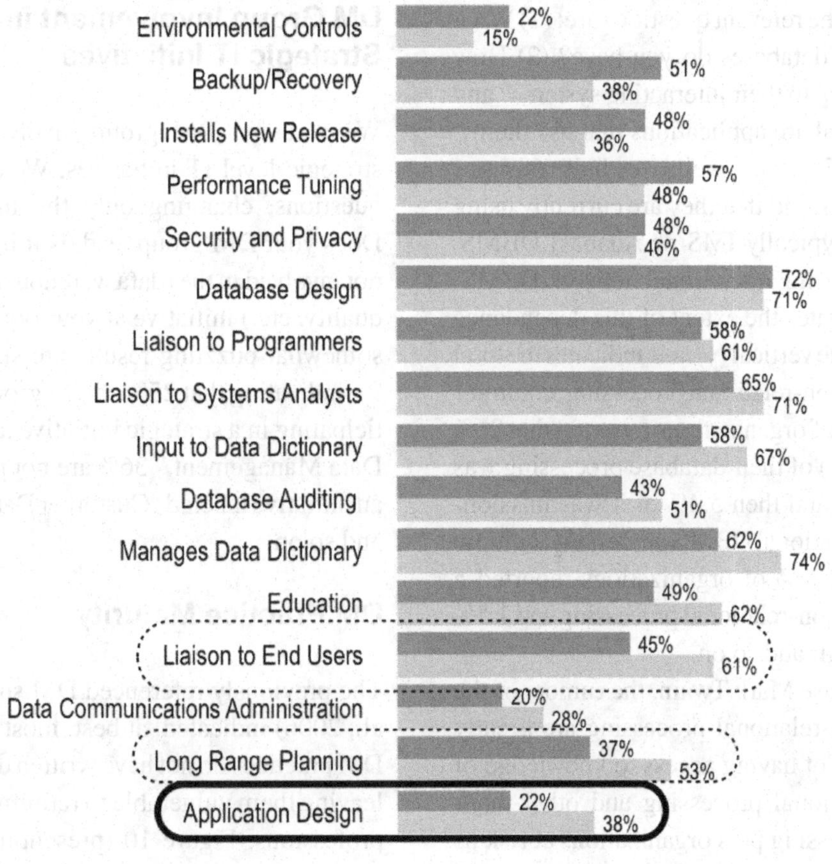

figures telling is that DM is projected to take on a clearly broader role within the IT environment, with DM becoming more and more a serious partner in the development of organizational information systems architectures.

Reliance on Non-Relational Database Processing

The world of database management in 1981 was limited to hierarchical and network "navigational" databases. Relational database was an emerging curiosity at that time. Given the progression that has led to relational database becoming the *de facto* standard today, statistical comparisons between database technology usage in 1981 and 2007 would be meaningless. Nevertheless, the technology usage responses proved to be interesting.

About one-third of the respondents in 1981 said that they were dealing with non-database flat files, in addition to their key navigational databases. Today, the relevant questions are: (1) What non-relational databases do you have? (2) How integral are they to their interacting systems? and (3) How critical are applications that use them?

In the 2007 survey, well over half (68%) of the respondents said that they are currently using hierarchical (typically IMS or Adabas) DBMS, with 20% reporting operational network DBMS. Figure 8 illustrates the extent of this dependence [Q15-Q17]. The vertical (y) axis indicates the total percentage of non-relational processing; column 1 indicates 10% of organizations reported that 26% (5.4% + 20.5%) of their database processing was non-relational and then 5.4% of it was mission-critical non-relational DBMS processing; column 2 records that 20% of organizations reported a total of 17.2% non-relational processing and 1.5% mission-critical; and so on.

To paraphrase Mark Twain, the rumors of the demise of non-relational processing are greatly exaggerated. Not having access to knowledge of both organizational processing and other-than-RDBMS processing puts organizations at risk as critical architectural decisions are made poorly and/or without access to all the facts. Major organizational technological disasters have occurred when organizations abandon working technologies to adopt "more modern" solutions – see for examples in GAO (2001) and many other examples from http://gao.gov.

Many good computer science/computer engineering/information systems (CSCEIS) students become IT workers who are not knowledgeable of these capabilities. Chapters on hierarchical/network databases have been removed from University-level textbooks – dismissed as "legacy" and are relegated now to companion textbook websites (Elmasri & Navathe, 2006). For CSCEIS beneficiaries, the world consists of relational database management systems (RDBMS) and some legacy "stuff." This is clearly something for companies to keep in mind as their existing DM practitioners continue to age.

DM Group Involvement in Strategic IT Initiatives

We assessed DM group involvement in new, strategic-level IT initiatives. We asked identical questions, changing only the initiative name: Does your DM group lead, is it involved, or is it not involved in the (data warehousing, XML, data quality, etc.) initiative at your organization? The somewhat puzzling results are shown in Figure 9 – indicating that 25% of DM groups are not participating in a strategic initiative labeled "Master Data Management," 36% are not participating in an initiative labeled "Customer Data Integration," and so on.

DM Practice Maturity

The previously referenced DM survey (Aiken et al., 2006) indicated, at best, most organizational DM practices do not have written documentation, leaving them vulnerable to retirements that hit all professions. Figure 10 (presenting summarized

Figure 8. Organizational dependence on non-relational database processing

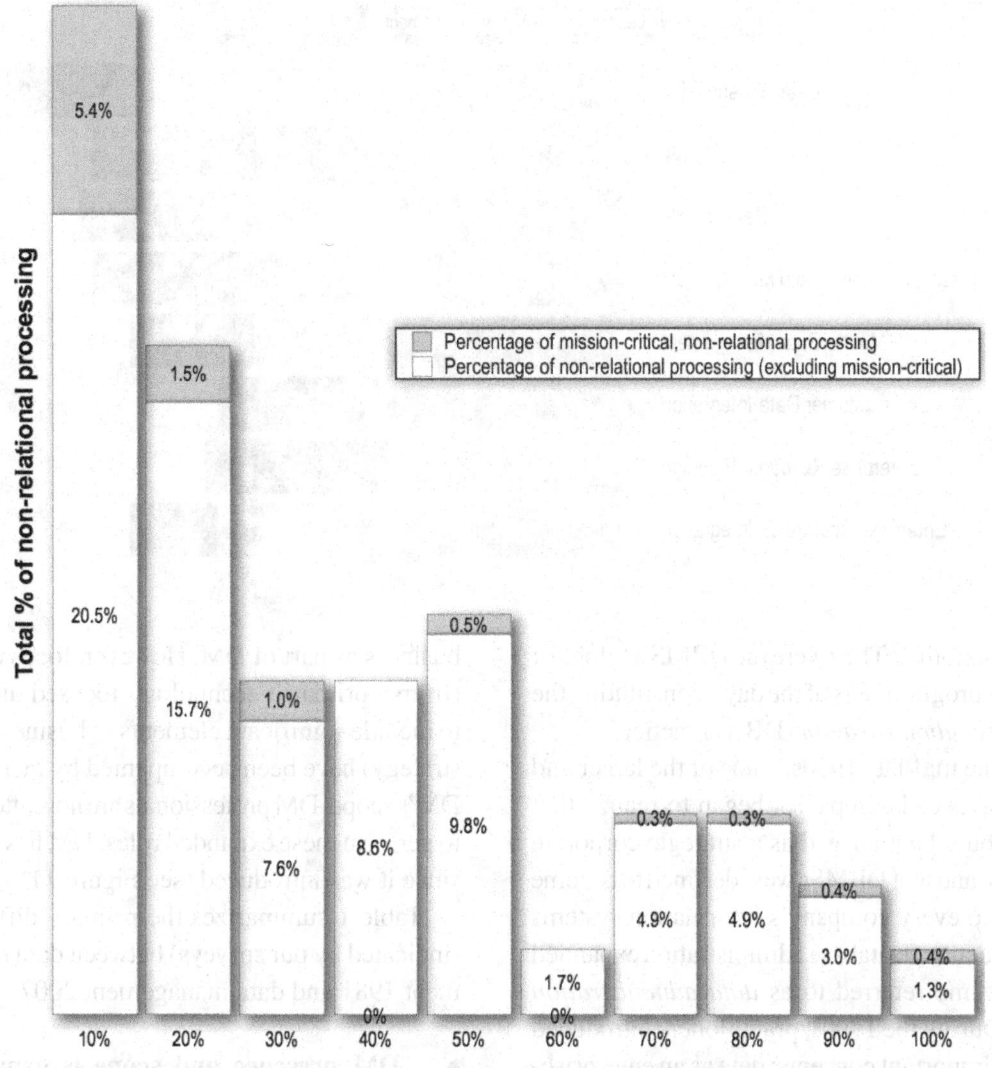

results from that survey) reports that repeatable DM practices (CMM Level-2) did not exist at most organizations. This indicates a potential challenge as organizations attempt to pass along organizational DM knowledge.

ANALYSIS SUMMARY: DM SCOPE CHANGES AND TRENDS

This section describes DM's scope changes and presents some DM trends. The earliest *database management systems* (DBMS) were developed in the late-1950s and popularized as commercial products around 1970. As they were incorporated into organizations, a need became apparent for professionals with skills such as logical and physical database design, performance monitoring, and

Figure 9. Relative amount of DM involvement in various data-dependent, strategic initiatives

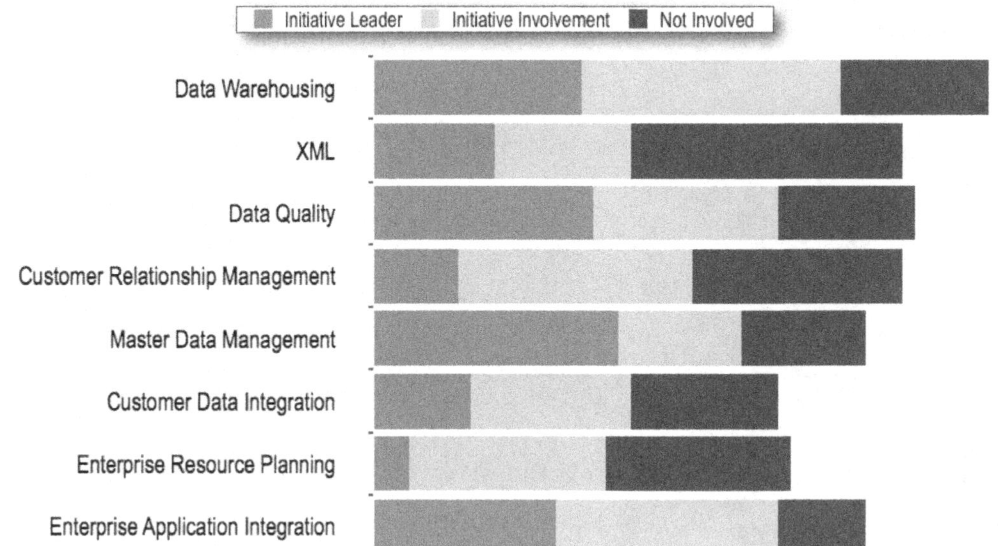

troubleshooting. They were the DBMS analogs of systems programmers of the day – constituting the *database administration* (DBA) practice.

By the mid-late 1970s, some of the larger and more advanced companies began to realize that data should be managed as a strategic corporate resource and that DBMSs were destined to become central to every company's information systems infrastructure. Database administration expanded and became referred to as *data administration* (DA). During the 1990s, practitioners introduced several important concepts: data as an enterprise-wide resource; the value of maintaining metadata; and the concept of shared data with all of its advantages. This set of practices became known as *enterprise data administration* (EDA).

Most recently EDA practices have yet again expanded as organizations have been forced to accept new responsibilities such as governance, compliance, and security. Each of these phases has increased the scope and responsibilities of DA and this, more broadly defined set of practices, is now referred to as *data management* (DM).

The original practices of database design and operation are still clearly seen by both IT and the business as part of DM. However, focus changes (from a primarily technology-focused discipline to include significant elements of business and IT strategy) have been accompanied by increases in DM's scope. DM professionals are now attempting to perform these expanded roles. DM has evolved since it was introduced (see Figure 11).

Table 1 summarizes the primary differences (indicated by our surveys) between data management 1981 and data management 2007.

- **DM presence and scope is expanding:** During the survey period, organizational DM practice has increased its overall presence in organizations (see Figure 6). Simultaneously, DM scope has expanded from a technical discipline focused on creating and operating database technologies to include more in-depth technical foci (advanced analytics, technical data discovery, warehouse and delivery optimization, etc.) and also includes a wide-range of socially based responsibilities (governance/compliance, security, stewardship, etc.) (see Figure 3, Figure 7, Figure 8, and Figure 9).

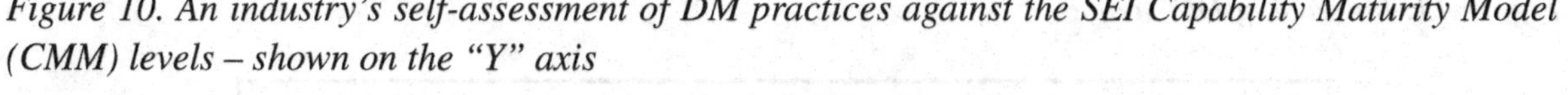

Figure 10. An industry's self-assessment of DM practices against the SEI Capability Maturity Model (CMM) levels – shown on the "Y" axis

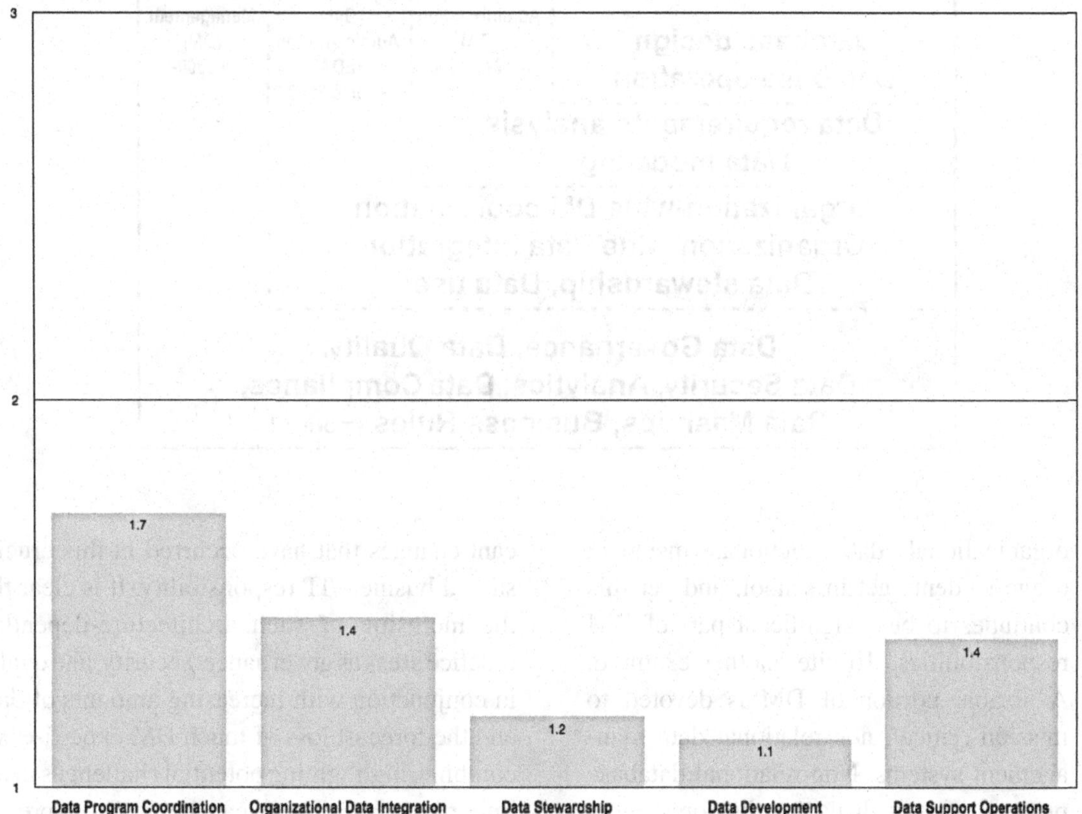

- **DM requirements are increasing:** DMs are further away from top IT management than they were 25 years ago; DM groups are less often involved in strategic technology initiatives; and DM is no longer a strictly centralized operation. The DM reporting level, footprint (see Figure 2), and last position profiles indicate growing demand and fragmenting solution delivery ability.
- **DM perception of self-success is not expanding:** Fewer DM organizations view themselves as successful (see Figure 4) and there appears to be mounting frustration at the lack of DM involvement in data-dependent strategic initiatives. The world of today's data manager is more varied and complex than the relatively orderly (by comparison) mainframe world of 1981. Perhaps this explains the worsening perception and measures of DM success (see Figure 5 and Figure 10). Data managers believe their jobs will evolve dramatically in the future (see Figure 3 and Figure 7) further strengthening requirements for mature DM practices.
- **DM education may need to be scrutinized:** Examining objective criteria, such as DM origin, non-relational database requirements, data dictionary use, and many interviews, we are able to discern a structural imbalance between organizational requirements and academic teachings. Consider how little exposure to

Figure 11. Increasing DM scope

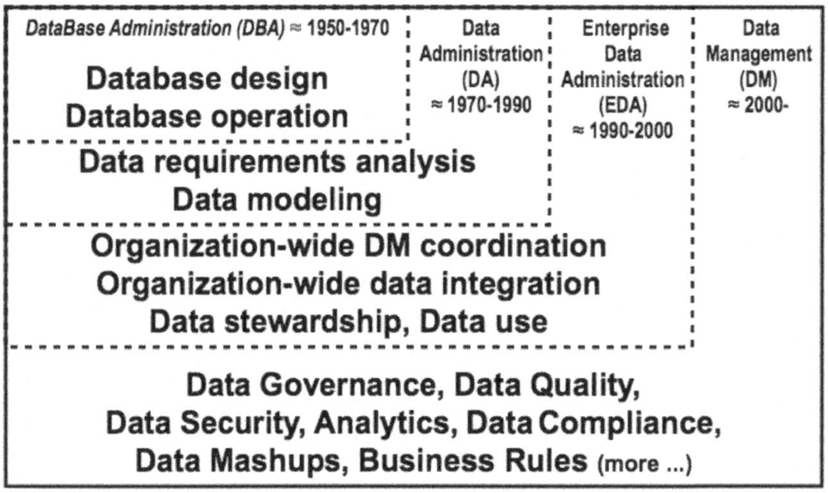

DataBase Administration (DBA) ≈ 1950-1970
Database design
Database operation
Data Administration (DA) ≈ 1970-1990
Data requirements analysis
Data modeling
Enterprise Data Administration (EDA) ≈ 1990-2000
Organization-wide DM coordination
Organization-wide data integration
Data stewardship, Data use
Data Management (DM) ≈ 2000-
Data Governance, Data Quality,
Data Security, Analytics, Data Compliance,
Data Mashups, Business Rules (more ...)

organizational data dictionary/metadata usage students get in school, and yet this continues to be a significant part of DM responsibilities. To cite another example: A sizable portion of DM is devoted to mission-critical, non-relational data management systems. Non-relational database processing is with us for the foreseeable future and we should continue to treat it as a relevant DM topic. Yet curricula are deemphasizing non-relational processing (often to website-only chapters) and as a result, IT professionals and organizations are unable to adequately evaluate valid alternatives. We have witnessed many organizations attempt to re-host applications from hierarchical and network style databases to relational processing because they were not "modern" solutions. The majority of these re-hostings have failed to achieve objectives.

CONCLUSION

We are certain that the evolution of DM in not complete. However, we have highlighted significant changes that have occurred in this crucial, shared business/IT responsibility. It is clear that the inclusion of such architecture-dependent practice areas as governance, security, and quality in conjunction with increasing amounts of data, and the forecast loss of much DM expertise will combine, highlighting potential challenges in this important area. These can be easily expressed in Figure 12 – our collective judgment that of surveyed DM investments:

- 10% achieve parity and (potentially positive returns);
- 30% (including the previously mentioned 10%) achieve tangible returns; and
- 70% have very small or no tangible return on their DM investments.

It is not possible at this stage of understanding to identify "the answer" to this challenge – our mission has been to raise awareness of it as an issue. Clearly the profession is still investigating what will work for organizations, which leads to directions for future research. A better understanding of DM organizational maturity is required so that we can provide guidance to organizations wishing to grow their DM practices in a predict-

Table 1. Summary of primary differences between 1981 and 2007 data management

Category	1981 Findings	2007 Findings
DM Existence	29% didn't have DM groups	<5% didn't have DM groups
DM Organization Footprint	90% centralized	50% centralized 17% divisionally centralized
DM Reporting Level	74% reported to CIO 26% reported 3-levels down	43% reported to CIO 57% reported 3-levels down
Perception of DM Success	43% Successful 5% Unsuccessful	15% Successful 21% Unsuccessful
DM Challenges	40% lacked management support	16% lacked management support
DM Origin	26% forming DM group before purchasing DBMS	9% forming DM group before purchasing DBMS
Changes in DM Responsibilities		Increased database auditing Decreased environmental control, backup/recover, liaison to programmers/systems analysts, data dictionary interaction

Several evolutionary DM trends are also evident (1981–2007).

able manner. Reasonable conditions for success need to be defined giving existing practice managers something to target. Finally, we need to understand more specifically what role DM can reasonably expect to play in an increasingly complex environment without greatly expanding the DM expertise and increasing the workload facing organizations in future years. For example, should DM be the focal point for a company's efforts to use data for competitive advantage through data mining and other techniques and is there evidence that this has been tried and worked well? Has DM proven to be more or less helpful in Enterprise Resource Planning (ERP) environments than in other environments? Does DM have a role in the use of social media to achieve competitive advantage? What is the role of DM regarding the acquisition of external data sources (Petschulat, 2010)?

While there is more work to be done, we can provide certain concrete recommendations to practitioners from our current results. Management should recognize that DM is continuing to move towards a model in which it is moving away from the inclusion of low-level operations and towards more managerial functions. Management should be sensitive to the DM perceptions of having too heavy of a workload and not enough management support. Management should recognize that with the pervasive use of data in today's organizations, it is feasible and often desirable to have DM functions organized on a decentralized basis through the various divisions and sites of organizations,

Figure 12. Largely unproductive DM investments

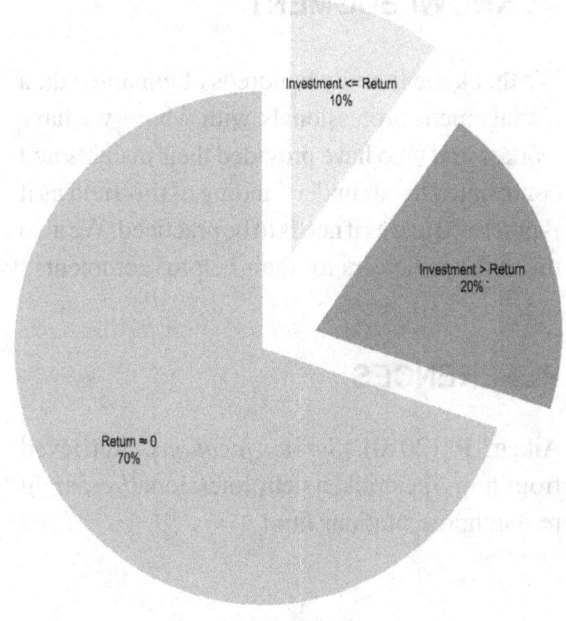

although central coordination for planning and setting standards should be considered. Management should be flexible in assessing DM success, since demands on the DM function have increased as the use of data in organizations has become more pervasive. Management should pay close attention to the DM function of database auditing as a natural response to the requirements of laws such as Sarbanes-Oxley.

A recent *Communications of the ACM* (CACM) article reported organizations would invest at least $4 billion USD in DM in 2012 and they would continue to invest in DM at an 8.7% annual rate (Bernstein and Haas, 2008). This investment may not be enough given that the cost of poor quality data was estimated to be more than $600 billion USD in 2002 (Eckerson, 2002) and that through 2007, at least 25% of critical data within Fortune 1000 companies continued to be inaccurate (Friedman, Gassman, & Newman, 2005). We look to our research community to continue to collectively focus on how best to deliver qualified data management-aware professionals to organizations and through them, improve organizational DM practices.

ACKNOWLEDGMENT

We thank the literally hundreds of unnamed data management professionals with whom we have worked and who have provided their insights and contributed to our understanding of this field as it is practiced and as it needs to be practiced. We also thank the reviewers for their helpful comments.

REFERENCES

Aiken, P. (2010). *Survey locations.* Retrieved from http://peteraiken.net/professional/research/researchpresentations.html

Aiken, P., Allen, M. D., Parker, B., & Mattia, A. (2006). Measuring data management's maturity: A community's self-assessment. *IEEE Computer, 40*(4), 42–50.

Bernstein, P., & Haas, L. (2008). Information integration in the enterprise. *Communications of the ACM, 51*(9), 72–79. doi:10.1145/1378727.1378745

Data, data everywhere - A special report on managing information. (2010, February 27). *The Economist*, pp. 1-14.

Eckerson, W. W. (2002). *Data quality and the bottom line: Achieving business success through a commitment to high quality data.* Chatsworth, CA: Data Warehousing Institute.

Elmasri, R., & Navathe, S. (2006). *Fundamentals of database systems* (5th ed.). Reading, MA: Addison-Wesley.

Even, A., & Shankaranarayanan, G. (2009). Utility cost perspectives in data quality management. *Journal of Computer Information Systems, 50*(2), 127–135.

Friedman, T., Gassman, B., & Newman, D. (2005). *Gartner report - Predicts 2006: Emerging data management drivers and imperatives.* Retrieved from http://www.gartner.com/DisplayDocument?doc_cd=136320

GAO. (2001). *Information technology: DLA should strengthen business systems modernization architecture and investment activities* (Tech. Rep. No. GAO-01-631). Washington, DC: U.S. Government Accountability Office.

Gillenson, M. L. (1982). The state of practice of data administration - 1981. *Communications of the ACM, 25*(10), 699–706. doi:10.1145/358656.358664

Gillenson, M. L. (1985). Trends in data administration. *Management Information Systems Quarterly, 9*(4), 317–325. doi:10.2307/249232

Gillenson, M. L. (1991). Database administration at the crossroads: The era of end-user oriented, decentralized data processing. *Journal of Database Administration*, *2*(4), 1–11.

Goodhue, D. L., Kirsch, L. J., Quillard, J. A., & Wybo, M. D. (1992). Strategic data planning: Lessons from the field. *Management Information Systems Quarterly*, *16*(1), 11–34. doi:10.2307/249699

Goodhue, D. L., Quillard, J. A., & Rockart, J. F. (1988). Managing the data resource: A contingency perspective. *Management Information Systems Quarterly*, *12*(3), 373–392. doi:10.2307/249204

Kahn, B. K. (1983). Some realities of data administration. *Communications of the ACM*, *26*(10), 794–799. doi:10.1145/358413.358431

Khatri, V., & Brown, C. V. (2010). Designing data governance. *Communications of the ACM*, *53*(1), 148–152. doi:10.1145/1629175.1629210

McCririck, I. B., & Goldstein, R. C. (1980). What do data administrators really do? *Datamation*, *26*(8), 131–134.

Munzenberger, H. (1980, September 25-26). Database administration – Experience from a European survey. In *Proceedings of the European Conference on Evaluation and Implementation of Database Systems*, Brussels, Belgium (pp. 85-94).

Perez, A. (2006). *The elusive species of the information age: The data management professional*. Retrieved from http://www.midsouthdama.org/pdf/2006_surveyart.pdf

Petschulat, S. (2010). Other people's data. *Communications of the ACM*, *53*(1), 53–57. doi:10.1145/1629175.1629196

Sun, S. X., Zhao, J. L., Nunamaker, J. F., & Sheng, O. R. L. (2006). Formulating the data-flow perspective for business process management. *Information Systems Research*, *17*(4), 374–391. doi:10.1287/isre.1060.0105

Swartz, N. (2007). Data management problems widespread. *Information Management Journal*, *41*(5), 28–30.

Trauth, E. M. (1989). The evolution of information resource management. *Information & Management*, *16*(5), 257–268. doi:10.1016/0378-7206(89)90003-7

Wang, R. Y., & Strong, D. M. (1996). Beyond accuracy: What data quality means to data consumers. *Journal of Management Information Systems*, *12*(4), 5–34.

Weldon, J.-L. (1979a). *Organizing for data base administration*. New York, NY: Center for Research on Information Systems, Graduate School of Business Administration, New York University.

Weldon, J.-L. (1979b). *The changing role of data base administration*. New York, NY: Center for Research on Information Systems, Graduate School of Business Administration, New York University.

APPENDIX

List of Survey Questions

Q1. How many DA groups are within the overall enterprise?
One
One per division
One per data center
One per division plus one at the corporate level
One per data center plus one at the corporate level
Other (please specify)

Q2. Consider "data management" in its broadest possible scope (including data quality, governance, data modeling, enterprise architecture, etc). How much total effort (in full-time equivalents) is currently devoted to data management by your organization?
0 | 1 | 2-4 | 5-8 | 9-24 | 25-50 | 51-100 | 201+0

Q3. How many levels are there from the DA managers to the **CIO**?
1 | 2 | 3 | 4 | 5 | 6 | 7 | 8 | 9 | 10 | 11-25 | 26 and more

Q4. To whom does the DA manager report (this one probably derived from the organization chart)?
The chief data processing officer
The manager of "services" or "support"
The overall manager of application development or one of the submanagers of application development
Other (please specify)

Q5. What are the current and future DA organization responsibilities (check all that apply)?
Controls IMS/DL/I Environment
Gens IMS/DL/I Control Blocks
IMS/DL/I Backup/Recovery
Performance Tuning
Installs New Release
Liaison to Systems Analysts
Liaison to Programmers
Liaison to End Users
Database Design
Application Design
Education
Manages Data Dictionary
Input to Data Dictionary
Security and Privacy
Long Range Planning
Database Auditing
Data Communications Administration

Q6. Does the data administration organization feel that the data administration concept has been successful?
Yes
Partially successful

Don't know, too soon to tell
No
No DA organization exists

Q7. What challenges does your DA organization face (check all that apply)?
Too heavy a workload
Responsibilities without the corresponding power
Resistance by others to changing job responsibilities
Lack of strong enough management support
DA group not placed high enough in the organization
Resistance to data sharing by users or system people
No enough responsibilities
Inadequate salaries
Other (please specify)

Q8. Do you use a data dictionary?
Yes | No

Q9. Do you use any metadata catalog tools?
Yes | No

Q10. Does your organization use or plan to use a repository?
last year (2006) | this year (2007) | next year (2008)

Q11. If yes, does your organization use a structured or formal approach to repository technology?
Yes | No

Q12. What was the data administration manager's last position before becoming involved in data administration?

Q13. Which was established first: the data administration organization or the database management system?
Data administration organization was first
Database management system was first
Simultaneously

Q14. What year was your data administration organization established?
Before 1990 | 1991 | 1992 | 1993 | 1994 | 1995 | 1996 | 1997 | 1998 | 1999 | 2000 | 2001 | 2002 | 2003 | 2004 | 2005 | 2006 | 2007 | not established

Q15. Do you currently use any Non-Relational Databases (hierarchical or network)?
Hierarchical | Network | OO | other ______

Q16. If so, approximately what percentage of your application processing uses them?
0% | 0-10% | 11-20% | 21-30% | 31-40% | 41-50% | 51-60% | 61-70% | 71-80% | 81-90% | 91-100%

Q17. Approximately what percentage of these are mission critical?
0% | 0-10% | 11-20% | 21-30% | 31-40% | 41-50% | 51-60% | 61-70% | 71-80% | 81-90% | 91-100%

This work was previously published in the Journal of Database Management, Volume 22, Issue 3, edited by Keng Siau, pp. 24-45, copyright 2011 by IGI Publishing (an imprint of IGI Global).

Chapter 12
A Systematic Literature Review on the Quality of UML Models

Marcela Genero
University of Castilla-La Mancha, Spain

H. James Nelson
Southern Illinois University, USA

Ana M. Fernández-Saez
University of Castilla-La Mancha, Spain

Geert Poels
Faculty of Economics & Business Administration, Ghent University, Belgium

Mario Piattini
University of Castilla-La Mancha, Spain

ABSTRACT

The quality of conceptual models directly affects the quality of the understanding of the application domain and the quality of the final software products that are ultimately based on them. This paper describes a systematic literature review (SLR) of peer-reviewed conference and journal articles published from 1997 through 2009 on the quality of conceptual models written in UML, undertaken to understand the state-of-the-art, and then identify any gaps in current research. Six digital libraries were searched, and 266 papers dealing specifically with the quality of UML models were identified and classified into five dimensions: type of model quality, type of evidence, type of research result, type of diagram, and research goal. The results indicate that most research focuses on semantic quality, with relatively little on semantic completeness; as such, this research examines new modeling methods vs. quality frameworks and metrics, as well as quality assurance vs. understanding quality issues. The results also indicate that more empirical research is needed to develop a theoretical understanding of conceptual model quality. The classification scheme developed in this paper can serve as a guide for both researchers and practitioners.

DOI: 10.4018/978-1-4666-2044-5.ch012

INTRODUCTION

Software is becoming increasingly complex. So complex, in fact, that it is widely acknowledged that it is impossible to test every aspect of system software or application programs before release. One method of increasing understanding between the software developer and the customer, of deepening the understanding of how software works, and ultimately of reducing the complexity of software, is through the use of models (Thomas, 2004). Over the years, we have come to understand that modeling offers benefits to different stakeholders in software projects (Selic, 2003). In the very early stages of a project, models aid in understanding and communicating requirements. During development, architecture and design models guide the implementation of the system. Finally, models are used for test-generation (Offutt & Abdurazik, 1999) and for easing maintenance activities (Dzidek, Arisholm, & Briand, 2008).

Software development itself is becoming more model-centric (Mohagheghi, Dehlen, & Neple, 2009). The OMG Model Driven Architecture (OMG, 2003) and the recent growth of the Model-Driven Development (MDD) software engineering paradigm (Atkinson & Kühne, 2003) emphasizes the role of modeling in the development of software systems. MDD treats software development as a set of transformations between successive models from requirements to analysis, to design, to implementation, and to deployment (Thomas, 2004). MDD's defining characteristic is that software development's primary focus and products are models rather than computer programs.

The dominant question is no longer "Should we do modeling?" but "*How* should we do modeling?" This new focus on the modeling process, rather than on the software product resulting from the development activities, puts model quality in the forefront. There has been increasing interest, both in industry and academia, on methods and techniques for quality assessment, assurance, and improvement of models in software development and maintenance (Mohagheghi, Dehlen, & Neple, 2009). While there has been a great deal of research on software quality, there has been relatively little work on the quality of models, and the concept of model quality is poorly understood. Existing knowledge on software quality has limited applicability to model quality. Models have very different characteristics than source code: models have multiple views, may be used informally and casually rather than formally and with precision, can be used throughout all phases of the project, and so on.

In an effort to bring together the wide variety of modeling methods and forms, the *Unified Modeling Language* (UML) emerged in the 1990s as a standard modeling language for a wide spectrum of application domains (Rumbaugh, Booch, & Jacobson, 1998). This standardization has driven the advancement of modeling methods and tools and has enabled academics and practitioners alike to improve on the core structure of UML and engage in a healthy debate about the use, advancement, and basic beliefs about the modeling process. However, modeling research has tended to be more about improving UML to deal with special modeling cases than with improving model quality (Dobing & Parsons, 2006; Grossman, Aronson, & McCarthy, 2005).

In order to advance the field of conceptual modelling quality research, it is useful to explore the history of the field and to determine its current state of the art by locating, evaluating, and interpreting relevant research to date that is related to model quality with a focus on UML. This paper presents a systematic literature review (SLR) of papers dealing with the quality of UML models. A proper systematic literature review follows a rigorous and systematic approach, in particular that described by Brereton, Kitchenham, Budgen, Turner, and Khalil (2007), Kitchenham (2004), and Kitchenham and Charters (2007).

Six digital libraries containing thousands of academic research papers were searched, producing 266 papers dealing exclusively with UML model quality. These papers were classified in five dimensions (see Table 3): quality type, type of evidence, research results, type of UML diagram, and research goals. These dimensions were chosen on the basis of previous research on model quality (though not necessarily restricted to UML) and conceptual frameworks that help define the concept of model quality. These dimensions are also useful to position new research activities appropriately, and the classified library of UML model quality research papers can serve as a valuable resource both for researchers and for practitioners.

An analysis of the papers shows the progress made in advancing UML model quality and identifies where gaps exist that could be areas for further investigation. The results indicate that there is no clear view of the real state of the field, although quality of models used in software development is a "hot topic" that needs further investigation (Wand & Weber, 2002). Quality assurance techniques for software, such as testing, inspections, analysis, and measurement, are well established, but their application in the domain of UML models and MDD is still in an embryonic phase. However, starting in the year 2002 and continuing to the present, the topic has been well represented in international conferences such as ER (International Conference on Conceptual Modeling) and MODELS (International Conference on Model Driven Engineering Languages and Systems) and in various associated workshops, such as QiM (Quality in Modeling), MoDEVA (Model Validation), IWCMQ (International Workshop on Conceptual Modelling Quality), and QoIS (Quality of Information Systems).

The remainder of the paper is structured as follows. The next section presents a brief discussion of related work. This is followed by the SLR outline, a description of the activities of the SLR process, and a discussion of the results and their implications. The paper concludes with an analysis of the threats to validity of the results, the lessons learned with respect to performing the SLR, and finally a discussion of future research possibilities.

RELATED WORK

In related work, Moody (2005) performed a review of research on conceptual model quality using two literature search engines: Ingenta and Proquest. The objective of this review was to investigate the possible ways of structuring, developing, and empirically validating conceptual model quality frameworks. Moody's review identified forty approaches and considered the following issues: level of generality, scope, origin, and empirical validation. The study described some initial efforts towards developing a common standard for data model quality which may provide a model for future standardisation efforts.

Genero, Piattini, and Calero (2005a) performed an exploratory review of measures for UML class diagrams. This paper described the goal of each measure, indicating whether it has any theoretical or empirical validation, and indicated if there were any tools that support the measure's use. A total of nine metrics sets for UML class diagrams were identified. Some were defined specifically for UML class diagrams, while others were originally defined for measuring specific types of Object-Oriented design models, but could be tailored for use with UML class diagrams. The study revealed that even though a plethora of metrics exists for measuring different properties of UML class diagrams (such as size, cohesion, complexity, coupling, etc.) empirical evidence of their utility in practice is scarce. Moreover, the theoretical validation (i.e., the test that the metrics really measure the attribute they purport to measure following principles of Measurement Theory) was neglected in most of the proposals.

Pretorius and Budgen (2008) reviewed 33 papers published between 2001 and 2008 reporting empirical evidence on the use of UML models and forms. Using only the abstracts, they found that comprehension and metrics were the major topics for experimentation. The authors concluded that model quality and adoption experiences deserve further study.

Mohagheghi, Dehlen, and Neple (2009) reviewed 40 primary studies (including books, a PhD thesis, journals, workshops, proceedings, and published online) published between 2000 and 2007 and focused on model quality within the domain of model-driven and model-based software development. Their research examined quality goals, quality practices, and the types of models and modeling approaches discussed in the literature. The authors identified six quality goals in their literature: correctness, completeness, consistency, comprehensibility by humans and tools, confinement, and changeability. They also identified six quality practices, and that most models discussed were UML Models.

Lucas, Molina, and Toval (2009) reviewed 44 papers published between 2001 and 2007, focusing only on consistency within UML models. That is, across two or more UML diagrams that makes up a complete UML model. Their conclusion is that UML model consistency is a highly active and promising line of research, but that there are some important gaps in the literature. The authors address these gaps by introducing a formal consistency management language.

This SLR differs from the previous literature reviews presented above in three ways: a different goal, a more extensive and a more systematic review, and a more refined classification. The goal of our review is to identify "what has been done" and "what needs to be addressed in the future" in the context of quality of UML models. This contrasts with previous SLRs that have a rather narrow focus, such as measures for UML class diagrams, quality frameworks, empirical research, MDA, and consistency. The reviews presented in Genero, Piattini, and Calero (2005a) and Moody (2005) do not describe a systematic selection process, nor do they state clear criteria for inclusion or exclusion. Pretorius and Budgen (2008) present a systematic review but on a fairly small scale with only 33 papers considered. The review of Mohagheghi, Dehlen, and Neple (2009) used fewer digital resources, had only 40 primary studies, and the review process was not strictly systematic.

Our extensive literature review is based on a systematic search of six digital libraries, following the procedure described in Brereton, Kitchenham, Budgen, Turner, and Khalil (2007), Kitchenham (2004), and Kitchenham and Charters (2007) producing 266 papers for analysis. This study uses a more refined classification system that classifies each paper along five dimensions, producing a finer-grained classification. It identifies additional analysis possibilities, and may provide deeper insights into UML model quality and modelling quality in general.

SLR OUTLINE

The SLR research method consists of three activities: planning, execution, and reporting (Kitchenham & Charters, 2007). Each of these activities is divided into several steps. Planning includes dividing the workload amongst the researchers, determining how the researchers will interact and conduct the review, and developing the review protocol itself. The execution activity includes data retrieval, study selection, data extraction, and data synthesis. Finally, the reporting activity presents and interprets the results. The next sections contain a detailed description of the SLR activities.

PLANNING THE REVIEW

The planning activity includes defining the research questions and developing the search strategy, the inclusion/exclusion criteria, and the data extraction form.

Five research questions were proposed, based on previous research by Piattini, Genero, Poels, and Nelson (2005). The underlying motivation for the research questions was the goal of determining the amount of coverage of the UML model quality research area and these questions guided the design of the review process (Jørgensen & Shepperd, 2007). The research questions and the motivation for each are described in Table 1.

Although there are many collections of research papers available to choose from in both electronic and physical (paper) form, we limited the search to only electronic collections and considered only peer-reviewed journals, conferences, and workshops. While there is a great deal of additional conceptual modeling literature in books, working papers, web pages, magazine articles, white papers, and trade journals, the content of these sources has not been subjected to peer review and so their quality cannot be reliably determined.

We chose electronic collections that contain a wide variety of computer science and management information systems journals: SCOPUS database, Science@Direct with the subject Computer Science, Wiley InterScience with the subject of Computer Science, IEEE Digital Library, ACM Digital Library, and SPRINGER database. The search was restricted to only the first level. That is, the references of the selected papers were not searched to obtain more papers on the subject. There are two reasons for this: relevant papers would have been found in the initial search process, and the references contain only the author and title, which may or may not indicate UML quality-related research.

The search terms used were constructed using the following steps (Brereton, Kitchenham, Budgen, Turner, & Khalil, 2007):

- Define the major terms
- Identify alternative spellings, synonyms or related terms for major terms.
- Check the keywords in any relevant papers we already had.
- Use the Boolean OR to incorporate alternative spellings, synonyms or related terms.
- Use the Boolean AND to link the major terms

The major search terms are "UML" and "Quality". The alternative spellings, synonyms or terms related to the major terms are shown in Table 2.

Whenever a database or digital library did not allow the use of complex Boolean search strings, we designed different search strings for each of these databases and manually manipulated the searches in order to obtain the same results that had been achieved using the original search string. The search was performed on the full text of the article, except in those libraries that did not provide

Table 1. Research questions

Research questions	Main motivation
RQ1 Which types of UML model quality are investigated by researchers?	To discover the different types of model quality and specific quality characteristics that have been addressed by research.
RQ2 Which research methods are used in research on UML model quality?	To determine if the field has generally more applied or more basic research as well as to identify opportunities for future research.
RQ3 What is the nature of the research results on UML model quality?	To find the kind of outputs produced by UML model quality research and to assess the state of the field.
RQ4 What are the UML model quality research goals?	To determine where most of the research interest lies and which areas may be under-studied: exploring basic concepts, gathering knowledge of current practices, or aiming at advancing practice through design science.
RQ5 Which types of UML diagrams are the focus of the research on UML model quality?	To discover the UML diagrams that research has focused upon, to reveal the parts of UML that are considered more important than others, as well as to identify opportunities for further research.

Table 2. Search string

Major terms	Alternative terms
Quality	quality OR consistency OR maintainability OR understandability OR completeness OR comprehension OR comprehensibility OR testability OR defect OR effectiveness OR complexity OR readability OR metric OR measure OR efficiency OR validation OR verification OR layout
UML	UML OR Unified Modeling Language
Representation	Representation OR diagram OR model

Table 3. Summary of the classification scheme

Dimensions	Categories
Type of Quality	Syntactic quality: correctness Semantic quality: consistency, completeness, correctness Pragmatic quality: maintainability, analyzability, understandability, testability, functionality, executability, reusability, complexity, dependability.
Type of Evidence/ Research Method	Argumentation, example, experiment, case study, survey
Type of Research Result	Quality model, notation, method (technique, methodology, process, approach, or strategy).or algorithm, tool, metric, confirmation of knowledge, pattern, view, checklist (guideline, rule or modeling convention)
Research goal	Understanding, measuring, evaluating, assuring, improving
Type of Diagram	Structure diagrams, behavior diagrams interaction diagrams

this capability. In that case, the search was restricted to the title and the abstract.

Papers were included that dealt with UML and the tangible results of the modelling process (the UML diagram), were written in English, and were published from 1997 through 2009. As UML was adopted by the Object Management Group in 1997 (OMG, 1997) it made no sense to search for papers before 1997. The final search was performed in March 2010, to allow as much time as possible for papers to appear in the digital libraries.

The following papers were excluded: pure discussion and opinion papers, studies available only in the form of abstracts or PowerPoint presentations, duplicates (for example, the same paper included in more than one database or in more than one journal), research focusing on issues other than UML model quality, or where quality is mentioned only as a general introductory term in the paper's abstract, an approach or other type of proposal related to quality not being amongst the paper's contributions. Papers were also excluded if they dealt with complexity of UML as a language (for example, how to make the UML language itself simpler) rather than on the quality of the models produced by UML, and finally if the paper was a summary of a workshop presentation.

The extracted papers were tracked on a two-part form. The first part contained the general "demographic" information, such as title, authors, publication, year, and so on. The second part contained the multidimensional classification scheme. A set of five dimensions was used to classify the research, based on the research questions described above which, in turn, are based on work by Piattini, Genero, Poels, and Nelson (2005). This work has its foundations in Krogstie (1998), Lindland, Sindre, and Sølvberg (1994), and Nelson, Monarchi, and Nelson (2001). These dimensions are shown in Table 3 and a detailed description of the classification scheme is presented in the Appendix.

A similar classification scheme to the one used in this paper was employed in Poels, Nelson, Genero, and Piattini (2003) to categorize the papers published in the first edition of The International Workshop on Quality in Conceptual Modeling (IWQCM) held within the ER conference, and in Piattini, Genero, Poels, and Nelson (2005) to classify the chapters of the book "Quality of Software Conceptual Models" (Genero, Piattini, & Calero, 2005b). Matulevicius and Heymans (2007) and Matulevicius, Heymans, and Sindre (2006) used a similar classification scheme to evaluate modeling languages for contextualizing their research on conceptual modeling quality.

CONDUCTING THE REVIEW

The review process and timeline is shown in Table 4. Planning for the SLR began in July 2007 and papers dealing with UML model quality published between 1997 and the extraction date were retrieved in September 2007. Over 1500 papers were extracted, duplicates were removed, and data was analyzed over the next ten months. The title and abstract of each of the papers was examined and all papers not dealing with UML model quality research were excluded, reducing the total to

Table 4. Chronology of the development of activities in the SLR

Time	Planning	Conducting	Reporting	Outcomes
First phase				
July 2007	Protocol development			Review protocol.
Sept 2007		Data retrieval (until Sept 2007)		Form with the general information of the papers (1500 papers).
		Study selection upon abstracts and titles		Form with the general information of the selected papers (483 papers).
Mar 2008		Retrieval of the files of the primary studies		Repository of papers (483 papers).
Apr 2008		Remove duplicates		Form with the general information of the papers (399 papers).
Jul 2008	Protocol improvement	Pilot data extraction		Data extraction form with the classification scheme refined.
Aug 2008		Study selection and Data extraction upon the full text		Data extraction form completed with the classification of 215 primary studies.
Feb 2009		Resolution of doubts in classification of primary studies in group		Revisited data extraction form with classification of the primary studies **(193).**
Mar 2009		Data synthesis		
July 2009			Report the results of the SLR	Pilot report
Second phase				
Mar 2010		Update of searches Data retrieval (until Dec 2009)		Form with the general information of the papers (979).
Mar 2010		Study selection upon abstracts and titles		Form with the general information of the selected papers (140).
		Retrieval of the files of the primary studies		Repository of papers 140).
		Remove duplicates		Form with the general information of the papers (103).
Feb 2010		Study selection and Data extraction upon the full text		Data extraction form completed with the classification of primary studies (103)
Mar 2010		Resolution of doubts in classification of primary studies in group		Revisited data extraction with the classification of primary studies **(73)**
Apr 2010		Data synthesis		
Jul 2010			Report the results of the SLR	Final report

483. 144 duplicate papers were discarded, and the inclusion and exclusion criteria were then applied by reading the full text of each of the 339 remaining papers. Amongst the excluded papers were a number related to functional size measurement based on UML diagrams, as functional size is not related to model quality. Based on this analysis, the extraction and classification schemes were refined, primary studies were identified, follow-up studies were eliminated, and final classifications were made. The final 193 papers were then analyzed and the results were interpreted.

However, by this point, considerable time had passed, so a second phase was planned and executed. This phase began in March 2010 and included all UML quality papers published in 2008 and 2009. 979 additional papers were extracted, analyzed, and classified using the same process as described in the first phase. 74 papers remained after the second phase. Finally, the results of the two selection phases were joined, resulting in 266 papers as primary studies to be analyzed in this SLR. The complete list of papers is available at http://alarcos.esi.uclm.es/SLR-QualityUMLModels

DATA SYNTHESIS AND RESULTS

For the purpose of the review analysis, i.e., addressing the research questions listed in Table 1, the 266 primary studies selected were classified according to the dimensions detailed in the classification scheme presented in Table 3. Based on this classification, the analysis reported in this section was aimed at finding answers to the research questions.

Model Quality (RQ1)

There are three main quality types: syntactic, semantic, and pragmatic (Lindland, Sindre, & Sølvberg, 1994; Unhelkar, 2005) with several subtypes defined under each type. The results of classifying the 266 research papers are shown in Table 5. Most of the research effort has concentrated on semantic quality (50.75%) followed by pragmatic quality (38.72%) with relatively little research effort on syntactic quality (5.64%). There are a few papers that cross quality types. Six papers deal with both syntactic and semantic quality, six deal with both semantic and pragmatic quality, and one addresses all three quality types.

Table 5. Percentage of papers addressing different quality types

Type of quality	Number	Percent
Syntactic	15	5.64%
Semantic	135	50.75%
Pragmatic	103	38.72%
Syntactic + Semantic	6	2.26%
Syntactic + Pragmatic	0	0.00%
Semantic + Pragmatic	6	2.26%
Syntactic + Semantic + Pragmatic	1	0.38%
Total	**266**	**100.00%**

Each quality type has associated with it a number of subtypes, described in Table 3. The count of research papers in each subtype is shown in Table 6. As with quality type, a paper may address more than one subtype, so the numbers will add up to more than 266, the actual number of papers in the study.

Semantic consistency is by far the semantic quality subtype that has been researched most. The papers that fall within this category investigate primarily issues of consistency that may arise when models are constructed using different types of UML diagrams. Next in line comes model correctness, whereas only 14 papers that deal with semantic quality address model completeness.

For pragmatic quality, understandability is a clear leader with maintainability coming in at a distant second place. Apart from complexity (11 papers), the other pragmatic quality subtypes are addressed in only a very few papers.

Table 6. Number of papers per quality characteristics

Syntactic	Number	
Correctness	21	100.00%
	Total	**21**
Semantic	**Number**	
Consistency	113	62.09%
Completeness	14	7.69%
Correctness	55	30.22%
	Total	**182**
Pragmatic	**Number**	
Maintainability	24	19.35%
Analyzability	1	0.81%
Understandability	78	62.90%
Testability	2	2.61%
Functionality	4	3.23%
Executability	2	1.61%
Reusability	1	0.81%
Complexity	11	8.87%
Dependability	1	0.81%
	Total	**124**

Research Method (RQ2)

There are many research methods to choose from when performing investigations into model quality. The results of the research method classification effort are shown in Table 7. Note that the total of the numbers (278) is higher than the total number of papers in the SLR (266). This is due to some papers falling into more than one category. For example, one paper is both a survey and a case study. In our classification, research methods can be empirical or non-empirical. The former category contains 29.86% of the papers and the latter 70.14%. The non-empirical category includes papers that use models only to illustrate the proposals made (e.g., methods, metrics, or guidelines).

Although more than half of the papers in the SLR (60.79%) used examples to clarify the proposal made, there were relatively few empirical research papers, with experiments being the empirical research method that was used most often. Survey and literature review methods are (almost) absent in the selected papers. Breaking this down further (not shown in Table 7), 71.67% of these papers focused on the impact on model understandability of different modeling methods or styles. Experimental research tended to be carried out with Computer Science Students (72.22%) who are in their third, fourth or fifth year. Less frequent are subjects that are academic staff members (5.56%) or practitioners (22.22%). In addition, the use of students as subjects, as well as "toy" problems makes generalizability a serious concern. Combining this research question with model quality type (RQ1), we see that 55 of these

Table 7. Number of papers per type of evidence

Research method	Number	Percent	Syntactic		Semantic		Pragmatic	
Empirical	**83**	**29.86%**	**2**	**9.09%**	**19**	**12.84%**	**62**	**57.41%**
Experiment	66	23.74%	2	9.09%	9	6.08%	55	50.93%
Case study	15	5.40%	0	0.00%	9	6.08%	6	5.56%
Survey	2	0.72%	0	0.00%	1	0.68%	1	0.93%
Non empirical	**195**	**70.14%**	**20**	**90.91%**	**129**	**87.16%**	**46**	**42.59%**
Speculation	26	9.35%	2	9.09%	19	12.84%	5	4.63%
Example	169	60.79%	18	81.82%	110	74.32%	41	37.96%
Literature Review	0	0.00%	0	0.00%	0	0.00%	0	0.00%
Total	**278**		**22**		**148**		**108**	

papers used controlled experiments to test hypotheses on pragmatic quality.

Most of the papers in the SLR, by far, were non-empirical research on semantic quality. The most common of these was research that proposed model quality related modifications or that extended UML and demonstrated the problem and/or the utility of the research using one or more examples. Of the research on semantic quality that used examples, 70.27% of the papers focus on consistency issues.

Research Results (RQ3)

The papers were also classified by the kind of research output that was produced. The results of the SLR are shown in Table 8. Again, the total number is greater than 266, as some papers fall into more than one category. By far the most common research output is a new method. These methods can be quite varied, as we find methods for model validation, verification, transformation, and so on. The second most common paper, but far behind methods, is that which produces new knowledge. These are largely papers that employ empirical research methods (RQ2), as the testing of hypotheses can be seen as knowledge production.

Table 8. Number of papers per type of research result

Type of Result	Number	Percent
Formal semantics	3	1.01%
Framework	3	1.01%
Knowledge	55	18.46%
Method	119	39.93%
Metrics	28	9.40%
Notation	10	3.36%
Pattern	4	1.34%
Quality model	1	0.34%
Tool	50	16.78%
View	3	1.01%
Checklist, rules, modeling conventions, and guidelines	22	7.38%
Total	**298**	**100.0%**

Closely following Knowledge and in third place are papers that propose new tools: tools for automatic consistency checking between diagrams within a UML model, model-based checking tools, visualization tools, and so on. Metrics papers present a variety of metrics and techniques for measuring different model characteristics, such as size, complexity, consistency, and so on. The fifth most common type of paper presents rules, modeling conventions, guidelines and checklists. Other types of research results are scarce.

If we focus on the five categories noted, we can see that the proposal of methods, tools, and rules relates mostly to semantic quality, whereas the knowledge and metrics research output relates mostly to the pragmatic quality. For the knowledge-producing studies, this result is consistent with the finding that these employ mostly experiments which focus on pragmatic quality and specifically on understandability.

Of the methods that deal with semantic quality issues, we can see that the majority are approaches to improve the consistency of UML diagrams. The same observation holds for tools that are proposed for semantic quality issues. Most of them focus on consistency, although a substantial percentage of the tools proposed in the papers relate to semantic correctness. In addition, most of the rules, modeling conventions, guidelines and checklists are related to semantic quality, especially to consistency.

Most pragmatic quality metrics papers propose metrics for assessing or predicting the maintainability of UML models, while the next largest percentage focuses on measuring understandability. These two categories are closely related; before a diagram can be modified, it must be understood. It is noteworthy that 76% of the papers in these two categories include a validation of the metrics through one or more controlled experiments or a case study in addition to the metrics definition (see Table 9).

Table 9. Crossing type of result with type of quality and quality characteristic

	Method	Knowledge	Tool	Metrics	Rule, modeling convention, checklist, guideline
Pragmatic	**18.25%**	**76.06%**	**22.03%**	**91.18%**	**24.0%**
Dependability	0.73%	0.00%	0.00%	0.00%	0.0%
Executability	0.73%	0.00%	3.39%	0.00%	0.0%
Functionality	1.46%	2.82%	0.00%	2.94%	0.0%
Maintainability	3.65%	9.86%	3.39%	26.47%	0.0%
Reusability	0.73%	0.00%	0.00%	0.00%	0.0%
Complexity	0.00%	1.41%	1.69%	23.53%	4.0%
Testability	0.00%	0.00%	1.69%	2.94%	0.0%
Understandability	10.95%	60.56%	11.86%	35.29%	20.0%
Analyzability	0.00%	1.41%	0.00%	0.00%	0.0%
Semantic	**74.45%**	**19.72%**	**62.71%**	**8.82%**	**72.0%**
Completeness	4.38%	7.04%	3.39%	0.00%	8.0%
Consistency	55.47%	9.86%	38.98%	5.88%	48.0%
Correctness	14.60%	2.82%	20.34%	2.94%	16.0%
Syntactic	**7.30%**	**4.23%**	**15.25%**	**0.00%**	**4.0%**
Correctness	7.30%	4.23%	15.25%	0.00%	4.0%

Research Goals (RQ4)

The purpose of investigating the goals of the research papers is to determine where UML model quality research interest lies and to determine which areas may be under-studied. As shown in Table 10, there are 121 papers (which represents 45.49% of the total) related to assuring quality, 85 papers (31.95%) are related to evaluating quality, and 38 papers (14.29%) to measuring quality. The other two categories, improving and understanding, together account for less than 9% of the papers.

Table 10. Results of papers per research goal

Research Goal	Number	Percent
Improving	15	5.64%
Assuring	122	45.49%
Measuring	38	14.29%
Evaluating	85	31.95%
Understanding	7	2.63%
Total	**266**	**100.0%**

Research on applied areas of UML quality assurance techniques and the evaluation of UML quality account for more than three-quarters (77.44%) of the papers published. This is not surprising, as quality assurance is a critically important topic. The other basic research topics are important for advancing the state of the art of UML model quality but they are much less well-represented in the survey. This can mean that a given topic is under-studied or that it has yet to find acceptance with journals, or it may be that both of these states are the case for the topic in question.

UML Diagram (RQ5)

While over 65% of the papers in the survey focused on the quality of a specific kind of UML diagram, nearly 30% examined UML diagrams as a whole. The original 1997 version of UML had nine differ-

Table 11. Number of papers per type of diagram

Type of diagram	Number	Percent
Class diagrams	83	25.30%
Sequence diagrams	34	10.37%
Activity diagrams	15	4.57%
Use case diagrams	21	6.40%
Statechart diagrams	55	16.77%
Collaboration diagrams	8	2.44%
Component diagrams	3	0.91%
Object diagrams	2	0.61%
Package diagrams	3	0.91%
Deployment diagrams	1	0.30%
No specific diagram	103	31.40%
UML 2.0 new diagrams	0	0.0%
Total	**328**	**100.0%**

ent kinds of diagrams that allowed systems to be modelled from many different viewpoints. UML 2.0 introduced four new diagrams, making a total of 13 diagrams. One of these, the communication diagram, was renamed from the original UML collaboration diagram. We use the name of the original version, as it is more widespread.

The type of diagram that has been studied most is the class diagram, followed by statechart diagrams and sequence diagrams. Research on UML model quality has placed much less attention on use case diagrams and activity diagrams. Very few papers found take as their focus collaboration, component or package diagrams. This is an interesting result, as class diagrams, state-transition diagrams, and sequence diagrams have had a long history before the introduction of UML. Use case diagrams, for example, are relatively newer. One would expect that older diagrams would have less research and that more research would be required on understanding and on improving the quality of the newer diagrams. The literature review found no references to any of the four new diagrams of UML 2.0. These results can be seen in Table 11.

Additional Results

Beyond the investigation into the state of research into the quality of UML models, it is useful for producers and consumers of research to be aware of the various outlets for the research and the growth of the field.

As shown in Figure 1, there is a clear progression in the number of publications that appear each year. This figure may show that interest in this subject has been growing over time, reaching its highest point in 2007.

When analysing the types of publication, we found that 63.53% of the papers (169 papers) were published in conferences, 22.93% in journals (61 papers) and 13.53% in workshops (36 papers). Without a doubt, the quality of UML models has been considered a "hot topic", given the number of publications dealing with it.

Table 12 shows the publications with the largest number of papers on UML model quality. The first three, the International Conference on Model Driven Engineering Languages and Systems (MODELS), which formerly was called UML, Electronic Notes in Theoretical Computer Science, and Information and Software Technology have 16, 15 and 9 papers each, together representing 15.04% of the total. The next one, the International Conference on Software Engineering (ICSE), has 8 papers, representing 3.01% of the total.

DISCUSSION

This systematic literature review discovered 266 papers in peer-reviewed journals, conferences, and workshops and classified them into five dimensions represented by the five research questions presented above. In this section we discuss the results and draw implications from the classifications.

Research Question 1 asked, "Which types of UML model quality have been investigated by researchers?" The results show a clear ordering

Figure 1. Number of papers per year

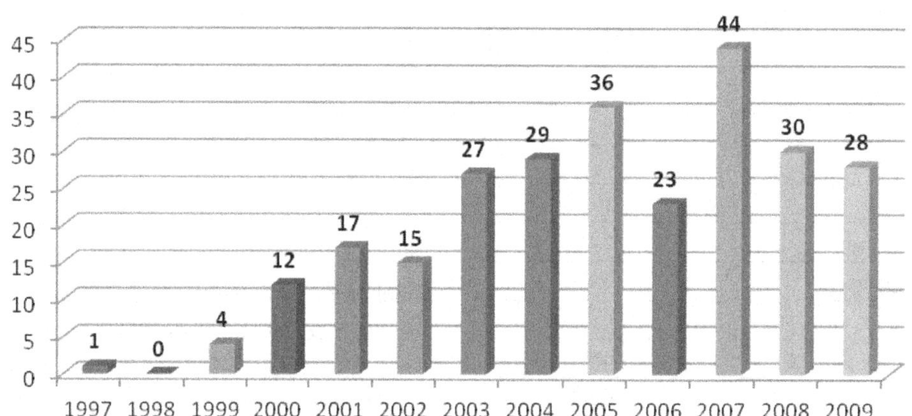

Table 12. Number of papers per type of publication

Publication	Number	Percent
International Conference on Model Driven Engineering Languages and Systems (MODELS, formerly UML)	16	6.04%
Electronic Notes in Theoretical Computer Science	15	5.66%
Information and Software Technology	9	3.40%
International Conference on Software Engineering (ICSE)	8	3.02%
ER Workshops	7	2.64%
ACM SIGSOFT Software Engineering Notes	6	2.26%
Journal of Systems and Software	6	2.26%
ACM symposium on software visualization (SoftVis)	5	1.89%
Empirical Software Engineering	5	1.89%
International Conference on Automated software engineering (ASE)	5	1.89%
Asia-Pacific Software Engineering Conference (APSEC)	4	1.51%
Australian Software Engineering Conference (ASWEC)	4	1.51%

which may indicate the relative importance that researchers attach to each quality type. The order is: (1) semantic quality (i.e., correctness and completeness of the model with regard to the system to be modelled), (2) pragmatic quality (i.e., aspects relating to the use of the model), and (3) syntactic quality (i.e., syntactical correctness of the model). Whereas it is difficult to explain why semantic quality has received more research attention than pragmatic quality, except perhaps for the focus on model consistency found in the papers (113 out of 266 papers), which we try to interpret below, less than ten percent of the papers address syntactic quality, but this result is not surprising. That is because most, if not all, modelling tools enforce syntactic correctness automatically, so that if a particular element is not syntactically correct, the tool will not allow it to be placed.

Semantic quality research has mainly focused upon consistency issues. A plausible reason for the attention paid to consistency issues is that UML offers 13 types of diagrams, some of which have overlapping semantics and purpose. Moreover, little guidance is offered on when to use these different diagram types. It seems logical that researchers have investigated ways to cope with possible inconsistencies that may arise when multiple diagrams (of different types) are used to model the same system, from different (though sometimes related, even overlapping) points of view. Research on semantic quality has paid less attention to issues of semantic correctness (i.e., is the system correctly modelled?), and especially semantic completeness (i.e., are all relevant elements of the system modelled?). This result may be due to the considerable difficulty of proposing new approaches to ensuring that a model is complete and correct when compared against a domain, raw descriptions of system requirements or process structure and flows, and so on. While ensuring inter-diagram consistency is an important topic for UML model quality research, it can be argued that without proper attention for model completeness and correctness, consistency will not help in building a "good" information system.

With respect to pragmatic quality, research has emphasized the understandability, and, to a lesser extent, the maintainability of UML models. There are several possible reasons for this. Firstly, these quality characteristics can relatively easily be operationalized in research, compared to other pragmatic quality characteristics like functionality, complexity, and reusability; for example through comprehension questions and modification tasks. Secondly, the research on pragmatic quality issues has focused mainly on the use of UML models to facilitate the communication between stakeholders. Models are thus seen as instruments carrying information over from one party to another (which means that they need to be easy to understand). This observation can be caused 'by construction', as originally pragmatic quality was defined by Lindland, Sindre, and Sølvberg (1994) and Unhelkar (2005) as being "the extent to which a model is understood." Once understood, modifications can be made, so the next logical step is to investigate the maintainability of models.

Research Question 2 asked, "Which research methods are used in research on UML model quality?" The finding that only 29.86% of the papers back up their claims with an empirical study is remarkable. Most of the other papers do employ one or more examples to illustrate the problem researched and the solution proposed, but these examples cannot be seen as evaluations of the proposals made. A plausible reason for the low presence of empirical studies is that the SLR also looked at conference and workshop papers, for which demands of completeness of the research are less stringent than with journal papers. It is common that in conference and workshop papers (which must often adhere to strict limits on length) only a problem statement is given, followed by the development of a solution, but that the empirical evaluation of the solution is mentioned as future work. Most of the papers that present an empirical evaluation are studies employing experiments. The use of other methods (surveys, literature review) is rare. Studies aimed at evaluating proposals made with regard to quality issues are an obvious opportunity for further research. An increasing number of such studies would also indicate that the field is maturing. Good case-study research is another opportunity, as yet seldom exploited by research on UML model quality.

Research Question 3 asked, "What is the nature of the research results on UML model quality?" Nearly half the reviewed papers propose a method related to some UML model quality issue or action, mostly with respect to semantic quality, and model consistency in particular. Other typical research outputs include (in decreasing order of frequency) tools, metrics, and what could be described as instruments providing guidance to modelers (rules, modeling conventions, guidelines and checklists). Tools and instruments also largely aim at semantic quality, while most metrics measure pragmatic quality characteristics related to maintainability and understandability. A minority of papers, less than one out of five, had as a goal to increase or confirm existing knowledge on UML model quality. These papers mostly report on experiments that evaluate the effectiveness or efficiency of research outputs related to pragmatic quality, in particular understandability, or they aim at validating metrics and finding relationships between UML model quality variables.

We believe that these results are an indication that research on UML model quality is primarily conducted in a design science tradition, focusing on the development of new artifacts that advance the state-of-the-practice and aim at providing solutions to real-world problems experienced by modelers (e.g., the problem of how to ensure the consistency between different UML diagrams that compose a model). The lack of evaluation studies for these artifacts could be a consequence of the decision to also include conference and workshop papers in the SLR, as noted before. Nevertheless, if such evaluation is not present (i.e., not taken up in the complete research publications in journal papers), then this would indicate an incomplete design science research cycle, which could be interpreted as an indication of immaturity. The lack of 'knowledge gathering' studies may then indicate a premature focus on providing instruments to deal with quality issues, without a profound knowledge of the nature of UML model quality and its influencing factors.

Research Question 4 asked, "What are the UML model quality research goals?" The most important goal is quality assurance, which examines how to ensure that the modelling process actually produces a quality model. This is followed closely by quality evaluation, which compares quality measurements against real world experiences. This is most likely related to a tendency to propose new methods, tools and other quality instruments (RQ3) via non-empirical research methods (RQ2).

Only three percent of the papers had as a goal increasing knowledge about model quality. This follows the results of RQ3 where the research results also had relatively few papers regarding knowledge. The goal of understanding appears to be of little direct importance, though measuring and evaluating are important and may also help to acquire a better understanding.

Research Question 5 asked, "Which types of UML diagrams are the focus of the research on UML model quality?" Forty percent of the reviewed papers did not look at any UML diagram in particular, so the research presented in these papers is on a general level. If specific diagram types were targeted, these were then, in order of frequency, structure diagrams (almost exclusively class diagrams), behavior diagrams (mainly statechart diagrams) and interaction diagrams (mainly sequence diagrams). The types of diagram that were newly introduced in UML 2.0 have not been investigated yet from a quality perspective, and interaction diagrams (for example, collaboration diagrams) have received very little research attention.

These results reflect how frequent the various diagrams are used in practice, with one significant difference. Research indicates that the diagrams that are used most in modelling software systems are, in order of decreasing frequency: use case diagrams, class diagrams, sequence diagrams, and statechart diagrams (Dobing & Parsons, 2006; Erickson & Siau, 2007; Grossman, Aronson, & McCarthy, 2005). Erickson and Siau (2007) conclude that the most important UML diagrams are: class, use cases, sequence and statechart diagrams, and they should comprise a UML kernel. Significantly, the diagram that is used most in practice, the use case diagram, has received little attention from UML model quality research. A possible reason for this is that model quality research in general has mainly investigated structural diagrams or data models, and much less attention has been given to models that represent system behavior and interaction (Recker, Rosemann, & Krogstie, 2007).

Our results parallel the results of Moody (2005). Moody's review of forty papers identified twelve major theoretical and practical issues in existing research: proliferation of proposals, different levels of generality, lack of empirical testing, of adoption in practice, of agreement on concepts and terminology, of consistency with related fields and standards, of measurement, of evaluation procedures, of guidelines for improvement, of knowledge about practices, and a focus on static models and on product quality. Our results indicate that the issues identified by Moody for conceptual modelling quality research in general have applicability to UML quality research in particular.

THREATS TO VALIDITY

The main threats to the validity of a SLR are publication selection bias, inaccuracy in data extraction, and misclassification (Sjøberg et al., 2005). We acknowledge that it is impossible to achieve complete coverage of everything written on a topic. We used six digital sources, including journals, conferences and workshops which are relevant to software engineering. The scope of journals and conferences covered in this SLR is sufficiently wide to attain reasonable completeness in the field studied. We did not include additional papers such as grey literature (technical reports, books, etc.) as these tend to be secondary sources. Most grey literature either has its source in peer-reviewed papers or will become peer-reviewed papers, or both conditions may be true for a given piece of work. Some relevant papers may therefore have not been included, but our knowledge of the subject leads us to believe that there are not many such cases.

To help ensure an unbiased selection process, we defined research questions in advance, organized the selection of articles as a multistage process, involved five researchers in this process, and documented the reasons for inclusion/exclusion as suggested in Liu, Dehlinger, and Lutz (2007). As was discussed above, the decisions to select the papers to be included as primary studies in this SLR were made by multiple researchers and the process followed rigorous rules. A further challenge was that there is no keyword standard that we are aware of which distinguishes between different quality characteristics, or methods in empirical software engineering that could be used to extract quality characteristics and research methods in a consistent manner.

Moreover, article duplication is a potential threat to frequency counts and the statistics in this SLR. The structure of the database is designed to handle duplication, but one threat would be that of duplication going undetected. However, at least two people have read through all the relevant articles and have not detected any further duplicates.

The data was extracted from the papers by one researcher (the first author of the paper) and checked by the second author. When necessary, disagreements were resolved through discussion, involving the rest of authors. Data extraction and classification from prose is difficult at the outset; the lack of standard terminology and standards for reporting empirical studies and for defining quality characteristics in software engineering may have resulted in some inaccuracies in the data extraction and this may have resulted in a misclassification. However, we believe that the extraction and selection process was rigorous and that it followed the guidelines provided in Brereton, Kitchenham, Budgen, Turner, and Khalil (2007), Kitchenham (2004), and Kitchenham and Charters (2007). We also judge that the use of multiple experts performing the classification reduced the risk of misclassification. The classification scheme that we provide in this paper may be used as a starting point by future researchers.

LESSONS LEARNED WITH RESPECT TO PERFORMING THE SLR

It is usually not possible to judge the relevance of a study from a review of the abstract alone. The standard of IT and software engineering abstracts is too poor to rely on when selecting primary studies; it is therefore necessary to review the full text. When used properly, structured abstracts are very useful for improving the quality and usefulness of the abstract. Structured abstracts must contain the following sections: 1) Context (the importance and relevance of the research), 2) Objectives (the main objectives pursued), 3) Methods (the research method followed and the proposal provided to attain the objectives), and 4) Results (the main findings and conclusions obtained).

The search string is extremely long. Due to the limitation of the search engines, we observed that such a long string could not be searched directly. It was therefore necessary to tailor the search string to each digital library by splitting the original and combining the results manually. Current search engines are not designed to support systematic literature reviews. Unlike medical researchers, software engineering researchers need to perform resource-dependent searches (Brereton, Kitchenham, Budgen, Turner, & Khalil, 2007).

CONCLUSION AND FUTURE WORK

This paper reviews UML model quality papers published in journals, conferences and workshops found in six digital libraries and tries to support other researchers and practitioners through a library of papers on UML model quality which have been classified according to the following dimensions: type of quality, context of study, type of diagram, type of research result, research method and research goal, based on Piattini, Genero, Poels, and Nelson (2005). The SLR was carried out following the guidelines in Brereton, Kitchenham, Budgen, Turner, and Khalil (2007), Kitchenham (2004), and Kitchenham and Charters (2007) making this study both rigorous and fair.

Only 29.86% of the proposals collected carried out some kind of empirical validation. This fact reveals the need for further validation, i.e., replications made by other researchers different from the ones that make the proposals. In addition, we encourage experimental material to be available for encouraging replication. The repository of models proposed in the context of the MiSE workshops will contribute to carrying out empirical studies, proving UML models taken from real projects (France, Bieman, & Cheng, 2007).

Based on our (to some extent subjective) interpretation of the review results, we have several recommendations. First of all, that much more effort be spent on empirical research into conceptual model quality in general and UML quality in particular. There is a proliferation of tools and extensions for UML, but little indication that these tools and extensions really improve the quality of UML models. A coordinated effort of empirical research, the use of meta-analysis for integrating experiments, and experimentation using diagrams from real-world projects is needed in order to build a solid body of knowledge. Secondly, more interaction is needed between academia and industry. Somewhat paralleling the lack of empirical evidence, academic research does seem to be "ivory tower" research, with little input from real-world problems and issues. Problems, diagrams, and projects need to inform research, and basic research needs to be able to be easily applied. Thirdly, UML model quality research seems to concentrate on three types of quality (syntactic, semantic, pragmatic), yet there is no consensus on the quality characteristics addressed nor on their definitions. Finally, the topic needs to mature, with many more peer-reviewed articles published in leading journals.

Conceptual modelling quality is an important topic, with academia and industry both recognizing that it is critical to "get the model right." If the model is not correct and complete, it will be very difficult for the software systems based on that model to be correct and complete as well. We hope that this paper can serve as a guide to the contributions from past research in the area, as well as being useful as a foundation for future research.

ACKNOWLEDGMENT

This research is part of the following projects: MEDUSAS (CDTI-MICINN and FEDER IDI-20090557), ORIGIN (CDTI-MICINN and FEDER IDI-2010043(1-5), PEGASO/MAGO (MICINN and FEDER, TIN2009-13718-C02-01), EECCOO (MICINN TRA2009_0074), MECCA (JCMM PII2I09-0075-8394) and IMPACTUM (JCCM PEII11-0330-4414).

REFERENCES

Atkinson, C., & Kühne, T. (2003). Model-driven development: A metamodeling foundation. *IEEE Software*, *20*(5), 36–41. doi:10.1109/MS.2003.1231149

Brereton, P., Kitchenham, B., Budgen, D., Turner, M., & Khalil, M. (2007). Lessons from applying the systematic literature review process within the software engineering domain. *Journal of Systems and Software*, *80*(4), 571–583. doi:10.1016/j.jss.2006.07.009

Dobing, B., & Parsons, J. (2006). How UML is used. *Communications of the ACM*, *49*(5), 109–113. doi:10.1145/1125944.1125949

Dzidek, W. J., Arisholm, E., & Briand, L. C. (2008). A realistic empirical evaluation of the costs and benefits of UML in software maintenance. *IEEE Transactions on Software Engineering*, *34*(3), 407–432. doi:10.1109/TSE.2008.15

Erickson, J., & Siau, K. (2007). Theoretical and practical complexity of modeling methods. *Communications of the ACM*, *50*(8), 46–51. doi:10.1145/1278201.1278205

Fenton, N., Pfleeger, S. L., & Glass, R. L. (1994). Science and Substance: A Challenge to Software Engineers. *IEEE Software*, *11*(4), 86–95. doi:10.1109/52.300094

France, R., Bieman, J., & Cheng, B. (2007). Repository for model driven development (ReMoDD). In *Proceedings of the MoDELS Workshops* (pp. 311-317).

Genero, M., Piattini, M., & Calero, C. (2005a). A survey of metrics for UML class diagrams. *Journal of Object Technology*, *4*(9), 59–92. doi:10.5381/jot.2005.4.9.a1

Genero, M., Piattini, M., & Calero, C. (2005b). *Metrics for software conceptual models*. London, UK: Imperial College Press. doi:10.1142/9781860946066

Grossman, M., Aronson, J. E., & McCarthy, R. V. (2005). Does UML make the grade? Insights from the software development community. *Information and Software Technology*, *47*(6), 383–397. doi:10.1016/j.infsof.2004.09.005

International Organization for Standardization. (1998). *ISO/IEC 9126: Information Technology - Software product quality*. Geneva, Switzerland: International Organization for Standardization.

Jørgensen, M., & Shepperd, M. J. (2007). A systematic review of software development cost estimation studies. *IEEE Transactions on Software Engineering*, *33*(1), 33–53. doi:10.1109/TSE.2007.256943

Kitchenham, B. (2004). *Procedures for performing systematic reviews* (Tech. Rep. No. TR/SE-0401). Staffordshire, UK: Keele University.

Kitchenham, B., & Charters, S. (2007). *Guidelines for performing systematic literature reviews in software engineering*. Staffordshire, UK: Keele University.

Krogstie, J. (1998). Integrating the understanding of quality in requirements specification and conceptual modeling. *ACM SIGSOFT Software Engineering Notes*, *23*(1), 86–91. doi:10.1145/272263.272285

Lindland, O. I., Sindre, G., & Sølvberg, A. (1994). Understanding quality in conceptual modeling. *IEEE Software*, *11*(2), 42–49, 267. doi:10.1109/52.268955

Liu, J., Dehlinger, J., & Lutz, R. (2007). Safety analysis of software product lines using state-based modeling. *Journal of Systems and Software*, *80*(11), 1879–1892. doi:10.1016/j.jss.2007.01.047

Lucas, F. J., Molina, F., & Toval, A. (2009). A systematic review of UML model consistency management. *Information and Software Technology*, *51*(12), 1631–1645. doi:10.1016/j.infsof.2009.04.009

Matulevicius, R., & Heymans, P. (2007). Comparing goal modelling languages: An experiment. In *Proceedings of the Conference on Requirements Engineering: Foundation for Software Quality* (pp. 18-32).

Matulevicius, R., Heymans, P., & Sindre, G. (2006). Comparing goal-modelling tools with the re-tool evaluation approach. *Information Technology and Control*, *35*(3A), 276–284.

Mohagheghi, P., Dehlen, V., & Neple, T. (2009). Definitions and approaches to model quality in model-based software development - A review of literature. *Information and Software Technology*, *51*(12), 1646–1669. doi:10.1016/j.infsof.2009.04.004

Moody, D. L. (2005). Theoretical and practical issues in evaluating the quality of conceptual models: current state and future directions. *Data & Knowledge Engineering*, *55*(3), 243–276. doi:10.1016/j.datak.2004.12.005

Nelson, H., Monarchi, D., & Nelson, K. (2001). Ensuring the "goodness" of a conceptual representation. In *Proceedings of the 4th European Conference on Software Measurement and ICT Control*, Heidelberg, Germany.

Neto, A. D., Subramanyan, R., Vieira, M., Travassos, G. H., & Shull, F. (2008). Improving Evidence about Software Technologies: A Look at Model-Based Testing. *IEEE Software*, *25*(3), 10–13. doi:10.1109/MS.2008.64

Offutt, J., & Abdurazik, A. (1999). Generating tests from UML specifications. In R. France & B. Rumpe (Eds.), *Proceedings of the Conference on Unified Modeling Language* (LNCS 1723, pp. 416-429).

OMG. (1997). *Object Management Group - UML*. Retrieved from http://www.uml.org/

OMG. (2003). *MDA guide (Vol. version 1.0.1)*. Retrieved from http://www.omg.org/docs/omg/03-06-01.pdf.

OMG. (2005). *The Unified Modeling Language. Documents associated with UML Version 2.0*. Retrieved from http://www.omg.org/spec/UML/2.0

Piattini, M., Genero, M., Poels, G., & Nelson, J. (2005). Towards a framework for conceptual modelling quality. In Genero, M., Piattini, M., & Calero, C. (Eds.), *Metrics For software conceptual models* (pp. 1–18). London, UK: Imperial College Press. doi:10.1142/9781860946066_0001

Poels, G., Nelson, J., Genero, M., & Piattini, M. (2003). Quality in conceptual modeling - New research directions. In A. Olivé, M. Yoshikawa, & E. S. K. Yu (Eds.), *Proceedings of the Conference on Advanced Conceptual Modeling Techniques* (LNCS 2784, pp. 243-250).

Pretorius, R., & Budgen, D. (2008). A mapping study on empirical evidence related to the models and forms used in the UML. In *Proceedings of the 2nd ACM-IEEE International Symposium on Empirical Software Engineering and Measurement*, Kaiserslautern, Germany (pp. 342-344).

Recker, J., Rosemann, M., & Krogstie, J. (2007). Ontology- versus pattern-based evaluation of process modeling languages: A comparison. *Communications of the Association for Information Systems*, *20*(48), 774–799.

Rumbaugh, J., Booch, G., & Jacobson, I. (1998). *Unified modeling language reference manual*. Reading, MA: Addison-Wesley.

Selic, B. (2003). The pragmatics of model-driven development. *IEEE Software*, *20*, 19–25. doi:10.1109/MS.2003.1231146

Shull, F., Singer, J., & Sjøberg, D. I. K. (2008). *Guide to Advanced Empirical Software Engineering*. Berlin, Germany: Springer. doi:10.1007/978-1-84800-044-5

Sjøberg, D. I., Hannay, J. E., Hansen, O., Kampenes, V. B., Karahasanovic, A., Liborg, N., & Rekdal, A. C. (2005). A survey of controlled experiments in software engineering. *IEEE Transactions on Software Engineering*, *31*, 733–753. doi:10.1109/TSE.2005.97

Thomas, D. (2004). MDA: Revenge of the modelers or UML utopia? *IEEE Software*, *21*, 15–17. doi:10.1109/MS.2004.1293067

Unhelkar, B. (2005). *Verification and validation for quality of UML 2.0 models*. New York, NY: Wiley Interscience. doi:10.1002/0471734322

Wand, Y., & Weber, R. (2002). Research commentary: Information systems and conceptual modeling - A research agenda. *Information Systems Research*, *13*(4), 363–376. doi:10.1287/isre.13.4.363.69

Wohlin, C., Runeson, P., Höst, M., Ohlsson, M. C., Regnell, B., & Wesslén, A. (2000). *Experimentation in Software Engineering: An Introduction*. Norwell, MA: Kluwer Academic Publishers.

Zelkowitz, M., & Wallace, D. (1997). Experimental validation in software engineering. *Information and Software Technology*, *39*, 735–743. doi:10.1016/S0950-5849(97)00025-6

Zelkowitz, M., Wallace, D., & Binkley, D. W. (2003). Experimental validation of new software technology. In *Lecture Notes on Empirical Software Engineering* (pp. 229–263). Singapore: World Scientific Publishing. doi:10.1142/9789812795588_0006

APPENDIX

Classification Scheme

The following is a detailed description of the classification scheme used to analyze the extracted papers. This classification scheme was developed prior to the first round of data extraction and was subsequently refined after the pilot data was extracted and analyzed.

Type of Diagram

This dimension refers to the UML diagram that is the focus of the research in question. From UML 2.0 (OMG, 2003) onwards there are 13 different kinds of diagrams that compose UML. These 13 diagrams are a superset of the diagrams contained in previous versions of UML (referred to as UML 1.x here). The 13 types of diagrams are combined into three broad categories:

Structure diagrams emphasize the elements that must exist in the modeled system: class diagram, component diagram, object diagram, composite structure diagram (UML 2.0), deployment diagram, and package diagram.

Behavior diagrams emphasize what must happen in the modeled system: activity diagram, use case diagram, and state diagrams.

Interaction diagrams are a subset of behavior diagrams, which emphasize the control and data flow between the modeled system elements: sequence diagram, communication diagram, which is a simplified version of the collaboration diagram (UML 1.x), time diagrams (UML 2.0), and light interaction diagram (UML 2.0).

Type of Quality

There are three main model quality types: syntactic quality, semantic quality, and pragmatic quality (Lindland, Sindre, & Solvberg, 1994; Unhekkar, 2005). Each of these quality types contains some additional quality characteristics, described below. Most of these definitions are taken from (International Organization for Standardization, 1998) which is related to software product quality, or from the definitions drawn from the papers that we found during the review process related to the topic. It should be borne in mind that the definitions have been adapted to define model quality instead of software quality.

Syntactic quality refers to how well the model adheres to the rules of the language. It is also known as *syntactic correctness*. The word *correctness* refers to the absence of syntactic errors, meaning that the model is a valid instantiation of the metamodel that defines the UML type of diagram considered.

Semantic quality refers to how faithfully the modeled system is represented. There are two semantic goals: *validity* which means that all statements made in the model are correct and relevant to describe/specify the modelled system and *completeness* which means that the model contains all the statements which would be correct and relevant for describing or specifying the modelled system. There are several quality characteristics that are related to semantic quality:

- *Consistency.* The coherence between the elements of a collection. There are two types of consistency in UML: intra-model and inter-model. Intra-model consistency is all elements in a model being internally consistent and not contradicting each other. Inter-model consistency is all models in the same system being consistent with one another.

- *Completeness.* The quality that something is complete or finished. A UML model is complete when all requirements for the system being developed have been represented.
- *Correctness.* The diagram represents the system requirements adequately, without ambiguities and without redundancies in the expression.

Pragmatic quality refers to how well the model is understood. In a more general sense, pragmatics refers to the use that is made of something. The quality characteristics related to pragmatic quality are the following:

- *Maintainability.* The capability of the model to be modified. Modifications may include corrections, improvements, or adaptation of the model to changes in the system or in the system requirements. We consider this to be synonymous with the concepts of modifiability and evolvability.
- *Analyzability.* The capability of the model to be diagnosed for deficiencies or for the parts to be modified to be identified.
- *Understandability.* How well the model enables the user to understand whether the model is suitable and how it can be used for particular tasks and conditions of use. In the case of UML diagrams, understanding is related to readability, layout, and comprehension.
- *Testability.* In engineering, this refers to the capability of equipment or system to be validated. Here, whether the model can be validated to be correct.
- *Functionality.* The model's "suitability." The ability of the model to provide functions which meet stated and implied needs when the model is used under specified conditions.
- *Executability.* The executability of a model can be understood as the ability to transform a model into a software product that is executable. For example, to transform a graphical model into an executable model in XML, OWL, and so on.
- *Reusability.* The ability of some or all of an existing model to be used in the construction of a model for another system. This takes advantage of previous work, saving time and reducing redundancy.
- *Complexity.* Whether something is complex, complicated, or difficult. The complexity of a UML model is directly related to the complexity of the system that tries it tries to represent. Complex models are generally difficult to understand, reducing the ease of implementation of the final system.
- *Dependability.* It is the ability to deliver service that can justifiably be trusted. It is a term used to describe the availability performance and its influencing factors: reliability performance, maintainability performance and maintenance support performance.

Type of Evidence

In Software Engineering (SE) it is very important to increase the level of rigor and evidence in research; more importance is given to research methods that provide a scientific basis to findings (Fenton, Pfleeger, & Glass, 1994; Zelkowitz & Wallace, 1997; Zelkowitz, Wallace, & Binkley, 2003). As there are many research methods and each one provides different levels of evidence, this classification was developed using a bottom-up approach. An initial list of research methods was developed, and after reading all the papers considered in the current SLR the classification was subsequently refined. Finally, the classification was refined further by considering a similar classification described in Neto, Subramanyan, Vieira, Travassos, and Shull (2008). The different research methods are ordered by the level of evidence they support, making it possible to determine to what extent the research results are supported by empirical evidence.

- *Speculation.* These papers describe a proposal or approach for addressing UML model quality without presenting any study or example that would indicate the feasibility of the proposal and the usefulness of the research results in practice.
- *Example.* Consists of the description of a proposal for addressing UML model quality, where its use or application is illustrated by an example. Examples might be "toy" examples taken from books or UML models developed in real projects.
- *Literature review.* Consists of the review of prior research to propose general frameworks, new proposals or topics for future research.
- *Experiment.* A controlled experiment is an investigation of a testable hypothesis where one or more independent variables are manipulated to measure their effect on one or more dependent variables. Controlled experiments allow determining in precise terms how the variables are related and, specifically, whether a cause-effect relationship exists between them. Experiments are sometimes referred to as research-in-the-small, since they are concerned with a limited scope and most often are run in a laboratory setting. They are often highly controlled and hence also occasionally referred to as controlled experiments (Shull, Singer, & Sjøberg, 2008; Wohlin et al., 2000).
- *Case study.* There is much confusion in the SE literature over what constitutes a case study. The term is often used to mean a "worked example." As an empirical method, a case study is something very different. Yin (2003) introduces the case study as "an empirical inquiry that investigates a contemporary phenomenon within its real-life context, especially when the boundaries between phenomenon and context are not clearly evident." Case studies offer in-depth understanding of how and why certain phenomena occur, and can reveal the mechanisms by which cause-effect relationships occur. Case studies are observational studies used for monitoring projects, activities and assignments. The case study is normally aimed at tracking a specific attribute or establishing relationships between different attributes. The level of control is lower in a case study than in an experiment (Shull et al., 2008; Wohlin et al., 2000).
- *Survey.* The survey is referred to as research-in-the-large (and past) since it is possible to send a questionnaire to or interview a large number people covering whatever target population is needed. Thus, a survey is often an investigation performed in retrospect, when (for example) a tool or technique has been in use for a period of time. The primary means of gathering qualitative and quantitative data are interviews or questionnaires through a sample that is representative of the population to be studied. The results from the survey are then analyzed to derive descriptive and explanatory conclusions and are then generalized to the population from which the sample was taken (Shull et al., 2008; Wohlin et al., 2000).

The first three research methods are considered non-empirical methods, whilst the rest are considered empirical methods. Empirical methods allow researchers to determine the empirical validity of the usefulness of the research results in practice.

Type of Research Result

This dimension refers to the outcome or the "product" of the research on UML model quality. Most of the following definitions are taken from (International Organization for Standardization, 1998), which is related to software product quality, or the definitions are drawn from the papers found during the paper analysis process.

A *quality model* defines a set of characteristics, and of relationships between them, which provides a framework for specifying quality requirements and evaluating quality.

A *notation* is a system of symbolic representations of objects and ideas; it is a writing system (in fact, a formal language) used for recording concepts related with the construction of a system. Some notations that support the UML modeling can increase its expressiveness, which improves the representation of requirements and the understanding of the reader.

A *method* or algorithm is a finite sequence of instructions used to prevent or detect and delete deficiencies in models. "Method" can also be considered a technique, methodology, process, approach, or strategy.

A *tool* gives automatic support to the evaluation or assurance of quality considering different techniques (metrics, checklist, etc.).

A *metric* is a measurement scale and the method used for assessment. Metrics can be internal or external. Metrics include methods for categorizing qualitative data.

In theoretical computer science, *formal semantics* is the field concerned with the rigorous mathematical study of the meaning of programming languages and models of computation. This can be used to perform validations on models, such as consistency checking.

We consider other types of results that are not "tangible", for example a confirmation of *knowledge* (e.g., a confirmation of a theory). For example, when we replicate an experiment to confirm the findings of the original one, in reality the outcome is not "tangible," but we are confirming the knowledge acquired previously.

A *pattern* is a type of theme of recurring events or objects, sometimes referred to as elements of a set. These elements repeat in a predictable manner. It can be a template or model which can be used to generate high-quality models.

A *view* is a representation of a whole system from the perspective of a related set of concerns. The view model provides guidance and rules for structuring, classifying, and organizing architectures. Each view provides the reader with a different perspective of the system to model, which can improve the understandability of the final product.

A *checklist*, *guideline*, *rule* or *modeling convention* guides the creation of models. Such techniques attempt to obtain better models by promoting best practices, either empirically-based or scientifically proven.

Research Goal

There are several goals; in fact every researcher or organization pursues his/her/its own goals. In general, we can distinguish five different goals: understanding, measuring, evaluating, assuring, and improving the quality of UML models. These goals are:

Research into *understanding* quality seeks to define the various dimensions of quality. This research also aims at understanding the factors that impact UML model quality.

Measuring quality is concerned with developing and evaluating scales that can be used to characterise (qualitatively or quantitatively) UML model quality.

Research that *evaluates* quality investigates the relationship between quality measurements and real-world experiences with the UML model. The goal is to attach a value judgment to quality measurements.

Quality *assurance* research examines how to ensure that the process that produces the UML model actually does produce a high-quality UML model.

Finally, the research into *improving* quality examines how to increase the current quality of UML models.

This work was previously published in the Journal of Database Management, Volume 22, Issue 3, edited by Keng Siau, pp. 46-70, copyright 2011 by IGI Publishing (an imprint of IGI Global).

Chapter 13
Semi-Automatic Composition of Situational Methods

Anat Aharoni
Kinneret College, Israel

Iris Reinhartz-Berger
University of Haifa, Israel

ABSTRACT

Situational methods are approaches to the development of software systems that are designed and constructed to fit particular circumstances that often refer to project characteristics. One common way to create situational methods is to reuse method components, which are the building blocks of development methods. For this purpose, method components must be stored in a method base, and then retrieved and composed specifically for the situation in hand. Most approaches in the field of situational method engineering require the expertise of method engineers to support the retrieval and composition of method components. Furthermore, this is usually done in an ad-hoc manner and for pre-defined situations. In this paper, the authors propose an approach, supported by a tool that creates situational methods semi-automatically. This approach refers to structural and behavioral considerations and a wide variety of characteristics when comparing method components and composing them into situational methods. The resultant situational methods are stored in the method base for future usage and composition. Based on an experimental study of the approach, the authors show that it provides correct and suitable draft situational methods, which human evaluators have assessed as relevant for the given situations.

INTRODUCTION

Method engineering deals with the design, construction, and adaption of approaches, techniques, and tools for the development of information and software systems (Brinkkemper, 1996). Siau, Long, and Ling (2010) claim that development methods are one of the key factors for the success of information systems development. However, since projects vary in their characteristics, standard development methods in a textbook or manual may require specific adaptations so that they will support all software development properly. Situational method engineering (SME), which is a sub-field of method engineering, focuses on

DOI: 10.4018/978-1-4666-2044-5.ch013

in-house construction of organization- or project-specific development methods (Kumar & Welke, 1992; Brinkkemper, 1996; Domíngueza & Zapata, 2007; Henderson-Sellers & Ralyté, 2010). The main terms used in SME are method components, situations, and situational methods (Mirbel & Ralyté, 2006; Henderson-Sellers & Ralyté, 2010). *Method components*, the building blocks of SME, are development methods, or any coherent parts of them. A *situation* can be defined as a vector of characteristics that relate to various entities in software development, such as the project in hand, the software development organization, the software development team, and so on. Finally, a *situational method* is an approach used in the development of software systems that is designed and constructed to fit particular situations.

In their review of twenty method engineering approaches, Becker, Janiesch, and Pfeiffer (2007) found five important mechanisms for composing method components into situational methods. The most utilized mechanism is *aggregation*, which combines independent method components to create a "larger" method component. This mechanism, which is also called assembly, construction, or integration, appeared in 70% of the reviewed approaches. *Specialization*, which is sometimes called tailoring, was found to be the second most popular mechanism, appearing in 45% of the approaches. *Analogy construction* (van Offenbeek & Koopman, 2006; Ralyté & Rolland, 2001; Raylte, Deneckere, & Rolland, 2003), *configuration* (Karlsson & Ågerfalk, 2005; Becker, Knackstedt, Pfeiffer, & Janiesch, 2007), and *instantiation* (Nuseibeh, 1994) were utilized much less frequently and usually in addition to aggregation or specialization. Becker et al. (2007) further claim that aggregation and specialization, which are classified by Ralyté et al. (2003) as assembly-based method engineering, can be used in a much wider variety of situations than the other mechanisms, as they provide flexible means to adapt a solution to the specific needs of a given situation.

Recently, due to the increasing number and variety of development methods and the emerging requirements of development processes (e.g., in the form of the CMMI model) (Chrissis, Konrad, & Shrum, 2003), efforts have been made to standardize the area of method engineering. These efforts have yielded the OPEN Process Framework (OPF) (Firesmith & Henderson-Sellers, 2001; Henderson-Sellers & Serour, 2005), OMG's Software Process Engineering Metamodel (SPEM) (OMG, 2005), and ISO/IEC 24744 (Gonzalez-Perez, 2007; ISO, 2007). These frameworks and approaches specify the core terminology of development methods and divide method components primarily into structural and behavioral ones. Structural method components, also called products or work products, represent the different possible artifacts in the development methods, such as documents, while behavioral method components, which are also called work units or processes, represent tasks, techniques, and activities in the development lifecycles. Other aspects, e.g., the stakeholder's involvement in software development, temporal aspects, and the language and modeling units, are also handled in these frameworks and approaches.

In order to guide the retrieval and composition of situational methods, the method components are associated with various situational characteristics, i.e., features that characterize certain situations. Examples of situational characteristics mentioned in the literature are: type of development, stakeholder cohesion or contention, project scale, distribution of project organization, domain experience of development team, degree of novelty, technical complexity, management complexity, architectural risk, incremental method evolution, company conditions, and organizational culture (Park, Na, Park, & Sugumaran, 2006; van de Weerd, Versendaal, & Brinkkemper, 2006). Mirbel and Ralyté (2006) propose what they term a 'reuse frame' for aggregating different situational characteristics relevant to a single critical development aspect. According to their proposal, situational characteristics are primarily divided into human-related, organizational, and application domains. The different characteristics in the reuse frames are organized in a tree of successively refined aspects, such that the actual characteristics appear in the leaves of the tree. A software development organization may adopt only the portion of this tree that fits its requirements.

While the different approaches in situational method engineering concentrate on providing representation and measuring aids to assist method engineers to create situational methods, these methods are usually actually composed and created manually by method engineers, who base their work on their experience and understanding of the situations and of the various method components. Furthermore, they usually compose the methods utilizing structural considerations only, in an ad-hoc manner, and for pre-defined situations. In this work, we present an approach, supported by a tool, the objective of which is to retrieve the most suitable method components for given situations and compose them semi-automatically into situational methods. The method components and resultant situational methods are represented in an XML-based notation, visualized by Object-Process Methodology (OPM) (Dori, 2002), and stored in a method base. Four similarity metrics, which refer to both the structural and the behavioral aspects of the method components as well as to additional meta-information regarding their role and essence, are identified. Having calculated the similarity between different method components, the approach defines two structural composition operations (merging and generalization) and five behavioral composition operations (sequential, concurrent, incremental, iterative, and alternative compositions) that can be used for creating situational methods. An experimental study of the suggested approach has shown that the popular aggregation and specialization mechanisms are supported at a satisfactory level, yielding situational methods that suit the given situations.

The main contribution of the study is two-fold. First, it enhances the retrieval and the composition of method components with both structural and behavioral aspects, and utilizes them in a semi-automatic manner, thus providing method engineers with a systematic tool. Secondly, the study compares the recommendations of humans (advanced and graduate students of information systems) and of an automatic tool for the same situations, and analyzes the differences between them and the possible reasons for these differences.

The structure of the rest of the paper is as follows. First, we provide an overview of the approach, presenting its method component model. We then elaborate on retrieval issues and the composition capabilities of the approach in separate sections. A report of our experience with the approach follows. Finally, we refer to related work, highlight the benefits and shortcomings of the suggested approach, summarize the work, and suggest future research directions.

The Approach Overview

The automatic creation of situational development methods requires the existence of a *method base*, which stores models of method components or of complete methods that are commonly used or can be used in a certain software development organization (Saeki, Iguchi, Wen-yin, & Shinohara, 1993; Ralyté, 1999). A possible scenario of such an automatic creation may include the following four steps (depicted in Figure 1): (1) specifying the situation query for which a development method is required; (2) retrieving potential or relevant method components from the method base; (3) applying different composition operations in order to satisfy completely or partially the situation query; and (4) representing and ranking the suggested situational methods according to their suitability to the query in hand. The situational methods thus created are then recorded in the method base for future use.

Figure 1. A possible scenario of automatic creation of situational development methods

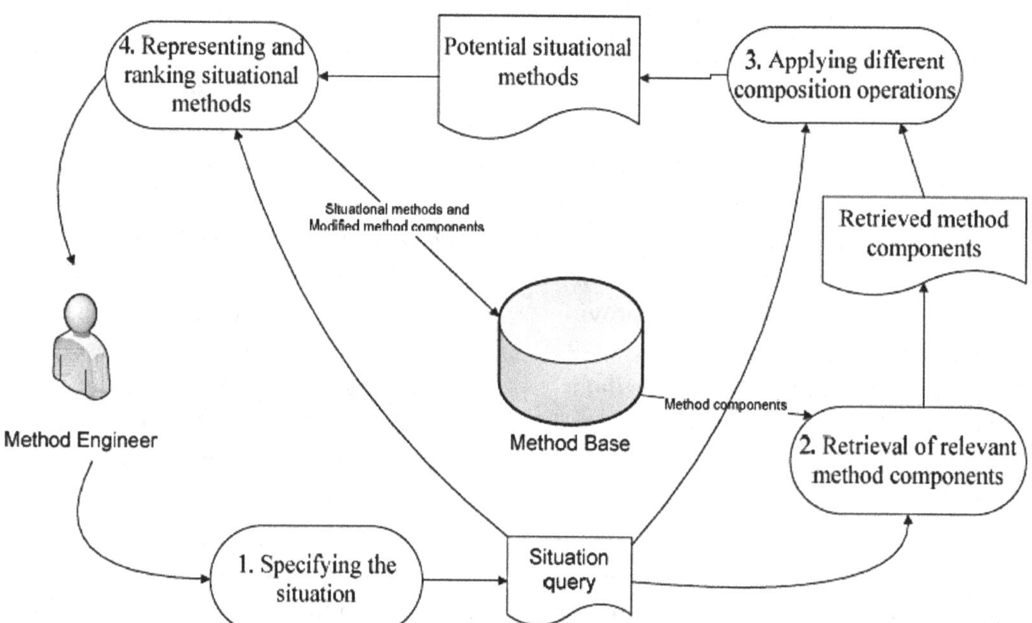

Before these activities can be carried out, a method component model first has to be defined. This model must support different types of method component, including: fragments, which can be product or process parts of development methods (Harmsen, Lubbers, & Wijers, 1995); chunks, which are autonomous and coherent parts of methods that support the realization of some specific information systems development activities (Kornyshova, Deneckere, & Salinesi, 2007); method services, which incorporate assistance-based utilities into method components [0]; road maps, each of which is composed of one or more coherent sequences of method chunks (Rolland, 2009); and patterns, which suggest domain-specific guidance to the creation of process or product fragments (Rolland, Nurcan, & Grosz, 2000). Thus, we use the following general definition for a method component model.

Definition 1 (Method Component Model)

A *method component model*, *MC*, is a quintuplet, <*n*, *r*, *Str*, *Bhv*, *SC*>, where:

- *n* is the name of the method component;
- *r* is the role the method component plays in the context of method engineering (e.g., a document, a technique, or a model unit).
- *Str* represents the structure of the method component;
- *Bhv* represents the behavior of the method component;
- *SC* represents the situation which the method component fits. In other words, *SC* is a set of pairs <*f*, *v*>, where *f* is a situational feature and *v* is its value in the particular method component.

The role of the method component is taken from a method engineering framework, such as ISO/IEC 24744 (ISO, 2007), which defines a metamodel for development methodologies. This standard refers primarily to five methodological aspects: (1) work units describing behaviors; (2) work products describing structures and artifacts; (3) producers specifying human-related aspects; (4) model units specifying the language aspect of development methods; and (5) stages specifying the temporal aspect of method components. Each aspect is further specialized to represent particular methodological concepts, such as tasks, techniques, and processes, all of which are work units. As will be explained later, the role of the method component is used when measuring the similarity between method components.

The structure and behavior of a method component are now defined.

Definition 2 (Structure of Method Component)

The structure, *Str*, of a method component, *MC*, is a triple <Exh, Agg, Rel>, where:

1. *Exh* is the set of features and attributes of MC, and is called its *exhibition set*;
2. *Agg* is the set of parts of MC, and is called its *aggregation set*;
3. *Rel* is the set of the method components to which MC is related, and is called its *relation set*.

Note that the elements in the aggregation and relation sets are method components in their own right, whereas the elements in the exhibition set may not be method components. Nevertheless, we refer to all the members in these three sets as elements that can be composed according to similarity metrics, i.e., as method components.

Definition 3 (Behavior of Method Component)

The behavior, *Bhv*, of a behavioral method component *MC* is a triple <Inp, Out, Tri>, where:

1. *Inp* is the set of inputs of MC, and is called its *input set*;
2. *Out* is the set of outputs of MC, and is called its *output set*;
3. *Tri* is the set of triggers of MC, as is called its *trigger set*.

Here again, the elements in these sets are method components. The inputs and the outputs of a work unit, for example, may be work products, whereas its triggers may be producers or work products.

In order to visualize the method component model described above, we use a simplified version of Object-Process Methodology (OPM) (Dori, 2002), which is a holistic approach for the modeling, study, development, and evolution of software systems. It combines ideas from object-oriented and process-oriented approaches into a single frame of reference, making it possible to express mutual relationships and effects between objects (structure) and processes (behavior). The main reasons for choosing OPM for the purpose of representing method components are: its balanced treatment of structure and behavior, and the mutual relationships between them; its scalability, which is achieved through refinement and abstraction mechanisms that enable recursive specification of the modeled element to any desired level of detail without losing the legibility, comprehension, and consistency of the complete model; its formality expressed by a metamodel (Reinhartz-Berger & Dori, 2005); and its accessibility to different types of users, as has been examined by Peleg and Dori (2000) and Reinhartz-Berger and Dori (2005). More details about the visual representation of method components in OPM can be found in the work of Aharoni and Reinhartz-Berger (2008).

As an example of the proposed method component model, consider the processes "Requirements Extraction" and "Manage User Stories," represented in Figure 2. As noted, a process in ISO/IEC 24744 is a large-grained work unit operating within a given area of expertise. The "Requirements Extraction" process, which is taken from the Rational Unified Process (RUP) (Kruchten, 2000), supports the procedure of discovering the requirements of a software system through communication with clients. The main artifacts of this process are requirements documents and business domain glossaries. The process is triggered by the requirements engineers and the systems analysts who use the client's initial information, follow the contract (and modify it if required), and also utilize various requirement templates. The clients themselves may be involved in this process too. In addition, this model specifies the situations for which the entire "Requirements Extraction" process is suitable: the minimal requested capability level is 2, the level of the project's flexibility to changes is low, and the project duration is at least one year. These situational characteristics, which appear in grey in the figure, are classified according to the reuse frame proposed in [0], and recorded in the upper left corner of the shapes as roles. Situational characteristics that do not appear in this reuse frame, such as Method Source, are classified as general.

The model also specifies that the process comprises three tasks: (1) obtain an initial understanding of the domain, (2) draw up a set of requirements, and (3) delimit the domain scope. Each task is a method component into which the relevant inputs, outputs, and triggers are percolated. The model of the method component "draw up a set of requirements" (not shown here), for example, includes its trigger (the end of the task "obtain an initial understanding of the domain"), its inputs ("Client's Initial Information," "Contract," "Requirements Templates," and "Business Domain Glossary"), and its outputs ("Business Domain Glossary," which may be modified by this task, and "Requirements Document"), as well as additional specific situational characteristics and recommended techniques for performing this task. Rules are defined and maintained in OPM in order to preserve consistency between diagrams that contain the same element (method component), describing its different aspects (Dori, 2002).

The "Manage User Stories" process, taken from eXtreme Programming (XP) (Beck and Andres, 2004), comprises the tasks "Write User Stories" and "Create Acceptance Tests". The techniques "Write 3 Sentences in Customer's Terminology" and "Focus on User Needs and Benefits" are recommended for composing user stories; customers and developers are required to participate in this task.

RETRIEVAL CAPABILITIES

For the purpose of retrieving relevant method components, we define four types of similarities between method components, linguistic, meta-informational, structural, and behavioral, each of which is described in the following sub-sections. The general (overall) similarity is a weighted average of the relevant linguistic, meta-informational, structural, and behavioral similarities, and is formally defined in Definition 9. The weights are set and maintained by the method engineers, according to different characteristics of the models in the method base. A discussion of these weights, as well as reference to the usage of situational characteristics and the definition of situation queries in the retrieval process, are given later in this section.

Linguistic Similarity

The similarity between elements is commonly defined in terms of the measured distance between their names. Different similarity metrics have been proposed for calculating the distances between terms and sentences (see a summary of WordNet-related metrics by Budanitsky & Hirst, 2006). In this work, we adopted Dao and Simpson's (2005) similarity metric between two sentences, using WordNet, which is a large, general-purpose lexical database of English. We chose this metric

Figure 2. The Requirements Extraction process taken from RUP: (a) an OPM model and (b) a formal specification. The Manage User Stories process taken from XP: (c) an OPM model and (d) a formal specification. The method components in the aggregation, input, output, trigger, and situational characteristics sets are represented by their names.

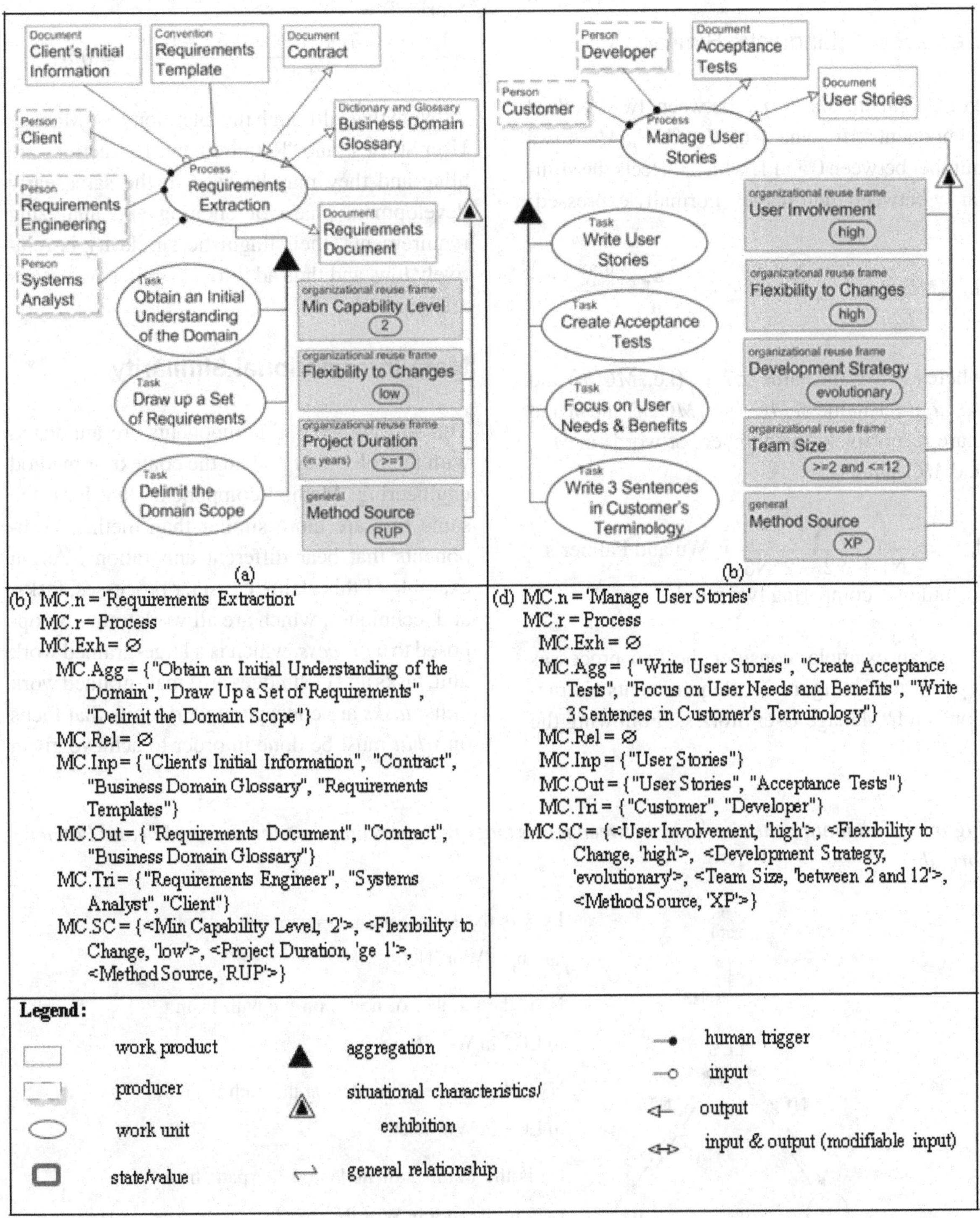

since it is simple, straightforward, and does not require a large corpus of statistics. This metric is based on Wu and Palmer's (1994) formula for comparing two words.

Definition 4 (Linguistic Similarity)

The *linguistic similarity* between two method components MC_1 and MC_2, $L_{sim}(MC_1, MC_2)$ is a number between 0 and 1, which reflects the similarity between their names. Formally expressed:

$$L_{sim}\left(MC_1, MC_2\right) = \frac{\sum_{i=1}^{m} \max_{j=1..n} l_{t_i,u_j} + \sum_{j=1}^{n} \max_{i=1..m} l_{t_i,u_j}}{m+n},$$

where $t_1 \ldots t_m$ is the name of MC_1 (i.e., $MC_1.n$) and $u_1 \ldots u_n$ is the name of MC_2 (i.e., $MC_2.n$) and m and n are respectively the numbers of words in MC_1 and MC_2 names.

$l_{ti,\,uj} = \dfrac{2^*N3}{N1 + N2 + 2^*N3}$ is Wu and Palmer's formula for comparing two words.

As an example, consider the two processes represented in Figure 2, "Requirements Extraction" and "Manage User Stories." Following the calculations in Table 1, the linguistic similarity between these method components is:

L_{sim}("Requirements Extraction", "Manage User Stories") =

$$\frac{(0.54 + 0.5) + (0.5 + 0.54 + 0.46)}{2 + 3} = 0.51.$$

Note that, although the intentions of "Manage User Stories" and "Requirements Extraction" are alike and they may be used in the same early development phase of eliciting and analyzing requirements, their linguistic similarity is relatively low, and thus additional similarity metrics are required.

Meta-Informational Similarity

The various method components are annotated with the roles they play in the context of method engineering. Method components that have the same role are more similar than method components that bear different annotations. As an example of this claim, consider processes, tasks, and techniques, which are all work units. As opposed to a *process*, which is a large-grained work unit, tasks and techniques are small-grained work units: *tasks* are conceptual work units that focus on *what* must be done in order to achieve given

Figure 3. Calculating the similarity between terms that are hierarchically related using Wu and Palmer's formula

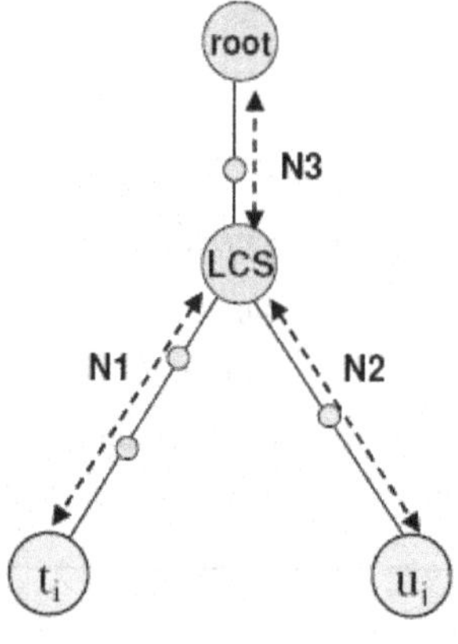

LCS is the least common super-concept of t_i and u_j in WordNet.

N_1 is the number of nodes on the path from t_i to LCS in WordNet.

N_2 is the number of nodes on the path from u_j to LCS in WordNet.

N_3 is the number of nodes on the path from LCS to the root in WordNet.

Table 1. The linguistic similarity between "requirements extraction" and "manage user stories"

	Manage	User	Stories
Requirements	0.5	0.54	0.46
Extraction	0.4	0.5	0.43

purposes, while *techniques* are technical work units that refer to *how* to achieve these purposes (ISO, 2007). We would like to be able to say, for example, that two processes with similar characteristics (e.g., name, structure, and behavior) are more similar than a process and a task that have the same goal.

Like the linguistic similarity, the meta-informational similarity is calculated using Wu and Palmer's formula. However, here the formula is calculated on the hierarchy of method engineering concepts, as derived from standard frameworks, such as ISO/IEC 24744.

Definition 5 (Meta-Informational Similarity)

The *meta-informational similarity* between two method components, MC_1 and MC_2, $MI_{sim}(MC_1, MC_2)$, is a number between 0 and 1 that reflects the similarity between the method engineering roles of the compared method components. Formally expressed:

$MI_{sim}(MC_1, MC_2) = 1_{MC1.r, MC2.r} = \frac{2*N3'}{N1' + N2' + 2*N3'}$, where $MC_i.r$, i=1, 2, is the role of method component MC_i.

In other words, $MI_{sim}(MC_1, MC_2)$ is Wu and Palmer's metric applied to the roles associated with MC_1 and MC_2, where only inheritance relations are taken into consideration for this calculation (in order to imitate a lexicon or a thesaurus). Note that $MI_{sim}(MC_1, MC_2)=1$ if and only if the two method components have the same role.

As an example of meta-informational similarity calculation, consider the partial hierarchy of ISO/IEC 24744, depicted in Figure 4. The main method engineering concepts, namely work products, producers, modeling units, stages, and work units, appear in this figure on the same level (the third). They are further divided into sub-concepts. Work units, for example, are specialized into processes, tasks, and techniques. In addition, since work products, producers, and modeling units are mainly structural in concept (triggering, providing inputs, or being produced as outputs of work units), an upper level that includes the distinction between structural and behavioral concepts is added, and the various method-engineering concepts are divided accordingly. The top element in this hierarchy is 'Method Engineering Concept'; it is added in order to create a single tree of concepts. According to the resultant tree, the meta-informational similarity between a process and a task, for example, is 0.67, whereas the meta-information similarity between a stage and a process is 0.4. The meta-informational similarity between method components that belong to completely different branches of this tree (e.g., work units and work products) is 0.

Structural Similarity

The internal structure of method components, as well as their external relationships to other method components, can be used to measure their similarity. Method components that exhibit similar features and parts and are connected to similar method components are considered more similar than method components that do not share a similar structure. As noted, the structure of a method component in our model consists of three sets: exhibition, aggregation, and relation sets. For simplicity, we assume that the method component model includes no generalization-specialization

Figure 4. The top level hierarchy derived from ISO/IEC 24744

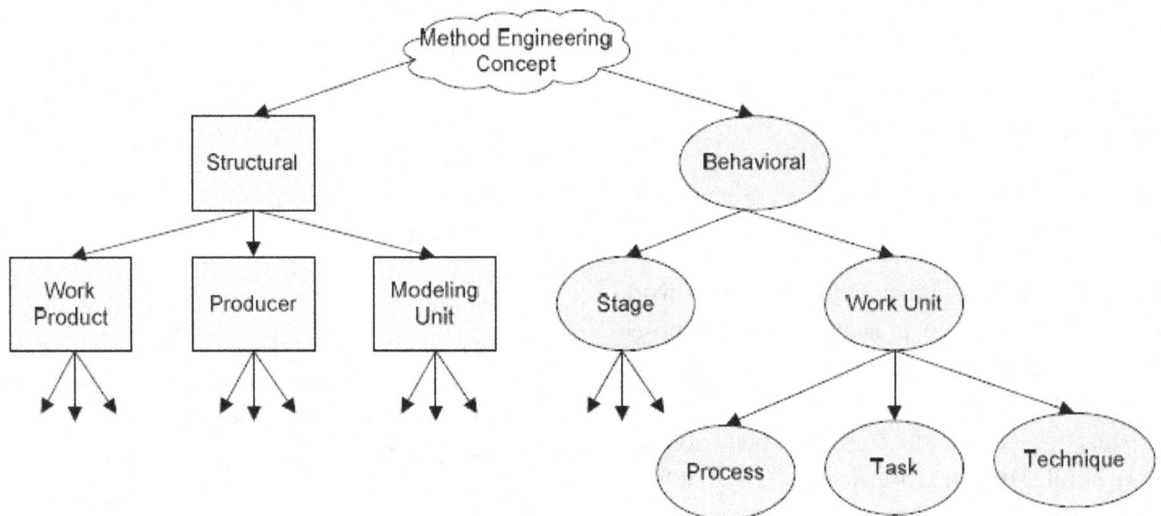

(inheritance) relations. If this is not the case, a pre-processing in which all the structural and behavioral relationships are percolated to the specialized method components has to be performed prior to similarity calculation. The following definitions describe structural similarity calculation. These definitions use the notion of general similarity, which is defined later in Definition 9. If the models include cycles of relationships, then the formula must traverse the model a fixed number of steps or until a cycle is detected.

Definition 6 (Set Similarity)

The *set similarity* between two sets of method components, $MCS_1=\{MC_{1i}\}$ and $MCS_2=\{MC_{2j}\}$, $SS(MCS_1, MCS_2)$, is a number between 0 and 1 that reflects the general similarity between the sets' members. Formally expressed,

$$SS(MCS_1, MCS_2) =$$

$$\frac{\sum_{i=1}^{MCS_1} \max_{j=1..MCS_2} G(MC_{1i}, MC_{2j}) + \sum_{j=1}^{MCS_2} \max_{i=1..MCS_1} G(MC_{1i}, MC_{2j})}{MCS_1 + MCS_2},$$

where $MC_{1i} \in MCS_1$, $MC_{2j} \in MCS_2$, $|MCS_1|$ and $|MCS_2|$ are respectively the numbers of method components in MCS_1 and MCS_2, and $G_{sim}(MC_{1i}, MC_{2j})$ is the general similarity between method components MC_{1i} and MC_{2j}.

Definition 7 (Structural Similarity)

The *structural similarity* between two method components, MC_1 and MC_2, $ST_{sim}(MC_1, MC_2)$, is a number between 0 and 1, which is calculated as a weighted average of the set similarities between the method components' exhibition, aggregation, and relation sets. Formally expressed,

$$ST_{sim}(MC_1, MC_2) = w_{exh}*SS(MC_1.Exh, MC_2.Exh)+w_{agg}*SS(MC_1.Agg, MC_2.Agg)+ w_{rel}*SS(MC_1.Rel, MC_2.Rel),$$

where $MC_k.Exh$, $MC_k.Agg$, and $MC_k.Rel$ are respectively the exhibition, aggregation, and relation sets of method component MC_k (k=1,2), w_{exh}, w_{agg}, w_{rel} are respectively the weights assigned to the similarity between the exhibition, aggregation, and relation sets in the structural similarity, and $w_{exh}+w_{agg}+w_{rel}=1$.

The structural similarity between "Requirements Extraction" and "Manage User Stories," depicted in Figure 2, is 0.56. This calculation is based on the aggregation sets only, since the exhibition and relation sets of these method components are empty. As can be seen, although the purpose of the two components is similar, in terms of eliciting requirements their structure is different, yielding a relatively low similarity value. Furthermore, since the different parts of these components are not detailed, the calculation of the general similarity between the parts takes into consideration only their linguistic and the meta-information similarity.

Behavioral Similarity

The behavior of work units and stages can be described through their interfaces, i.e., their inputs, outputs, and triggers. Method components that have similar inputs, outputs, and triggers may perform the same activity in different ways and, thus, may be considered as alternative method components. The following definition refers to the calculation of the similarity between method components based on their behaviors. Here again, the definition implicitly uses the notion of general similarity, which is defined later in Definition 9. If the models include cycles of triggers, then the formula must traverse the model a fixed number of steps or until a cycle is detected.

Definition 8 (Behavioral Similarity)

The *behavioral similarity* between two (behavioral) method components, MC_1 and MC_2, $BH_{sim}(MC_1, MC_2)$, is a number between 0 and 1, which is calculated as a weighted average of the set similarity between the behavioral methods' input, output, and trigger sets. Formally expressed,

$$BH_{sim}(MC_1, MC_2)=w_{Inp}*SS(MC_1.Inp, MC_2.Inp)+w_{out}*SS(MC_1.Out, MC_2.Out)+w_{Tri}*SS(MC_1.Tri, MC_2.Tri),$$

where $MC_k.Inp$, $MC_k.Out$, and $MC_k.Tri$ are respectively the input, output, and trigger sets of MC_k (k=1,2), w_{inp}, w_{out}, w_{tri} are respectively the weights assigned to the similarity between input, output, and trigger sets in the behavioral similarity, and $w_{inp}+w_{out}+w_{tri}=1$.

Assuming the process inputs, outputs, and triggers are of equal importance, the behavioral similarity between "Requirements Extraction" and "Manage User Stories" is 0.7, which is quite a high similarity level, potentially justifying considering the two processes as interchangeable method components.

Weights and Suitability

As mentioned, the general similarity between method components is defined as a weighted average of the relevant linguistic, meta-informational, structural, and behavioral similarities.

Definition 9 (General Similarity)

The *general similarity* between two method components, MC_1 and MC_2, $G_{sim}(MC_1, MC_2)$, is a number between 0 and 1 that is calculated as a weighted average of their linguistic, meta-informational, structural, and behavioral similarity metrics. Formally expressed,

$$G_{sim}(MC_1, MC_2)= w_{ling}*L_{sim}(MC_1, MC_2) + w_{meta}*MI_{sim}(MC_1, MC_2) + w_{str}*ST_{sim}(MC_1, MC_2) + w_{bhv}*BH_{sim}(MC_1, MC_2),$$

where $L_{sim}(MC_1, MC_2)$, $MI_{sim}(MC_1, MC_2)$, $ST_{sim}(MC_1, MC_2)$, and $BH_{sim}(MC_1, MC_2)$ are respectively the linguistic, meta-informational, structural, and behavioral similarities, w_{ling}, w_{meta}, w_{str}, and w_{bhv} are respectively the weights assigned to linguistic, meta-informational, structural, and behavioral similarities, and $w_{ling}+w_{meta}+w_{str}+w_{bhv}=1$.

The structural and behavioral similarities are further defined as the weighted averages of the similarity between their constituent sets. The initial values of these weights are: $w_{ling}=w_{meta}=w_{str}=w_{bhv}=0.25$ and $w_{exh}=w_{agg}=w_{rel}=w_{inp}=w_{out}=w_{tri}=0.33$. However, they can be controlled by the method engineers, who are enabled to take into consideration both their own previous experiences and the characteristics of the various components in the method base. A high weight given to the linguistic similarity, for example, may indicate the existence of an established, relatively homogenous vocabulary for the different method components. Still, there may be similar method components, whose intentions are alike but whose calculated linguistic similarity is low. Furthermore, utilizing a general vocabulary in the form of WordNet may lead to skewed results. In this case, one should consider reducing the weight of the linguistic similarity or using a specific method engineering-related vocabulary. Increasing the weights of behavioral and structural similarities is advisable in cases where the method base includes detailed method components that specify the structure and the behavior of the various method components. In the example that we have used to introduce and explain the different similarity types, we have seen that the linguistic similarity between the method components "Requirements Extraction" and "Manage User Stories" is 0.51, their meta-informational similarity is 1, their structural similarity is 0.56, and their behavioral similarity is 0.7. If all these similarity types are given the same weights (i.e., $w_{ling}=w_{meta}=w_{str}=w_{bhv}=0.25$), the general similarity between these method components is 0.69. However, since these processes are derived from two different development paradigms (RUP and XP) that use different vocabularies, it may be reasonable to reduce the weight of the linguistic similarity (e.g., $w_{ling}=0.1$ and $w_{meta}=w_{str}=w_{bhv}=0.3$). In this case, the general similarity between the two method components will increase to 0.73.

It is important to understand that these weights are set for the entire method base. However, when calculating the similarity between particular method components, whose models do not include certain sets relevant to similarity calculation, the weights are proportionally divided into the other (existing) sets. If, for example, $w_{exh}=w_{agg}=w_{rel}=0.33$, but the compared method components have no exhibition sets, their structural similarity will be calculated assuming $w_{agg}=w_{rel}=0.5$ (and $w_{exh}=0$).

Note that usually the method base used by a software development company is relatively fixed and rarely changes. Thus, defining and tuning the different weights should seldom be necessary. However, the software projects in which the company is involved may have a wide variety of characteristics, requiring a more frequent creation of situational methods. For each such project, a situation query has to be defined. The method component model can be used for this purpose. Figure 5, for example, specifies the following situation query as a "regular" method component: create a method component for eliciting project requirements, which is triggered by a systems analyst, receives the client's information and agreement as inputs, and produces requirement specifications. Furthermore, the retrieved method components should suit situations in which the level of flexibility to changes in the project requirements is low and the project duration is at least one year. Once the situation query has been specified, the approach retrieves an initial set of method components whose general measure of similarity to the situation query is the greatest. The absolute values of these general similarity metrics may, however, be low, requiring several method components to be composed. Furthermore, the method engineers can control the number of method components in this initial set and even specify that it should be the number of method components in the method base. The retrieved method components must satisfy the situational characteristics modeled in the situation query. The initial set of the retrieved method components is then extended using different composition operations, as described next.

Figure 5. Specification of a situation query: (a) in OPM and (b) in a formal manner

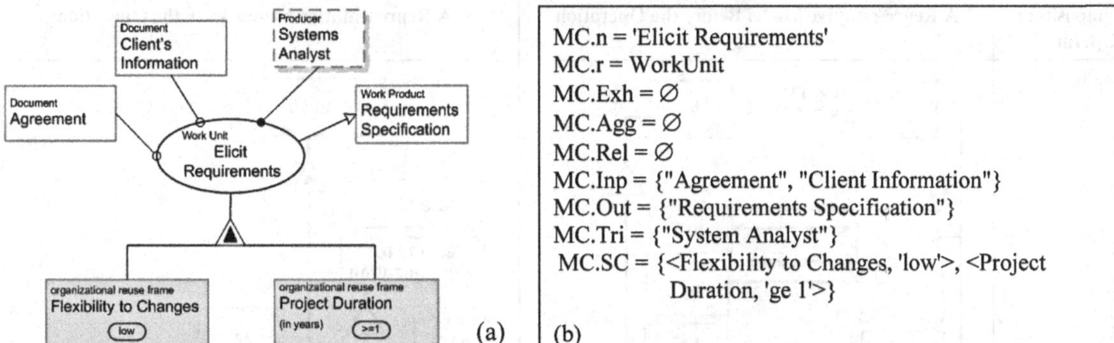

COMPOSITION CAPABILITIES

In order to create situational development methods, different method components have to be combined to create larger method components that will eventually become the requested situational development methods. We elaborate here on the structural composition of method components (both structural and behavioral) and on the behavioral composition of method components. For simplicity, we give an example of these different composition operations applied concurrently on two method components; however, these operations can be applied successively. Finally, we also refer in this section to the general composition algorithm and its complexity.

Structural Composition

The structural composition of method components can be applied to both structural and behavioral method components. It focuses on the structural aspects of the method components, i.e., their internal structure and their external relationships with other method components. We can differentiate between two structural composition operations: merging and generalization. *Merging* combines all the method components into a single one, unifying the exhibition, aggregation, relation, input, output, trigger, and situational characteristics sets of the method components and associating the unified sets with the resultant method component. When merging two method components and unifying their sets, the elements in these sets are also structurally composed, applying merge or generalization operations.

Generalization enables one to abstract away aspects that differ between method components. While the merging operation can be applied to "very similar" method components, i.e., method components whose general similarity is greater than a high similarity threshold (hTH), specialization can be applied to "similar enough" method components, i.e., method components whose general similarity is greater than a different similarity threshold (sTh) which satisfies $sTh < hTh < 1$. Table 2 summarizes the types and conditions of the structural composition operations. In this table, exhibition links are representative of all structural relations. However, they can also be replaced by other structural links.

As can be seen, the name of the new structural composition that resulted from applying a merging or generalization operation, is derived from the constituents (i.e., the method components) and the operation: the merged method components are named 'MC_1 and MC_2', while the generalized method components are named 'MC_1 and MC_2 generalization', where MC_1 and MC_2 are

Table 2. Structural composition of method components

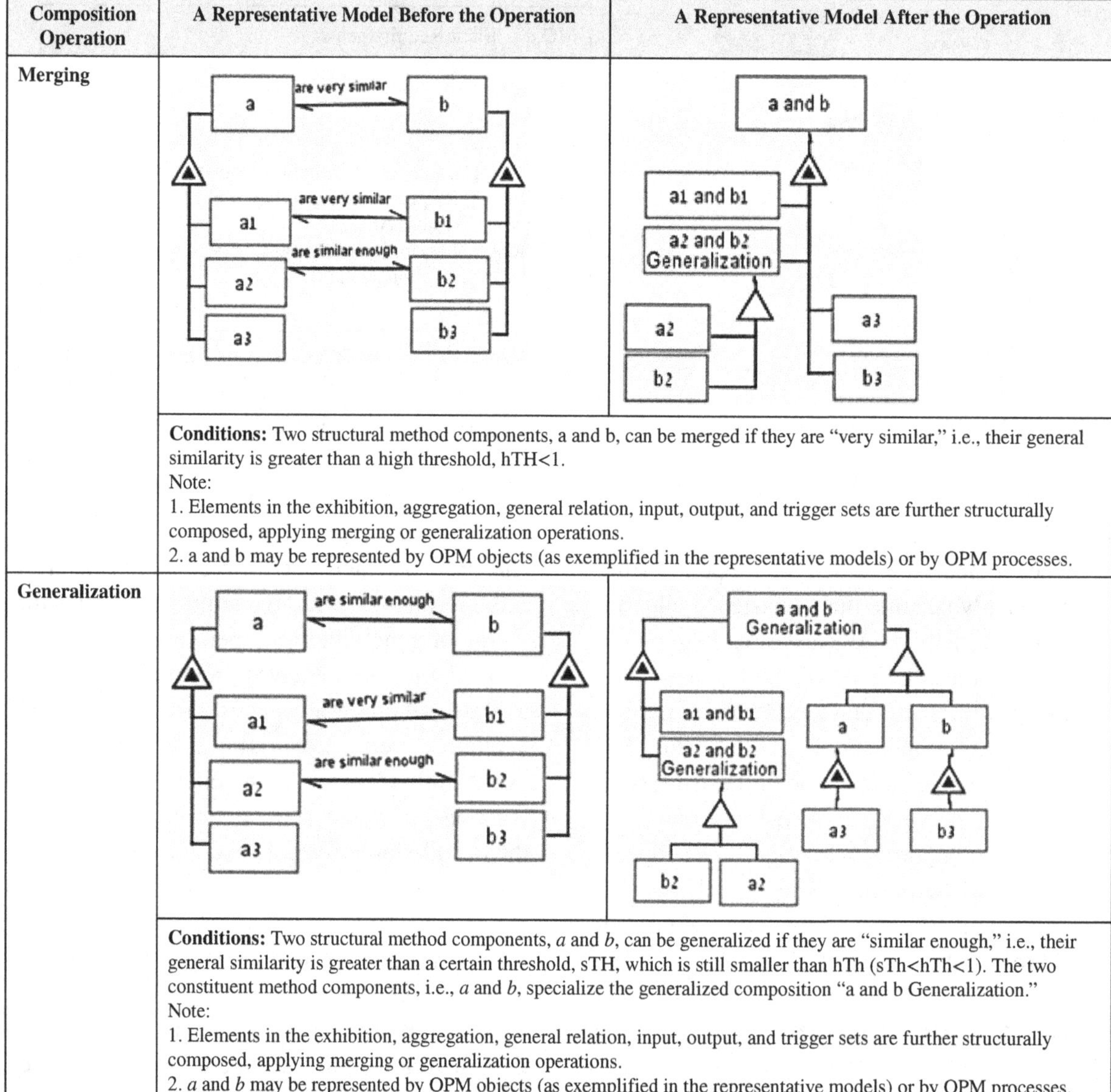

Composition Operation	A Representative Model Before the Operation	A Representative Model After the Operation
Merging		
	Conditions: Two structural method components, a and b, can be merged if they are "very similar," i.e., their general similarity is greater than a high threshold, hTH<1. Note: 1. Elements in the exhibition, aggregation, general relation, input, output, and trigger sets are further structurally composed, applying merging or generalization operations. 2. a and b may be represented by OPM objects (as exemplified in the representative models) or by OPM processes.	
Generalization		
	Conditions: Two structural method components, *a* and *b*, can be generalized if they are "similar enough," i.e., their general similarity is greater than a certain threshold, sTH, which is still smaller than hTh (sTh<hTh<1). The two constituent method components, i.e., *a* and *b*, specialize the generalized composition "a and b Generalization." Note: 1. Elements in the exhibition, aggregation, general relation, input, output, and trigger sets are further structurally composed, applying merging or generalization operations. 2. *a* and *b* may be represented by OPM objects (as exemplified in the representative models) or by OPM processes.	

the names of the constituents. In any case, the role of the structurally composed method components is the least common super-element in the hierarchy of method engineering concepts, derived, for example, from ISO/IEC 24744. If, for instance, MC_1 is a 'process' and MC_2 is a 'task', then the role of the composed method component will be 'work unit'.

Behavioral Composition

Behavioral composition deals with combining two or more method components into one composite method component, taking temporal aspects into consideration. As such, behavioral composition can be applied on behavioral method components, i.e., work units. The five behavioral composition operations used in different development methods

Table 3. Behavioral composition of method components

Composition Operation	A Representative Model Before the Operation	A Representative Model After the Operation
Alternative	a1, b1, are similar, A, B, a2, b2, are similar	A or B, Alternative Stage, Process Selection, Work Product Selected process, 1, 2, A, B, a1 and b1, a2 and b2
	Conditions: Two behavioral method components *A* and *B* are considered as alternatives if the behavioral similarity between them is greater than a certain threshold. Note that the internal structure, names, and even roles of *A* and *B* may be different, but their similar interfaces indicate that they may have similar purposes.	
Sequential	B, b, are similar, A, a	Sequential Stage, B before A, B, A, a and b
	Conditions: Two method components, *A* and *B*, can be sequentially composed if they are not alternatives and one produces an output that may be used as an input by the other. Formally expressed, ∃a∈A.Inp, b∈B.Out such that the general similarity between a and b is greater than a certain threshold. In this case, *B* should be executed *before A*.	
Concurrent	a, are similar, b, A, B	Concurrent Stage, A with B, A, B, a and b
	Conditions: Two method components, A and B, can be concurrently composed if they are not alternatives; they cannot be sequentially composed (in either order); and they are triggered in similar conditions (formally expressed, ∃a∈A.Tri, b∈B.Tri such that the general similarity between a and b is greater than a certain threshold).	

continued on following page

are: (1) alternative, in which the constituent behavioral components are substituted and perform similar tasks; (2) sequential, in which the constituent behavioral components perform consecutively; the preceding behavioral component results in (structural) method components that serve as inputs to the following behavioral component; (3) concurrent, in which the constituent behavioral components perform in parallel or independently; (4) iterative, in which the constituent behavioral components are repeated and in each cycle the produced products are detailed and refined; and (5) incremental, in which the constituent behavioral components are repeated and in each cycle new increments are added to the produced products. Table 3 summarizes the conditions for carrying

Table 3. Continued

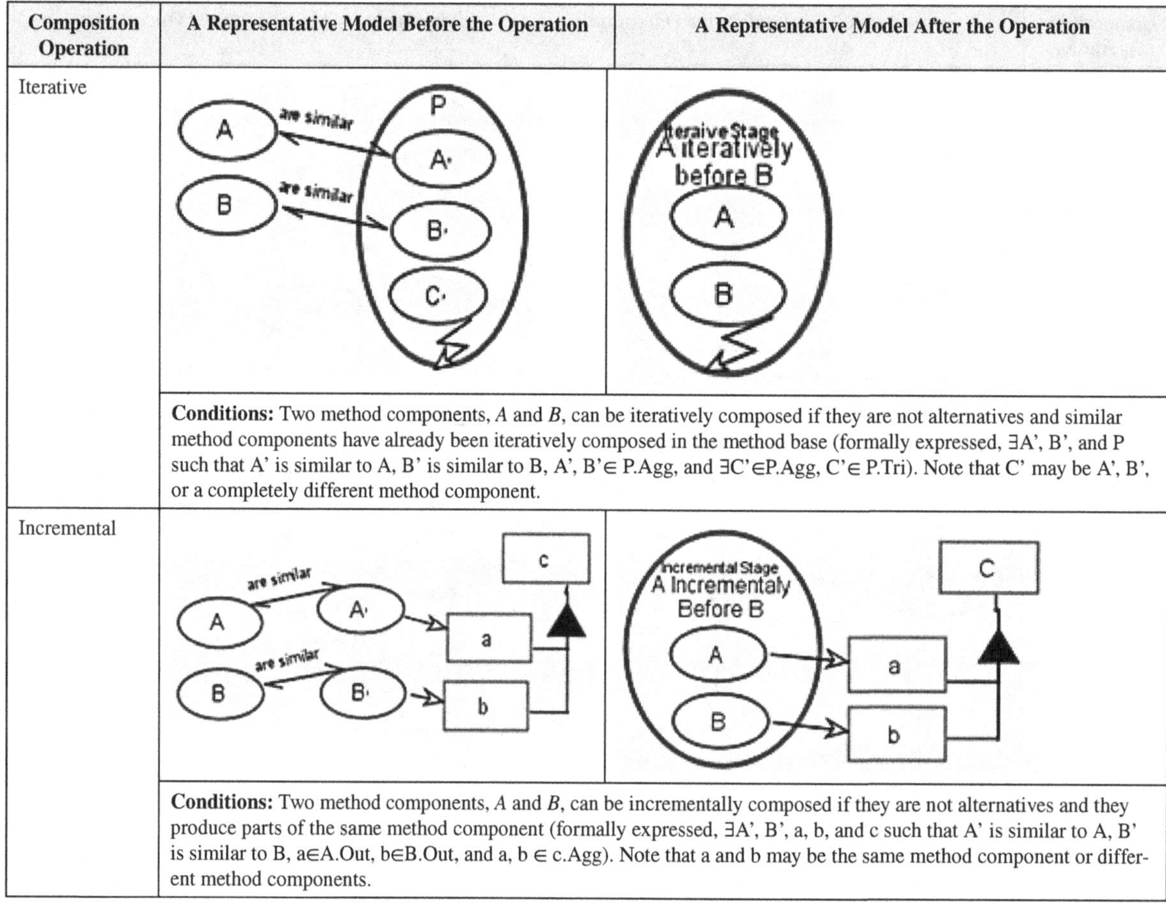

Composition Operation	A Representative Model Before the Operation	A Representative Model After the Operation
Iterative		
	Conditions: Two method components, *A* and *B*, can be iteratively composed if they are not alternatives and similar method components have already been iteratively composed in the method base (formally expressed, ∃A', B', and P such that A' is similar to A, B' is similar to B, A', B'∈ P.Agg, and ∃C'∈P.Agg, C'∈ P.Tri). Note that C' may be A', B', or a completely different method component.	
Incremental		
	Conditions: Two method components, *A* and *B*, can be incrementally composed if they are not alternatives and they produce parts of the same method component (formally expressed, ∃A', B', a, b, and c such that A' is similar to A, B' is similar to B, a∈A.Out, b∈B.Out, and a, b ∈ c.Agg). Note that a and b may be the same method component or different method components.	

out these operations, along with representative associated models for each operation. The composed method component can be represented, for example, via the 'Stage' concept from ISO/IEC 24744, which specifies the temporal aspect of development methods.

As can be seen in Table 3, the name of the resultant composite method component is derived from the operation (e.g., 'or' for alternatives and 'before' for sequential composition) and the names of the method components that it comprises. The aggregation set of the composite method component includes the method components that comprise it, whereas the input, output, and trigger sets of all the method components that comprise them are percolated to the new composite method component. Finally, the situational characteristics are also percolated from the constituent method components to the composite method component, but if different constituent method components have the same situational feature, f, with different values, $v_1, \ldots v_n$, then the situational characteristics set of the composite method component will include the pair <f, 'v_1 or … or v_n'>.

As an example, consider the composition of the two method components depicted in Figure 2, "Requirements Extraction" and "Manage User Stories." As already noted, the level of behavioral similarity between these method components is relatively high, justifying their composition as alternatives. Figure 6 depicts the resultant composite method component. Note that merged and generalized inputs, outputs, and triggers are percolated to the wrapping stage (the alternative stage in this case), preserving OPM consistency rules between diagrams. "Requirements Document and User Stories Generalization," for example, is an output for Requirements Extraction, and both an input and an output for Manage User Stories. Thus, it is considered both an input and an output for the alternative stage. Furthermore, OPM enables implicit specification of aggregation and exhibition relationships: processes that appear within the frame of a process define aggregation relationships between the processes, whereas objects that appear within the frame of a process define exhibition relationships between the elements. Therefore, for Requirements Extraction, MC.Exh = {"Selected Process"} and MC.Agg = {"Process Selection", "Requirements Extraction", "Manage User Stories"}.

An examination of the five behavioral composition operations reveals that the last four can be classified as aggregation according to Becker et

Figure 6. Composition of Requirement Extraction and Manage User Stories as alternatives: (a) the OPM model and (b) the formal specification

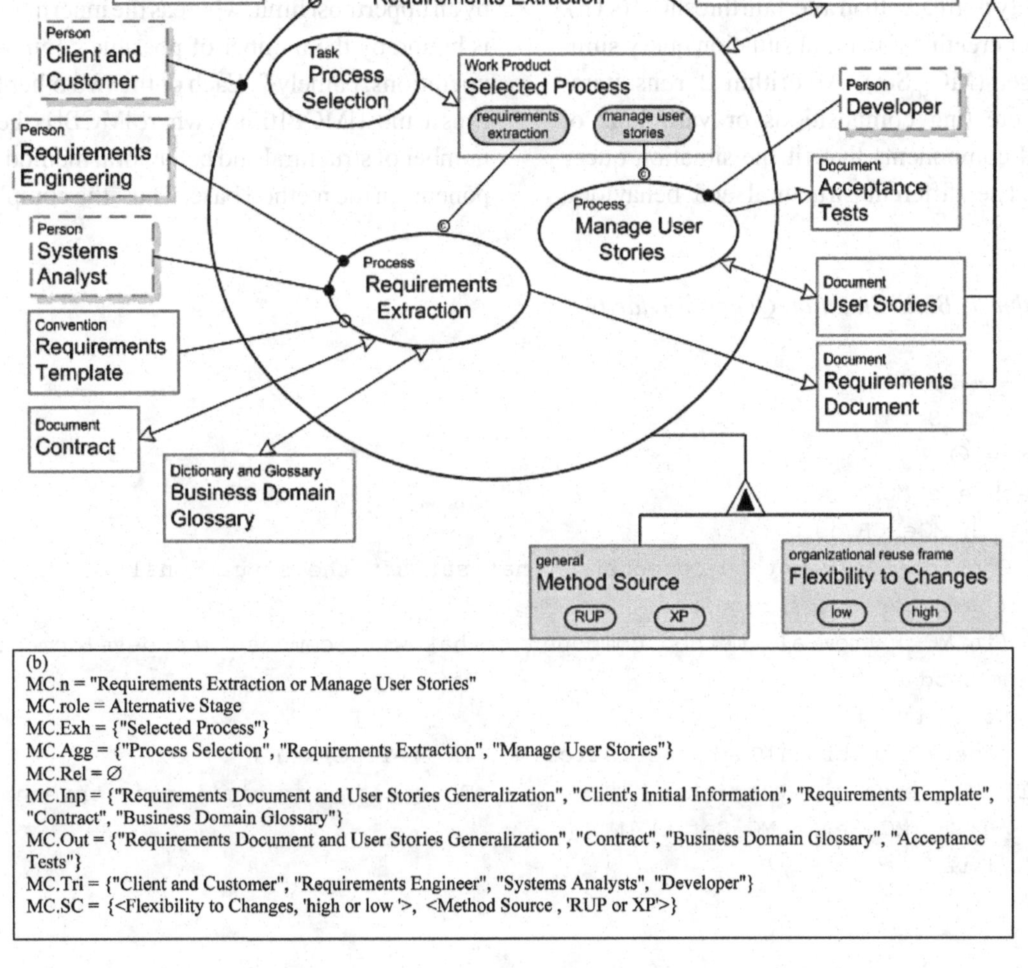

(b)
MC.n = "Requirements Extraction or Manage User Stories"
MC.role = Alternative Stage
MC.Exh = {"Selected Process"}
MC.Agg = {"Process Selection", "Requirements Extraction", "Manage User Stories"}
MC.Rel = ∅
MC.Inp = {"Requirements Document and User Stories Generalization", "Client's Initial Information", "Requirements Template", "Contract", "Business Domain Glossary"}
MC.Out = {"Requirements Document and User Stories Generalization", "Contract", "Business Domain Glossary", "Acceptance Tests"}
MC.Tri = {"Client and Customer", "Requirements Engineer", "Systems Analysts", "Developer"}
MC.SC = {<Flexibility to Changes, 'high or low '>, <Method Source , 'RUP or XP'>}

al.'s classification (2007), whereas the alternative operation can be classified as specialization: the two constituents (i.e., method components) can be generalized to a single method component.

The General Composition Algorithm

As noted, the creation of a situational method requires the definition of a situation query, the retrieval of suitable method components from a method component base, and the composition of method components (denoted in the following as MC_{SQ}, MCB, and MC_{SQ}Set, respectively). Algorithm 1 describes how the initial set of retrieved method components is achieved: for each element in the situation query, the algorithm associates similar method components from the method base, where similar elements are those whose general similarity is greater than a certain threshold (sTh).

After creating the initial situation query similarity set (MC_{SQ}Set), Algorithm 2 runs iteratively, creating compositions or variations of method components that fit the situation query better. The different structural and behavioral composition operations are applied on the initial situation query similarity set (MC_{SQ}Set) and the method components base (MCB), in an effort to compose larger method components that suit the situation query in hand better, until no composition is applicable or the maximum number of iterations is reached. Note that any created composition (newMC) is checked against the situational characteristics specified by the method engineer in the situation query, MC_{SQ}. Only if it satisfies these situational characteristics, as a whole composite method component, is it inserted into the resultant method components set, MC_{SQ}Set.

An analysis of the complexity of the Create Situational Composition algorithm (Algorithm 2) shows that it contains four loops, two of which are bound by constants; the outermost loop is bound by an uppermost limit, whereas the innermost loop is bound by the number of possible composition operations, namely 7. Each of the two other loops runs at most |MCB| times, where |MCB| is the total number of structural and behavioral method components in the method base. Thus, the complexity

Algorithm 1. Build Situation Query Similarity Set

```
Input:  MCB, MC_SQ
Output: MC_SQ Set
MC_SQ Set = Ø
For each e ∈ MC_SQ
  For each MC∈MCB do
    // Consider only method components that satisfy the situational
       characteristics required
    // (in MC_SQ) from all method components that will compose the development
       method
    // to be built
    If (checkSituationalCharacteristics(MC, MC_SQ)=True) then
      If (G_sim(e, MC) > sTh) then         // sTh stands for similarity threshold
            MC_SQ Set = MC_SQ Set ∪ {MC}
      End if
    End if
  End for
End for
Return MC_SQ Set
```

Algorithm 2. Create Situational Composition

```
Input:  MCB, MC_SQSet, MC_SQ
Output: MC_SQSet
Do
  MC_SQSetTemp = ∅
  For each MC ∈ MC_SQSet do
    For each MC' ∈ MCB do
      For each strategy∈{seq, iter, inc, conc, alter, merge, generalize} do
        // possibleOperation and createCompositeMethodComponent follow
        // Table 3 rules
        If possibleOperation (MC, MC', strategy) then
          newMC= createCompositeMethodComponent(MC, MC', strategy)
          If (checkSituationalCharacteristics(newMC, MC_SQ)=True) then
            MC_SQSetTemp = MC_SQSetTemp ∪ newMC
        End if
      End for
    End for
    Delete MC from MC_SQSet
  End for
  MC_SQSet = MC_SQSet ∪ MC_SQSetTemp
Until MC_SQSetTemp = ∅ or the number of iterations reaches an uppermost limit
Return  MC_SQSet
```

of the Create Situational Composition algorithm is $O(|MCB|^2)$. Prior to this algorithm, the Situation Query Similarity Set has to be built (Algorithm 1). The complexity of this preprocessing is also bound by $|MCB|^2$. The complexity of the overall automatic method components composition is therefore $O(|MCB|^2)$.

EVALUATING THE AUTOMATIC CREATION OF SITUATIONAL METHODS

In order to evaluate it, the proposed approach has been implemented as a tool called ADOM-ME. This tool enables the creation, modification, retrieval, and composition of method components that are stored in a method base. The experimental method base consisted of 244 structural and behavioral method components, organized in 15 OPM models, which were derived from four well known methods, namely XP (Beck & Andres, 2004), Scrum (Schwaber & Beedle, 2002), RUP (Kruchten, 2000), and OPF (Firesmith & Henderson-Sellers, 2001). The selection of these methods was not arbitrary: XP and Scrum represented "agile" methods, while RUP and OPF represented "traditional" ones. The method components were taken from different development phases, including business modeling, requirements analysis, software design, and software implementation. Having analyzed the characteristics of this method base, we set the different weights and thresholds as described in Table 4; the reasons for setting these values are presented in the fourth column.

We compared the results received from the ADOM-ME tool with the recommendations of

Table 4. The values assigned to the different weights and thresholds for the experiment

Parameter	Description	Value	Reasons for Setting
w_{ling}	The linguistic similarity weight	0.15	The weight of the linguistic similarity was reduced with respect to the other weights, due to the variability of the method components in the method base (different development approaches, different development phases).
w_{meta}	The meta-informational similarity weight	0.283	
w_{str}	The structural similarity weight	0.283	
w_{bhv}	The behavioral similarity weight	0.283	
w_{exh}	The exhibition set similarity weight	0.4	The weight of the relation set similarity was reduced with respect to the other weights, since the method components used were rarely structurally related.
w_{agg}	The aggregation set similarity weight	0.4	
w_{rel}	The relation set similarity weight	0.2	
w_{inp}	The input set similarity weight	0.33	Equal values were assigned to these weights, since no bias was detected.
w_{out}	The output set similarity weight	0.33	
w_{tri}	The trigger set similarity weight	0.33	
hTh	The high threshold for defining "very similar" components	0.60	These values were experimentally set, after running different queries on the method base and analyzing the tool's results.
sTh	The low threshold for defining "similar enough" components	0.55	

humans for the same different situation queries in order to evaluate our retrieval and composition considerations. Due to difficulties in conducting such a comparison in industrial settings, because it would require considerable time, effort, and resources (Carver, Jaccheri, Morasca, & Shull, 2003), the human recommenders who participated in this comparison were a dozen advanced undergraduate (final year) and graduate information systems students at the University of Haifa, Israel, who took a seminar in method engineering in the academic year 2008-2009. The students were familiar with method engineering and situational method engineering concepts and activities, as well as with OPM. We further claim that the academic and industrial background of these students render them comparable to junior method engineers. The students were familiar with all the method components in the method base and had worked with them during the semester on different occasions. The rest of this section elaborates on the comparison settings, results, conclusions, and validity threats.

Comparison Settings

The tasks were divided into three categories, each of which consisted of two to four representative tasks. The first category consisted of *comprehension tasks*, which required the students to understand the intentions of the models of the different method components. The students were asked to justify the selection of specific method components for given situation queries. The second category consisted of *retrieval tasks*, which required the students to suggest suitable method components (from the method base) for given situation queries, and justify their choices. Finally, the third category consisted of *composition tasks*, which required the students to suggest appropriate compositions for sets of retrieved method components and given situation queries. The full questionnaire is provided in ADOM-ME web site (http://mis.hevra.haifa.ac.il/~iris/research/ME/). Table 5 details the classification of the different tasks in that questionnaire into the three aforementioned categories.

So that the results of the automatic tool would not influence the human recommenders (i.e., the

Table 5. Classification of the different questionnaire tasks into comprehension, retrieval, and composition categories

Part	Question No.	Category	Question Format
A	1	Comprehension	For each listed method component, explain the reasons for its selection in the context of the given situation. Indicate all possible reasons.
A	2	Composition	Identify pairs of elements relevant to both "Requirements Extraction" and "Manage User Stories" that in your opinion indicate the relationships between these method components. For each pair, briefly explain the relationships and your reasons for composition.
A	3		Rank the level of suitability of the two method components to the situation in hand (1 indicates "not suitable at all" and 5 indicates "very suitable"). The objective of this question is to attain additional insights into questions A1 and A2.
B	1		Identify and mark the words in the given text that may influence the retrieval of relevant method components. The objective of this question is to aid situation query definition (for questions B2 and B3).
B	2	Retrieval	Identify the method components (from the method base) that are suitable for the given situation. For each component, indicate the reasons for your selection.
B	3	Composition	Which of the method components you retrieved (in question B2) should be incrementally or iteratively composed? Explain your choice.
C	1	Comprehension	Indicate the level of suitability of each listed component for the situation in hand (scale 1-5), and give the factors that you think led to its selection.
C	2	Composition	Suggest compositions of the components retrieved for question C1 that are suitable to the described situation. Refer to sequential and concurrent compositions only.
C	3	Retrieval + Composition	The situation has been changed <description of the change>. State which components you would pick in order to support this change. How would you integrate these components with the prior components? Refer to sequential and concurrent compositions only.

students), the latter were not provided with the tool outcomes, but rather were required to make their suggestions independently, and justify each suggestion. Since this process is time-consuming, error-prone, and influenced by the students' knowledge and understanding of the development methods used, the tasks were very concrete and the students were given unlimited time to conclude their tasks.

Independently, we modeled each situation query related to these tasks and ran the ADOM-ME tool to obtain its suggestions of suitable method components or compositions. We limited the number of the iterations of the tool, so that the tool outcome would be comparable with the results of the manual processing of the students.

Comparison Results

In each question, the answers given by the students were sorted according to the number of students who provided them and the number of supplied justifications, whereas the outputs of ADOM-ME were presented as an ordered list of method components sorted according to their descending general similarity with the situation query. We then compared pairs of relevant student and tool responses, classifying each pair into complete match, partial match, or mismatch. A pair was considered as a 'complete match' when both its location in the ordered lists of answers and its justifications were alike (we used the different similarity metrics as "justifications" of the tool); the pair of responses was considered as 'partial mismatch' when either its location in the ordered lists of answers or its justifications were differ-

Table 6. The comparison results

Category	Comparison Results		Reasons for Differences
Comprehension	complete match partial match mismatch	68% 9% 23%	1. The level of detail of the models in the method base 2. Behavioral similarity between structural method components (students only) 3. Differences in the work nature (manual vs. automatic) 4. Justification according to different criteria (linguistic, meta-informational, structural, and behavioral)
Retrieval	complete match partial match mismatch	52% 11% 37%	1. Differences in the work nature (manual vs. automatic) 2. Students relied on previous knowledge that was not explicitly specified in the models
Composition	complete match partial match mismatch	61% 11% 28%	1. Students paid no attention to the linguistic similarity between work products, especially when their specification spanned different diagrams 2. Students searched mainly for compositions of behavioral method components and merged only similar work products that they ran across 3. Students were influenced by the level of detail of work unit models and the number of similar associated work products and producers 4. Students relied on previous knowledge that was not explicitly specified in the models 5. Students missed options due to their manual work

ent; otherwise, i.e., when both its location in the ordered lists of answers and justifications were different, it was considered as 'mismatch'. Student or tool responses that had no counterpart were classified as mismatches. Table 6 summarizes the comparison results in each category, namely comprehension, retrieval, and composition, along with possible reasons for differences. These differences are elaborated next.

Comprehension Results

In 77% of the cases, the students correctly comprehended the method component models, providing responses that were similar to those of the tool. Only in 23% of the results was a complete mismatch between the answers of the students and of the tool detected. An analysis of the students' responses and the tool's outputs revealed four main reasons for these mismatches. First, the level of detail of the models in the method base influenced the performance of the students. The "Requirement Extraction" process, for example, had a very detailed model, which spanned across three different diagrams. As a result, the general similarity that was calculated by the tool between this method component and the situation query was relatively low, but the students ranked this method component high due to the similarity between its behavioral aspects and the given situation. This outcome may indicate that the importance of behavioral similarity in the creation of situational methods is greater than that of the structural aspects, justifying a reduction in the structural weight (w_{str}) with respect to the behavioral weight (w_{bhv}).

Secondly, the students referred to the behavioral similarity between structural method components, especially those of producers. They took into consideration the behavioral components that are triggered by the producers, while measuring the similarity between the producers. This outcome may raise a question concerning our decision to refer to behavioral aspects of behavioral components only, and thus suggests a subject for future research.

Thirdly, we detected differences that we believe originate in the differences in the nature of the work (manual vs. automatic). While the students had to establish their decisions manually in a large method base, the tool did so automatically and systematically, taking into consideration all the method components in the method base, and thus its results were more consistent and more explicable.

Finally, in a few cases, we found different justifications for the same decision, e.g., the tool made recommendations mainly according to linguistic considerations while the students focused on behavioral justifications. The reason for this outcome may be the fact that English was not the first language of the students and they could not recognize the linguistic similarity between the method component names in these cases.

Despite these differences, when the students were asked to give an overall recommendation (question 3 in Part A), they reached conclusions similar to those of the tool.

Retrieval Results

In 63% of the cases, the tool and the students retrieved quite similar method components or provided similar justifications for their selection. However, in 37% of the cases, mismatches were found. The higher percentages of mismatches in this category may be attributed mainly to differences in the nature of the work (manual vs. automatic). The tool retrieved five suitable method components that were not mentioned in the students' responses at all. The linguistic and behavioral similarity metrics of these method components justify their retrieval for the given situation queries. The students, who were required to search the entire method base manually, seemed to miss these method components: two out of the five method components were sub-processes of method components that had already been discussed in another part of the questionnaire, while two other method components handled requirements that satisfied only a small part of the goal of the situation query. Another finding is that the students relied on previous knowledge that was not explicitly specified in the models and thus could not be used by the tool. This finding points to the importance of including detailed models in the method base in order to obtain relevant situational methods.

Composition Results

In 72% of the cases, the tool and the students recommended similar compositions, while 28% of the cases were classified as mismatches. An analysis of the justifications of the tool and the students showed that the differences in ranking compositions that involve work products occurred when the linguistic aspect of these work products reflected no similarity and the specification of the method components spanned across different diagrams. This outcome is in line with our observation that throughout the questionnaire the students searched mainly for compositions of behavioral method components and only merged similar work products that they encountered.

The main reasons for the differences in composing work units are the detail level of the models and the number of similar associated work products and producers. According to our analysis of incremental vs. iterative compositions (Question 2 in Part B of the questionnaire), more than half of the students' recommendations on incremental compositions (6 out of 10) were in line with the rule implemented for incremental compositions in the tool. Two out of the four recommendations that did not follow this rule were based on previous knowledge that was not explicitly specified in the models, whereas each one of the other two method components was retrieved by only one student. Regarding iterative compositions, the students based their recommendations mainly on linguistic aspects (expressed in the method component names or roles), rather than on the method components structure. While this strategy may work well on pre-defined method components in a relatively small method base, it may be problematic in the general case. Nevertheless, this result raises the question whether linguistic aspects should be examined in addition to the iterative composition rule – an issue that should be investigated in the future.

An examination of the recommendations of the student and the tool concerning sequential vs. concurrent compositions (Questions 1 and 3 in Part C) revealed that almost all the recommendations concerning the same method components yielded the same composition operation. The two exceptions were method components that could be concurrently composed, but (some of) the students tried ordering them into a sequential composition, utilizing their "previous knowledge." In addition, the tool found one to two compositions that were not found by the students, probably due to the manual nature of their work, whereas the students suggested several compositions that were not detected by the tool, based on their "previous knowledge."

General Conclusions and Threats to Validity

Based on the comparison above, ignoring differences that we believe were due to the manual work of the students, we can draw four general conclusions. First, the different similarity metrics we have identified for comparing method components, namely, linguistic, meta-informational, structural, and behavioral similarities, correlated in most cases with the students' selection and justification in the same situations. Differences were discovered mainly when: (1) students used previous knowledge that was not explicitly modeled in the method base, and (2) students referred to behavioral aspects while evaluating the similarity between structural method components, especially producers. Secondly, the rules for sequential, concurrent, and increment composition were in line with the students' recommendations. Nevertheless, the students offered more compositions than were suggested by the tool, following a more flexible policy for composition, based mainly on their previous knowledge. Thirdly, the students recommended iterative composition, considering linguistic aspects alone. This may be due to a confusion between incremental and iterative compositions and because they did not have a clear criterion for distinguishing between these types of composition. Finally, the students seem to comprehend the method components model.

The main threats to the validity of the results can be divided into threats to internal, construct, external, and conclusion validity (Wohlin, Runeson, Höst, Ohlsson, Regnell, & Wesslén, 2000). Regarding internal validity, we compared the manual work of humans (students) with the automatic and systemic work of ADOM-ME. It is well known that manual work is more time-consuming and error-prone, and less consistent. Thus, we took the following actions: (1) the scope of each task was limited and the goal was very concrete; (2) we limited the number of iterations of the tool, preventing it from examining complicated cases (such as compositions of three method components); and (3) we required justifications for each selection (of a method component or a composition) and we used this information in addition to the ranking.

The representativeness of the method components can also be questioned. We chose four well-known methods, two of which are classified as 'agile' (XP and Scrum) and the others as 'traditional' (RUP and OPF). From each method, we selected both structural and behavioral method components that had been developed by different individuals in various levels of detail. Nevertheless, further evaluations of additional method components and approaches have to be made.

The main external threat to validity stems from the type of subject who performed the tasks. In our case, the subjects were advanced undergraduate (final year) and graduate information systems students who were familiar with method engineering and situational method engineering. However, as already noted, we claim that their academic and industrial background makes them comparable to junior method engineers. Furthermore, we made an effort to ensure that staff members would accompany the students throughout the seminar course and provide detailed guidance for their tasks. Nevertheless, an additional evaluation of the approach is required; in particular, method engineers should be requested to provide feedback concerning the tool's outcome for the different situations.

Regarding construct threats to validity, the tasks in this comparison were objective, such as retrieving and composing method components according to pre-defined rules, and subjective, such as ranking. However, the subjects were requested to justify each subjective task; their ranking correlated with the provided justifications.

Finally, the small number of participants in the comparison (about a dozen), which prevented us from carrying out a statistical analysis, may raise concerns about the validity of the conclusions. To overcome this concern, we provide the raw results, as well as detailed explanations of the analysis and conclusions, on the ADOM-ME web site (http://mis.hevra.haifa.ac.il/~iris/research/ME/).

RELATED WORK

Retrieving method components and composing them into situational development methods are time-consuming, error-prone, and subjective tasks. To make these tasks more systemic, different heuristic methods have been proposed for determining similarity metrics between method components. These approaches generally measure the closeness between entities of different conceptual schemas by evaluating the common properties and links with other entities. Ralyté and Rolland (2001), for example, define semantic and structural criteria for measuring the similarity between method components. The similarity between product-related components is measured using name affinity metrics and links calculation. The process models of the method components are represented as maps that provide a non-deterministic ordering of intentions and strategies. When measuring the similarity between these maps, the semantic affinity and structural similarity between intentions and sections (i.e., intention-strategy-intention edges) are taken into consideration. Further, Ralyté and Rolland suggest two strategies for assembling method components: association and integration. Association is applicable for method components that correspond to different functionalities and do not have common elements, while integration is suitable for method components that have similar engineering goals, but provide different ways to satisfy them. In addition to these strategies, extension-based and paradigm-based operations can be performed. In comparison to this work, our approach refers to behavioral and meta-informational considerations when retrieving relevant method components, and allows additional composition possibilities, namely concurrent, iterative, and incremental compositions.

The Situation-Success-Scenario (S3) model (Harmsen, Lubbers, & Wijers, 1995) lists aggregated situation factors, performance indicators, and scenario aspects. The method components are then selected in four steps: (1) determination of the project goal, (2) determination of a preliminary scenario, (3) adaptation of the preliminary scenario, resulting in a project scenario, and (4) selection of the method components containing the aspects of the project scenario. All tasks are performed manually by method engineers or project managers.

Mirbel (2006) provides ways to qualify each method component using meaningful keywords for the critical organizational, technical, and human-related aspects. This is done in order to allow each project to share its best practices with other projects without imposing a unique organization-wide method on all of them. Similarity metrics are proposed for measuring the distances between a given situation, which is specified as a set of at least one pertinent keyword and forbidden keywords, and a method component reuse context, depicting the situations to which the method component is applicable.

Kornyshova et al. (2007) introduced multi-criteria techniques for improved guidance in the retrieval of method components. These techniques allow the selected method components to be prioritized according to multiple criteria in order to guide the method engineers in the final selection process. As opposed to mono-criterion approaches, this approach allows a more in-depth analysis of problems that takes various aspects into consideration. Two groups of techniques are used: outranking and weighting. Outranking techniques are inspired by the theory of social choice and serve as a means for indicating the degree of dominance of one alternative over the other. Weighting techniques assign weights to the different decision criteria. A project characteristics typology is suggested in order to identify all the relevant critical aspects. The final selection is then realized using similarity metrics that measure the distances between different work products and various work units. The approach does not take into consideration the structure and behavior of the method components.

Pirro (2009) compares several approaches for assessing similarity, according to the source of information they exploit. Ontology-based approaches (e.g., Rada, Mili, Bicknell, & Blettner, 1989; Hirst & St-Onge, 1998) assess semantic similarity by counting the number of nodes or edges separating two concepts. These approaches suffer from the limitation that, in order to perform properly, they require consistent and rich ontologies. Information theory approaches (e.g., Lin, 1998; Rodríguez & Egenhofer, 2002) exploit the notion of information content, defined as a measure of the informativeness of concepts and computed by counting the occurrence of words in large corpora. The drawbacks here are that these approaches require time-consuming analysis of corpora, and that Information Content values usually depend on the kind of corpora being considered. Hybrid approaches (e.g., Li, Bandar, & McLean, 2003) combine multiple information sources. They typically require some "configuration knobs" to be adjusted (e.g., weights used to set the contribution of each information source).

SUMMARY AND FUTURE WORK

As the variety of development projects increases, so does the importance of approaches that support the retrieval and composition of method components for use in given situations. However, at present most approaches in this area support manual work in which retrieval is basically structural and composition is usually sequential. Furthermore, the resultant situational methods are not recorded, managed, and potentially cataloged for future 'similar' situations. The objective of the approach suggested here is to increase the spectrum of semi-automatically created situational methods, taking behavioral aspects into consideration, and introducing additional assembling operations. The similarity between the method components is measured according to linguistic, meta-informational, structural, and behavioral considerations. Composition is enabled using two structural operations (merging and generalization) and five behavioral operations (sequential, concurrent, incremental, iterative, and alternative compositions). The resultant situational methods are inserted into the method base for future use in similar situations. Nevertheless, the creation of situational methods is not a completely automatic process and may require the involvement of method engineers to bridge the gaps between method components that are only similar enough, but not identical.

We have developed an automatic tool for the creation of situational methods and compared the outcomes of the tool with the evaluation of information systems students. The analysis of the results of this comparison highlights the importance of behavioral aspects in the retrieval and composition of method components, especially when different development paradigms are involved. In such cases, the vocabulary used for modeling the method components is diverse, the linguistic similarity value may be low, and the behavioral and structural aspects become dominant. For the purpose of retrieving reasonable method components and compositions, it is important to detail the structure and behavior of method components.

The proposed approach is adaptable and can be extended. In particular, the weights of the different similarity metrics, as well as the different thresholds, can be modified according to the diversity of the available method components. Nevertheless, the determination of the different parameters (weights and thresholds) needs further investigation. Moreover, guidelines for the determination process of these parameters should be developed, and the involvement of a team of method engineers in this process should be considered.

Further research is required to investigate the different similarity metrics and composition operations, and to consider new kinds of similarity and composition operations. In particular, the following questions can be examined. Should behavioral aspects be taken into consideration when measuring the similarity between structural method components, such as producers and work products? Should linguistic aspects be taken into consideration when applying iterative (and other) composition operations? Should the indirect context of method components be taken into consideration for retrieval and composition purposes? In addition, experimental studies of the approach in industrial settings are required. This way, the tool outcome can be examined by experienced method engineers and their feedback can be used to improve the tool and its framework.

REFERENCES

Aharoni, A., & Reinhartz-Berger, I. (2008). A domain engineering approach for situational method engineering. In Q. Li, S. Spaccaapietra, E. Yu, & A. Olivé (Eds.), *Proceedings of the 27th International Conference on Conceptual Modeling* (LNCS 5231, pp. 455-468).

Beck, K., & Andres, C. (2004). *Extreme programming explained: Embrace change* (2nd ed.). Reading, MA: Addison-Wesley.

Becker, J., Janiesch, C., & Pfeiffer, D. (2007). Reuse mechanisms in situational method engineering. In *Proceedings of the IFIP WG 8.1 Working Conference on Situational Method Engineering: Fundamentals and Experiences* (Vol. 244, pp. 79-93).

Becker, J., Knackstedt, R., Pfeiffer, D., & Janiesch, C. (2007). Configurative method engineering: On the applicability of reference modeling mechanisms in method engineering. In *Proceedings of the 13th Americas Conference on Information Systems.*

Brinkkemper, S. (1996). Method engineering: engineering of information systems development methods and tools. *Information and Software Technology*, *38*, 275–280. doi:10.1016/0950-5849(95)01059-9

Budanitsky, A., & Hirst, G. (2006). Evaluating WordNet-based measures of lexical semantic relatedness. *Computational Linguistics*, *32*(1), 13–47. doi:10.1162/coli.2006.32.1.13

Carver, J., Jaccheri, L., Morasca, S., & Shull, F. (2003). Issues in using students in empirical studies in software engineering education. In *Proceedings of the 9th International Software Metrics Symposium* (pp. 239-249).

Chrissis, M. B., Konrad, M., & Shrum, S. (2003). *CMMI: Guidelines for process integration and product improvement*. Reading, MA: Addison-Wesley.

Dao, T. N., & Simpson, T. (2005). *Measuring similarity between sentences*. Retrieved from http://wordnetdotnet.googlecode.com/svn/trunk/Projects/Thanh/Paper/WordNetDotNet_Semantic_Similarity.pdf

Domíngueza, E., & Zapata, M. A. (2007). Noesis: Towards a situational method engineering technique. *Information Systems, 32*(2), 181–222. doi:10.1016/j.is.2005.07.001

Dori, D. (2002). *Object-process methodology – A holistic system paradigm*. Berlin, Germany: Springer-Verlag.

Firesmith, D., & Henderson-Sellers, B. (2001). *The OPEN process framework: An introduction*. Reading, MA: Addison-Wesley.

Gonzalez-Perez, C. (2007). Supporting situational method engineering with ISO/IEC 24744 and the work product pool approach. In *Proceedings on Situational Method Engineering: Fundamentals and Experiences* (pp. 7-18).

Harmsen, F., Lubbers, I., & Wijers, G. (1995). Success-driven selection of fragments for situational methods: The S3 model. In *Proceedings of the 2nd International Workshop on Requirements Engineering: Foundations of Software Quality* (pp. 104-115).

Henderson-Sellers, B., & Ralyté, J. (2010). Situational method engineering: State-of-the-art review. *Journal of Universal Computer Science, 16*(3), 424–478.

Henderson-Sellers, B., & Serour, M. K. (2005). Creating a dual-agility method: The value of method engineering. *Journal of Database Management, 16*(4), 1–24. doi:10.4018/jdm.2005100101

Hirst, G., & St-Onge, D. (1998). Lexical chains as representations of context for the detection and correction of malapropisms. In Fellbaum, C. (Ed.), *WordNet: An electronic lexical database* (pp. 305–323). Cambridge, MA: MIT Press.

International Organization for Standardization (ISO). (2007). *ISO/IEC 24744: Software engineering – Metamodel for development methodologies*. Retrieved from http://www.iso.org/iso/catalogue_detail.htm?csnumber=38854

Karlsson, F., & Ågerfalk, P. J. (2009). Towards structured flexibility in information systems development: Devising a method for method configuration. *Journal of Database Management, 20*(3), 51–75. doi:10.4018/jdm.2009070103

Kornyshova, E., Deneckere, R., & Salinesi, C. (2007). Method chunks selection by multicriteria techniques: an extension of the assembly-based approach. In *Proceedings of the IFIP WG 8.1 Working Conference on Situational Method Engineering: Fundamentals and Experiences* (Vol. 244, pp. 64-78).

Kruchten, P. (2000). *The rational unified process: An introduction* (2nd ed.). Reading, MA: Addison-Wesley.

Kumar, K., & Welke, R. J. (1992). Method engineering – A proposal for situation-specific methodology construction. In Cotterman, W. W., & Senn, J. A. (Eds.), *Challenges and strategies for research in systems development* (pp. 257–268). New York, NY: John Wiley & Sons.

Li, Y., Bandar, A., & McLean, D. (2003). An approach for measuring semantic similarity between words using multiple information sources. *IEEE Transactions on Knowledge and Data Engineering, 15*(4), 871–882. doi:10.1109/TKDE.2003.1209005

Lin, D. (1998). An information-theoretic definition of similarity. In *Proceedings of the Conference on Machine Learning* (pp. 296-304).

Mirbel, I. (2006). Method chunk federation. In *Proceedings of the Workshop on Exploring Modeling Methods for Systems Analysis and Design* (pp. 407-418).

Mirbel, I., & Ralyté, J. (2006). Situational method engineering: Combining assembly-based and roadmap-driven approaches. *Requirements Engineering, 11*, 58–78. doi:10.1007/s00766-005-0019-0

Nuseibeh, B. A. (1994). *A multi-perspective framework for method integration*. Unpublished doctoral dissertation, University of London, London, UK.

Object Management Group (OMG). (2005). *Software process engineering metamodel specification - Version 1.1*. Retrieved from http://www.omg.org/docs/formal/05-01-06.pdf

Park, S., Na, H., Park, S., & Sugumaran, V. (2006). A semi-automated filtering technique software process tailoring using neural network. *Expert Systems with Applications, 30*(2), 179–189. doi:10.1016/j.eswa.2005.06.023

Peleg, M., & Dori, D. (2000). The model multiplicity problem: Experimenting with real-time specification methods. *IEEE Transactions on Software Engineering, 26*(8), 742–759. doi:10.1109/32.879812

Pirro, G. (2009). A semantic similarity metric combining features and intrinsic information content. *Data & Knowledge Engineering, 68*(11), 1289–1308. doi:10.1016/j.datak.2009.06.008

Rada, R., Mili, H., Bicknell, M., & Blettner, E. (1989). Development and application of a metric on semantic nets. *IEEE Transactions on Systems, Man, and Cybernetics, 19*(1), 17–30. doi:10.1109/21.24528

Ralyté, J. (1999). Reusing scenario based approaches in requirement engineering methods: CREWS method base. In *Proceedings of the 10th International Workshop on Database & Expert Systems Applications* (pp. 305-309).

Ralyté, J., & Rolland, C. (2001). An assembly process model for method engineering. In K. R. Dittrich, A. Geppert, & M. C. Norrie (Eds.), *Proceedings of the 13th International Conference on Advanced Information Systems Engineering* (LNCS 2068, pp. 267-283).

Raylte, J., Deneckere, R., & Rolland, C. (2003). Towards a generic model for situational method engineering. In J. Eder & M. Missikoff (Eds.), *Proceedings of the International Conference on Advanced Information Systems Engineering* (LNCS 2681, pp. 95-110).

Reinhartz-Berger, I., & Dori, D. (2005). A reflective metamodel of object-process methodology: The system modeling building blocks. In Green, P., & Rosemann, M. (Eds.), *Business systems analysis with ontologies* (pp. 130–173). Hershey, PA: Idea Group. doi:10.4018/978-1-59140-339-5.ch006

Reinhartz-Berger, I., & Dori, D. (2005). OPM vs. UML – Experimenting comprehension and construction of web application models. *Empirical Software Engineering, 10*(1), 57–80. doi:10.1023/B:EMSE.0000048323.40484.e0

Rodríguez, A., & Egenhofer, M. (2002). Determining semantic similarity among entity classes from different ontologies. *IEEE Transactions on Knowledge and Data Engineering, 15*(2), 442–456. doi:10.1109/TKDE.2003.1185844

Rolland, C. (2009). Method engineering: Towards methods as services. *Software Process Improvement and Practice, 14*, 143–164. doi:10.1002/spip.416

Rolland, C., Nurcan, S., & Grosz, G. (2000). A decision making pattern for guiding the enterprise knowledge development process. *Information and Software Technology*, *42*(5), 313–331. doi:10.1016/S0950-5849(99)00089-0

Saeki, M., Iguchi, K., Wen-yin, K., & Shinohara, M. (1993). A meta-model for representing software specification & design methods. In *Proceedings of the IFIP WG 8.1 Conference on Information Systems Development Process* (pp. 149-166).

Schwaber, K., & Beedle, M. (2002). *Agile software development with Scrum (Series in agile software development)*. Upper Saddle River, NJ: Prentice Hall.

Siau, K., Long, Y., & Ling, M. (2010). Toward a unified model if information systems development success. *Journal of Database Management*, *21*(1), 80–101. doi:10.4018/jdm.2010112304

van de Weerd, I., Versendaal, J., & Brinkkemper, S. (2006). A product software knowledge infrastructure for situational capability maturation: vision and case studies in product management. In *Proceedings of the 12th Working Conference on Requirements Engineering: Foundation for Software Quality* (pp. 97-112).

van Offenbeek, M. A. G., & Koopman, P. L. (1996). Scenarios for system development: Matching context and strategy. *Behaviour & Information Technology*, *15*(4), 250–265. doi:10.1080/014492996120175

Wohlin, C., Runeson, P., Höst, M., Ohlsson, M., Regnell, B., & Wesslén, A. (2000). *Experimentation in software engineering – An introduction*. Boston, MA: Kluwer Academic.

Wu, Z., & Palmer, M. (1994). Verb semantic and lexical selection. In *Proceedings of the 32nd Annual Meeting of the Association for Computational Linguistics* (pp. 133-138).

This work was previously published in the Journal of Database Management, Volume 22, Issue 4, edited by Keng Siau, pp. 1-29, copyright 2011 by IGI Publishing (an imprint of IGI Global).

Chapter 14
DocBase:
Design, Implementation and Evaluation of a Document Database for XML

Arijit Sengupta
Wright State University, USA

Ramesh Venkataraman
Indiana University, USA

ABSTRACT

This chapter introduces a complete storage and retrieval architecture for a database environment for XML documents. DocBase, a prototype system based on this architecture, uses a flexible storage and indexing technique to allow highly expressive queries without the necessity of mapping documents to other database formats. DocBase is an integration of several techniques that include (i) a formal model called Heterogeneous Nested Relations (HNR), (ii) a conceptual model XER (Extensible Entity Relationship), (ii) formal query languages (Document Algebra and Calculus), (iii) a practical query language (Document SQL or DSQL), (iv) a visual query formulation method with QBT (Query By Templates), and (v) the DocBase query processing architecture. This paper focuses on the overall architecture of DocBase including implementation details, describes the details of the query-processing framework, and presents results from various performance tests. The paper summarizes experimental and usability analyses to demonstrate its feasibility as a general architecture for native as well as embedded document manipulation methods.

MOTIVATION

The growth of electronic documents in the Internet era has been phenomenal. In early studies by Lawrence and Giles (1998, 1999) the approximate size of the web was reported to be about 320 million in 1997 and had grown to 800 million by 1999. With the explosive growth of the Internet that is understood to double about every five years following Moore's Law, it is hard to determine the current size of the Internet, one can easily assume that there over 10 billion unique web pages on the Internet. The primary markup language for documents on the Internet is HTML, but because

DOI: 10.4018/978-1-4666-2044-5.ch014

of its layout-driven nature and its limitations for use as a format for document interchange, new languages are being developed and used, primary among them being XML (eXtensible Markup Language) (Bray et al., 2008). XML is also being used to structure data-exchange among businesses, e.g., through the use of the ebXML standard (Grangard et al., 2001). Further, emerging web services standards such as SOAP (Gudgin et al., 2007), WSDL (Christensen et al., 2001) and UDDI (Clement et al., 2004) all use XML for achieving their required functionality. Hence, it is not surprising that XML is a key component of advanced software development frameworks such as Sun Microsystem's (now acquired by Oracle) J2EE and Microsoft's .NET, and is the backbone of emerging architectures such as Service Oriented Architecture (SOA).

Use of XML, however, is not limited to the "back end" of systems. XML is playing an increasing larger role in the area of document management. For example, many academic conferences now require that the final submissions are submitted as an XML document. This allows the proceedings to seamlessly be converted to various presentations formats (HTML, PDF etc.). At the same time, it allows for the creation of a searchable repository of these articles for use in electronic document databases, e.g., ABI/Inform or INSPEC. Thus, it is not surprising that XML documents are playing a significant role in modern day libraries (Tennant, 2002). XML is also being used to transform the way financial information is collected and reported. Extensible Business Reporting Language (XBRL) is a language to enable standardized communication of business and financial information around the world (http://www.xbrl.org). Many companies such as, Edgar Online, Reuters, Microsoft etc. are now reporting and archiving financial information using XBRL. A similar standard, XBITS (XML Book Industry Transaction Standards) is taking root in the book industry to enable "bi-directional electronic data interchanges within the book manufacturing supply chain" (http://www.idealliance.org/xbits).

With the growth in the use of XML, both in terms of quantity and variety of applications, it is important that techniques be developed that will allow for the flexible as well as efficient management of XML data and documents. In particular, there is a critical need to examine the issues surrounding the storage and retrieval of XML data.

With regard to storage, researchers have proposed techniques that range from storing XML documents using existing file-based systems (e.g., Gonnet & Tompa, 1987) to storing them in object-oriented and relational databases (e.g., Christophides et al., 1994). Native XML data management (Fiebig et al., 2002) has also emerged as a viable alternative to relational or object-oriented databases. From a querying perspective, the most common method for searching information in XML databases is using the standard released by the World Wide Web Consortium (W3C) - XQuery (Boag et al., 2007). However, given the popularity of declarative languages like SQL for querying databases, the jury is still out on whether a query language like XQuery can serve the needs of all constituencies.

Let us use a motivating example which in fact started this research. Suppose a reference librarian has acquired the Chadwyck-Healey English poetry database (Chadwyck-Healey, 1994) and needs to make the data available to patrons who have no background in XML and related standards such as XQuery, XPath, etc. A simple option would be to index the documents using a standard web search engine that will immediately allow keyword searches through the collection. However, the poems have an interesting meta-data structure that a standard web search cannot easily perform, unless the documents are converted into other formats. DocBase was designed from this perspective, with the goal that the librarian can drop the XML documents into a file system folder and start treating the documents as a database that can be queried using an SQL-based language.

DocBase was designed ground up to enable users of structured documents to store, index and retrieve information from the documents much in the same way one uses a database system. Although it is designed with usability in mind, DocBase represents a complete formal methodology for designing and implementing databases for any type of structured documents. The complete stream of research based on DocBase provides several contributions to the field of databases for documents[1]:

- A conceptual model for designing XML-based applications (Sengupta et al., 2003) allowing users to design XML databases using visual and conceptual techniques;
- A formal model for structured documents (covered in this paper), allowing databases to build internal representations of the data based on the users' conceptual models;
- A system of equivalent low-complexity query languages combining first order logic with structured text retrieval, including DSQL, a conservative extension to SQL (Sengupta & Ramesh, 2009) – allowing users to write ad-hoc queries on the data easily and without the need to learn any new technologies;
- A generalized visual query language and interface for document queries (Sengupta & Dillon, 2006) – allowing users to search data using an intuitive visual method;
- A flexible architecture for storage and query processing on structured documents *in place*, i.e., without conversion (covered in this paper) – allowing databases to store the documents securely that allows efficient execution of the queries;
- A methodology of securing the documents and providing strategies for access control into various components of the document (Mohan et al., 2007);
- An experimental setup and evaluation for document databases using well-known benchmarks as well as information retrieval models (covered in this paper) to demonstrate that all the above can be performed with reasonable performance.

The paper follows the design science methodology prescribed in Hevner et al. (2004). The artifact in question in this paper is the overall system itself and more specifically the formal model for documents and flexible architecture. In addition to presenting the details of these pieces, we specifically evaluate this artifact by a series of experiments that demonstrate the performance, viability and scalability of the system.

The rest of this paper is structured as follows. The next section reviews the literature on prior work in the area of XML document storage and retrieval, both in academic research and in industry, with a particular focus on native XML databases. We then introduce the key philosophies underlying the DocBase system and present the architectural overview of the system. We then start with the storage layer of DocBase, detail the logical component, and then finally describe the actual query processing techniques. Next, we compare the performance of DocBase with some existing systems and demonstrate the benefits of the query capabilities available in DocBase. Finally, we present some concluding comments and future research directions.

RELATED WORK

Increased usage of XML both as a media for exchange and as the native data format creates a need to store, manage and query the information. There are essentially three different ways in which this can be done:

- **Store XML as Files:** XML documents and data are treated similar to text files and are stored either directly using the file system supported by an operating system or by using the "BLOB" and "CLOB" datatypes seen in a relational database. External indexes and other query optimization strategies are generally used to improve the efficiency of query access.

- ***XML* Data in Relational Tables:** In this approach, the XML document is parsed and the information is automatically converted into a series of tables in a relational database. Two popular approaches for storing XML data in relational databases are the structure-mapping and model-mapping approaches (Yoshikawa et al., 2001). In the structure-mapping approach, the logical structure of documents (from available DTDs or schemas, or generated from content) is mapped to an equivalent database schema, and the documents are transformed into the host database. In the model-mapping approach, a fixed database model is used to represent any document structure, and the documents are decomposed to the target structure, primarily using path traversal and other graph-theoretic properties.
- **Native XML Database:** With this approach, the XML document is stored in a database that understands the structure of the XML document and is able to perform queries and retrieve the data taking advantage of the knowledge of its XML structure.

Although various File-based systems exist for XML query processing (Fankhauser, 2002; Fernandez & Simeon, 2004), these systems are primarily for the purpose of demonstrating XML querying capabilities with XQuery, and do not demonstrate all the requirements of XML database systems.

Translating XML into database systems using either structure-mapping or model-mapping is fairly common. Structure-mapping approach is followed in Verso from INRIA (Abiteboul et al., 1993; Abiteboul & Viannu, 1997; Christophides et al., 1994) using the Object-oriented database system O_2 (Bancilhon et al., 1988). Some of the translation mechanisms require an object (or table) to be created for every element type of XML documents (structure-mapping approach) which in turn requires the tables to be joined to process queries. Model-mapping approaches often show highly efficient query processing capabilities, often because of the relational structure involves pre-computing some of the paths (Yoshikawa et al., 2001; Zhang, 1995). Commercial relational database management systems such as IBM DB2, Oracle 10g and Microsoft SQL Server, also support several extensions to help store and query XML.

Although our methodology can support existing database systems for storage, because of its direct handling of XML documents in the storage, it falls under the category of native XML systems. In the rest of the section, we provide further details on some well-known native XML databases. Native XML systems are databases that have been designed keeping XML specific requirements and features in mind. Similar to traditional databases, native XML databases have to support features like transaction management, multi-user access, query languages and so on. The rest of the section briefly describes research efforts in academia and industry and other open source collaborations in the development of native XML databases.

Research Based Systems

One common method followed by native XML databases is to model the document structure using a grammar and the actual documents as words in the language described by the grammar. Querying methods in this approach include:(i) operations based on the grammar which governs the database schema (Desai et al., 1986; Gonnet & Tompa, 1987; Colby, 1990); (ii) use of existing database systems to implement an equivalent database schema to store the documents; or (iii) use of special structures such as Patricia trees (Gonnet & Baeza-Yates, 1991). Although limited in their storage capabilities, insights to efficient querying of documents without complete re-mapping can be derived from much of this work. Systems like Sgrep (Jaakkola & Kilpelainen, 1996), Open Text Search Server (previously Open Text 5.0) (OpenText, 2010) have been commonly used for highly efficient queries on documents, using proprietary query languages based on structure traversal. The following are some of the recently developed systems found in literature:

1. **Lore:** Lore (Abiteboul et al., 1997) was one of the first proponents for using a semi-structured view for structured documents. Structured documents are treated as edge-labeled graphs with links between nodes belonging to different substructures. The query language *Lorel* supported by Lore provides mechanisms for structure traversing as well as pointer constructs for processing queries.
2. **Natix:** Natix (Fiebig et al., 2002) is a database management system designed from scratch to provide storage and processing mechanisms for XML data. Natix includes features for a full-fledged database system including efficient storage, transaction management and retrieval, all optimized for XML data. The data is stored using an internal logical model that has an equivalent mapping from an XML schema, and it can be used for fragmenting large trees into segments for the purpose of fitting into small disk pages for storage. Natix supports powerful index structures including inverted file full text indexes as well as a new structure called XASR (Fiebig & Moerkotte, 2001) specially designed for Natix.
3. **Timber:** Timber (Jagadish et al., 2002) is a native XML database system with an architecture similar to relational databases that uses an algebra for XML called TAX (Jagadish et al., 2001). Queries formulated in XQuery can be evaluated in Timber by parsing into the TAX algebraic representation which is then used to generate multiple query plans using the query optimizer. Cost based query optimization techniques have been introduced to estimate answer sizes and to count twig matches in Timber and help select the most optimal query plan. New access methods and join algorithms have been introduce to increase the effectiveness and efficiency of query evaluation. Transaction management is also supported in Timber using Shore (Carey et al., 1994).
4. **Db4XML:** Db4XML (Sipani et al., 2004) is an open source native XML database that supports the XPath and XQuery query languages. Db4XML is a high performance, main memory resident database engine and provides the ability to add documents, schemas and run queries on the stored documents. It includes a query tool for user interaction, and a query processor for parsing queries and generating an optimized query evaluation plan for the engine. It also supports path and value indexes to increase the efficiency of query processing. Db4XML supports transaction management and full recovery in the event of a system crash.

Commercial Systems

In addition to the research-oriented systems, several commercial systems have been designed to provide querying support for XML. The premier ones amongst these include TextML from Ixiasoft (http://www.ixiasoft.com), a system that stores the data in a proprietary managed format and allows fast access using APIs. Other similar systems include Open_Text's Opentext/Pat 5.0 (http://www.opentext.com) based on the Patricia Tree structure (Gonnet & Baeza-Yates, 1991), Infonyte's XML Query processing system (http://

www.infonyte.com/en/products.html), etc. Two systems deserve special attention in this category:

1. **Tamino XML Server:** Tamino from Software AG (http://www1.softwareag.com/corporate/products/tamino/default.asp) is a native XML database system that provides transactions, security, multi-user access, scalability and other typical database features, including support for XQuery. The Tamino Database consists of multiple collections, each of which is a group of documents associated with a schema description. Tamino supports three different types of indexing - (i) value based indices as in relational databases for searching elements or attributes having certain values, (ii) text indices for efficient text retrieval and (iii) XML specific index called structure index with information about all paths that occur in documents. Data stored in relational databases can be transparently integrated into documents stored in Tamino by explicitly describing the correspondence between the documents and relational data.
2. **eXist:** eXist is an Open Source effort (http://exist.sourceforge.net/) to develop a native XML database system capable of keyword searches on text, queries on the proximity of terms and regular expression-based search patterns. The search engine of eXist has been designed to provide fast XPath queries, using indexes (based on path join algorithms) for all element, text and attribute notes. Inside the database, documents are managed in hierarchical collections that can be arbitrarily nested and not bound to predefined schema. eXist uses a numerical indexing scheme to identify XML nodes in the index. The indexing scheme links index entries to the actual DOM nodes in the XML store and also provides a quick identification of possible relationships between nodes in the document node tree. eXist's query engine uses path join algorithms to evaluate XPath expressions.

XML Information Retrieval Systems

While not directly related to the objectives of this paper, a plethora of research has been performed on information retrieval from XML documents. In its simplest form, primitive information retrieval techniques extract lines containing specified keywords from a document. It is often useful to restrict the searches to specific portions of the document. The most common method for searching information in a document repository is by using *Boolean searches* (Salton, 1991). The problem with this type of search is that all matching documents in the resulting document set are given the same importance. To avoid this, one can use the *weighted keyword search*, in which the search items are assigned weights based on their importance, and the retrieved documents can be ordered by the most relevant to the least relevant based on the number of matches and the weights of the matched terms. Typically such searches are supported via indexes built on the documents for improving search performance. In addition to Boolean searches, top-k searches, designed to find the top *k* most relevant documents (or document fragments). Such search techniques include search methods involving document structure (Li et al., 2009a), and often documents from heterogeneous sources and structures (Li et al., 2009b).

In this section we looked at various strategies (in academic and commercial sectors) that have been used to store and retrieve XML data. In the following section, we present our approach to document management, which provides native XML processing in a completely formalized model capable of handling standard and emerging storage and indexing methods. With DocBase, we propose the creation of a database solution for XML that is based on usability. In prior research (Sengupta & Dillon, 2006; Sengupta & Ramesh, 2009) we have demonstrated that XML can be queried using languages that are based on human factors and usability criteria. In this paper we demonstrate that a working solution can be built based on these standards that can take advantage of existing solutions and perform credibly.

REQUIREMENTS FOR AN XML DATABASE SYSTEM

Research on XML data repositories, like research in other data management fields, has focused on data storage and efficient data retrieval methods, with emphasis on XML query algebras (Frasincar et al., 2002, Jagadish et al., 2001, Paparizos et al., 2004), XML query languages (Braga et al., 2005; Erwig, 2003; Funderburk et al., 2002), new physical operators (Wu et al., 2002), query rewrite (Amer-Yahia et al., 2002; Wu et al., 2004), and query optimization (Amer-Yahia et al., 2002, Balmin et al., 2004, Fernandez & Suciu, 1998; Wu et al., 2003). The solution architecture presented here is not yet another foray into introducing a specific solution to a data management problem, but a unified methodology to incorporate native XML and relational data within a single system, with the capability of incorporating current and emerging storage and indexing techniques.

The design of DocBase was based on well-accepted requirements for XML database systems. A set of 6 criteria for XML databases were proposed by Salminen and Tompa (2001). These requirements include (R1) Data independence, (R2) Logical data model, (R3) Full support of XML data standards, (R4) Indexing structures at different levels of granularity, (R5) Security support, and (R6) Data manipulation. These requirements need to be supported at various degrees by database systems that claim to fully support XML. In the subsequent sections, we are going to refer back to these requirements and demonstrate how DocBase aims to fulfill these requirements.

The aspect of DocBase that sets it apart from the extant systems discussed in the previous section is that it has been designed ground up from the perspective of structured documents, and not just for XML. As such, DocBase can be applied equally to any form of tagged document structure, including, SGML, HTML, even other forms of tagged structures. While the implementation is targeted towards SGML and XML, the concepts in this paper and the theory behind DocBase are fully generalizable because of its data model. Table 1 compares DocBase against some of the systems with respect to the requirements.

DocBase is part of a stream of research that aims to develop a database system based on these requirements. The conceptual data model, query language and security aspects of the system have been covered in previous work. This paper presents the systems aspects of the paper, focusing only on the storage and retrieval aspects of the system, and demonstrating that a database system based on a relational influence can provide adequate performance and provide a high usability and familiarity to relational database users.

THE DOCBASE ARCHITECTURE

The architecture of DocBase involves a "component-based design" method (Szyperski, 2000; Szyperski et al., 1999), which is known as an advanced object-oriented design of complex systems using several small independent components. We closely follow the theory of design and analysis of component-based software (Gibson et al., 2000) in developing the architecture of DocBase. In the conceptual layer, database objects take their logical form as relations. Access to the raw storage is limited only to the lowermost physical layer, which handles the storage and retrieval of the data from the disk. The query processing layer involving query parsing, translation and optimization is built on top of the storage layer, while users interact only with a presentation view of the data and the query results.

Table 1. Comparison of DocBase against other XML databases (✔ indicates full support, ☐ indicates partial support, and blank indicates no documented support)

	R1	R2	R3	R4	R5	R6
DocBase	✔	✔	☐	✔	✔	✔
Lore	☐	✔	☐	✔	☐	✔
Natix		☐	✔	☐	☐	☐
Timber	☐	✔	✔	✔	☐	✔
Db4XML			✔	☐		✔
eXist			✔	☐		☐
Tamino			✔	✔	☐	☐

While the architectural platform of DocBase shown in Figure 1 is fairly typical of 3-layer database systems, the design of these loosely coupled layers allows DocBase to take advantage of current research in various aspects of database systems. The query processing layer (discussed in detail later in this paper) allows DocBase to use component-based development, allowing existing components to be incorporated into the system via a set of interfaces. For example, Figure 1 shows DocBase using Exodus (Carey et al., 1986) as a storage manager and the Patricia Tree index structure as the indexing mechanism for query processing. The design goal of the DocBase architecture was to allow testing of different components in the various roles to determine the best possible performance of the overall system. In addition, the loose coupling between the three layers ensures the *data independence requirement* (R1) as discussed in the previous section.

The Physical Layer

DocBase is designed to be a modular system, in which users can incorporate existing storage and indexing techniques. The primary advantage of this modular design is the possibility of incorporating emerging as well as legacy technology as needed. From a programming perspective, this is achieved using an API using which new subclasses can be created for interfacing with other systems if they provide their own API, or via message passing through I/O sockets if they do not. Full details of the coding are beyond the scope of this paper, but we present an overview of the storage and index management components in this section. The current implementation has the capability of either a UNIX file system or Sybase as a storage manager; and the Open Text (OpenText, 2010) indexing system as the index manager.

Storage Manager Component

The storage manager is needed to provide storage management functionality to the managed data in DocBase. The following storage managers are supported in the current implementation of DocBase:

1. **Flat file storage:** In this type of storage management, documents are stored as files

Figure 1. Architecture of DocBase showing the three-layer design

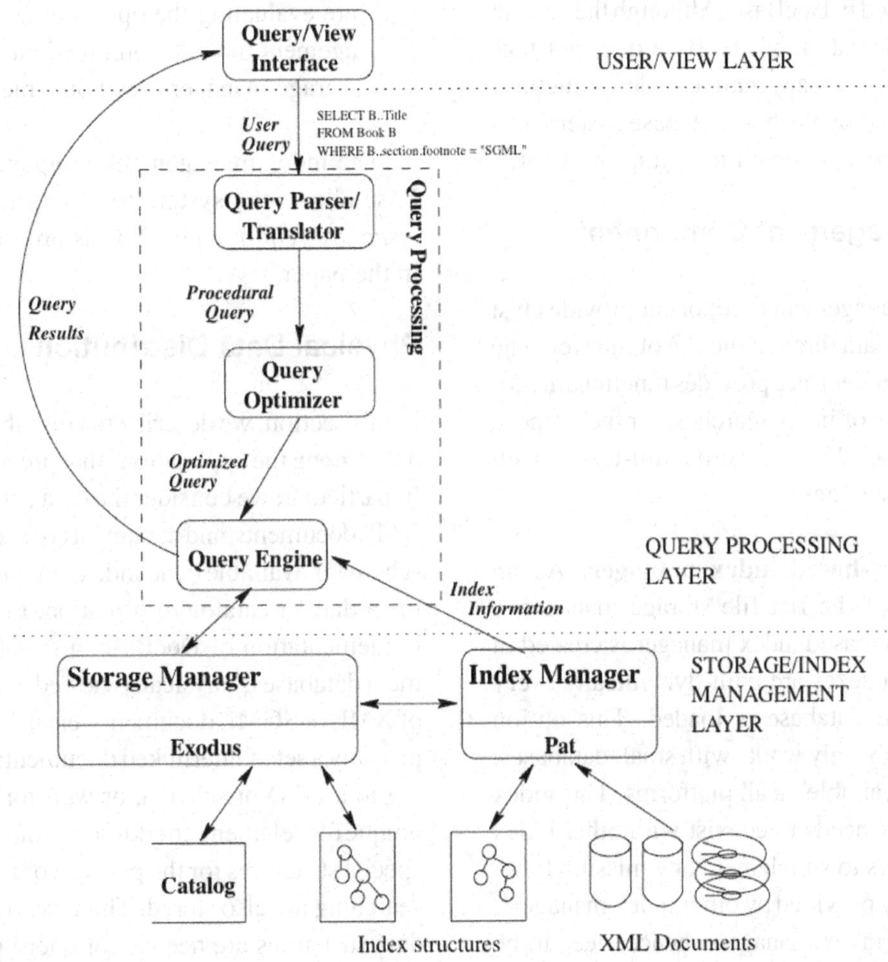

in the operating system, so all the file management is left to the Operating system. This is the simplest of the storage management facilities - in this mode, all the security and concurrency control (if any) are provided by the operating system. DocBase keeps track of modification times for the managed files, and re-indexes any time files have been modified. Obviously this is the least effective storage management solution, but the reason it is implemented this way is that it is guaranteed to work on any platform, and is always available.

2. **Independent storage managers:** Two independent storage managers have been used with DocBase with mixed results. These are Exodus (Carey et al., 1986) and Shore (Carey et al., 1994). Both have extensive storage management functionalities including concurrency control and logging, and require the DML statements to create and alter controlled objects. Shore has the capability of being mounted as an operating system partition, a feature that would enable users to create and modify objects as in flat file storage, and yet provide management functionality through the storage manager.
3. **Database storage managers:** A database storage manager uses a database CLOB column in a table for the XML components.

Currently Sybase and Oracle databases are supported in DocBase. Although the current implementation of DocBase does not take advantage of any native index structures supported by the host database system, this would be a possible future improvement.

Index Management Component

The index management component provides fast access to the data through the use of indexes. The index manager interface provides functionality for different types of index searches, for the purpose of retrieval based on keywords, full-text as well as structure searches.

1. **Memory-based index manager:** As an analog of the flat file storage manager, a memory-based index manager is created in which indexes are built dynamically every time the database is loaded. This option obviously only works with small databases, but is available on all platforms. This index manager needs to coexist with other index managers to supplement any missing functionality provided by other index managers. Special index managers, hence, need to be built as a subclass of this memory-based index manager.
2. **PAT index manager:** The only functional index manager currently available with DocBase is the Patricia Tree (PAT) (Gonnet & Baeza-Yates, 1991) index manager. This index is only available for demonstration and cannot be distributed, but shows how an external indexing software can be used with DocBase. PAT does not have a standard API for interfacing its query language with an external system, so this component uses IPC (Inter-process communication) mechanisms through to drive PAT commands through sockets.
3. **Database index manager:** Given the capabilities of direct querying of XML using Oracle's InterMedia/Text component, we are evaluating the option of an index management module combined into a database storage manager based on Oracle.

The index management component of DocBase allows the system to satisfy the *indexing structure requirement* (R4) as presented earlier in the paper.

Physical Data Distribution

In this section, we describe the distribution of the data among the applications that process the data. In particular, we consider the data (in the form of XML documents, and document type definitions or schema if available), the index structures and the meta-data or catalog information. In the current implementation of DocBase, a structured document database is physically viewed as a collection of XML or SGML documents, each document (or possibly a set of interlinked documents) conforming to a DTD or schema, or well-formed with a unique root element. In addition to the documents, special structures for the purpose of indexing and searching are also stored. Three primary types of data structures are needed for query processing: (i) a hierarchical structure for the actual parse tree for document instances, (ii) a hierarchical structure for the catalog (representing the DTD), and (iii) optional auxiliary index structures on the meta-data for the purpose of efficient query processing (see Figure 2).

- **Note:** The data structures can be generalized to any XML DTD or schema, including recursive structures. The indexes include starting and ending offsets for every region bound by a start tag and end tag. Since XML is a normalized structure, these regions in an instance document will always be completely contained within one another, even if there is a structural recursion. For example, in Figure 2(c) if the *sec-*

Figure 2. A simple representation of the data structures: (a) the document (b) the catalog structure and (c) the parse tree and auxiliary indices

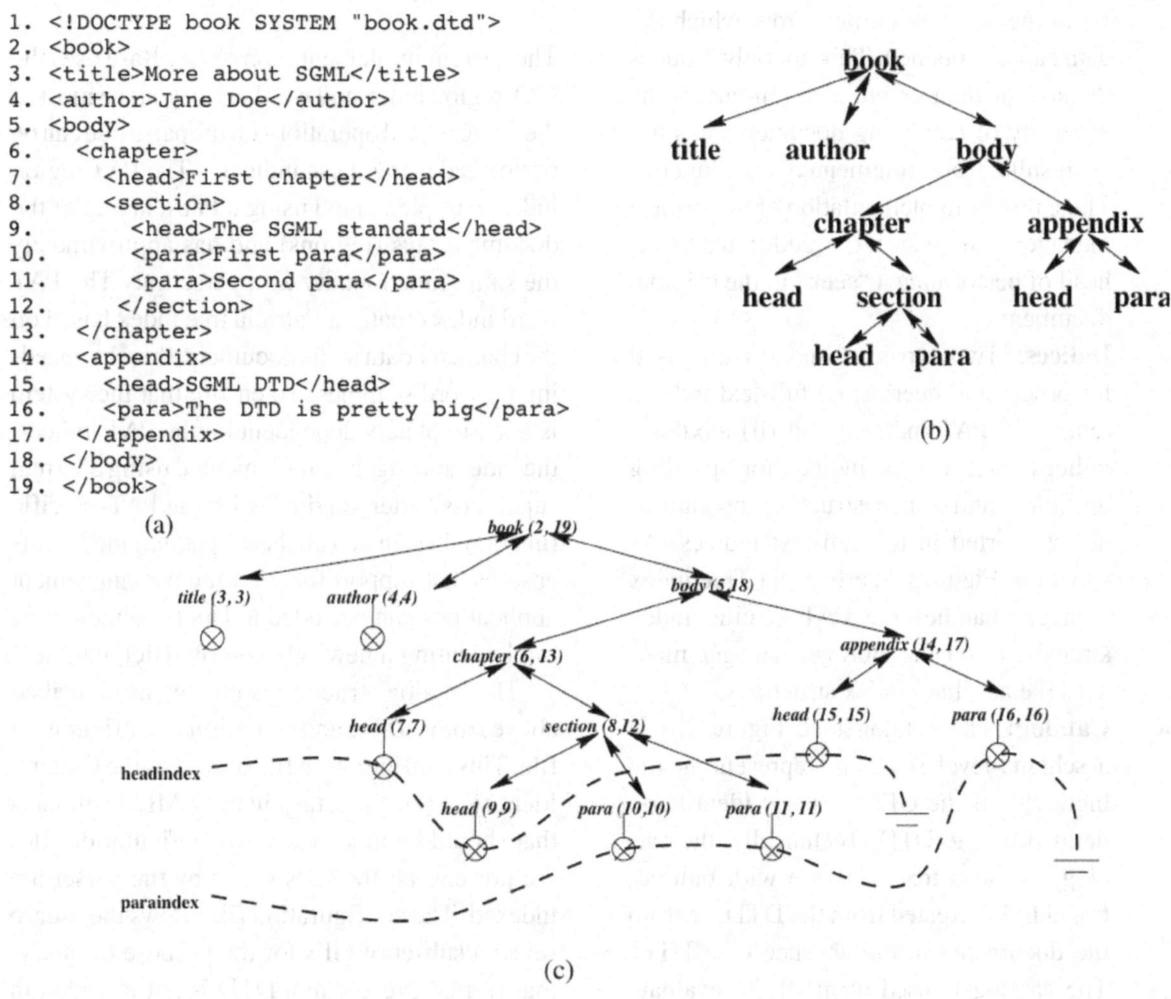

tion tag is recursive, it may have a section inside it, but it is guaranteed to be completely inside the outer section boundaries.

- **Data:** In the current prototype, the data is stored in the form of structured documents in a file system (using the flat-file storage manager). In addition, in order to keep a correspondence between the documents and their physical storage, documents conforming to the same DTD are stored in the same distinct directory of the file system.
- **The Parse Tree:** The parse tree shown in Figure 2(c) is an instance-level structure representing the hierarchical structure of the actual document instances. Prior to the incorporation into the database, every document needs to be parsed by a validating parser to assure the conformance of the document to a DTD. The structure created by the parser is the parse tree generated from that particular document instance. This parse tree contains all the information about the structure of the document, but does not replicate the actual text present

in the document. Instead, each node in the parse tree contains information on the *offset* in the actual document from which the data can be obtained. This not only reduces the size of the tree but also eliminates the necessity of recreating documents as query results from fragmented components. Thus, proper implementation of the storage manager can reduce the additional overhead of performing a "seek" in the original document.

- **Indices:** Two types of indices are used for processing queries: (i) full-text indices (currently PAT indices) and (ii) auxiliary indices such as join indices for speeding up joins and other structure operations not supported in the full-text indices. As shown in Figure 1, the Patricia Tree index manager handles the PAT-specific index structures and the storage manager manages the auxiliary index structures.
- **Catalog:** The catalog (see Figure 2b) is a schema-level structure representing the hierarchy of the GI's (Generic Identifiers) defined by the DTD. Technically, the catalog is also a tree structure with bidirectional links, created from the DTD, or from the documents in the absence of a DTD. The catalog is used primarily to evaluate and optimize path expression queries. The current implementation of DocBase also creates a detailed catalog of objects in the database, including a binary representation of the document structure and a list of the different types of objects (e.g., documents, DTDs, stored queries, auxiliary join indices and temporary structures). Currently auxiliary join indices are implemented only in the database storage manager for performing join queries. As shown in Figure 1, the storage manager has full control over this catalog information.

Implementation of the Data Structures

The current implementation of DocBase uses the PAT region index and word indices, since most of the navigational operations on the parse tree can be performed using these indices[2] . The PAT region index is implemented using a Patricia tree of the document tags (regions) and has approximately the same functionality as a parse tree. The PAT word index creates a Patricia tree index based on the character data in the document, thereby speeding up word searches. To ensure that the system is not completely dependent on the PAT indices, the index manager is implemented using a virtual superclass "Hier_engine" with the PAT-specific functionality in a subclass "pat_engine". This ensures that support for other index management applications can be added to DocBase merely by implementing a new subclass of "Hier_engine."

The catalog structure is created as described above from a DTD and an optional configuration file. This configuration file describes the Generic Identifiers (GI), i.e., tags in the XML documents that should be indexed. If no configuration files are present, all the GI's found by the parser are indexed. The configuration file allows the user to select a subset of GI's for the purpose of querying. If a GI present in a DTD is not included in the configuration file, no queries can use that GI in a term. However, the elements in the instances corresponding to the non-indexed GI's are still available in the parse tree (implemented using the region index of PAT) and can still be used for generating query outputs.

Once the configuration file is created for a specific XML schema, documents in that schema can be easily included in the database as well as queried through the DSQL query language that we will present shortly. The underlying logical model of DocBase and the query processing methods are presented in the next sections.

The Logical Layer

The topmost layer in the DocBase design architecture is the *user layer* which facilitates user interaction with the system. Presently DocBase supports two query languages, both based on a formal document model. The first query language is a textual query language called DSQL (Document SQL) (Sengupta & Ramesh, 2009). The second query language is a graphical language called QBT (Query By Templates) (Sengupta & Dillon, 2006). The availability of multiple query languages is important since it serves the needs of different types of users. For example, novices may prefer a QBT style interface while people comfortable with SQL would prefer to use DSQL. We begin by describing the logical model that forms the basis for DocBase and the query languages it supports. DSQL is a theoretically sound language, and can be used as ad-hoc querying frontend to XQuery. The complete languages and their comparison with XQuery are beyond the scope of this paper, and can be obtained from (Sengupta & Dillon, 2006; Sengupta & Ramesh, 2009).

A Logical Model for Documents

The document model used by DocBase is an extension of the Nested relational model (Jaeschke & Schek, 1982; Levene & Loizou, 1993) that we call Heterogeneous Nested Relations (HNR). In this model, the collection of documents is viewed as a set of complex document relations. Each document relation is a set of documents of a particular type. The ordering within this set is not important, but inside each document, the structure is implicitly or explicitly ordered. To define the notion of structured document databases, we first define a few sets: gi is a countably infinite set of generic identifiers (GI's) that form the schema of the documents. $\mathrm{doc} \subseteq \mathrm{gi}$ is the set of document types that represent the top-level relations in the database. We also define dom, which is a countably infinite set of constant character strings, and var, a countably infinite set of variables.

Types

We only consider two types:

1. **Basic type** β : The base type comprises of character strings, with dom being the range of values. The basic type can be augmented to support data types other than character strings as well.
2. **Complex type** τ : The complex types form the set gi. Within this set, the subset doc defines document types which are special complex types in the database. In the presence of a DTD (or schema), any GI in a DTD defines a complex type, and various operations in the language create new productions to generate a new DTD or schema.

Documents and Databases

Documents form the core component in a document database system. We define the concepts documents and document databases as follows:

- **Document:** Conceptually, a document is a strictly hierarchical structure with a root GI that defines its type. If a DTD or schema is available, the document type can be modeled as a grammar represented by a quadruple $d = (\tau, G, C, P)$ where $\tau \in \mathrm{doc}$ is a document type, $G \subset \mathrm{gi}$ is a set of generic identifiers, and $C \subset \mathrm{dom}$ is a set of constants. P is a set of production rules describing the structure of conforming document instances.
- **Document relations:** A document relation can now be viewed as a set of documents of a given document type.

A database, in this setting, is a set of Document relations.

Note: A document conceptually does not coincide with a physical document file. A single file may include multiple documents, or a single document. A set of documents can be in one file, or spread over multiple files.

- **Path expressions:** Because of the complex document structure, the model needs to allow expressions to traverse the tree structure. While standard path expression languages such as XPath (Clark & DeRose, 1999) exist for such purposes, for the clarity of the presentation of the formalism we use the notion of a "Simple Path Expression" (SPE). SPEs include only two operators, the standard "." operator to traverses to a child node, and a new ".." operator that traverses to a descendant. So Book.title returns titles directly underneath book, whereas Book..title returns titles reachable by traversing down from book, which may lead to chapter titles, section titles, figure titles, etc.

The logical model used in DocBase ensures that the XML data is stored and retrieved in a consistent form implied by the storage engines, query languages and indexing applications, and at the same time, allows DocBase to fulfill the *logical data model requirement* (R2).

Query Languages in DocBase

Since the emphasis of DocBase is in the processing of complex queries on complex structures, and not on developing a new processor for XQuery, we chose to use a correlated set of languages Document Algebra (DA), Document Calculus (DC) and Document SQL (DSQL) as described in Sengupta and Ramesh (2009). Based on the theoretical basis of the calculus and algebraic languages, the DSQL query language provides a true SQL semantics for structured queries on XML documents, maintaining the low complexity, closure and safety properties of SQL.

For the purpose of this article, we augment DSQL as described in Sengupta and Ramesh (2009) with limited data definition and manipulation capabilities as described.

DSQL DDL (Document Definition Language): We define the CREATE RELATION statement that allows a user to create a document relation essentially in the same sense of creating a table in a relational database. The structure is specified using an XML schema or a DTD (Document Type Definition). Once a relation is created, the DTD (or schema) is loaded in the database. In order to change the structure, an ALTER RELATION statement can be issued that changes the schema or DTD. Any inserted document must conform to the new structure in order for the ALTER RELATION to succeed. Analogous to the notion of micro-documents (McFadden, 1997), documents are stored in fragments, where the level of fragmentation can be controlled by the user.

```
CREATE|ALTER RELATION <relation_name>
[USING DTD <dtd_name> | USING SCHEMA
<schema_name>]
[FRAGMENT BY <gi>
[ORDERED|UNORDERED]]
```

To insert documents in a relation, the insert statement needs to be issued:

```
INSERT INTO <relation_name>[FRAGMENT]
< DOCUMENT <document_name> | TEXT
<marked_up_data> >
```

The above statement can insert a document into a previously created relation or relation fragment. Every document is given a document identifier docid and every fragment is given a fragment identifier fragid which is unique in the relation context. Obviously, this method of inserts into the database allows only a limited amount of inserts and updates to the system. The top layer (view layer) of an implementation needs to allow the user editing capabilities similar to the types of edits that are possible in a document editor. The DDL component in DSQL allows DocBase to fulfill the *data manipulation requirement* (R6).

The Query component of DSQL: DSQL has the same basic structure as SQL, with the SELECT, FROM and WHERE clauses for retrieval, and GROUP BY, HAVING and ORDER BY clauses for grouping and ordering of the results. The GROUP BY clause in DSQL, unlike that of SQL is actually an integral part of the querying method, since GROUP BY turns out to be an elegant way of restructuring the results. Every DSQL query has the following basic syntax:

```
SELECT output_structure
FROM input_specification
WHERE conditions
grouping_specs
ordering_specs
```

As in SQL, only the SELECT and the FROM clauses are required. The other clauses are optional. Also, multiple SELECT queries can be combined using the standard set operations (Union, Intersect, Minus). The SELECT clause in DSQL has the same major structure of SQL, with the main difference being that the SELECT clause can create complex structures, and can traverse paths[3] in retrieved structures. The WHERE conditions in DSQL are similar to those in SQL, except some differences in semantics with the use of path expressions. Since path expressions typically retrieve sets of nodes, comparison operators in the WHERE clause are mostly set operators. More details on DSQL can be obtained from Sengupta and Ramesh (2009).

QBT: A Visual Query Language for DocBase

DocBase includes a method for interactive retrieval from the database using a semi-visual language called QBT (Query By Templates) (Sengupta & Dillon, 2006) - a language based on the relational counterpart QBE (Query By Example) (Zloof, 1977). As a language, the set of possible queries that can be written using QBT is a proper subset of those using DSQL, since QBT does not allow nested subqueries. QBT is capable of expressing queries without the knowledge of the internal document structure. In QBT, users specify their queries by entering relevant information in different parts of a template that resembles the data. Search clauses are indicated directly on "hot" areas of the template, and immediate feedback to the user is provided that displays the current number of matches for the query. The theoretical expressiveness of QBT is the same as core DSQL (DSQL without nesting and aggregate functions).

QUERY PROCESSING IN DOCBASE

As indicated earlier, queries are formulated in DocBase using either an ad-hoc query language (DSQL), or a graphical query language (QBT). These queries are then processed by a parser which then validates the query and translates it into an algebraic form to be processed by the query engine. Once all the query fragments have been processed, the query engine determines the structure and format of the output and then combines the query fragments. In this section, we briefly describe the parser and the translation routines, highlighting the query processing algorithms in details.

The Parser and Translator

DSQL has been implemented using a parser generated using the Unix tools Lex and YACC. The parser is capable of validating the syntax of a DSQL query as well as performing query evaluation tasks such as (i) translation into an internal algebra for query processing or (ii) translation into XQuery for processing by an external XQuery engine. In the internal processing mode, the parser receives the DSQL query in the standard input and creates instances of the storage management, index management and query engine modules of DocBase to evaluate and process the query.

Although the parser is written for the complete DSQL language, the current implementation provides support for a subset of DSQL which excludes nested queries, grouping and ordering operations. Since the infrastructure is very similar to the relational query implementations, techniques used in relational databases for evaluating nested queries, such as tuple substitution, can also be used for nested queries. Moreover, grouping, ordering and aggregate operations can be implemented using filters on the result of the queries. We demonstrate here that a reasonably self-contained subset of queries can be implemented using the proposed model and structures, and propose implementation methods for the rest of the queries as future work. The details on the evaluation of queries are described in the next section.

Query Evaluation

The current implementation of DocBase uses an accumulator-based evaluation method. An accumulator here is an internal representation of a document relation used in the query, and can be thought of as a container for temporary results. One or more accumulators may be needed depending on the number of relations used in the FROM clause of the query. The accumulator denotes a list of virtual documents rooted at a particular element or GI (Generic Identifier). Hence every accumulator corresponds to a GI (we will refer to this GI as *accumregn* in the following discussion).

For normal evaluation, we assume that the accumulator is sorted in document order. System R style optimization techniques are built into the evaluation mechanism - selection operations are performed as early as possible in the life cycle of the query, using index structures whenever possible. Joins are performed only if necessary and at the last stage of the query processing. The accumulator carries only links to the original document and hence can be implemented in memory. The bulk of the query processing is in the traversal of the embedded tree structure. Here we present a synopsis of the algorithms for traversal and path selection in the DocBase query engine.

Given an accumulator, it is possible to traverse the document structures upwards or downwards from the accumulator. Given an accumulator and its corresponding GI *accumregn*, a traversal down to a target GI results in an accumulator associated with the target GI, containing a list of document components rooted at the target GI that are descendants of *accumregn*. Similarly, an upward traversal results in an accumulator, with elements rooted at the target GI that are ancestors of *accumregn*. In addition, given an accumulator and a path expression, it is often necessary to only retain the elements that match a path expression P so that *accumregn* matches $last(P)$. Note that the accumulators can be implemented in the persistent storage as well, to avoid limitations posed by limited amount of available RAM. These three algorithms are described in Figure 3.

The algorithms in Figure 3 constitute the basis of the query engine. Given any parsed query, the algebraic operations are performed as ordered by the query plan generator in the optimization process. The temporary results are stored in accumulators that are then combined using union or intersection. If a join is necessary, a standard sort-merge join is performed, and a new accumulator is created with the result of the join operation. The final accumulator is processed to retrieve components of the document(s) to generate the results of the query. To demonstrate the execution of these algorithms, we show the actual steps involved in the execution of a sample query. The

Figure 3. Upward and downward traversal algorithms

```
traverseup(list accumulator, GI accumregn, GI targetgi:input)
begin
  if ((accumregn == targetgi) ||(targetgi==null)) return;
  templist = empty
  for each element e in accumulator do
  | repeat
  | | follow the parent of e upwards
  | | if parent node has GI targetgi
  | | if parent not already in templist
  | | append parent to templist
  | | endif
  | | endif
  | until no more parents
  endfor
  return (templist, targetgi)
end traverseup

traversedown(list accumulator, GI accumregn, GI targetgi:input)
begin
  if ((accumregn == targetgi)||(targetgi==null)) return;
  templist = empty
  for each element e in accumulator do
    starting for e, do breadth-first search for nodes labeled targetgi
    during search, do not add nodes that can never reach targetgi
       using the catalog
    append  matched nodes not yet visited to templist
  endfor
  return (templist, targetgi)
end traversedown

selectpath(list accumulator, GI accumregn, string pathexp)
begin
  if (first(pathexp) == root GI of the DTD)
    create a finite automaton for pathexp
  else
    rootgi = root GI of the active DTD
    create a finite automaton for rootgi..pathexp
  endif
  for each element e in accumulator do
    construct path by traversing from e up to the root and reversing it
    if the constructed path is accepted by the FA, retain e
    else reject e
  endfor
  return (accumulator, accumregn);
end
```

following query uses the Shakespeare plays collection in XML (Bosak, 1999). This is query # 8 among the queries that were used for performance testing.

```
SELECT s.TITLE
FROM shakes.PLAY.ACT.SCENE s
WHERE s.SPEAKER="steward"
```

Given the above query, the following steps are performed to execute the query.

Step 1. Algebratization: In the first step, the query is first converted to an algebraic equivalent using DA (Document Algebra). The DA equivalent for the above query is:

$$\left(\sigma_{s.SPEAKER='steward'}\left(\rho_s\left(shakes.PLAY.ACT.SCENE\right)\right)\right).TITLE$$

Step 2. Optimization: Since there are no joins and multiple selections in this query, the above algebra is already the most optimal version. Most common algebraic optimization principles like the System R optimization can be applied to DA because of its similarity to relational algebra. More specific query optimization process is part of the future work in this research.

Step 3. Execution: The accumulator-based execution starts here, beginning from the innermost component of the optimized algebra. The following is the sequence of calls made to the algorithms mentioned earlier:

```
accumulator = (shakes, 'PLAY')
accumulator =
traversedown(accumulator, 'PLAY',
'ACT')
accumulator =
traversedown(accumulator, 'ACT',
'SCENE')
accumulator =
traversedown(accumulator, 'SCENE',
'SPEAKER')
accumulator = restrict(accumulator,
'equals', 'steward')
accumulator = traverseup(accumulator,
'SPEAKER', 'SCENE')
accumulator = selectpath(accumulator,
'SCENE', 'SCENE.TITLE')
```

In the above steps, the call to restrict is an index operation which uses a word index to select only the items from the current accumulator that satisfies the given condition.

Step 4. Retrieval: The accumulator at the end of the query processing stage contains a set of node offsets. The documents are accessed at this point to extract the appropriate fragments to construct the final result, which is then returned as a well-formed XML document wrapped within a root element 'RESULT' since no root element was specified in the query.

EVALUATION OF DOCBASE

DocBase was evaluated in several different methods with respect to the following measures: performance, expressiveness and scalability. The results of these experiments are reported here.

Performance Results

To determine the effectiveness of DocBase as an architecture for storage and retrieval of XML documents, we compared the retrieval speed of DocBase with that of XRel discussed earlier (Yoshikawa et al., 2001). XRel was identified as the most appropriate comparison since it is the only system that reports specific queries and performance results, based on a commonly available set of XML documents which makes it conducive for comparative evaluations. Same tests as in Yoshikawa et al. were run, with the same Bosak Shakespeare play data collection. Similar hardware was used in the experiments – Yoshikawa et al. used a SUN Enterprise 4000 (4 * UltraSPARC - II 248 MHz CPU, 32 GB U320 SCSI disk and 2048MB memory) running Solaris 2.5.1 and a commercial relational database system.

The performance data shows the superiority of DocBase (see Tables 2 and 3) for processing

Table 2. Performance evaluation queries

Q	XPath	DSQL
1	/PLAY/ACT	SELECT PLAY.ACT FROM shakes
2	/PLAY/ACT/SCENE/SPEECH/LINE/STAGEDIR	SELECT PLAY.ACT.SCENE.SPEECH.LINE.STAGEDIR FROM shakes
3	//SCENE/TITLE	SELECT SCENE.TITLE FROM shakes
4	//ACT//TITLE	SELECT ACT..TITLE FROM shakes
5	/PLAY/ACT[2]	SELECT PLAY.ACT[2] FROM shakes
6	(/PLAY/ACT)[2]/Title	SELECT (PLAY.ACT)[2].TITLE FROM shakes
7	/PLAY/ACT/SCENE/SPEECH [SPEAKER = 'CURIO']	SELECT * FROM shakes.PLAY.ACT.SCENE.SPEECH s WHERE s.SPEAKER="CURIO"
8	/PLAY/ACT/SCENE [.//SPEAKER = 'Steward']/TITLE	SELECT s.TITLE FROM shakes.PLAY.ACT.SCENE s WHERE s.SPEAKER="steward"

Table 3. Query Performance Comparison between DocBase and XRel. Performance data for XRel reported verbatim from (Yoshikawa et al., 2001)

Qno	DocBase	DocBaseTuples	XRel	XReltuples
1	0.098	185	0.021	185
2	0.252	618	0.024	618
3	0.096	750	0.320	750
4	0.099	951	0.304	766
7	0.169	4	2.748	4
8	0.129	2	9.687	6

standard selection queries on a moderately sized database. The fact that we ran DocBase on inferior hardware further establishes the superiority of our system. The speedup in query processing performance can be attributed to DocBase's handling of storage, indexing, and optimization. DocBase we ran these test queries using the standard file system storage manager, and the OpenText Patricia tree index manager, with full query optimization. The optimization routines ensured that all the selection operations are performed as early in the query processing as possible, and combination of separate branches delayed as much as possible.

INEX Participation and Information Retrieval Queries

We participated in the 2004 Initiative for the Evaluation of XML Retrieval (INEX) to determine DocBase's ability for information retrieval queries. Fifty nine organizations from different parts of the world submitted queries for the purpose of evaluation based on a common data set consisting of about 500MB of full-text publication data. Two types of queries were used for evaluation purposes: content-only (CO) or content-and-structure (CAS) queries. CO queries are free text queries, like those used in TREC, for which the retrieval system should retrieve relevant XML elements of

Table 4. CO topics and equivalent DSQL queries

	Candidate Topic	DSQL Equivalent
162	Text and Index "Compression Algorithms"	Select i From inex.article i Where i="text" and i="index" and i="compression algorithm"
166	+ "tree edit distance" + XML	Select i From inex.article i Where i=" tree edit distance" and (i= "XML" or i = "xml")
178	"Multimedia Retrieval"	Select i.fm.tig.atl From inex.article i Where i="multimedia retrieval"

Figure 4. INEX Content only queries on DocBase

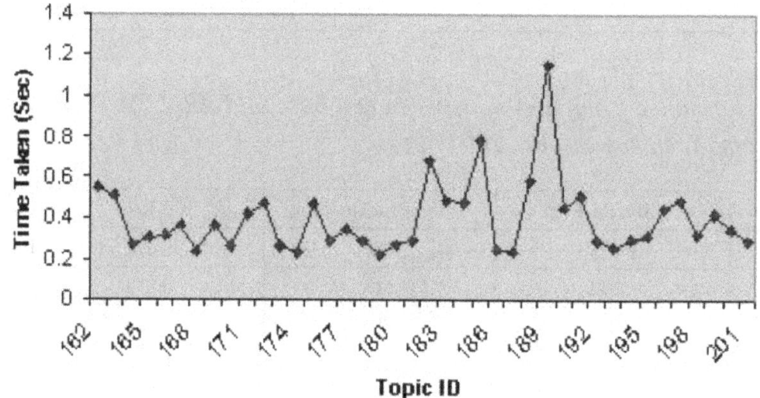

varying granularity, while CAS queries contain explicit structural constraints, such as containment conditions. Different queries were submitted by the 59 organization which took part in INEX and from the pooled set of candidate topics INEX selected a final set of topics to form part of the INEX test collection[4].

In order to run content-only queries using DocBase, the queries were translated to find the articles with the given keywords and their combinations. Table 4 shows how a Boolean keyword query in INEX can be translated to DSQL. This translation process has two primary implications. First, the retrieved region is not the "point of match" for the keyword, but the complete article. This may seem incorrect for a single keyword, retrieving the document that matches a Boolean combination seems more correct. Secondly, the number of matches reported by the DSQL query would be the number of articles retrieved and not the number of times the keyword(s) matched the data. The second observation is essentially a by-product of the first. Some of the other IR-specific issues involve ranking and approximation. As standard with database systems, every item in the database has the same rank and hence the retrieved documents are in the order they are stored (or indexed). Also, SQL searches are quite literal and do not perform any approximation (such as retrieving documents matching only one keyword) unless the query explicitly specifies it. Other than these observations, DocBase and DSQL are quite capable of handling the keyword searches due to

Figure 5. INEX content and structure queries on DocBase

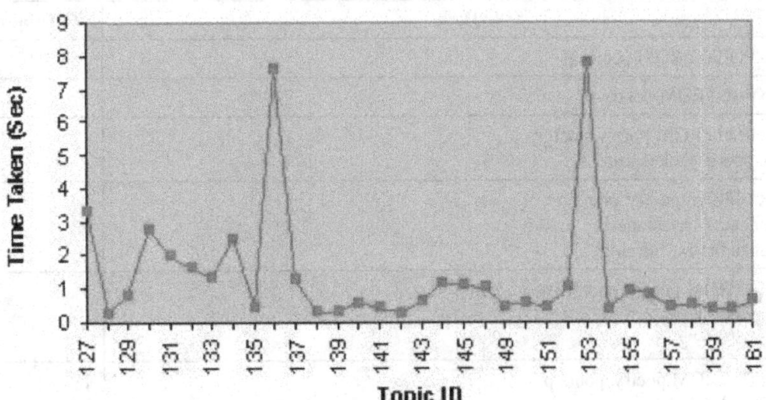

IR queries because of the deep structure searches embedded in the language.

For the INEX evaluation, we were able to convert all the 75 Queries (40 CO and 35 CAS) successfully into DSQL revealing the capability and applicability of DSQL and DocBase as a querying platform for XML databases. The timing results from these studies are presented in Figure 4 and Figure 5. On average CAS queries took 1.33 seconds while CO queries took 0.395 seconds. The standard deviations for the same were 1.80 and 0.179 seconds respectively. Most of the queries performed within the acceptable range except for two queries which took approximately 7 seconds to execute. These queries are also responsible for the slightly elevated mean of CAS queries. Careful analysis of the topics in question reveals that those queries had a conjunction of very specific search conditions on widely different structures.

DocBase was tested using the INEX initiative to test the suitability of using database systems to run IR queries. Although the evaluation did show the limitations of database query languages for classic information retrieval tasks, it also demonstrated that several interesting results can be obtained by using database query languages for information retrieval, especially for queries involving both content and structure. Our results demonstrate the adaptability and scalability of a database system for processing IR queries. More details of the tests and the translation algorithms for converting CO and CAS topics to DSQL queries can obtained from (Mohan & Sengupta, 2005).

Scalability Results

We have run queries of similar and higher complexity on databases of much larger sizes and obtained highly encouraging results. For example, we tested DocBase on the Chadwyck Healey English Poetry database (Chadwyck-Healey, 1994), a database greater than 850MB in size containing over 160,000 poems. Table 5 shows the results of some of the queries that we tested on this database. The results clearly demonstrate the scalability of DocBase and its ability to handle very large document repositories.

We also tested DocBase using the XMark Benchmark system (Schmidt et al., 2002). A brief report on the results of benchmark tests are given here. The XMark suite consists of the "xmlgen" data generator which produces XML documents modeling an auction web site, a typical user scenario. The "xmlgen" tool has the ability to generate well formed documents with support for recursion to the tune of several gigabytes. The size of the documents can be easily controlled by the

Table 5. Performance evaluation on a large database

Qno	DSQL	Tuples	Time
1	SELECT p.POEM FROM poetry p	165904	0.105
2	SELECT p.poet FROM poetry p	5705	0.101
3	SELECT p.head FROM poetry..poetgrp p WHERE p..poet="shakespeare"	175	0.129
4	SELECT P.* FROM poetry..poem p WHERE p.head="casabianca" AND p..stanza.firstl="burning"	1	0.676
5	SELECT P.* FROM poetry..poetgrp a, a.poem p WHERE a.poet="keats" AND p.head="ode"	9	0.571
6	SELECT (p.*) FROM poetry..poem p WHERE p.head="test" AND p..stanza="love"	18	1.502

scaling factor. We evaluated DocBase on the standard XMark Benchmark queries on different scaling factor ranging from 0.1(Document size is 10 MB) to 1.0 (Document Size is .1GB). The time taken by DocBase to evaluate the queries compares favorably to those reported in Schmidt et al. (2002) where six unidentified systems were tested as a part of the XMark Benchmarking process. The data demonstrates that the performance of DocBase scales very well as the size of the database increases from 10 MB. DocBase currently has the ability to evaluate 16 of the 20 queries. Of the four queries for which results are not reported, 3 of them result in combination of multiple branches in the output. DSQL supports this feature but the current implementation of DocBase has support for generating a single tree output. The last query for which the results were not reported needs support for user defined functions, a capability not supported by DSQL. The results of the evaluation are shown in Figure 6 and the evaluation time in Table 6.

Analysis of the evaluation times shows that a collection of queries (q9 - q12) take a slightly longer time to execute than other queries. This is due to the fact that these queries require that a Join be performed. Joins in DocBase are not handled internally but are instead achieved by using an external relational database manager. The time taken to evaluate these queries can be significantly reduced once the Join operation is implemented internally in DocBase. Further, the running time analysis shows that the time taken for evaluating queries (q2, q9-12) increases exponentially as the scaling factor increases. This is due to the characteristics of the document generated by XMark. These benchmark queries attempt to retrieve significant parts of the document whose relative size ratio with the document size grows exponentially.

Empirical Usability Experiments

We have also experimentally evaluated the need for multiple forms of querying with XML. In one study Sengupta and Ramesh (2009) compared the performance of users writing multiple queries using DSQL and XQuery on two types of XML schema - flat as well as nested. This study showed for ad hoc queries, users performed better with regard to both efficiency and accuracy using DSQL than using XQuery. The results were consistent in both the flat and nested schema. Detailed analysis of the results indicated that the users using XQuery had the most problems in specifying the data sources in XQuery, as well as in specifying

Figure 6. XMark benchmark queries on docbase

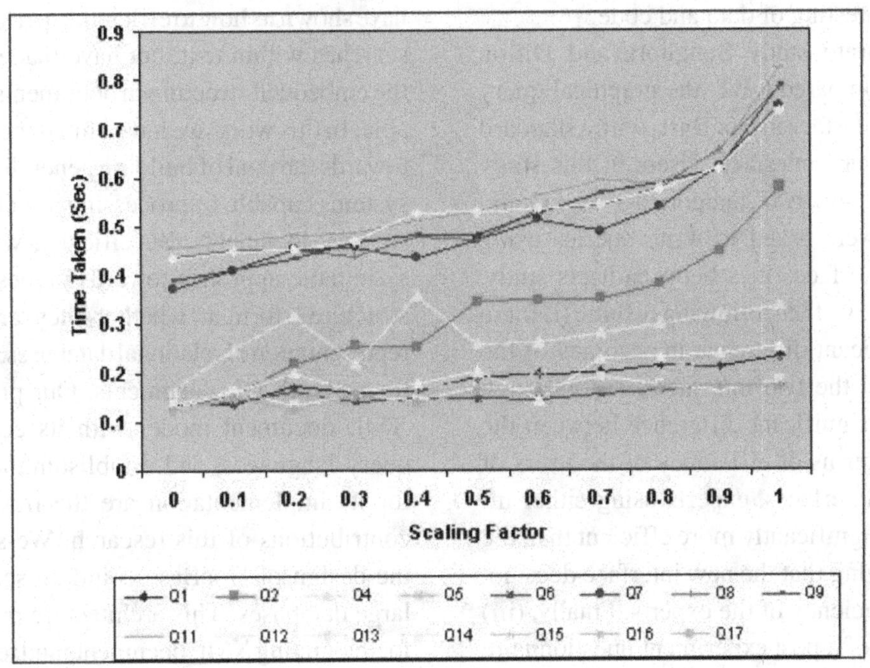

Table 6. XMark timing results

	0.0	0.1	0.2	0.3	0.4	0.5	0.6	0.7	0.8	0.9	1.0
Q1	0.136	0.136	0.170	0.158	0.161	0.188	0.195	0.200	0.215	0.209	0.231
Q2	0.126	0.152	0.218	0.254	0.251	0.343	0.347	0.351	0.379	0.448	0.577
Q4	0.164	0.247	0.317	0.218	0.357	0.258	0.262	0.278	0.297	0.317	0.335
Q5	0.131	0.178	0.194	0.195	0.166	0.183	0.195	0.214	0.220	0.198	0.224
Q6	0.134	0.139	0.161	0.140	0.145	0.145	0.143	0.154	0.161	0.168	0.178
Q7	0.372	0.410	0.453	0.456	0.435	0.473	0.512	0.487	0.538	0.621	0.745
Q8	0.437	0.453	0.452	0.439	0.477	0.473	0.533	0.539	0.578	0.654	0.782
Q9	0.390	0.412	0.433	0.467	0.481	0.480	0.523	0.567	0.589	0.613	0.789
Q11	0.456	0.473	0.481	0.483	0.512	0.527	0.563	0.593	0.589	0.646	0.821
Q12	0.436	0.451	0.453	0.469	0.523	0.527	0.535	0.543	0.573	0.617	0.737
Q13	0.138	0.165	0.132	0.155	0.143	0.168	0.164	0.188	0.174	0.160	0.180
Q14	0.126	0.160	0.198	0.161	0.177	0.202	0.143	0.226	0.229	0.235	0.252
Q15	0.120	0.153	0.181	0.173	0.218	0.241	0.286	0.250	0.268	0.286	0.302
Q16	0.126	0.146	0.151	0.150	0.159	0.172	0.168	0.167	0.170	0.172	0.175
Q17	0.117	0.150	0.125	0.154	0.136	0.161	0.159	0.163	0.163	0.168	0.168

the output structure and mapping the conceptual output into a nesting of data and code.

In a separate study Sengupta and Dillon (2006), we compared QBT, the graphical query formulation interface in DocBase, with a standard web-based query interface. Users in this study were divided into two categories - expert and novice, and were asked to write queries using one of the interfaces in a between-users study. This study showed the following results: (i) there was no significant difference in accuracy of the users between the two interfaces, (ii) although there was no significant difference between the interfaces in terms of efficiency of the users of the different interfaces, experts using either interface were significantly more efficient than the novices, showing that the new interface does not hinder the efficiency of the experts. Finally, (iii) with the help of a post experiment questionnaire we determined that the users of QBT were more satisfied and more confident of their results than the users of the web interface.

These results demonstrate the utility of the two query processing approaches that we allow in DocBase. In particular, they show that XQuery may not be the answer to all the query processing requirements. A viable option for database vendors could be to use a language such as DSQL or QBT as an ad-hoc querying front-end-end to XQuery. DSQL is a proper subset of XQuery, and DocBase includes a parser which translates DSQL queries into equivalent XQuery queries. Such a translation process could be used to provide an ad-hoc querying support to systems that already implement XQuery.

CONTRIBUTIONS AND CONCLUSION

Traditionally databases have always been viewed as highly structured discrete sets of data. Although databases may contain extensive textual information in text or "memo" fields, such information has not been efficiently searchable and indexable. On the other hand, information retrieval systems have shown us how to efficiently perform keyword searches within text, but have made little use of the embedded structure in documents when available. In this work, we have united these two fields towards the goal of building generalized database systems capable of processing structured data as well as documents. Specifically, we describe a systematic approach towards processing data in structured format, whether they are document representation of relational databases, or databases for native XML documents. Our proposal for a XML document model with its corresponding query languages, and establishing a framework for its implementation are the most important contributions of this research. We showed how the design of DocBase could be scaled to very large databases. This architecture paves the way for integrating XML documents and relational data consistently under the same database or a set of distributed databases, with the ability to combine data from disparate sources in one query. The design of DocBase also fulfills all requirements of XML databases – Requirements R1, R2, R4 and R6 have been demonstrated in this paper. R5 (Security requirements) have been demonstrated in Mohan et al. (2007). Using standard XML parsers, requirement R3 is fulfilled. The query languages do not directly support specific XML features such as namespaces, because of our commitment to all marked-up document formats such as SGML, HTML, but incorporating namespaces will be considered in future work.

Our future work in this area is primarily focused on three main areas:

1. Enhancing the capabilities of the existing system, including support for other database systems for storage and index management, full incorporation of DSQL including nested queries, and improving the implementation of QBT to allow more complex queries.
2. Establishing a formal relationship between DSQL and XQuery, and providing support

for processing XQuery queries in DocBase through an inverse translation to DSQL.

3. Establishing methods for optimizing queries in the absence of a specialized index structure such as PAT.

Without question XML is emerging as the de-facto standard for document description and exchange because of its flexibility and simplicity. The capability of XML for representing both data and meta-data gives it the power that can be harnessed with query languages and processing technologies that certainly would constitute major subjects of research in the forthcoming decade. The biggest contribution of this work is a theoretically sound foundation for the forthcoming design and development of document database systems.

REFERENCES

Abiteboul, S., Cluet, S., & Milo, T. (1993). Querying and updating the file. In *Proceedings of the 19th International Conference on Very Large Data Bases*, Dublin, Ireland (pp. 73-84).

Abiteboul, S., Quass, D., McHugh, J., Widom, J., & Wiener, J. (1997). The Lorel query language for semistructured data. *International Journal on Digital Libraries*, *1*, 68–88.

Abiteboul, S., & Viannu, V. (1997). Regular path queries with constraints. In *Proceedings of the ACM SIGACT-SIGMOD-SIGART Symposium on Principles of Database Systems*, Tucson, AZ (pp. 122-133).

Amer-Yahia, S., Cho, S., Lakshmanan, L. V. S., & Srivastava, D. (2002). Tree pattern query minimization. *Very Large Data Base Journal*, *11*(4), 315–331. doi:10.1007/s00778-002-0076-7

Balmin, A., Ozcan, F., Beyer, K. S., Cochrane, R. J., & Pirahesh, H. (2004). A framework for using materialized XPath views in XML query processing. In *Proceedings of the Thirtieth International Conference on Very Large Data Bases*, Toronto, ON, Canada (Vol. 30).

Bancilhon, F., Barbedette, G., Benzaken, V., Delobel, C., Gamerman, S., & Lecluse, C. (1988). The design and implementation of O2, an object-oriented database system. *Advances in Object-Oriented Database Systems*, *6*(1), 1–22.

Boag, S., Chamberlin, D., Fernandez, M., Florescu, D., Robie, J., & Simeon, J. (2007). *XQuery 1.0: An XML query language*. Retrieved from http://www.w3.org/TR/xquery/

Bosak, J. (1999). *The plays of Shakespeare in XML*. Retrieved from http://xml.coverpages.org/bosakShakespeare200.html

Braga, D., Campi, A., Ceri, S., & Raffio, A. (2005). XQBE: a visual environment for learning XML query languages. In *Proceedings of the ACM SIGMOD International Conference on Management of Data*, Baltimore, MD (pp. 903-905).

Bray, T., Paoli, J., Sperberg-McQueen, C. M., Maler, E., & Yergeau, F. (2008). *Extensible markup language (XML) 1.0* (5th ed.). Retrieved from http://www.w3.org/TR/REC-xml/

Carey, M., & DeWitt, J. D. J., Franklin, M., Hall, N., AcAuliffe, M., Naughton, J., et al. (1994). Shoring up persistent applications. In *Proceedings of the ACM SIGMOD International Conference on Management of Data*, Minneapolis, MN (pp. 383-394).

Carey, M. J., DeWitt, D. J., Frank, D., Graefe, G., Muralikrishna, M., Richardson, J. E., & Shikita, E. J. (1986). The architecture of the EXODUS extensible DBMS. In *Proceedings of the International Workshop on Object-Oriented Database Systems* (pp. 52-65).

Chadwyck-Healey. (1994). *The English poetry full-text database. The works of more than 1,250 poets from 600 to 1900.* Retrieved from http://eresources.lib.unc.edu/eid/

Christensen, E., Curbera, F., Meredith, G., & Weerawarana, S. (2001). *Web services description language (WSDL) 1.1*. Retrieved from http://www.w3.org/TR/wsdl

Christophides, V., Abiteboul, S., Cluet, S., & Scholl, M. (1994). From structured documents to novel query facilities. *SIGMOD Record*, *23*(2), 313–324. doi:10.1145/191843.191901

Clark, J., & DeRose, S. (1999). *XML path language XPath version 1.0.* Retrieved from http://www.w3.org/TR/xpath

Clement, L., Hately, A., von Riegen, C., & Rogers, T. (2004). *Universal description discovery and integration (UDDI) specifications, version 3.0.2.* Retrieved from http://www.uddi.org/pubs/uddi_v3.htm

Colby, L. S. (1990). A recursive algebra for nested relations. *Information Systems*, *15*(5), 567–582. doi:10.1016/0306-4379(90)90029-O

Desai, B. C., Goyal, P., & Sadri, F. (1986). A data model for use with formatted and textual data. *Journal of the American Society for Information Science American Society for Information Science*, *37*(3), 158–165.

Erwig, M. (2003). Xing: A visual XML query language. *Journal of Visual Languages and Computing*, *14*, 5–45. doi:10.1016/S1045-926X(02)00074-5

Fankhauser, P. (2002). XQuery by the book = an implementation based on rigid formal semantics. In *Proceedings of the XML Conference*.

Fernandez, M., & Simeon, J. (2004). Building an extensible XQuery engine: Experiences with Galax. In Z. Bellahsene, T. Milo, M. Rys, D. Suciu, & R. Unland (Eds.), *Proceedings of the Second International Conference on Database and XML Technologies* (LNCS 3186, pp. 1-14).

Fernandez, M. F., & Suciu, D. (1998). Optimizing regular path expressions using graph schemas. In *Proceedings of the International Conference on Data Engineering* (pp. 14-23).

Fiebig, T., Helmer, S., Kanne, C., Moerkotte, G., Neumann, J., Schiele, R., & Westmann, T. (2002). Anatomy of a native XML base management system. *Very Large Data Base Journal*, *11*(4), 292–314. doi:10.1007/s00778-002-0080-y

Fiebig, T., & Moerkotte, G. (2001). Evaluating queries on structure with extended access support relations. In G. Goos, J. Hartmanis, J. van Leeuwen, D. Sciu, & G. Vossen (Eds.), *Proceedings of the Third International Workshop on the World Wide Web and Databases* (LNCS 1997, pp. 125-136).

Frasincar, F., Houben, G.-J., & Pau, C. (2002). XAL: an algebra for XML query optimization. In *Proceedings of the 13th Australasian Database Conference* (Vol. 5, pp. 49-56).

Funderburk, J. E., Malaika, S., & Reinwald, B. (2002). XML programming with SQL/XML and XQuery. *IBM Systems Journal*, *41*(4), 642–665. doi:10.1147/sj.414.0642

Gibson, D. S., Weide, B. W., Pike, S. M., & Edwards, S. H. (2000). Toward a normative theory for component-based system design and analysis. In Leavens, G. T., & Sitaraman, M. (Eds.), *Foundations of component-based systems* (pp. 211–230). Cambridge, UK: Cambridge University Press.

Gonnet, G. H., & Baeza-Yates, R. (1991). *Lexicographical indices for text: Inverted files vs. pat trees*. Waterloo, ON, Canada: University of Waterloo.

Gonnet, G. H., & Tompa, F. W. (1987). Mind your grammar: a new approach to modeling text. In *Proceedings of the 13th International Conference on Very Large Data Bases*, Brighton, UK (pp. 339-346).

Grangard, A., Eisenberg, B., & Nickull, D. (2001). *ebXML technical architecture specification v1.0.4*. Retrieved from http://www.ebxml.org/specs/ebTA.pdf

Gudgin, M., Hadley, M., Mendelsohn, N., Moreau, J., Nielsen, H. F., Karmakar, A., & Lafon, Y. (2007). *SOAP version 1.2 part 1: Messaging framework* (2nd ed.). Retrieved from http://www.w3.org/TR/soap12-part1/

Hevner, A. R., March, S. T., Park, J., & Ram, S. (2004). Design science in information system research. *Management Information Systems Quarterly*, *28*(1), 75–105.

Jaakkola, J., & Kilpelainen, P. (1996). *The Sgrep online manual*. Retrieved from http://www.cs.helsinki.fi/u/jjaakkol/sgrepman.html

Jaeschke, G., & Schek, H. (1982). Remarks on the algebra on non first normal form relations. In *Proceedings of the ACM SIGACT-SIGMOD Symposium on Principles of Database Systems*, Los Angeles, CA (pp. 124-138).

Jagadish, H. V., Al-Khalifa, S., Chapman, A., Lakshmanan, L. V. S., Nierman, A., & Paparizos, S. (2002). TIMBER: A native XML database. *Very Large Data Base Journal*, *11*(4), 274–291. doi:10.1007/s00778-002-0081-x

Jagadish, H. V., Lakshmanan, L. V. S., Srivastava, D., & Thompson, K. (2001). TAX: A tree algebra for XML. In G. Ghelli & G. Grahne (Eds.), *Proceedings of the 8th International Workshop on Database Programming Languages* (LNCS 2397, pp. 149-164).

Lawrence, S., & Giles, C. L. (1998). Searching the World Wide Web. *Science*, *280*, 98–100. doi:10.1126/science.280.5360.98

Lawrence, S., & Giles, C. L. (1999). Accessibility of information on the Web. *Nature*, *400*, 107–109. doi:10.1038/21987

Levene, M., & Loizou, G. (1993). Semantics for null extended nested relations. *ACM Transactions on Database Systems*, *18*(3), 415–459. doi:10.1145/155271.155275

Li, G., Li, C., Feng, J., & Zhou, L. (2009a). SAIL: Structure-aware indexing for effective and progressive top-k keyword search over XML documents. *Information Sciences*, *179*(21), 3745–3762. doi:10.1016/j.ins.2009.06.025

Li, J., Liu, C., Yu, J., & Zhou, R. (2009b). Efficient top-k search across heterogeneous XML data sources. In *Proceedings of the 13th International Conference on Database Systems for Advanced Applications*, Brisbane, Australia (pp. 314-329).

McFadden, J. (1997). Micro document architectures (MDOC): A new concept beyond full-text & document management systems. In *Proceedings of the SGML Conference*.

Mohan, S., & Sengupta, A. (2005). DocBase - the INEX evaluation experience. In N. Fuhr, M. Lalmas, S. Malik, & Z. Szlávik (Eds.), *Proceedings of the Third International Workshop on Advances in XML Information Retrieval* (LNCS 3493, pp. 261-275).

Mohan, S., Sengupta, A., & Wu, Y. (2007). A rewrite based approach for enforcing access constraints for XML. In B. Apolloni, R. J. Howlett, & L. Jain (Eds.), *Proceedings of the 11th International Conference on Knowledge-Based Intelligent Information and Engineering Systems* (LNCS 4694, pp. 1081-1089).

OpenText. (2010). *Open text search server, eDOCS edition.* Retrieved from http://www.opentext.com/2/sso_download_open?docpath=product/livelink/edocs/edocs_searchserver_po.pdf

Paparizos, S., Wu, Y., Lakshmanan, L. V. S., & Jagadish, H. V. (2004). Tree logical classes for efficient evaluation of XQuery. In *Proceedings of the ACM SIGMOD International Conference on Management of Data*, Paris, France (pp. 71-82).

Salminen, A., & Tompa, F. (2001). Requirements for XML document database systems. In *Proceedings of the ACM Symposium on Document Engineering*, Atlanta, GA (pp. 85-94).

Schmidt, A. R., Waas, F., Kersten, M. L., Carey, M. J., Manolescu, I., & Busse, R. (2002). XMark: A benchmark for XML data management. In *Proceedings of the International Conference on Very Large Data Bases* (pp. 974-985).

Sengupta, A., & Dillon, A. (2006). Query by templates: Using the shape of information to search next generation databases. *IEEE Transactions on Professional Communication*, *49*(2), 128–144. doi:10.1109/TPC.2006.875073

Sengupta, A., Mohan, S., & Doshi, R. (2003). XER - Extensible entity relationship modeling. In *Proceedings of the XML Conference*.

Sengupta, A., & Ramesh, V. (2009). Designing document SQL (DSQL)- an accessible yet comprehensive ad-hoc querying frontend for XQuery. *Journal of Database Management*, *20*(4), 25–51. doi:10.4018/jdm.2009062502

Sipani, S., Verma, K., Miller, J. A., & Aleman-Meza, B. (2004). Designing a high-performance database engine for the 'Db4XML' native XML database system. *Journal of Systems and Software*, *69*(1-2), 87–104. doi:10.1016/S0164-1212(03)00077-3

Szyperski, C. (2000). Component software and the way ahead. In Leavens, G. T., & Sitaraman, M. (Eds.), *Foundations of component-based systems* (pp. 1–20). Cambridge, UK: Cambridge University Press.

Szyperski, C. A., Bosch, J., & Weck, W. (1999). Component-oriented programming. In *Proceedings of the Workshop on Object-Oriented Technology* (pp. 184-192).

Tennant, R. (Ed.). (2002). *XML in libraries*. New York, NY: Neal-Schuman.

Wu, Y., Al-Khalifa, S., Jagadish, H. V., Patel, J. M., Koudas, N., & Srivastava, D. (2002). Structural joins: A primitive for efficient XML query pattern matching. In *Proceedings of the IEEE International Conference on Data Engineering*.

Wu, Y., Paparizos, S., Lakshmanan, L. V. S., & Jagadish, H. V. (2004). Tree logical classes for efficient evaluation of XQuery. In *Proceedings of the SIGMOD Conference* (pp. 71-82).

Wu, Y., Patel, J. M., & Jagadish, H. V. (2003). Structural join order selection for XML query optimization. In *Proceedings of the IEEE International Conference on Data Engineering* (pp. 443-454).

Yoshikawa, M., Amagasa, T., Shimura, T., & Uemura, S. (2001). XRel: A path-based approach to storage and retrieval of XML documents using relational databases. *ACM Transactions on Internet Technology*, *1*(1), 110–141. doi:10.1145/383034.383038

Zhang, J. (1995). OODB and SGML techniques in text database: An electronic dictionary system. *SIGMOD Record*, *24*(1), 3–8. doi:10.1145/202660.202661

Zloof, M. M. (1977). Query by example: A database language. *IBM Systems Journal*, *16*(4), 324–343. doi:10.1147/sj.164.0324

ENDNOTES

1. Some of the items have been published elsewhere as indicated, and not covered in complete detail in this paper
2. Not all tree traversal operations can be performed using the PAT indices. Because of the way PAT flattens the structure to perform its queries, it is not possible to obtain an immediate child or immediate parent of a node using the PAT indices. Navigation can only be performed on named ancestors and descendants.
3. Basic paths such as p1.p2 where p2 is an immediate child of p1 or abbreviated paths such as p1..p2 where p2 is a descendant of p1
4. The INEX document collection is made up of the full-texts, marked up in XML, of 12,107 articles of the IEEE Computer Society's publications from 12 magazines and 6 transactions, covering the period of 1995-2002, and totaling 494 megabytes in size. The collection has a suitably complex XML structure (192 different content models in DTD) and contains scientific articles of varying length. On average an article contains 1,532 XML nodes, where the average depth of a node is 6.9.

This work was previously published in the Journal of Database Management, Volume 22, Issue 4, edited by Keng Siau, pp. 30-56, copyright 2011 by IGI Publishing (an imprint of IGI Global).

Chapter 15
A Meta-Analysis Comparing Relational and Semantic Models

Keng Siau
University of Nebraska – Lincoln, USA

Fiona Fui-Hoon Nah
University of Nebraska – Lincoln, USA

Qing Cao
Texas Tech University, USA

ABSTRACT

Data modeling is the sine quo non of systems development and one of the most widely researched topics in the database literature. In the past three decades, semantic data modeling has emerged as an alternative to traditional relational modeling. The majority of the research in data modeling suggests that the use of semantic data models leads to better performance; however, the findings are not conclusive and are sometimes inconsistent. The discrepancies that exist in the data modeling literature and the relatively low statistical power in the studies make meta-analysis a viable choice in analyzing and integrating the findings of these studies.

1. INTRODUCTION

Databases are used in every sector of the industry including business, health care, education, government, and libraries (Liao & Palvia, 2000; Firat *et al.*, 2009; Aiken *et al.*, 2011; Siau & Rossi, 2011). As databases continue to become ever more critical components of both large and small systems, the success of development projects will become increasingly dependent on the accuracy of the data models (Ramakrishnan & Gehrke, 2002; Siau *et al.*, 2010). We have witnessed enormous growth in the number and importance of database applications in the last three decades. Aiken *et al.* (2011) stressed that the amount of data available these days and the value from information that organizations must derive from these data have made data modeling and database management a critical

DOI: 10.4018/978-1-4666-2044-5.ch015

and vital issue for the competitiveness and survival of organizations. Data modeling techniques have continued to evolve since the first database management system was introduced in the 1960s (Watson, 2005). Subsequently, hierarchical and network database models were introduced in the 1970s. The relational data model and semantic data models, such as entity-relationship model (ER) and extended entity-relationship model (EER), have been widely used in practice since the early 1980s (Hoffer *et al.*, 2010) and the trend continues even today.

Object oriented modeling became popular in the late 1990s and early 2000s. Studies on object oriented approaches (e.g., Siau & Cao, 2001; Siau & Loo, 2006; Taha & Elmasri, 2009; Gemino & Parker, 2009; VanderMeer & Dutta, 2009; Evermann & Wand, 2009; Siau & Tian, 2009; Shank *et al.*, 2010; Siau, 2010; Tan *et al.*, 2011) started to appear in academic publications in the 2000s. Despite the emergence of object oriented modeling techniques, relational and ER/EER models and their query languages continue to be important and widely studied (e.g., Sengupta & Ramesh, 2009; Niu *et al.*, 2009; Sakr, 2009; Ayanso *et al.*, 2009; Huh *et al.*, 2010; An *et al.*, 2010; Bera *et al.*, 2010; Shlezinger *et al.*, 2010). Further, relational database management systems are widely used and relational data model is still the dominant model in industry.

In the relational data model, a relation is a subset of the Cartesian product of an ordered list of domains (Codd, 1970). The power of the relational data model lies in its rigorous mathematical foundations and simple user-level paradigm. Semantic models use the concepts of entities or objects and relationships among them. Semantic models provide flexible structuring capabilities and allow data constraints to be specified explicitly. Object-oriented data models, dynamic data models, and active data models are the new trends in data modeling (Embley, 1998). Despite much research interest in semantic and object oriented data modeling, the relational database is still the predominant database used in the industry (Coronel *et al.*, 2009), while ER modeling remains highly popular as a tool for conceptual data modeling (Post, 2004).

Many empirical studies have examined the effect of relational versus semantic data modeling on user performance (Batra *et al.*, 1990; Carlis & March, 1983; Chan *et al.*, 1993; Chan & Lim, 1998; Hardgrave & Dalal, 1995; Jarvenpaa & Machesky, 1989; Juhn & Naumann, 1985; Kim & March, 1995; Leitheiser *et al.*, 1996; Shoval & Even-Chaime, 1987; Siau *et al.*, 1995, 2004). Much of the research in data modeling suggests that the use of semantic data models leads to better performance; however, the findings are not conclusive and are sometimes inconsistent. The discrepancies in the data modeling literature and the relatively low statistical power of the studies make meta-analysis a viable choice in analyzing and integrating the findings of these studies (Chan & Lim, 1998).

The objective of this research is twofold. First, a narrative review was carried out to compile empirical studies that compared relational data modeling and semantic data modeling. This provided a basis for an assessment of inconsistencies in the data modeling literature. Second, a meta-analysis was carried out as it offers powerful tests for detecting significant relationships by increasing the statistical power.

The rest of the paper is organized as follows: Section 2 provides a comprehensive literature review on relational and semantic data modeling, and summarizes prior studies comparing relational and semantic data modeling. Section 3 presents the research questions and model. Section 4 discusses the theories used in this research and lists the hypotheses for this study. Section 5 describes the research methodology and details the research procedure. Section 6 presents the results and discussion. The last section, Section 7, lists the limitations of the research and concludes the paper.

2. LITERATURE REVIEW

This section of the paper reviews the basic concepts of relational and semantic data modeling and provides a narrative review of the data modeling literature.

2.1. Relational and Semantic Models

Numerous data modeling approaches have been introduced in the last three decades. Two of the most popular approaches are the relational and semantic models. The relational data model is the most popular technique for managing large collections of data (Watson, 2005). A data relational model consists of a set of relations, where a relation is a two-dimensional table arranged in rows and columns. A distinguishing characteristic of the relational data model is that there is no explicit linkage between tables. The major advantages of the relational model are its simplicity in data presentation and the ease with which complex queries can be expressed.

Semantic data models emerged in the mid 1970s as an alternative to relational data modeling. Semantic data models refer to models that have been employed for conceptual database design activities. They possess characteristics such as expressiveness, simplicity, minimality, formality, and unique interpretation (Hoffer *et al.*, 2010). The main advantages of the semantic data model are that it captures more semantic information of the world than the relational model and it gives users an easily understandable visual representation of the data and relationships. The most widely used semantic data model is the entity-relationship (ER) model (Chen, 1976).

An ER model provides a detailed, logical representation of the data. The ER model is expressed in terms of entities, relationships among entities, and attributes of both entities and relationships. The basic ER model was subsequently extended to include more advanced concepts such as generalization/specialization and aggregation. These improved ER models are known as Extended or Enhanced ER (EER) models (Hoffer *et al.*, 2010).

Empirical studies, especially experimental studies, are widely used in comparing semantic and relational data modeling. Two of the most widely used constructs in data modeling research are user performance and perceived ease-of-use. In the context of this research, user performance comprises model understanding and model comprehension time (Juhn & Naumann, 1985; Shoval & Even-Chaime, 1987). Perceived ease-of-use indicates the degree of effort needed to use the data model (Batra *et al.*, 1990).

2.2. Narrative Review

Through a search of various databases including ABI/Inform, INFORTAC, and ORMS-WEB, we found a number of studies that compared the relational and semantic models in terms of data model understanding. Although the majority of these studies suggest that the use of semantic data models leads to better performance, the findings are neither conclusive nor consistent. On one hand, some studies (e.g., Jarvenpaa & Machesky, 1986; Leitheiser *et al.*, 1996; Chan *et al.*, 1993; Siau *et al.*, 2004) have shown that semantic models were better than the relational model in terms of model understanding, comprehension time, and/or perceived ease of use. On the other hand, other studies (e.g., Jih *et al.*, 1989; Chan & Lim, 1998) found that there were no significant differences between the semantic and relational models.

It should be noted that not all data modeling languages represent the same information in the same manner and this can be one of the factors contributing to the differences in the findings. This is one of the issues facing meta-analysis and there are ways to alleviate this problem, which will be discussed in Section 7. The next two subsections review the existing literature on the comparisons between relational and semantic data modeling.

2.2.1. Literature Favoring Semantic Models Over Relational Model

A number of studies suggest that semantic models outperform the relational model (Jarvenpaa & Machesky, 1986, 1989; Juhn & Naumann, 1985; Leitheiser *et al.,* 1996; Siau *et al.*, 1995, 2004). Some research findings also indicate that semantic models are perceived to be easier to use than the relational model.

Juhn and Naumann (1985) studied end-user model comprehension. They found that semantic data models – the entity-relationship model (ER) and the logical data structure (LDS) – were easier for users to understand than the relational data model for relationship existence-finding and cardinality-finding tasks.

Jarvenpaa and Machesky (1989) examined the ways in which formalisms support naive analysts' comprehension of data analysis skills. The results suggest that, for structured tasks, novices were able to more quickly understand LDS than the relational model.

Chan *et al.* (1993) conducted an experiment with a customized ER language for users of the ER model. Users of the relational model used SQL. The results showed significantly better performance by users of the ER model. The higher performance, however, may be attributed to the use of a language designed for the ER model.

Siau *et al.* (1995, 2004) compared both the relational and the ER model using visual languages. They found that users of the semantic model took less time than users of the relational model to understand the model and to formulate the queries.

Leitheiser *et al.* (1996) studied end-user model comprehension. He found that the semantic model (LDS) was easier to comprehend and resulted in higher recall of database schema than the relational model.

2.2.2. Literature Favoring Relational Model Over Semantic Models

In spite of the claims by many researchers that semantic models are superior to the relational model, some studies (e.g., Juhn & Naumann, 1985; Shoval & Even-Chaime, 1987) showed that the relational model outperformed the semantic model in both user performance and perceived ease of use.

According to Juhn and Naumann (1985), although relationships in semantic data models were more intuitive and easier to understand than relationships in the relational data model, the relational model outperformed semantic data models with respect to recognizing relationship identifiers.

Shoval and Even-Chaime (1987) studied database schema designs by comparing the relational model and the ER model. Their findings suggest that users of the relational model took less time to understand the model than users of the ER model. The study also suggests that the relational model rendered better model understanding of unary relationships than the ER model.

2.2.3. Studies with Non-Significant Results

Some research findings show no significant difference between the relational and semantic data models in user performance and perceived ease of use. For example, in Juhn and Naumann's (1985) study, the EER model was not perceived to be easier to use than the relational model.

Another example is the study by Jih *et al.* (1989). This study compared the relational and entity-relationship models. In the experiment, users of both the relational and ER models used the same query language, SQL. The results did not show any significant difference between the two groups of users.

2.2.4. Justification for Meta-Analysis

The discrepancies that exist in the literature indicate that a meta-analysis is warranted. Several researchers have advocated the use of meta-analysis to resolve inconsistent results in the literature (King & He, 2005). For example, Chan and Lim (1998) argued that the seemingly contradictory results in the data modeling literature prompted the need for meta-analysis. Pickardaa *et al.* (1998) investigated empirical software engineering research by combining the results of independent studies using a meta-analysis. Their analysis focuses on the relationship between project effort and product size in software companies. They suggest that meta-analysis is appropriate for homogeneous studies where the raw data or quantitative summary information is available.

3. RESEARCH MODEL AND QUESTIONS

A commonly used research model for data modeling comparisons is shown in Figure 1. The original model was proposed by Jenkins (1982) to study end-user's query writing ability as measured by syntax errors, semantic errors, and time needed to write queries. This model was later adapted for studies on other aspects of data modeling performance, i.e., model understanding, modeling correctness, and perceived ease-of-use (Batra *et al.*, 1990; Bock & Ryan, 1993; Hardgrave & Dalal, 1995; Siau *et al.*, 2004).

The model consists of the following variables: data model (independent variable), user (controlled), task (controlled), and modeling performance. Modeling performance, as the dependent variable, consists of ease of use, model understanding, and comprehension time.

Research Questions

In this meta-analysis research, we are interested in the following research questions:

1. Do semantic data models, when compared to the relational model, lead to better user performance (model understanding) – for unary relationships, binary one-many relationships, binary many-many relationships, ternary one-many-many relationships, and

Figure 1. Research model

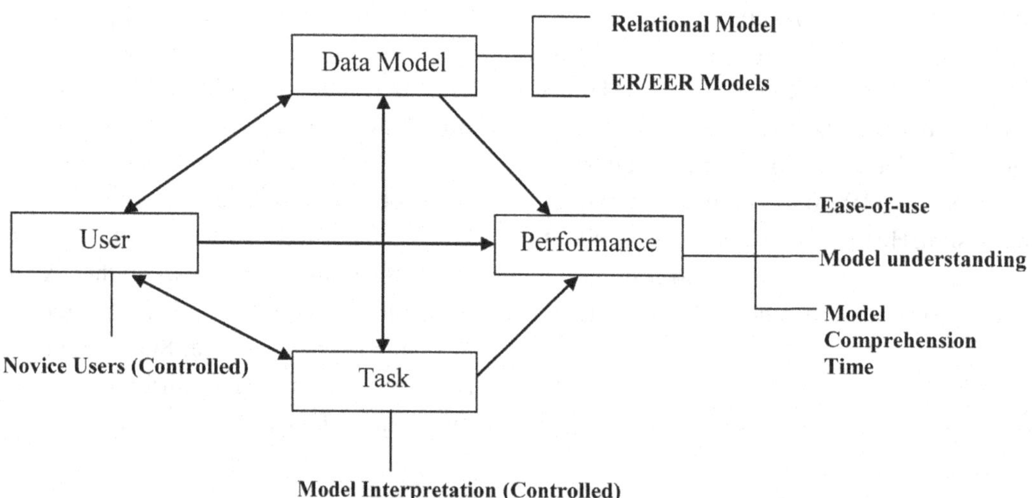

ternary many-many-many relationships? (A ternary relationship is a simultaneous relationship among the instances of three entity types).

2. Do users of semantic data models take less time to comprehend a data model than users of the relational data model?
3. Do users perceive semantic data models to be easier to use, when compared to the relational model?

Control Variables

In this meta-analysis, both user and task variables were controlled – since the goal of this research is to compare user performance of relational and semantic models. For the user variable, novice users were used for this meta-analysis since there were not enough studies on expert users to carry out a meta-analysis. The task in this study is model interpretation.

Independent Variable

The independent variable has two levels – the relational and semantic data models, where the latter includes both ER and EER models. The ER model was chosen in this study because of its widespread use and acceptance (Hoffer *et al.*, 2010). The EER model was also included since it is an extension of the ER model. Moreover, EER models capture important business rules such as constraints in supertype/subtype relationships (Ramakrishnan & Gehrke, 2002), which are an important component of semantic data models.

Dependent Variables

The dependent variables (modeling performance) for this study are: 1) model understanding, 2) model comprehension time, and 3) perceived ease-of-use. Model understanding refers to the accuracy of model interpretation, and model comprehension time refers to the time taken to understand a data model. Perceived ease-of-use indicates the degree of effort needed to use the data model.

Modeling of relationships in semantic data models is multi-faceted (e.g., unary, binary relationships). The facets measured in this study are: unary, binary one-many, binary many-many, ternary many-many-many, and ternary one-many-many.

The instrument used to measure perceived ease-of-use in the studies included in this meta-analysis was adopted from Batra *et al.* (1990), Davis (1989), and Hardgrave and Dalal (1995).

4. THEORIES AND HYPOTHESES

Two human-computer interaction (HCI) theories are used as the theoretical foundation for this study. First, the cognitive theory on HCI serves as the theoretical foundation for data modeling performance. This theory is widely used to explain the difference in performance between semantic models and the relational model. Next, Larkin and Simon's (1987) theory is used to predict and explain differences in perceived ease of use of semantic and relational modeling.

4.1. Cognitive Theory on HCI

According to the human-computer-interface model proposed by Booth (1992) (see Figure 2), psychological variables do not map directly onto the physical system (i.e., data models). The gulf of evaluation is the degree to which the system provide representations that can be directly perceived and interpreted in terms of the expectations and intentions of the user.

A gulf of execution exists when a user, with a goal in mind, knows what needs to be achieved, but does not know which physical variables to adjust or in what ways to adjust them. Thus, the gulf of execution directly determines the amount of cognitive effort it takes for a user to manipulate and evaluate a system.

Figure 2. Human-computer-interface model

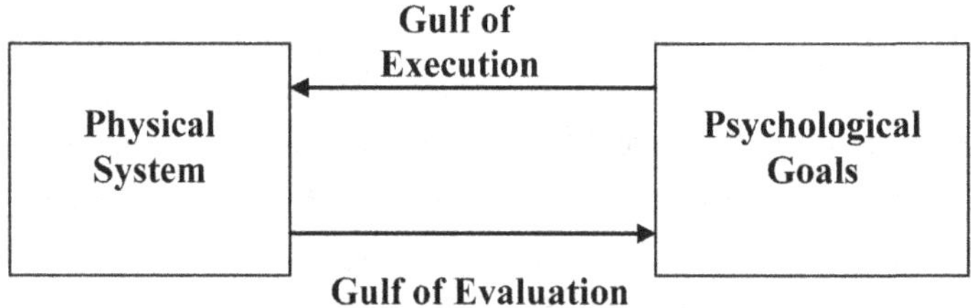

4.1.1. Proposed Hypotheses based on Cognitive Theory on HCI

Noran (1981) described the semantic gulf of execution. To the user, the semantic level consists of conceptual entities and conceptual operations on these entities. In the context of database design, the semantic gulf of execution is the distance between the meaning as depicted by the conceptual model and the user's knowledge of the real world data. While the ER/EER models use special symbols to capture the degree and connectivity of relationships, the relational model captures relationships in a more implicit manner. Since semantic models (ER/EER) capture and explicitly represent the characteristics of the relationship between entities in a more direct fashion (i.e., more direct mapping), it is logical to assume that the semantic models would render a narrower semantic gulf of execution when compared to the relational model. Examples of relational and ER models are shown in Figure 3.

Relationships are the "glue" that holds the various components of a semantic data model together. In order to compare semantic models to the relational model, we need to look at the main relationship types. In this study, five types of relationships are investigated: unary, binary one-many, binary many-many, ternary one-many-many, and ternary many-many-many. Ternary one-one-many relationship is excluded in this research because there are not enough existing studies to carry out a meta-analysis. Based on the cognitive theory on HCI, semantic models would yield a shorter gulf of execution due to the explicit representation of relationships. Therefore, we hypothesize that users of semantic data models will outperform users of the relational model in model understanding.

Hence, the following hypotheses for model understanding are proposed:

Users of semantic data models (ER/EER), when compared to users of the relational model, will perform better in model understanding:

H1: In unary relationships
H2: In binary one-many relationships
H3: In binary many-many relationships
H4: In ternary one-many-many relationships
H5: In ternary many-many-many relationships

4.2. Larkin and Simon's Theory

According to Larkin and Simon (1987), diagrams are superior to text for representing complex problems or scenarios. First, diagrams can group related information together, thus avoiding lengthy searches for the elements needed to make a problem-solving inference. Second, diagrams automatically support a large number of perceptual inferences, which are easier for humans to understand and comprehend. In the case of data modeling, the relational model uses a tabular format while the ER/EER models use a pictorial representation. A data modeling technique that uses graphical formalisms (e.g., ER/EER) is easier to use than one that uses a tabular format (e.g., the relational model), as indicated in the study by

Figure 3. ER model versus relational model

ER Model

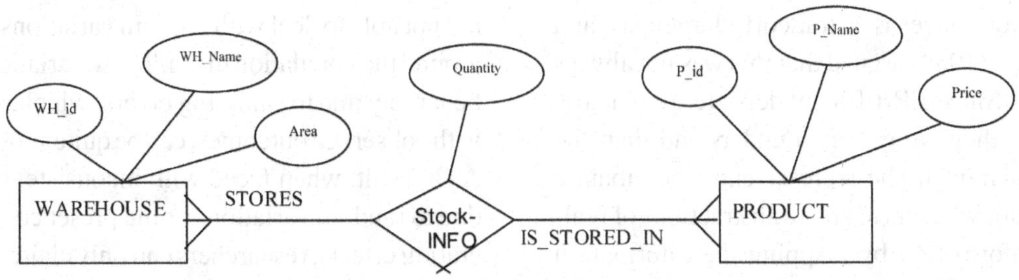

The Relational Model

WAREHOUSE
PK: Primary key

WH_id	WH_Name	Area

PRODUCT
PK: Primary key

P_id	P_Name	Price

STOCK_INFO
FK: WAREHOUSE.WH_id FK:PRODUCT.P_id

WH_id	P_id	Quantity

* FK: Foreign key

Kim and March (1995). The reason for this argument is because, in an ER/EER representation, a relationship is shown explicitly. A relational model represents a relationship by associating the identifiers of objects. In other words, in relational model, the relationship is not depicted explicitly. Thus, the relationships between the objects are more direct in an ER/EER model than a relational model (Hoffer *et al.*, 2010).

4.2.1. Hypotheses Based on Larkin and Simon's Theory

Perceived ease-of-use is defined as the degree to which a person believes that using a particular system would be free of effort. In the context of data modeling, ease-of-use specifies the degree of cognitive effort needed to use a data model. Users are perceived to perform better if the data model they are using requires less mental effort. Since the relational model is based on mathematical theory and represents data in a tabular form, relationships appear to be most difficult for users to comprehend. On the other hand, the ER/EER models are perceived by users to be easier to use because they provide a more direct approach to representing relationships. Hence, we hypothesize that:

H6: Semantic data models are perceived to be easier to use than the relational data model.

The time required to understand a data model is another important measure of modeling performance. While previous studies considered time and performance as a tradeoff, Jarvenpaa and Machesky (1989) argued that this was not always the case. Since ER/EER models are graphically oriented, they are easier to understand than the relational model. The expressiveness of semantic models allows users to create abstractions of real-world information by mapping the information onto basic human concepts (Tsichritzis & Lochovsky, 1992). It is, therefore, reasonable to suggest that it requires less time for users to comprehend semantic models than the relational model.

H7: Users of semantic data models, when compared to users of the relational data model, require less time to comprehend the data model.

5. RESEARCH METHODOLOGY AND PROCEDURE

Meta-analysis involves the statistical integration of the results of independent studies. It is a rigorous approach for integrating and aggregating research studies that examine the same (or similar) phenomenon. This quantitative approach is widely used in research fields such as business, education, and psychology. The use of meta-analysis to integrate research findings is popular in established subareas of MIS such as DSS (Alavi & Joachimsthaler, 1992; Montazemi & Wang, 1989), GSS (Dennis *et al.*, 2001; Dennis & Wixom, 2002; McLeod, 1992), IT acceptance (Wu & Lederer, 2009), and natural database languages (Chan & Lim, 1998).

Although both traditional narrative reviews and meta-analysis share the same goals, narrative reviews are not as effective as meta-analysis in providing answers to research questions. For instance, two narrative reviews on the same domain may not end up with the same conclusion due to the inarticulate and subjective rules that guide the narrative reviews. The meta-analysis approach is more objective than narrative reviews.

Another pitfall of narrative reviews is that they are not able to deal with random variations of data around the population mean. These variations may be largely due to sampling errors, which, relative to the observed outcomes, can be quite substantial. As a result, when faced with inconsistent results due to random variations or the presence of moderating effects, researchers can only claim that the research results are inconclusive and call for more research to explain the differences. Meta-analysis provides an opportunity to account for sampling errors or moderating effects, which results in a more reliable and accurate aggregated summary of the literature. Finally, the quantitative measures derived from the meta-analysis indicate the significance and magnitude of the phenomenon under study and the variability of these study outcomes.

5.1. Statistical Power Analysis

Statistical power analysis describes the relationship between significance level (α), sample size, effect size, and statistical power ($1-\beta$). A smaller α decreases statistical power. Effect size is an index, which measures the strength of association between the populations of interest (Cohen, 1988). Effect size is important because it helps researchers distinguish between a meaningful effect and a trivial one, and between the relative magnitudes of effects. Power increases as the value of effect size increases. As sample size increases, statistical power also increases. Generally speaking, a larger sample size is needed for higher statistical power.

5.2. Procedure for Meta-Analysis

Since the statistical procedures used in the independent studies included in this meta-analysis may vary, common metrics for significance levels and effect sizes must be established. In this study, the *p* value is used to present the significance level. The two most commonly used effect size measures in meta-analysis are Cohen's *d* and Pearson's *r*. Pearson's *r* was chosen in this study because it is the most commonly used measure for effect size in data modeling research. In this research, Pearson's *r* was either obtained from the findings of the individual studies or derived from other statistical tests such as *F*, *t*, or k^2.

All findings were then grouped by hypotheses, and the standard deviations were calculated using the formulae proposed by Hunter *et al.* (1990):

$$\text{Mean effect size (R)} = \frac{\sum N_i r_i}{\sum N_i}$$

$$\text{Sample variance (Var(R))} = \frac{\sum N_i (r_i - R)^2}{\sum N_i}$$

$$\text{Standard deviation (SD)} = \frac{Var(R)}{M}$$

where N_i = sample size of study *i*, r_i = effect size of study *i*, and *M* = number of studies included in the meta-analysis.

A rule of thumb for judging the magnitude of effect sizes was suggested by Cohen (1977) – an effective size of 0.2 represents a small effect, an effective size of 0.5 constitutes a medium effect, and an effective size of 0.8 indicates a large effect.

6. RESULTS AND DISCUSSION

In this section, we present the results of the meta-analysis and discuss the findings. The research findings provide insights into the differences between relational and semantic data modeling. It resolves some inconsistencies in the data modeling literature and boosts the statistical power of the findings.

6.1. Results

The results of the meta-analysis are displayed in Table 1. For each hypothesis, Table 1 shows the number of studies and sample size included in the meta-analysis, average effect of the independent studies, mean effect of the meta-analysis, standard deviation of the meta-analysis, and the significance level (*p*-value).

6.1.1. Hypothesis 1

Hypothesis 1 (model understanding in unary relationships) renders a significant result ($p<0.05$) indicating that users understand semantic models (ER/ERR) better than the relational model when unary relationships are involved. This result is consistent with most of the findings in the literature (e.g., Chan *et al.*, 1993; Siau *et al.*, 1995, 2004). However, this result is not in line with the findings of the study by Shoval and Even-Chaime (1987). We believe that this inconsistency arises due to the relatively small sample size (42 subjects) in their study as compared to our meta-analysis (289 subjects). Our analysis suggests that users of semantic data models will perform better in model understanding than users of the relational model because of the smaller "gulf of execution" in semantic modeling (Larkin & Simon, 1987). Our finding is also consistent with Larkin and Simon's (1987) argument that diagrams are superior to text expressions.

6.1.2. Hypotheses 2, 3, and 4

Results for hypotheses 2, 3, and 4 (model understanding in binary one-many relationships, binary many-many relationships, and ternary one-many-many relationships) not only concur with the findings of numerous research studies (i.e., that semantic models outperform the relational model for binary and ternary one-many-many relationships), but the meta-analysis technique also increases the effect size by an average of

Table 1. Results of meta-analysis

Hypothesis	Number of Studies	Sample Size	Average Effect	Mean Effect (Ri)	Standard Deviation	P Value
Unary relationship (H1)	5	289	0.390	0.508	0.025	0.0478
Binary 1:M relationship (H2)	7	452	0.684	0.801	0.019	0.0002
Binary M:M relationship (H3)	7	407	0.625	0.714	0.008	0.0001
Ternary 1:M:M relationship (H4)	7	414	0.621	0.740	0.006	0.0000
Ternary M:M:M relationship (H5)	6	352	0.472	0.529	0.009	0.1020
Perceived ease-of-use (H6)	7	442	0.420	0.623	0.048	0.0616
Model comprehension time (H7)	5	225	0.437	0.615	0.150	0.0190

0.751. Thus, the meta-analysis results are more convincing and support the cognitive model proposed by Booth (1992) and the argument by Larkin and Simon (1987) that a picture is worth 10,000 words.

6.1.3. Hypothesis 5

As for hypothesis 5 (model understanding in ternary many-many-many relationships), our meta-analysis does not produce any significant result ($p = 0.102 > 0.05$). Since the studies included in this meta-analysis involved subjects who were novice end users of data models, it is likely that ternary many-many-many relationships were too difficult for them to comprehend.

6.1.4. Hypothesis 6

For hypothesis 6 (perceived ease of use of data models), our findings indicate that there is no significant difference in perceived ease of use between semantic data models and the relational model ($p = 0.062 > 0.05$). The underlying reason is two-fold. First, it indicates that even though our findings suggest that users of semantic models perform better than users of the relational model, the users may not perceive semantic models to be easier to use than the relational model. Second, the small number of studies available for this meta-analysis may not yield enough power to detect the difference.

6.1.5. Hypothesis 7

Our findings on hypothesis 7 (time required to understand data models) suggest that the time required to understand semantic models is significantly shorter ($p = 0.019 < 0.05$) than the time needed to understand the relational model. The result is consistent with HCI theories in that semantic modeling is easier to comprehend than relational modeling due to the smaller "gulf of execution" and the "graphical nature" of semantic modeling.

6.2. Effect Size and Power Analysis

Table 2 shows the increase in effect size for each hypothesis.

As indicated in Table 2, the effect size of each hypothesis has increased. This result shows the benefit of meta-analysis – increasing the statistical power.

Table 2. Increase in effect sizes

Hypothesis	Average Effect	Mean Effect (Ri)	Increase in Mean Effect (%)
Unary relationship (H1)	0.390	0.508	30%
Binary 1:M relationship (H2)	0.684	0.801	17%
Binary M:M relationship (H3)	0.625	0.714	14%
Ternary 1:M:M relationship (H4)	0.621	0.740	19%
Ternary M:M:M relationship (H5)	0.472	0.529	12%
Perceived Ease-of-use (H6)	0.420	0.623	48%
Comprehension time (H7)	0.437	0.615	41%

For the performance measures with unary relationship, the effect size increased by 30%. More importantly, the result shows that there is a significant difference ($p = 0.0478 < 0.05$) between the relational and semantic models in users' data modeling performance for unary relationships.

For performance measures in binary one-many, binary many-many, and ternary one-many-many relationships, the findings indicate that the effect sizes increased by 17%, 14%, and 19% respectively. The implication is two-fold. First, the increased effect sizes in the meta-analysis indicate that the magnitudes of the treatments have been improved. Second, the increased effect sizes also result in higher statistical power – the probability that the test will correctly reject the null hypothesis. The effect size obtained in binary one-many relationships exceeds 0.8 – the mark for large effect size.

Even with an increase of 14% in effect size (higher magnitude of treatment and higher statistical power), the performance measure for ternary many-many-many relationships is still not statistically significant ($p = 0.102 > 0.05$).

As for perceived ease-of-use, there is a 48% increase in effect size, which means higher magnitude of treatment and higher statistical power. However, the p value ($p = 0.0616 > 0.05$) of this hypothesis does not indicate significance of the result.

The time required in model comprehension is significantly shorter for semantic modeling ($p = 0.019 < 0.05$). The effect size was increased by 41% from 0.437 (small size effect) to 0.615 (medium effect size). As such, the meta-analysis renders higher magnitude of treatment and higher statistical power.

7. LIMITATIONS AND CONTRIBUTIONS

Meta-analysis is not a panacea for all research problems. Certain limitations must be handled properly when using meta-analysis. The "apples and oranges" criticism – the mixing of data that come from studies in diverse settings – is the most widely cited problem in meta-analysis. Nevertheless, we tried to alleviate this problem by selecting studies that had compatible research themes. However, some degree of heterogeneity is inevitable in a meta-analysis. When utilizing meta-analysis, there is a trade-off between avoiding comparing apples with oranges and limiting the available sample size, which is another problem of meta-analysis (Hunter *et al.*, 1990). Since we include only studies that are very closely related in terms of the phenomenon studied (i.e., to try to avoid comparing apples with oranges), only eight studies were included in our meta-analysis.

Our research has contributed to the understanding of the pros and cons of two popular data modeling techniques. For practitioners, the results show that relationships in semantic models are generally easier to understand than relationships in the relational model. This suggests that users will understand semantic models better than the relational model. Therefore, it is better to communicate with users (e.g., end-users) using semantic models than the relational model.

For researchers, this research suggests that meta-modeling is a viable technique that is potentially useful for aggregating multiple studies in a narrow area of research. In this study, the meta-analysis has not only resolved some inconsistencies in the current literature but also produces larger effect sizes across the board. It also results in higher statistical power. As such, this study's findings provide a more general and accurate picture of comparative studies on data modeling.

REFERENCES

Aiken, P., Gillenson, M., Zhang, X., & Rafner, D. (2011). Data management and data administration: Assessing 25 Years of practice. *Journal of Database Management*, *22*(3), 24–45. doi:10.4018/jdm.2011070102

Alavi, M., & Joachimsthaler, E. A. (1992). Revisiting DSS implementation research: a meta-analysis of the literature and suggestions for researchers. *Management Information Systems Quarterly*, *16*(1), 95–116. doi:10.2307/249703

An, Y., Hu, X., & Song, I. (2010). Maintaining mappings between conceptual models and relational schemas. *Journal of Database Management*, *21*(3), 36–68. doi:10.4018/jdm.2010070102

Ayanso, A., Goes, P. B., & Mehta, K. (2009). A cost-based range estimation for mapping top-k selection queries over relational databases. *Journal of Database Management*, *20*(4), 1–25. doi:10.4018/jdm.2009062501

Batra, D., Hoffer, J. A., & Bostrom, R. P. (1990). A comparison of user performance between the relational and the extended entity relationship models in the discovery phase of database design. *Communications of the ACM*, *33*(2), 126–139. doi:10.1145/75577.75579

Bera, P., Krasnoperova, A., & Wand, Y. (2010). Using ontology languages for conceptual modeling. *Journal of Database Management*, *21*(1), 1–28. doi:10.4018/jdm.2010112301

Bock, D. B., & Ryan, T. (1993). Accuracy in modeling with extended entity relationship and object-oriented data models. *Journal of Database Management*, *4*(4), 30–39.

Booth, P. (1992). *An Introduction to Human-Computer Interaction*. Mahwah, NJ: Lawrence Erlbaum.

Carlis, J. V., & March, S. T. (1983). Computer-aided physical database design methodology. *Computer Performance*, *4*(4), 198–214.

Chan, H. C., & Lim, L. H. (1998). Database interfaces: a conceptual framework and a meta-analysis on natural language studies. *Journal of Database Management*, *9*(3), 25–32.

Chan, H. C., Wei, K. K., & Siau, K. L. (1993). User-database interface: The effect of abstraction levels on query performance. *Management Information Systems Quarterly*, *17*(4), 441–464. doi:10.2307/249587

Chen, P. (1976). The entity-relationship model: Towards a unified view of data. *ACM Transactions on Database Systems*, *1*(1), 9–36. doi:10.1145/320434.320440

Codd, E. F. (1970). A relational model of data for large shared data banks. *Communications of the ACM*, *13*(6), 377–387. doi:10.1145/362384.362685

Cohen, J. (1977). *Statistical Power Analysis for the Behavioral Sciences*. New York, NY: Academic Press.

Cohen, J. (1988). *Statistical Power Analysis*. Mahwah, NJ: Lawrence Erlbaum.

Coronel, C., Morris, S., & Rod, P. (2009). *Database Systems: Design, Implementation, and Management* (9th ed.). Florence, KY: Course Technology.

Davis, F. D. (1989). Perceived usefulness, perceived ease of use, and user acceptance of information technology. *Management Information Systems Quarterly*, *13*(3), 318–339. doi:10.2307/249008

Dennis, A. R., Haley, B. J., & Vandenberg, R. J. (2001). Understanding fit and appropriation effects in group support systems via meta-analysis. *Management Information Systems Quarterly*, *25*(2), 167–193. doi:10.2307/3250928

Dennis, A. R., & Wixom, B. H. (2002). Investigating the moderators of the group support systems use with meta-analysis. *Journal of Management Information Systems*, *18*(3), 235–258.

Embley, D. W. (1998). *Object Database Development Concepts and Principles*. Reading, MA: Addison-Wesley.

Evermann, J., & Wand, Y. (2009). Ontology based object-oriented domain modeling: Representing behavior. *Journal of Database Management*, *20*(1), 48–77. doi:10.4018/jdm.2009010103

Firat, A., Wu, L., & Madnick, S. (2009). General strategy for querying web sources in a data federation environment. *Journal of Database Management*, *20*(2), 1–18. doi:10.4018/jdm.2009092201

Gemino, A., & Parker, D. (2009). Use case diagrams in support of use case modeling: Deriving understanding from the picture. *Journal of Database Management*, *20*(1), 1–24. doi:10.4018/jdm.2009010101

Hardgrave, B. C., & Dalal, N. P. (1995). Comparing object oriented and extended entity relational data model. *Journal of Database Management*, *6*(3), 15–21.

Hoffer, J. A., Venkataraman, R., & Topi, H. (2010). *Modern Database Management* (10th ed.). Upper Saddle River, NJ: Prentice Hall.

Huh, S., Moon, K., & Park, J. (2010). An integrated query relaxation approach adopting data abstraction and fuzzy relation. *Journal of Database Management*, *21*(4), 35–59. doi:10.4018/jdm.2010100103

Hunter, J. E., Schmidt, F. L., & Jackson, F. B. (1990). *Meta-Analysis: Cumulating Research Finding Across Studies*. Thousand Oaks, CA: Sage.

Jarvenpaa, S. L., & Machesky, J. J. (1986). End user learning behavior in data analysis and data modeling tools. In *Proceedings of the 7th International Conference on Information Systems* (pp. 152-167).

Jarvenpaa, S. L., & Machesky, J. J. (1989). Data analysis and learning: An experimental study of data modeling tools. *International Journal of Human-Computer Studies*, *31*(4), 367–391.

Jenkins, A. M. (1982). *MIS Decision Variables and Decision Making Performance*. Ann Arbor, MI: UI Research Press.

Jih, K., Bradbard, D., Snyder, C., & Thompson, N. (1989). The effects of relational and entity-relational models on query performance of end users. *International Journal of Man-Machine Studies*, *31*(3), 257–267. doi:10.1016/0020-7373(89)90007-2

Juhn, S., & Naumann, J. (1985). The effectiveness of data representation characteristics on user validation. In *Proceedings of the 6th International Conference on Information Systems* (pp. 212-226).

Kim, Y., & March, S. T. (1995). Comparing data modeling formalisms. *Communications of the ACM*, *38*(6), 123–113. doi:10.1145/203241.203265

King, W. R., & He, J. (2005). Understanding the Role and Methods of Meta-Analysis in IS Research. *Communications of the Association for Information Systems*, *16*, 32. Retrieved from http://aisel.aisnet.org/cais/vol16/iss1/32.

Larkin, J. H., & Simon, H. A. (1987). Why a diagram is (sometimes) worth ten thousand words. *Cognitive Science*, *11*, 65–99. doi:10.1111/j.1551-6708.1987.tb00863.x

Leitheiser, R. L., & March, S. T. (1996). The influence of database structure representation on database system learning and use. *Journal of Management Information Systems*, *12*(4), 187–213.

Liao, C., & Palvia, P. C. (2000). The impact of data models and task complexity on end-user performance: An experimental investigation. *International Journal of Human-Computer Studies*, *52*(5), 831–845. doi:10.1006/ijhc.1999.0358

McLeod, P. L. (1992). An assessment of the experimental literature on electronic support of group work: Results of a meta-analysis. *Human-Computer Interaction*, *7*(3), 257–280. doi:10.1207/s15327051hci0703_1

Montazemi, A. R., & Wang, S. (1989). The effects of models of information presentation on decision-making: A review and meta-analysis. *Journal of Management Information Systems*, *5*(3), 121–127.

Mullen, B. (1989). *Advanced Basic Meta-Analysis*. Mahwah, NJ: Lawrence Erlbaum.

Niu, B., Martin, P., & Powley, W. (2009). Towards autonomic workload management in DBMSs. *Journal of Database Management*, *20*(3), 1–17. doi:10.4018/jdm.2009070101

Noran, T. P. (1981). The Command Language Grammar: A representation for the user interface of interactive computer systems. *International Journal of Man-Machine Studies*, *15*(1), 3–50. doi:10.1016/S0020-7373(81)80022-3

Pickardaa, L. M., Kitchenhamaa, B. A., & Jonesbb, P. W. (1998). Combining empirical results in software engineering. *Information and Software Technology*, *40*(14), 811–821. doi:10.1016/S0950-5849(98)00101-3

Post, G. V. (2004). *Database Management Systems: Designing and Building Business Applications* (3rd ed.). New York, NY: McGraw-Hill/Irwin.

Ramakrishnan, R., & Gehrke, J. (2002). *Database Management Systems* (3rd ed.). New York, NY: McGraw-Hill.

Sakr, S. (2009). Cardinality-aware purely relational xQuery processor. *Journal of Database Management*, *20*(3), 76–125. doi:10.4018/jdm.2009070104

Sengupta, A., & Ramesh, V. (2009). Designing Document SQL (DSQL): An accessible yet comprehensive ad-hoc querying frontend for query. *Journal of Database Management*, *20*(4), 26–53. doi:10.4018/jdm.2009062502

Shanks, G., Moody, D., Nuredini, J., Tobin, D., & Weber, R. (2010). Representing classes of things and properties in general in conceptual modelling: An empirical evaluation. *Journal of Database Management*, *21*(2), 1–25. doi:10.4018/jdm.2010040101

Shlezinger, G., Reinhartz-Berger, I., & Dori, D. (2010). Modeling design patterns for semi-automatic reuse in system design. *Journal of Database Management*, *21*(1), 29–57. doi:10.4018/jdm.2010112302

Shoval, P., & Even-Chaime, M. (1987). Database schema design: An experimental comparison between normalization and information analysis. *Database*, *18*(3), 30–39.

Siau, K. (2010). An analysis of Unified Modeling Language (UML) graphical constructs based on BWW ontology. *Journal of Database Management*, *21*(1), i–viii.

Siau, K., Long, Y., & Ling, M. (2010). Toward a unified model of information systems development success. *Journal of Database Management*, *21*(1), 80–101. doi:10.4018/jdm.2010112304

Siau, K., & Loo, P. (2006). Identifying difficulties in learning UML. *Information Systems Management*, *23*(3), 43–51. doi:10.1201/1078.10580530/46108.23.3.20060601/93706.5

Siau, K., & Rossi, M. (2011). Evaluation techniques for systems analysis and design modelling methods: A review and comparative analysis. *Information Systems Journal*, *21*(3), 249–268. doi:10.1111/j.1365-2575.2007.00255.x

Siau, K., Tan, X., & Sheng, H. (2010). Important characteristics of software development team members: An empirical investigation using repertory grid. *Information Systems Journal*, *20*(6), 563–580. doi:10.1111/j.1365-2575.2007.00254.x

Siau, K., & Tian, Y. (2009). A semiotics analysis of UML graphical notations. *Requirements Engineering*, *14*(1), 15–26. doi:10.1007/s00766-008-0071-7

Siau, K. L., & Cao, Q. (2001). Unified Modeling Language – A Complexity Analysis. *Journal of Database Management*, *12*(1), 26–34. doi:10.4018/jdm.2001010103

Siau, K. L., Chan, H. C., & Wei, K. K. (1995). The effects of conceptual and logical interfaces on visual query performance of end-users. In *Proceedings of the 16th Annual International Conference on Information Systems*, Amsterdam, The Netherlands.

Siau, K. L., Chan, H. C., & Wei, K. K. (2004). Effects of query complexity and learning on novice user query performance with conceptual and logical database interfaces. *IEEE Transactions on Systems, Man, and Cybernetics*, *34*(2), 276–281. doi:10.1109/TSMCA.2003.820581

Taha, K., & Elmasri, R. (2009). OOXKSearch: A search engine for answering XML keyword and loosely structured queries using OO techniques. *Journal of Database Management*, *20*(3), 18–50. doi:10.4018/jdm.2009070102

Tan, X., Alter, S., & Siau, K. (2011). Using service responsibility tables to supplement UML in analyzing e-service systems. *Decision Support Systems*, *51*(3), 350–360. doi:10.1016/j.dss.2011.01.001

Tsichritzis, D. C., & Lochovsky, F. H. (1982). *Data Models*. Upper Saddle River, NJ: Prentice Hall.

VanderMeer, D., & Dutta, K. (2009). Applying learner-centered design principles to UML sequence diagrams. *Journal of Database Management*, *20*(1), 25–47. doi:10.4018/jdm.2009010102

Watson, R. T. (2005). *Data Management: Databases and Organizations* (5th ed.). New York, NY: John Wiley & Sons.

Wu, J., & Lederer, A. (2009). A meta-analysis of the role of environment-based voluntariness in information technology acceptance. *Management Information Systems Quarterly*, *33*(2), 419–432.

This work was previously published in the Journal of Database Management, Volume 22, Issue 4, edited by Keng Siau, pp. 57-72, copyright 2011 by IGI Publishing (an imprint of IGI Global).

Chapter 16
Extending Agile Principles to Larger, Dynamic Software Projects: A Theoretical Assessment

Dinesh Batra
Florida International University, USA

Debra VanderMeer
Florida International University, USA

Kaushik Dutta
National University of Singapore, Singapore

ABSTRACT

The article evaluates the feasibility of extending agile principles to larger, dynamic, and possibly distributed software development projects by uncovering the theoretical basis for agile values and principles for achieving agility. The extant literature focuses mainly on one theory – complex adaptive systems – to support agile methods, although recent research indicates that the control theory and the adaptive structuration theory are also applicable. This article proposes that at least three other theories exist that are highly relevant: transaction cost economics, social exchange theory, and expectancy theory. By employing these theories, a rigorous analysis of the Agile Manifesto is conducted. Certain agile values and principles find theoretical support and can be applied to enhance agility dynamic projects regardless of size; some agile principles find no theoretical support while others find limited support. Based on the analysis and the ensuing discussion, the authors propose a framework with five dimensions of agility: process, design, people, outcomes, and adaptation.

DOI: 10.4018/978-1-4666-2044-5.ch016

INTRODUCTION

As business and technology environments change at an unprecedented rate, software development agility to respond to changing user requirements has become increasingly critical for software development performance (Lee & Xia, 2010). Software development agility is the ability of an information system development (ISD) method to create change, or proactively, reactively, or inherently embrace change in a timely manner, through its internal components and relationships with its environment (Conboy, 2009). Agility is an organization's ability to sense and respond swiftly to technical changes and new business opportunities (Lyytinen & Rose, 2006). At its core, agility means to strip away as much of the heaviness, commonly associated with traditional software-development methodologies, as possible to promote quick response to changing environments, changes in user requirements, and accelerated project deadlines (Erickson, Lyytinen, & Siau, 2005). In response to the need for agility, lightweight agile software development methods have emerged as alternatives to process-heavy plan-based methodologies as organizations seek to deliver software more quickly (Abrahamsson, Conboy, & Wang, 2009), while simultaneously ensuring that the delivered software is of high quality and is closely aligned to the needs of the customer (Larman, 2003).

The call for such methods arose in 2001, with the publication of the Agile Manifesto (http://agilemanifesto.org), which has remained unchanged in a decade even as several agile methods have been proposed. The manifesto is based on four values: "individuals and interactions over processes and tools, working software over comprehensive documentation, customer collaboration over contract negotiation, and responding to change over following a plan." These values are accompanied by a set of twelve agile principles that provide guidance toward agile practice in development.

The manifesto was written by a group of practitioners interested in bringing together a number of lightweight methodologies, most of which now fall into the agile camp (Boehm & Turner, 2003; Qumer & Henderson-Sellers, 2008), including Scrum (Schwaber & Beedle, 2002), Extreme Programming or XP (Beck, 2000), Adaptive Software Development (Highsmith, 1999), and others. The agile movement grew out of practitioners' impatience with heavier, plan-based methods, and their belief that there must be a better way. Indeed, the use of the word "manifesto," a highly-charged word associated with revolutionary change, in the title was probably intentional – the authors wanted to highlight the radical differences between their agile methods and traditional plan-based approaches.

A decade later, the impact of the Agile Manifesto and its associated ideas is clear: agile methods have taken their place alongside more traditional approaches and are widely used (McAvoy & Butler, 2009). Thousands of practitioners have signed their names in support of the Agile Manifesto (http://agilemanifesto.org/sign/display.cgi), while a 2008 survey by Dr. Dobb's Digest suggests that up to 69% of responding organizations have adopted agile methods in some form, from pilot projects to full deployment of agile methods, and that respondents believe that their use of agile methods result in higher quality deliverables, more productive developers, and more satisfied stakeholders (Ambler, 2008).

However, there is evidence that supports the widely-held view that agile development has been applied only to small projects (Henderson-Sellers & Serour, 2005). Dyba and Dingsoyr (2008) present an extensive review of agile case study reports in the literature. Of the 33 projects referenced in this study, only four project teams had 20 or more members, and only one project team had a size greater than 23, at 60 members. Chow and Cao (2008) examined critical success factors in 109 agile projects. Of these projects, nearly 80% of project teams had fewer than 20 members. The Scrum methodology recommends projects teams of no more than six members (Schwaber, 2005). Beck (2005) states: "You probably couldn't run an XP project with a hundred programmers. Not fifty. Nor twenty, probably. Ten is definitely doable."

It is widely accepted that agile development does, indeed, enhance agility although the supporting evidence is generally restricted to small projects (Boehm & Turner, 2003; Turk, France, & Rumpe, 2005). However, small projects account for only 17% of programming code (Beck & Boehm, 2003). Even free open-source software can be large and significant enough to disrupt commercial incumbents (Brydon & Vining, 2008).

Nevertheless, agile values and principles can provide a starting point to examine agility for large, dynamic projects. A few studies (e.g., Lindvall et al., 2004; Eckstein, 2004; Cao, Mohan, Xu, & Ramesh, 2009; Heeager & Nielsen, 2009; Batra, Xia, VanderMeer, & Dutta, 2010) have examined attempts to introduce agile methods in large development organizations. Lindvall et al. (2002) defines a large software project as one requiring 20-40 or more developers. In this paper, we prefer the term "larger" project, which is meant as a project that does not have fewer than 20 developers.

Traditionally, larger and more distributed projects tend to follow more formal models and methods, such as those described in the Project Management Body of Knowledge (PMBOK) (Project Management Institute, 2004). These methods have their early roots in research in logistics and operations management theory (Kelley, 1961; Malcolm, Roseboom, Clark, & Fazar, 1959), and constitute a large and active area of research today. Although the discipline-oriented PMBOK practices have been popular, many experts (e.g., Boehm & Turner, 2003) question the effectiveness of the bureaucratic nature of discipline approaches in today's dynamic business world. Many practitioners (e.g., Highsmith, 1999) have persuasively argued that excessive planning may run counter to the uncertainty-marked nature of the contemporary software project.

An important research issue, therefore, is to evaluate the feasibility of extending agile values and principles to large and potentially distributed information systems development projects to come up with a more balanced approach (Fernandez & Fernandez, 2008; Fitzgerald, Hartnett, & Conboy, 2006; Nord & Tomayko, 2006). Vinekar, Slinkman, and Nerur (2006) report that there is some empirical evidence that systems development organizations are attempting to employ both agile and organizational approaches. However, there are no guidelines that specify which agile principles are applicable for large projects. In fact, there is some uncertainty about the efficacy of agile methods. After a thorough evaluation of empirical studies in agile development, Dyba and Dingsoyr (2008) remarked (p. 852): "For agile software development, we believe the current state of theory and research on methods is clearly nascent." One way to determine the applicability of agile values and principles is to examine each agile value and principle in the context of relevant theories, and determine the extent to which each is supported by theory. We posit that principles with strong theoretical support will scale well as projects grow larger and, perhaps, become more distributed. Principles with weak or no theoretical support have probably not been challenged because smaller projects are likely to succeed simply because of lower complexity. After all, as Hilkka, Tuure, and Matti (2005) point out, excellent designers should be able to handle any small project.

Based on the supported principles, we propose a set of agility dimensions designed to serve as an *agility support framework* for larger, dynamic software projects where the traditional agility methods have not sufficed. Practitioners involved in large dynamic projects can select the agility dimensions most appropriate for their specific scenarios, balancing these with plan-based methods to enhance the agility of their projects. Researchers can extend this framework through empirical studies and case studies to develop a comprehensive framework for balancing agile and plan-based approaches.

The remainder of this paper is organized as follows. We first introduce key theories that are relevant to the discussion of the agile values. We then consider each of the twelve agile principles, searching for its theoretical support. For principles that are only partially supported, we suggest possible modified applications for larger, dynamic projects. We also point out principles that are largely not supported. Finally, we summarize the analysis and propose the agility support framework.

AGILE VALUES AND ORGANIZATIONAL THEORIES

The agile manifesto lists four essential values: individuals and interactions over processes and tools, working software over comprehensive documentation, customer collaboration over contract negotiation, and responding to change over following a plan. It is assumed that when a value is presented as A over B, that there is a significantly more emphasis for A than for B, and not just a subtle preference for A over B.

A literature search to unearth the theoretical basis of agile development revealed only one theory: *Complex Adaptive Systems* (CAS). The CAS theory (Highsmith, 1999; Vidgen & Wang, 2009) states that complex systems are like living organisms, and are made up of multiple interconnected elements and have the capacity to change and learn. These systems should not be viewed as dead, mechanistic, and linear machines. The CAS theory suggests that adaptation is significantly more important than optimization because complex systems cannot be predicted because of their emergent behavior (Meso & Jain, 2006). Emergence is a property of complex adaptive systems that creates some greater property of the whole, and can, thus, cause lack of predictability. Although the CAS theory supports some agile principles, and this discussion is covered in a later section, the theory cannot be used to explain the majority of the principles. For example, the CAS theory cannot explain why customers should be allowed to make changes late in the project (unless the customers compensate the vendors accordingly). The CAS theory does not address key indicators of the projects such as meeting budgetary goals, ensuring cost-benefit of the project, and completing the project in time.

Just as information systems development success is not a narrow dimension (Siau, Long, & Ling, 2010), information systems development agility is a wider notion than that proposed by the Agile Manifesto, which is employed only as an initial benchmark. As an example, a statement like the agile value "individual and interactions over processes and tools" can be interpreted by examining the agile principles that exemplify the value as well as by how the value is explicated in literature and practice. If the premise is that motivated developers can trump processes and tools, then the principle should be adapted based on theories that address motivation instead of assuming that only motivated individuals are allowed in the project. Similarly, the value "customer collaboration over contract negotiation" would necessitate examining theories related to trust between principal and agent as well as on contracts. A software development method that does not address the issue pertaining to legal agreements on budget and time cannot work for projects that are large. By using agile values and principles as a starting point, examining the applicable theories, and adapting the values and principles, we can come up with a more relevant agility framework.

The Agile Manifesto covers both values and principles. Theories relevant to the agile values are examined first.

Individuals and Interactions over Processes and Tools

The underlying notion in this value is that motivated individuals can adapt processes and tools successfully and that teams should dynamically organize as needed. While evaluating agile practices, Turk, France, and Rumpe (2005) remark that motivation is one of the most important properties humans need in order to achieve ambitious goals with good quality results. There are several motivation theories, but the spirit of the Agile Manifesto is, perhaps, closely related to the *Expectancy Theory* (Vroom, 1964), which suggests that motivation can be increased by organizational rewards if efforts can lead to outcomes, outcomes can lead to the rewards, and the rewards are valued. One of the agile principles detailed later, states: "Build projects around motivated individuals. Give them the environment and support they need, and trust them to get the job done." While the agile principle expects that the individuals are intrinsically motivated, which can be considered somewhat dubious, the Expectancy Theory is more specific in how to motivate individuals because it recognizes individual preferences on reward designs. Further, under the aegis of this theory, processes and tools can work alongside individuals and interactions.

Although motivation is important, equally important is control: should the control be formal or informal, and should it be guided by outcome, behavior, clan, or self-control? Maruping, Venkatesh, and Agarwal (2009) used Ouchi's (1981) ideas and used the *Control theory* to examine how agile methodology use interacted with requirement changes and the mode of control. A similar approach was used to determine control mechanisms in open-source software (Lin, Xu, & Xu, 2011). Other researchers have indirectly considered the issue of control (McAvoy & Butler, 2009).

Working software over comprehensive documentation: The software project may be considered as a complex adaptive system (Highsmith, 1999), which contains complex interactions that lead to emergent results. Requirement changes may result simply because of a communication gap - what was documented by the analyst may be different from what was desired by the customer - or it may result because the complex interactions are better revealed when there is an actual product. Working software provides a concrete product to the customer, and the feedback can be used to intervene and make corrections early in the project. As explained earlier, the *complex adaptive system (CAS) theory* (Holland, 1992) can address the uncertain nature of dynamic software projects.

Customer Collaboration over Contract Negotiation

Two theories are related to this principle: one supports contract negotiation while the other supports customer collaboration in specific situations. The stakes are greater in a large project and the default scenario favors contract negotiation. The *Transaction Costs Economic theory* considers the transaction costs as the costs of contracting, and admits that the measurement of transactions costs poses formidable difficulties (Williamson, 1979). Two key determinants of transaction costs are bounded rationality (Simon, 1957) and opportunistic behavior. A contract is always incomplete because of the limitations of human mind (Williamson, 1979). However, a deliberately loose and incomplete contract, or no contract, will likely result in opportunistic behavior. The agile manifesto eschews the contract placing the customer at an advantageous position, and the software vendor at a distinct disadvantage. The "customer collaboration over contract negotiation" value, thus, needs to be revisited especially for large, distributed projects where contracts cannot be avoided because the agreements underlying a contract actually protect both the software firm and the customer. A contract can cover some but not all contingent situations especially relating to the dynamic aspect of the project.

In long term relationships, however, the *Social Exchange Theory* (Blau, 1986), which states that social behavior can entail an exchange of goods, both material and non-material (e.g., symbols of approval or prestige), predicts that customer collaboration is possible. Thus, the goodwill and reputation engendered as both customer and vendor collaborate in addressing unforeseen situations can foster agility. Overall though, the agile value – customer collaboration over contract negotiation – is applicable only under narrow circumstances in large projects.

Responding to Change over Following a Plan

The *complex adaptive system (CAS) theory* (Holland, 1992), based on responding to emergent effects resulting from change, is an important underlying theory here. Another lens to examine this agile principle is the adaptive structuration theory (AST), which examines organizational change facilitated by different types of structures provided by advanced technologies, tasks, and organizational environments, as well as structures that actually emerge in social action (DeSanctis & Poole, 1994). A key concept of this theory is appropriation, which refers to the application of the structures in a particular context. Appropriation creates 'structures in use' when groups select and interpret specific structures from the 'structural potential' afforded to them by the artifact in consideration. The act of appropriation is a continual reflection, interpretation, and adjustment of structures in use.

In summary, the key theories that form the theoretical support for our framework, based on the agile values, are: Complex Adaptive System (CAS) theory, Expectancy theory, Control theory, Transaction Costs Economic theory, Social Exchange theory, and Adaptive Structuration theory. These theories are further examined by analyzing the agile principles, which are detailed and fine-grained explication of the agile values.

A THEORY-BASED ANALYSIS OF AGILE MANIFESTO PRINCIPLES

In the previous section, we identified key theories related to agile values. In this section, we assess each agile principle and evaluate if it can be supported by existing theories, and under what conditions. We summarize our analysis in Table 1. In many cases, theoretical guidelines indicate the need for modifying the principle to make it applicable to larger, dynamic projects.

1. **Our highest priority is to satisfy the customer through early and continuous delivery of valuable software:** This principle is supported by the CAS theory. When a software project that has significant anticipated change is proposed, the customer may not be able to describe the requirements in concrete detail. Neither the user (i.e., customer), nor the analyst can predict emergent effects from interactions of parts of the system. Continual development and feedback can steer the project in the right direction (Baskerville & Pries-Heje, 2004) invariant of the project type – large or small, co-located or distributed. The availability of working in-progress software provides the customer with a tangible base from which to describe emergent requirements in greater detail. Problems in specifying exact user requirements, which are a key reason for system failure, can be mitigated by early and continuous delivery of software, which can facilitate agility in larger, dynamic projects.
2. **Welcome changing requirements, even late in development. Agile processes harness change for the customer's competitive advantage:** This principle is largely not supported when applied to larger projects. Transaction Cost Economics theory suggests that applying such a principle can encourage opportunistic behavior on the

Table 1. Theoretical assessment of agile manifesto principles

Agile Manifesto Principle	Applicable Theory	Scalability to Large Projects
1. Our highest priority is to satisfy the customer through early and continuous delivery of valuable software.	Complex Adaptive Systems	Emergence is a property of complex adaptive systems that creates some greater property of the whole. In large projects, continual delivery of working software facilitates assessment and feedback by the customer.
2. Welcome changing requirements, even late in development. Agile processes harness change for the customer's competitive advantage.	Transaction Cost Economics (works against the principle) Social Exchange	In large projects, Transaction Cost Economics theory predicts opportunistic behavior on the part of customer. However, Social Exchange theory can accommodate changing requirements, even late in development, if there is trust between the customer and the vendor.
3. Deliver working software frequently, from a couple of weeks to a couple of months, with a preference to the shorter timescale.	Complex Adaptive Systems	In large projects, the build cycles for customer and for internal purposes need to have different time frames.
4. Business people and developers must work together daily throughout the project.	None	There is no theory that supports "daily" interactions between business people and developers.
5. Build projects around motivated individuals. Give them the environment and support they need, and trust them to get the job done.	Expectancy Theory (partial support)	Expectancy Theory can be used to define appropriate incentives to motivate individual members of the project, rather than building projects only around motivated individuals.
6. The most efficient and effective method of conveying information to, and within, a development team is face-to-face conversation.	None	Face-to-face conversation is not an efficient mechanism in large, distributed projects.
7. Working software is the primary measure of progress.	Complex Adaptive Systems	Similar to (1) and (3) above.
8. Agile processes promote sustainable development. The sponsors, developers, and users should be able to maintain a constant pace indefinitely.	Expectancy Theory (partial support)	Quality of life is an important issue that needs to be considered as a motivation tool in all projects. However, this agile principle may conflict with agile principle (2).
9. Continuous attention to technical excellence and good design enhances agility.	None; the principle is too generic	Systems concepts such as decomposition, minimization of dependency between subsystems, and refactoring need to be considered.
10. Simplicity – the art of maximizing the amount of work not done – is essential.	Complex Adaptive Systems	Adaptation is significantly more important than optimization in large projects.
11. The best architectures, requirements, and designs emerge from self-organizing teams.	Control theory (partial support)	The agile literature does *not* indicate how self-organizing teams can form in large groups.
12. At regular intervals, the team reflects on how to become more effective, then tunes and adjusts its behavior accordingly.	Adaptive structuration	Continual reflection and assessment is needed to reconfigure internal and external competencies to address rapidly changing environments.

part of the customer (Williamson, 1979). In large projects, major changes made late in software development can be expensive (Boehm, 1981; Nuseibeh & Easterbrook, 2000). To curb opportunistic behavior and account for cost escalations for late-stage changes, a large project is expected to involve a detailed contractual agreement, which in turn may necessitate process-heavy change-management methods that account for the repercussions of requirements changes late in the project timeline.

A contingent look at Transaction Cost Economics Theory (Williamson, 1979), however, reveals a possibility for agility, even in large and distributed projects. Normally, this theory considers transactions costs in the absence of trust between organizations. As an organization does repeated business with a customer or partner, trust and reputation ensue, which lowers transaction costs (Gulati, 1995). Trust can be examined through the Social Exchange Theory (Blau, 1986), which states that social behavior can entail an exchange of goods, both material and non-material (e.g., symbols of approval or prestige). Parties that give much to others generally expect to get much from them, and parties that get much from others are frequently under pressure to give much back to them. This process of influence tends toward equilibrium in the exchanges, and is one of the reasons that companies frequently have preferred relationships with their vendors.

In social exchange scenarios, a loss in a single project is not necessarily tantamount to an overall loss of profit for the vendor, given that customer and vendor satisfaction can lead to trust, goodwill, and dependency, and can increase switching costs. The key here is that repeated opportunistic behavior, especially on the part of the customer, needs to be prevented. When referring to relationships in contemporary times, Drucker (1997) notes: "these relationships have to be based on a common understanding of objectives, policies, and strategies; on teamwork; and on persuasion – or they do not work at all" (p. 2). Anecdotal evidence from industry supports the need for trust from both the client (Armour, 2007; Layman, Williams, Damian, & Bures, 2006; Ramesh, Cao, Mohan, & Xu, 2006) and the vendor (Groise & Mangin, 2007; Jain, 2006) perspectives.

If there is trust in the customer-vendor relationship, it might be possible to support this principle – "welcome changing requirements – even late in development" – in large, distributed projects. Conversations about changing requirements should be structured around "reprioritization" rather than "new, additional requirements". However, both customers and vendors need to acknowledge that major change, especially late in development, involves costs across several dimensions: time, budget, functionality, and sustainability. A contract, therefore, is indispensable. Thus, transaction cost economics and social exchange provide theoretical lens to examine changes, especially late, in software development.

3. Deliver working software frequently, from a couple of weeks to a couple of months, with a preference to the shorter timescale.

This principle is similar to the first agile principle, and is supported by the Complex Adaptive Systems theory. The developer needs a discrete time frame to deliver functionality, and the customer similarly needs a reasonable time interval for evaluation. In a large, distributed project with multiple integration points, however, preparing a fully-integrated and customer-friendly build (e.g., one that includes installers and other release-oriented features) may itself require a week or more to prepare, and in a way, represents an opportunity cost that is much better spent on software development. On a two-week release cycle, too large a fraction of time is spent in releasing software rather than building increasing functionality. In such a cycle, the customer might see little change between releases, which may incur a large opportunity cost for a small benefit. This suggests that the timeframes cited in this agile principle might require slight relaxation in large and distributed projects. The actual timeframe will depend on how soon a customer can observed a discrete change so that feedback can be provided for the complex system to adapt.

Frequent build cycles have two main goals: (a) to ensure that the overall system remains consistently in a close-to-integrated state; and (b) to provide the customer with the means to evaluate overall progress and give feedback. To ensure that each customer-oriented release includes sufficient additional functionality to justify the work of the build, the build cycle can be separated into two parts: a frequent internal build cycle for each module, perhaps every two weeks, to ensure integration over time, and a slightly longer customer feedback cycle, perhaps every four weeks. Overall, it is evident that this agile principle, somewhat of a repeat of the first principle, has considerable theoretical appeal and can lead to agility in large projects.

4. Business people and developers must work together daily throughout the project.

There is no theory to support "daily" interaction of business people and developers. One way to examine this principle is from the notion of marginal value, which indicates that the marginal return decreases as more of a service is added (O'Connor & Faille, 2000). The amount of time a customer provides to the software developers may be highly useful in the beginning or at certain intervals of a project, but will result in diminishing returns if the interaction is on a daily basis, especially if the predominant activity in a project is coding. There is a definite value in customer-developer interaction as dictated by the needs of a project, but working together on a daily basis may be overkill. Dyba and Dingsoyr (2008) note that the role of on-site customer seems to be unsustainable for long periods. Moreover in a distributed development team, where various development teams are working in different time zones, daily interaction with the customer may add quite a bit of overhead, in time, money, and reduced quality of life. This principle, therefore, cannot be applied in larger projects.

5. Build projects around motivated individuals. Give them the environment and support they need, and trust them to get the job done.

This principle has two statements – the first is somewhat vague, while the second has some theoretical support. One cannot embark on a software project hoping that only the most motivated individuals are available. In large and distributed projects, there will be individuals with both high and low intrinsic motivation levels. Thus, one cannot magically "build projects around motivated individuals." Expectancy Theory (Vroom, 1964) suggests that motivation can be increased by organizational rewards if the rewards can be earned and are valued. The theory considers motivation resulting from expectancy (the probability that effort leads to performance), instrumentality (the probability that performance leads to work outcomes), and valence (the value attached by the individual to the work outcomes). Motivation can be increased by giving the developers "the environment and support they need" assuming there are adequate organizational resources. Suitable hiring procedures and training can ensure expectancy and instrumentality. To facilitate valence, the rewards have to be flexible enough to support individual preferences. One person may favor monetary awards, the second may favor recognition, the third may favor interesting work, the fourth may prefer travel, the fifth may abhor travel, and the sixth may prefer flexible working time and working from home. A project manager has to be sensitive to such individual differences and, within the organizational constraints, customize the reward structure.

However, the mere fact that an individual is provided incentives does not guarantee performance. There is no theory that supports the hypothesis that rewarding employees alone will result in better performance. Accountability is a key tenet of performance evaluation and the issue of control is paramount; otherwise, an agile method can quickly disintegrate into chaos. The Control theory (Ouchi, 1985) is, therefore, relevant and is discussed in more detail under the agile principle 11 on self-organizing teams.

This agile principle, taken as a whole, has little theoretical support. The agile principle assumes that only motivated developers engage in software development. A better principle that indicates how work and rewards are linked and distributed, and control is established, is needed.

6. The most efficient and effective method of conveying information to, and within, a development team is face-to-face conversation.

This principle is effective in small, co-located group situations; however, it can be an inefficient method in several situations. There is no theoretical support for the principle. Schermerhorn, Osborn, and Hunt (2003) consider two aspects of communication – effectiveness, which pertains to accuracy, and efficiency, which pertains to its cost. Face-to-face conversation is clearly effective because of feedback and its clarifying effect, trust facilitation, and because of kinesics or nonverbal cues. In a large, distributed project, face-to-face conversation is not always an efficient mechanism, which can also be severely mitigated by temporal, geographic, and cultural distances (Ågerfalk & Fitzgerald, 2006). "Face-to-face" connotes physical proximity, which is sometimes difficult in large projects and mostly not feasible in distributed development scenarios. "Face-to-face" may be very useful at an early stage to establish familiarity and trust; otherwise, there are a number of efficient communication mechanisms such as video conferencing, email, phone conferencing, discussion forums, text messaging, and phone calls that may be more efficient. Therefore, the "face-to-face" agile principle lacks theoretical support and needs a broader interpretation to make it applicable in larger, especially distributed projects, and should include personal and impersonal as well as synchronous and asynchronous methods of coordination and communication.

Using a common albeit diverse set of tools and practices for the entire project organization, including all multisourcing partners and customer stakeholders, reduces the need for synchronous communication. Communication in software development projects falls primarily into two categories: activity coordination (e.g., assigning tasks to developers, keeping track of bugs and test results) and decision-making (e.g., design discussions, requirements elicitation, and customer feedback). Technology can assist communication in both categories, providing the team with the support needed to get the job done (suggested by agile principle #5). A wide range of software is now available to support coordination, and to some extent, decision-making for projects in general and software development projects in particular. Anecdotal industry experience strongly supports the use of shared communication environments, in many cases (Jain, 2006; Layman et al., 2006; Ramesh et al., 2006), citing it as a significant positive influence on project success, and in one case, citing non-use (Korkala & Abrahamsson, 2007) as contributing to project failure.

7. **Working software is the primary measure of progress:** This principle is quite similar to the agile principles (1) and (3), and is supported by the CAS theory.
8. **Agile processes promote sustainable development:** The sponsors, developers, and users should be able to maintain a constant pace indefinitely.

This principle usually translates to the XP-espoused forty-hour work-week rule to manage work-related stress and strain. This principle aims to protect the quality of life of developers and other participants. However, this agile principle is not consistent with some other agile principles. Transaction Cost Economics theory (Williamson, 1979) suggests that an over-emphasis on customer satisfaction, as suggested in agile principle #2, can result in a loose contract that could result in opportunistic behavior on the part of the customer. The desire to satisfy the client can disrupt sustainable development as developers rush to meet project deadlines that result in long and stressful days for developers (Batra et al., 2010). The software development industry suffers from a higher rate of burnout than other industries (Procaccino, Verner, Overmyer, & Darter, 2002). Client satisfaction and employee wellness do not seem consistent in this industry. Hence this principle may be meaningless given that the agile manifesto ascribes so much emphasis on the client especially on allowing changes late in development through principle #2.

Quality of life should be an important aspect when considering developer motivation, as is implicit in principle #5. Expectancy theory (Vroom, 1964) is again applicable here and needs to focus on work stress, which does not merely arise from task demands and long hours of working, but can also be caused by role ambiguities, role conflicts, ethical dilemmas, interpersonal problems, career development, and physical setting (Schermerhorn, Hunt, & Osborn, 2003). For example, in a distributed work environment, time differences can cause sleep deprivation since regular cross-continent meetings are likely to be held during the night time for one of the two parties. Overall, the agile principle is a reminder that today's project managers need to find ways to manage developer stress so that burnout is minimized and sustainable development becomes feasible; however, the principle needs to be harmonized with other principles.

9. Continuous attention to technical excellence and good design enhances agility.

This principle is almost axiomatically true – technical excellence and good design will make any project better, regardless of size or level of distribution. However, the principle is rather generic and not suitable for theoretical evaluation; it should be made more specific. Good design is important, but so are many other facets such as good requirements, good coding, and good communication.

The more important issue is: how do you achieve good design in a large project? The intended purpose of the agile proponents is that refactoring should be done continually to ensure that the resulting code can be reused and easily maintained. Refactoring refers to the structuring of software to remove duplication, improve communication, simplify, or add flexibility without changing its behavior. Refactoring may be possible in large projects if two prerequisite activities are completed before refactoring is actualized: the project is decomposed into smaller parts, and dependencies are minimized between subsystems.

Projects suitable for agile development generally have one or few parts; however, a large software project is automatically complex because invariably it has many interacting parts (Reeves, 1999). A project viewed as a system can be decomposed into subsystems, which may be recursively divided into smaller subsystems, where the subsystems are less complex because they contain fewer components and relationships. Each module exposes a clear and unchanging interface through which other modules can access its functionality. When integrated, the full set of modules work together to provide the overall functionality of the system. Although the decomposition principle is well-known, it is rarely discussed in agile development references. This may be so because the agile projects are usually small in size.

Principles of good design dictate that low coupling, i.e., the degree of dependency between modules, and high cohesion, i.e., the degree of focus in a module's responsibility, are desirable characteristics (Stevens, Myers, & Constantine, 1999). Low coupling is of particular interest, since this minimizes dependencies among modules. These dependencies are realized in the module interface implementations (Brechner, 2005). Minimizing dependencies between modules at the time of interface design enables module encapsulation (Blaha & Rumbaugh, 2005), which makes a large distributed project more amenable to agility principles. Maruping, Venkatesh, and Agarwal (2009) report a project that had 151 teams working on an enterprise-wide project; each team was responsible for developing a single module. Kahkonen (2004) suggests various methods that teams can use to communicate and coordinate with each other.

Many organizations have recently restructured their operations, replacing isolated departments with teams of people that are expected to be more flexible and creative in accomplishing work tasks (Eisenberg, Goodall, & Trethewey, 2006). A number of small, agile teams, potentially working at different locations, can work semi-independently on separate subsystems (Beavers, 2007). Modular design allows an organization to scale agile principles. For example, Scrum can be managed as a hierarchy of Scrum of Scrums (Schwaber, 2005). Each agile team can then actively engage in continual refactoring. In fact, developers should anticipate changes and enhancements, and incorporate design agility through parameterization.

10. Simplicity – the art of maximizing the amount of work not done – is essential.

This principle is supported by the CAS theory and can be scaled to large, distributed projects. The notion of simplicity is borrowed from the Lean Software Development (Poppendieck & Poppendieck, 2003) practices and represents a deliberate effort at identifying and reducing wasteful work. Achieving optimization necessitates clear and fixed specification of parameters such as user requirements and quality; however, in dynamic situations, cost and time become more important, and the need for adaptation requires that extraneous work be minimized. Simplicity allows adjusting the scope and even quality if time and cost are the more important attributes of the project. Thus, this principle has theoretical support, and should scale very well to large, distributed projects.

11. The best architectures, requirements, and designs emerge from self-organizing teams.

This agile principle has limited theoretical support. Self-organization is an underlying precept in CAS for enabling adaptation. As the environment changes, organisms evolve and restructure to adapt to address the changing conditions. However, it is not clear how self-organization can be facilitated in large projects. The issue is one of control – how much control should be attributed to the project manager, to the team, and to the individual developer. Outcome, behavior, clan, and self-control are mechanisms to ensure that developers achieve the objectives of a project. Maruping, Venkatesh, and Agarwal (2009) used Ouchi's (1981) ideas and used the Control theory to examine how agile methodology use interacted with requirement changes and the mode of control. McAvoy and Butler (2009) found that the high level of empowerment of a cohesive software development team undertaking an agile project may be one of these negative factors, as empowered, cohesive teams can exhibit problems such as groupthink or the Abilene Paradox.

A self-organizing team is not always the best structure (Schermerhorn, Osborn, & Hunt, 2003, p. 207), because the characteristics of any self-managing team – high involvement, participation, and empowerment – must be consistent with the values and culture of the organization. Eisenberg and Goodall (2004) state that there is such as a thing as too much autonomy, and that most employees do not want complete control over and accountability for their day-to-day decision making. Further, if the group size is large, it is plausible that some group members may attempt to get a free-ride by coasting while the work is done by others (Jensen & Meckling, 1976).

Jacques (1996) argues that hierarchy is necessary to ensure accountability, and that group authority without group accountability is dysfunctional. He states that "managerial hierarchy will remain the only way to structure unified working systems with hundreds, thousands, or tens of thousands of employees" (p. 248). Each team in a large project, therefore, should have a manager or coordinator that is responsible for meeting the goals. Some degree of hierarchy is necessary even in a fairly decentralized project structure, especially for larger and more distributed projects.

Another aspect that determines the team structure is the set of cultural norms of the organization, which in turn, is affected by the cultural norms of the region and country where the organization is located. Thus, the offshore office of an American or a British company may not find the same success with self-managing team structures as the central office. Hofstede and Hofstede (2005) have identified five dimensions of national culture: power distance, uncertainty avoidance, individualism-collectivism, masculinity-femininity, and long-term/short-term orientation. An offshore office located in a country with high power distance (how rigidly divides between supervisor/supervisee roles are maintained) may find the self-organizing team notion novel, if not downright strange.

Hierarchy is inevitable today given that a large number of software companies in countries such as the US and the UK have Asian offshore offices that carry out the programming tasks. In the latter countries, hierarchy is the preferred structure although it seems that at least in software companies, hierarchy is not resulting in undue bureaucracy. While it is generally accepted that in today's software development environment the traditional authority-heavy role of the project manager needs to give away to director and co-ordinator role (Nerur, Mahapatra, & Mangalaraj, 2005), self-organization in large projects does not seem to be a viable structure in the near future.

12. At regular intervals, the team reflects on how to become more effective, then tunes and adjusts its behavior accordingly.

More than one theory can support this principle. For example, if one takes an organizational learning perspective, then the Action Learning Theory, which focuses on double-loop learning (Argyris, 1982; Nerur & Balijepally, 2007), may be applicable. In double-loop learning, the entities involved (individuals, groups or organization) question the values, assumptions and policies that led to the actions in the first place.

A related but more appropriate lens to examine this agile principle is the adaptive structuration theory (AST), which examines organizational change facilitated by different types of structures provided by advanced technologies, tasks, and organizational environments, as well as structures that actually emerge in social action (DeSanctis & Poole, 1994). Cao et al. (2009) consider agile methods as artifacts that facilitate an adapted structure due to social action of the participants in the process. The artifact itself, the task that uses the artifact and the organizational environment can be potential sources of structure. In essence, AST highlights structuration, which refers to the act of bringing rules, resources, and other structures into action, and appropriation, which refers to the application of the structure in a particular context. Appropriation creates 'structures in use' when groups select and interpret specific structures from the 'structural potential' afforded to them by the artifact in consideration. The act of appropriation is a continual reflection, interpretation, and adjustment of structures in use.

IMPLICATIONS FOR THEORY

Table 2 summarizes our evaluation of the theoretical support for the agile principles. A few patterns emerge from this analysis. Principles 4, 6, and 9 do not have theoretical support while principles 2, 5, 8, and 11 have limited theoretical support. Principles 1, 3, and 7, all based on the CAS theory, point to iterative development modes. Principles 10 and 12 are also theoretically supported: principle 10 underscores simplicity in analysis, design, and coding, and principle 12 advocates appropriation and adaptation of structures brought out by interaction of artifacts, tasks, and organizational environment.

The Agile Manifesto has four values and twelve principles. As may be evident from the discussions in this paper, there is overlap between agile values and principles, and among principles. Five principles have full theoretical support, four have partial theoretical support, and the remaining three have no theoretical support. Underlying the manifesto, there are just three agility-enhancing theoretically-supported themes: iterative development, simplicity, and adaptation. Various agile

Table 2. Agility dimensions

Agility Dimension	Theory Base	Justification
Process	Complex Adaptive Systems	Iterative test-driven process facilitates agility. Simple methods enhance agility.
Design	Complex Adaptive Systems	Decomposition, minimization of dependency between subsystems, parameterization, and refactoring enhance agility.
People	Expectancy Theory Control Theory	Motivation mechanisms need to be flexible and somewhat customized to the individual. Controls should be based more on informal mechanisms backed up by formal rules.
Outcomes	Transaction Cost Economics Social Exchange Theory Complex Adaptive Systems	Trust enhances agility while contracts prevent opportunistic behavior. Within this framework, the decision-maker is able to juggle costs, time, scope, and quality. Simplicity enhances the ability to make such trade-offs.
Adaptation	Adaptive Structuration Theory	The ability to reflect and learn during a project enables agility methods to be adapted and appropriated.

methods have emerged, and while the practices employed in these methods usually follow the Agile Manifesto, it seems that even newer principles such as pair programming, which have no theoretical support, are added. The Agile Manifesto has remained unchanged since it was proposed about a decade ago. Perhaps, it is time to revisit the manifesto, and extend it so that its dimensions not only have theoretical support, but also provide specific guidelines for enhancing agility in projects of all sizes.

In the spirit of establishing more rigorous facets of agility, a few researchers have proposed agility dimensions. Meredith and Francis (2000) proposed four dimensions of organizational agility (but not software development in particular): agile strategy, agile processes, agile linkages, and agile people. For outsourcing environments, Sarker and Sarker (2009) proposed three dimensions with sub- dimensions in each dimension: resource agility (people, technology), process agility (methodology, environment awareness, temporal-bridge), and linkage agility (cultural mutuality, communicative relationship). For software development, we propose an *agility support framework* along five dimensions.

Process Agility: This dimension pertains to the iterative delivery method, which is supported by the CAS theory. The iterative delivery mechanism supports both the customer as well as the developer. Developing and testing software components frequently, internally, keep the overall system in a close-to-integrated state at all times. However, delivering integrated, customer-ready software at the same frequency may hamper project progress; instead, a frequency approved by the customer may be more useful. Methods and processes that are simpler are more likely to foster agility.

Design Agility: This dimension pertains to incorporating agility in the software through design techniques such as decomposition, minimization of dependency between subsystems, parameterization, and refactoring.

People Agility: This dimension pertains to motivating developers and other personnel as well as their teams, and is supported by the expectancy theory. The dimension also addresses quality of life issues of the personnel. The creative energies of developers need to be harnessed to direct them to the project goals; however, informal control mechanisms need to be established while the formal control mechanisms need to be used as back-up or in situations that resonate with the culture of the team.

Outcomes Agility: This dimension considers the customers and providers and addresses how the various outcomes such as cost, schedule, scope, and quality are balanced and adapted. Decision time is an important success factor in agile development (Misra, Kumar, & Kumar, 2009).

Responsive trade-off decisions by an authorized body like a steering committee can enhance agility. Trade-offs should consider cost-benefit rather than a bureaucratic commitment to initial success indicators. Simplicity enhances the ability to make such trade-offs. To prevent opportunistic behavior, a contract can establish the framework and benchmark for these outcomes. Within this framework that protects both the customers and the providers, trust can provide a catalyst for fostering agility.

Adaptation Agility: There is empirical evidence that even agile methods need to undergo adaptation (Aydin, Harmsen, Slooten, & Stegwee, 2005). "Agility mindset" may be defined as the ability to reflect and learn during a project so that methods can be adapted and appropriated. Eventually, methods are guidelines that are placed in a complex web of requirements, outcomes, constraints, social interactions, developer capabilities, tools, and culture. Adaptation can be incorporated in any project by setting aside milestones for "agility retreats" where the focus is on reflection, learning, and appropriation.

IMPLICATIONS FOR PRACTICE

The agile manifesto was proposed by practitioners; thus, it is inevitable that the agility dimensions proposed in the paper will have significant implications for practice. In fact, agile development issues have been largely discussed in the practitioner arena but the theoretical analysis has largely been missing. Although the original authors of the Agile Manifesto defined their values and principles in opposition to planning-oriented approaches, the results of our study here suggest that there may be no reason to adopt a "pure" agile or plan-oriented approach; rather, elements of both may be judiciously combined to meet the needs of a software development project. This proposition, even as it awaits definitive empirical support, is very significant for practitioners.

The agility dimensions provide a more comprehensive view of agility, which can be applied to larger, dynamic projects. For example, project managers and team leads always need to keep an eye on project management aspects such as the quality, the cost (and the incremental benefit with respect to an incremental cost), and the project duration. Agile development does not directly focus on these attributes but practitioners are accountable on these measures of success, which can be tricky because of the trade-offs. A strategic project, for instance, has cost and quality targets but these attributes may sometimes pale in comparison to being first in the market. In addition, a large project that needs to be completed quickly may require an assessment of people and process agility. The project manager, team leads, and stakeholders may ask: Do we have skills required to complete this project? How long will our developers be able to work sixty-hour weeks? What might motivate our developers? Can we outsource a portion or phase of the project? What might be a practical time interval for iteration? Will we have a calcified mindset or one that is open to learning as the project proceeds? How can we ensure that the change control process is not an adversarial, legalistic process but involves a transparent prioritization process that recognizes all stakeholders and allows for mutually agreeable trade-offs in the development schedule?

Agile development principles deserve a lot of credit for invoking the kind of thinking that leads to agility. In a large, dynamic project, however, a systems and comprehensive approach is required to evaluate a number of dimensions and achieve trade-offs. The five factors proposed in this paper - process, design, people, outcomes, and adaptation – provide a useful template for practitioners to analyze the complex nature and requirements of contemporary software development projects.

CONCLUSION

We believe that this paper is unique in its attempt to assess and adapt the agile principles for agility for larger and dynamic projects by employing a multi-theory based approach. We have examined the values and principles defined in the Agile Manifesto for theoretical support, and have proposed an agility support framework that can facilitate agility in large, dynamic software projects. This framework suggests five agility dimensions: process, design, people, outcomes, and adaptation.

Future research can employ this framework to study software development agility. The immediate step is to verify the dimensions using empirical research. As an example, multiple case interviews can be conducted involving projects that involve more than twenty developers and have witnesses a fair amount of requirement changes. The questions can be generated based on the five agility dimensions. Further, open-ended questions can be asked on critical success factors that enhanced agility in a project. The transcripts can be analyzed to assess if the five dimensions were critical in enhancing agility. Similar questionnaire-based studies may also reveal such factors. Another approach is to examine case studies to identify factors considered in adapting a development method to facilitate agility.

Overall, our analysis of the Agile Manifesto reveals that it does not have strong theoretical support. Although about seven out of ten organizations have adopted agile methods, it is likely that these organizations have not figured what aspects of these methods actually facilitate agility. Theoretically-based empirical research is needed to identify the true dimensions of software development agility.

REFERENCES

Abrahamsson, P., Conboy, K., & Wang, X. (2009). 'Lots done, more to do': the current state of agile systems development research. *European Journal of Information Systems*, *18*(4), 281–284. doi:10.1057/ejis.2009.27

Ågerfalk, P. J., & Fitzgerald, B. (2006). Flexible and distributed software processes: Old petunias in new bowls? *Communications of the ACM*, *49*(10), 26–34.

Ambler, S. W. (2008). Has agile peaked? Scott crunches the numbers to find out. *Dr. Dobb's Digital Digest.* Retrieved September 22, 2011, from http://www.drdobbs.com/architecture-and-design/207600615

Argyris, C. (1982). *Reasoning, learning, and action: Individual and organizational*. San Francisco, CA: Jossey-Bass.

Armour, P. G. (2007). Agile… and offshore. *Communications of the ACM*, *50*(1), 13–16. doi:10.1145/1188913.1188930

Aydin, M. N., Harmsen, F., Stegwee, R. A., & van Slooten, K. (2005). On the adaptation of an agile information systems development method. *Journal of Database Management*, *16*(4), 24–40. doi:10.4018/jdm.2005100102

Baskerville, R., & Pries-Heje, J. (2004). Short cycle time systems development. *Information Systems Journal*, *14*(3), 237–264. doi:10.1111/j.1365-2575.2004.00171.x

Batra, D., Xia, W., VanderMeer, D., & Dutta, K. (2010). Balancing agile and structured approaches to manage large distributed software projects: A case study from the cruise line industry. *Communications of the AIS*, *27*(1), 379–394.

Beavers, P. A. (2007). Managing a large "agile" software engineering organization. In *Proceedings of the IEEE AGILE Conference* (pp. 296-303).

Beck, K. (2000). *Extreme programming explained: Embrace change*. Reading, MA: Addison-Wesley.

Beck, K. (2005). The XP geography: mapping your next step, a guide to planning your journey. In H. Baumeister, M. Marchesi, & M. Holcombe (Eds.), *Proceedings of the 6th International Conference on Extreme Programming and Agile Processes in Software Engineering* (LNCS 3556, pp. 287-287).

Beck, K., & Boehm, B. (2003). Agility through discipline: A debate. *Computer, 36*(6), 44–46. doi:10.1109/MC.2003.1204374

Blaha, M., & Rumbaugh, J. (2005). *Object-oriented modeling and design with UML* (2nd ed.). Upper Saddle River, NJ: Pearson Education.

Blau, P. M. (1986). *Exchange and power in social life*. New Brunswick, NJ: Transaction Books.

Boehm, B. W. (1981). *Software engineering economics*. Upper Saddle River, NJ: Prentice Hall.

Boehm, B. W., & Turner, R. (2003). *Balancing agility and discipline: A guide for the perplexed*. Reading, MA: Addison-Wesley.

Brechner, E. (2005). *Journey of enlightenment: the evolution of development at Microsoft*. Paper presented at the 27th International Conference on Software Engineering, St. Louis, MO.

Brydon, M., & Vining, A. R. (2008). Adoption, improvement, and disruption: predicting the impact of open source applications in enterprise software markets. *Journal of Database Management, 19*(2), 73–94. doi:10.4018/jdm.2008040104

Cao, L., Mohan, K., Xu, P., & Ramesh, B. (2009). A framework for adapting agile development methodologies. *European Journal of Information Systems, 18*(4), 332–343. doi:10.1057/ejis.2009.26

Chow, T., & Cao, D. B. (2008). A survey study of critical success factors in agile software projects. *Journal of Systems and Software, 81*(6), 961–971. doi:10.1016/j.jss.2007.08.020

Conboy, K. (2009). Agility from first principles: Reconstructing the concept of agility in information systems development. *Information Systems Research, 20*(3), 329–354. doi:10.1287/isre.1090.0236

DeSanctis, G., & Poole, M. S. (1994). Capturing the complexity in advanced technology use: Adaptive structuration theory. *Organization Science, 5*(2), 121–147. doi:10.1287/orsc.5.2.121

Drucker, P. F. (1997). Toward the new organization. In Hesselbein, F., Goldsmith, M., & Beckhard, R. (Eds.), *The organization of the future* (pp. 1–5). San Francisco, CA: Jossey-Bass.

Dyba, T., & Dingsoyr, T. (2008). Empirical studies of agile software development: A systematic review. *Information and Software Technology, 50*(9-10), 833–859. doi:10.1016/j.infsof.2008.01.006

Eckstein, J. (2004). *Agile software development in the large: Diving into the deep*. New York, NY: Dorset House.

Eisenberg, E. M., Goodall, H. L., & Trethewey, A. (2006). *Organizational communication: Balancing creativity and constraint* (5th ed.). New York, NY: St. Martin's.

Erickson, J., Lyytinen, K., & Siau, K. (2005). Agile modeling, agile software development, and extreme programming: the state of research. *Journal of Database Management, 16*(4), 88–100. doi:10.4018/jdm.2005100105

Fernandez, D. J., & Fernandez, J. D. (2008). Agile project management—Agilism versus traditional approaches. *Journal of Computer Information Systems, 49*(2), 10–17.

Fitzgerald, B., Hartnett, G., & Conboy, K. (2006). Customising agile methods to software practices at Intel Shannon. *European Journal of Information Systems, 15*(2), 200–213. doi:10.1057/palgrave.ejis.3000605

Groise, E., & Mangin, N. (2007). Octopus: Agile software development facing our imperfect world. In *Proceedings of the IEEE AGILE Conference* (pp. 344-350).

Gulati, R. (1995). Does familiarity breed trust? The implications of repeated ties for contractual choice in alliances. *Academy of Management Journal, 38*(1), 85–112. doi:10.2307/256729

Heeager, L. T., & Nielsen, P. A. (2009). *Agile software development and its compatibility with a document-driven approach? A case study.* Paper presented at the Australasian Conference on Information Systems.

Henderson-Sellers, B., & Serour, M. K. (2005). Creating a dual-agility method: The value of method engineering. *Journal of Database Management, 16*(4), 1–23. doi:10.4018/jdm.2005100101

Highsmith, J. A. III. (1999). *Adaptive software development: A collaborative approach to managing complex systems*. New York, NY: Dorset House.

Hilkka, M.-R., Tuure, T., & Matti, R. (2005). Is extreme programming just old wine in new bottles: a comparison of two cases. *Journal of Database Management, 16*(4), 41–61. doi:10.4018/jdm.2005100103

Hofstede, G., & Hofstede, G. J. (2005). *Cultures and organizations: Software for the mind*. New York, NY: McGraw-Hill.

Holland, J. H. (1992). Complex adaptive systems. *Daedalus, 121*(1), 17–30.

Jacques, E. (1996). In praise of hierarchy. In Shafritz, J. M., & Ott, J. S. (Eds.), *Classics of organizational theory* (pp. 245–253). Orlando, FL: Harcourt Brace.

Jain, N. (2006). Offshore agile maintenance. In *Proceedings of the IEEE AGILE Conference*, Minneapolis, MN.

Jensen, M. C., & Meckling, W. H. (1976). Theory of the firm: Managerial behavior, agency costs and ownership structure. *Journal of Financial Economics, 3*(4), 305–360. doi:10.1016/0304-405X(76)90026-X

Kahkonen, T. (2004). Agile methods for large organisations - Building communities of practice. In *Proceedings of the AGILE Development Conference*, Salt Lake City, UT.

Kelley, J. E. (1961). Critical-path planning and scheduling: Mathematical basis. *Operations Research, 9*(3), 296–320. doi:10.1287/opre.9.3.296

Korkala, M., & Abrahamsson, P. (2007). Communication in distributed agile development: A case study. In *Proceedings of the 33rd EUROMICRO Conference on Software Engineering and Advanced Applications* (pp. 203-210).

Larman, C. (2003). *Agile and iterative development: A manager's guide*. Reading, MA: Addison-Wesley.

Layman, L., Williams, L., Damian, D., & Bures, H. (2006). Essential communication practices for Extreme Programming in a global software development team. *Information and Software Technology, 48*(9), 781–794. doi:10.1016/j.infsof.2006.01.004

Lee, G., & Xia, W. (2010). Toward agile: An integrated analysis of quantitative and qualitative field data. *Management Information Systems Quarterly, 34*(1), 87–114.

Lin, Z., Xu, B., & Xu, Y. (2011). A study of open source software development from control perspective. *Journal of Database Management, 22*(1), 26–42. doi:10.4018/jdm.2011010102

Lindvall, M., Basili, V., Boehm, B., Costa, P., Dangle, K., Shull, F., et al. (2002). *Empirical findings in agile methods.* Paper presented at the Second XP Universe and First Agile Universe Conference, Chicago, IL.

Lindvall, M., Muthig, D., Dagnino, A., Wallin, C., Stupperich, M., & Kiefer, D. (2004). Agile software development in large organizations. *Computer, 37*(12), 26–34. doi:10.1109/MC.2004.231

Lyytinen, K., & Rose, G. M. (2006). Information system development agility as organizational learning. *European Journal of Information Systems, 15*, 181–199. doi:10.1057/palgrave.ejis.3000604

Malcolm, D. G., Roseboom, J. H., Clark, C. E., & Fazar, W. (1959). Application of a technique for research and development program evaluation. *Operations Research, 7*(5), 646–669. doi:10.1287/opre.7.5.646

Maruping, L. M., Venkatesh, V., & Agarwal, R. (2009). A control theory perspective on agile methodology use and changing user requirements. *Information Systems Research, 20*(3), 377–399. doi:10.1287/isre.1090.0238

McAvoy, J., & Butler, T. (2009). The role of project management in ineffective decision making within Agile software development projects. *European Journal of Information Systems, 18*(4), 372–383. doi:10.1057/ejis.2009.22

Meredith, S., & Francis, D. (2000). Journey towards agility: The agile wheel explored. *The TQM Magazine, 12*(2), 137–143. doi:10.1108/09544780010318398

Meso, P., & Jain, R. (2006). Agile software development: Adaptive system principles and best practices. *Information Systems Management, 23*(5), 19–29. doi:10.1201/1078.10580530/46108.23.3.20060601/93704.3

Misra, S. C., Kumar, V., & Kumar, U. (2009). Identifying some important success factors in adopting agile software development practices. *Journal of Systems and Software, 82*, 1869–1890. doi:10.1016/j.jss.2009.05.052

Nerur, S., & Balijepally, V. G. (2007). Theoretical reflections on agile development methodologies. *Communications of the ACM, 50*(3), 79–83. doi:10.1145/1226736.1226739

Nerur, S., Mahapatra, R., & Mangalaraj, G. (2005). Challenges of migrating to agile methodologies. *Communications of the ACM, 48*(5), 72–78. doi:10.1145/1060710.1060712

Nord, R. L., & Tomayko, J. E. (2006). Software architecture-centric methods and agile development. *IEEE Software, 23*(2), 47–53. doi:10.1109/MS.2006.54

Nuseibeh, B., & Easterbrook, S. (2000). *Requirements engineering: A roadmap.* Paper presented at the International Conference on Software Engineering, Limerick, Ireland.

O'Connor, D. E., & Faille, C. C. (2000). *Basic economic principles: A guide for students.* Westport, CT: Greenwood Press.

Ouchi, W. G. (1979). A conceptual framework for the design of organizational control mechanisms. *Management Science, 25*(9), 833–848. doi:10.1287/mnsc.25.9.833

Poppendieck, M., & Poppendieck, T. (2003). *Lean software development: An agile toolkit.* Reading, MA: Addison-Wesley.

Procaccino, J. D., Verner, J. M., Overmyer, S. P., & Darter, M. E. (2002). Case study: Factors for early prediction of software development success. *Information and Software Technology, 44*(1), 53–62. doi:10.1016/S0950-5849(01)00217-8

Project Management Institute. (2004). *A guide to the project management body of knowledge.* Newtown Square, PA: Project Management Institute.

Qumer, A., & Henderson-Sellers, B. (2008). An evaluation of the degree of agility in six agile methods and its applicability for method engineering. *Information and Software Technology, 50*(4), 280–295. doi:10.1016/j.infsof.2007.02.002

Ramesh, B., Cao, L., Mohan, K., & Xu, P. (2006). Can distributed software development be agile? *Communications of the ACM*, *49*(10), 41–46. doi:10.1145/1164394.1164418

Reeves, W. W. (1999). *Learner-centered design: A cognitive view of managing complexity in product, information, and environmental design*. Thousand Oaks, CA: Sage.

Sarker, S., & Sarker, S. (2009). Exploring agility in distributed information systems development teams: an interpretive study in an offshoring context. *Information Systems Research*, *20*(3), 440–461. doi:10.1287/isre.1090.0241

Schermerhorn, J. R., Hunt, J. G., & Osborn, R. N. (2003). *Organizational behaviour*. New York, NY: John Wiley & Sons.

Schwaber, K. (2005). Agile project management. In H. Baumeister, M. Marchesi, & H. Holombe (Eds.), *Proceedings of the 6th International Conference on Extreme Programming and Agile Processes in Software Engineering* (LNCS 3556, pp. 277-277).

Schwaber, K., & Beedle, M. (2002). *Agile software development with Scrum*. Upper Saddle River, NJ: Prentice Hall.

Siau, K., Long, Y., & Ling, M. (2010). Toward a unified model of information systems development success. *Journal of Database Management*, *21*(1), 80–101. doi:10.4018/jdm.2010112304

Simon, H. A. (1957). *Models of man: Social and rational; Mathematical essays on rational human behavior in a social setting*. New York, NY: John Wiley & Sons.

Stevens, W. P., Myers, G. J., & Constantine, L. L. (1999). Structural design. *IBM Systems Journal*, *38*(2-3), 231–256. doi:10.1147/sj.382.0231

Turk, D., France, R., & Rumpe, B. (2005). Assumptions underlying agile software-development processes. *Journal of Database Management*, *16*(4), 62–87. doi:10.4018/jdm.2005100104

Vidgen, R., & Wang, X. (2009). Coevolving systems and the organization of agile software development. *Information Systems Research*, *20*(3), 355–376. doi:10.1287/isre.1090.0237

Vinekar, V., Slinkman, C. W., & Nerur, S. (2006). Can Agile and traditional systems development approaches coexist? An ambidextrous view. *Information Systems Management*, *25*(3), 31–42. doi:10.1201/1078.10580530/46108.23.3.20060601/93705.4

Vroom, V. H. (1964). *Work and motivation*. New York, NY: John Wiley & Sons.

Williamson, O. E. (1979). Transaction-cost economics: The governance of contractual relations. *The Journal of Law & Economics*, *22*(2), 233–261. doi:10.1086/466942

This work was previously published in the Journal of Database Management, Volume 22, Issue 4, edited by Keng Siau, pp. 73-92, copyright 2011 by IGI Publishing (an imprint of IGI Global).

Compilation of References

Abelló, A., Samos, J., & Saltor, F. (2002, November 8). On relationships offering new drill-across possibilities. In *Proceedings of the ACM Fifth International Workshop on Data Warehousing and OLAP,* McLean, VA (pp. 7-13).

Abelló, A., Samos, J., & Saltor, F. (2006). YAM2: a multidimensional conceptual model extending UML. *Information Systems, 31*(6), 541–567. doi:10.1016/j.is.2004.12.002

Abiteboul, S., Cluet, S., & Milo, T. (1993). Querying and updating the file. In *Proceedings of the 19th International Conference on Very Large Data Bases*, Dublin, Ireland (pp. 73-84).

Abiteboul, S., Quass, D., McHugh, J., Widom, J., & Wiener, J. (1997). The Lorel query language for semistructured data. *International Journal on Digital Libraries, 1*, 68–88.

Abiteboul, S., & Viannu, V. (1997). Regular path queries with constraints. In *Proceedings of the ACM SIGACT-SIGMOD-SIGART Symposium on Principles of Database Systems*, Tucson, AZ (pp. 122-133).

Abiteboul, S., Vianu, V., Fordham, B. S., & Yesha, Y. (2000). Relational Transducers for Electronic Commerce. *Journal of Computer and System Sciences, 61*, 236–269. doi:10.1006/jcss.2000.1708

Abrahamsson, P., Conboy, K., & Wang, X. (2009). 'Lots done, more to do': the current state of agile systems development research. *European Journal of Information Systems, 18*(4), 281–284. doi:10.1057/ejis.2009.27

Aburub, F., Odeh, M., & Beeson, I. (2007). Modelling non-functional requirements of business processes. *Information and Software Technology, 49*(11), 1162–1171. doi:10.1016/j.infsof.2006.12.002

Ågerfalk, P. J., & Fitzgerald, B. (2006). Flexible and distributed software processes: Old petunias in new bowls? *Communications of the ACM, 49*(10), 26–34.

Agerfalk, P. J., & Fitzgerald, B. (2008). Outsourcing to an unknown workforce: Exploring opensourcing as a global sourcing strategy. *Management Information Systems Quarterly, 32*(2), 385–409.

Aguilar-Saven, R. S. (2004). Business process modelling: Review and framework. *International Journal of Production Economics, 90*, 129–149. doi:10.1016/S0925-5273(03)00102-6

Aharoni, A., & Reinhartz-Berger, I. (2008). A domain engineering approach for situational method engineering. In Q. Li, S. Spaccaapietra, E. Yu, & A. Olivé (Eds.), *Proceedings of the 27th International Conference on Conceptual Modeling* (LNCS 5231, pp. 455-468).

Aiken, P. (2010). *Survey locations.* Retrieved from http://peteraiken.net/professional/research/researchpresentations.html

Aiken, P., Allen, M. D., Parker, B., & Mattia, A. (2006). Measuring data management's maturity: A community's self-assessment. *IEEE Computer, 40*(4), 42–50.

Aiken, P., Gillenson, M., Zhang, X., & Rafner, D. (2011). Data management and data administration: Assessing 25 Years of practice. *Journal of Database Management, 22*(3), 24–45. doi:10.4018/jdm.2011070102

Ajzen, I. (2002). Perceived Behavioral Control, Self-Efficacy, Locus of Control, and the Theory of Planned Behavior. *Journal of Applied Social Psychology, 32*(4), 665–683. doi:10.1111/j.1559-1816.2002.tb00236.x

Alavi, M., & Joachimsthaler, E. A. (1992). Revisiting DSS implementation research: a meta-analysis of the literature and suggestions for researchers. *Management Information Systems Quarterly, 16*(1), 95–116. doi:10.2307/249703

Aleman-Meza, B., Halaschek-Wiener, C., Arpinar, I. B., & Sheth, A. (2003). Context-aware semantic association ranking. In *Proceedings of the Semantic Web and Database Workshop,* Berlin (pp. 33-50).

Aleman-Meza, B., Halaschek-Wiener, C., Arpinar, I. B., Ramakrishnan, C., & Sheth, A. (2005). Ranking complex relationships on the Semantic Web. *IEEE Internet Computing, 9*(3), 37–44. doi:10.1109/MIC.2005.63

Allcock, W., Bresnahan, J., Kettimuthu, R., Link, M., Dumitrescu, C., Raicu, I., & Foster, I. (2005, November). The globus striped gridFTP framework and server. In *Proceedings of the IEEE/ACM Conference on Supercomputing.*

Allen, G. N., & March, S. T. (2006). The Effects of State-Based and Event-Based Data Representation on User Performance in Query Formulation Tasks. *Management Information Systems Quarterly, 30*(2), 269–290.

Al-Masri, E., & Mahmoud, Q. H. (2007). Qos-based discovery and ranking of Web Services. In *Proceedings of the International Conference on Computer Communications and Networks* (pp. 529–534). Los Alamitos, CA: IEEE Computer Society.

Alonso, G., Agrawal, D., Abbadi, A. E., & Mohan, C. (1997). Functionality and Limitations of Current Workflow Management Systems. *IEEE Expert, 12*(5), 68–74.

Alonso, G., Casati, F., Kuno, H., & Machiraju, V. (2004). *Web Services - Concepts, Architectures and Applications.* Berlin, Germany: Springer-Verlag.

Alonso, G., Vingralek, R., Agrawal, D., Breitbart, Y., El Abbadi, A., Schek, H.-J., & Weikum, G. (1994). Unifying Concurrency Control and Recovery of Transactions. *Information Systems, 19,* 101–115. doi:10.1016/0306-4379(94)90029-9

Alves, A., Arkin, A., Askary, S., Barreto, C., Bloch, B., & Curbera, F. (2007). *Web Services Business Process Execution Language Version 2.0.* Burlington, MA: OASIS.

Ambler, S. W. (2008). Has agile peaked? Scott crunches the numbers to find out. *Dr. Dobb's Digital Digest.* Retrieved September 22, 2011, from http://www.drdobbs.com/architecture-and-design/207600615

Amer-Yahia, S., Cho, S., Lakshmanan, L. V. S., & Srivastava, D. (2002). Tree pattern query minimization. *Very Large Data Base Journal, 11*(4), 315–331. doi:10.1007/s00778-002-0076-7

Amir, R., & Zeid, A. (2004, October). A UML profile for service oriented architectures. In *Proceedings of the ACM SIGPLAN Conference on Object-Oriented Programming, Systems, Languages, and Applications.*

An, Y., Hu, X., & Song, I. (2010). Maintaining mappings between conceptual models and relational schemas. *Journal of Database Management, 21*(3), 36–68. doi:10.4018/jdm.2010070102

Ang, J. S. K., Sum, C. C., & Chung, W. F. (1995). Critical Success Factors in Implementing MRP and Government Asistance: A Singapore Context. *Information & Management, 29*(2), 63–70. doi:10.1016/0378-7206(95)00017-Q

Ansari, N., Rusinkiewicz, L., & Sheth, A. (1992). Using flexible transaction to support multi-system telecommunication applications. In *Proceedings of the 18th VLDB Conference,* Vancouver, BC, Canada (pp. 65-76).

Antkiewicz, M., & Czarnecki, K. (2004, October). Featureplugin: Feature modeling plug-in for eclipse. In *Proceedings of the ACM SIGPLAN Conference on Object-Oriented Programming, Systems, Languages, and Applications, Workshop on Eclipse Technology Exchange.*

Antkiewicz, M., & Czarnecki, K. (2006, October). Framework-specific modeling languages with round-trip engineering. In *Proceedings of the ACM/IEEE International Conference on Model Driven Engineering Languages and Systems.*

Antony, S., & Mellarkod, V. (2004). A Methodology for using Data-modeling Patterns. In D. Batra, J. Parsons, & V. Ramesh (Eds.), *Proceedings of the 3rd Symposium on research in Systems Analysis and Design.* St. John's, NL, Canada.

Anyanwu, K., Maduko, A., & Sheth, A. (2005). SemRank: Ranking complex relationship search results on the Semantic Web. In *Proceedings of the International World Wide Web Conference Committee (IW3C2),* Chiba, Japan (pp. 117-127).

Argyris, C. (1982). *Reasoning, learning, and action: Individual and organizational.* San Francisco, CA: Jossey-Bass.

Armour, P. G. (2007). Agile... and offshore. *Communications of the ACM*, *50*(1), 13–16. doi:10.1145/1188913.1188930

Armstrong, J. S., & Overton, T. S. (1977). Estimating nonresponse bias in mail surveys. *Journal of Marketing Research*, *14*, 396–402. doi:10.2307/3150783

Atkinson, C., & Kühne, T. (2003). Model-driven development: A metamodeling foundation. *IEEE Software*, *20*(5), 36–41. doi:10.1109/MS.2003.1231149

Ayanso, A., Goes, P. B., & Mehta, K. (2009). A cost-based range estimation for mapping top-k selection queries over relational databases. *Journal of Database Management*, *20*(4), 1–25. doi:10.4018/jdm.2009062501

Aydin, M. N., Harmsen, F., Stegwee, R. A., & van Slooten, K. (2005). On the adaptation of an agile information systems development method. *Journal of Database Management*, *16*(4), 24–40. doi:10.4018/jdm.2005100102

Bagozzi, R. P., & Dholakia, U. M. (2006). Open source software user communities: a study of participation in Linux user groups. *Management Science*, *52*(7), 1099–1115. doi:10.1287/mnsc.1060.0545

Baligand, F., & Monfort, V. (2004, December). A concrete solution for web services adaptability using policies and aspects. In *Proceedings of the ACM SIGSOFT/ACM SIGWEB International Conference on Service Oriented Computing.*

Balmin, A., Ozcan, F., Beyer, K. S., Cochrane, R. J., & Pirahesh, H. (2004). A framework for using materialized XPath views in XML query processing. In *Proceedings of the Thirtieth International Conference on Very Large Data Bases*, Toronto, ON, Canada (Vol. 30).

Bamba, B., & Mukherjea, S. (2004). Utilizing resource importance for ranking Semantic Web query results. In C. Bussler et al. (Eds.), *Proceedings of the Second Toronto International Workshop on Semantic Web Databases (SWDB),* Toronto, ON, Canada (pp. 185-198). Berlin: Springer-Verlag.

Bancilhon, F., Barbedette, G., Benzaken, V., Delobel, C., Gamerman, S., & Lecluse, C. (1988). The design and implementation of O2, an object-oriented database system. *Advances in Object-Oriented Database Systems*, *6*(1), 1–22.

Bandura, A. (1997). *Self-Efficacy: The Excercise of Control.* New York: W.H. Freeman.

Barros, A. P., Dumas, M., & ter Hofstede, A. H. M. (2005). Service Interaction Patterns. In *Proceedings of the 3rd International Conference on Business Process Management* (pp. 302-318). Berlin, Germany: Springer.

Baskerville, R., & Pries-Heje, J. (2004). Short cycle time systems development. *Information Systems Journal*, *14*(3), 237–264. doi:10.1111/j.1365-2575.2004.00171.x

Basten, T., & van der Aalst, W. M. P. (2001). Inheritance of Behavior. *Journal of Logic and Algebraic Programming*, *47*(2), 47–145. doi:10.1016/S1567-8326(00)00004-7

Batra, D. (2005). Conceptual Data Modeling Patterns: Representation and Validation. *Journal of Database Management*, *16*(2), 84–106.

Batra, D., Hoffer, J. A., & Bostrom, R. P. (1990). A comparison of user performance between the relational and the extended entity relationship models in the discovery phase of database design. *Communications of the ACM*, *33*(2), 126–139. doi:10.1145/75577.75579

Batra, D., & Sin, T. (2008). The READY Model: Patterns of Dynamic Behavior in REA-Based Accounting Applications. *Information Systems Management*, *25*, 200–210. doi:10.1080/10580530802151103

Batra, D., & Wishart, N. A. (2004). Comparing a rule-based approach with a pattern-based approach at different levels of complexity of conceptual data modelling tasks. *International Journal of Human-Computer Studies*, *61*, 397–419. doi:10.1016/j.ijhcs.2003.12.019

Batra, D., Xia, W., VanderMeer, D., & Dutta, K. (2010). Balancing agile and structured approaches to manage large distributed software projects: A case study from the cruise line industry. *Communications of the AIS*, *27*(1), 379–394.

Battle, S. (2003). *Boxes: black, white, grey and glass box view of web-services* (Tech. Rep. No. HPL-2003-30). Bristol, UK: HP Laboratories Bristol.

Beavers, P. A. (2007). Managing a large "agile" software engineering organization. In *Proceedings of the IEEE AGILE Conference* (pp. 296-303).

Beck, K. (2000). *Extreme programming explained: Embrace change*. Reading, MA: Addison-Wesley.

Beck, K. (2005). The XP geography: mapping your next step, a guide to planning your journey. In H. Baumeister, M. Marchesi, & M. Holcombe (Eds.), *Proceedings of the 6th International Conference on Extreme Programming and Agile Processes in Software Engineering* (LNCS 3556, pp. 287-287).

Beck, K., & Boehm, B. (2003). Agility through discipline: A debate. *Computer*, *36*(6), 44–46. doi:10.1109/MC.2003.1204374

Becker, J., Janiesch, C., & Pfeiffer, D. (2007). Reuse mechanisms in situational method engineering. In *Proceedings of the IFIP WG 8.1 Working Conference on Situational Method Engineering: Fundamentals and Experiences* (Vol. 244, pp. 79-93).

Becker, J., Knackstedt, R., Pfeiffer, D., & Janiesch, C. (2007). Configurative method engineering: On the applicability of reference modeling mechanisms in method engineering. In *Proceedings of the 13th Americas Conference on Information Systems.*

Bera, P., Krasnoperova, A., & Wand, Y. (2010). Using ontology languages for conceptual modeling. *Journal of Database Management*, *21*(1), 1–28. doi:10.4018/jdm.2010112301

Bergquist, M., & Ljungberg, J. (2001). The power of gifts: organizing social relationships in open source communities. *Information Systems Journal*, *11*, 305–320. doi:10.1046/j.1365-2575.2001.00111.x

Berners-Lee, T. (2005). *Semantic Web stack*. Retrieved October 13, 2008, from http://www.w3.org/2005/Talks/0511-keynote-tbl/#[17]

Berners-Lee, T., Hendler, J., & Lassila, O. (2001). The Semantic Web. *Scientific American Magazine*. Retrieved March 26, 2008, from http://www.sciam.com/article.cfm?id=the-semantic-web&print=true

Bernstein, P., & Haas, L. (2008). Information integration in the enterprise. *Communications of the ACM*, *51*(9), 72–79. doi:10.1145/1378727.1378745

Bézivin, J. (2006, July 4-8). Model Driven Engineering: An Emerging Technical Space. In *Proceedings of the Generative and Transformational Techniques in Software Engineering, International Summer School*, Braga, Portugal (LNCS 4143, pp. 36-64).

Bhiri, S. (2005). *Approche transactionnelle pour assurer des compositions fiables*. Nancy, France: University Henri Poincar - Nancy 1, LORIA.

Bhiri, S., Perrin, O., & Godart, C. (2005). Ensuring required failure atomicity of composite web services. In A. Ellis & T. Hagino (Eds.), *Proceedings of the 14th International Conference on World Wide Web* (pp. 138-147). New York, NY: ACM.

Bichler, M., & Lin, K. (2006). Service-oriented computing. *IEEE Computer*, *39*(3), 99–101.

Bieberstein, N., Bose, S., Fiammante, M., Jones, K., & Shah, R. (2005). *Service-oriented architecture (soa) compass: Business value, planning, and enterprise roadmap*. Boston, MA: IBM Press.

Birukou, A., Blanzieri, E., D'Andrea, V., Giorgini, P., & Kokash, N. (2007). Improving Web Service discovery with usage data. *IEEE Software*, *24*(6), 47–54. doi:10.1109/MS.2007.169

Blaha, M., & Rumbaugh, J. (2005). *Object-oriented modeling and design with UML* (2nd ed.). Upper Saddle River, NJ: Pearson Education.

Blau, P. M. (1986). *Exchange and power in social life*. New Brunswick, NJ: Transaction Books.

Boag, S., Chamberlin, D., Fernandez, M., Florescu, D., Robie, J., & Simeon, J. (2007). *XQuery 1.0: An XML query language*. Retrieved from http://www.w3.org/TR/xquery/

Bock, D. B., & Ryan, T. (1993). Accuracy in modeling with extended entity relationship and object-oriented data models. *Journal of Database Management*, *4*(4), 30–39.

Bodart, F., Patel, A., Sim, M., & Weber, R. (2001). Should Optional Properties Be Used in Conceptual Modelling? A Theory and Three Empirical Tests. *Information Systems Research*, *12*, 384–405. doi:10.1287/isre.12.4.384.9702

Boehm, B. W. (1981). *Software engineering economics*. Upper Saddle River, NJ: Prentice Hall.

Boehm, B. W., & Turner, R. (2003). *Balancing agility and discipline: A guide for the perplexed*. Reading, MA: Addison-Wesley.

Bonifati, A., Cattaneo, F., Ceri, S., Fuggetta, A., & Paraboschi, S. (2001). Designing Data Marts for Data Warehouses. *ACM Transactions on Software Engineering and Methodology*, *10*(4), 452–483. doi:10.1145/384189.384190

Booth, P. (1992). *An Introduction to Human-Computer Interaction*. Mahwah, NJ: Lawrence Erlbaum.

Bosak, J. (1999). *The plays of Shakespeare in XML*. Retrieved from http://xml.coverpages.org/bosakShakespeare200.html

Bouguettaya, A., Malik, Z., Rezgui, A., & Korff, L. (2004). A scalable middleware for web databases. *Journal of Database Management, 17*, 20–46.

BPM Initiative. (2004, May). *Business process modeling notation (bpmn) 1.0*. Needham, MA: Object Management Group.

Braga, D., Campi, A., Ceri, S., & Raffio, A. (2005). XQBE: a visual environment for learning XML query languages. In *Proceedings of the ACM SIGMOD International Conference on Management of Data*, Baltimore, MD (pp. 903-905).

Bray, K. (2002). *An introduction to requirements engineering*. Reading, MA: Addison-Wesley.

Bray, T., Paoli, J., Sperberg-McQueen, C. M., Maler, E., & Yergeau, F. (2008). *Extensible markup language (XML) 1.0* (5th ed.). Retrieved from http://www.w3.org/TR/REC-xml/

Brechner, E. (2005). *Journey of enlightenment: the evolution of development at Microsoft*. Paper presented at the 27th International Conference on Software Engineering, St. Louis, MO.

Brereton, P., Kitchenham, B., Budgen, D., Turner, M., & Khalil, M. (2007). Lessons from applying the systematic literature review process within the software engineering domain. *Journal of Systems and Software, 80*(4), 571–583. doi:10.1016/j.jss.2006.07.009

Breslin, M. (2004). Data Warehousing Battle of the Giants: Comparing the Basics of the Kimball and Inmon Models. *Business Intelligence Journal, 9*(1), 6–20.

Bretthauer, D. (2002). Open source software: A history. *Information Technology and Libraries, 21*(1), 3–10.

Breyfogle, F. W. (2003). *Implementing six sigma: Smarter solutions using statistical methods*. New York, NY: John Wiley & Sons.

Brickley, D., & Guha, R. V. (Eds.). (2004). *RDF vocabulary description language 1.0: RDF schema*. Retrieved October 15, 2008, from http://www.w3.org/TR/rdf-schema/

Brin, S., Motwani, R., Page, L., & Winograd, T. (1998). What can you do with a Web in your pocket. *Bulletin of the IEEE Computer Society Technical Committee on Data Engineering, 21*(2), 37–47.

Brin, S., & Page, L. (1998). The anatomy of a large-scale hypertextual Web search engine. *Special Issue of the 7th International World Wide Web Conference on Computer Networks and ISDN Systems, 30*(1-7), 107-117.

Brinkkemper, S. (1996). Method engineering: engineering of information systems development methods and tools. *Information and Software Technology, 38*, 275–280. doi:10.1016/0950-5849(95)01059-9

Britton, C., & Bye, P. (2004). *IT Architectures and Middleware: Strategies for Building Large, Integrated Systems* (2nd ed.). Boston, MA: Addison-Wesley Professional.

Brogi, A., Corfini, S., & Popescu, R. (2008). Semantics-based composition-oriented discovery of Web services. *ACM Transactions on Internet Technology, 8*, 1–39. doi:10.1145/1391949.1391953

Bruijn, J. D. (2005). *D16.1v0.21 the web service modeling language wsml*. Retrieved from http://www.wsmo.org/TR/d16/d16.1/v0.21/.

Brydon, M., & Vining, A. R. (2008). Adoption, improvement, and disruption: predicting the impact of open source applications in enterprise software markets. *Journal of Database Management, 19*(2), 73–94. doi:10.4018/jdm.2008040104

Budanitsky, A., & Hirst, G. (2006). Evaluating WordNet-based measures of lexical semantic relatedness. *Computational Linguistics, 32*(1), 13–47. doi:10.1162/coli.2006.32.1.13

Bultan, T., Fu, X., Hull, R., & Su, J. (2003). Conversation Specification: A New Approach to Design and Analysis of E-Service Composition. In *Proceedings of the International World Wide Web Conference 2003 (WWW 2003)* (pp. 403-410).

Bunge, M. (1977). Treatise on basic philosophy: *Vol. 3. Ontology I: The furniture of the world*. Boston, MA: Reidel.

Bunge, M. (1979). Treatise on basic philosophy: *Vol. 4. Ontology II: A world of systems*. Boston, MA: Reidel.

Burden, R. L., & Faires, J. D. (2001). *Numerical Analysis*. Pacific Grove, CA: Brooks/Cole.

Burton-Jones, A., & Meso, P. N. (2008). The Effects of Decomposition Quality and Multiple Forms of Information on Novices' Understanding of a Domain from a Conceptual Model. *Journal of the Association for Information Systems*, *9*(12), 748–802.

Burton-Jones, A., & Weber, R. (1999). Understanding Relationships with Attributes in Entity-Relationship Diagrams. In *Proceedings of the Twentieth International Conference on Information Systems* (pp. 214-228).

Burton-Jones, A., & Weber, R. (2003). Properties do not have properties: Investigating a questionable conceptual modelling practice. In D. Batra, J. Parsons, & V. Ramesh (Eds.), *Proceedings of the 2nd Annual Symposium on Research in Systems Analysis and Design.*

Cabibbo, L., & Torlone, R. (2004, June 21-23). On the Integration of Autonomous Data Marts. In *Proceedings of the 16th International Conference on Scientific and Statistical Database Management,* Santorini Island, Greece (pp. 223-231). Washington, DC: IEEE Computer Society.

Cabibbo, L., & Torlone, R. (2001). An Architecture for Data Warehousing Supporting Data Independence and Interoperability. *International Journal of Cooperative Information Systems*, *10*(3), 377–397. doi:10.1142/S0218843001000394

Cao, L., Mohan, K., Xu, P., & Ramesh, B. (2009). A framework for adapting agile development methodologies. *European Journal of Information Systems*, *18*(4), 332–343. doi:10.1057/ejis.2009.26

Cardinal, L. B. (2001). Technological innovation in the pharmaceutical industry: The use of organizational control in managing research and development. *Organization Science*, *12*(1), 19–36. doi:10.1287/orsc.12.1.19.10119

Cardinal, L. B., Sitkin, S. B., & Long, C. P. (2004). Balancing and rebalancing in the creation and evolution of organizational control. *Organization Science*, *15*(4), 411–431. doi:10.1287/orsc.1040.0084

Cardoso, J., & Sheth, A. (2003). Semantic e-workflow composition. *Journal of Intelligent Information Systems*, *21*(3), 191–225. doi:10.1023/A:1025542915514

Carey, M., & DeWitt, J. D. J., Franklin, M., Hall, N., AcAuliffe, M., Naughton, J., et al. (1994). Shoring up persistent applications. In *Proceedings of the ACM SIGMOD International Conference on Management of Data*, Minneapolis, MN (pp. 383-394).

Carey, M. J., DeWitt, D. J., Frank, D., Graefe, G., Muralikrishna, M., Richardson, J. E., & Shikita, E. J. (1986). The architecture of the EXODUS extensible DBMS. In *Proceedings of the International Workshop on Object-Oriented Database Systems* (pp. 52-65).

Carlis, J. V., & March, S. T. (1983). Computer-aided physical database design methodology. *Computer Performance*, *4*(4), 198–214.

Carver, J., Jaccheri, L., Morasca, S., & Shull, F. (2003). Issues in using students in empirical studies in software engineering education. In *Proceedings of the 9th International Software Metrics Symposium* (pp. 239-249).

Casati, F., Ceri, S., Paraboschi, S., & Pozzi, G. (1999). Specification and implementation of exceptions in workflow management systems. *ACM Transactions on Database Systems*, *24*(3), 405–451. doi:10.1145/328939.328996

Casati, F., & Dayal, U. (Eds.). (2002). Special Issue on Web Services. *IEEE Bulletin of the Technical Committee on Data Engineering*, *25*(4).

Casati, F., Ilnicki, S., Jin, L., Krishnamoorthy, V., & Shan, M.-C. (2000). Adaptive and Dynamic Service Composition in eFlow, HP Labs Report HPL-2000-39.

Chadwyck-Healey. (1994). *The English poetry full-text database. The works of more than 1,250 poets from 600 to 1900.* Retrieved from http://eresources.lib.unc.edu/eid/

Chan, H. C., & Lim, L. H. (1998). Database interfaces: a conceptual framework and a meta-analysis on natural language studies. *Journal of Database Management*, *9*(3), 25–32.

Chan, H. C., Wei, K. K., & Siau, K. L. (1993). User-database interface: The effect of abstraction levels on query performance. *Management Information Systems Quarterly*, *17*(4), 441–464. doi:10.2307/249587

Chan, V. C. T., Chiu, D. K. W., Chow, S., & Hung, P. C. K. (2007). e-Monitoring of Outsourcing IS Project in Financial Institutions: A Case Study on Mandatory Provident Fund Projects in Hong Kong. In *Proceedings of the 2007 IEEE International Conference on e-Business Engineering* (pp. 460-465). Washington, DC: IEEE Computer Society.

Charfi, A., Schmeling, B., Heizenreder, A., & Mezini, M. (2006, December). Reliable, secure, and transacted web service compositions with ao4bpel. In *Proceedings of the IEEE European Conference on Web Services.*

Chaudhuri, S., & Dayal, U. (1997). An Overview of Data Warehousing and OLAP Technology. *SIGMOD Record, 26*(1), 65–74. doi:10.1145/248603.248616

Chen, P. (1976). The entity-relationship model: Towards a unified view of data. *ACM Transactions on Database Systems, 1*(1), 9–36. doi:10.1145/320434.320440

Chen, Y., Zhou, L., & Zhang, D. (2006). Ontology-supported Web Service composition: An approach to service-oriented knowledge management in corporate services. *Journal of Database Management, 17*(1), 67–84.

Cheung, S. C., Chiu, D. K. W., & Till, S. (2003). Data-driven methodology to extending workflows to e-services over the internet. In *Proceedings of the 36th Annual Hawaii International Conference on System Sciences (HICSS 2003),* Big Island, HI. Washington, DC: IEEE Computer Society.

Chin, W. W. (1998). Issues and options on structural equation modeling. *Management Information Systems Quarterly, 1,* 7–16.

Chitchyan, R., Rashid, A., Sawyer, P., Garcia, A., Alarcon, M. P., & Bakker, J. (2005). *Survey of aspect-oriented analysis and design approaches.* Lancaster, UK: AOSD-Europe.

Chiu, D. K. W., Cheung, S. C., Kafeza, E., & Ho-Fung, L. (2003). A three-tier view-based methodology for M-services adaptation. Systems. *IEEE Transactions on Man and Cybernetics. Part A, 33*(6), 725–741.

Chiu, D. K. W., Cheung, S. C., Till, S., Karlapalem, K., Li, Q., & Kafeza, E. (2004). Workflow View Driven Cross-Organizational Interoperability in a Web Service Environment. *Information Technology Management, 5*(3-4), 221–250. doi:10.1023/B:ITEM.0000031580.57966.d4

Chiu, D. K. W., Cheung, S. C., Till, S., Narupiyakul, L., & Hung, P. C. K. (2010). Enhancing E-service Collaboration with Enforcement and Relationship Management: a Methodology from Requirements to Event Driven Realization. *International Journal of Organizational and Collective Intelligence, 1*(1), 15–43. doi:10.4018/joci.2010100802

Chiu, D. K. W., Kafeza, K., Cheung, S. C., Kafeza, E., & Hung, P. C. K. (2009). Alerts in Healthcare Applications: Process and Data Integration. *International Journal of Healthcare Information Systems and Informatics, 4*(2), 36–56. doi:10.4018/jhisi.2009040103

Chiu, D. K. W., Karlapalem, K., & Li, Q. (2001). Views for Inter-organization Workflow in an E-commerce Environment. In *Semantic Issues in E-Commerce Systems: Proceedings of the IFIP TC2/WG2.6 9th Working Conference on Database Semantics,* Hong Kong (pp. 137-151). Dordrecht, The Netherlands: Kluwer.

Chiu, D. K. W., Karlapalem, K., Li, Q., & Kafeza, E. (2002). Workflow View Based E-Contracts in a Cross-Organizational E-Services Environment. *Distributed and Parallel Databases, 12*(2-3), 193–216. doi:10.1023/A:1016503218569

Chiu, D. K. W., Li, Q., & Karlapalem, K. (2000). Web Interface-Driven Cooperative Exception Handling in ADOME Workflow Management System. *Information Systems, 26*(2), 93–120. doi:10.1016/S0306-4379(01)00012-6

Choudhury, V., & Sabherwal, R. (2003). Portfolios of control in outsourced software development projects. *Information Systems Research, 14*(3), 291–314. doi:10.1287/isre.14.3.291.16563

Chow, T., & Cao, D. B. (2008). A survey study of critical success factors in agile software projects. *Journal of Systems and Software, 81*(6), 961–971. doi:10.1016/j.jss.2007.08.020

Chrissis, M. B., Konrad, M., & Shrum, S. (2003). *CMMI: Guidelines for process integration and product improvement.* Reading, MA: Addison-Wesley.

Christensen, E., Curbera, F., Meredith, G., & Weerawarana, S. (2001). *Web services description language (WSDL) 1.1.* Retrieved from http://www.w3.org/TR/wsdl

Christophides, V., Hull, R., Karvounarakis, G., Kumar, A., Tong, G., & Xiong, M. (2001). Beyond Discrete E-Services: Composing Session-Oriented Services in Telecommunications. In *Proceedings of the 2nd International Workshop on Technologies for E-Services (TES) 2001* (LNCS 2193, pp. 58-73).

Christophides, V., Abiteboul, S., Cluet, S., & Scholl, M. (1994). From structured documents to novel query facilities. *SIGMOD Record*, *23*(2), 313–324. doi:10.1145/191843.191901

Chung, L., Nixon, B., Yu, E., & Mylopoulos, J. (1999). *Non-functional requirements in software engineering*. Dordrecht, The Netherlands: Kluwer Academic Publishers.

Church, K., & Smith, R. (2008). REA Ontology-Based Simulation Models for Enterprise Strategic Planning. *Journal of Information Systems*, *22*(2), 301–329. doi:10.2308/jis.2008.22.2.301

Clark, J., & DeRose, S. (1999). *XML path language XPath version 1.0.* Retrieved from http://www.w3.org/TR/xpath

Clement, L., Hately, A., von Riegen, C., & Rogers, T. (2004). *Universal description discovery and integration (UDDI) specifications, version 3.0.2.* Retrieved from http://www.uddi.org/pubs/uddi_v3.htm

Codd, E. F. (1970). A relational model of data for large shared data banks. *Communications of the ACM*, *13*(6), 377–387. doi:10.1145/362384.362685

Cohen, J. (1977). *Statistical Power Analysis for the Behavioral Sciences*. New York, NY: Academic Press.

Colby, L. S. (1990). A recursive algebra for nested relations. *Information Systems*, *15*(5), 567–582. doi:10.1016/0306-4379(90)90029-O

Colombo, E., Francalanci, C., & Pernici, B. (2002). Modeling Coordination and Control in Cross-Organizational Workflows. In *Proceedings of the CoopIS-DOA-ODBASE 2002 Conference* (LNCS 2519, pp. 91-106).

Conboy, K. (2009). Agility from first principles: Reconstructing the concept of agility in information systems development. *Information Systems Research*, *20*(3), 329–354. doi:10.1287/isre.1090.0236

Connolly, T. M., & Begg, C. E. (2005). *Database Systems: a Practical Approach to Design, Implementation, and Management* (4th ed.). New York: Addison-Wesley.

Coronel, C., Morris, S., & Rod, P. (2009). *Database Systems: Design, Implementation, and Management* (9th ed.). Florence, KY: Course Technology.

Correal, D., & Casallas, R. (2007, October). Using domain specific languages for software process modeling. In *Proceedings of the ACM SIGPLAN Conference on Object-Oriented Programming, Systems, Languages, and Applications, Workshop on Domain-Specific Modeling*.

Courbis, C., & Finkelstein, A. (2005, October). Weaving aspects into web service orchestrations. In *Proceedings of the IEEE International Conference on Web Services*.

Crasso, M., Zunino, A., & Campo, M. (2008). Easy Web Service discovery: a Query-by-Example approach. *Science of Computer Programming*, *71*(2), 144–164. doi:10.1016/j.scico.2008.02.002

Crasso, M., Zunino, A., & Campo, M. (2009). Combining query-by-example and query expansion for simplifying Web Service discovery. In *Information Systems Frontiers*.

Crasso, M., Zunino, A., & Campo, M. (2009). Semantic Web: Standards, Tools and Ontologies. In *An Approach to Assist Developers to Annotate Web Services with Ontologies* (pp. 195-229). Hauppauge, NY: Nova Science Publishers.

Cronbach, L. J. (1951). Coefficient alpha and the internal structure of tests. *Psychometrika*, *16*, 297–334. doi:10.1007/BF02310555

Crowston, K., & Howison, J. (2005). The social structure of free and open source software development. *First Monday*, *10*(2).

Curbera, F., Duftler, M. J., Khalaf, R., Nagy, W. A., Mukhi, N., & Weerawarana, S. (2005). Colombo: Lightweight middleware for service-oriented computing. *IBM Systems Journal*, *44*(4), 799–820. doi:10.1147/sj.444.0799

Curbera, F., Khalaf, R., Leymann, F., & Weerawarana, S. (2003). Exception handling in the BPEL4WS language. In *Proceedings of the International Conference on Business Process Management (BPM 2003)*, Eindhoven, The Netherlands (pp. 276-290). Berlin, Germany: Springer.

Czarnecki, K., & Antkiewicz, M. (2005, September). Mapping features to models: A template approach based on superimposed variants. In *Proceedings of the International Conference on Generative Programming and Component Engineering.*

Czarnecki, K., & Eisenecker, U. (2000). *Generative programming: Methods, tools and applications.* Reading, MA: Addison-Wesley.

Czarnecki, K., Helsen, S., & Eisenecker, U. (2005). Formalizing cardinality-based feature models and their specialization. *Software Process Improvement and Practice, 10*(1), 7–29. doi:10.1002/spip.213

Dao, T. N., & Simpson, T. (2005). *Measuring similarity between sentences.* Retrieved from http://wordnetdotnet.googlecode.com/svn/trunk/Projects/Thanh/Paper/WordNetDotNet_Semantic_Similarity.pdf

Data, data everywhere - A special report on managing information. (2010, February 27). *The Economist*, pp. 1-14.

Davis, F. D. (1989). Perceived usefulness, perceived ease of use, and user acceptance of information technology. *Management Information Systems Quarterly, 13*(3), 318–339. doi:10.2307/249008

De Antonellis, V., Melchiori, M., Pernici, B., & Plebani, P. (2003). A Methodology for e-Service Substitutability in a Virtual District Environment. In *Advanced Information Systems Engineering: Proceedings of CAiSE '03,* Klagenfurt, Austria (LNCS 2681, pp. 552-567).

de Bruijn, J., Lausen, H., Polleres, A., & Fensel, D. (2006). The Web Service modeling language WSML: An overview. In *ESWC* (LNCS 4011, pp. 590–604).

De Sousa Saraiva, J., & da Silva, A. R. (2008). Evaluation of mde tools from a metamodeling perspective. *Journal of Database Management, 19*(4), 21–46.

Dedene, G., & Snoeck, M. (1995). Formal Deadlock Elimination in an Object-Oriented Conceptual Schema. *Data & Knowledge Engineering, 15*(1), 1–30. doi:10.1016/0169-023X(94)00031-9

Dehnert, J., & Rittgen, P. (2001). Relaxed soundness of business processes. In K. R. Dittrich, A. Geppert, & M. C. Norrie (Eds.), *Proceedings of the 13th International Conference on Advanced Information Systems Engineering* (LNCS 2068, pp. 157-170).

Dehnert, J., & van der Aalst, W. M. P. (2004). Bridging the gap between business models and workflow specifications. *International Journal of Cooperative Information Systems, 13*(3), 289–332. doi:10.1142/S0218843004000973

Demil, B., & Lecocq, X. (2006). Neither market nor hierarchy nor network: The emergence of bazaar governance. *Organization Studies, 27*(10), 1447–1466. doi:10.1177/0170840606067250

Dennis, A. R., Haley, B. J., & Vandenberg, R. J. (2001). Understanding fit and appropriation effects in group support systems via meta-analysis. *Management Information Systems Quarterly, 25*(2), 167–193. doi:10.2307/3250928

Dennis, A. R., & Wixom, B. H. (2002). Investigating the moderators of the group support systems use with meta-analysis. *Journal of Management Information Systems, 18*(3), 235–258.

Desai, B. C., Goyal, P., & Sadri, F. (1986). A data model for use with formatted and textual data. *Journal of the American Society for Information Science American Society for Information Science, 37*(3), 158–165.

DeSanctis, G., & Poole, M. S. (1994). Capturing the complexity in advanced technology use: Adaptive structuration theory. *Organization Science, 5*(2), 121–147. doi:10.1287/orsc.5.2.121

Ding, L., Finin, T., Joshi, A., Pan, R., Cost, R. S., Peng, Y., et al. (2004). Swoogle: A semantic Web search and metadata engine. In *Proceedings of the 13th ACM Conference on Information and Knowledge Management* (pp. 652-659).

Ding, L., Finin, T., Joshi, A., Peng, Y., Pan, R., & Reddivari, P. (2005). Search on the Semantic Web. *Computer, 38*(10), 62–69. doi:10.1109/MC.2005.350

Ding, L., Pan, R., Finin, T., Joshi, A., Peng, Y., & Kolari, P. (2005). Finding and ranking knowledge on the Semantic Web. In *Proceedings of the 4th Galway IE International Semantic Web Conference,* Galway, Ireland (pp. 156-170). Berlin: Springer-Verlag.

Dobing, B., & Parsons, J. (2006). How UML is used. *Communications of the ACM, 49*(5), 109–113. doi:10.1145/1125944.1125949

Domíngueza, E., & Zapata, M. A. (2007). Noesis: Towards a situational method engineering technique. *Information Systems, 32*(2), 181–222. doi:10.1016/j.is.2005.07.001

Dong, Z., Halevy, A. Y., Madhavan, J., Nemes, E., & Zhang, J. (2004). Similarity search for Web Services. In *Proceedings of the Thirtieth International Conference on Very Large Data Bases*, Toronto, ON, Canada (pp. 372–383). San Francisco: Morgan Kaufmann.

Dongen, B. F., van der Aalst, W. M. P., & Verbeek, H. M. W. (2005). Verification of EPCs: Using reduction rules and petri nets. In A. Pastor & J. Falcao e Cunha (Eds.), *Proceedings of the 17th International Conference on Advanced Information Systems Engineering* (LNCS 3520, pp. 372-386).

Dori, D. (2002). *Object-process methodology – A holistic system paradigm*. Berlin, Germany: Springer-Verlag.

Drucker, P. F. (1997). Toward the new organization. In Hesselbein, F., Goldsmith, M., & Beckhard, R. (Eds.), *The organization of the future* (pp. 1–5). San Francisco, CA: Jossey-Bass.

Dunn, C. L., Cherrington, J. O., & Hollander, A. S. (2005). *Enterprise Information Systems: A Pattern Based Approach*. New York: McGraw-Hill.

Dunn, C., & Grabski, S. (2001). An Investigation of Localization as an Element of Cognitive Fit in Accounting Model Representations. *Decision Sciences, 32*(1), 55–94. doi:10.1111/j.1540-5915.2001.tb00953.x

Dyba, T., & Dingsoyr, T. (2008). Empirical studies of agile software development: A systematic review. *Information and Software Technology, 50*(9-10), 833–859. doi:10.1016/j.infsof.2008.01.006

Dzidek, W. J., Arisholm, E., & Briand, L. C. (2008). A realistic empirical evaluation of the costs and benefits of UML in software maintenance. *IEEE Transactions on Software Engineering, 34*(3), 407–432. doi:10.1109/TSE.2008.15

Eaddy, M., Aho, A., & Murphy, G. C. (2007, May). *Identifying, assigning, and quantifying crosscutting concerns*. Paper presented at the AOSD-Europe International Workshop on Assessment of Contemporary Modularization Techniques.

Eckerson, W. W. (2002). *Data quality and the bottom line: Achieving business success through a commitment to high quality data*. Chatsworth, CA: Data Warehousing Institute.

Eckstein, J. (2004). *Agile software development in the large: Diving into the deep*. New York, NY: Dorset House.

Ehrlich, L. W. (1969). *Rate of Convergence Proofs of the Method for Finding Roots of Polynomials (or Eigenvalues of Matrices) by the Power and Inverse Power Methods* (Tech. Rep. No. AD707331). Alexandria, VA: National Technical Information Service.

Eisenberg, E. M., Goodall, H. L., & Trethewey, A. (2006). *Organizational communication: Balancing creativity and constraint* (5th ed.). New York, NY: St. Martin's.

Eisenhardt, K. M. (1985). Control: organizational and economic approaches. *Management Science, 31*(2), 134–149. doi:10.1287/mnsc.31.2.134

Elmagarmid, A. (1992). *Transaction models for advanced database applications*. San Francisco, CA: Morgan-Kaufmann.

Elmagarmid, A., Leu, Y., Litwin, W., & Rusinkiewicz, M. (1990). A multi-database transaction model for interbase. In *Proceedings of the VLDB Conference* (pp. 507-518). San Francisco, CA: Morgan-Kaufmann.

Elmasri, R., & Navathe, S. (2006). *Fundamentals of database systems* (5th ed.). Reading, MA: Addison-Wesley.

Elrad, T., Aldawud, O., & Bader, A. (2002, October). Aspect-oriented modeling - bridging the gap between design and implementation. In *Proceedings of the ACM International Conference on Generative Programming and Component Engineering*.

Embley, D. W. (1998). *Object Database Development Concepts and Principles*. Reading, MA: Addison-Wesley.

Erickson, J., Lyytinen, K., & Siau, K. (2005). Agile modeling, agile software development, and extreme programming: the state of research. *Journal of Database Management, 16*(4), 88–100. doi:10.4018/jdm.2005100105

Erickson, J., & Siau, K. (2007). Theoretical and practical complexity of modeling methods. *Communications of the ACM, 50*(8), 46–51. doi:10.1145/1278201.1278205

Erickson, J., & Siau, K. (2008). Web Service, Service-Oriented Computing, and Service-Oriented Architecture: Separating hype from reality. *Journal of Database Management, 19*(3), 42–54.

Erl, T. (2006). *Service-Oriented Architecture: Concepts, Technology, and Design*. Upper Saddle River, NJ: Prentice-Hall.

Erwig, M. (2003). Xing: A visual XML query language. *Journal of Visual Languages and Computing*, *14*, 5–45. doi:10.1016/S1045-926X(02)00074-5

Eshuis, R., & Grefen, P. (2008). Constructing customized process views. *Data & Knowledge Engineering*, *64*(2), 419–438. doi:10.1016/j.datak.2007.07.003

Euzenat, J., & Shvaiko, P. (2007). *Ontology Matching*. New York: Springer-Verlag.

Even, A., & Shankaranarayanan, G. (2009). Utility cost perspectives in data quality management. *Journal of Computer Information Systems*, *50*(2), 127–135.

Evermann, J. (2008). Theories of meaning in schema matching: A review. *Journal of Database Management*, *19*(3), 55–82.

Evermann, J., & Wand, Y. (2009). Ontology based object-oriented domain modeling: Representing behavior. *Journal of Database Management*, *20*(1), 48–77. doi:10.4018/jdm.2009010103

Fankhauser, P. (2002). XQuery by the book = an implementation based on rigid formal semantics. In *Proceedings of the XML Conference*.

Fauvet, M.-C., Dumas, M., Benatallah, B., & Paik, H.-Y. (2001). Peer-to-Peer Traced Execution of Composite Services. In *Proceedings of the 2nd International Workshop on Technologies for E-Services (TES) 2001* (LNCS 2193, pp. 103-117).

Fellbaum, C. (Ed.). (1989). *WordNet: An Electronic Lexical Database*. Cambridge, MA: MIT Press.

Feller, J., & Fitzgerald, B. (2002). *Understanding Open Source Software Development*. Reading, MA: Addison-Wesley.

Fenton, N., Pfleeger, S. L., & Glass, R. L. (1994). Science and Substance: A Challenge to Software Engineers. *IEEE Software*, *11*(4), 86–95. doi:10.1109/52.300094

Fernandez, D. J., & Fernandez, J. D. (2008). Agile project management—Agilism versus traditional approaches. *Journal of Computer Information Systems*, *49*(2), 10–17.

Fernandez, M., & Simeon, J. (2004). Building an extensible XQuery engine: Experiences with Galax. In Z. Bellahsene, T. Milo, M. Rys, D. Suciu, & R. Unland (Eds.), *Proceedings of the Second International Conference on Database and XML Technologies* (LNCS 3186, pp. 1-14).

Fernandez, M. F., & Suciu, D. (1998). Optimizing regular path expressions using graph schemas. In *Proceedings of the International Conference on Data Engineering* (pp. 14-23).

Fiebig, T., Helmer, S., Kanne, C., Moerkotte, G., Neumann, J., Schiele, R., & Westmann, T. (2002). Anatomy of a native XML base management system. *Very Large Data Base Journal*, *11*(4), 292–314. doi:10.1007/s00778-002-0080-y

Fiebig, T., & Moerkotte, G. (2001). Evaluating queries on structure with extended access support relations. In G. Goos, J. Hartmanis, J. van Leeuwen, D. Sciu, & G. Vossen (Eds.), *Proceedings of the Third International Workshop on the World Wide Web and Databases* (LNCS 1997, pp. 125-136).

Fielding, R. (1999). Shared leadership in the apache project. *Communications of the ACM*, *42*(4), 42–43. doi:10.1145/299157.299167

Finin, T., & Ding, L. (2006). Search engines for Semantic Web knowledge. In *Proceedings of XTech 2006: Building Web 2.0*, Amsterdam, The Netherlands.

Firat, A., Wu, L., & Madnick, S. (2009). General strategy for querying web sources in a data federation environment. *Journal of Database Management*, *20*(2), 1–18. doi:10.4018/jdm.2009092201

Firesmith, D., & Henderson-Sellers, B. (2001). *The OPEN process framework: An introduction*. Reading, MA: Addison-Wesley.

Fischer, L. (Ed.). (2007). *Methods, concepts, case studies and standards in business process management and workflow*. Lighthouse Point, FL: Future Strategies.

Fitzgerald, B. (2006). The transformation of open source software. *Management Information Systems Quarterly*, *30*(3), 587–598.

Fitzgerald, B., Hartnett, G., & Conboy, K. (2006). Customising agile methods to software practices at Intel Shannon. *European Journal of Information Systems*, *15*(2), 200–213. doi:10.1057/palgrave.ejis.3000605

France, R., Bieman, J., & Cheng, B. (2007). Repository for model driven development (ReMoDD). In *Proceedings of the MoDELS Workshops* (pp. 311-317).

Francisco, C., Rania, K., Nirmal, M., Stefan, T., & Sanjiva, W. (2003). The Next Step in Web Services. *Communications of the ACM*, *46*(10), 29–34. doi:10.1145/944217.944234

Franz, T., Schultz, A., Sizov, S., & Staab, S. (2009). TripleRank: Ranking Semantic Web Data By Tensor Decomposition. In *Proceedings of the 8th International Semantic Web Conference* (pp. 213-228). Berlin: Springer-Verlag.

Frasincar, F., Houben, G.-J., & Pau, C. (2002). XAL: an algebra for XML query optimization. In *Proceedings of the 13th Australasian Database Conference* (Vol. 5, pp. 49-56).

Friedman, T., Gassman, B., & Newman, D. (2005). *Gartner report - Predicts 2006: Emerging data management drivers and imperatives.* Retrieved from http://www.gartner.com/DisplayDocument?doc_cd=136320

Fu, X., Bultan, T., & Su, J. (2002). Formal Verification of e-Services and Workflows. In *Proceedings of the International Workshop on Web Services, E-Business, and the Semantic Web (WES) 2002* (LNCS 2512, pp. 188-202).

Funderburk, J. E., Malaika, S., & Reinwald, B. (2002). XML programming with SQL/XML and XQuery. *IBM Systems Journal*, *41*(4), 642–665. doi:10.1147/sj.414.0642

Gailly, F., Laurier, W., & Poels, G. (2008). Positioning and Formalizing the REA enterprise ontology. *Journal of Information Systems*, *22*(2), 219–248. doi:10.2308/jis.2008.22.2.219

Gallivan, M. J. (2001). Striking a balance between trust and control in a virtual organization: a content analysis of open source software case studies. *Information Systems Journal*, *11*, 277–304. doi:10.1046/j.1365-2575.2001.00108.x

GAO. (2001). *Information technology: DLA should strengthen business systems modernization architecture and investment activities* (Tech. Rep. No. GAO-01-631). Washington, DC: U.S. Government Accountability Office.

Garcia-Molina, H., Gawlick, D., Klein, J., Kleissner, K., & Salem, K. (1991). Modeling long-running activities as nested sagas. *A Quarterly Bulletin of the Computer Society of the IEEE Technical Committee on Data Engineering*, *14*(1), 14–18.

Garcia-Molina, H., & Salem, K. (1987, May 27-29). Sagas. In U. Dayal & I. L. Traiger (Eds.), *Proceedings of the ACM SIGMOD Conference,* San Francisco, CA (pp. 249-259). New York, NY: ACM.

Garofalakis, J. D., Panagis, Y., Sakkopoulos, E., & Tsakalidis, A. K. (2006). Contemporary Web Service Discovery Mechanisms. *Journal of Web Engineering*, *5*(3), 265–290.

Geerts, G., & McCarthy, W. E. (2002). An Ontological Analysis of the Economic Primitives of the Extended-REA Enterprise Information Architecture. *International Journal of Accounting Information Systems*, *3*(1), 1–16. doi:10.1016/S1467-0895(01)00020-3

Geerts, G., & McCarthy, W. E. (2006). Policy-Level Specification in REA Enterprise Information Systems. *Journal of Information Systems*, *20*(2), 37–63. doi:10.2308/jis.2006.20.2.37

Gemino, A., & Parker, D. (2009). Use case diagrams in support of use case modeling: Deriving understanding from the picture. *Journal of Database Management*, *20*(1), 1–24. doi:10.4018/jdm.2009010101

Gemino, A., & Wand, Y. (2003). Foundations for Empirical Comparisons of Conceptual Modelling Techniques. In D. Batra, J. Parsons, & V. Ramesh (Eds.), *Proceedings of the 2nd Symposium on Research in Systems Analysis and Design.*

Gemino, A., & Wand, Y. (2005). Complexity and clarity in conceptual modeling: Comparison of mandatory and optional properties. *Data & Knowledge Engineering*, *55*(3), 301–326. doi:10.1016/j.datak.2004.12.009

Genero, M., Piattini, M., & Calero, C. (2005). A survey of metrics for UML class diagrams. *Journal of Object Technology*, *4*(9), 59–92. doi:10.5381/jot.2005.4.9.a1

Genero, M., Piattini, M., & Calero, C. (2005). *Metrics for software conceptual models.* London, UK: Imperial College Press. doi:10.1142/9781860946066

Genero, M., Poels, G., & Piattini, M. (2008). Defining and Validating Metrics for Assessing the Understandability of Entity-Relationship Diagrams. *Data & Knowledge Engineering*, *64*(3), 534–557. doi:10.1016/j.datak.2007.09.011

Gentner, D., & Medina, J. (1998). Similarity and the development of rules. *Cognition*, *65*, 263–297. doi:10.1016/S0010-0277(98)00002-X

Georgakopoulos, D., Hornick, M. F., Krychniak, P., & Manola, F. (1994, February 14-18). Specification and management of extended transactions in a programmable transaction environment. In *Proceedings of the ICDE Conference,* Houston, TX (pp. 462-473). Washington, DC: IEEE Computer Society.

Georgakopoulos, D., Hornick, M. F., & Manola, F. (1996). Customizing transaction models and mechanisms in a programmable environment supporting reliable workflow automation. *IEEE Transactions on Knowledge and Data Engineering*, *8*(4), 630–649. doi:10.1109/69.536255

Georgakopoulos, D., Hornick, M. F., & Sheth, A. P. (1995). An overview of workflow management: From process modeling to workflow automation infrastructure. *Distributed and Parallel Databases*, *3*(2), 119–153. doi:10.1007/BF01277643

Gerard, G. J. (2005). The REA Pattern, Knowledge Structures and Conceptual Modeling Performance. *Journal of Information Systems*, *19*(1), 57–77. doi:10.2308/jis.2005.19.2.57

Gibson, D. S., Weide, B. W., Pike, S. M., & Edwards, S. H. (2000). Toward a normative theory for component-based system design and analysis. In Leavens, G. T., & Sitaraman, M. (Eds.), *Foundations of component-based systems* (pp. 211–230). Cambridge, UK: Cambridge University Press.

Gillenson, M. L. (1982). The state of practice of data administration - 1981. *Communications of the ACM*, *25*(10), 699–706. doi:10.1145/358656.358664

Gillenson, M. L. (1985). Trends in data administration. *Management Information Systems Quarterly*, *9*(4), 317–325. doi:10.2307/249232

Gillenson, M. L. (1991). Database administration at the crossroads: The era of end-user oriented, decentralized data processing. *Journal of Database Administration*, *2*(4), 1–11.

Gioldasis, N., & Christodoulakis, S. (2002). UTML: Unified transaction modeling language. In *Proceedings of the 3rd International Conference on Web Information Systems Engineering* (pp. 115-126). Washington, DC: IEEE Computer Society.

Giorgini, P., Rizzi, S., & Garzetti, M. (2005). GRAnD: A goal-oriented approach to requirement analysis in data warehouses. *Decision Support Systems*, *45*(1), 4–21. doi:10.1016/j.dss.2006.12.001

Golfarelli, M., Maio, D., & Rizzi, S. (1998). The Dimensional Fact Model: A Conceptual Model for Data Warehouses. *International Journal of Cooperative Information Systems*, *7*(2-3), 215–247. doi:10.1142/S0218843098000118

Golub, G., & Van Loan, C. F. (1989). *Matrix Computations*. Baltimore, MD: Johns Hopkins University Press.

Gonnet, G. H., & Baeza-Yates, R. (1991). *Lexicographical indices for text: Inverted files vs. pat trees*. Waterloo, ON, Canada: University of Waterloo.

Gonnet, G. H., & Tompa, F. W. (1987). Mind your grammar: a new approach to modeling text. In *Proceedings of the 13th International Conference on Very Large Data Bases*, Brighton, UK (pp. 339-346).

Gonzalez-Perez, C. (2007). Supporting situational method engineering with ISO/IEC 24744 and the work product pool approach. In *Proceedings on Situational Method Engineering: Fundamentals and Experiences* (pp. 7-18).

Goodhue, D. L., Kirsch, L. J., Quillard, J. A., & Wybo, M. D. (1992). Strategic data planning: Lessons from the field. *Management Information Systems Quarterly*, *16*(1), 11–34. doi:10.2307/249699

Goodhue, D. L., Quillard, J. A., & Rockart, J. F. (1988). Managing the data resource: A contingency perspective. *Management Information Systems Quarterly*, *12*(3), 373–392. doi:10.2307/249204

Goodhue, D. L., & Thompson, R. L. (1995). Task-Technology Fit and Individual-Performance. *Management Information Systems Quarterly*, *19*(2), 213–236. doi:10.2307/249689

Gotthelf, P., Zunino, A., & Campo, M. A. (2008). Peer-To-Peer communication infrastructure for groupware applications. *International Journal of Cooperative Information Systems, 17*(4), 523–554. doi:10.1142/S0218843008001920

Grabski, S. V., Reneau, J. H., & West, S. G. (1987). A comparison of judgment, skills, and prompting effects between auditors and systems analysts. *Management Information Systems Quarterly, 11*(2), 151–162. doi:10.2307/249356

Grangard, A., Eisenberg, B., & Nickull, D. (2001). *ebXML technical architecture specification v1.0.4.* Retrieved from http://www.ebxml.org/specs/ebTA.pdf

Graves, A., Adali, S., & Hendler, J. (2008). A method to rank nodes in an RDF graph. In *Proceedings of the 7th International Semantic Web Conference (ISWC2008)* (Vol. 401). CEUR-WS.

Grewal, R., Lilien, G. L., & Mallapragada, G. (2006). Location, location, location: How network embeddedness affects project success in open source systems. *Management Science, 52*(7), 1043–1056. doi:10.1287/mnsc.1060.0550

Groise, E., & Mangin, N. (2007). Octopus: Agile software development facing our imperfect world. In *Proceedings of the IEEE AGILE Conference* (pp. 344-350).

Grossman, M., Aronson, J. E., & McCarthy, R. V. (2005). Does UML make the grade? Insights from the software development community. *Information and Software Technology, 47*(6), 383–397. doi:10.1016/j.infsof.2004.09.005

Gruber, T. R. (1993). A Translation Approach to Portable Ontology Specifications. *Knowledge Acquisition, 5*, 199–220. doi:10.1006/knac.1993.1008

Gudgin, M., Hadley, M., Mendelsohn, N., Moreau, J., Nielsen, H. F., Karmakar, A., & Lafon, Y. (2007). *SOAP version 1.2 part 1: Messaging framework* (2nd ed.). Retrieved from http://www.w3.org/TR/soap12-part1/

Guinan, P. J., Cooprider, J. G., & Faraj, S. (1998). Enabling software development team performance during requirements definition: A behavioral versus technical approach. *Information Systems Research, 9*(2), 101–125. doi:10.1287/isre.9.2.101

Gulati, R. (1995). Does familiarity breed trust? The implications of repeated ties for contractual choice in alliances. *Academy of Management Journal, 38*(1), 85–112. doi:10.2307/256729

Haddad, J. E., Manouvrier, M., & Rukoz, M. (2007). A hierarchical model for transactional web service composition in p2p networks. In *Proceedings of the ICWS Conference* (pp. 346-353). Washington, DC: IEEE Computer Society.

Hagan, D., Watson, O., & Barron, K. (2007). Ascending into order: A reflective analysis from a small open source development team. *International Journal of Information Management, 27*(6), 397–405. doi:10.1016/j.ijinfomgt.2007.08.011

Hagen, C., & Alonso, G. (2000). Exception handling in workflow management systems. *IEEE Transactions on Software Engineering, 26*(10), 943–958. doi:10.1109/32.879818

Halaschek, C., Aleman-Meza, B., Arpinar, I. B., & Sheth, A. (2004). Discovering and ranking semantic associations over a large RDF metabase. In *Proceedings of the 30th VLDB Conference,* Toronto, ON, Canada (pp. 1317-1320). VLDB Endowment.

Hardgrave, B. C., & Dalal, N. P. (1995). Comparing object oriented and extended entity relational data model. *Journal of Database Management, 6*(3), 15–21.

Harmsen, F., Lubbers, I., & Wijers, G. (1995). Success-driven selection of fragments for situational methods: The S3 model. In *Proceedings of the 2nd International Workshop on Requirements Engineering: Foundations of Software Quality* (pp. 104-115).

Hars, A., & Ou, S. (2002). Working for free? Motivations for participation in open source projects. *International Journal of Electronic Commerce, 6*(3), 25–39.

Hauck, F. J., Kapitza, R., Reiser, H. P., & Schmied, A. I. (2005). A flexible and extensible object middleware: Corba and beyond. In *SEM '05: Proceedings of the 5th International Workshop on Software Engineering and Middleware* (pp. 69–75). New York: ACM.

Haugen, R., & McCarthy, W. E. (2000). *REA, a semantic model for Internet supply chain collaboration.* Retrieved from https://www.msu.edu/user/mccarth4/paplist1.html

Haveliwala, T. H. (1999). *Efficient Computation of PageRank (Tech. Rep.)*. Stanford, CA: Stanford University.

Hee, K., Oanea, O., Serebrenik, A., Sidorova, N., & Voorhoeve, M. (2008). History-based joins: Semantics, soundness and implementation. *Data & Knowledge Engineering, 64*, 24–37. doi:10.1016/j.datak.2007.06.005

Heeager, L. T., & Nielsen, P. A. (2009). *Agile software development and its compatibility with a document-driven approach? A case study.* Paper presented at the Australasian Conference on Information Systems.

Henderson, J. C., & Lee, S. (1992). Managing IS design teams: A control theories perspective. *Management Science, 38*(6), 757–777. doi:10.1287/mnsc.38.6.757

Henderson-Sellers, B., & Ralyté, J. (2010). Situational method engineering: State-of-the-art review. *Journal of Universal Computer Science, 16*(3), 424–478.

Henderson-Sellers, B., & Serour, M. K. (2005). Creating a dual-agility method: The value of method engineering. *Journal of Database Management, 16*(4), 1–24. doi:10.4018/jdm.2005100101

Hertel, G., Niednerand, S., & Herrmann, S. (2003). Motivations of software developers in open source projects: an internet-based survey of contributors to the Linux kernel. *Research Policy, 32*(7), 1159–1177. doi:10.1016/S0048-7333(03)00047-7

Hevner, A. R., March, S. T., Park, J., & Ram, S. (2004). Design science in information system research. *Management Information Systems Quarterly, 28*(1), 75–105.

Highsmith, J. A. III. (1999). *Adaptive software development: A collaborative approach to managing complex systems*. New York, NY: Dorset House.

Hilkka, M.-R., Tuure, T., & Matti, R. (2005). Is extreme programming just old wine in new bottles: a comparison of two cases. *Journal of Database Management, 16*(4), 41–61. doi:10.4018/jdm.2005100103

Hirst, G., & St-Onge, D. (1998). Lexical chains as representations of context for the detection and correction of malapropisms. In Fellbaum, C. (Ed.), *WordNet: An electronic lexical database* (pp. 305–323). Cambridge, MA: MIT Press.

Hoffer, J. A., Venkataraman, R., & Topi, H. (2010). *Modern Database Management* (10th ed.). Upper Saddle River, NJ: Prentice Hall.

Hofstede, G., & Hofstede, G. J. (2005). *Cultures and organizations: Software for the mind.* New York, NY: McGraw-Hill.

Holland, J. H. (1992). Complex adaptive systems. *Daedalus, 121*(1), 17–30.

Hollingsworth, D. (1995). *Workflow Management Coalition: The Workflow Reference Model.* Retrieved from http://www.wfmc.org/standards/docs/tc003v11.pdf

Horner, J., Song, I. Y., & Chen, P. P. (2004, November 12-13). An analysis of additivity in OLAP systems. In *Proceedings of the ACM Seventh International Workshop on Data Warehousing and OLAP,* Washington, DC (pp. 83-91).

Hruby, P., Kiehn, J., & Scheller, C. V. (2006). *Model-Driven Design Using Business Patterns*. New York: Springer.

Huh, S., Moon, K., & Park, J. (2010). An integrated query relaxation approach adopting data abstraction and fuzzy relation. *Journal of Database Management, 21*(4), 35–59. doi:10.4018/jdm.2010100103

Huhns, M. N., & Singh, M. P. (2005). Service-Oriented Computing: Key Concepts and Principles. *IEEE Internet Computing, 9*(1), 75–81. doi:10.1109/MIC.2005.21

Hull, R., Benedikt, M., Christophides, V., & Su, J. (2003). E-Services: A Look Behind the Curtain. In *Proceedings of the 22nd ACM Symposium on Principles of Database Systems (PODS) 2003*, San Diego, CA.

Hull, R., & Su, J. (2005). Tools for Composite Web Services: A Short Overview. *SIGMOD Record, 34*(2), 86–95. doi:10.1145/1083784.1083807

Hung, P. C. K., & Chiu, D. K. W. (2004). Developing workflow-based information integration (WII) with exception support in a web services environment. In *Proceedings of the 37th Annual Hawaii International Conference on System Sciences (HICSS 2004),* Big Island, HI. Washington, DC: IEEE Computer Society.

Hunter, J. E., Schmidt, F. L., & Jackson, F. B. (1990). *Meta-Analysis: Cumulating Research Finding Across Studies*. Thousand Oaks, CA: Sage.

Hurtado, C. A., Mendelzon, A. O., & Vaisman, A. A. (1999, November 6). Updating OLAP Dimensions. In *Proceedings of the ACM Second International Workshop on Data Warehousing and OLAP,* Kansas City, MO (pp. 60-66).

Hurtado, C. A., Poulovassilis, A., & Wood, P. T. (2009). Ranking Approximate Answers to Semantic Web Queries. In *Proceedings of the 6th European Semantic Web Conference* (pp. 263-277). Berlin: Springer-Verlag.

Hüsemann, B., Lechtenbörger, J., & Vossen, G. (2000). Conceptual Data Warehouse Modeling. In *Proceedings of the 2nd International Workshop on Design and Management of Data Warehouses (DMDW'00),* Stockholm, Sweden (pp. 6.1-6.11).

IBM. (2007). *Business Process Execution Language for Web Services version 1.1.* Retrieved from http://www-106.ibm.com/developerworks/library/ws-bpel/

Inmon, W. H. (2005). *Building the Data Warehouse.* New York: Wiley.

International Organization for Standardization. (1998). *ISO/IEC 9126: Information Technology - Software product quality.* Geneva, Switzerland: International Organization for Standardization.

International Organization for Standardization (ISO). (2007). *ISO/IEC 24744: Software engineering – Metamodel for development methodologies.* Retrieved from http://www.iso.org/iso/catalogue_detail.htm?csnumber=38854

Irwin, G. (2002). The Role of Similarity in the Reuse of Object-Oriented Analysis Models. *Journal of Management Information Systems, 19*(2), 219–248.

Jaakkola, J., & Kilpelainen, P. (1996). *The Sgrep online manual.* Retrieved from http://www.cs.helsinki.fi/u/jjaakkol/sgrepman.html

Jablonski, S., & Bussler, C. (1996). *Workflow Management: Modeling Concepts, Architecture, and Implementation.* Itp New Media.

Jacques, E. (1996). In praise of hierarchy. In Shafritz, J. M., & Ott, J. S. (Eds.), *Classics of organizational theory* (pp. 245–253). Orlando, FL: Harcourt Brace.

Jaeschke, G., & Schek, H. (1982). Remarks on the algebra on non first normal form relations. In *Proceedings of the ACM SIGACT-SIGMOD Symposium on Principles of Database Systems,* Los Angeles, CA (pp. 124-138).

Jagadish, H. V., Al-Khalifa, S., Chapman, A., Lakshmanan, L. V. S., Nierman, A., & Paparizos, S. (2002). TIMBER: A native XML database. *Very Large Data Base Journal, 11*(4), 274–291. doi:10.1007/s00778-002-0081-x

Jagadish, H. V., Lakshmanan, L. V. S., Srivastava, D., & Thompson, K. (2001). TAX: A tree algebra for XML. In G. Ghelli & G. Grahne (Eds.), *Proceedings of the 8th International Workshop on Database Programming Languages* (LNCS 2397, pp. 149-164).

Jain, N. (2006). Offshore agile maintenance. In *Proceedings of the IEEE AGILE Conference,* Minneapolis, MN.

James, L., Demaree, R., & Wolf, G. (1984). Estimating within-group interrater reliability with and without response bias. *The Journal of Applied Psychology, 69*(1), 85–98. doi:10.1037/0021-9010.69.1.85

Jarke, M., Jeusfeld, M. A., Quix, C., & Vassiliadis, P. (1999). Architecture and Quality in Data Warehouses: An Extended Repository Approach. *Information Systems, 24*(3), 229–253. doi:10.1016/S0306-4379(99)00017-4

Jarvenpaa, S. L., & Machesky, J. J. (1986). End user learning behavior in data analysis and data modeling tools. In *Proceedings of the 7th International Conference on Information Systems* (pp. 152-167).

Jarvenpaa, S. L., & Machesky, J. J. (1989). Data analysis and learning: An experimental study of data modeling tools. *International Journal of Human-Computer Studies, 31*(4), 367–391.

Jaworski, B. J. (1988). Toward a theory of marketing control: Environmental context, control types, and consequences. *Journal of Marketing, 52*(3), 23–39. doi:10.2307/1251447

Jaworski, B. J., & MacInnis, D. J. (1989). Marketing jobs and management controls: Toward a framework. *JMR, Journal of Marketing Research, 26*(4), 406–419. doi:10.2307/3172761

Jaworski, B. J., Stathakopoulos, V., & Krishnan, H. S. (1993). Control combinations in marketing: Conceptual framework and empirical evidence. *Journal of Marketing, 57,* 57–69. doi:10.2307/1252057

Jenkins, A. M. (1982). *MIS Decision Variables and Decision Making Performance.* Ann Arbor, MI: UI Research Press.

Jensen, M. C., & Meckling, W. H. (1976). Theory of the firm: Managerial behavior, agency costs and ownership structure. *Journal of Financial Economics*, *3*(4), 305–360. doi:10.1016/0304-405X(76)90026-X

Jih, K., Bradbard, D., Snyder, C., & Thompson, N. (1989). The effects of relational and entity-relational models on query performance of end users. *International Journal of Man-Machine Studies*, *31*(3), 257–267. doi:10.1016/0020-7373(89)90007-2

Jones, M. E., & Song, I. Y. (2008). Dimensional modeling: Identification, classification, and evaluation of patterns. *Decision Support Systems*, *45*(1), 59–76. doi:10.1016/j.dss.2006.12.004

Jones, R. A., Tsay, J. E., & Griggs, K. (2005). An Empirical Investigation of the Task Specific Relative Strengths of Selected Accounting and Information Systems Diagramming Techniques. *Journal of Computer Information Systems*, *46*, 99–114.

Jordan, D., Evdemon, J., Alves, A., Arkin, A., Askary, S., Bareto, C., et al. (2007). *Business process execution language for web services version 2.0*. Retrieved from http://docs.oasis-open.org/wsbpel/2.0/OS/wsbpel-v2.0-OS.pdf

Jørgensen, M., & Shepperd, M. J. (2007). A systematic review of software development cost estimation studies. *IEEE Transactions on Software Engineering*, *33*(1), 33–53. doi:10.1109/TSE.2007.256943

Juhn, S., & Naumann, J. (1985). The effectiveness of data representation characteristics on user validation. In *Proceedings of the 6th International Conference on Information Systems* (pp. 212-226).

Jukic, N. (2006). Modeling Strategies and Alternatives for Data Warehousing Projects. *Communications of the ACM*, *49*(4), 83–88. doi:10.1145/1121949.1121952

Jürjens, J. (2002, October). UMLsec: Extending UML for secure systems development. In *Proceedings of the ACM/IEEE International Conference on Unified Modeling Language*.

Kafeza, E., Chiu, D. K. W., Cheung, S. C., & Kafeza, M. (2004). Alerts in mobile healthcare applications: requirements and pilot study. *IEEE Transactions on Information Technology in Biomedicine*, *8*(2), 173–181. doi:10.1109/TITB.2004.828888

Kahkonen, T. (2004). Agile methods for large organisations - Building communities of practice. In *Proceedings of the AGILE Development Conference*, Salt Lake City, UT.

Kahn, B. K. (1983). Some realities of data administration. *Communications of the ACM*, *26*(10), 794–799. doi:10.1145/358413.358431

Kambayashi, Y., & Peng, Z. (1996). An Object Deputy Model for Realization of Flexible and Powerful Objectbases. *Journal of Systems Integration*, *6*, 329–362. doi:10.1007/BF02265083

Kang, K., Kim, S., Lee, J., & Lee, K. (1999, December). Feature-oriented engineering of pbx software. In *Proceedings of the Asia-Pacific Software Engineering Conference*.

Karlsson, F., & Ågerfalk, P. J. (2009). Towards structured flexibility in information systems development: Devising a method for method configuration. *Journal of Database Management*, *20*(3), 51–75. doi:10.4018/jdm.2009070103

Kaul, D., Kogekar, A., Gokhale, A., Gray, J., & Gokhale, S. (2007, January). Posaml: A visual modeling framework for middleware provisioning. In *Proceedings of the Hawaiian International Conference on System Sciences*.

Kavantzas, N., Burdett, D., Ritzinger, G., & Lafon, Y. (2004). *Web services choreography description language version 1.0*. Retrieved from http://www.w3.org/TR/ws-cdl-10

Kawamura, T., Hasegawa, T., Ohsuga, A., Paolucci, M., & Sycara, K. (2005). Web Services lookup: A matchmaker experiment. *IT Professional*, *7*(2), 36–41. doi:10.1109/MITP.2005.45

Kelley, J. E. (1961). Critical-path planning and scheduling: Mathematical basis. *Operations Research*, *9*(3), 296–320. doi:10.1287/opre.9.3.296

Khatri, V., & Brown, C. V. (2010). Designing data governance. *Communications of the ACM*, *53*(1), 148–152. doi:10.1145/1629175.1629210

Khatri, V., Vessey, I., Ramesh, V., Clay, P., & Park, S.-J. (2006). Understanding Conceptual Schemas: Exploring the Role of Application and IS Domain Knowledge. *Information Systems Research*, *17*, 81–99. doi:10.1287/isre.1060.0081

Kiczales, G., Lamping, J., Mendhekar, A., Maeda, C., Lopes, C., Loingtier, J. M., et al. (1997, June). Aspect-oriented programming. In *Proceedings of the European Conference on Object-Oriented Programming*.

Kim, Y. G., & March, S. T. (1995). Comparing Data Modeling Formalisms. *Communications of the ACM, 38*(6), 103–115. doi:10.1145/203241.203265

Kimball, R. (2003). *The Soul of the Data Warehouse, Part Two: Drilling Across*. Intelligent Enterprise Magazine.

Kimball, R., & Ross, M. (2002). *The Data Warehouse Toolkit: The Complete Guide to Dimensional Modeling*. New York: Wiley.

Kindler, E. (2004). On the semantics of EPCs: A framework for resolving the vicious circle. In J. Desel, B. Pernici, & M. Weske (Eds.), *Proceedings of the 2nd International Conference on Business Process Management* (LNCS 3080, pp. 82-97).

Kindler, E. (2006). On the semantics of EPCs: Resolving the vicious circle. *Data & Knowledge Engineering, 56*, 23–40. doi:10.1016/j.datak.2005.02.005

King, W. R., & He, J. (2005). Understanding the Role and Methods of Meta-Analysis in IS Research. *Communications of the Association for Information Systems, 16*, 32. Retrieved from http://aisel.aisnet.org/cais/vol16/iss1/32.

Kirsch, L. J. (1996). The management of complex tasks in organizations: controlling the systems development process. *Organization Science, 7*(1), 1–21. doi:10.1287/orsc.7.1.1

Kirsch, L. J. (1997). Portfolios of control modes and IS project management. *Information Systems Research, 8*(3), 215–239. doi:10.1287/isre.8.3.215

Kirsch, L. J. (2004). Deploying Common Systems Globally: The Dynamics of Control. *Information Systems Research, 15*(4), 374–395. doi:10.1287/isre.1040.0036

Kirsch, L. J., Sambamurthy, V., Ko, D., & Purvis, R. L. (2002). Controlling information systems development projects: The view from the client. *Management Science, 48*(4), 484–498. doi:10.1287/mnsc.48.4.484.204

Kitchenham, B. (2004). *Procedures for performing systematic reviews* (Tech. Rep. No. TR/SE-0401). Staffordshire, UK: Keele University.

Kitchenham, B., & Charters, S. (2007). *Guidelines for performing systematic literature reviews in software engineering*. Staffordshire, UK: Keele University.

Kiwata, K., Nakano, A., Yura, S., Uchihashi, T., & Kanai, A. (2007). Scenario-based service composition method in the open service environment. In *Proceedings of the 5th International Symposium on Autonomous Decentralized Systems* (pp. 135-140). Washington, DC: IEEE Computer Society.

Kleinberg, J. (1999). Authoritative sources in a hyperlinked environment. *Journal of the ACM, 46*(5), 604–632. doi:10.1145/324133.324140

Klyne, G., & Carroll, J. (Eds.). (2004). *Resource description framework (RDF): Concepts and abstract syntax*. Retrieved October 15, 2008, from http://www.w3.org/TR/rdf-concepts/

Kokash, N. (2006, August 28-29). A comparison of Web Service interface similarity measures. In *Proceedings of the 3rd European Starting AI Researcher Symposium*, Riva del Garda, Italy (pp. 220–231). IOS Press.

Kokash, N., van den Heuvel, W.-J., & D'Andrea, V. (2006, December 4-7). Leveraging Web Services discovery with customizable hybrid matching. In *Proceedings of the International Conference on Service-Oriented Computing*, Chicago (LNCS 4294, pp. 522–528).

Korfhage, R. R. (1997). *Information Storage and Retrieval*. New York: John Wiley & Sons.

Korkala, M., & Abrahamsson, P. (2007). Communication in distributed agile development: A case study. In *Proceedings of the 33rd EUROMICRO Conference on Software Engineering and Advanced Applications* (pp. 203-210).

Kornyshova, E., Deneckere, R., & Salinesi, C. (2007). Method chunks selection by multicriteria techniques: an extension of the assembly-based approach. In *Proceedings of the IFIP WG 8.1 Working Conference on Situational Method Engineering: Fundamentals and Experiences* (Vol. 244, pp. 64-78).

Kozlenkov, A., Spanoudakis, G., Zisman, A., Fasoulas, V., & Sanchez Cid, F. (2007). Architecture-driven service discovery for service centric systems. *International Journal of Web Services Research, 4*(2), 82–113.

Krogh, G., Spaeth, S., & Lakhani, K. R. (2003). Community, joining, and specialization in open source software innovation: a case study. *Research Policy, 32*(7), 1217–1241. doi:10.1016/S0048-7333(03)00050-7

Krogstie, J. (1998). Integrating the understanding of quality in requirements specification and conceptual modeling. *ACM SIGSOFT Software Engineering Notes, 23*(1), 86–91. doi:10.1145/272263.272285

Kruchten, P. (2000). *The rational unified process: An introduction* (2nd ed.). Reading, MA: Addison-Wesley.

Kumar, K., & Welke, R. J. (1992). Method engineering – A proposal for situation-specific methodology construction. In Cotterman, W. W., & Senn, J. A. (Eds.), *Challenges and strategies for research in systems development* (pp. 257–268). New York, NY: John Wiley & Sons.

Lai, A., & Murphy, G. C. (1999). *The Structure of Features in Java Code: An exploratory investigation.* Paper presented at the 1st International Workshop on Multi-dimensional Separation of Concerns (OOPSLA'99), Denver, CO.

Larkin, J. H., & Simon, H. A. (1987). Why a diagram is (sometimes) worth ten thousand words. *Cognitive Science, 11*, 65–99. doi:10.1111/j.1551-6708.1987.tb00863.x

Larman, C. (1997). *Applying UML and Patterns.* Upper Saddle River, NJ: Prentice-Hall.

Larman, C. (2003). *Agile and iterative development: A manager's guide.* Reading, MA: Addison-Wesley.

Lawrence, S., & Giles, C. L. (1998). Searching the World Wide Web. *Science, 280*, 98–100. doi:10.1126/science.280.5360.98

Lawrence, S., & Giles, C. L. (1999). Accessibility of information on the Web. *Nature, 400*, 107–109. doi:10.1038/21987

Layman, L., Williams, L., Damian, D., & Bures, H. (2006). Essential communication practices for Extreme Programming in a global software development team. *Information and Software Technology, 48*(9), 781–794. doi:10.1016/j.infsof.2006.01.004

Lee, G., & Xia, W. (2010). Toward agile: An integrated analysis of quantitative and qualitative field data. *Management Information Systems Quarterly, 34*(1), 87–114.

Lee, G. K., & Cole, R. E. (2003). From a firm-based to a community-based model of knowledge creation: the case of the Linux kernel development. *Organization Science, 14*(6), 633–649. doi:10.1287/orsc.14.6.633.24866

Lee, K.-H., Lee, M.-Y., Hwang, Y.-Y., & Lee, K.-C. (2007, April 26-28). A framework for XML Web Services retrieval with ranking. In *Proceedings of the International Conference on Multimedia and Ubiquitous Engineering*, Seoul, Korea (pp. 773–778). Washington, DC: IEEE Computer Society.

Leite, J. C. S. P., Cappelli, C., Batista, T., & Silva, L. (2009, March). An aspect-oriented approach to business process modeling. In *Proceedings of the ACM International Conference on Aspect-Oriented Software Development, Workshop on Early Aspects.*

Leitheiser, R. L., & March, S. T. (1996). The influence of database structure representation on database system learning and use. *Journal of Management Information Systems, 12*(4), 187–213.

Lerner, J., & Tirole, J. (2002). Some Simple Economics of Open Source. *The Journal of Industrial Economics, 5*, 197–234.

Lertnattee, V., & Theeramunkong, T. (2004). Effect of term distributions on centroid-based text categorization. *Information Sciences, 158*, 89–115. doi:10.1016/j.ins.2003.07.007

Levene, M., & Loizou, G. (1993). Semantics for null extended nested relations. *ACM Transactions on Database Systems, 18*(3), 415–459. doi:10.1145/155271.155275

Leymann, F., & Roller, D. (1999). *Production workflow: Concepts and techniques.* Upper Saddle River, NJ: Prentice Hall PTR.

Li, G., Li, C., Feng, J., & Zhou, L. (2009). SAIL: Structure-aware indexing for effective and progressive top-k keyword search over XML documents. *Information Sciences, 179*(21), 3745–3762. doi:10.1016/j.ins.2009.06.025

Li, J., Liu, C., Yu, J., & Zhou, R. (2009). Efficient top-k search across heterogeneous XML data sources. In *Proceedings of the 13th International Conference on Database Systems for Advanced Applications*, Brisbane, Australia (pp. 314-329).

Li, K., Verma, K., Mulye, R., Rabbani, R., Miller, J., & Sheth, A. P. (2006). Designing semantic web processes: The WSDL-S approach. In *Semantic Web Services* (pp. 161–193). Processes and Applications.

Li, S.-H., Huang, S.-M., Yen, D. C., & Chang, C.-C. (2007). Migrating legacy information systems to Web Services architecture. *Journal of Database Management, 18*(4), 1–25.

Li, X., Madnick, S., Zhu, H., & Fan, Y. (2009). An Approach to Composing Web Services with Context Heterogeneity. In *Proceedings of the IEEE International Conference on Web Services* (pp. 695-702). Washington, DC: IEEE Computer Society.

Li, Y., Bandar, A., & McLean, D. (2003). An approach for measuring semantic similarity between words using multiple information sources. *IEEE Transactions on Knowledge and Data Engineering, 15*(4), 871–882. doi:10.1109/TKDE.2003.1209005

Liao, C., & Palvia, P. C. (2000). The impact of data models and task complexity on end-user performance: An experimental investigation. *International Journal of Human-Computer Studies, 52*(5), 831–845. doi:10.1006/ijhc.1999.0358

Limthanmaphon, B., & Zhang, Y. (2004). Web service composition transaction management. In *Proceedings of the 15th Australasian Database Conference* (pp. 171-179).

Lin, D. (1998). An information-theoretic definition of similarity. In *Proceedings of the Conference on Machine Learning* (pp. 296-304).

Lin, Z., Xu, B., & Xu, Y. (2011). A study of open source software development from control perspective. *Journal of Database Management, 22*(1), 26–42. doi:10.4018/jdm.2011010102

Lindland, O. I., Sindre, G., & Solvberg, A. (1994). Understanding quality in conceptual modeling. *IEEE Software, 11*(2), 42–49. doi:10.1109/52.268955

Lindvall, M., Basili, V., Boehm, B., Costa, P., Dangle, K., Shull, F., et al. (2002). *Empirical findings in agile methods.* Paper presented at the Second XP Universe and First Agile Universe Conference, Chicago, IL.

Lindvall, M., Muthig, D., Dagnino, A., Wallin, C., Stupperich, M., & Kiefer, D. (2004). Agile software development in large organizations. *Computer, 37*(12), 26–34. doi:10.1109/MC.2004.231

Little, M. (2007). Ws-caf: Contexts, coordination and transactions for web services. In R. Meersman & Z. Tari (Eds.), *On the Move to Meaningful Internet Systems 2007: CoopIS, DOA, ODBASE, GADA, and IS Conferences* (LNCS 4803, pp. 439-453).

Liu, A., Liu, H., Lin, B., Huang, L., Gu, N., & Li, Q. (2010). A Survey of Web Services Provision. *International Journal of Systems and Service-Oriented Engineering, 1*(1), 26–45. doi:10.4018/jssoe.2010092102

Liu, D.-R., & Shen, M. (2003). Workflow modeling for virtual processes: an order-preserving process-view approach. *Information Systems, 28*(6), 505–532. doi:10.1016/S0306-4379(02)00028-5

Liu, J., Dehlinger, J., & Lutz, R. (2007). Safety analysis of software product lines using state-based modeling. *Journal of Systems and Software, 80*(11), 1879–1892. doi:10.1016/j.jss.2007.01.047

Ljungberg, J. (2000). Open source movements as a model for organizing. *European Journal of Information Systems, 9*, 208–216. doi:10.1057/palgrave/ejis/3000373

Lodderstedt, T., Basin, D., & Doser, J. (2002, October). Secureuml: A UML-based modeling language for model-driven security. In *Proceedings of the ACM/IEEE International Conference on Unified Modeling Language.*

Lohmann, D., Scheler, F., Preikschat, W. S., & Spinczyk, O. (2006, July). Pure embedded operating systems - ciao. In *Proceedings of the IEEE International Workshop on Operating System Platforms for Embedded Real-Time Applications.*

Lohmann, N., Massuthe, P., Stahl, C., & Weinberg, D. (2008). Analyzing interacting WS-BPEL processes using flexible model generation. *Data & Knowledge Engineering, 64*, 38–54. doi:10.1016/j.datak.2007.06.006

Long, Y., & Siau, K. (2007). Social network structures in open source software development teams. *Journal of Database Management, 18*(2), 25–40.

Lucas, F. J., Molina, F., & Toval, A. (2009). A systematic review of UML model consistency management. *Information and Software Technology*, *51*(12), 1631–1645. doi:10.1016/j.infsof.2009.04.009

Luján-Mora, S., & Trujillo, J. (2006). Applying the UML and the Unified Process to the design of Data Warehouses. *Journal of Computer Information Systems*, *17*(2), 12–42.

Luján-Mora, S., & Trujillo, J. (2006). Physical modeling of data warehouses using uml component and deployment diagrams: Design and implementation issues. *Journal of Database Management*, *17*(2), 12–42.

Luján-Mora, S., Trujillo, J., & Song, I. Y. (2006). A UML profile for multidimensional modeling in data warehouses. *Data & Knowledge Engineering*, *59*(3), 725–769. doi:10.1016/j.datak.2005.11.004

Lyytinen, K., & Rose, G. M. (2006). Information system development agility as organizational learning. *European Journal of Information Systems*, *15*, 181–199. doi:10.1057/palgrave.ejis.3000604

Maedche, A., & Staab, S. (2002). Measuring similarity between ontologies. In *Proceedings of the European Conference of Knowledge Acquisition and Management (EKAW2002),* Madrid, Spain (LNCS 2473, pp. 15-21).

Maedche, A., Staab, S., Stojanovic, N., Studer, R., & Sure, Y. (2001). SEAL-A Framework for Developing SEmantic Web PortALs. In *Advances in Databases* (LNCS 2097, pp. 1-22).

Maes, A., & Poels, G. (2007). Evaluating Quality of Conceptual Modelling Scripts Based on User Perceptions. *Data & Knowledge Engineering*, *63*(3), 701–724. doi:10.1016/j.datak.2007.04.008

Mahmood, M. A. (1987). System development methods – A comparative investigation. *Management Information Systems Quarterly*, *11*(3), 292–311. doi:10.2307/248674

Makris, C., Panagis, Y., Sakkopoulos, E., & Tsakalidis, A. (2006). Efficient and adaptive discovery techniques of Web Services handling large data sets. *Journal of Systems and Software*, *79*(4), 480–495. doi:10.1016/j.jss.2005.06.002

Malcolm, D. G., Roseboom, J. H., Clark, C. E., & Fazar, W. (1959). Application of a technique for research and development program evaluation. *Operations Research*, *7*(5), 646–669. doi:10.1287/opre.7.5.646

Malinowski, E., & Zimányi, E. (2006). Hierarchies in a multidimensional model: From conceptual modeling to logical representation. *Data & Knowledge Engineering*, *59*(2), 348–377. doi:10.1016/j.datak.2005.08.003

Manola, F., & Miller, E. (Eds.). (2004). *RDF primer.* Retrieved October 15, 2008, from http://www.w3.org/TR/rdf-primer/

Manz, C. C., Mossholder, K. W., & Luthans, F. (1987). An integrated perspective of self-control in organizations. *Administration & Society*, *19*(1). doi:10.1177/009539978701900101

Marchiori, M. (1997). The quest for correct information on the Web: Hyper Search Engines. In *Proceedings of the 6th International WWW Conference,* Santa Clara, CA (pp. 1225-1235). Amsterdam, The Netherlands: Elsevier Science Publishers Ltd.

Markus, M. L., Manville, B., & Agres, C. E. (2000). What makes a virtual organization work? *Sloan Management Review*, *42*(1), 13–26.

Martin, D. (2004). *Owl-s: Semantic markup for web services.* Retrieved from http://www.w3.org/Submission/OWL-S/

Martin, D., Burstein, M., Mcdermott, D., Mcilraith, S., Paolucci, M., & Sycara, K. (2007). Bringing semantics to Web Services with owl-s. *World Wide Web (Bussum)*, *10*(3), 243–277. doi:10.1007/s11280-007-0033-x

Maruping, L. M., Venkatesh, V., & Agarwal, R. (2009). A control theory perspective on agile methodology use and changing user requirements. *Information Systems Research*, *20*(3), 377–399. doi:10.1287/isre.1090.0238

Matulevicius, R., & Heymans, P. (2007). Comparing goal modelling languages: An experiment. In *Proceedings of the Conference on Requirements Engineering: Foundation for Software Quality* (pp. 18-32).

Matulevicius, R., Heymans, P., & Sindre, G. (2006). Comparing goal-modelling tools with the re-tool evaluation approach. *Information Technology and Control*, *35*(3A), 276–284.

Mazón, J. N., Pardillo, J., & Trujillo, J. (2006, September 4-8). Applying Transformations to Model Driven Data Warehouses. In *Proceedings of the 8th International Conference on Data Warehousing and Knowledge Discovery*, Krakow, Poland (LNCS 4081, pp. 13-22).

Mazón, J. N., Pardillo, J., & Trujillo, J. (2007, November 5-9). A Model-Driven Goal-Oriented Requirement Engineering Approach for Data Warehouses. In *Proceedings of the International Workshop on Requirements, Intentions and Goals in Conceptual Modelling*, Auckland, New Zealand (LNCS 4802, pp. 255-264).

Mazón, J. N., & Trujillo, J. (2007, November 5-9). A Model Driven Modernization Approach for Automatically Deriving Multidimensional Models in Data Warehouses. In *Proceedings of the 26th International Conference on Conceptual Modeling (ER 2007)*, Auckland, New Zealand (LNCS 4801, pp. 56-71).

Mazón, J. N., & Trujillo, J. (2008). An MDA approach for the development of data warehouses. *Decision Support Systems*, *45*(1), 41–58. doi:10.1016/j.dss.2006.12.003

Mazón, J.-N., & Trujillo, J. (2009). A Hybrid Model Driven Development Framework for the Multidimensional Modeling of Data Warehouses. *SIGMOD Record*, *28*(2), 12–17. doi:10.1145/1815918.1815920

Mazón, J. N., Trujillo, J., & Lechtenbörger, J. (2007). Reconciling requirement-driven data warehouses with data sources via multidimensional normal forms. *Data & Knowledge Engineering*, *63*(3), 725–751. doi:10.1016/j.datak.2007.04.004

McAvoy, J., & Butler, T. (2009). The role of project management in ineffective decision making within Agile software development projects. *European Journal of Information Systems*, *18*(4), 372–383. doi:10.1057/ejis.2009.22

McCarthy, W. E. (1982). The REA Accounting Model: A Generalized Framework for Accounting Systems in A Shared Data Environment. *Accounting Review*, *57*, 554–578.

McCarthy, W. E. (2004). The Evolution toward REA Accountability Infrastructures for Enterprise Systems. In *Proceedings of the First International Conference on Enterprise Systems and Accounting*, Thesaloniki, Greece (pp. 1-2).

McConnell, S. (2006). *Software Estimation: Demystifying the Black Art*. Redmond, CA: Microsoft Corporation.

McCool, R. (2006). Rethinking the Semantic Web, part II. *IEEE Internet Computing*, *10*(1), 93–96. doi:10.1109/MIC.2006.18

McCririck, I. B., & Goldstein, R. C. (1980). What do data administrators really do? *Datamation*, *26*(8), 131–134.

McFadden, J. (1997). Micro document architectures (MDOC): A new concept beyond full-text & document management systems. In *Proceedings of the SGML Conference*.

McLeod, P. L. (1992). An assessment of the experimental literature on electronic support of group work: Results of a meta-analysis. *Human-Computer Interaction*, *7*(3), 257–280. doi:10.1207/s15327051hci0703_1

Mecella, M., Presicce, F. P., & Pernici, B. (2002). Modeling E-Service Orchestration through Petri Nets. In *Proceedings of the 3rd International Workshop on Technologies for E-Services (TES) 2002* (LNCS 2444, pp. 38-47).

Medjahed, B., Benatallah, B., Bouguettaya, A., Ngu, A. H. H., & Elmagarmid, A. K. (2003). Business-to-business interactions: issues and enabling technologies. *The VLDB Journal*, *12*(1), 59–85. doi:10.1007/s00778-003-0087-z

Mehrotra, S., Rastogi, R., Korth, H. F., & Silberschatz, A. (1992). A transaction model for multidatabase systems. In *Proceedings of the 12th International Conference on Distributed Computing Systems* (pp. 56-63).

Mendenhall, W., Wackerly, D. D., & Scheaffer, R. L. (1990). *Mathematical Statistics with Applications*. Boston: PWS Publishers.

Mendling, J., & van der Aalst, W. M. P. (2007). Formalization and verification of EPCs with OR-joins based on state and context. In J. Krogstie, A. L. Opdahl, & J. Sindre (Eds.), *Proceedings of the 19th International Conference on Advanced Information Systems Engineering* (LNCS 4495, pp. 439-453).

Mendling, J., Verbeek, H. M. W., van Dongen, B. F., van der Aalst, W. M. P., & Neumann, G. (2008). Detection and prediction of errors in EPCs of the SAP reference model. *Data & Knowledge Engineering*, *64*, 312–329. doi:10.1016/j.datak.2007.06.019

Merchant, K. A. (1988). Progressing toward a theory of marketing control: A comment. *Journal of Marketing*, *52*, 40–44. doi:10.2307/1251448

Meredith, S., & Francis, D. (2000). Journey towards agility: The agile wheel explored. *The TQM Magazine*, *12*(2), 137–143. doi:10.1108/09544780010318398

Meso, P., & Jain, R. (2006). Agile software development: Adaptive system principles and best practices. *Information Systems Management*, *23*(5), 19–29. doi:10.1201/1078.10580530/46108.23.3.20060601/93704.3

Michael, P. P. (2003). Web Services and Business Transactions. *World Wide Web (Bussum)*, *6*(1), 49–91. doi:10.1023/A:1022308532661

Miguel, V., & Charoy, F. (2003). *Bonita: Workflow cooperative system*. Retrieved from http://bonita.objectweb.org

Mikalsen, T., Tai, S., & Rouvellou, I. (2002). *Transactional Attitudes: Reliable Composition of Autonomous Web Services*. Paper presented at the Workshop on Dependable Middleware-based Systems (WDMS '02), Washington, DC.

Milanovic, N., & Malek, M. (2004). Current Solutions for Web Service Composition. *IEEE Internet Computing*, *8*(6), 51–59. doi:10.1109/MIC.2004.58

Mirbel, I. (2006). Method chunk federation. In *Proceedings of the Workshop on Exploring Modeling Methods for Systems Analysis and Design* (pp. 407-418).

Mirbel, I., & Ralyté, J. (2006). Situational method engineering: Combining assembly-based and roadmap-driven approaches. *Requirements Engineering*, *11*, 58–78. doi:10.1007/s00766-005-0019-0

Misra, S. C., Kumar, V., & Kumar, U. (2009). Identifying some important success factors in adopting agile software development practices. *Journal of Systems and Software*, *82*, 1869–1890. doi:10.1016/j.jss.2009.05.052

Mohagheghi, P., Dehlen, V., & Neple, T. (2009). Definitions and approaches to model quality in model-based software development - A review of literature. *Information and Software Technology*, *51*(12), 1646–1669. doi:10.1016/j.infsof.2009.04.004

Mohan, S., & Sengupta, A. (2005). DocBase - the INEX evaluation experience. In N. Fuhr, M. Lalmas, S. Malik, & Z. Szlávik (Eds.), *Proceedings of the Third International Workshop on Advances in XML Information Retrieval* (LNCS 3493, pp. 261-275).

Mohan, S., Sengupta, A., & Wu, Y. (2007). A rewrite based approach for enforcing access constraints for XML. In B. Apolloni, R. J. Howlett, & L. Jain (Eds.), *Proceedings of the 11th International Conference on Knowledge-Based Intelligent Information and Engineering Systems* (LNCS 4694, pp. 1081-1089).

Montazemi, A. R., & Wang, S. (1989). The effects of models of information presentation on decision-making: A review and meta-analysis. *Journal of Management Information Systems*, *5*(3), 121–127.

Moody, D. (2002). Comparative Evaluation of Large Data Representation Methods: The Analyst's Perspective. In *Conceptual Modeling* (LNCS 2503, pp. 214-231).

Moody, D. (2009). The "Physics" of Notations: Towards a Scientific Basis for Constructing Visual Notations in Software Engineering. *IEEE Transactions on Software Engineering*, *35*(6), 756–779. doi:10.1109/TSE.2009.67

Moody, D., & Shanks, G. (2003). Improving the quality of data models: empirical validation of a quality management framework. *Information Systems*, *28*, 619–650. doi:10.1016/S0306-4379(02)00043-1

Moody, D. L., & Kortink, M. A. R. (2000). From enterprise models to dimensional models: a methodology for data warehouse and data mart design. In *Proceedings of the 2nd International Workshop on Design and Management of Data Warehouses (DMDW'00)*, Stockholm, Sweden (pp. 5.1-5.11).

Moody, D. L. (2005). Theoretical and practical issues in evaluating the quality of conceptual models: current state and future directions. *Data & Knowledge Engineering*, *55*(3), 243–276. doi:10.1016/j.datak.2004.12.005

Moon, J., Kim, R., Song, B., & Cho, H. (2005). Transformation algorithms between WSCI and BPEL4WS for the collaborative business process. In *Proceedings of the 7th International Conference on Advanced Communication Technology* (pp. 285-290). Washington, DC: IEEE Computer Society.

Moon, J., Lee, D., Park, C., & Cho, H. (2004). Transformation algorithms between BPEL4WS and BPML for the executable business process. In *Proceedings of the 13th IEEE International Workshops on Enabling Technologies: Infrastructure for Collaborative Enterprises* (pp. 135-140). Washington, DC: IEEE Computer Society.

Moss, E. B. (1981). *Nested transactions: An approach to reliable distributed computing*. Cambridge, MA: MIT Press.

Mukherjea, S., & Bamba, B. (2004). BioPatentMiner: An information retrieval system for biomedical patents. In *Proceedings of the 30th Toronto Conference on Very Large Databases (VLDB)* (pp. 1066-1077).

Mukherjea, S., Bamba, B., & Kankar, P. (2005). Information retrieval and knowledge discovery utilizing a biomedical patent Semantic Web. *IEEE Transactions on Knowledge and Data Engineering*, *17*(8), 1099–1110. doi:10.1109/TKDE.2005.130

Mullen, B. (1989). *Advanced Basic Meta-Analysis*. Mahwah, NJ: Lawrence Erlbaum.

Munzenberger, H. (1980, September 25-26). Database administration – Experience from a European survey. In *Proceedings of the European Conference on Evaluation and Implementation of Database Systems*, Brussels, Belgium (pp. 85-94).

Mylopoulos, J. (1992). Conceptual modeling and telos. In Locoupoulos, P., & Zicari, R. (Eds.), *Conceptual modeling, databases, and cases*. New York, NY: John Wiley & Sons.

Nakamura, Y., Tatsubori, M., Imamura, T., & Ono, K. (2005, July). Model-driven security based on a web services security architecture. In *Proceedings of the IEEE International Conference on Services Computing*.

National Research Council. (2003). *Assessing research-doctorate programs: A methodology study*. Retrieved October 15, 2008, from http://www7.nationalacademies.org/resdoc/ranking_and_ratings.html

Nelson, H., Monarchi, D., & Nelson, K. (2001). Ensuring the "goodness" of a conceptual representation. In *Proceedings of the 4th European Conference on Software Measurement and ICT Control*, Heidelberg, Germany.

Nerur, S., & Balijepally, V. G. (2007). Theoretical reflections on agile development methodologies. *Communications of the ACM*, *50*(3), 79–83. doi:10.1145/1226736.1226739

Nerur, S., Mahapatra, R., & Mangalaraj, G. (2005). Challenges of migrating to agile methodologies. *Communications of the ACM*, *48*(5), 72–78. doi:10.1145/1060710.1060712

Neto, A. D., Subramanyan, R., Vieira, M., Travassos, G. H., & Shull, F. (2008). Improving Evidence about Software Technologies: A Look at Model-Based Testing. *IEEE Software*, *25*(3), 10–13. doi:10.1109/MS.2008.64

Newcomer, E. (2002). *Understanding Web Services: XML, WSDL, SOAP, and UDDI*. Harlow, MA: Addison-Wesley.

Newcomer, E., Robinson, I., Feingold, M., & Jeyaraman, R. (2007). *Web services coordination version 1.1*. Retrieved from http://docs.oasis-open.org/ws-tx/wstx-wscoor-1.1-spec-os.pdf

Newcomer, E., Robinson, I., Freund, T., & Little, M. (2007). *Web services business activity version 1.1*. Retrieved from http://docs.oasis-open.org/ws-tx/wstx-wsba-1.1-spec-errata-os.pdf

Newcomer, E., Robinson, I., Little, M., & Wilkinson, A. (2007). *Web services atomic transaction version 1.1*. Retrieved from http://docs.oasis-open.org/ws-tx/wstx-wsat-1.1-spec-os.pdf

Nickerson, J. V., Corter, J. E., Tversky, B., Zahner, D., & Rho, Y. J. (2008). *The Spatial Nature of Thought: Understanding Systems Design Through Diagrams*. Paper presented at the 2008 International Conference on Information Systems.

Nidumolu, S. R., & Subramani, M. R. (2003). The matrix of control: Combining process and structure approaches to managing software development. *Journal of Management Information Systems*, *20*(3), 159–196.

Niemi, T., Nummenmaa, J., & Thanisch, P. (2001, November 9). Constructing OLAP Cubes Based on Queries. In *Proceedings of the Fourth International Workshop on Data Warehousing and OLAP*, Atlanta, GA (pp. 9-11).

Niu, B., Martin, P., & Powley, W. (2009). Towards autonomic workload management in DBMSs. *Journal of Database Management*, *20*(3), 1–17. doi:10.4018/jdm.2009070101

Noran, T. P. (1981). The Command Language Grammar: A representation for the user interface of interactive computer systems. *International Journal of Man-Machine Studies*, *15*(1), 3–50. doi:10.1016/S0020-7373(81)80022-3

Nord, R. L., & Tomayko, J. E. (2006). Software architecture-centric methods and agile development. *IEEE Software*, *23*(2), 47–53. doi:10.1109/MS.2006.54

Nunally, J. C. (1978). *Psychometric Theory*. New York: McGraw-Hill.

Nuseibeh, B. A. (1994). *A multi-perspective framework for method integration*. Unpublished doctoral dissertation, University of London, London, UK.

Nuseibeh, B., & Easterbrook, S. (2000). *Requirements engineering: A roadmap*. Paper presented at the International Conference on Software Engineering, Limerick, Ireland.

O'Leary, D. E. (2004). On the relationship between REA and SAP. *International Journal of Accounting Information Systems*, *5*, 65–81. doi:10.1016/j.accinf.2004.02.004

O'Mahony, S., & Ferraro, F. (2007). The emergence of governance in an open source community. *Academy of Management Journal*, *50*(5), 1079–1105.

OASIS. (2003). *Web services business process execution language*.

OASIS. (n.d.). *OASIS Business Transaction Protocol*. Retrieved from http://www.oasis-open.org/committees/business-transactions/documents/primer/Primerhtml/

Object Management Group (OMG). (2005). *Software process engineering metamodel specification - Version 1.1*. Retrieved from http://www.omg.org/docs/formal/05-01-06.pdf

Object Management Group (OMG). (2008). *Model Driven Architecture (MDA), Unified Modeling Language (UML), Common Warehouse Metamodel (CWM), Query/View/Transformation Language (QVT), MOF Model to Text Transformation Language (Mof2Text)*. Retrieved from http://www.omg.org

O'Connor, D. E., & Faille, C. C. (2000). *Basic economic principles: A guide for students*. Westport, CT: Greenwood Press.

Offutt, J., & Abdurazik, A. (1999). Generating tests from UML specifications. In R. France & B. Rumpe (Eds.), *Proceedings of the Conference on Unified Modeling Language* (LNCS 1723, pp. 416-429).

Oh, S.-C., & Lee, D. (2009). Wsben: A Web Services discovery and composition benchmark toolkit. *International Journal of Web Services Research*, *6*(1), 1–19.

Oh, W., & Jeon, S. (2007). Membership herding and network stability in the open source community: The ising perspective. *Management Science*, *53*(7), 1086–1101. doi:10.1287/mnsc.1060.0623

Oldham, N., Thomas, C., Sheth, A. P., & Verma, K. (2004). METEOR-S Web Service annotation framework with machine learning classification. In *Proceedings of SWSWPC* (LNCS 3387, pp. 137–146).

Olivé, A. (2007). *Conceptual Modeling of Information Systems*. New York: Springer.

OMG. (1997). *Object Management Group - UML*. Retrieved from http://www.uml.org/

OMG. (2003). *MDA guide (Vol. version 1.0.1)*. Retrieved from http://www.omg.org/docs/omg/03-06-01.pdf.

OMG. (2005). *The Unified Modeling Language. Documents associated with UML Version 2.0*. Retrieved from http://www.omg.org/spec/UML/2.0

OpenText. (2010). *Open text search server, eDOCS edition*. Retrieved from http://www.opentext.com/2/sso_download_open?docpath=product/livelink/edocs/edocs_searchserver_po.pdf

Oracle. (2008). *Oracle Fusion Middleware*. Retrieved April 4, 2009, from http://www.oracle.com/technology/products/middleware/index.html

Orriens, B., Yang, J., & Papazoglou, M. P. (2003). A framework for business rule driven service composition. In *Proceedings of the 4th VLDB Workshop on Technologies for E-Services* (pp. 14-27). London, UK: Springer-Verlag.

Ortiz, G., & Hernändez, J. (2006, September). Toward UML profiles for web services and their extra-functional properties. In *Proceedings of the IEEE International Conference on Web Services*.

Ossher, H., & Tarr, P. (2001). Using multidimensional separation of concerns to (re)shape evolving software. *Communications of the ACM*, *44*(10), 43–50. doi:10.1145/383845.383856

Ouchi, W. G. (1977). The relationship between organizational structure and organizational control. *Administrative Science Quarterly*, *22*, 95–113. doi:10.2307/2391748

Ouchi, W. G. (1978). The transmission of control through organizational hierarchy. *Academy of Management Journal*, *21*(2), 173–192. doi:10.2307/255753

Ouchi, W. G. (1979). A conceptual framework for the design of organizational control mechanisms. *Management Science*, *25*(9), 833–848. doi:10.1287/mnsc.25.9.833

Ouchi, W. G. (1980). Markets, bureaucracies, and clans. *Administrative Science Quarterly*, *25*(1), 129–141. doi:10.2307/2392231

Overhage, S., & Thomas, P. (2003). Ws-specification: Specifying Web Services using uddi improvements. In *Revised Papers from the NODe 2002 Web and Database-Related Workshops on Web, Web-Services, and Database Systems*, London (LNCS 2593, pp. 100–119).

Page, L., Brin, S., Motwani, R., & Winograd, T. (1998). *The PageRank Citation Ranking: Bringing Order to the Web* (Tech. Rep. No. SIDL-WP-1999-0120). Stanford, CA: Stanford University.

Paim, F. R. S., & Castro, J. (2002). Enhancing Data Warehouse Design with the NFR Framework. In *Proceedings of the Workshop em Engenharia de Requisitos (WER)*, Valencia, Spain (pp. 40-57).

Paolucci, M., Kawamura, T., Payne, T. R., & Sycara, K. P. (2002). Semantic matching of Web Services capabilities. In *ISWC '02: Proceedings of the First International Semantic Web Conference on The Semantic Web*, London (pp. 333–347). Berlin: Springer-Verlag.

Paolucci, M., & Sycara, K. (2003). Autonomous semantic Web Services. *IEEE Internet Computing*, *7*(5), 34–41. doi:10.1109/MIC.2003.1232516

Paolucci, M., Sycara, K. P., Nishimura, T., & Srinivasan, N. (2003). Using DAML-S for P2P discovery. In *Proceedings of IWCS* (pp. 203–207). CSREA Press.

Paparizos, S., Wu, Y., Lakshmanan, L. V. S., & Jagadish, H. V. (2004). Tree logical classes for efficient evaluation of XQuery. In *Proceedings of the ACM SIGMOD International Conference on Management of Data*, Paris, France (pp. 71-82).

Papazoglou, P., & Yang, J. (2002). Design Methodology for Web Services and Business Processes. In *Proceedings of the 3rd International Workshop on Technologies for E-Services (TES) 2002* (LNCS 2444, pp. 54-64).

Papazoglou, M., & Heuvel, W. (2007). Service oriented architectures: Approaches, technologies and research issues. *International Journal on Very Large Data Bases*, *16*(3), 389–415. doi:10.1007/s00778-007-0044-3

Papazoglou, M. P. (2003). Web services and business transactions. *World Wide Web (Bussum)*, *6*(1), 49–91. doi:10.1023/A:1022308532661

Papazoglou, M. P., & Georgakopoulos, D. (2003). Service-Oriented Computing: Introduction. *Communications of the ACM*, *46*(10), 24–28. doi:10.1145/944217.944233

Papazoglou, M. P., & van den Heuvel, W.-J. (2007). Service-oriented computing: concepts, characteristics and directions. *The VLDB Journal*, *16*(3), 389–415. doi:10.1007/s00778-007-0044-3

Pardillo, J., Mazón, J. N., & Trujillo, J. (2008, July 7-10). Model-driven OLAP Metadata for Data Warehouses. In *Proceedings of the 25th British National Conference on Databases, BNCOD 25*, Cardiff, UK (LNCS 5071, pp. 203-206).

Pardillo, J., & Trujillo, J. (2008, October 20-24). Integrated Model-Driven Development of Goal-Oriented Data Warehouses and Data Marts. In *Proceedings of the 27th International Conference on Conceptual Modeling (ER 2008)*, Barcelona, Spain (LNCS 52I31, pp. 426-439).

Park, S., Na, H., Park, S., & Sugumaran, V. (2006). A semi-automated filtering technique software process tailoring using neural network. *Expert Systems with Applications*, *30*(2), 179–189. doi:10.1016/j.eswa.2005.06.023

Parsons, J. (2003). Effects of Local versus Global Schema Diagrams on Verification and Communication in Conceptual Data Modelling. *Journal of Management Information Systems*, *19*(3), 155–183.

Parsons, J. (2005). Empirical Research in Conceptual Modeling - Using Experiments to Understand Semantic Expression. *Wirtschaftsinformatik, 47*(2), 155–156.

Parsons, J., & Cole, L. (2005). What do the pictures mean? Guidelines for experimental evaluation of representation fidelity in diagrammatical conceptual modeling techniques. *Data & Knowledge Engineering, 55*(3), 327–342. doi:10.1016/j.datak.2004.12.008

Patil, A. A., Oundhakar, S. A., Sheth, A. P., & Verma, K. (2004). METEOR-S Web Service annotation framework. In *WWW '04: Proceedings of the 13th International Conference on World Wide Web*, New York (pp. 553–562). New York: ACM Press.

Pedersen, T. B. (2004, September 1-3). How Is BI Used in Industry?: Report from a Knowledge Exchange Network. In *Proceedings of the 6th International Conference on Data Warehousing and Knowledge Discovery*, Zaragoza, Spain (LNCS 3181, pp. 179-188).

Peleg, M., & Dori, D. (2000). The model multiplicity problem: Experimenting with real-time specification methods. *IEEE Transactions on Software Engineering, 26*(8), 742–759. doi:10.1109/32.879812

Perez, A. (2006). *The elusive species of the information age: The data management professional.* Retrieved from http://www.midsouthdama.org/pdf/2006_surveyart.pdf

Perron & Frobenius. (2003). *Perron-frobenius theory.* Retrieved October 15, 2008, from http://www.win.tue.nl/~aeb/srgbk/node4.html

Perry, D. E., Romanovsky, A., & Tripathi, A. (2000). Current trends in exception handling. *IEEE Transactions on Software Engineering, 26*(10), 921–922. doi:10.1109/TSE.2000.879816

Petre, M. (1995). Why Looking Isn't Always Seeing - Readership Skills and Graphical Programming. *Communications of the ACM, 38*(6), 33–44. doi:10.1145/203241.203251

Petschulat, S. (2010). Other people's data. *Communications of the ACM, 53*(1), 53–57. doi:10.1145/1629175.1629196

Piattini, M., Genero, M., Poels, G., & Nelson, J. (2005). Towards a framework for conceptual modelling quality. In Genero, M., Piattini, M., & Calero, C. (Eds.), *Metrics For software conceptual models* (pp. 1–18). London, UK: Imperial College Press. doi:10.1142/9781860946066_0001

Pickardaa, L. M., Kitchenhamaa, B. A., & Jonesbb, P. W. (1998). Combining empirical results in software engineering. *Information and Software Technology, 40*(14), 811–821. doi:10.1016/S0950-5849(98)00101-3

Pires, P. F., Benevides, M. R. F., & Mattoso, M. (2002). Building Reliable Web Services Compositions. In *Proceedings of the Workshop on the Web, Web-Services, and Database Systems 2002* (LNCS 2593, pp. 59-72).

Pirro, G. (2009). A semantic similarity metric combining features and intrinsic information content. *Data & Knowledge Engineering, 68*(11), 1289–1308. doi:10.1016/j.datak.2009.06.008

Platzer, C., & Dustdar, S. A. (2005, November). vector space search engine for Web Services. In *Proceedings of the 3rd European Conference on Web Services* (pp. 62–71). Washington, DC: IEEE Computer Society.

Poels, G., Gailly, F., Maes, A., & Paemeleire, R. (2005). Object Class or Association class? Testing the User Effect on Cardinality Interpretation. In *Perspectives in Conceptual Modeling* (LNCS 3770, pp. 33-42).

Poels, G., Maes, A., Gailly, F., & Paemeleire, R. (in press). The pragmatic quality of Resources-Events-Agents diagrams: an experimental evaluation. *Information Systems Journal, 21*(1).

Poels, G., Nelson, J., Genero, M., & Piattini, M. (2003). Quality in conceptual modeling - New research directions. In A. Olivé, M. Yoshikawa, & E. S. K. Yu (Eds.), *Proceedings of the Conference on Advanced Conceptual Modeling Techniques* (LNCS 2784, pp. 243-250).

Poppendieck, M., & Poppendieck, T. (2003). *Lean software development: An agile toolkit.* Reading, MA: Addison-Wesley.

Post, G. V. (2004). *Database Management Systems: Designing and Building Business Applications* (3rd ed.). New York, NY: McGraw-Hill/Irwin.

Prakash, N., & Gosain, A. (2008). An approach to engineering the requirements of data warehouses. *Requirements Engineering, 13*(1), 49–72. doi:10.1007/s00766-007-0057-x

Pretorius, R., & Budgen, D. (2008). A mapping study on empirical evidence related to the models and forms used in the UML. In *Proceedings of the 2nd ACM-IEEE International Symposium on Empirical Software Engineering and Measurement*, Kaiserslautern, Germany (pp. 342-344).

Procaccino, J. D., Verner, J. M., Overmyer, S. P., & Darter, M. E. (2002). Case study: Factors for early prediction of software development success. *Information and Software Technology*, *44*(1), 53–62. doi:10.1016/S0950-5849(01)00217-8

Project Management Institute. (2004). *A guide to the project management body of knowledge*. Newtown Square, PA: Project Management Institute.

Prud'hommeaux, E., & Seaborne, A. (Eds.). (2007). *SPARQL query language for RDF*. Retrieved October 15, 2008, from http://www.w3.org/TR/rdf-sparql-query/

Purao, S., Storey, V. C., & Han, T. D. (2003). Improving analysis pattern reuse in conceptual design: Augmenting automated processes with supervised learning. *Information Systems Research*, *14*(3), 269–290. doi:10.1287/isre.14.3.269.16559

Qumer, A., & Henderson-Sellers, B. (2008). An evaluation of the degree of agility in six agile methods and its applicability for method engineering. *Information and Software Technology*, *50*(4), 280–295. doi:10.1016/j.infsof.2007.02.002

Rada, R., Mili, H., Bicknell, M., & Blettner, E. (1989). Development and application of a metric on semantic nets. *IEEE Transactions on Systems, Man, and Cybernetics*, *19*(1), 17–30. doi:10.1109/21.24528

Ralyté, J. (1999). Reusing scenario based approaches in requirement engineering methods: CREWS method base. In *Proceedings of the 10th International Workshop on Database & Expert Systems Applications* (pp. 305-309).

Ralyté, J., & Rolland, C. (2001). An assembly process model for method engineering. In K. R. Dittrich, A. Geppert, & M. C. Norrie (Eds.), *Proceedings of the 13th International Conference on Advanced Information Systems Engineering* (LNCS 2068, pp. 267-283).

Ramakrishnan, R., & Gehrke, J. (2002). *Database Management Systems* (3rd ed.). New York, NY: McGraw-Hill.

Ramesh, B., Cao, L., Mohan, K., & Xu, P. (2006). Can distributed software development be agile? *Communications of the ACM*, *49*(10), 41–46. doi:10.1145/1164394.1164418

Ran, S. (2003). A model for Web Service discovery with QoS. *SIGecom Exchanges*, *4*(1), 1–10. doi:10.1145/844357.844360

Raylte, J., Deneckere, R., & Rolland, C. (2003). Towards a generic model for situational method engineering. In J. Eder & M. Missikoff (Eds.), *Proceedings of the International Conference on Advanced Information Systems Engineering* (LNCS 2681, pp. 95-110).

Raymond, E. (2001). *The Cathedral and the Bazaar: Musings on Linux and Open Source by an Accidental Revolutionary*. Cambridge, MA: O'Reilly & Associates.

Recker, J. (2007). A socio-pragmatic constructionist framework for understanding quality in process modelling. *Australasian Journal of Information Systems*, *14*(2), 43–63.

Recker, J., Rosemann, M., & Krogstie, J. (2007). Ontology- versus pattern-based evaluation of process modeling languages: A comparison. *Communications of the Association for Information Systems*, *20*(48), 774–799.

Recker, J., Rosemann, M., & van der Aalst, W. M. P. (2005). On the user perception of configurable reference process models – Initial insights. In *Proceedings of the 16th Australian Conference on Information Systems*, Sydney, NSW, Australia.

Reed, J. W., Jiao, Y., Potok, T. E., Klump, B., Elmore, M. T., & Hurson, A. R. (2006). TF-ICF: A new term weighting scheme for clustering dynamic data streams. In *ICMLA '06: Proceedings of the 5th International Conference on Machine Learning and Applications*, (pp. 258–263). Washington, DC: IEEE Computer Society.

Reeves, W. W. (1999). *Learner-centered design: A cognitive view of managing complexity in product, information, and environmental design*. Thousand Oaks, CA: Sage.

Reinhartz-Berger, I., & Dori, D. (2005). A reflective metamodel of object-process methodology: The system modeling building blocks. In Green, P., & Rosemann, M. (Eds.), *Business systems analysis with ontologies* (pp. 130–173). Hershey, PA: Idea Group. doi:10.4018/978-1-59140-339-5.ch006

Reinhartz-Berger, I., & Dori, D. (2005). OPM vs. UML – Experimenting comprehension and construction of web application models. *Empirical Software Engineering*, *10*(1), 57–80. doi:10.1023/B:EMSE.0000048323.40484.e0

Reisig, W. (1985). *Petri Nets, an Introduction*. Berlin, Germany: Springer Verlag.

Ren, J., & Taylor, R. N. (2007). Automatic and versatile publications ranking for research institutions and scholars. *Communications of the ACM*, *50*(6), 81–85. doi:10.1145/1247001.1247010

Riehle, D., & Zullighoven, H. (1996). Understanding and using patterns in software development. *Theory and Practice of Object Systems*, *2*(1), 3–13. doi:10.1002/(SICI)1096-9942(1996)2:1<3::AID-TAPO1>3.0.CO;2-#

Roberts, J., Hann, I., & Slaughter, S. (2006). Understanding the motivations, participation, and performance of open source software developers: A longitudinal study of the Apache Projects. *Management Science*, *52*(7), 984–999. doi:10.1287/mnsc.1060.0554

Robillard, M. P., & Murphy, G. C. (2007). Representing Concerns in Source Code. *ACM Transactions on Software Engineering and Methodology*, *16*(1), 3. doi:10.1145/1189748.1189751

Robinson, W. N., & Purao, S. (2009). Specifying and monitoring interactions and commitments in open business processes. *IEEE Software*, *26*(2), 72–79. doi:10.1109/MS.2009.48

Rodriguez, J. M., Crasso, M., Zunino, A., & Campo, M. (2009). Discoverability anti-patterns: frequent ways of making undiscoverable Web Service descriptions. In *Proceedings of the 10th Argentine Symposium on Software Engineering (ASSE2009) - 38th JAIIO* (pp. 1–15).

Rodriguez, J. M., Crasso, M., Zunino, A., & Campo, M. (2010). Improving Web Service descriptions for effective service discovery. *Science of Computer Programming*.

Rodríguez, A., & Egenhofer, M. (2002). Determining semantic similarity among entity classes from different ontologies. *IEEE Transactions on Knowledge and Data Engineering*, *15*(2), 442–456. doi:10.1109/TKDE.2003.1185844

Rolland, C. (2009). Method engineering: Towards methods as services. *Software Process Improvement and Practice*, *14*, 143–164. doi:10.1002/spip.416

Rolland, C., Nurcan, S., & Grosz, G. (2000). A decision making pattern for guiding the enterprise knowledge development process. *Information and Software Technology*, *42*(5), 313–331. doi:10.1016/S0950-5849(99)00089-0

Roman, D., Lausen, H., & Keller, U. (2006). *D2v1.3. web service modeling ontology (WSMO)*. Retrieved from http://www.wsmo.org/TR/d2/v1.3/

Roman, D., Keller, U., Lausen, H., de Bruijn, J., Lara, R., & Stollberg, M. (2005). Web Service Modeling Ontology. *Applied Ontology*, *1*(1), 77–106.

Rosenberg, J., & Remy, D. (2004). *Securing Web Services with WS-Security: Demystifying WS-Security, WS-Policy, SAML, XML Signature, and XML Encryption*. Sebastopol, CA: Sams.

Rosli, K., Ahmi, A., & Mohamad, L. (2009). Resource-Event-Agent (REA) Modelling in Revenue Information System (RiS) Development: Smart Application for Direct-Selling Dealers and SMEs. *Journal for the Advancement of Science & Arts*, *1*(1), 43–62.

Rumbaugh, J., Booch, G., & Jacobson, I. (1998). *Unified modeling language reference manual*. Reading, MA: Addison-Wesley.

Rusinkiewicz, M., & Sheth, A. P. (1995). Specification and execution of transactional workflows. In Kim, W. (Ed.), *Modern database systems: the object model, interoperability, and beyond* (pp. 592–620).

Ryan, S. D., Bordoloi, B., & Harrison, D. A. (2000). Acquiring Conceptual Data Modeling Skills: The Effect of Cooperative Learning and Self-Efficacy on Learning Outcomes. *The Data Base for Advances in Information Systems*, *31*, 9–24.

Sadiq, S., Orlowska, M., Sadiq, W., & Cameron, F. (2004). Data flow and validation in workflow modelling. In *Proceedings of the 15th Australasian Database Conference*, Dunedin, New Zealand.

Saeki, M., Iguchi, K., Wen-yin, K., & Shinohara, M. (1993). A meta-model for representing software specification & design methods. In *Proceedings of the IFIP WG 8.1 Conference on Information Systems Development Process* (pp. 149-166).

Sagan, H. (1994). *Space-Filling Curves*. New York: Springer-Verlag.

Sakr, S. (2009). Cardinality-aware purely relational xQuery processor. *Journal of Database Management, 20*(3), 76–125. doi:10.4018/jdm.2009070104

Salminen, A., & Tompa, F. (2001). Requirements for XML document database systems. In *Proceedings of the ACM Symposium on Document Engineering*, Atlanta, GA (pp. 85-94).

Salton, G., Wong, A., & Yang, C. S. (1975). A vector space model for automatic indexing. *Communications of the ACM, 18*(11), 613–620. doi:10.1145/361219.361220

Samos, J., Saltor, F., Sistac, J., & Bardés, A. (1998, August 24-28). Database Architecture for Data Warehousing: An Evolutionary Approach. In *Proceedings of the 9th International Conference on Database and Expert Systems Applications (DEXA),* Vienna, Austria (LNCS 1460, pp. 746-756).

Sant'Anna, C. N., Garcia, A. F., Chavez, C., Lucena, C. J. P., & Staa, A. (2003, October). *On the reuse and maintenance of aspect-oriented software: An assessment framework*. Paper presented at the Brazilian Symposium on Software Engineering.

SAP. (n.d.). *SAP NetWeaver Technology Platform*. Retrieved April 4, 2009, from http://www.sap.com/platform/netweaver/index.epx

Sapkota, B., Vasiliu, L., Toma, I., Roman, D., & Bussler, C. (2005). Peer-to-Peer technology usage in Web Service discovery and matchmaking. In *Proceedings of the 6th International Conference on Web Information Systems Engineering (WISE)* (pp. 418–425).

Sarker, S., & Sarker, S. (2009). Exploring agility in distributed information systems development teams: an interpretive study in an offshoring context. *Information Systems Research, 20*(3), 440–461. doi:10.1287/isre.1090.0241

Sarshar, K., & Loos, P. (2005). Comparing the control-flow of EPC and petri net from the end-user perspective. In W. M. P. van der Aalst, B. Benatallah, F. Casati, & F. Curbera (Eds.), *Proceedings of the 3rd International Conference on Business Process Management* (LNCS 3649, pp. 434-439).

Sawilowsky, S. (1990). Nonparametric tests of interaction in experimental design. *Review of Educational Research, 60*(1), 91–126.

Scacchi, W. (2002). Understanding the requirements for developing open source software systems. *IEEE Proceedings on Software, 149*(1), 24–39. doi:10.1049/ip-sen:20020202

Scheer, A. W. (1998). *ARIS-Business process modeling*. Berlin, Germany: Springer-Verlag.

Schek, H.-J., Weikum, G., & Ye, H. (1993). Towards a Unified Theory of Concurrency Control and Recovery. In *Proceedings of the 12th ACM SIGACT-SIGMOD-SIGART Symposium on Principles of Database Systems* (pp. 300-311).

Schermerhorn, J. R., Hunt, J. G., & Osborn, R. N. (2003). *Organizational behaviour*. New York, NY: John Wiley & Sons.

Schmidt, A. R., Waas, F., Kersten, M. L., Carey, M. J., Manolescu, I., & Busse, R. (2002). XMark: A benchmark for XML data management. In *Proceedings of the International Conference on Very Large Data Bases* (pp. 974-985).

Schmit, B. A., & Dustdar, S. (2005). Systematic design of web service transactions. In *Technologies for E-Services* (LNCS 3811, pp. 23-33).

Schmit, B. A., & Dustdar, S. (2005). Towards Transactional Web Services. In *Proceedings of the 7th IEEE International Conference on E-Commerce Technology Workshops* (pp. 12-20). Washington, DC: IEEE Computer Society.

Schmidt, C., & Parashar, M. A. (2004). Peer-to-Peer approach to Web Service discovery. *World Wide Web (Bussum), 7*(2), 211–229. doi:10.1023/B:WWWJ.0000017210.55153.3d

Schneider, P., Hayes, P., & Horrocks, I. (Eds.). (2004). *OWL Web ontology language semantics and abstract syntax*. Retrieved October 15, 2008, from http://www.w3.org/TR/owl-semantics/

Schuldt, H., Alonso, G., Beeri, C., & Schek, H. J. (2002). Atomicity and isolation for transactional processes. *ACM Transactions on Database Systems, 27*(1), 63–116. doi:10.1145/507234.507236

Schuler, C., Schuldt, H., & Schek, H. J. (2001). Supporting Reliable Transactional Business Processes by Publish-Subscribe Techniques. In *Proceedings of the 2nd International Workshop on Technologies for E-Services (TES) 2001* (LNCS 2193, pp. 118-131).

Schulz, K. A., & Orlowska, M. E. (2004). Facilitating cross-organisational workflows with a workflow view approach. *Data & Knowledge Engineering, 51*(1), 109–147. doi:10.1016/j.datak.2004.03.008

Schwaber, K. (2005). Agile project management. In H. Baumeister, M. Marchesi, & H. Holombe (Eds.), *Proceedings of the 6th International Conference on Extreme Programming and Agile Processes in Software Engineering* (LNCS 3556, pp. 277-277).

Schwaber, K., & Beedle, M. (2002). *Agile software development with Scrum (Series in agile software development)*. Upper Saddle River, NJ: Prentice Hall.

Sebastiani, F. (2002). Machine learning in automated text categorization. *ACM Computing Surveys, 34*(1), 1–47. doi:10.1145/505282.505283

Selic, B. (2003). The pragmatics of model-driven development. *IEEE Software, 20*, 19–25. doi:10.1109/MS.2003.1231146

Sen, A., & Sinha, A. P. (2005). A Comparison of Data Warehousing Methodologies. *Communications of the ACM, 48*(3), 79–84. doi:10.1145/1047671.1047673

Sengupta, A., & Dillon, A. (2006). Query by templates: Using the shape of information to search next generation databases. *IEEE Transactions on Professional Communication, 49*(2), 128–144. doi:10.1109/TPC.2006.875073

Sengupta, A., Mohan, S., & Doshi, R. (2003). XER - Extensible entity relationship modeling. In *Proceedings of the XML Conference.*

Sengupta, A., & Ramesh, V. (2009). Designing document SQL (DSQL)- an accessible yet comprehensive ad-hoc querying frontend for XQuery. *Journal of Database Management, 20*(4), 25–51. doi:10.4018/jdm.2009062502

Serrano, M., Trujillo, J., Calero, C., Luján, S., & Piattini, M. (2004, June 7-11). Empirical Validation of Metrics for Conceptual Models of Data Warehouses. In *Proceedings of the 16th International Conference on Advanced Information Systems Engineering (CAiSE 2004),* Riga, Latvia (LNCS 3084, pp. 506-520).

Serrano, M., Trujillo, J., Calero, C., & Piattini, M. (2007). Metrics for data warehouse conceptual models understandability. *Information and Software Technology, 49*(8), 851–870. doi:10.1016/j.infsof.2006.09.008

Shadbolt, N., Berners-Lee, T., & Hall, W. (2006). The Semantic Web revisited. *IEEE Intelligent Systems, 21*(3), 96–101. doi:10.1109/MIS.2006.62

Shah, D. A., & Madden, L. V. (2004). Nonparametric analysis of ordinal data in designed factorial experiments. *Phytopathology, 94*(1), 33–43. doi:10.1094/PHYTO.2004.94.1.33

Shan, Z., Li, Q., Luo, Y., & Peng, Z. (2005). Deputy Mechanism for Workflow Views. In *Proceedings of the 10th International Conference on Database Systems for Advanced Applications (DASFAA 2005)* (pp. 816-827). Berlin, Heidelberg: Springer.

Shankar, R. P., & Armando, F. (2004). Interoperability among independently evolving web services. In *Proceedings of the 5th ACM/IFIP/USENIX International Conference on Middleware* (pp. 331-351). New York, NY: ACM.

Shanks, G., Moody, D., Nuredini, J., Tobin, D., & Weber, R. (2010). Representing classes of things and properties in general in conceptual modelling: An empirical evaluation. *Journal of Database Management, 21*(2), 1–25. doi:10.4018/jdm.2010040101

She, W., Yen, I., Thuraisingham, B., & Bertino, E. (2009). The SCIFC Model for Information Flow Control in Web Service Composition. In *Proceedings of the IEEE International Conference on Web Services* (pp. 1-8). Washington, DC: IEEE Computer Society Press.

Sheth, A. P., & Rusinkiewicz, M. (1993). On transactional workflows. *Data Engineering Bulletin, 16*(2), 37–40.

Sheth, A., Aleman-Meza, B., Arpinar, I. B., Halaschek, C., & Ramakrishnan, C. (2005). Semantic association identification and knowledge discovery for national security applications. *Journal of Database Management, 16*(1), 33–53.

Shlezinger, G., Reinhartz-Berger, I., & Dori, D. (2010). Modeling design patterns for semi-automatic reuse in system design. *Journal of Database Management*, *21*(1), 29–57. doi:10.4018/jdm.2010112302

Shoval, P., & Even-Chaime, M. (1987). Database schema design: An experimental comparison between normalization and information analysis. *Database*, *18*(3), 30–39.

Shull, F., Singer, J., & Sjøberg, D. I. K. (2008). *Guide to Advanced Empirical Software Engineering*. Berlin, Germany: Springer. doi:10.1007/978-1-84800-044-5

Siau, K. (2004). Informational and Computational Equivalence in Comparing Information Methods. *Journal of Database Management*, *15*(1), 73–86.

Siau, K. (2010). An analysis of Unified Modeling Language (UML) graphical constructs based on BWW ontology. *Journal of Database Management*, *21*(1), i–viii.

Siau, K., & Cao, Q. (2001). Unified modeling language: A complexity analysis. *Journal of Database Management*, *12*(1), 26–34.

Siau, K., Long, Y., & Ling, M. (2010). Toward a unified model of information systems development success. *Journal of Database Management*, *21*(1), 80–101. doi:10.4018/jdm.2010112304

Siau, K., & Loo, P. (2006). Identifying difficulties in learning UML. *Information Systems Management*, *23*(3), 43–51. doi:10.1201/1078.10580530/46108.23.3.20060601/93706.5

Siau, K., & Rossi, M. (2011). Evaluation techniques for systems analysis and design modelling methods: A review and comparative analysis. *Information Systems Journal*, *21*(3), 249–268. doi:10.1111/j.1365-2575.2007.00255.x

Siau, K., & Rossi, M. (in press). Evaluation techniques for systems analysis and design modelling methods – a review and comparative analysis. *Information Systems Journal*, *21*(1).

Siau, K., & Tan, X. (2005). Improving the quality of conceptual modeling using cognitive mapping techniques. *Data & Knowledge Engineering*, *55*, 343–365. doi:10.1016/j.datak.2004.12.006

Siau, K., Tan, X., & Sheng, H. (2010). Important characteristics of software development team members: An empirical investigation using repertory grid. *Information Systems Journal*, *20*(6), 563–580. doi:10.1111/j.1365-2575.2007.00254.x

Siau, K., & Tian, Y. (2009). A semiotics analysis of UML graphical notations. *Requirements Engineering*, *14*(1), 15–26. doi:10.1007/s00766-008-0071-7

Siau, K., Wand, Y., & Benbasat, I. (1997). The relative importance of structural constraints and surface semantics in information modeling. *Information Systems*, *22*(2-3), 155–170. doi:10.1016/S0306-4379(97)00009-4

Siau, K. L., & Cao, Q. (2001). Unified Modeling Language – A Complexity Analysis. *Journal of Database Management*, *12*(1), 26–34. doi:10.4018/jdm.2001010103

Siau, K. L., Chan, H. C., & Wei, K. K. (1995). The effects of conceptual and logical interfaces on visual query performance of end-users. In *Proceedings of the 16th Annual International Conference on Information Systems*, Amsterdam, The Netherlands.

Siau, K. L., Chan, H. C., & Wei, K. K. (2004). Effects of query complexity and learning on novice user query performance with conceptual and logical database interfaces. *IEEE Transactions on Systems, Man, and Cybernetics*, *34*(2), 276–281. doi:10.1109/TSMCA.2003.820581

Silicon.com. (n.d.). *Latest white papers*. Retrieved from http://whitepapers.silicon.com

Simon, H. A. (1957). *Models of man: Social and rational; Mathematical essays on rational human behavior in a social setting*. New York, NY: John Wiley & Sons.

Singh, M. P., & Huhns, M. N. (2005). *Service-Oriented Computing: Semantics, Processes, Agents*. Hoboken, NJ: John Wiley & Sons.

Sipani, S., Verma, K., Miller, J. A., & Aleman-Meza, B. (2004). Designing a high-performance database engine for the 'Db4XML' native XML database system. *Journal of Systems and Software*, *69*(1-2), 87–104. doi:10.1016/S0164-1212(03)00077-3

Sivashanmugam, K., Verma, K., Sheth, A. P., & Miller, J. A. (2003). Adding semantics to Web Services standards. In *Proceedings of the 2003 International Conference on Web Services*, Las Vegas, NV (pp. 395–401). CSREA Press.

Sjøberg, D. I., Hannay, J. E., Hansen, O., Kampenes, V. B., Karahasanovic, A., Liborg, N., & Rekdal, A. C. (2005). A survey of controlled experiments in software engineering. *IEEE Transactions on Software Engineering, 31*, 733–753. doi:10.1109/TSE.2005.97

Slevin, D. P., & Pinto, J. K. (1987). Balancing Strategy and Tactics in Project Implementation. *Sloan Management Review, 29*(1), 33–41.

Smith, D. K., Chang, J., & Moores, T. T. (2003). *Comparing Self-Efficacy and Meta-Cognition as Indicators of Learning.* Paper presented at the 9th Americas Conference on Information Systems.

Snell, S. A. (1992). Control theory in strategic human resource management: The mediating effect of administrative information. *Academy of Management Journal, 35*(2), 292–327. doi:10.2307/256375

Soffer, P., Kaner, M., & Wand, Y. (2008). Assigning ontology-based semantics to process models: The case of petri nets. In Z. Bellahsene & M. Leonard (Eds.), *Proceedings of the International Conference on Advanced Information Systems Engineering* (LNCS 5074, pp. 16-31).

Soffer, P., & Wand, Y. (2004). Goal-driven analysis of process model validity. In A. Pearsson & J. Stirna (Eds.), *Proceedings of the International Conference on Advanced Information Systems Engineering* (LNCS 3084, pp. 521-535).

Soffer, P., & Wand, Y. (2005). On the notion of soft goals in business process modeling. *Business Process Management Journal, 11*(6), 663–679. doi:10.1108/14637150510630837

Soffer, P., & Wand, Y. (2007). Goal-driven multi-process analysis. *Journal of the Association for Information Systems, 8*(3), 175–203.

Soler, E., Villarroel, R., Trujillo, J., Medina, E. F., & Piattini, M. (2006, April). Representing security and audit rules for data warehouses at the logical level by using the common warehouse metamodel. In *Proceedings of the International Conference on Availability, Reliability and Security.*

Sommerville, I. (2007). *Software engineering* (8th ed.). Harlow, UK: Addison-Wesley.

Song, H., Cheng, D., Messer, A., & Kalasapur, S. (2007, July). Web Service discovery using general-purpose search engines. In *Proceedings of the IEEE International Conference on Web Services (ICWS)* (pp. 265–271).

Steinmetz, R., & Wehrle, K. (2005). *Peer-to-Peer Systems and Applications.* New York: Springer-Verlag. doi:10.1007/11530657

Stevens, W. P., Myers, G. J., & Constantine, L. L. (1999). Structural design. *IBM Systems Journal, 38*(2-3), 231–256. doi:10.1147/sj.382.0231

Stewart, K. J., Ammeter, A. P., & Maruping, L. M. (2006). Impacts of license choice and organizational sponsorship on user interest and development activity in open source software projects. *Information Systems Research, 17*(2), 126–144. doi:10.1287/isre.1060.0082

Stewart, K. J., & Gosain, S. (2006). The impact of ideology on effectiveness in open source software development teams. *Management Information Systems Quarterly, 30*(2), 291–314.

Stoica, I., Morris, R., Liben-Nowell, D., Karger, D. R., Kaashoek, M. F., & Dabek, F. (2003). Chord: A scalable Peer-to-Peer lookup service for internet applications. *IEEE/ACM Transactions on Networking, 11*(1), 17–32. doi:10.1109/TNET.2002.808407

Stroulia, E., & Wang, Y. (2005). Structural and semantic matching for assessing Web Service similarity. *International Journal of Cooperative Information Systems, 14*(4), 407–438. doi:10.1142/S0218843005001213

Subramaniam, C., Sen, R., & Nelson, M. (2009). Determinants of open source software project success: A longitudinal study. *Decision Support Systems, 46*(2). doi:10.1016/j.dss.2008.10.005

Sun, S. X., Zhao, J. L., Nunamaker, J. F., & Sheng, O. R. L. (2006). Formulating the data-flow perspective for business process management. *Information Systems Research, 17*(4), 374–391. doi:10.1287/isre.1060.0105

Sutton, J. S. M., & Rouvellou, I. (2002). Modeling of software concerns in cosmos. In *Proceedings of the 1st International Conference on Aspect-oriented Software Development (AOSD'02)* (pp. 127-133). New York: ACM.

Swartz, N. (2007). Data management problems widespread. *Information Management Journal, 41*(5), 28–30.

Szyperski, C. (2000). Component software and the way ahead. In Leavens, G. T., & Sitaraman, M. (Eds.), *Foundations of component-based systems* (pp. 1–20). Cambridge, UK: Cambridge University Press.

Szyperski, C. A., Bosch, J., & Weck, W. (1999). Component-oriented programming. In *Proceedings of the Workshop on Object-Oriented Technology* (pp. 184-192).

Taha, K., & Elmasri, R. (2009). OOXKSearch: A search engine for answering XML keyword and loosely structured queries using OO techniques. *Journal of Database Management, 20*(3), 18–50. doi:10.4018/jdm.2009070102

Tan, X., Alter, S., & Siau, K. (2011). Using service responsibility tables to supplement UML in analyzing e-service systems. *Decision Support Systems, 51*(3), 350–360. doi:10.1016/j.dss.2011.01.001

Tennant, R. (Ed.). (2002). *XML in libraries*. New York, NY: Neal-Schuman.

Thomas, D. (2004). MDA: Revenge of the modelers or UML utopia? *IEEE Software, 21*, 15–17. doi:10.1109/MS.2004.1293067

Toma, I., Iqbal, K., Moran, M., Roman, D., Strang, T., & Fensel, D. (2005, September 19-22). An evaluation of discovery approaches in Grid and Web Services environments. In *Proceedings of the 2nd International Conference on Grid Services Engineering and Management*, Erfurt, Germany (LNI 69, pp. 233–247). Bonner Köllen Verlag.

Topi, H., & Ramesh, V. (2002). Human Factors research on Data Modeling: A review of Prior Research, An extended Framework and Future Research Directions. *Journal of Database Management, 13*(2), 3–19.

Tran, H., Zdun, U., & Dustdar, S. (2007). View-based and Model-driven Approach for Reducing the Development Complexity in Process-Driven SOA. In *Proceedings of the International Working Conference on Business Process and Services Computing (BPSC'07)* (LNI 116, pp. 105-124).

Trauth, E. M. (1989). The evolution of information resource management. *Information & Management, 16*(5), 257–268. doi:10.1016/0378-7206(89)90003-7

Tsichritzis, D. C., & Lochovsky, F. H. (1982). *Data Models*. Upper Saddle River, NJ: Prentice Hall.

Turk, D., France, R., & Rumpe, B. (2005). Assumptions underlying agile software-development processes. *Journal of Database Management, 16*(4), 62–87. doi:10.4018/jdm.2005100104

Turner, C. R., Fuggetta, A., Lavazza, L., & Wolf, A. L. (1998). Feature engineering software development. In *Proceedings of the 9th International Workshop on Software Specification and Design* (pp. 162-164). New York, NY: ACM.

Unhelkar, B. (2005). *Verification and validation for quality of UML 2.0 models*. New York, NY: Wiley Interscience. doi:10.1002/0471734322

van Breugel, F., & Koshkina, M. (2005). Dead-path-elimination in BPEL4WS. In *Proceedings of the 5th International Conference on Application of Concurrency to System Design* (pp. 192-201). Los Alamitos, CA: IEEE Computer Society.

van de Weerd, I., Versendaal, J., & Brinkkemper, S. (2006). A product software knowledge infrastructure for situational capability maturation: vision and case studies in product management. In *Proceedings of the 12th Working Conference on Requirements Engineering: Foundation for Software Quality* (pp. 97-112).

van der Aalst, W. M. P. (1998). The application of petri nets to workflow management. *Journal of Circuits. Systems and Computers, 8*(1), 21–66.

van der Aalst, W. M. P. (1999). Formalization and verification of event-driven process chains. *Information and Software Technology, 41*(10), 639–650. doi:10.1016/S0950-5849(99)00016-6

van der Aalst, W. M. P. (1999). Interorganizational Workflows: An Approach based on Message Sequence Charts and Petri Nets. *Systems Analysis - Modelling - Simulation, 34*(3), 335-367.

van der Aalst, W. M. P. (2002). Making work flow: On the application of petri nets to business process management. In J. Esparza & C. Lakos (Eds.), *Proceedings of the 23rd International Conference on Application and Theory of Petri Nets* (LNCS 2360, pp. 1-22).

van der Aalst, W. M. P., Desel, J., & Kindler, E. (2002). On the semantics of EPCs: A vicious circle. In Nüttgens, M., & Rump, F. (Eds.), *Geschäftsprozessmanagement mit Ereignisgesteuerten Prozessketten* (pp. 71–79). Trier, Germany: Springer-Verlag.

van der Aalst, W. M. P., Dumas, M., Gottschalk, F., Hofstede, A. H. M., La Rosa, M., & Mendling, J. (2009). Preserving correctness during business process model configuration. *Formal Aspects of Computing*, *22*(3-4), 459–482.

van der Aalst, W. M. P., Dumas, M., & ter Hofstede, A. H. M. (2003). Web Service Composition Languages: Old Wine in New Bottles? In *Proceedings of the 29th Euromicro Conference* (pp. 298-305). Los Alamitos, CA: IEEE Computer Society.

van der Aalst, W. M. P., & Kumar, A. (2003). XML Based Schema Definition for Support of Inter-organizational Workflow. *Information Systems Research*, *14*(1), 23–46. doi:10.1287/isre.14.1.23.14768

van der Aalst, W. M. P., ter Hofstede, A. H. M., Kiepuszewski, B., & Barros, A. P. (2003). Workflow patterns. *Distributed and Parallel Databases*, *14*(1), 5–51. doi:10.1023/A:1022883727209

van der Aalst, W. M. P., & van Hee, K. M. (2002). *Workflow management: models, methods and tools*. Cambridge, MA: MIT Press.

van der Aalst, W. M. P., & Weske, M. (2001). The P2P Approach to Interorganizational Workflows. In *Proceedings of the 13th International Conference Advanced Information Systems Engineering* (pp. 140-156). Berlin, Germany: Springer.

van Offenbeek, M. A. G., & Koopman, P. L. (1996). Scenarios for system development: Matching context and strategy. *Behaviour & Information Technology*, *15*(4), 250–265. doi:10.1080/014492996120175

van Thanh, D., & Jorstad, I. (2005). A Service-Oriented Architecture Framework for Mobile Services. In *Proceedings of the Advanced Industrial Conference on Telecommunications / Service Assurance with Partial and Intermittent Resources Conference/ E-Learning on Telecommunications Workshop* (pp. 65-70). Los Alamitos, CA: IEEE Computer Society Press.

Vanderfeesten, I., Reijers, H. A., Mendling, J., van der Aalst, W. M. P., & Cardoso, J. (2008). On a quest for good process models: The cross-connectivity metric. In Z. Bellahsene & M. Leonard (Eds.), *Proceedings of the International Conference on Advanced Information Systems Engineering* (LNCS 5074, pp. 480-494).

VanderMeer, D., & Dutta, K. (2009). Applying learner-centered design principles to UML sequence diagrams. *Journal of Database Management*, *20*(1), 25–47. doi:10.4018/jdm.2009010102

Vassiliadis, P. (2000). Gulliver in the land of data warehousing: practical experiences and observations of a researcher. In *Proceedings of the 2nd International Workshop on Design and Management of Data Warehouses (DMDW'00),* Stockholm, Sweden (pp. 12.1-12.11).

Verbeek, H. M. W., & van der Aalst, W. M. P. (2006). *On the verification of EPCs using T-invariants* (Tech. Rep. No. BPM-06-05). Eindhoven, The Netherlands: BPM Center.

Verbeek, H. M. W., van der Aalst, W. M. P., & Hofstede, A. H. M. (2007). Verifying workflows with cancellation regions and OR-joins: An approach based on relaxed soundness and invariants. *The Computer Journal*, *50*(3), 294–314. doi:10.1093/comjnl/bxl074

Verma, K., Sivashanmugam, K., Sheth, A., Patil, A., Oundhakar, S., & Miller, J. (2005). METEOR-S WSDI: A scalable Peer-to-Peer infrastructure of registries for semantic publication and discovery of Web Services. *Information Technology Management*, *6*(1), 17–39. doi:10.1007/s10799-004-7773-4

Vidgen, R., & Wang, X. (2009). Coevolving systems and the organization of agile software development. *Information Systems Research*, *20*(3), 355–376. doi:10.1287/isre.1090.0237

Vidyasankar, K., Radha Krishna, P., & Karlapalem, K. (2007). A Multi-Level Model for Activity Commitments in E-contracts. In *Proceedings of CoopIS 2007* (LNCS 4803, pp. 300-317).

Vinekar, V., Slinkman, C. W., & Nerur, S. (2006). Can Agile and traditional systems development approaches coexist? An ambidextrous view. *Information Systems Management*, *25*(3), 31–42. doi:10.1201/1078.10580530/46108.23.3.20060601/93705.4

Vokäc, M. (2005, October). Using a domain-specific language and custom tools to model a multi-tier service-oriented application–experiences and challenges. In *Proceedings of the ACM/IEEE International Conference on Model Driven Engineering Languages and Systems.*

von Hippel, E., & von Krogh, G. (2003). Open source software and the "private-collective" innovation model: issues for organization science. *Organization Science, 14*(2), 209–223. doi:10.1287/orsc.14.2.209.14992

Vossen, G. (2006). Have Service-Oriented Architectures Taken a Wrong Turn Already? In A. Min Tjoa, L. Xu, & S. Chaudhry (Eds.), *Research and Practical Issues of Enterprise Information Systems: Proceedings of the IFIP TC 8 International Conference on Research and Practical Issues of Enterprise Information Systems (CONFENIS) 2006,* Vienna, Austria (Vol. 205, pp. xxiii-xxix). International Federation for Information Processing.

Vroom, V. H. (1964). *Work and motivation.* New York, NY: John Wiley & Sons.

Wada, H., Suzuki, J., & Oba, K. (2006, September). Modeling non-functional aspects in service oriented architecture. In *Proceedings of the IEEE International Conference on Services Computing.*

Wada, H., Suzuki, J., & Oba, K. (2007, July). A feature modeling support for non-functional constraints in service oriented architecture. In *Proceedings of the IEEE International Conference on Services Computing.*

Wada, H., Suzuki, J., & Oba, K. (2008). A model-driven development framework for non-functional aspects in service oriented architecture. *Journal of Web Services Research, 5*(4), 1–31. doi:10.4018/jwsr.2008100101

Wand, Y., Storey, V. C., & Weber, R. (1999). An Ontological Analysis of the Relationship Construct in Conceptual Modeling. *ACM Transactions on Database Systems, 24,* 494–528. doi:10.1145/331983.331989

Wand, Y., & Weber, R. (1990). An ontological model of an information system. *IEEE Transactions on Software Engineering, 16*(11), 1282–1292. doi:10.1109/32.60316

Wand, Y., & Weber, R. (1995). Towards a theory of deep structure of information systems. *Journal of Information Systems, 5*(3), 203–223. doi:10.1111/j.1365-2575.1995.tb00108.x

Wand, Y., & Weber, R. (2002). Research Commentary: Information Systems and Conceptual Modeling - A Research Agenda. *Information Systems Research, 13*(4), 363–377. doi:10.1287/isre.13.4.363.69

Wang, G., Chen, A., Wang, C., Fung, C., & Uczekaj, S. (2004). Integrated quality of service (QOS) management in service-oriented enterprise architectures. In *Proceedings of the IEEE Enterprise Distributed Object Computing Conference.*

Wang, L., & Lee, L. (2005). UML-based modeling of web services security. In *Proceedings of the IEEE European Conference on Web Services.*

Wang, S., Zhang, L., & Ma, N. (2008). A quantitative measurement for reputation of Web Service and providers based on cloud model. In *Proceedings of the International Conference on Computational Intelligence for Modelling, Control and Automation* (pp. 500–505). Los Alamitos, CA: IEEE Computer Society.

Wang, R. Y., & Strong, D. M. (1996). Beyond accuracy: What data quality means to data consumers. *Journal of Management Information Systems, 12*(4), 5–34.

Wang, Y., & Stroulia, E. (2003). Flexible interface matching for Web Service discovery. In *WISE '03: Proceedings of the Fourth International Conference on Web Information Systems Engineering* (p. 147). Washington, DC: IEEE Computer Society.

Wang, Y., & Vassileva, J. (2007). A review on trust and reputation for Web Service selection. *International Transactions on Systems Science and Applications, 3*(2), 118–132.

Warmer, J., & Kleppe, A. (2003). *The object constraint language: Getting your models ready for mda* (2nd ed.). Reading, MA: Addison-Wesley.

Wätcher, H., & Reuter, A. (1992). The contract model. In Elmagarmid, A. K. (Ed.), *Database transaction models for advanced applications* (pp. 219–263).

Watson, H. J., Annino, D. A., Wixom, B. H., Avery, K. L., & Rutherford, M. (2001). Current Practices in Data Warehousing. *Information Systems Management, 18*(1), 1–9. doi:10.1201/1078/43194.18.1.20010101/31264.6

Watson, R. T. (2005). *Data Management: Databases and Organizations* (5th ed.). New York, NY: John Wiley & Sons.

Weber, R. (2004). Conceptual modelling and ontology: Possibilities and pitfalls. *Journal of Database Management, 14*(3), 1–20. doi:10.4018/jdm.2003070101

Weikum, G., & Schek, H. J. (1992). Concepts and applications of multilevel transactions and open nested transactions. In Elmagarmid, A. K. (Ed.), *Database transaction models for advanced applications* (pp. 515–553).

Weikum, G., & Vossen, G. (2002). *Transactional Information Systems: Theory, Algorithms, and the Practice of Concurrency Control and Recovery*. San Francisco, CA: Morgan-Kaufmann Publishers.

Weldon, J.-L. (1979). *Organizing for data base administration*. New York, NY: Center for Research on Information Systems, Graduate School of Business Administration, New York University.

Weldon, J.-L. (1979). *The changing role of data base administration*. New York, NY: Center for Research on Information Systems, Graduate School of Business Administration, New York University.

White, J., Schmidt, D., Czarnecki, K., Wienands, C., Lenz, G., Wuchner, E., et al. (2007, October). Automated model-based configuration of enterprise java applications. In *Proceedings of the IEEE International Conference on Enterprise Distributed Object Computing*.

White, S. A. (2008). *BPMN Modeling and Reference Guide*. Lighthouse Point, FL: Future Strategies.

Williamson, O. E. (1979). Transaction-cost economics: The governance of contractual relations. *The Journal of Law & Economics, 22*(2), 233–261. doi:10.1086/466942

Wohed, P., Van Der Aalst, W. M. P., Dumas, M., & ter Hofstede, A. H. M. (2003). Analysis of Web Services Composition Languages: The Case of BPEL4WS. In *Proceedings of the 22nd International Conference on Conceptual Modeling (ER 2003)* (pp. 200-215). Berlin, Germany: Springer.

Wohlin, C., Runeson, P., Höst, M., Ohlsson, M., Regnell, B., & Wesslén, A. (2000). *Experimentation in software engineering – An introduction*. Boston, MA: Kluwer Academic.

Worah, D., & Sheth, A. P. (1997). Transactions in transactional workflows. In Jajodia, S., & Kerschberg, L. (Eds.), *Advanced transaction models and architectures* (pp. 3–34).

Wu, C. G., Gerlach, J. H., & Young, C. E. (2007). An empirical analysis of open source software developers' motivations and continuance intentions. *Information & Management, 44*(3), 231–352. doi:10.1016/j.im.2006.12.006

Wu, G., & Li, J. (2007). SWRank: An Approach for Ranking Semantic Web Reversely and Consistently. In *Proceedings of the Third International Conference on Semantics, Knowledge and Grid (SKG 2007)* (pp. 116-121).

Wu, J., & Lederer, A. (2009). A meta-analysis of the role of environment-based voluntariness in information technology acceptance. *Management Information Systems Quarterly, 33*(2), 419–432.

Wu, J., & Wu, Z. (2005. July 11-15). Similarity-based Web Service matchmaking. In *Proceedings of the IEEE International Conference on Services Computing,* Orlando, FL (Vol. 1, pp. 287–294). Washington, DC: IEEE Computer Society.

Wu, Y., Al-Khalifa, S., Jagadish, H. V., Patel, J. M., Koudas, N., & Srivastava, D. (2002). Structural joins: A primitive for efficient XML query pattern matching. In *Proceedings of the IEEE International Conference on Data Engineering*.

Wu, Y., Paparizos, S., Lakshmanan, L. V. S., & Jagadish, H. V. (2004). Tree logical classes for efficient evaluation of XQuery. In *Proceedings of the SIGMOD Conference* (pp. 71-82).

Wu, Y., Patel, J. M., & Jagadish, H. V. (2003). Structural join order selection for XML query optimization. In *Proceedings of the IEEE International Conference on Data Engineering* (pp. 443-454).

Wu, Z., & Palmer, M. (1994). Verb semantic and lexical selection. In *Proceedings of the 32nd Annual Meeting of the Association for Computational Linguistics* (pp. 133-138).

Xu, B., & Jones, D. R. (2010). Volunteers' Participation in Open Source Software Development: A Study from the Social-Relational Perspective. *The Data Base for Advances in Information Systems, 41*(3), 69–84.

Xu, B., Jones, D. R., & Shao, B. (2009). Volunteers' involvement in online community based software development. *Information & Management, 46*(3), 151–158. doi:10.1016/j.im.2008.12.005

Xu, L., Ziv, H., Richardson, D., & Liu, Z. (2005, March). Towards modeling non-functional requirements in software architecture. In *Proceedings of the ACM International Conference on Aspect-Oriented Software Development, Early Aspects Workshop*.

Yang, B., & Garcia-Molina, H. (2001). Comparing hybrid Peer-to-Peer systems. In *VLDB '01: Proceedings of the 27th International Conference on Very Large Data Bases* (pp. 561–570). San Francisco: Morgan Kaufmann Publishers.

Yang, J., Papazoglou, M. P., & van den Heuvel, W. J. (2002). Tackling the challenges of service composition in e-marketplaces. In *Proceedings of the 12th International Workshop on Research Issues in Data Engineering: Engineering E-Commerce/E-Business Systems* (pp. 125-133). Los Alamitos, CA: IEEE Computer Society Press.

Yoshikawa, M., Amagasa, T., Shimura, T., & Uemura, S. (2001). XRel: A path-based approach to storage and retrieval of XML documents using relational databases. *ACM Transactions on Internet Technology, 1*(1), 110–141. doi:10.1145/383034.383038

Yu, E. S. K., & Mylopoulos, J. (1994, May 16-21). Understanding "Why" in Software Process Modelling, Analysis, and Design. In *Proceedings of the 16th International Conference on Software Engineering (ICSE),* Sorrento, Italy (pp. 159-168).

Yu, M., Taleb-Bendiab, A., & Reilly, D. (2004). A polyarchical middleware for self-regenerative invocation of multi-standard ubiquitous services. In *Proceedings of the 2004 IEEE International Conference on Web Services* (pp. 410-417). Los Alamitos, CA: IEEE Computer Society Press.

Yu, Q., Liu, X., Bouguettaya, A., & Medjahed, B. (2008). Deploying and managing Web Services: issues, solutions, and directions. *The International Journal on Very Large Data Bases, 17*(3), 537–572. doi:10.1007/s00778-006-0020-3

Zelkowitz, M., & Wallace, D. (1997). Experimental validation in software engineering. *Information and Software Technology, 39*, 735–743. doi:10.1016/S0950-5849(97)00025-6

Zelkowitz, M., Wallace, D., & Binkley, D. W. (2003). Experimental validation of new software technology. In *Lecture Notes on Empirical Software Engineering* (pp. 229–263). Singapore: World Scientific Publishing. doi:10.1142/9789812795588_0006

Zhang, A., Nodine, M., Bhargava, B., & Bukhres, O. (1994). Ensuring relaxed atomicity for flexible transactions in multidatabase systems. In *Proceedings of the ACM SIGMOD Conference* (pp. 67-78). New York, NY: ACM.

Zhang, J. (1995). OODB and SGML techniques in text database: An electronic dictionary system. *SIGMOD Record, 24*(1), 3–8. doi:10.1145/202660.202661

Zhao, L., & Siau, K. (2007). Information mediation using metamodels: An approach using XML and Common Warehouse Metamodel. *Journal of Database Management, 18*(3), 69–82.

Zhao, Z., Wei, J., Lin, L., & Ding, X. (2008). A concurrency control mechanism for composite service supporting user-defined relaxed atomicity. In *Proceedings of the COMPSAC Conference* (pp. 275-278). Washington, DC: IEEE Computer Society.

Zhou, C., Chia, L.-T., & Lee, B.-S. (2004). QoS-aware and federated enhancement for UDDI. *International Journal of Web Services Research, 1*(2), 58–85.

Zhuge, H., & Liu, J. (2004). Flexible retrieval of Web Services. *Journal of Systems and Software, 70*(1-2), 107–116. doi:10.1016/S0164-1212(03)00003-7

Zloof, M. M. (1977). Query by example: A database language. *IBM Systems Journal, 16*(4), 324–343. doi:10.1147/sj.164.0324

Zou, Y., Xiao, H., & Chan, B. (2007, September). Weaving business requirements into model transformations. In *Proceedings of the ACM/IEEE International Conference on Model Driven Engineering Languages and Systems, Workshop on Aspect-Oriented Modeling*.

Zur-Muehlen, M., & Rosemann, M. (2004). Multi-paradigm process management. In *Proceedings of the Workshop on Business Process Modeling, Development and Support* (pp. 169-175).

About the Contributors

Keng Siau is the Chair of the Department of Business and Information Technology at the Missouri University of Science and Technology. Prior to joining the Missouri University of Science and Technology in June 2012, he was the Edwin J. Faulkner Chair Professor and Full Professor of Management at the University of Nebraska-Lincoln. Professor Siau is the Editor-in-Chief for the *Journal of Database Management*, North America Regional Editor for the *Requirements Engineering Journal*, and Co-Editor-in-Chief for the *Advances in Database Research* series. He is the Vice President of Education for the Association for Information Systems and serves on the Board of Partnership for Advancing Computing Education (PACE). He received his PhD in Business Administration (major: Management Information Systems; minor: Psychology) from the University of British Columbia in 1996. His MSc and BSc (honors) degrees are in Computer and Information Sciences from the National University of Singapore. Professor Siau has more than 250 academic publications. According to the ISI Web of Science and Google Scholar, he has more than 1600 and 4000 citation counts respectively. His h-index, according to Harzing's Publish or Perish, is 33. In 2011, he was ranked as one of the top researchers in his field based on h-index and productivity rate. In 2006, he was ranked as one of the top ten e-commerce researchers in the world (Arithmetic Rank of 7, Geometric Rank of 3). In the same year, the citation count for his paper "Building Customer Trust in Mobile Commerce" is ranked in the top 1% within the field as reported by Essential Science Indicators.

* * *

Anat Aharoni is a faculty member at the department of Information Systems Engineering, The School of Engineering, Kinneret College, Israel and a lecturer at the University of Haifa, Israel. She received her BS degree in computer science from the Tel Aviv University, Israel in 1989. She obtained an MS degree in 2001 from the department of education in technology and science, Technion, Israel Institute of Technology, and a PhD in 2010 in information systems, from the University of Haifa, Israel. Her research interests include method engineering and methodologies for information systems development. She had worked as a programmer and project manager in different software companies focusing on development of information systems.

Peter Aiken is an award-winning, internationally recognized thought leader in the area of organizational data management, architecture, and engineering. As a practicing data manager, consultant, author and researcher, he has been actively performing and studying these areas for more than twenty-five years. He has published extensively in the research literature and is author/co-author of seven books. He has held leadership positions with the US Department of Defense and consulted with more than 50 organizations in 17 different counties. He is an Associate Professor in Virginia Commonwealth University's Information Systems Department and the Founding Director of datablueprint.com.

Dinesh Batra is a professor in the decision sciences and information systems in the College of Business Administration at the Florida International University. His publications have appeared in *Management Science, Journal of MIS, Communications of the ACM, Communications of the Association for Information Systems, European Journal of Information Systems, International Journal of Human Computer Studies, Journal of Database Management, Computers and Operations Research, Data Base, Information and Management, Decision Support Systems, Requirements Engineering Journal, Information Systems Management,* and others. He is a co-author of the book *Object-Oriented Systems Analysis and Design* published by Pearson Prentice-Hall. He has served as the President of the AIS SIG on Systems Analysis and Design (SIGSAND).

Sami Bhiri is the leader of the SOA research unit at DERI - the National University of Ireland, Galway. Before joining DERI, he was a research and teaching assistant in the University of Nancy 1 and in the ECOO team of the LORIA-INRIA research laboratory. His research interests are in the area of applying semantics to B2B Integration, Service Oriented Computing and Business Process Management.

Marcelo Campo received a Ph.D. degree in Computer Science from the Universidade Federal do Rio Grande do Sul, Porto Alegre, Brazil, in 1997 and the Systems Engineer degree from the UNICEN, in 1988. He is an Associate Professor at UNICEN, Head of the ISISTAN, and member of the CONICET. His research interests include intelligent aided software engineering, software architecture and frameworks, agent technology and software visualization.

Qing Cao is the Jerry Rawls professor of management information systems at the Rawls College of Business, Texas Tech University. He holds a PhD from the college of business administration at the University of Nebraska-Lincoln (2001). He received an MBA from the University of Wisconsin system and a BS in mechanical engineering from the Shanghai JiaoTong University. Dr. Cao has eight years of industrial experiences in engineering, operations management and IT consulting before entering the academic field in 1997. Before joining Texas Tech in fall of 2008, he was an associate professor of Management Information Systems at the University of Missouri - Kansas City. Dr. Cao has also served as a business consultant to multi-national corporations and healthcare systems (e.g., Sprint, Honeywell, YRC Worldwide Inc., and St. Luke's Hospital Systems).

S.C. Cheung received his Ph.D. from the Imperial College London. He is currently an Associate Professor of Computer Science at the Hong Kong University of Science and Technology. He is a member of the ACM SIGSOFT executive committee, and an editor of the IEEE Transactions on Software Engineering (TSE), the Journal of Computer Science and Technology (JCST), and International Journal of RF Technologies: Research and Application. He is leading an industrial project on RFID benchmarking, and has helped to establish the Global RF Lab Alliance (GRFLA). He participates actively in the program and organizing committees of major international conferences on software engineering and services computing. His work has been disseminated at major international journals and conferences, which include TOSEM, TSE, ASE, DSS, TR, ICSE, FSE, ESEC, ICDCS, ER and ICWS. He is a Chartered Fellow of the British Computer Society and a senior member of the IEEE. His research interests include services computing, context-aware computing, object design patterns, software testing, ubiquitous computing, wireless sensor networks and RFID.

Dickson K.W. Chiu received the B.Sc. (Hons.) degree in Computer Studies from the University of Hong Kong in 1987. He received the M.Sc. (1994) and the Ph.D. (2000) degrees in Computer Science from the Hong Kong University of Science and Technology, where he worked as a Visiting Assistant Lecturer after graduation. He also started his own computer company while studying part-time. From 2001 to 2003, he was an Assistant Professor at the Department of Computer Science and Engineering, the Chinese University of Hong Kong. He was a Visiting Assistant Professor in 2006 at the Computing Department, Hong Kong Polytechnic University for teaching M.Sc. courses. His research results have been published in over 120 papers in international journals and conference proceedings, including practical results of many master and undergraduate projects. He received a best paper award in the 37th Hawaii International Conference on System Sciences in 2004. He is the founding Editor-in-chief of the International Journal on Systems and Service-Oriented Engineering and serves in the editorial boards of several international journals.

Marco Crasso received a Ph.D. degree in Computer Science from the UNICEN in 2010. He holds a Systems Engineer degree from the UNICEN. He is a member of the ISISTAN. His research interests include the application of machine learning and data mining to ease the development of Service-oriented applications, and programming models for Web Service consumption.

Wassim Derguech is a researcher at DERI – the National University of Ireland, Galway towards completion of his Ph.D. He is member of the SOA research unit. His main research interests are in the area of semantic services and business process management.

Kaushik Dutta is an associate professor of information systems in the school of computing at the National University of Singapore. His research interest is enterprise IT Infrastructure and software development. He has published articles in journals such as *Management Science, Journal of Computing,* and *ACM Transactions on Database Systems*. Dr. Dutta also has several publications in various IEEE and ACM conference proceedings. He is the area editor (Database and Data Management) for Elsevier Journal of Systems and Software. Prior to joining FIU, Dr. Dutta was Director of Engineering for Chutney Technologies, funded by KPCB Venture Capital, which developed solutions to improve the scalability and performance of enterprise Web applications. He received his doctorate in Information Systems from the Georgia Institute of Technology.

Matthias Farwick received his B. Sc. at the University of Innsbruck. He is currently working as a research assistant at the research group Quality Engineering at the Computer Science Institute of the University of Innsbruck. He has worked as the software architect for several large SOA projects that focus on Web- service security, privacy and inter-organizational business processes. His research interests include service oriented architectures, location-based access control and domain specific modeling languages.

Ana M. Fernández-Sáez has a MSc in Computer Science from the University of Castilla-La Mancha, Ciudad Real, Spain (2009). She is member of the Alarcos research group and Ph.D student at the Department of Technologies and Information Systems at the same university. Her research interests include: UML model quality, quality in model-driven development, software measures and empirical software engineering.

Walid Gaaloul is an assistant professor in TELECOM & Management SudParis. He was an adjunct lecturer in the National University of Ireland, Galway (NUIG) and a postdoctoral researcher at the Digital Enterprise Research Institute (DERI). He holds an M.S. (2002) and a Ph.D. (2006) in computer science from the University of Nancy-France. His research interests lie in the area of Business Process Management, Process intelligence, Process reliability, Service Oriented Computing and semantics for B2B Integration.

Marcela Genero is Associate Professor in the Department of Technologies and Information Systems at the University of Castilla-La Mancha, Ciudad Real, Spain. She received her MSc. degree in Computer Science in the Department of Computer Science of the University of the South, Argentina, in 1989, and her Ph.D. at the University of Castilla-La Mancha, Ciudad Real, Spain in 2002. She has published in prestigious journals (Information and Software Technology, Journal of Software Maintenance and Evolution: Research and Practice, Data and Knowledge Engineering, Empirical Software Engineering, European Journal of Information Systems, etc.). Along with Mario Piattini and Coral Calero she edited the books entitled ''Data and Information Quality'' (Kluwer, 2001), and ''Metrics for Software Conceptual Models'' (Imperial College, 2005). She is a member of the International Software Engineering Research Network (ISERN). Her research interests are: empirical software engineering, software metrics, conceptual models quality, quality in model-driven development, etc.

Mark L. Gillenson is Professor of Management Information Systems in the Fogelman College of Business and Economics of the University of Memphis. He received his B.S. degree from Rensselaer Polytechnic Institute and his M.S. and Ph.D. degrees in Computer and Information Science from the Ohio State University. Dr. Gillenson worked for the IBM Corp. for 15 years and has consulted for major corporations and government organizations. Dr. Gillenson's research has appeared in *MIS Quarterly*, *Communications of the ACM*, *Information & Management*, and other leading journals. His latest book is *Fundamentals of Database Management Systems*, 2005, John Wiley & Sons.

Claude Godart is full time Professor at Nancy University, France and member of the INRIA team SCORE. His centre of interest concentrates on the consistency maintenance of the data mediating the cooperation between several partners. This encompasses advanced transaction models, user centric workflow and web services composition models. He has been implicated in several transfer projects with industries (France, Europe, and Japan) for a wide range of applications including e-commerce, software processes and e-learning.

Patrick C. K. Hung is an Associate Professor and IT Director at the Faculty of Business and Information Technology in UOIT and an Adjunct Faculty Member at the Department of Electrical and Computer Engineering in University of Waterloo. He is an executive committee member of the IEEE Computer

Society's Technical Steering Committee for Services Computing, a steering member of EDOC "Enterprise Computing," and an associate editor/editorial board member/guest editor in several international journals such as the IEEE Transactions on Services Computing (TSC), International Journal of Web Services Research (JWSR) and International journal of Business Process and Integration Management (IJBPIM).

Maya Kaner is a senior lecturer in operations and production management at the Ort Braude College in Israel. She received her PhD (2004) and MSc (1999) in Industrial Engineering and her BSc in Applied Mathematics (1996) from the Technion–Israel Institute of Technology. Dr. Kaner's current research interests include service system design, business process modeling and knowledge management in project environments. She has reported on her research in books and journals such as *Knowledge and Process Management, Information Knowledge Systems Management* and *Technological Forecasting and Social Change*.

Qing Li received the PhD degree in computer science from USC. He is a Professor at the City University of Hong Kong where he has been in the Department of Computer Science since 1998. Prior to that, he has taught at the Hong Kong Polytechnic University, the Hong Kong University of Science and Technology, and the Australian National University (Canberra, Australia). Professor Li is an author/coauthor of more than 280 published papers in peer-reviewed journals and conferences in the areas of data modeling, multimedia database, data mining/warehousing, Web services, and e-learning systems. He has been actively involved in the research community by serving as an associate editor including the ACM Transactions on Internet Technology (TOIT), the IEEE Transactions on Knowledge and Data Engineering (TKDE), and World Wide Web, and as an organizer/co-organizer of numerous international conferences including APWeb-WAIM'09, ER'08, ICWL'07, EDOC'06, WAIM'04, VLDB'02, WISE'00, etc. In addition, he served as a program committee member for over 70 international conferences and workshops. He is currently a senior member of the IEEE, a member of ACM-SIGMOD, and the IEEE Technical Committee on Data Engineering. He is the chairperson of the Hong Kong Web Society, vice chairman of the international Web Information Systems Engineering (WISE) society, and also served/is serving as an executive committee member of the IEEE-Hong Kong Computer Chapter and the ACM Hong Kong Chapter.

Zhangxi Lin is an associate professor at the Rawls College of Business Administration, Texas Tech University. His research interests include electronic commerce, data communications, information economics, and IT strategy. He has published papers in *Information Systems Research, Decision Support Systems, Information Sciences, Communications of AIS, Information Technology and Management, Journal of Organization Computing and electronic Commerce, Journal of Global Information Management,* and others more.

Jose-Norberto Mazón is Assistant Professor at the Department of Software and Computing Systems in the University of Alicante (Spain). He obtained his Ph.D. in Computer Science from the University of Alicante (Spain) within the Lucentia Research Group. He has published several papers about data warehouses and requirement engineering in national and international workshops and conferences, (such as DAWAK, ER, DOLAP, BNCOD, JISBD and so on) and in several journals such as Decision Support Systems (DSS), SIGMOD Record or Data and Knowledge Engineering (DKE). He has also been co-organizer of the International Workshop on Business intelligencE and the WEB (BEWEB 2010) and the International Workshop on The Web and Requirements Engineering (WeRE 2010). His research interests are: business intelligence, design of data warehouses, multidimensional databases, requirement engineering and model driven development. Contact him at jnmazon@dlsi.ua.es.

Fiona Fui-Hoon Nah is a full professor of management information systems (MIS) at the University of Nebraska-Lincoln. Her research interests include human-computer interaction, 3D virtual worlds, mobile and ubiquitous commerce, knowledge-based and decision support systems, and enterprise resource planning. She is a senior editor of Journal of the Association for Information Systems (JAIS) and AIS Transactions on Human-Computer Interaction (THCI), and an Associate Editor of several other journals including International Journal of Human-Computer Studies (IJHCS), Information and Management (I&M), and Journal of Electronic Commerce Research (JECR). She also serves on the editorial board of more than ten other MIS journals. She is a co-Founder and Past Chair of the Association for Information Systems Special Interest Group on Human-Computer Interaction (SIGHCI). She received her Ph.D. in MIS from the University of British Columbia and was previously on the faculty of the Krannert School of Management at Purdue University.

Jim Nelson is an assistant professor of Management Information Systems at Southern Illinois University, Carbondale. He received his BS in Computer Science from California Polytechnic State University, San Luis Obispo, and his MS and PhD in Information Systems from the University of Colorado, Boulder. His research interests include the quality of conceptual models, investigating how people make IT paradigm shifts, and determining the business value of information technology. Dr. Nelson generally teaches the more technical courses in information systems including object oriented technology, systems analysis and design, database theory and practice, and business data communications.

Katsuya Oba received the Bachelor of Arts degree from Osaka University, Osaka, Japan in 1989. He joined Osaka Gas Information System Research Institute Co., Ltd. (OGIS-RI) as a systems engineer. From 2000 to 2005, he worked for OGIS International, Inc. in Palo Alto, California as General Manager and leaded several software product development and R&D projects. He returned to OGIS-RI in 2006, and is leading R&D and business development relating to Service Oriented Architecture (SOA). His research interests include software architecture, business and systems modeling and software development processes. He is a member of Information Processing Society of Japan.

Jesús Pardillo graduated with honours in Information Systems Engineering in 2006 and obtained his Ph.D. in Computer Science in 2010 from the University of Alicante. He currently enjoys a research grant from the Spanish Ministry of Education and Science and works at the University of Montreal. He has publications on software engineering in international conferences such as MODELS, DOLAP, QUATIC, ER, DaWaK, or JISBD, and journals such as the Journal of Systems and Software, the International Journal of Intelligent Systems, Information Sciences, or Information and Software Technology. His research interests include: conceptual data modelling, programming languages, formal methods in software engineering, and information & software visualisation. Contact him at research@jesuspardillo.com or follow him at www.jesuspardillo.com.

Hyunjung Park is a researcher of the Institute of Management Research at the Seoul National University. She got a PhD of Management Information System from the Graduate School of Business at the Seoul National University. Her doctoral dissertation deals with the ranking problem of Semantic Web resources based on link structure, and her research interests include ontology development and application, knowledge management, U-learning, and social network services. She had an experience working at Korea Telecom, where she has participated in many projects related with the optimization of telecommunication systems and policies.

Jinsoo Park is Associate Professor of Information Systems in the Graduate School of Business at Seoul National University. He was formerly on the faculties of the Department of Information and Decision Sciences in the Carlson School of Management at the University of Minnesota and the Department of Management Information Systems in the College of Business Administration at Korea University. He received a Ph.D.degree in Management Information Systems from the University of Arizona in 1999. His research interests are in the areas of ontology, semantic interoperability and metadata management in interorganizational information systems, and data modeling. His research has been published in *MIS Quarterly*, *IEEE Transactions on Knowledge and Data Engineering* (TKDE), *IEEE Computer*, *ACM Transactions on Information Systems* (TOIS), *Information Systems Frontiers*, *Communications of the AIS*, *Journal of Global Information Technology Management* (JGITM), *International Journal of Electronic Business*, and several other journals and conference proceedings.

Olivier Perrin is an assistant professor at Nancy University (University Nancy 2) since 1995, and works at LORIA in the SCORE project. He received his Ph.D. from University Henri Poincaré Nancy 1 in 1994. His research interests include various topics in virtual organizations, Web services compositions, workflow management, and enterprise application integration. He has published several articles in international journals and conferences, and he was involved in many international and European projects. His current work is on extending Web services and Grid computing with temporal and security properties.

Mario Piattini has an MSc. and PhD in Computer Science from the Technical University of Madrid and is CISA, CISM and CGEIT by ISACA (Information System Audit and Control Association), and CSQE by the ASQ. He is a professor in the Department of Computer Science at the University of Castilla-La Mancha, in Ciudad Real, Spain, where he leads the ALARCOS research group. His research interests are: Information system quality, software metrics, software maintenance and security.

Geert Poels is a professor with the rank of senior lecturer at the Department of Management Information Science and Operations Management, within the Faculty of Economics and Business Administration of Ghent University. He heads the Management Information Systems research group which focuses on conceptual modeling, business ontology, business process management, and Service Science. He is also a part-time professor in software project management at the Center of Industrial Management of the Katholieke Universiteit Leuven. His research was published in IEEE Transactions on Software Engineering, Information Sciences, Information Systems Journal, Data & Knowledge Engineering, and other academic journals within the information systems and computer science domains.

David Rafner oversees Research and Technology at Richmond Group Fund Co., Ltd., an institutional hedge fund. He was previously a graduate student in Virginia Commonwealth University's Information Systems Department and Director of Technology at Data Blueprint. He holds a M.S. in Software Design and Development from the University of St. Thomas in St. Paul, Minnesota. His career spans positions in commercial real estate, aerospace, biotechnology, alternative energy, and telecommunications.

Iris Reinhartz-Berger is a faculty member in the department of information systems, University of Haifa, Israel. She received her BS degree in applied mathematics and computer science from the Technion, Israel Institute of Technology in 1994. She was awarded an MS degree in 1999 and a PhD in 2003 in information management engineering from the Technion, Israel Institute of Technology. Her research interests include conceptual modeling, analysis and design of information systems, software product line engineering, and method engineering. Her work has been published in international journals and conferences and she has chaired a series of domain engineering workshops and presented tutorials on domain engineering and variability management.

Sangkyu Rho is Professor in Information Systems, Graduate School of Business, Seoul National University. Rho received his BBA from Seoul National University, and his MBA and PhD from the University of Minnesota. His research interests include Internet business, ontology development and mining. He has published papers in such journals as *IEEE Transactions on Knowledge and Data Engineering, Annals of Operations Research, Strategic Management Journal,* and *Long Range Planning*.

Arijit Sengupta is associate professor of information systems and operations management at the Raj Soin College of Business at Wright State University, Dayton, Ohio. He received his PhD in computer science from Indiana University. Prior to joining Wright State, Dr. Sengupta served as faculty at Kelley School of Business at Indiana University and the Robinson College of Business at Georgia State University. Dr. Sengupta's current primary research interest is in the efficient use and deployment of RFID (Radio Frequency Identification) for business applications. His other research interests are in databases and XML, specifically in modeling, query languages, data mining, and human-computer interaction.

Zhe Shan received his B.Sc. from Nanjing University in 2000 and his M.Phil. from City University of Hong Kong in 2003. He is currently a Ph.D. candidate in the Department of Supply Chain and Information Systems at the Pennsylvania State University. His major research interests include business process management, Web services, and service science. He is a student member of the AIS, the ACM, the IEEE and the INFORMS.

Pnina Soffer is a senior lecturer at the management information systems department, University of Haifa. Her PhD (2002) and MSc (1994) were in the Faculty of Industrial Engineering and Management at the Technion, Israel Institute of Technology. Her research areas are business processes and conceptual modeling, including ontological foundations of both.

Junichi Suzuki received a Ph.D. in computer science from Keio University, Japan, in 2001. He joined the University of Massachusetts, Boston in 2004, where he is currently an associate professor of computer science. From 2001 to 2004, he was with the University of California, Irvine (UCI), as a postdoctoral research fellow. Before joining UCI, he was with Object Management Group Japan, Inc., as Technical

Director. He served as a program co-chair for the 2009 International Conference on Service Oriented Computing and served as the general chair for the 2010 International Conference on Bio-Inspired Models of Network, Information and Computing Systems. His research interests include service-oriented computing, search-based software engineering, model-driven software/performance engineering and autonomous adaptive distributed systems. He is a member of IEEE and ACM.

Juan Trujillo is a Full-time Professor at the Department of Software and Computing Systems in the University of Alicante (Spain). His main research topics include business intelligence applications, data warehouses' development, OLAP, data mining, UML, MDA, data warehouses security and quality, etc. He has published more than a 120 papers in different national and international highly impact conferences such as the ER, UML, ADBIS or CaiSE, and more than 30 papers in highly ranked international journals indexed by JCR such as the DKE, DSS, ISOFT, IS, or JDBM. He has also been co-editor of five special issues in different JCR journals (e.g. DKE). He has also been PC member of different events and JCR journals such as ER, DAWAK, CIKM, ICDE, DOLAP, DSS, JDM, ISOFT or DKE, and PC Chair of DOLAP'05, DAWAK'05-'06 and FP-UML'05-'09. Further information on his main research publications can be found on: http://www.informatik.uni-trier.de/~ley/db/indices/a-tree/t/Trujillo:Juan.html. Contact him at: jtrujillo@dlsi.ua.es.

Debra VanderMeer is an assistant professor in the college of business at Florida International University. Her research interests focus on applying concepts developed in computer science and information systems to solve real-world problems. She is widely published in well-known journals, such as *Management Science, ACM Transactions on Database Systems,* and *IEEE Transactions on Knowledge and Data Engineering*, as well as prestigious conference proceedings, including the International Conference on Data Engineering, International Conference on Distributed Computing Systems, and the Very Large Database Conference. She also has significant professional experience in the software industry. She has served in software engineering and managerial roles in large companies, as well as early-stage venture-funded software enterprises. She received her doctorate from the Georgia Institute of Technology.

Ramesh Venkataraman is associate professor in the information systems department and Ford Motor Company Teaching Fellow at Indiana University's Kelley School of Business where he also serves as Director of the MS in Information Systems program. His research interests are in data modeling, heterogeneous databases, virtual teams and groupware, usability in mobile systems and software engineering. Ramesh has published over 25 papers in leading journals, book and conferences, such as *Communications of the ACM, Journal of Management Information Systems, ACM Transactions on Information Systems, Information Systems* and *IEEE Expert*. His teaching interests include Database Design, Object-oriented Design and Programming (Java and VB.NET), Web Applications Development (JSP/Servlets, ASP.NET), E-business Infrastructure.

K. Vidyasankar is a Professor in the Department of Computer Science, Memorial University, St. John's, Newfoundland, Canada. He received his B.E. and M.Tech. in Electrical Engineering from India, and Ph.D. in Computer Science from University of Waterloo, Canada, in 1968, 1970 and 1976, respectively. His research areas include (i) transactional aspects in database and information systems, Web services, and e-contracts and (ii) shared variable constructions, mutual exclusion problems and transactional memory in distributed computing.

Gottfried Vossen is a Professor of Computer Science in the Department of Information Systems at the University of Muenster in Germany. He received his master's and Ph.D. degrees as well as the German habilitation in 1981, 1986, and 1990, resp., all from the Technical University of Aachen in Germany. He has held visiting positions at the University of California in San Diego, at several German universities including the Hasso-Plattner-Institute for Software Systems Engineering in Potsdam near Berlin, at Karlstad University in Sweden and at The University of Waikato in Hamilton, New Zealand. In 2004 he became the European Editor-in-Chief of Elsevier's Information Systems - An International Journal, and a Director of the European Research Center for Information Systems (ERCIS) in Muenster. His research interests include conceptual as well as application-oriented problems concerning databases and information systems, electronic learning, process management, and the Web 2.0 context.

Hiroshi Wada is a researcher at the Business Process and Interoperation research group, National ICT Australia. He is also a conjoint lecturer at the School of Computer Science and Engineering, University of New South Wales. He received a Ph.D. in computer science from University Massachusetts Boston in 2009. His research interests include model-driven software engineering, performance engineering, search-based software engineering and distributed computing. In these areas, he has published over 25 refereed papers including four award papers. Before pursuing a Ph.D., he was with Object Technology Institute, Inc., Japan and engaged various consulting and educational services to enhance clients' enterprise systems.

Bo Xu is an assistant professor at School of Management, Fudan University in Shanghai, China. He received Ph.D. degree in Management Information Systems from Texas Tech University, USA. His research interests include electronic commerce, open source software, and online community. He has published papers in *Decision Support Systems, Information & Management*, *Database for Advances in Information Systems*, *Journal of Global Information Technology Management*, and some major information systems conferences.

Yan Xu is an instructor of Computer Science and Information Technology at Del Mar College, Texas. He received master degree of Computer Science from Texas Tech University in 2002. His research interests include controls in open source software, self-healing software component and architecture, software security modeling, network security, and software product line. Mr. Xu has published technical papers in the related areas.

Yu Yang is a M. Phil. graduate of Department of Computer Science, City University of Hong Kong. His research interests are in data indexing and multimedia data management.

Maciej Zaremba is a researcher at DERI Galway working towards completion of his Ph.D. under supervision of Prof. Manfred Hauswirth. He is a member of USOA unit. He holds a M.Sc. degree from Wroclaw University of Technology. His main research interests are on semantic services, service discovery, service middleware, sensors and business process management. He worked in a number of EU projects including DIP, SWING and SUPER as well in national projects.

Xihui Zhang is an Assistant Professor of Computer Information Systems in the College of Business at the University of North Alabama. He earned a Ph.D. in Business Administration with a concentration on Management Information Systems from the University of Memphis. His teaching and research interests include technical, behavioral, and managerial aspects of Information Systems. He has published numerous articles in refereed journals and conference proceedings. He serves on the Editorial Review Board for several academic IS journals such as *Journal of Computer Information Systems* and *Journal of Information Technology Education*. Additional information about him can be found at http://sites.google.com/site/xihuizhang/.

Alejandro Zunino received a Ph.D. degree in Computer Science from the UNICEN, in 2003, his M.Sc. in Systems Engineering in 2000 and the Systems Engineer degree in 1998. He is an Adjunct Professor at UNICEN, a member of ISISTAN Research Institute, and of the CONICET. His research interests are Grid computing, Service-oriented computing, Semantic Web Services, Agent development tools/frameworks, Mobile agents, and Reactive mobility.

Index

A

B

C

D

E

F

G

H

I

L

M

N

O

P

Q

R

S

T

U

V

W

X